Peace Process

WILLIAM B. QUANDT

Peace Process

AMERICAN DIPLOMACY AND
THE ARAB-ISRAELI CONFLICT
SINCE 1967

THE BROOKINGS INSTITUTION
Washington, D.C.

UNIVERSITY OF CALIFORNIA PRESS
Berkeley and Los Angeles

Library of Congress Cataloging-in-Publication data

Quandt, William B.
  Peace process : American diplomacy and the Arab-
Israeli conflict since 1967 / William B. Quandt.
    p.   cm.
  Includes bibliographical references and index.
  ISBN 0-520-08388-1 (alk. paper)—
ISBN 0-520-08390-3 (pbk. : alk. paper)
   1. Jewish-Arab relations—1967–1973. 2. Jewish-
Arab relations—1973–   3. United States—Foreign
relations—Middle East.   4. Middle East—Foreign
relations—United States.   5. United States—Foreign
relations—20th century.   I. Title.
DS119.7.Q69   1993
327.73056—dc20   93-18804
                                                      CIP

9 8 7 6 5 4 3 2 1

The paper used in this publication meets the minimum
requirements of the American National Standard for
Information Sciences—Permanence of paper for Printed
Library Materials, ANSI Z39.48-1984

Foreword

Each of the past six presidents became deeply involved in the diplomacy surrounding the Arab-Israeli conflict. The same will doubtless be true of President Bill Clinton. The hopeful message of this book is that the United States, if it plays its role of mediator skillfully, can contribute to a resolution of the dispute between Israel and its Arab neighbors. Just as often, however, presidents and their advisers have misread the realities of the Middle East, have pursued flawed policies, and have contributed to a worsening of the conflict. They did so particularly when they viewed the Middle East through a cold war lens.

This study provides a detailed analytical account of American policy toward the Arab-Israeli conflict since the crisis that resulted in the June 1967 war. Each administration's initial approach to the problem of peacemaking is assessed, along with the evolution of policy as it confronted the stubborn realities of the region and the mine fields of domestic political controversy.

Given the complexity of the challenge, American policy has shown remarkable consistency and surprising successes. Egypt and Israel are at peace with each other and are both close friends of the United States. More recently, other Arab parties have begun to negotiate with Israel under American auspices. One point on which presidents of both political parties have agreed is that a U.S. role in support of Arab-Israeli peace is consistent with U.S. national interests.

William B. Quandt, a senior fellow in the Foreign Policy Studies program at Brookings, participated in the policymaking process as a member of the National Security Council staff in both the Nixon and the Carter administrations. He brings his direct experience to bear on the analysis of how decisions are made on a particularly sensitive foreign-policy issue.

In 1977 Quandt published a book called *Decade of Decisions: American Policy toward the Arab-Israeli Conflict, 1967–1976*. The University of California Press published that study. The current work is, in part, a revision and updating of *Decade of Decisions*, and Brookings is pleased to copublish it with the University of California Press.

In revising the early chapters on the Johnson, Nixon, and Ford administrations, Quandt was assisted by a number of former American officials, including Alfred L. Atherton, Jr., Lucius Battle, Richard Helms, Robert Oakley, Richard Parker, Harold Saunders, Joseph Sisco, Eugene Rostow, and Walt Rostow. Ephraim Evron was also especially helpful on the 1967 crisis.

For the Carter period, the author was assisted by Zbigniew Brzezinski, Jimmy Carter, Hermann Eilts, Samuel Lewis, Gary Sick, and Cyrus Vance. For the Reagan period, he benefited from discussions with Geoffrey Kemp, William Kirby, Daniel Kurtzer, Richard Murphy, and Nicholas Veliotes. Former secretary of state George Shultz generously shared an early draft of the Middle East chapters of his memoirs. On the Bush administration, the author was helped by Richard Haass, Aaron Miller, and Dennis Ross, among others. Throughout, Helena Cobban was a supportive critic and adviser.

The author also wishes to thank Elisa Barsoum for staff assistance; Marlin Dick, Susanne Lane, and Deborah Rivel for research support; Agnieska Paczynska for verification; Leila Rached for proofreading; Caroline Lalire for editing the manuscript; and L. Pilar Wyman for preparing the index. Professor L. Carl Brown, William Kirby, and John Steinbruner provided helpful reviews of the manuscript.

Brookings gratefully acknowledges the financial support of the John D. and Catherine T. MacArthur Foundation.

The views expressed in this book are those of the author and should not be ascribed to any of the persons whose assistance is acknowledged above, to the sources of funding support, or to the trustees, officers, or other staff members of the Brookings Institution.

Bruce K. MacLaury
President

March 1993
Washington, D.C.

Author's Note

In one way or another, I have been studying and writing about American policy toward the Arab-Israeli conflict since 1968. Mostly I have been an outsider, trying to figure out how policy is made by looking at the results, talking to those in positions to know, reading the records when they become available. Twice I have been close enough to events, as a member of the National Security Council staff in 1972–74 and in 1977–79, to observe the process up close and to play some part in it.

This book was designed to revise and bring up to date my earlier study, *Decade of Decisions: American Policy toward the Arab-Israeli Conflict, 1967–1976* (University of California Press, 1977). About one-half the material in the present book is new. Only chapters 4 through 9 are essentially unchanged from their counterparts in *Decade of Decisions*. Even there, however, I have incorporated any new material that has come to light, especially in the various memoirs of participants.

Chapter 1 is an essentially new introduction, although the analytical scheme is similar to that used in the earlier volume. I still find that an emphasis on the president and his inner circle is essential, although I now emphasize more than before the on-the-job learning that seems to take place and that produces a degree of convergence in the policies of administrations after they have encountered the realities of the Middle East region and of Washington.

The chapters on the 1967 war (2 and 3) are almost entirely new. In recent years the Lyndon Baines Johnson Library in Austin, Texas, has released a large quantity of material that helps to answer questions of how Johnson saw the crisis. As a result, my present interpretation of those important events is somewhat different from what it was when I published in 1977.

The three chapters on the Carter period (10, 11, and 12) are derived from previous writing I did on the subject, primarily my *Camp David: Peacemaking and Politics* (Brookings, 1986) and a chapter entitled "The American Strategy in the Camp David Negotiations," in S. Seikaly, R.

Baalbaki, P. Dodd, eds., *Quest for Understanding: Arabic and Islamic Studies in Memory of Malcolm H. Kerr* (American University of Beirut Press, 1991). Chapter 13, on the early Reagan years, is a heavily revised version of a chapter that appeared in a book I edited called *The Middle East: Ten Years after Camp David* (Brookings, 1988). Chapters 14, 15, and 16 are entirely new.

Inevitably the latter chapters of a book of this sort must be somewhat speculative. Less is known about how decisions were made in the Reagan and Bush administrations. In due course memoirs will be written and gaps will be filled. But for now, much of the narrative must be derived from publicly available sources. I recognize that this creates something of an imbalance between the in-depth treatment of the earlier periods and the less-detailed accounting of the later ones. But because much of the logic and the approaches to Arab-Israeli peacemaking were forged in the Johnson through Carter periods, I feel that the detailed accounts of those periods are warranted.

W.B.Q.

To Lorna

Contents

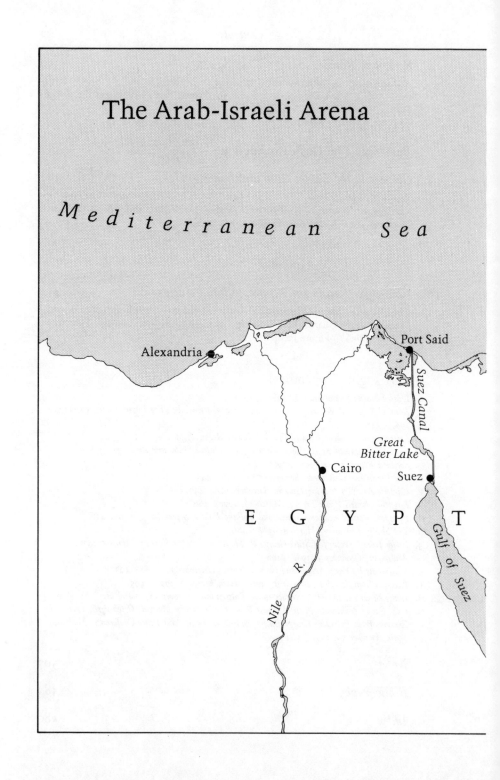

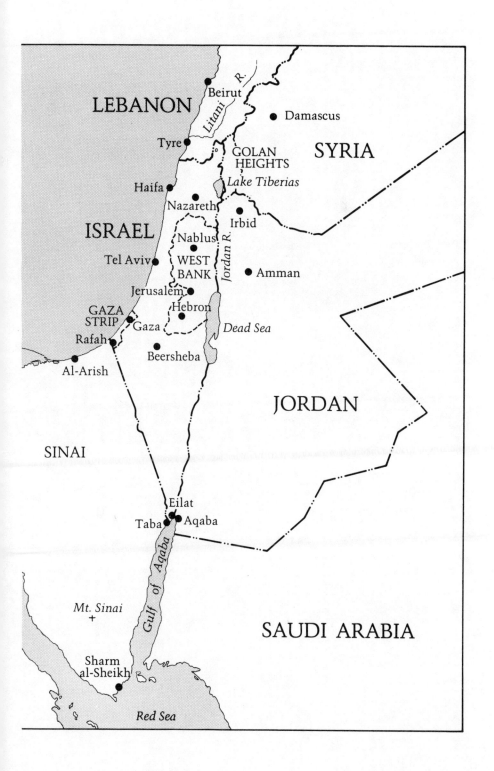

Peace Process

CHAPTER ONE

Introduction

Sometime in the mid-1970s the term *peace process* began to be widely used to describe the American-led efforts to bring about a negotiated peace between Israel and its Arab neighbors. The phrase stuck, and ever since it has been synonymous with the gradual, step-by-step approach to resolving one of the world's most difficult conflicts.

In the years since 1967 the emphasis in Washington has shifted from the spelling out of the ingredients of "peace" to the "process" of getting there. This procedural bias, which frequently seems to characterize American diplomacy, reflects a practical, even legalistic side of American political culture. Procedures are also less controversial than substance, more susceptible to compromise, and thus easier for politicians to deal with. Much of U.S. constitutional theory focuses on how issues should be resolved—the process—rather than on substance—what should be done.

Whenever progress has been made toward Arab-Israeli peace through American mediation, there has always been a joining of substance and procedure. The United States has provided both a sense of direction and a mechanism. That, at its best, is what the "peace process" has been about. At worst, it has been little more than a slogan used to mask the marking of time.

THE PRE-1967 STALEMATE

The stage was set for the contemporary Arab-Israeli peace process by the 1967 Six-Day War. Until then, the conflict between Israel and the Arabs had seemed almost frozen, moving neither toward resolution nor toward war. The ostensible issues in dispute were still those left unresolved by the armistice agreements of 1949. At that time, it had been widely expected that those agreements would simply be a step toward final peace talks. But the issues in dispute were too complex for the many mediation efforts of the early 1950s, and by the mid-1950s the cold war rivalry between Moscow and Washington had left the Arab-Israeli conflict suspended somewhere between war and peace. For better or worse, the armistice agreements had provided a semblance of stability from 1949 to 1967.

During this long truce the Israelis had been preoccupied with questions of an existential nature. Would the Arabs ever accept the idea of a Jewish state in their midst? Would recognition be accompanied by security arrangements that could be relied on? Would the Arabs insist on the return of the hundreds of thousands of Palestinian refugees who had fled their homes in 1948–49, thereby threatening the Jewishness of the new state? And would the Arabs accept the 1949 armistice lines as recognized borders, or would they insist on an Israeli withdrawal to the indefensible lines of the 1947 United Nations partition agreement? As for tactics, would Israel be able to negotiate separately with each Arab regime, or would the Arabs insist on a comprehensive approach to peacemaking? Most Israelis felt certain that the Arabs would not provide reassuring answers to these questions, and therefore saw little prospect for successful negotiations, whether with the conservative monarchs or the new brand of nationalistic army officers.

From the Arab perspective, the conflict also seemed intractable, but the interests of existing regimes and the interests of the Palestinians, who had lost most from the creation of Israel, were by no means identical. The regimes struck the pose of defending the rights of the Palestinians to return to their homes or to be compensated for their losses. They withheld recognition from the Jewish state, periodically engaging in furious propaganda attacks against the "Zionist entity." The more militant Arabs sometimes coupled their harsh rhetoric with support for guerrilla attacks on Israel. But others, such as Jordan and Lebanon, were fairly content with the armistice arrangements and even maintained under-the-table contacts with the Israelis. "No war, no peace" suited them well.

The Palestinians, not surprisingly, used all their moral and political capital to prevent any Arab regime from recognizing the Jewish state, and by the mid-1950s they had found a champion for their cause in Egypt's president Gamal Abdel Nasser. From that point on, Arab nationalism and the demand for the restoration of Palestinian rights were Nasser's most potent weapons as he sought to unify the ranks of the Arab world. But Nasser also sought to steer a course between war and peace, at least until the momentous days of May 1967. Then, as tensions rose, Palestinian radicals, who had hoped to draw the Arab states into conflict with Israel on their behalf, rallied to Nasser's banner and helped to cut off any chance that he might retreat from the brink to which he had so quickly advanced.

THE 1967 WATERSHED

The 1967 war transformed the frozen landscape of the Arab-Israeli conflict in dramatic ways. Israel revealed itself to be a military power able to outmatch all its neighbors. By the end of the brief war, Israel was in control of the Sinai desert; the West Bank of the Jordan River, including all of East Jerusalem; Gaza, with its teeming refugee camps; and the strategically important Golan Heights. More than a million Palestinians came under the control of the Israeli military, creating an acute dilemma for Israel. None of the post-1921 British mandate of Palestine was now free of Israeli control. If Israel kept the newly conquered land and granted the people full political rights, Israel would become a binational state, which few Israelis wanted. If it kept the land but did not grant political rights to the Palestinians, it would come to resemble other colonial powers, with predictable results. Finally, if Israel relinquished the land, it would retain its Jewish character, but could it live in peace and security? These were the alternatives debated within the fractious, often boisterous Israeli democracy.

Given the magnitude of their victory in the 1967 war, some Israelis seemed to expect right afterwards that the Arabs would have no option but to sue for peace. But that did not happen. So, confident of its military superiority, and assured of American support, Israel decided to wait for the Arabs to change their position. But what would happen to the occupied territories while Israel waited? Would they be held in trust, to be traded for peace and security at some future date? Or would they gradually and selectively be incorporated into Israel, as the nationalists on the right demanded? Jerusalem, at least, would not be returned, and almost immediately Israel announced the unilateral expansion of the municipal boundaries and the annexation of the eastern parts of the city. Palestinians living there would have the right to become Israeli citizens, but few took up the offer. Apart from Jerusalem, Israel signaled its willingness to return most of the occupied territories, although the passage of time and changing circumstances gradually eroded that position.

The 1967 war was a shock to Arabs who had believed Nasser could end their sense of weakness and humiliation at the hands of the West. Indeed, although Nasser lived on for another three years after the war, his prestige was shattered. Arab nationalism of the sort he preached would never again be such a powerful force. Instead, regimes came to look more and more after their own narrow interests, and the Palestinians followed suit by organizing their own political movement, free of control by any Arab government. One of the few dynamic developments in the Arab world after the 1967 war was the emergence of a new generation of Palestinians leading the fight for their rights.

The Palestine Liberation Organization (PLO), originally supported by Arab regimes to keep the Palestinians under control, quickly became an independent actor in the region. It symbolized the hopes of many Palestinians and caused much concern among established Arab regimes, which were not used to seeing the Palestinians take matters into their own hands.

In theory, these changes in the Arab world might have opened the way for an easing of the Arab-Israeli conflict. A certain amount of self-criticism took place in Arab intellectual circles. Political realism began to challenge ideological sloganeering. But no one made any serious peace effort immediately after the 1967 war, and by September of that year the Arab parties had all agreed there would be no negotiations with Israel, no peace, and no recognition. Once again, "neither war nor peace" seemed to be a tolerable prospect for both Arabs and Israelis.

THE NEED FOR A MEDIATOR

With the parties to the conflict locked into mutually unacceptable positions, the chance for diplomatic movement seemed to depend on others, especially the United States. Because of the close U.S.-Israeli relationship, many Arabs looked to Washington to press Israel for concessions. The example of President Dwight D. Eisenhower, who had pressured Israel to relinquish its gains from the Suez war of 1956, was still a living memory. The two main areas of Arab concern were the return of territories seized in the 1967 war and some measure of justice for the Palestinians. In return, it was implied, something short of peace would be offered to Israel, perhaps an end to belligerency or strengthened armistice arrangements.

The Arab regimes were still reluctant to promise full peace and recognition for Israel unless and until the Palestinians were satisfied, and that would require more than Israeli withdrawal from occupied territories. As time went by, and the PLO gained in prestige, it became more and more difficult for the Arab states to pursue their narrowly defined interests with no regard for Palestinian claims. And the Arabs were reluctant to deal directly with Israel. If a deal was to be struck, it would be through the efforts of the two superpowers—the United States and the Soviet Union—and the United Nations.

By contrast, Israel was adamant that territory would not be returned for less than peace, recognition, and security. And the means for getting to a settlement would have to include direct negotiations by each Arab party with Israel. For most Israelis, the claims of the Palestinians were impossible to deal with. At best, Jordan could act as a stand-in for the Palestinians, who would have to be satisfied with some form of internationally supported rehabilitation and compensation scheme. Above all, Palestinians would not be allowed to return to their homes, except in very special circumstances of family reunions and in very small numbers.

AMERICAN AMBIVALENCE: POSITIONS AND POLICIES

Confronted with these almost contradictory positions, the United States was reluctant to get deeply involved in Arab-Israeli diplomacy. The Vietnam War was still raging in 1967, and the needs of the Middle East seemed less compelling than the daily demands of an ongoing war in Southeast Asia. Still, from the outset the United States staked out a position somewhere in between the views of Israelis and Arabs. Israel, it was believed, was entitled to more than a return to the old armistice arrangements. Some form of contractually binding end to the state of war should be achieved, and Israeli security concerns would have to be met. On the other hand, if the Arabs were prepared to meet those conditions, they should recover most, if not all, of the territory lost in 1967. These views were spelled out by President Lyndon Johnson soon after the war and became the basis for UN Resolution 242, of November 22, 1967, which thereafter provided the main reference point, with all its ambiguities, for peacemaking.

In the years from 1967 through 1992 every American president—Lyndon Johnson, Richard Nixon, Gerald Ford, Jimmy Carter, Ronald Reagan, and George Bush—was drawn into the intricacies of the Arab-Israeli conflict, often much more than he had intended to be. American mediation became essential to the diplomatic effort.

The basic American position adopted in 1967 has remained remarkably consistent. For example, each American president since 1967 has formally subscribed to the following points:

—Israel should not be required to relinquish territories captured in 1967 without a quid pro quo from the Arab parties involving peace, security, and recognition. This position, summarized in the formula "land for peace," and embodied in UN Resolution 242, applies to each front of the conflict.

—East Jerusalem is legally considered to be occupied territory whose status should eventually be settled in peace negotiations. Whatever its final political status, Jerusalem should not be physically redivided. Reflecting the legal American position on the city, the American embassy has remained in Tel Aviv, despite promises by many presidential candidates to move the embassy to Jerusalem.

—Israeli settlements beyond the 1967 armistice lines—the "green line"—are obstacles to peace. Until 1981 they were considered illegal under international law, but the Reagan administration reversed position and declared they were not illegal. But Reagan, and especially Bush, continued to oppose the creation of settlements. No American funds are to be used by Israel beyond the green line.

—However Palestinian rights may eventually be defined, they do not include the right of unrestricted return to homes within the 1967 lines, nor do they entail the automatic right of independence. All administrations have opposed the creation of a fully independent Palestinian state, preferring some form of association of the West Bank and Gaza with Jordan. Over time, however, the Jordan option—the idea that Jordan should speak for the Palestinians—has faded, and since 1988 the United States has agreed to deal directly with Palestinian representatives.

—Israel's military superiority, its technological edge, against any plausible coalition of Arab parties has been maintained through American military assistance. Each U.S. administration has tacitly accepted the existence of Israeli nuclear weapons, with the understanding that they will not be brandished and can be regarded only as an ultimate deterrent, not as a battlefield weapon. American conventional military aid is provided, in part, to ensure that Israel will not have to rely on its nuclear capability for anything other than deterrence.

With minor adjustments, every president from Lyndon Johnson to Bill Clinton has subscribed to each of these positions. They have been so fundamental that they are rarely even discussed. To change any one of these positions would entail costs, both domestic and international. These positions represent continuity and predictability. But they do not always determine policy. Policy, unlike these positions, is heavily influenced by tactical considerations, and here presidents and their advisers differ with one another, and sometimes with themselves from one moment to the next.

Policies involve judgments about what will work. How can a country be best influenced? What levers exist to influence a situation? Should aid be offered or withheld? Will reassurance or pressure—or both—be most effective? When is the optimal time to launch an initiative? Should it be done in public or private? How much prior consultation should take place, and with whom? On these matters, there is no accepted received wisdom. Each president and his top advisers must evaluate the realities of the Middle East, of the international environment, of the domestic front, and of human psychology before reaching a subjective judgment. While positions tend to be predictable, policies are not. They are the realm where leadership makes all the difference. And part of leadership is knowing when a policy has failed and should be replaced with another.

HOW POLICY IS MADE: ALTERNATIVE MODELS

More than any other regional conflict, the Arab-Israeli dispute has consistently competed for top priority on the American foreign-policy agenda. This study tries to account for the prominence of the Arab-Israeli peace process in American policy circles since 1967. It seeks to analyze the way in which perceived national interests have interacted with domestic political considerations to ensure that Arab-Israeli peacemaking has become the province of the president and his closest advisers.

Because presidents and secretaries of state—not faceless bureaucrats—usually set the guidelines for policy on the Arab-Israeli dispute, it is important to try to understand how they come to adopt the views that guide them through the labyrinthine complexities of Arab-Israeli diplomacy. Here several models compete for attention.

One model would have us believe that policies flow from a cool deliberation of national interest. This *strategic* model assumes that decisions are made by rational decisionmakers. Such a perspective implies that it does not much matter who occupies the Oval Office. The high degree of continuity in several aspects of the American stance toward the conflict since 1967 would serve as evidence that broad interests and rational policy processes provide the best explanation for policy.

But anyone who has spent time in government will testify that policymaking is anything but orderly and rational. As described by the *bureaucratic politics* model, different agencies compete with one another, fixed organizational procedures are hard to change, and reliable information is difficult to come by. This perspective places a premium on bureaucratic rivalries and the "game" of policymaking. Policy outcomes are much less predictable from this perspective. Instead, one needs to look at who is influencing whom. Microlevel analysis is needed, in contrast to the broad systemic approach favored by the strategic model. Much of the gossip of Washington is based on the premise that the insiders' political game is what counts in setting policy. Embassies try desperately to convince their governments back home that seemingly sinister policy outcomes are often simply the result of the normal give and take of everyday bureaucratic struggles, the compromises, the foul-ups, the trading of favors that are part of the Washington scene. If conspiracy theorists thrive on the strategic model—there must be a logical explanation for each action taken by the government—political cynics and comics have a field day with the bureaucratic politics model.[1]

A third model, one emphasizing the importance of *domestic politics*, is also injected into the study of American policy toward the Arab-Israeli conflict. Without a doubt Arab-Israeli policymaking in Washington does get tangled up in internal politics. Congress, where support for Israel is usually high, and where pro-Israeli lobbies tend to concentrate their efforts, can frequently exert influence over foreign policy, largely through its control over the budget.[2] While some senators and representatives no doubt do consider the national interest, for many others positions taken on the Arab-Israeli conflict are little more than part of their domestic reelection strategy. Some analysts have maintained that American Middle East policy is primarily an expression of either the pro-Israeli lobby or the oil lobby. Little evidence will be found here for such an extreme view, even though in some circumstances the lobbies can be influential.

Besides considering the role of Congress, one must also take into account the effect of the workings of the American political system, especially the four-year cycle of presidential elections. This cycle imposes some regular patterns on the policymaking process that have little to do with the world outside but a great deal to do with the way power is pursued and won through elections.[3] One should hardly be surprised to find that every four years the issue of moving the American embassy to Jerusalem reemerges, arms sales to Arab countries are deferred, and presidential contenders emphasize those parts of their program that are most congenial to the supporters of Israel. Nor should one be surprised to find that once the election is over, policy returns to a more evenhanded course.

THE MIND OF THE PRESIDENT

As much as each of these approaches—strategic-rational analysis, bureaucratic politics, and domestic politics—can illuminate aspects of how the United States has engaged in the Arab-Israeli peace process,[4] the most important factor, as this book argues, is the view of the conflict—the definition of the situation—held by the president and his closest advisers, usually including the secretary of state. The president is more than just the first among equals in a bureaucratic struggle or in domestic political debates. And he is certainly not a purely rational, strategic thinker.

More than anything else, an analyst studying American policy toward the Arab-Israeli conflict should want to know how the president—and the few key individuals to whom he listens—makes sense of the many arguments, the mountain of "facts," the competing claims he hears whenever his attention turns to the Arab-Israeli conflict. To a large degree he must impose order where none seems to exist; he must make sense out of something he may hardly understand; he must simplify when complexity becomes overwhelming; and he must decide to authorize others to act in his name if he is not interested enough, or competent enough, to formulate the main lines of policy.

What, then, do the president and his top advisers rely on if not generalized views that they bring with them into office? No senior policymaker in American history has ever come to power with a well-developed understanding of the nuances of the Arab-Israeli dispute, the intricacies of its history, or even much knowledge of the protagonists. At best policymakers have general ideas, notions, inclinations, biases, predispositions, fragments of knowledge. To some extent "ideology" plays a part, although there has never really been a neat liberal versus conservative, Democrat versus Republican divide over the Arab-Israeli conflict. Only when it came to dealing with the Soviet Union as a power in the Middle East region—up until 1990—did the cold war ideological divide between conservatives and liberals seem to make a difference, and even then the evidence is not conclusive.

Any account of policymaking would, however, be incomplete if it did nothing more than map the initial predispositions of key decisionmakers. As important as these are in setting the broad policy guidelines for an administration, they are not enough. Policy is not static, set once and forever after unchanged. Nor is policy reassessed every day. But over time views do change, learning takes place, and policies are adjusted. As a result, a process of convergence seems to take place, whereby the views of senior policymakers toward the Arab-Israeli conflict differ most with those of their predecessors when they first take office, and tend to resemble them by the end of their terms. Ford and Carter disagreed on Middle East policy in 1976–77 but were later to coauthor articles on what should be done to resolve the Arab-Israeli conflict. Even Reagan in his later years seemed closer to his predecessor's outlook than to his own initial approach to Arab-Israeli diplomacy.

It is this process of adjustment, modification, and adaptation to the realities of the Middle East and to the realities of Washington that allows each administration to deal with uncertainty and change. Without this on-the-job learning, American foreign policy would be at best a rigid, brittle affair.

What triggers a change in attitudes? Is the process of learning incremental, or do changes occur suddenly because of crises or the failure of previous policies? When change takes place, are core values called into account, or are tactics merely revised? The evidence presented here suggests that change rarely affects deeply held views. Presidents and their advisers seem reluctant to abandon central beliefs. Basic positions are adhered to with remarkable tenacity, accounting for the stability in the stated positions of the United States on the issues in dispute in the Arab-Israeli conflict. They represent a deep consensus. But politicians and diplomats have no trouble making small adjustments in their understanding of the Arab-Israeli conflict, and that is often enough to produce a substantial change in policy, if not in basic positions or in overall strategy. One simple change in judgment—that President Anwar Sadat of Egypt should be taken seriously—was enough to lead to a major reassessment of American policy in the midst of the October 1973 war.

Since most of the American-led peace process has been geared toward procedures, not substance, the ability of top decisionmakers to experiment with various approaches as they learn more about the conflict has imparted an almost experimental quality to American foreign policy in the Middle East. Almost every conceivable tactic is eventually considered, some are tried, and some even work. And if one administration does not get it right, within a matter of years another team will be in place, willing to try other approaches. Although American foreign policy is sometimes maddening in its lack of consistency and short attention span, this ability to abandon failed policies and move on has often been the hallmark of success.

Foreign-policy making seems to involve an interplay among the initial predispositions of top policymakers, information about the specific issues being considered, the pull of bureaucratic groupings, the weight of domestic political considerations, the management of transitions from one presidency to the next, and the impact of events in the region of concern. It is often in the midst of crises that new policies are devised, that the shortcomings of one approach are clearly seen, and that a new definition of the situation is imposed. And it is in the midst of crises that presidential powers are at their greatest.

Only rarely are crises anticipated and new polices adopted to ward them off. As a result, American policy often seems to run on automatic pilot until jolted out of its inertial course by an event beyond its control. Critics who find this pattern alarming need to appreciate how complex it is to balance the competing perspectives that vie for support in the Oval Office and how difficult it is to set a course that seems well designed to protect the multiple interests of a global power like the United States—and to do all this without risking one's political life.

NATIONAL INTERESTS

To get a sense of the difficulty, consider the nature of American interests in the Middle East, as seen from the perspective of the White House. An assessment of these interests almost always takes place at the outset of a new administration, or just after a crisis, in the belief, usually unjustified, that light will be shed on what should be done to advance the prospects of Arab-Israeli peace at the least risk to American interests.

Politicians and some analysts like to invoke the national interest because it seems to encompass tangible, hard-headed concerns as opposed to sentimental, emotional considerations. There is something imposing about cloaking a decision in the garb of national security interests, as if no further debate were needed.

In the real world of policymaking, interests are indeed discussed, but most officials understand that any definition of a national interest contains a strong subjective element. Except for limited areas of foreign affairs, such as trade policy, alternative courses of action cannot readily be tested against an objective yardstick to determine how well they serve the national interest.

In discussions of the Arab-Israeli conflict, several distinct, often competing, national interests confound the problem of relating interests to policy. For example, most policymakers until about 1990 would have said that a major American interest in the Middle East, and therefore related to the handling of Arab-Israeli diplomacy, was the *containment of Soviet influence* in the region. This interest derived from a broader strategy of containment that had been initially developed for Europe but was gradually universalized during the cold war.

In Europe the strategy of containment had led to the Marshall Plan and the North Atlantic Treaty Organization (NATO). But the attempt to replicate these mechanisms of containment in the Middle East had failed, in part because of the unresolved Arab-Israeli conflict. So, however much American policymakers might worry about the growth of Soviet influence in the region, they rarely knew what should be done about it. In the brief period of a few months in 1956–57, the United States opposed the Israeli-French-British attack on Egypt (the Suez war), announced the Eisenhower Doctrine of support to anticommunist regimes in the area, forced the Israelis to withdraw from Sinai, and criticized Nasser's Egypt for its intervention in the affairs of other Arab countries. How all that contributed coherently to the agreed-upon goal of limiting Soviet influence was never quite clear.

Over the years many policies toward the Arab-Israeli conflict have been justified, at least in part, by this concern about the Soviet Union. Arms sales have been made and denied in pursuit of this interest; and the Soviets have been excluded from, and included in, discussions on the region, all as part of the goal of trying to manage Soviet influence in the region.

One might think that a strategy of challenging the Soviets in the region would have led the United States to adopt belligerent, interventionist policies, as it did in Southeast Asia. But in the Middle East the concern about overt Soviet military intervention was high, especially from the mid-1960s on, and therefore any American intervention, it was felt, might face a comparable move by the Soviets. Indeed, on several occasions, in the June 1967 war, in 1970 in Jordan, during the October 1973 war, and to a lesser degree in 1982 in Lebanon, the United States feared a possible military confrontation with the Soviet Union. Thus, however ardently American officials might want to check Soviet advances, they wanted to do so without much risk of direct military confrontation with Moscow. In brief, the Soviet angle was never far from the minds of policymakers, but it did little to help clarify choices. With the collapse of the Soviet

Union in 1990–91, this interest suddenly disappeared, leaving oil and Israel as the two main American concerns in the Middle East.

Oil has always been a major reason for the United States to pay special attention to the Middle East, but its connection to the Arab-Israeli conflict has not always been apparent. American companies were active in developing the oil resources of the area, especially in Saudi Arabia; the industrialized West was heavily dependent on Middle East oil; and American import needs began to grow from the early 1970s on.[5]

The basic facts about oil in the region were easy to understand. Saudi Arabia, Iraq, and Iran, along with the small states of the Persian Gulf littoral, sat atop about two-thirds of the known reserves of oil in the world. The least expensive place to produce oil was also the Middle East. Production costs were remarkably low. Thus Middle East stability seemed to go hand in hand with access to relatively inexpensive supplies of oil.

Throughout most of the 1950s and 1960s Middle East oil was readily available for the reconstruction of Europe and Japan. American companies made good profits. And threatened disruptions of supply had little effect. A conscious effort to keep Persian Gulf affairs separate from the Arab-Israeli conflict seemed to work quite well.

But by the late 1960s the British had decided to withdraw their military presence from east of Suez. How, if at all, would that affect the security of Gulf oil supplies? Should the United States try to fill the vacuum with forces of its own, or should it try to build up regional powers, such as Iran and Saudi Arabia? If arms were sold to Saudi Arabia to help ensure access to oil supplies, how would the Israelis and the other Arab countries react? What would the Soviets do? In short, how could an interest, which everyone agreed was important, be translated into concrete policies?

American calculations about oil were further complicated by the fact that the United States is both a large producer of oil and a large importer. For those concerned with enhancing domestic supplies, the low production costs of Middle East oil are always a potential threat. Texas oil producers argue for quotas to protect them from "cheap" foreign oil. But consumers want cheap oil and will therefore resist gasoline taxes, tariffs, or quotas designed to prop up the domestic oil industry. No American president would know how to answer the question of the proper price of Middle East oil. If forced to give an answer, he would have to mumble something like "not too high and not too low." In practice, the stability and predictability of oil supplies have been seen as more important than a specific price. This perception has reinforced the view that the main American interest is in reliable access to Middle East oil, and therefore in regional stability. Still, price cannot be ignored. In the early 1990s the annual import bill for oil from the Middle East exceeded $10 billion, out of a total oil import bill of $35 billion. Each one dollar increase in the price of oil added more than $1 billion to the oil import bill.

The other main interest that has dominated discussion of the Arab-Israeli conflict is the *special American commitment to Israel*. The United States had been an early and enthusiastic supporter of the idea of a Jewish state in part of Palestine. That support was clearly rooted in a sense of moral commitment to the survivors of the holocaust, as well as in the intense attachment of American Jews to Israel. During the 1980s a "strategic" rationale was added to the traditional list of reasons for supporting Israel, although this view was never universally accepted.

Support for Israel was always tempered by a desire to maintain some interests in surrounding Arab countries, because of either oil or competition with the Soviet Union. As a result, through most of the years from 1949 until the mid-1960s, the United States provided few arms and only modest amounts of aid. As Eisenhower demonstrated in 1956, support for Israel did not mean offering a blank check.

Even though each of these perceived interests was readily accepted as important by successive administrations—and there was little argument over the list—what the implications for policy were of any one, to say nothing of all three, of these interests was not clear. To take the most difficult case, what should be done when one set of interests seemed to be at variance with another? Which should get more weight, the economic interest of oil, or the strategic interest of checking Soviet advances, or the moral interest of supporting Israel?

Without a common yardstick, the interests were literally incommensurate. How could arms for the Saudis or Jordanians be squared with support for Israel? How could Soviet inroads in a country like Egypt be checked? Was it better to oppose Nasser to teach him a lesson about the costs of relying on the Soviets, or should an effort be made to win him away from dependence on Moscow? And what would either of these approaches mean for relations with Israel and Saudi Arabia?

In brief, U.S. national interests were clearly involved in the Middle East and would be affected by every step of the Arab-Israeli peace process. But there was almost no agreement on what these interests meant in terms of concrete policies. Advocates of different perspectives, as will be seen, were equally adept at invoking national interests to support their preferred courses of action. Often policy preferences seemed to come first, and then the interests were found to justify the policy. Precisely because of these dilemmas, policymaking could not be left to bureaucrats. The stakes were too high, the judgments too political. Thus Arab-Israeli policy, with remarkable frequency, landed in the lap of the president or his secretary of state. More than for most issues of foreign policy, presidential leadership became crucial to the Arab-Israeli peace process.

Insofar as presidents and their advisers saw a way to resolve the potential conflict among American interests in the Middle East, it was by promoting the Arab-Israeli peace process. This policy is the closest equivalent to that of containment toward the Soviet Union—a policy with broad bipartisan support that promises to protect a range of important American interests. If Arab-Israeli peace could be achieved, it was thought, Soviet influence in the region would decline, Israeli security would be enhanced, and American relations with key Arab countries would improve. Regional stability would therefore be more easily achieved, and oil supplies would be less threatened. Obviously, other sources of trouble would still exist in the region, but few disagreed on the desirability of Arab-Israeli peace, or the need for American leadership to achieve it. The differences, and they were many, came over the feasibility of a peace settlement and over the appropriate tactics. In making these judgments, presidents made their most important contribution to the formulation of policy.

PRESIDENTIAL LEADERSHIP AND POLICYMAKING

In U.S. politics, there is a strong presumption that who is president matters. Huge sums are spent on electoral campaigns to select the president. That office receives immense respect and deference, and most writers of American political history assume that the man occupying the White House can shape events. Does this perspective merely reflect an individualism rooted in American culture, or does it contain a profound truth?

One can easily imagine situations in which it would be meaningless to explain a policy by looking at the individuals responsible for making the decisions. If no real margin for choice exists, individuals do not count for much. Other factors take precedence. For example, to predict the voting behavior of senators from New York on aid to Israel, one normally need not consider their identity. It is enough to know something about the constituency, the overwhelming support for Israel among New Yorkers, and the lack of countervailing pressures to be virtually certain about the policy choice of an individual senator.

If context can account for behavior, so can the nature of perceived interests or objectives. If we were studying Japan's policies toward the Arab-Israeli conflict, we would not be especially concerned with who was prime minister at any given moment. It would make more sense to look at the dependence of Japan on Arab oil and the lack of any significant cultural or economic ties to Israel to predict that Japan will adopt a generally pro-Arab policy. When interests easily converge on a single policy, individual choice can be relegated to the background.

Finally, if a nation has no capability to act in foreign policy, we will not be particularly interested in the views of its leaders. To ask why a small European country does not assume a more active role in promoting an Arab-Israeli settlement does not require us to examine who is in charge of policy. Instead, the lack of significant means to affect the behavior of Arabs and Israelis is about all we need to know. A country without important economic, military, or diplomatic assets has virtually no choices to make in foreign policy. Obviously none of these conditions hold for the United States in its approach to the Arab-Israeli conflict. Capabilities for action do exist. The nature of American interests, as generally understood by policymakers, does not predetermine a single course of action. And despite the obvious constraints imposed by the structure of the international system and domestic politics, choices do exist on most issues, even though at times the margin of choice may be narrow.

CONFRONTING COMPLEXITY AND UNCERTAINTY

Most political leaders, with no noteworthy alteration in personality or psychodynamics, are likely at some point to change positions on policy issues. Often such changes will be portrayed as opportunism or waffling. But they could instead be a reaction to a complicated situation, suggesting that people can learn as new information is acquired. Particularly when dealing with complex events and ambiguous choices, people may shift their positions quite suddenly, without altering the fundamental aspects of their approaches to policy. As Raymond Bauer said, "Policy problems are sufficiently complex that for the vast majority of individuals or organizations it is conceivable—given the objective features of the situation—to imagine them ending up on any side of the issue."[6]

Policymakers often find it difficult to recognize the difference between a good proposal and a bad proposal. In normal circumstances, bargaining and compromise may be rational courses for a politician to follow, but to do so assumes that issues have been defined according to some understood criteria. When such criteria are not obvious, what should one do?

On most issues of importance, policymakers operate in an environment in which uncertainty and complexity are dominant. Addressing an unknowable future with imperfect information about the past and present, policymakers must use guidelines and simplifications drawn from their own experience, the "lessons of history," or the consensus of their colleagues. The result is often a cautious style of decisionmaking that strives merely to make incremental changes in existing policies.[7] At times, however, very sudden shifts in policy may also take place. How can one account for both these outcomes?

Leadership is only rarely the task of selecting between good and bad policies. Instead, the anguish and challenge of leadership is to choose between equally plausible arguments about how best to achieve one's goals. For example, most presidents and their advisers have placed a very high value on achieving peace in the Middle East. But values do not easily translate into policy. Instead, several reasonable alternatives are likely to compete for presidential attention, such as the following:

—If Israel is to feel secure enough to make the territorial concessions necessary to gain Arab acceptance of the terms of a peace agreement, it must continue to receive large quantities of American military and economic aid.

—If Israel feels too strong and self-confident, it will not see the need for any change in the status quo. U.S. aid must therefore be used as a form of pressure.

Presidents Nixon, Ford, Carter, and Bush subscribed to both the foregoing views at different times.

Similarly, consider the following propositions, which were widely entertained by U.S. presidents until the breakup of the USSR:

—The Soviet Union has no interest in peace in the Middle East, because it would lose influence unless it could exploit tensions in the area. Hence the United States cannot expect cooperation from the Soviet Union in the search for a settlement.

—The Soviets, like ourselves, have mixed interests in the Middle East. They fear a confrontation and are therefore prepared to reach a settlement, provided they are allowed to participate in the diplomatic process. By leaving the Soviet Union out, the United States provides it with an incentive to sabotage the peacemaking effort. Therefore, U.S.-Soviet agreement will be essential to reaching peace in the Middle East.

Concerning the Arabs, one may also hear diverse opinions:

—Only when the Arabs have regained their self-respect and feel strong will they be prepared to make peace with Israel.

—When the Arabs feel that time is on their side, they increase their demands and become more extreme. Only a decisive military defeat will convince them that Israel is here to stay and that they must use political means to regain their territory.

Each of these propositions has been seriously entertained by recent American presidents and secretaries of state. One could almost say that all of them have been believed at various times by some individuals. The key element in selecting among these plausible interpretations of reality is not merely whether one is pro-Israeli or pro-Arab, or hard line or not so hard line on relations with Moscow. A more complex process is at work.

LESSONS OF HISTORY

In choosing among plausible, but imperfectly understood, courses of action, policymakers inevitably resort to simplifications. Guidelines emerge from recent experiences, historical analogies, wishful thinking, and group consensus.[8] Categorical inferences are thus made; confusing events are placed in comprehensible structures; reality is given a definition that allows purposive action to take place. Recent experience is a particularly potent source of guidance for the future. If a policy has worked in one setting, policymakers will want to try it in another context as well. Secretary of State Henry A. Kissinger, for example, apparently relied on his experiences in negotiating with the Chinese, Russians, and Vietnamese when he approached negotiations with the Arabs and Israelis in 1974–75. Step-by-step diplomacy was the result.

More general historical "lessons" may loom large in the thinking of policymakers as they confront new problems.[9] President Harry Truman was especially inclined to invoke historical analogies. He well understood that the essence of presidential leadership was the ability to make decisions in the face of uncertainty and to live with their consequences. By relying on history, he was able to reassure himself that his decisions were well founded.[10]

Several historical analogies have been notably effective in structuring

American views of reality. The lessons of Munich, for example, have been pointed to repeatedly over the years, principally that the appeasement of dictators serves only to whet their appetite for further conquest. Hence a firm, resolute opposition to aggression is required. The "domino theory" is a direct descendant of this perspective, as was the policy of containment.

A second set of guidelines for policy stems from President Woodrow Wilson's fourteen points after World War I, especially the emphasis on self-determination and opposition to spheres of influence. As embodied in the Atlantic Charter in 1941, these principles strongly influenced American policy during the Second World War.[11] Since the failure of U.S. policy in Southeast Asia, new "lessons" have been drawn, which warn against overinvolvement, commitments in marginal areas, excessive reliance on force, and risks of playing the role of world policeman. Whether these will prove as durable as the examples of Munich and Wilsonian idealism remains to be seen, but American policy continues to be discussed in terms of these historical analyses.

When recent experience and historical analogies fail to resolve dilemmas of choice, certain psychological mechanisms may come to the rescue. Wishful thinking is a particularly potent way to resolve uncertainty. When in doubt, choose the course that seems least painful, that fits best with one's hopes and expectations; perhaps it will turn out all right after all. In any event, one can almost always rationalize a choice after making it. Good reasons can be found even for bad policies, and often the ability to come up with a convincing rationale will help to overcome uncertainties.

Apart from such well-known but poorly understood aspects of individual psychology, the social dynamics of a situation often help to resolve uncertainty. If through discussion a group can reach consensus on the proper course of action, individuals are likely to suppress their private doubts. Above all, when a president participates in a group decision, a strong tendency toward consensus is likely. As some scholars have emphasized, presidents must go to considerable lengths to protect themselves from the stultifying effects of group conformity in their presence and the tendency to suppress divergent views.[12] Neither President Johnson's practice of inviting a large number of advisers to consult with him nor President Nixon's effort to use the National Security Council to channel alternatives to him are guarantees against the distortions of group consensus, in part because presidents value consensus as a way to resolve doubts.

At any given moment presidents and their key advisers tend to share fairly similar and stable definitions of reality. However such definitions emerge, whether through reference to experience or to history, through wishful thinking and rationalization, or through group consensus, they will provide guidelines for action in the face of uncertainty. Complexity will be simplified by reference to a few key criteria. In the Arab-Israeli setting, these will usually have to do with the saliency of issues, their amenability to solution, the role of the Soviet Union (up until late 1990), and the value of economic and military assistance to various parties.

CRISES AND THE REDEFINING OF ISSUES

Crises play an extremely important role in the development of these guidelines. By definition, crises involve surprise, threat, and increased uncertainty. Previous policies may well be exposed as flawed or bankrupt. Reality no longer accords with previous expectations. In such a situation a new structure of perceptions is likely to emerge, one that will reflect presidential perspectives to the degree the president becomes involved in handling the crisis. If the crisis is satisfactorily resolved, a new and often quite durable set of assumptions will guide policy for some time.

Often crises can produce significant policy changes without causing a sweeping reassessment of a decisionmaker's views. It may be only a greater sense of urgency that brings into play a new policy. Or it may be a slight shift in assumptions about the Soviet role, for example, or the advantages of pursuing a more conciliatory policy toward Egypt. Small adjustments in a person's perceptions, in the weight accorded to one issue as opposed to another, can lead to substantial shifts of emphasis, of nuance, and therefore of action. Again, policymakers do not change from being pro-Israeli to pro-Arab overnight, but crises may bring into focus new relations among issues or raise the importance of one interest, thus leading to changes in policy. Basic values will remain intact, but perceptions and understanding of relationships may quickly change.

In the case studies that follow, I explore the important role of crises in defining issues for presidents and their advisers. And I try to account for their views, to understand their reasoning, and to see situations from their standpoint. Between crises, as is noted, it is difficult to bring about changes in policies forged in the midst of crisis and having the stamp of presidential approval.

This approach shortchanges the role of Congress, public opinion, interest groups, the media, and the bureaucracy. All these are worthy subjects of study and undoubtedly have influenced American diplomacy toward the Arab-Israeli conflict. Nor do I discuss in this book why Arabs and Israelis took the decisions that they did. Only in passing do I deal with the protagonists in the conflict, describing their views but not subjecting them to the kind of analysis reserved for American policy.

Starting, then, with the key role of the president and his advisers in shaping policy, particularly in moments of crisis, when domestic and organizational constraints are least confining, the book examines how politics and bureaucratic habits affect both the formulation and implementation of policies in normal times. But at the center of the study are those rare moments when policymakers try to make sense out of the confusing flow of events, when they strive to relate action to purposes, for it is then that the promises and limitations of leadership are most apparent.

PART ONE

The Johnson Presidency

CHAPTER TWO

Yellow Light: Johnson and the Crisis of May–June 1967

Lyndon Baines Johnson brought to the presidency a remarkable array of political talents. An activist and a man of strong passions, Johnson seemed to enjoy exerting his power. As majority leader in the Senate, he had used the art of persuasion as few other leaders had; building consensus through artfully constructed compromises had been one of his strong suits. His political experience did not, however, extend to foreign-policy making, an area that demanded his attention, especially as American involvement in Vietnam grew in late 1964 and early 1965.

Fortunately for the new president, one part of the world that seemed comparatively quiet in the early 1960s was the Middle East. Long-standing disputes still simmered, but compared with the turbulent 1950s the situation appeared to be manageable. The U.S.-Israeli relationship had been strengthened by President Kennedy, and Johnson obviously was prepared to continue on this line, particularly with increases in military assistance. His personal sentiments toward Israel were warm and admiring. To all appearances he genuinely liked the Israelis he had dealt with, many of his closest advisers were well-known friends of Israel, and his own contacts with the American Jewish community had been close throughout his political career.[1]

Johnson's demonstrated fondness for Israel did not mean he was particularly hostile to Arabs, but it is fair to say that Johnson showed little sympathy for the radical brand of Arab nationalism expounded by Egypt's president Gamal Abdel Nasser. And he was sensitive to signs that the Soviet Union was exploiting Arab nationalism to weaken the influence of the West in the Middle East. Like other American policymakers before him, Johnson seemed to waver between a desire to try to come to terms with Nasser and a belief that Nasser's prestige and regional ambitions had to be trimmed. More important for policy than these predispositions, however, was the fact that Johnson, overwhelmingly preoccupied by Vietnam, treated Middle East issues as deserving only secondary priority.

U.S.-Egyptian relations had deteriorated steadily between 1964 and early 1967, in part because of the conflict in Yemen, in part because of quarrels over aid. By 1967, with Vietnam becoming a divisive domestic issue for Johnson, problems of the Middle East were left largely to the State Department. There the anxiety about increased tension between Israel and the surrounding Arab states was growing after the Israeli raid on the Jordanian town of Al-Samu' in November 1966 and especially after an April 1967 Israeli-Syrian air battle that resulted in the downing of six Syrian MiGs. Under Secretary of State Eugene Rostow was particularly concerned about the drift of events, suspecting as he did that the Soviets were seeking to take advantage in the Middle East of Washington's preoccupation with Vietnam.[2]

One indication of this mounting concern can be found in a report filed by the American ambassador in Cairo, Lucius Battle, after his last meeting with Nasser before returning to Washington to become the assistant secretary of state for Near Eastern affairs in the spring of 1967. He warned that Nasser was looking for some foreign-policy adventure to divert attention from his internal difficulties. Battle predicted that this would come in the form of heating up the Yemen crisis, trying to subvert the pro-Western regime in Libya, or, least likely, trying to heat up the Arab-Israeli conflict.[3] So great was the concern with the situation in Yemen that the National Security Council planned to hold a session on that crisis in late May. (As events unfolded, the meeting was held as scheduled on May 24, but by then the focus was on the mounting tension between Egypt and Israel.)

If the tensions on the Syrian-Israeli border provided the fuel for the early stages of the 1967 crisis, the spark that ignited the fuel came in the form of erroneous Soviet reports to Egypt on May 13 that Israel had mobilized some ten to thirteen brigades on the Syrian border. Against the backdrop of Israeli threats to take action to stop the guerrilla raids from Syria,[4] this disinformation apparently helped to convince Nasser the time had come for Egypt to take some action to deter any Israeli moves against Syria and to restore his own somewhat tarnished image in the Arab world.[5] The Soviets, he seemed to calculate, would provide firm backing for his position.

On May 14 Nasser made the first of his fateful moves. Egyptian troops were ostentatiously sent into Sinai, posing an unmistakable challenge to Israel, if not yet a serious military threat. President Johnson and his key advisers were quick to sense the danger in the new situation. Because of his well-known sympathy for Israel and his forceful personality, Johnson might have been expected to take a strong and unambiguous stand in support of Israel at the outset of the crisis, especially as such a stand might have helped to prevent Arab miscalculations. Moreover, reassurances to Israel would lessen the pressure on Prime Minister Levi Eshkol to resort to preemptive military action. Finally, a strong stand in the Middle East would signal the Soviet Union that it could not exploit tensions there without confronting the United States.

The reality of U. S. policy as the Middle East crisis unfolded in May was, however, quite different. American behavior was cautious, at times ambiguous, and ultimately unable to prevent a war that was clearly in the offing. Why was that the case? This is the central puzzle to solve in examining Johnson's reaction to the events leading up to the June 1967 war. Also, one must ask how hard Johnson really tried to restrain Israel. Some have alleged that, in fact, Johnson gave Israel a green light to attack, or in some way colluded with Israel to draw Nasser into a trap.[6] These charges need to be carefully assessed. And what role did domestic political considerations play in Johnson's thinking? Did the many pro-Israeli figures in Johnson's entourage influence his views? Finally, what is one to make of the specific allegations from anonymous sources that the United States sent a military team to Israel on the eve of the war which carried out reconnaissance missions on the Egyptian front after hostilities had begun?[7]

INITIAL REACTIONS TO THE CRISIS

Nasser's initial moves were interpreted in Washington primarily in political terms. Under attack by the conservative monarchies of Jordan and Saudi Arabia for being soft on Israel, Nasser was seen as attempting to regain prestige by appearing as the defender of the embattled and threatened radical regime in Syria. Middle East watchers in the State Department thought they recognized a familiar pattern. In February 1960 Nasser had sent troops into Sinai, postured for a while, claimed victory by deterring alleged Israeli aggressive designs, and then backed down.[8] All in all, a rather cheap victory, and not one that presented much of a danger to anyone. Consequently the initial American reaction to Nasser's dispatch of troops was restrained. Even the Israelis did not seem to be particularly alarmed.

On May 16, however, the crisis took on a more serious aspect as the Egyptians made their initial request for the removal of the United Nations

Emergency Force (UNEF).[9] This prompted President Johnson to sound out the Israelis about their intentions and to consult with the British and French. On May 17 Johnson sent Eshkol the first of several letters exchanged during the crisis in which he urged restraint and specifically asked to be informed before Israel took any action. "I am sure you will understand that I cannot accept any responsibilities on behalf of the United States for situations which arise as the result of actions on which we are not consulted."[10]

From the outset, then, Johnson seemed to want to avoid war, to restrain the Israelis, and to gain allied support for any action that might be taken. Two possible alternative courses of action seem not to have been seriously considered at this point. One might have been to stand aside and let the Israelis act as they saw fit, even to the extent of going to war.[11] The danger, of course, was that Israel might get into trouble and turn to the United States for help. Johnson seemed to fear this possibility throughout the crisis, despite all the intelligence predictions that Israel would easily win a war against Egypt alone or against all the surrounding Arab countries.

The second alternative not considered at this point was bold unilateral American action opposing Nasser's effort to change the status quo. Here the problems were twofold. A quarrel with Egypt might inflame the situation and weaken American influence throughout the Arab world. The Suez precedent, and what it had done to British and French positions in the region, was very much in the minds of key American officials. Nasser was not noted for backing down when challenged. Moreover, U.S. military assets were deeply committed in Vietnam, so that a full-scale military confrontation with Egypt was ruled out. But even if American forces had been available, Congress was in no mood to countenance unilateral military action, even in support of Israel. Therefore, the initial United States effort was directed toward restraining Israel and building a multilateral context for any American action, whether diplomatic or military.

Eshkol's reply to Johnson's letter reached Washington the following day, May 18. The Israeli prime minister blamed Syria for the increase in tension and stated that Egypt must remove its troops from Sinai. Then, appealing directly to Johnson, Eshkol requested that the United States reaffirm its commitment to Israeli security and inform the Soviet Union in particular of this commitment. Johnson wrote to Premier Aleksei Kosygin the following day, affirming the American position of support for Israel as requested, but suggesting in addition a "joint initiative of the two powers to prevent the dispute between Israel and the UAR [United Arab Republic, or Egypt] and Syria from drifting into war."[12]

After Egypt's initial request for the withdrawal of the UNEF on May 16, there was danger that Nasser might overplay his hand by also closing the Strait of Tiran to the Israelis. The opening of the strait to Israeli shipping was the one tangible gain made by Israel in the 1956 war. American commitments concerning the international status of the strait were explicit. It was seen as an international waterway, open for the free passage of ships of all nations, including Israel. The Israelis had been promised that they could count on U.S. support to keep the strait open. According to a February 11, 1957, aide-memoire presented to Israel, the United States undertook to "exercise the right of free and innocent passage [in the Strait of Tiran] and to join with others to secure general recognition of this right." In subsequent clarifications of the American position, Secretary of State John Foster Dulles recognized Israel's right, under article 51 of the United Nations Charter, to use force to open the strait if it was ever closed to Israeli ships by force.[13]

The UNEF had stationed troops at Sharm al-Shaykh since 1957, and shipping had not been impeded. If the UNEF withdrew, however, Nasser would be under great pressure to return the situation to its pre-1956 status. Israel had long declared that such action would be considered a casus belli.

In light of these dangers, one might have expected some action by the United States after May 16 aimed at preventing the complete removal of the UNEF. But the record shows no sign of an urgent approach to UN Secretary General U Thant on this matter, and by the evening of May 18 U Thant had responded positively to the formal Egyptian government request that all UNEF troops leave Egyptian territory.

The strait still remained open, however, and a strong warning by Israel or the United States about the consequences of its closure might conceivably have influenced Nasser's next move. From May 19 until midday on May 22, Nasser took no action to close the strait, nor did he make any threat to do so. Presumably he was waiting to see how Israel and the United States, among others, would react to the UNEF's withdrawal. The United States made no direct approach to Nasser until May 22, the day Nasser finally announced the closure of the strait. It issued no public statements reaffirming the American view that the strait was an international waterway, nor did the reputedly pro-Israeli president respond to Eshkol's request for a public declaration of America's commitment to Israel's security.

Some Israelis had feared that Nasser might view the cautious U.S. stand in this initial period as an invitation to interfere with free passage in the strait.[14] At that point, however, the Israeli position itself was not particularly strong, as Eshkol's May 22 speech showed, and made a restrained American position easier to justify. Instead of spelling out its position on the UNEF and the threatened closure of the Strait of Tiran during the period between May 16 and May 22, the United States continued to warn Israel not to act unilaterally. A preference for working within a UN framework was conveyed to the Israelis, including a suggestion that the UNEF troops might be moved to the Israeli side of the armistice lines.[15]

The day before Nasser's May 22 speech at Bir Gifgafa announcing the closure of the strait to Israeli shipping, Johnson sent a second letter to Eshkol reassuring him that the Soviet Union understood the U.S. commitment to Israel. At the same time, however, Johnson sought to explain why he could not make a public statement on the consequences of a blockade of the Gulf of Aqaba. In particular, he noted that any statement by him on the strait might complicate the mission of U Thant, who was on his way to Cairo. Johnson did, however, refer to the need for suitable measures inside or outside the UN to deal with the crisis.[16] Israeli Foreign Minister Abba Eban felt that this letter did not reflect Johnson's real views and must have been drafted by a "frightened bureaucrat."[17]

On May 22 Johnson finally sent a letter to the Egyptian leader. The thrust of the message was to assure Nasser of the friendship of the United States while urging him to avoid any step that might lead to war. In addition, Johnson offered to send Vice President Hubert Humphrey to Cairo. Johnson ended the letter with words he had personally added: "I look forward to our working out a program that will be acceptable and constructive for our respective peoples." The message was not delivered by ambassador-designate Richard Nolte until the following day, by which time the strait had already been declared closed to Israeli shipping and strategic cargoes bound for Israel.[18]

Johnson informed Eshkol the same day that he was writing to the Egyptian and Syrian leaders warning them not to take actions that might lead to hostilities.[19] In addition, another message from Johnson to Kosygin was also sent on May 22. Reiterating his suggestion of joint action to calm the situation, Johnson went on to state, "The increasing harassment of Israel by elements based in Syria, with attendant reactions within Israel and within the Arab world, has brought the area close to major violence. Your and our ties to nations of the area could bring us into difficulties which I am confident neither of us seeks. It would appear a time for each of us to use our influence to the full in the course of moderation, including our influence over action by the United Nations."[20]

These messages, which might have helped to calm the situation earlier, were rendered meaningless by the next major escalation of the crisis.[21] The well-intentioned American initiative of May 21–22 was too little and too late. Shortly after midnight May 22–23, Nasser's speech announcing the closure of the strait was broadcast.

THE CRISIS OVER THE STRAIT

If Johnson had feared that Israel might resort to force unilaterally before May 23, the danger now became acutely real. Therefore he requested that Israel not make any military move for at least forty-eight hours.[22] During the day of May 23 arrangements were made for Foreign Minister Eban to visit Washington for talks prior to any unilateral action. Johnson also decided to accede to an Israeli request for military assistance worth about $70 million, but he rejected an Israeli request for a U.S. destroyer to visit the port of Eilat.[23]

American diplomacy went into high gear. Johnson issued a forceful public statement to the effect that "the United States considers the gulf to be an international waterway and feels that a blockade of Israeli shipping is illegal and potentially disastrous to the cause of peace. The right of free, innocent passage of the international waterway is a vital interest of the international community."[24]

In Tel Aviv, U.S. Ambassador Walworth Barbour repeated the request for a forty-eight-hour delay before any unilateral Israeli action and raised the possibility of pursuing a British idea of a multinational naval force to protect maritime rights in the event that UN action failed to resolve the crisis. Eban's trip to Washington was designed in part to explore the feasibility of this idea.

In Washington, Israeli Ambassador Avraham Harman and Minister Ephraim Evron met with Under Secretary Eugene Rostow and were told that "the United States had decided in favor of an appeal to the Security Council. . . . The object is to call for restoring the status quo as it was before . . . the blockade announcement. Rostow explained that the congressional reaction compels a president to take this course."[25] Rostow reportedly referred to the realities created by the Vietnam War in describing Johnson's approach to the blockade.

As U.S. policy began to move toward consideration of multilateral action to break the blockade of the Gulf of Aqaba, Johnson understandably was concerned about Congress. On May 23 Secretary Rusk briefed the members of the Senate Foreign Relations Committee and reported back to Johnson that Congress would support Israel but was opposed to unilateral U.S. action.[26] In an effort to build public support for the administration, the president contacted former president Eisenhower, who confirmed that in 1957 the United States had recognized that if force was used to close the strait, Israel would be within its rights under article 51 of the UN Charter to respond with force.[27] George Meany, president of the AFL-CIO, was also asked to issue a statement in support of administration policy.

The basic elements of Johnson's approach to the crisis as of May 23 were the following:

—Try to prevent war by restraining Israel and warning the Egyptians and Soviets.

—Build public and congressional support for the idea of an international effort to reopen the Strait of Tiran. (Unilateral U.S. action was ruled out without much consideration.)

—Make an effort through the UN Security Council to open the strait. If that fails, as is anticipated, a multilateral declaration in support of free shipping will be drawn up. This will be followed, as the British suggested, by a multinational naval force transiting the strait.

Noteworthy was the continuing reluctance either to consider unilateral American action or to "unleash Israel," as a second option came to be known. These alternatives had been ruled out virtually from the beginning, and even the closure of the strait did not lead to a reevaluation of the initial policy. Instead, the two key elements of policy dating from May 17 were merely embellished as conditions changed.

A complex multilateral plan was designed that would surely be supported by Congress and public opinion, but could it produce results rapidly enough to ensure the other element in the U.S. approach—restraint of Israel? A dilemma clearly existed. To keep Israel from acting on its own, as even the United States acknowledged it had a right to do in order to reopen the strait, an acceptable alternative had to be presented.

The stronger the stand of the United States and the firmer its commitment to action, the more likely it was that Israel could be restrained; by the same token, the less likely it was that Nasser would probe further. Yet a strong American stand was incompatible with the desire for multilateral action, which had to be tried, in Johnson's view, to ensure congressional and public support. Such support was essential at a time of controversy over the U.S. role in Vietnam.

Johnson was mindful of the furor over his handling of the Gulf of Tonkin incident in 1964. Then he had seized on a small incident to broaden his power, with full congressional approval, to act in Vietnam. Subsequently, however, he had been charged with duplicity, with misleading Congress concerning the event, and with abusing the authority he had received. In mid-1967 Johnson was not about to lead the United States into another venture that might entail the use of force unless he had full congressional and public backing. Consequently he insisted on trying the United Nations first, and only then seeking a multilateral maritime declaration and sending ships through the strait. By moving slowly, cautiously, and with full support at home, Johnson would minimize the domestic political risks to his position.

The goals of restraining Israel and pursuing a multilateral solution were not necessarily incompatible, if sufficient time was available. For time to be available, perhaps as much as two to three weeks, the situation on the ground could not be allowed to change radically, nor could the balance of forces within Israel shift toward those who favored war. At a minimum, then, Nasser had to sit tight, the Soviet Union had to remain on the sidelines, and Eshkol had to be given something with which to restrain his hawks. If any of these conditions could not be met, the assumptions of U.S. policy would be undermined and war would probably ensue.

At the National Security Council meeting held on May 24, Rusk reviewed the broad strategy that had been decided upon. He noted that the Senate was unanimous in believing the United States should work through the UN and multilaterally. "The President then said he would like to hear views on what we do if all these other measures fail. We should play out the UN and other multilateral efforts until they are exhausted. 'I want to play every card in the UN, but I've never relied on it to save me when I'm going down for the third time. I want to see Wilson and De Gaulle out there with their ships all lined up too.' But all of these things have a way of falling apart. He mentioned, for instance, early congressional support for his actions in Vietnam. Therefore, we have to figure out what we can do if all these other courses fail." [28]

EBAN'S VISIT TO WASHINGTON

The impending visit of Israel's foreign minister served as a catalyst for the further definition of an American plan of action for dealing with the closure of the Strait of Tiran. If Israel was to refrain from forceful action, it needed to be given a credible alternative to war. But the process of moving from general principles—restrain Israel, act within a multilateral context—to a more detailed proposal revealed inherent contradictions and ambiguities, as well as bureaucratically rooted differences of opinion. What had initially been a fairly widespread consensus among Johnson's top advisers on how to deal with the crisis began to fragment as the crisis grew more acute. When Johnson felt most in need of broad support for his cautious, restrained approach, the viability of that position came under question.

The key to Johnson's policy on the eve of Eban's visit was the British idea of a multinational naval force. On May 24 Eugene Rostow met with the British minister of state for foreign affairs, George Thomson, and an admiral of the Royal Navy to discuss the British proposal. They agreed to try for a public declaration on freedom of shipping through the Strait of Tiran, to be signed by as many countries as possible. A multinational naval force would then be set up, composed of ships from as many maritime countries as were prepared to act, and a flotilla, soon to be known as the Red Sea Regatta, would then pass through the strait. [29] Rostow talked to Johnson later in the day about the plan and found the president receptive toward it.

Johnson was scheduled to make a trip to Canada on May 25, and he used the occasion to seek Prime Minister Lester Pearson's support for the multinational-fleet idea. [30] Meanwhile the Pentagon was charged with coming up with a concrete plan for forming a naval force. At this point, consensus began to erode. [31] Although some Pentagon analysts reported that the United States was capable of managing a crisis involving possible military intervention in the Middle East as well as Vietnam, most believed that Israel could deal with the Arab threat perfectly well on its own and that there was no need for a costly American commitment of forces. In any event, it would take time to get the necessary forces in place to challenge Nasser's blockade. At one point in the crisis, for example, the chairman of the Joint Chiefs stated that antisubmarine capabilities would be required and that two weeks would be needed to bring the appropriate ships to the area.[32]

The idea of a token display of U.S. force to reopen the strait did not have many fans in the Pentagon. What would happen if the Egyptians fired on an American ship? Would the United States respond with force? Would Egyptian airfields be attacked? Would ground troops be required? If so, how many? If the Egyptians held their fire, but did not back down, the U.S. Navy might find itself in the awkward position of having to patrol the strait indefinitely, under the guns of the Egyptians. Nothing would be solved politically, and the United States would simply find itself stuck with another commitment that diverted forces from other essential theaters. Furthermore, what could the Navy do about the growing numbers of Egyptian ground troops deployed along Israel's borders?

On balance, the military was not in favor of the use of U.S. force. Bureaucratic self-interest and a professional attitude that dictated the use of force only when success was assured and when superior power was available lay at the root of the opposition. The multinational fleet was a military man's nightmare. It was not the way the military would plan such an operation. It was too political. Deeming it undesirable, the military did little to make it feasible. Almost imperceptibly, Johnson was being deprived of his principal policy instrument because of the Pentagon's skepticism.

The State Department, at least at the top levels, was, by contrast, enthusiastic about the idea. Secretary Rusk endorsed it, and Under Secretary Rostow became its chief advocate. From their point of view, the fact that it was a flawed military concept was less important than its politically attractive features. First, it would associate other nations with the United States in defense of an important principle—freedom of navigation—and in the upholding of a commitment to Israel. Second, it would deflate Nasser's prestige, which was once again on the rise, without putting him into an impossible position. If Nasser wanted to back down from confrontation with Israel, the fleet would provide him with an honorable excuse to do so. The State Department therefore set out to find cosigners of the maritime declaration and donors of ships for the fleet. This essentially political task was what State was best at performing; the planning of the fleet was the province of Defense. Unfortunately, little coordination went on between the two.

Foreign Minister Eban arrived in Washington on the afternoon of May 25. His first talks were held at the State Department at 5:00 p.m. The result was to sow confusion among U.S. policymakers, who had just adjusted to the crisis and thought they saw a way out of it. Eban, who had left Israel with instructions to discuss American plans to reopen the Strait of Tiran, arrived in the United States to find new instructions awaiting him.[33] No longer was he to emphasize the issue of the strait. A more urgent danger, that of imminent Egyptian attack, had overshadowed the blockade. Eban was instructed to inform the highest authorities of this new threat to peace and to request an official statement from the United States that an attack on Israel would be viewed as an attack on the United States.[34] Despite his own skepticism, Eban followed his instructions in his first meeting with Secretary Rusk, Under Secretary Rostow, and Assistant Secretary Battle.

Rusk quickly ended the meeting so that he could confer with Johnson about the new situation. The meeting with Eban resumed at 6:00 p.m. for a working dinner, at which Eugene Rostow, Lucius Battle, Joseph Sisco (assistant secretary for international affairs), and Leonard Meeker (legal adviser) were present among the American group. The Israelis were told that U.S. sources could not confirm an Egyptian plan to attack. Nonetheless, the Egyptians would be warned against the use of force, and Moscow would be asked to make a parallel demarche. Discussion then shifted to the British proposal, including the declaration of maritime powers, its endorsement by the United Nations, and the multinational fleet. Israel was once again warned not to preempt.[35] The opinion was put forward on the American side that Egypt would not resist the fleet when the time came. But first the declaration of maritime powers must be issued and the debate in the UN proceed; only then could the ships move. American public opinion, it was stressed, must be convinced that all avenues had been explored before using force.

The conversation must have had an unreal quality about it, the Israelis being preoccupied with reports of imminent Egyptian attack and the Americans talking about declarations, the United Nations, Congress, and hypothetical naval forces.[36] After the talks ended, Israeli Ambassador Harman returned to the State Department at about midnight to reemphasize Israel's need for a concrete and precise statement of U.S. intentions.[37] He also warned that Israel could not accept any plan in which the strait might be opened to all ships except those of Israel.

American intelligence experts spent the night of May 25–26 analyzing the Israeli claim that an Egyptian attack was imminent. Several specific items had been presented by the Israelis in making their case, and by the morning of May 26 the intelligence community had analyzed each of these charges and concluded that an attack was not pending.[38] The Israelis suffered a loss of credibility at an important moment, and Johnson seems to have become suspicious that he was being pressured to make commitments that he either could not make, such as a statement that he would view an attack on Israel as an attack on the United States, or did not want to make yet, such as a precise plan on the multinational fleet. According to those who worked with him during this period, Johnson did not want to be crowded, he disliked ultimatums and deadlines, and he resented the mounting pressure on him to adopt Israel's definition of the situation. After all, as president he had to worry about the Soviet Union, about Congress and public opinion, and even about U.S.-Arab relations; he did not want to be stampeded, to use the imagery of his native Texas.[39]

Johnson was obviously reluctant to see Eban on Friday, May 26. He knew it would be an important, perhaps crucial meeting. The Israeli cabinet was to meet on Sunday, and what he told Eban might make the difference between war and peace. The Israelis were pressing for a specific commitment, for a detailed plan, for promises to act, and for understanding in the event Israel took matters into its own hands. Faced with these pressures, Johnson tried to stall. Rusk called Harman early in the morning to find out whether Eban could stay in Washington through Saturday. This would allow Johnson to learn the results of U Thant's mission to Cairo. Eban, stressing the importance of the Sunday cabinet meeting, said he had to leave Friday evening for Israel.[40]

During the morning of Friday, May 26, Eban went to the Pentagon, where he met with Secretary of Defense Robert McNamara, Chairman of the Joint Chiefs Earle Wheeler, and CIA Director Richard Helms. There he was given the results of the intelligence review of the previous night.[41] No evidence could be found that Egypt was planning to attack. Moreover, Eban was told, both the CIA and the Pentagon were convinced that Israel would easily win if hostilities were to begin, no matter who struck first. The fighting would not last a week. This assumption was probably more reassuring to the American military, which did not want to be called on to intervene, than it was to the Israelis.[42]

Meanwhile Secretary Rusk and Under Secretary Eugene Rostow had prepared a policy memorandum for the president. A meeting was

scheduled for noon to discuss it and to plan for the Eban meeting. Walt
Rostow called Evron during the morning to request a delay in Eban's
meeting with the president, claiming that Johnson was busy studying the
1957 documents on the American commitment concerning the strait.[43]

Rusk's memo to the president began with a review of his talk with
Eban the previous evening, including the Israeli information that an
Egyptian and Syrian attack was imminent and the request for a public
statement of American support for Israel against such aggression. Eban,
it was stated, would not press this point with Johnson, and the president's
talk could concentrate on the British proposal. Rusk then outlined two
basic options:

—"to let the Israelis decide how best to protect their own national
interests, in the light of the advice we have given them: i.e., to 'unleash'
them"; or

—"to take a positive position, but not a final commitment, on the
British proposal."

Rusk recommended strongly against the first option. Noting that the
British cabinet would meet on the multinational-fleet plan the following
day, Rusk endorsed the second option, which he then reviewed in some
detail. Included in his outline was the idea that a UN force should take
a position along both sides of the Israeli-Egyptian frontier. If Egypt
refused, Israel might accept.

Eban's need for a strong commitment from Johnson was made clear
in the Rusk memorandum. Congressional views were reviewed, and the
option of unilateral U.S. action was referred to with caution. A draft
joint resolution of the Congress was being prepared to support international
action on the strait. In closing, Rusk referred to the possibility of offering
Israel economic and military aid to help offset the strains of continuing
mobilization.[44]

On May 26, shortly after noon, President Johnson convened at the
White House the most important full-scale meeting of his advisers held
during the crisis. Present were Vice President Humphrey, Secretary
Rusk, Secretary McNamara, National Security Adviser Walt Rostow,
Under Secretary Eugene Rostow, Chairman of the Joint Chiefs of Staff
Wheeler, CIA Director Helms, Deputy Secretary of Defense Cyrus
Vance, Assistant Secretary Battle, Assistant Secretary Sisco, press secre-
tary George Christian, and unofficial advisers Supreme Court Justice Abe
Fortas, George Ball, and Clark Clifford. Wheeler began with a military
briefing, which included the evidence available on each side's force

postures. He expressed the judgment that Israel could stay at its present level of mobilization for two months without serious trouble. In a military sense, then, time did not seem to be running out. Rusk followed with a review of the diplomatic situation, especially his talks the previous night with Eban. Rusk told the group that he had cautioned Israel not to launch a preemptive strike. McNamara then spoke of his morning session with Eban in which the Israeli foreign minister had raised the issue of United States commitments made in 1957 as part of the negotiations that resulted in Israel's withdrawal from Sinai. These consisted of the aide-memoire of February 11, 1957, signed by Secretary Dulles, which stated that the United States considered the Strait of Tiran to be an international waterway. Eban was apparently trying to extend this and other statements made at the time into an American commitment to use force if necessary to reopen the strait. On the American side, the most that was acknowledged was that Dulles had said that the United States recognized Israel's right, under article 51 of the UN Charter, to use force to open the strait if it was closed by force.

One by one, each of Johnson's advisers then expressed his views to the president. Discussion turned to the idea of a multinational fleet, with McNamara stating his disapproval of the idea on military grounds.[45] Rusk then reported on U Thant's talks in Cairo, which had elicited from Nasser a promise not to take preemptive action and had led to some discussion of how the blockade might be modified. He then introduced a phrase that was to be repeated to the Israelis frequently in the coming two weeks: "Israel will not be alone unless it decides to go alone."[46] To Rusk, it clearly mattered who opened fire first.[47] Johnson, who seemed to be reassured by the judgment that the military situation would not deteriorate suddenly, spoke of the maritime effort approvingly, terming it his "hole card" for his talk with Eban. But he realized this might not be enough for Eban. He asked his advisers if they thought Eban would misinterpret this as a "cold shoulder." Johnson expressed his feeling that he could not make a clear commitment to use force, because of congressional sentiment.

Fortas joined the discussion, stating that the problem was to keep Israel from making a first strike. This required an American commitment that an Israeli ship would get through the strait. Fortas recommended that Johnson promise to use whatever force was necessary. Johnson said he was in no position to make such a promise. Eban was not going to get everything he wanted. Congress, he said, was unanimously against taking a stronger stand. He wondered out loud if he would regret on Monday not having given Eban more today. Then he left the meeting. The others talked on for a few minutes, with both McNamara and Rusk taking the strong stand that Israel would be on its own if it decided to strike first. Fortas countered by saying that Johnson could not credibly say to Israel that it would be alone. The president did not have a choice of standing on the sidelines.[48]

Thus were the two main schools of thought among Johnson's advisers presented. The president seemed to be taking his cues from McNamara and Rusk, but he no doubt was also attentive to what Fortas was saying. The drama of the next few days in American policy circles involved the gradual shift on Johnsons's part from supporting Rusk's "red light" views to siding with Fortas, who began to argue that Israel should be allowed to act on its own if the United States was unwilling or unable to use force to reopen the strait—the "yellow light" view.

By late afternoon the Israelis were becoming anxious to set a definite time for Eban's meeting with the president.[49] Minister Evron called Walt Rostow and was invited to come to the White House to talk. Johnson, he was told, did not want any leaks to the press from the meeting, and several details of the visit had to be discussed. While Evron was in his office, Rostow contacted Johnson, who, upon learning of Evron's presence, asked him in for an informal talk. Johnson knew and liked Evron, and presumably felt that it would be useful to convey his position through Evron before the more formal meeting with Eban. Johnson began by stressing that any American action would require congressional support of the president. He repeated this point several times. Talks in the UN, though not expected to produce anything, were an important part of the process of building support. On a more positive note, Johnson mentioned the multinational-fleet effort. He acknowledged that Israel, as a sovereign state, had the right to act alone, but in that case, the United States would feel no obligation for any consequences that might ensue.[50] He stated that he did not believe Israel would carry out such unilateral action. In closing, Johnson stressed that he was not a coward, that he did not renege on his promises, but that he would not be rushed into a course of action which might endanger the United States simply because Israel had set Sunday as a deadline.[51]

Eban arrived at the White House unannounced while Evron was with the president. After some confusion, their meeting began shortly after 7:00 p.m. The Americans present included Johnson, McNamara, Walt and Eugene Rostow, Joseph Sisco, and George Christian. In response to

Eban's appeal that the United States live up to its explicit commitments, Johnson emphasized that he had termed the blockade illegal and that he was working on a plan to reopen the strait. He noted that he did not have the authority to say that an attack on Israel would be considered an attack on the United States. He again stressed the two basic premises of American policy: any action must have congressional support, and it must be multilateral. He told Eban he was fully aware of what three past presidents had said, but their statements were "not worth five cents" if the people and Congress did not support the president.

Twice Johnson repeated the phrase that Rusk had coined: "Israel will not be alone unless it decides to go alone." He said he could not imagine Israel making a precipitate decision. In case Eban doubted his personal courage, Johnson stressed that he was "not a feeble mouse or a coward." Twice Eban asked the president if he could tell the cabinet that Johnson would do everything in his power to get the gulf open to all shipping, including that of Israel. Johnson replied "yes."[52] Eban was given an aide-memoire spelling out U.S. policy:

The United States has its own Constitutional processes which are basic to its action on matters involving war and peace. The Secretary-General has not yet reported to the UN Security Council and the Council has not yet demonstrated what it may or may not be able or willing to do, although the United States will press for prompt action in the UN.

I have already publicly stated this week our views on the safety of Israel and on the Strait of Tiran. Regarding the Strait, we plan to pursue vigorously the measures which can be taken by maritime nations to assure that the Strait and the Gulf remain open to free and innocent passage of the vessels of all nations.

I must emphasize the necessity for Israel not to make itself responsible for the initiation of hostilities. Israel will not be alone unless it decides to go alone. We cannot imagine that it will make this decision.

As Eban left the White House, Johnson turned to his advisers and stated: "I've failed. They'll go."[53]

PRELUDE TO THE JUNE 1967 WAR

Johnson obviously was aware of the awkwardness of the policy he was pursuing. The multinational-fleet effort would take time, and even then might fall through for any number of reasons. The alternative of unilateral American action was not seriously considered. Congress was obviously a major concern, and behind Congress lay the realities of the Vietnam conflict. Johnson understood that Israel was subject to a different set of pressures and might be forced to go to war. But if so, the United States, he had said, would not be committed to act. He apparently still wanted the Israelis to hold off on military action, but as time went by he seems to have become resigned to letting the Israelis take whatever action they felt was necessary. Above all, he was not prepared to give Israel the one thing that might have kept it from acting on its own—a firm guarantee to use force if necessary to reopen the strait. Eban had almost extracted such a promise, but in Johnson's mind it was clearly hedged by references to United States constitutional processes and "every means within my power."

What Johnson had asked for was time—time for the fleet idea to be explored, for passions to cool, for compromises to be explored. He had tried to pin the Israelis down with a commitment to give him two weeks, beginning about May 27. On that day the Soviets had told Johnson they had information that Israel was planning to attack. The president replied to Kosygin and sent a message to Eshkol, which reached him on May 28, repeating the information from Moscow and warning Israel against starting hostilities.[54] Meanwhile, the president decided to initiate further contacts with Nasser, and to that end Ambassador Charles Yost was sent to Cairo to assist ambassador-designate Nolte in his dealings with the Egyptians, and Robert Anderson, former secretary of the treasury, was requested to talk to Nasser privately to help set up an exchange of visits at the vice-presidential level.

Rusk followed up Johnson's message to Eshkol with one of his own to Ambassador Barbour, for transmittal to the Israelis:[55] "With the assurance of international determination to make every effort to keep the strait open to the flags of all nations, unilateral action on the part of Israel would be irresponsible and catastrophic." Rusk also paralleled Johnson's message to Kosygin, which had called for a U.S.-USSR effort to find a prompt solution to the Strait of Tiran issue, with a message to Foreign Minister Andrei Gromyko calling for a two-week moratorium on the Egyptian closure of the strait. The message to Eshkol had its intended effect. At its Sunday, May 28, meeting, the cabinet seemed evenly split on the issue of whether to go to war. Eshkol, reflecting on Johnson's letter and Eban's report of his talks, decided to accede to the president's request.

From this point on, many Washington officials began to act as if they had at least two weeks in which to work toward a solution. The critical period, it was felt, would begin after Sunday, June 11. Although there was reason to believe that the Israelis would stay their hand until that date, as Johnson had requested, clearly such a pledge would lose validity if the situation on the ground or within Israel changed substantially. And in the ensuing days, changes did indeed occur.

INFORMAL LINES OF COMMUNICATION

During this period, Justice Abe Fortas, presumably with Johnson's blessing, spoke frequently with Israel's respected ambassador, Avraham Harman.[56] Fortas and Harman were close personal friends, who met on a regular basis during late May and the first days of June. And with considerable regularity, Fortas talked to the president by telephone. The Israelis had every reason to assume they were dealing with one of Johnson's true confidants, although Harman reportedly did not view his talks with Fortas as constituting an alternative channel for dealing with the U.S. government. He and Evron, who also talked to Fortas, did know, of course, that they were dealing with someone who was close to Johnson and whose views deserved careful attention. They were also dealing with a man who was deeply committed to Israel and who seems to have been suspicious of the State Department and Dean Rusk in particular.[57] What they heard from Fortas would be one more piece of evidence they could use in trying to fathom Johnson's thinking.

Eban's report of Johnson's views was not universally credited in Israel. Some thought he had misunderstood the import of the phrase "Israel will not be alone unless its decides to go alone." It was not an absolute prohibition. In fact, Johnson had acknowledged that Israel had the right to act on its own. But he had urged them not to do so, at least not right away. And he had made it clear that he could not do much to help if they got into trouble. Over the next several days the Israelis mounted a major effort to check on exactly where Johnson stood and to signal that time was working against Israeli interests. Central to this effort was a visit by Meir Amit, the head of Israel's intelligence service (the Mossad), who traveled to Washington under an assumed name on May 31.

Just as the Israelis were setting out to determine Johnson's views with precision, he left town for a long weekend at his Texas ranch. None of his foreign policy advisers accompanied him, although they were able to stay in regular touch by telephone and cables. Much of his time over the Memorial Day weekend—which extended from Saturday, May 27, until his return to the White House very early Wednesday morning, May 31—was spent in the company of Arthur and Mathilde Krim, Mary Lasker, and Jake Jacobsen, a former legal adviser. All were involved in party politics, and the Krims and Mrs. Lasker were large contributors to the Democratic party. Johnson must have been thinking about the party that weekend, since he was scheduled to speak to a party fund-raising event on June 3. Arthur Krim was to preside that night, and the audience would certainly be keenly interested in what the president said about the Middle East and Israel. Robert Kennedy was also scheduled to be there, and Johnson may well have been concerned about Kennedy's efforts to win the party away from him.[58] In short, he had more than the Middle East and Vietnam on his mind as he raced around his ranch with his guests.[59]

Just before Amit's arrival in Washington, an extremely important change took place in the Middle East situation. Jordan's King Hussein, under great pressure to join the Arab-nationalist mainstream, had flown to Cairo and signed a mutual-defense pact with Nasser. He returned to Jordan with an Egyptian general in tow who would head the joint military command. Walt Rostow saw this as a major turning point, and underscored the military danger represented by the dispatch of Egyptian commandos to Jordan. From this point on, he believed, Arab actions were making war virtually inevitable. Unless the Arabs backed down, or unless enough time was available for American power to make itself felt, Israel was bound to take matters into its own hands.[60]

In Washington on May 30 and 31, mixed signals were being given precisely on this crucial issue of whether the United States had the means and the will, alone or with others, to break the blockade of the Strait of Tiran. A proposed joint declaration of maritime powers had been shown to the Israeli ambassador, but it made no mention of the use of force, if necessary, to break the blockade.[61]

Eshkol replied to Johnson's letter of May 28 on May 30, noting that American assurances to take "any and all measures to open the straits" had played a role in Israel's decisions not to go to war and to agree to wait for "a week or two."[62] Within that time frame, Eshkol urged, a naval escort must move through the strait. Apprised of this message on May 31, Johnson became angry, claiming he had not promised Israel that he would use "any and all measures," but rather had stressed that he would make every effort within his constitutional authority. Walt Rostow was told to contact Evron to ensure that there should be no misunderstanding on this point. Evron replied by warning of the implications of what seemed to be a weakening of the U.S. commitment.[63]

From Cairo, Yost reported on May 30 his impression that Nasser "cannot and will not retreat," that "he would probably welcome, but not seek, military showdown with Israel," and that any American effort to force the strait would "undermine, if not destroy, US position throughout Arab world."[64] The following day, Anderson met with Nasser and discussed the possibility that Egyptian Vice President Zakariyya Muhieddin would visit Washington on June 7.[65] Some officials in Washington suspected that Nasser might propose referring the dispute over the strait to the International Court of Justice. The United States might find such a proposal difficult to refuse; Israel would certainly find it impossible to accept.

Rumors began to circulate in Washington on May 31 that the United States was looking for possible compromises to end the crisis.[66] In fact, some consideration was being given in the State Department to such steps, and Rusk's consultations with Congress to this effect rapidly reached Israeli ears and caused alarm.[67] That same day the Israelis picked up a report that Rusk had told a journalist, "I don't think it is our business to restrain anyone," when asked if the United States was trying to restrain Israel.[68]

This was the atmosphere that Amit found when he filed his first report on his soundings in Washington. His advice was to wait a few more days, but he observed that the mood was beginning to change. In his opinion the fleet idea was increasingly seen as bankrupt. If Israel were to act on its own, and win decisively, no one in Washington would be upset. The source for these impressions, it is worth noting, was not the State Department or the president. Amit's talks on June 1 and the morning of June 2 were focused on the Pentagon, where he saw McNamara, and on the CIA, where he talked with Helms and James Angleton.[69]

On June 1 the simmering political crisis in Israel broke. Late in the day Moshe Dayan, hero of the 1956 Suez campaign, was brought into the cabinet as minister of defense. War now seemed likely in the near future. Some leaders in the Israeli military were eager to strike quickly. Eban, however, was mindful of the Suez experience, when Israel had gone to war without the blessing of the United States. He wanted Johnson's support, or at least acquiescence, if Israel took military action. And based on what he had heard on May 26 in the Oval Office, reinforced by Rusk's stern message of May 28, that support could not be taken for granted if Israel acted preemptively.

Then on June 1 Eban received a message that contributed to his change of position. It was an account of a meeting that Minister Evron had had with Fortas. Fortas reportedly said that "Eshkol and Eban did great service to Israel by giving the U.S. a chance to explore options other than Israeli force. If they had not done so, it would have been difficult to secure the President's sympathy."[70] Eban concluded that this was as near a green light as a president could safely give, and he then called on Generals Yitzhak Rabin and Aharon Yariv to tell them that he no longer saw any diplomatic necessity for further military restraint.[71]

June 2 was the last occasion for serious diplomatic efforts before Israel's decision to fight. The Israeli ambassador was scheduled to leave for Israel later that day, and another "fateful" cabinet meeting would be held on June 4. At about 11:00 a.m. on June 2, Minister Evron, without instructions from Jerusalem, called on Walt Rostow at the White House. He wanted to make sure Johnson understood that time was very short and that Israel might have to go to war. He was seeking further confirmation of Amit's impression that the United States would not object too strenuously if Israel acted on its own. Evron stressed that he was not conveying an official communication from his government, but his points were taken seriously. First he emphasized that time was working against Israel and that the military cost of war with Egypt was rising every day. He then asked what the American response would be if an Israeli ship tried to break the blockade, drawing Egyptian fire, and then Israel responded with an attack on Sharm al-Shaykh. Would the United States see this as a case of Israel's asserting its legitimate right of self-defense? What if the Soviet Union intervened?

Rostow said this scenario was very different from the one discussed with Eban, but was an alternative that might be considered. He would seek Johnson's views. He then asked Evron how much time remained, in reply to which Evron referred to June 11, although he stressed that there was nothing ironclad about that date.[72] Evron noted, and Rostow confirmed, that intelligence reports indicated Nasser would probably not fire on a U.S.-escorted probe of the strait.[73] Therefore, the issue of Israeli access to the Gulf of Aqaba might be left hanging indefinitely.

Evron then mentioned the 1957 commitment, emphasizing that it had two parts: an American commitment to assert the right of free passage in the strait, and acknowledgment of Israel's right to act with force if the strait was closed. It was this second track he was now exploring, the former having been discussed with Eban. Among other things, he noted, it would be better for U.S.-Arab and U.S.-Soviet relations if Israel acted alone rather than relying on the United States to use force to open the strait.[74] This was a point that several American ambassadors in Arab countries had also made, and it was not lost on Rostow, who urged Johnson to "urgently consider" Evron's suggestion.

Johnson's reaction to Evron's ideas is unknown, although he reportedly discussed them with Rusk.[75] But the letter he sent to Eshkol the following day shows little hint of a new approach. Evron noted, however, that the letter did specifically refer to him and also contained the following sentence: "We have completely and fully exchanged views with General Amit."[76] Johnson, in fact, had inserted the sentence on Amit by himself after having received on June 2 a full memorandum from Helms of his talks with Amit, coupled with a warning that Israel was on the verge of striking.[77] Otherwise, the letter, a reply to Eshkol's message of May 30, largely repeated what Eban had already been told. The text of the aide-memoire was quoted in full. Johnson promised to "provide as effective American support as possible to preserve the peace and freedom of your nation and of the area." He again referred to the need for the backing of Congress and for working through the UN. After mentioning the maritime-powers' declaration and the naval escort, Johnson added, "Our leadership is unanimous that the United States should not move in isolation."[78]

Ambassador Harman had a last talk on June 2 with Secretary Rusk before departing for Israel. Rusk had little new to report. Efforts to gain adherents to the maritime declaration were continuing. The necessary multilateral context for action in the Gulf of Aqaba did not yet exist. The question of which side fired first would be extremely important, and Rusk cautioned Harman against Israeli action.[79]

That same caution, however, was not heard when Harman called on Fortas just before leaving for the airport. According to Fortas's law clerk, who overheard the comments, Fortas, who had spoken to the president earlier in the day, said to Harman: "Rusk will fiddle while Israel burns. If you are going to save yourselves, do it yourselves."[80]

The following day, June 3, it was announced in Cairo that Muhieddin would visit the United States for talks on June 7.[81] Rusk had informed Harman of the planned visit the day before. The Israelis were obviously irritated. Such a visit could only work to their disadvantage. In Israel, both Harman and Amit, who had returned together, reported to Eshkol that there was no chance of unilateral U.S. action or of successful multilateral action. The conclusion was inescapable: Israel was on its own. Amit judged that the United States could not object if Israel opened the blockade in its own way.[82] Sensing that time was running out, Rusk

cabled ambassadors in the Arab world with the warning that Israel might
act soon. He underscored the American commitment to the political
independence and territorial integrity of all the nations of the area,
reminded them of American commitments made to Israel in 1957
concerning the strait, and urged that they send in any ideas on how to
avoid war.[83]

That same evening Johnson flew to New York for the Democratic
party event that had apparently been much on his mind over the previous
days. He referred to his "deep concern" about the situation in the Middle
East but did not elaborate. While at dinner, seated between Mathilde
Krim and Mary Lasker, Johnson was reportedly told that the Israelis had
made the decision to go to war. Abe Feinberg, a prominent banker and
fund-raiser for the Democratic party, leaned over and whispered in his
ear: "Mr. President, it can't be held any longer. It's going to be within
the next twenty-four hours."[84] Thus, it seems, the president learned war
was imminent.

In the twenty-four hours, more or less, remaining before the Israeli
attack, Johnson took no further action. He was not officially informed by
the Israelis of their decision, but he had no reason to be surprised when
he was awakened on the morning of June 5 with the news that war had
begun. After all, he had taken steps to assure the Israelis that the "red
light" of May 26 had turned yellow. Johnson, while far from instigating
the Israelis to attack, seemed to feel he had nothing to offer them. The
"yellow light," hinted at in his letter to Eshkol on June 3, and reiterated
in remarks from Fortas and Goldberg, meant "be careful," and "don't
count on the United States if you get into trouble." But, as for most
motorists, the yellow light was tantamount to a green one.

The Middle East would never again be the same. A war that might
have been avoided was soon to transform the politics and the map of the
region. American policy toward the region was about to be radically
overhauled. A conflict that Washington had tried to consign to the
"icebox" for the past decade could no longer be so casually ignored.

CHAPTER THREE

War and Its Aftermath

The outbreak of war on June 5 created a profoundly changed situation for U.S. policymakers. The premises of the preceding three weeks were invalidated overnight, and new issues assumed priority. How would President Johnson cope with the urgent problems that now confronted him? Would he hold Israel responsible for preempting, or would he recognize there really was no alternative? Secretary of State Rusk had repeatedly told the Israelis that it would matter who opened fire, but Johnson had hinted that he did not share this view. What about the territorial integrity of all countries in the region, which the United States had pledged to uphold? Would that now apply to Arab countries that had lost land to Israel? Fundamentally, would U.S. policy aim for a return to something like the status quo ante, or would an effort be made to devise a different basis for Arab-Israeli relations in the future? In short, were the armistice agreements of 1949 now obsolete? And, if so, what would take their place?

Johnson never blamed the Israelis for starting the war, although he did express his "disappointment" that they had not taken his advice.[1] And in a meeting with his advisers on June 7, when Israeli success on the battlefield was clearly evident, Johnson expressed his pessimism about the war solving deep-seated problems of the region.[2] His national security adviser, Walt Rostow, who talked to the president more frequently than anyone else during the crisis, maintained years later that Johnson had firmly opposed the Israeli decision to go to war.[3]

If Johnson had genuinely had qualms about Israel's resort to force, why did he become such an ardent supporter of Israel once the fighting began? Was he responding to pressures from pro-Israeli opinion in the United States, or to his own sympathy for the Jewish state? Certainly his sympathies did play a part, as did the fact that he knew he had been unable to solve the crisis for the Israelis. Only an early American commitment to use force to reopen the Strait of Tiran could have stayed Israel's hand, and that was more than he had been prepared to contemplate.

Perhaps his own bitter experience with Vietnam made him skeptical that military solutions could be found to complex political problems. Johnson had not quite given the Israelis a green light, but he had removed a veto on their actions. He had signaled that there would be no repeat of Suez. But what would there be? Would the United States underwrite Israel's occupation of sizable pieces of Arab land indefinitely? Would it seek an early political settlement? If so, on what terms? All these issues would soon have to be tackled. But once it had become clear that Israel had won an overwhelming victory, "there was a great sense of relief," because the United States would not have to get involved militarily.[4]

The United States quickly turned its attention to obtaining a cease-fire and ensuring that the Soviet Union would not intervene. The question of how the war had begun, which excited some interest in the early hours, was quickly overtaken by events. (Israeli Foreign Minister Eban told U.S. Ambassador Barbour that Egypt had attacked first. By midday on June 5, when it was known for sure that Israel had struck the first blow, it no longer seemed to matter.)[5]

Johnson was anxious to convey the impression that the United States was not involved in the fighting. This might help to minimize the danger to U.S. interests in the Arab world, reduce the likelihood of Soviet intervention, and facilitate a cease-fire. Here again the memory of the Suez crisis seemed to play a part. The United States did not want to be perceived in the Arab world as a co-conspirator with Israel, as Britain and France had been in 1956. When the war began, the Marine Battalion Landing Team was instructed to remain on shore leave in Malta.[6] Two carriers were on station near Crete, but they were not moved closer to the area of conflict. Once hostilities were under way, the United States imposed an embargo on new arms agreements to all countries of the Middle East, including Israel. The embargo remained in force through the end of the year, despite Israeli urgent requests to lift it.

The first news of the fighting reached Johnson early on the morning of June 5. Three hours after the start of hostilities, Secretary Rusk, after consultations with the president, sent a message through normal channels to Moscow expressing surprise at the outbreak of war and calling for an early end to the fighting.[7] At 7:47 a.m. Premier Kosygin replied over the "hot line"—the first use of this channel of communication in a crisis. He referred to the dangerous situation and the need for U.S.-Soviet cooperation in bringing about a cease-fire. Johnson's answer, sent by the hot line at 8:47 a.m., stated that both superpowers should stay out of the conflict and encourage a cease-fire. In all, twenty messages were exchanged over the hot line during the crisis.

The American position quickly became one of support for a cease-fire, but there was ambiguity about whether it would be linked to a provision for return to the prehostilities borders. Restoration of the immediate status quo ante of June 4 was clearly ruled out, inasmuch as that would have kept the strait closed; but a withdrawal of Israeli forces in conjunction with a lifting of the blockade might have found support in Washington if the Soviets or the Arabs had pressed the issue on the first day.

By June 6, however, the United States had come out in favor of a simple cease-fire in place.[8] Kosygin had communicated with Johnson during the day on the need for a cease-fire coupled with Israeli withdrawal, but by the end of the day the Soviets had agreed to accept the American position. The Egyptians, however, rejected a cease-fire in place. By that time Johnson was not in a mood to help President Nasser, who that day had falsely accused the United States of directly participating in the air attacks against Egypt. The result of his charge was that six Arab states broke off diplomatic relations with Washington, all of which created considerable bitterness toward Nasser, even among the State Department Arabists.

Apart from denying Nasser's accusations and continuing to support a cease-fire, the United States did little on the next day of the war, June 7.[9] On the 8th, however, an American intelligence ship stationed off the Sinai coast, the USS *Liberty*, was attacked by unidentified aircraft, which proved later to be Israeli. When news of the attack was flashed to Washington, Secretary of Defense McNamara and Johnson both feared that the Soviet Union might be responsible, and dark predictions of "World War III" were briefly heard in the White House situation room. The identity of the attackers was soon clarified, and Johnson informed Moscow by the hot line of the incident and the dispatch of aircraft from the Sixth Fleet to the scene of the attack.[10]

The incident shows the extraordinary degree to which Johnson was attuned to Soviet behavior once the war began. If during the May crisis he had been prepared to see the conflict primarily in terms of Arabs and Israelis, once hostilities were under way the main focus of his attention was the Soviet Union. With Israel secure from defeat by the Arabs, only Soviet behavior could trigger a direct American military response. The regional dispute paled in significance before the danger of superpower confrontation. The risk of Soviet intervention appeared once again before an effective cease-fire on all fronts went into effect on the sixth day, June

10. On the Syrian front, where fighting was particularly intense on June 9 and 10, the Israelis seemed capable of threatening Damascus. Although American officials were sure that Israel was on the verge of agreeing to a cease-fire once the Golan Heights had been secured, the Soviets were apparently less sanguine. At about 8:48 a.m. on June 10, Washington time, Kosygin sent a hot-line message to Johnson warning that they would take necessary actions, "including military," if Israel did not stop its advance.[11] Johnson responded by assuring the Soviets that Israel was prepared to stop and by instructing McNamara to turn the Sixth Fleet toward the Syrian coast to make certain that the Soviet Union would not underestimate Johnson's determination to meet any Soviet military move with one of his own. CIA Director Richard Helms, who participated in the meeting in the White House Situation Room, recalled that the conversation during the first couple of hours was in the lowest voices he had ever heard in a meeting of that kind. The atmosphere was tense. As the morning wore on, everyone relaxed a bit as it became clear that the fighting was petering out and that the two nuclear superpowers were not, in fact, heading toward confrontation.[12]

By noon the crisis was nearly over, a cease-fire soon went into effect, and the Sixth Fleet stopped its eastward movement. The war was over. Once again, a new situation existed and new policies were called for.

WAS THERE U.S.-ISRAELI COLLUSION?

Johnson publicly maintained after the war that he had done everything in his power to prevent it. He further claimed that he had opposed Israel's decision to go to war. Rusk asserted that he was shocked and "angry as hell" that the Israelis had launched their surprise offensive just before the Egyptian vice-president was to arrive in Washington. He added, with a note of caution, "To my knowledge, Israel had no undercover encouragement from the United States to start the war."[13] Others, however, have challenged this interpretation, and the documentary record does raise serious questions about its accuracy.

The extreme case against the Johnson version argues that the United States actively colluded with Israel during the crisis in the hope of weakening, perhaps even toppling, the Nasser regime. In brief, the critics see the 1967 crisis as a rerun of Suez 1956, but with the United States in the role of Britain and France. Mohamed Heikal's entrapment theory, and Mahmoud Riad's less extreme version of the same, stand out as Egyptian interpretations from this perspective.[14]

Stephen Green has given greatest credence to the conspiracy theory by asserting that the United States sent reconnaissance aircraft to Israel a few days before the war and that they continued to fly during the hostilities. He maintains that at least three sources confirm this secret exercise, but none has allowed his name to be used and no documentation has been produced.[15] The Johnson Library claims to have searched its files and come up with nothing. Moreover, none of the senior American officials interviewed for this study—Helms, McNamara, Lucius Battle, Harold H. Saunders (member of the National Security Council staff)—had any knowledge of this supposed American involvement in the 1967 war. One might have thought that the secretary of defense and the director of the CIA would have known of these events even if lower-ranking officials might not have. Nor has any Israeli source ever hinted at such collusion.

What, then, to make of the story? Johnson did have some forewarning that Israel was about to go to war. He had expressed some concern that Israel might need help, and he had approved a military assistance package on May 23. A small reconnaissance unit might have been seen as a useful, nonintrusive way of assisting the Israelis. But whatever plausibility this story may have, it does not meet the normal standards of historical evidence. Barring further disclosures, it should be rejected as unproved.[16]

From a thorough examination of all available sources, and many interviews, I conclude that there was no collusion between the United States and Israel before the crisis. The "entrapment" theory does not hold up. If anyone was trying to provoke a crisis in the Middle East in mid-May 1967, it was the Soviets.[17] The United States had its hands full in Vietnam. Nasser did not have many friends in Washington, but he was not such a big problem that Johnson, or anyone else in a top position, was out to get him.

Once the crisis began, Johnson, and especially Secretary of State Rusk, initially tried to prevent war. This remained Rusk's position throughout.[18] There seems little doubt from the stream of messages to Israel from May 17 to May 28 that Johnson was serious in urging restraint and pleading for time. But the Israelis are also correct in sensing a change in tone, if not in substance, by the first of June. Johnson, after his long weekend at his Texas ranch, and after Jordan had thrown in its lot with Egypt, seems to have concluded that war could no longer be avoided. No purpose would be served by trying to hold Israel back. Israel was free to act, but on its own. This is not quite the same as a green light—but certainly it was not a red one either. Johnson made sure the Israelis understood that the light had turned to yellow.[19] There was no U.S.-Israeli collusion, but there was acquiescence in what Johnson had come to believe was an inevitable Israeli resort to force to solve a problem for which the United States could offer no solution of its own.

POSTWAR DIPLOMACY

Johnson and his advisers were mindful of how Eisenhower had dealt with the Israelis after the Suez War. They were determined not to adopt the same strategy of forcing Israel to withdraw from conquered territories in return for little in the way of Arab concessions.[20] This did not mean that the United States endorsed Israel's indefinite hold on the occupied territories, but rather that the territories should be exchanged for a genuine peace agreement, something that had been missing in the Middle East since Israel's creation. This would take time, obviously, but time seemed to be on Israel's side. And the Israelis had officially made it clear that they did not intend to enlarge their borders as a result of the war.[21] The need, as American officials saw it, was to establish such a framework for a peace settlement and then to allow time to pass until the Arabs were prepared to negotiate to recover their territories. Apart from helping to establish the diplomatic framework, the United States need only ensure that the military balance not shift against Israel. Such a change was not likely in the near future, however, because the Egyptian, Syrian, and Jordanian armed forces lay in ruins.

In brief, a major shift in U.S. policy took place in the days following the war. But there is no record that this change was accompanied by much debate or consideration of alternative courses of action. Instead, it was almost as if the president and his top aides just assumed that they could not go back to the old, failed policy. Quite possibly, the intensely pro-Israeli tone of public opinion, the views of Congress, the private lobbying of Johnson's many Jewish friends, and Nasser's unfounded accusations all played a part. Perhaps. But Johnson also had his own memories of Suez. He had opposed Eisenhower's policy of forcing Israel to withdraw from Suez without peace in return. He would not emulate Eisenhower now, not when Israel's moral and legal case seemed so much stronger than in 1956.

Johnson apparently did not believe the United States should launch a high-level, intensive peacemaking effort immediately. Either he considered that such a move could not succeed, given the minimal influence of the United States in Arab capitals, or he did not feel he could sustain such an effort at a time when Vietnam was demanding so much of his attention. In either event, the option never seems to have been seriously considered. Instead, Johnson suggested a general outline of a settlement in a major policy statement on June 19, on the eve of his meeting with Soviet Premier Kosygin at Glassboro, New Jersey.[22]

In his June 19 statement, drafted in large measure by his special adviser McGeorge Bundy, Johnson clearly placed the major responsibility for the war on Egypt, terming the closure of the Strait of Tiran an "act of folly." He then stated that the United States would not press Israel to withdraw in the absence of peace. Five principles essential to such a peace were spelled out: the recognized right to national life, justice for the refugees, innocent maritime passage, limits on the arms race, and political independence and territorial integrity for all. In brief, Johnson contemplated a full settlement of all the issues stemming from 1947–49 and 1967.

In the course of the next five months, American diplomatic efforts were aimed at achieving a UN Security Council resolution that would incorporate Johnson's five points. The main areas of disagreement between Israel and the Arabs, as well as between the United States and the Soviet Union, rapidly emerged. The Arabs insisted on full Israeli withdrawal from newly occupied territory prior to the end of belligerency. Israel, on the other hand, held out for direct negotiations and a "package settlement" in which withdrawal would occur only after the conclusion of a peace agreement. The Soviet Union generally backed the Arab position, whereas the United States agreed with Israel on the "package" approach, but was less insistent on direct negotiations.

As to the withdrawal of Israeli forces, the American position changed between June and November.[23] Initially the United States was prepared to support a Latin American draft resolution that called on Israel to "withdraw all its forces from all territories occupied by it as a result of the recent conflict." The resolution was defeated, as was a tentative joint U.S.-Soviet draft in mid-July that was never considered because of radical Arab objections to provisions calling for an end of war with Israel. In late August the Arab position hardened further at the Khartoum conference, where Nasser and King Hussein of Jordan, in return for subsidies from the oil-producing Arab countries, were obliged to subscribe to guidelines for a political settlement with Israel based on no recognition, no negotiations, no peace agreement, and no abandonment of Palestinian rights.[24]

When the UN debate resumed in late October, the United States position, in part because of Eban's persuasive efforts with Goldberg, had shifted to support for "withdrawal of armed forces from occupied territories." The ambiguity was intentional and represented the maximum that Israel was prepared to accept. Even with this change, however, the United States made it clear in an early October minute of understanding signed with the British that the text "referring to withdrawal must similarly be understood to mean withdrawal from occupied territories of the UAR, Jordan and Syria, the details to be worked out between the parties taking security into account."[25] Finally, on November 22, 1967, a British compromise, known as UN Resolution 242, was passed. (See appendix A.) It incorporated all of Johnson's five points, along with a deliberately balanced call for "withdrawal of Israeli armed forces from territories occupied in the recent conflict" and "termination of all claims of belligerency and respect for and acknowledgement of the sovereignty, territorial integrity, and political independence of every state in the area and their right to live in peace within secure and recognized boundaries free from threats or acts of force." As a sop to the Arabs, the preambular language emphasized "the inadmissability of the acquisition of territory by war." But in UN documents, preambular language has no binding effect, so Eban raised only perfunctory objections.

In brief, the resolution fell just short of calling on Israel to withdraw from all territories and on the Arabs to make "full peace" with Israel. Note that the Palestinians were nowhere referred to by name, an omission much remarked upon in later years. But the United States did maintain from the outset that 242 did not mean that Israel should gain any significant amount of territory beyond the 1967 lines once peace was established.[26] Much of the diplomacy of the subsequent years revolved around efforts to make more precise and binding this deliberately vague wording. The resolution called for a UN-appointed representative to work with the parties to find a solution, a task that fell to Gunnar Jarring, Sweden's ambassador to Moscow, whose only Middle East experience was as a Turkic language specialist who had lived in Kashgar in the 1930s—a long way from the vicissitudes of the Arab-Israeli conflict.

During most of 1968 the Johnson administration assumed a comparatively low profile in Arab-Israeli diplomacy, leaving the main task to Jarring. In private, American officials consistently told the Israelis that a peace settlement would have to be based on virtually complete Israeli withdrawal, but in public nothing was said to modify the language of Resolution 242. Johnson was clearly preoccupied with Vietnam, especially after the Tet offensive in February, and in late March he announced his intention not to seek the presidency for another term, a decision that set off an intense political campaign within his own party and, after Hubert Humphrey's nomination, between the two parties. In this atmosphere major initiatives for peace in the Middle East could not be expected. Instead, Johnson acted to ensure that the post-1967 status quo would not be disrupted by Soviet arms shipments to Syria and Egypt. With a war on his hands in Vietnam, he was not anxious to see a resumption of fighting in the Middle East. In January 1968 he ended the American embargo on new arms shipments to the region.[27] Both Jordan and Israel were the beneficiaries, though on quite different scales.[28]

Johnson met with Prime Minister Eshkol in January 1968 to discuss Israeli arms requests. Topping the Israeli list was the high performance F-4 Phantom jet. Before 1967 the United States had not been a primary supplier of military equipment to Israel. The Israeli air force was of French origin, but France, because of Charles de Gaulle's Arab policy, was no longer a reliable arms supplier; hence the need for American arms.

Johnson reportedly assured Eshkol that Phantoms would be provided, but left unspecified the terms, timing, and possible conditions.[29] Within the bureaucracy many officials felt the United States should link the furnishing of F-4s to some concessions from Israel. Two possibilities were considered. First, to reverse Israel's growing appetite for territory, some felt that Israel should be asked to agree to the principle of full withdrawal in the context of peace in exchange for the jets. Others, fearful of Israeli nuclear development, argued that Israel should be required to sign the Nuclear Nonproliferation Treaty (NPT) before receiving U.S. arms.

The NPT issue was discussed at length with Israeli representatives. The most the Israelis would say was that they would not be the first ones to "introduce" nuclear weapons into the Middle East. In trying to clarify what this meant, U.S. officials discovered that Israeli Ambassador Rabin understood it to mean that Israel would not be the first to "test" such weapons or to reveal their existence publicly. Paul Warnke, assistant secretary of defense, then sent a letter to Rabin spelling out the American understanding of what nonintroduction of nuclear weapons meant: no production of a nuclear device. Before the issue was ever resolved, Johnson ordered the bureaucracy to end the search for a quid pro quo on the F-4s. Pressure was mounting for an affirmative United States response to the Israeli request. Political candidates were all endorsing the Israeli position, and in July the Senate passed a resolution calling for the sale of F-4s to Israel. Finally, on October 9 Johnson publicly announced that Israel would be allowed to purchase the Phantoms.[30] The two countries signed a deal for fifty F-4s in late December, providing for delivery of sixteen aircraft late in 1969 and the rest in 1970.

Perhaps in the hope of offsetting negative Arab reactions to the Phantom deal, Secretary of State Rusk, on his own initiative, informed the Egyptians on November 2 that the United States favored full Israeli withdrawal from Sinai as part of a peace settlement.[31] A year later, this position was publicly disclosed in the Rogers Plan, but in fact it had consistently been part of the American official consensus on the terms of an Israeli-Egyptian agreement. It did little, however, to win the confidence of the Israelis, and the last months of the Johnson administration were marked by a perceptible chill between the two countries.

In December, with the administration of Richard Nixon on the verge of taking office, the Soviet Union sent the United States a diplomatic note urging a more active search for an Arab-Israeli settlement. Britain and France were also pushing for a role in any Middle East peace talks. But time had run out on the Johnson presidency, and these issues would be passed on to Nixon, against a background of escalating violence and mounting guerrilla activity on the part of the Palestinian fedayeen.

ANALYZING JOHNSON'S MIDDLE EAST POLICY

The development of American policy before, during, and after the June 1967 Arab-Israeli war highlights the importance of a few key assumptions held by top decisionmakers, especially the president, at each stage of the crisis. The situation in the Middle East in May and June 1967 was extraordinarily complex. To make sense of the flow of events, decisionmakers needed some guidelines, some simplifying assumptions. They found them, not surprisingly, among the "lessons of the past" and the categorical inferences that had served well in other circumstances. An element of wishful thinking also existed. Together, several key principles provided a gyroscope of sorts for the decisionmaking process; order was perceived where it might have otherwise been missing. Little real discussion took place on these core assumptions.

The basic principles from which policy flowed in each of the phases of the crisis can be summarized as follows:

—Pre-war imperatives: do not commit American forces unilaterally, primarily because of Congress.

—Wartime policy: deter Soviet intervention; seek a cease-fire (but not a return to the status quo ante, which had been dangerous and unstable).

—Postwar policy: try for "full peace"; do not consider a Suez-like return to the status quo ante; insist that occupied territory would ultimately be traded for peace; keep Israel strong through arms shipments.

Several things about the decisionmaking process during the crisis are noteworthy. First is the obvious preeminence of the president. Crises, by their nature, bring the president to the center of the policymaking arena. His perceptions tend to define the situation for others; his needs tend to dominate the process. In May and June 1967 that meant a great sensitivity to congressional views, a desire not to become involved in another war, and a hope that time could be found to pursue the more cumbersome, but politically preferable, multilateral alternative. When this policy began to lose credibility, Johnson signaled his acquiescence to Israel's taking action on its own. When war began on June 5, it was primarily the president again who defined the stakes in the new game, as he did once more after the cease-fire went into effect on June 10.

Although Johnson's advisers did not completely agree on policy during the crisis, they nonetheless showed a remarkable degree of consensus. No one made a case for unilateral United States action; only a few voices were raised on behalf of "unleashing Israel"; little debate occurred over policy on a cease-fire in place as opposed to a cease-fire plus withdrawal; nor did anyone challenge the "package settlement" approach that emerged almost imperceptibly after the war. When divergent perceptions did appear, they seem to have been more deeply rooted in bureaucratic rivalries than anything else. For example, on political-diplomatic grounds, both Secretary Rusk and Under Secretary Rostow strongly favored the multinational fleet. McNamara and the professional military men were skeptical of the fleet on military grounds and were doubtless not anxious to see forces diverted from Vietnam or NATO for use in the Middle East. Small, politically motivated uses of force are not what the Pentagon tends to favor.

Advisers did not split primarily along pro-Israeli or pro-Arab lines. In fact, it was hard to say what course of action might be most dangerous for American interests in the Arab world. Some American ambassadors in the Arab countries, sensing that war was inevitable, hoped that Israel would act quickly, but on a limited scale, to break the blockade without involving the United States. Such a view came close to being the "unleash Israel" option that the Israelis were seeking by late May. The State Department, however, normally thought to tilt toward the Arabs, did not favor this option, at least not at the policymaking level of Rusk and Rostow.

An important lesson of the crisis, and one often encountered in Middle Eastern policymaking, is that American policy choices rarely come to be seen in simple pro-Israeli or pro-Arab terms. Thus individuals, whatever their particular sympathies, may find themselves in support of policies that to the outside observer seem inconsistent with those sympathies. In a crisis, however, policy evolves in complex circumstances, is defined under presidential directive, and comes to be rationalized in terms of principles that are easily supported by high-level policymakers.

Outside the circle of the president's official advisers, however, there were people in his entourage who were very committed to Israel and very close to its leaders. Johnson spoke frequently with Justice Abe Fortas, quite possibly in the knowledge that he could convey Johnson's real views to the Israelis.[32] The Israelis knew they had many friends around Johnson—U.S. Ambassador to the UN Arthur Goldberg, Fortas, Vice President Humphrey, Eugene and Walt Rostow, Arthur and Mathilde Krim, Abe Feinberg, and White House aides Joseph Califano, Harry McPherson, and John Roche, to mention just a few.[33]

What seems to have been missing from the policymaking process during the crisis was an explicit effort to relate policies to outcomes, as the rational decisionmaker is supposed to do. To a limited degree, of course, outcomes were discussed. But no one seems to have thought through the full implications of Israel's going to war, especially the problems this might cause in the long run. The future is indeed unknowable, but policymakers can be expected to consider consequences. They do so, however, in fairly simple ways. For example, Johnson gave serious consideration to the extremely low-probability event of Israel's being militarily defeated by the Arabs, to the point where it became one of the chief reasons for his effort to restrain Israel. He acknowledged the more likely outcome, predicted by the intelligence community, of rapid Israeli victory, but did not think through its consequences in detail. No one asked what Israel would do with Sinai, the West Bank, and the

Golan Heights after the war was over. Would East Jerusalem ever be returned to Jordan once it had been conquered in war?[34] What would happen to the Palestinians on the West Bank? These were all important questions and came to be seen as such after 1967, but they paled in comparison with the overriding question of what would happen if Israel faced defeat.

Noteworthy by their unimportance during the crisis were the allegedly powerful pro-Israeli interest groups and the oil lobby. Johnson was sympathetic to Israel already and did not need to be reminded of the U.S. interest in supporting the Jewish state. He paid no attention to the formal pro-Israel lobby, but he was in constant touch with Americans who were friendly to Israel, some of whom were also key personalities in the Democratic party. His desire to keep the fund-raisers of the party in his camp, and not see them drift toward his nemesis, Robert Kennedy, may have had some impact on his thinking about the crisis. During the crucial days of late May he spent many more hours in the close company of the Krims, for example, than he did with any of his top advisers. And we know from the official records that Mathilde Krim regularly passed messages, documents, and suggestions to him. To say the least, she had a strong pro-Israeli point of view.

More important, however, than the pro-Israeli personalities that surrounded him was Congress. This was the institution in which Johnson had spent most of his political life. And Congress did not want another open-ended unilateral commitment of American troops. More than any other single political fact, that seemed to weigh on Johnson and helped to turn this normally energetic and aggressive personality into a cautious, reluctant leader in this crisis.

Once the war had begun, and especially in its aftermath, the extremely pro-Israeli tone of American public opinion, coupled with Nasser's hostility, probably did make it easier for Johnson to adopt a policy of unquestioning support for Israel. Lobbying, however, was not a significant factor.

Oil was of only marginal significance to the formulation of policy. It was clear to some policymakers that any increase in Nasser's prestige would weaken the positions of the pro-Western oil-rich Arab countries, such as Saudi Arabia and Libya. Some officials also recognized that unilateral American use of force to open the strait could damage U.S. interests in the oil-producing Arab countries. And some feared that an oil embargo as part of an Arab-Israeli war might have dangerous consequences for NATO allies and Japan. But, on balance, oil was very much a secondary factor in presidential policy considerations in 1967.[35]

Finally, an important lesson of the policymaking process can be learned from the 1967 Arab-Israeli crisis: the initial definition of a situation tends to endure unless subjected to overwhelming disconfirming evidence from external sources. Between May 16 and the end of the month, Johnson and his key aides maintained essentially the same basic perceptions, adding details to a framework created in the initial stages of the crisis but not fundamentally altering policy. The president seems to have changed his views during the long weekend at the ranch. At least the signals the Israelis began to receive started to change. But the evidence is not clear as to what, precisely, the president was thinking as the possibility of war became more and more real. The available record, however, is certainly consistent with the Israeli belief that the red light that had been switched on in mid-May had turned to yellow by early June.

When war did occur, a new definition was required and was quickly provided. Not surprisingly, the Soviet Union assumed a much greater salience once war had begun.[36] Then, with the cease-fire achieved, the third basic policy framework emerged, which emphasized the need to pursue a full peace agreement. This last policy was largely a reaction to the 1956–57 approach of pressing Israel for immediate withdrawal. The war of 1967 had shown that the Eisenhower decision had not brought peace; Johnson had opposed Eisenhower's pressure on Israel at the time, and now he had the chance to try an alternative approach. With little discussion and no apparent dissent, the United States found itself supporting Israel's hold on the newly conquered territories pending Arab willingness to make peace. Such is the power of the lessons of history that accumulate in the minds of presidents. "No repeat of Suez" may have seemed to President Johnson as plausible as "no more Munichs," but it would not be long before the dilemmas of the new policy would become evident.

PART TWO

The Nixon Presidency

CHAPTER FOUR

Cross-Purposes: Nixon, Rogers, and Kissinger, 1969–70

Richard M. Nixon was, to say the least, an unusual president. By the time he resigned from office in disgrace on August 9, 1974, his domestic support had virtually disappeared. The Watergate scandal, exposed in exquisite detail by the press, Congress, and the tapes of the president's conversations, revealed a suspicious man in the White House who lied, who was vindictive, and who appeared to be strangely indecisive and incoherent when it came to dealing with important policy issues. Many Americans, as well as foreigners, had difficulty reconciling this image with that of the Richard Nixon who was overwhelmingly reelected in 1972 to a second term in office, a man whose achievements in the realm of foreign policy won him the grudging support of many former opponents.

These two faces of President Nixon were no doubt part of the same complex, unhappy personality, but it is Nixon as foreign-policy strategist who is of primary concern here. Nixon viewed his experience in international affairs as one of his strongest assets and foreign relations as a particularly important arena for presidential action. As Eisenhower's vice-president for eight years, Nixon had been on the margins of key foreign-policy decisions of the 1950s. He had earned a reputation as a tough-minded anticommunist and an advocate of a strong international role for the United States.

During his period of exile from elective politics, from 1961 through 1968, Nixon had traveled widely and had met many heads of state. By chance, he was in Morocco at the time of the June 1967 war. His cable to Secretary of State Dean Rusk gives a glimpse of his views, uncluttered by those of subsequent advisers, at that defining moment:

I hope that with the outbreak of the Arab-Israel hostilities, our government will bring all possible influence to bear to have all major powers stand up to their responsibility for the maintenance of peace. Let us make it clear that the key to peace in the Middle East is now in Moscow and that peace efforts in the United Nations and multilaterally up to this time have been blocked by the Soviet Union. I hope, too, that in considering our actions in this situation, we remember that while all Arabs have strong feelings on the subject of Israel, many are not in agreement with Nasser and his ambitions for the UAR [United Arab Republic] and leadership of the Arab world.

My fear in the present circumstances is that unless we can demonstrate that our attachment to peace is impartial, we will have given the Soviet Union an unparalleled opportunity to extend its influence in the Arab world to the detriment of vastly important United States and free world interests.[1]

These trips to the Middle East must have made an impression on Nixon, for he spoke of them frequently in later years. In discussions of the region, he would refer to his talks with Israeli, Egyptian, and Saudi leaders, emphasizing his personal knowledge of key individuals and their countries. His experience in foreign affairs, such as it was, came largely through his own firsthand experience and discussions. He had little patience with academic studies or lengthy briefing materials. Nixon was very much a loner, rarely reaching out to others to discuss his views.

Unlike President Johnson, Nixon never betrayed a strong desire to immerse himself in the day-to-day flow of events and information. He prided himself instead on his detachment and his analytical ability to see problems in their broad strategic context. He admired strength and toughness, and firmly believed that foreign policy should be formulated in secret, with only minimal contributions from Congress and public opinion. And Nixon prided himself on not being beholden to the pro-Israeli lobby, since relatively few Jews had voted for him.[2]

THE NIXON TEAM

From the outset it was clear that President Nixon intended to make the basic decisions in foreign policy. To ensure his control of the vast foreign-policy bureaucracy—which he distrusted as being a bastion of the Democrats—he decided to reinvigorate the National Security Council system.[3] Nixon's NSC evolved substantially over the years, but at the beginning it was designed for two purposes: to provide the president with genuine policy alternatives, or options; and to educate the bureaucracy concerning the new themes in Nixon's foreign policy. Toward both these ends, Nixon requested an unprecedented number of policy studies in his first few months in office, mostly in the form of National Security Study Memoranda (NSSMs). These were to be discussed by a Senior Review Group (SRG),[4] then referred to the full NSC for decision, after which a National Security Decision Memorandum (NSDM) would be issued. Overseeing this elaborate system was a former Harvard professor, Henry A. Kissinger, Nixon's national security affairs adviser.

Kissinger was a well-known foreign-policy analyst. He first gained public recognition with the publication of an influential book in 1957, *Nuclear Weapons and Foreign Policy*. Subsequently he became a consultant to both the Kennedy and Johnson administrations, but his closest ties were with his earliest patron, Nelson Rockefeller. Kissinger's acceptance of the national security affairs position was as unexpected as Nixon's offer. The two men seemed fundamentally different in temperament and character, but they quickly recognized in each other a remarkable intellectual compatibility. Nixon was instinctual and decisive; Kissinger was analytical and subtle. Nevertheless, they held similar views of the international role of the United States, of the need for strength wedded to diplomacy, of the intimate links between domestic and foreign policy, and of the danger of nuclear war.

Within a short time, the Nixon-Kissinger team was working smoothly, and Kissinger had ascended from the obscurity of the White House basement to a well-appointed office on the first floor of the west wing.[5] Nixon and Kissinger both had a keen sense for the symbols as well as the realities of power. Nonetheless, Nixon deliberately kept Kissinger from dominating Middle East policy during the first year and one-half, at least in part because of his Jewish origins.[6]

For the position of secretary of state, Nixon named a close personal friend, William P. Rogers, a lawyer by profession who had served as attorney general in Eisenhower's cabinet. He was not particularly experienced in foreign policy, nor was his a strong, assertive personality. He did, however, have an affable, reassuring style and a dignified bearing. Given the modest role that Nixon envisaged for him, these were perhaps enough. Nonetheless, Nixon decided to entrust Rogers with the Middle East dossier, perhaps realizing that success there was unlikely and domestic controversy could be deflected toward the State Department rather than the White House.[7]

If Rogers seemed unlikely to be a particularly aggressive secretary of state, some of his subordinates in the department were men of considerable talent, energy, and ambition. Elliot Richardson, during his brief tenure as under secretary, played an important role in the running of the department and in keeping lines open to the White House. Unlike Rogers, Richardson quickly developed a close working relationship with Kissinger.

The new assistant secretary of state for the Near East and South Asia was a controversial figure. Joseph Sisco, formerly assistant secretary of state for international organizations, was a Democrat and had never served overseas in his long career in the State Department. His knowledge of the Middle East came from his years in Washington. He was a consummate bureaucratic politician; he knew the ins and the outs of the State Department; he was a man of drive, a skillful speaker, and a shrewd tactician. Working closely with him was Alfred L. Atherton, Jr., first as office director for Israel and Arab-Israeli affairs and later as deputy assistant secretary for the Near East. Atherton represented continuity, experience, professional expertise. He was cool when Sisco was hot. The two were a formidable pair in Middle East policymaking circles.[8]

NIXON'S FOREIGN POLICY

President Nixon, with the assistance of Henry Kissinger and some parts of the State Department, quickly established a set of priorities and guidelines for American foreign policy. Some represented new departures; others reflected continuities and standard responses to long-standing problems. Inevitably, Vietnam stood at the top of Nixon's agenda of foreign policy issues. Domestic dissent over Vietnam had destroyed Lyndon Johnson's chances for reelection and had produced a grave crisis of confidence and of conscience within the United States. Nixon was no doubt less tempted by the prospects of "victory" in Vietnam than Johnson had been, but at the same time he was strongly opposed to a sudden withdrawal of American forces.[9]

In private, Nixon and Kissinger expressed the fear that a precipitate withdrawal from Vietnam, followed by a communist victory, might provoke a right-wing McCarthyite backlash in the United States and would reinforce latent isolationist sentiments. The art of managing the Vietnam commitment was to disengage American troops in such a way that, domestically and internationally, the United States would still be able to conduct an effective foreign policy in other parts of the world, such as the Middle East, where important interests were at stake.

Apart from Vietnam, Nixon and Kissinger were primarily concerned with the other major powers, especially the Soviet Union. Both men were preoccupied with the dangers of nuclear war; both were intrigued by the possibility of establishing a new relationship with the Soviet Union that would help to ensure global stability and to minimize the risks of confrontation; both were prepared to transcend the ideological rivalry of the cold war and to establish ties with adversaries based on mutual interest.

Part of Nixon's strategy of restructuring the relations between the superpowers involved China. In October 1967 Nixon had published an article entitled "Asia after Viet Nam."[10] In it he wrote, "Any American policy toward Asia must come urgently to grips with the reality of China." Little public notice was taken of China during Nixon's first two years in office, but it is clear in retrospect that the president and Kissinger were already laying the groundwork for a dramatic opening to Peking. Apart from intrinsic benefits from restoring U.S.-Chinese relations after a generation of hostility, Nixon recognized that an American-Chinese connection could have a moderating effect on Soviet foreign policy. In addition, improved ties to Moscow and Peking might help bring about a Vietnam settlement and ensure that the post-Vietnam era in Asia would be comparatively free of conflict. Consequently, Vietnam, the Soviet Union, and China came to be linked as priority concerns to the Nixon administration. Significantly, each was managed almost exclusively from the White House, the president providing general guidance and Kissinger and his staff working on the details of the new policies and overseeing their implementation.

One priority area remained for the State Department to deal with: the Middle East. The Arab-Israeli conflict was generally seen as potentially dangerous, although hopelessly complex and perhaps less urgent than the other tasks facing the administration. Some momentum had already been established under Johnson, and around it a modified policy might be constructed. The State Department was anxious to play a leading role and was able to call on impressive expertise. Thus, with some skepticism about the likelihood of immediate results, Nixon authorized the State Department to develop and carry forward a new American policy toward the Arab-Israeli conflict. If it should succeed, there would be credit enough for everyone; if it were to fail, Nixon and Kissinger would be relatively free of blame.

Nixon's own views on the Middle East, as reflected in his cable to Rusk on the opening day of the June 1967 war, seemed to combine a strong dose of cold war assumptions about the role of the Soviets, along with an expressed belief that the United States could best compete with Moscow by being "impartial" in the Arab-Israeli conflict. The concern with the Soviets was similar to Kissinger's, but Nixon's "evenhandedness" was closer to the conventional State Department position. In short, Nixon embodied in his own mind the two competing paradigms for how best to tackle the Arab-Israeli conflict. What came to be seen as a great battle between Kissinger and Rogers was also, apparently, an unresolved debate within Nixon's own mind.[11]

By contrast, Kissinger had well-developed, if not well-informed, views on the Middle East. This was not a part of the world he knew well. His inclination was to look at issues in the Middle East in terms of the broader U.S.-Soviet rivalry. His views may have crystallized at the time of the Suez crisis, when he concluded that Eisenhower's policy of checking the British-French move against Nasser was misguided. One should not, he believed, weaken friends and help adversaries who depended on Soviet support.[12] In terms of the realities of 1969, this led Kissinger to advocate strong backing for Israel until such time as the Arabs decided to break with Moscow. The normal State Department instinct of launching initiatives was anathema to his way of thinking, and he did what he could to persuade Nixon of the correctness of his views. For the first year or so, he did not always get his way, but that did not stop him from trying to undermine State's preferred strategies.

Nixon's initial approach to foreign-policy issues did not center on the Middle East. His big themes were aimed at managing America's extrication from Vietnam without upsetting the global balance of power. To these ends, he spoke frequently of "linkage," a "structure of peace," "détente," and "negotiations," all against the backdrop of keeping the United States strong and restoring domestic consensus behind broad foreign policy goals.

A favorite Nixon-Kissinger concept was linkage. This meant that issues would not be negotiated with Moscow in isolation from one another. Rather, the United States in its talks with the Soviet Union would aim for a global settlement of issues. Progress should be made across the board on Vietnam, strategic-arms talks, and the Middle East. Simultaneous negotiations in each of these areas would mean that trade-offs could be made, thus adding flexibility and nuance to the negotiations. A Soviet concession on Vietnam might be reciprocated by an American move in the Middle East. As an intellectual construct, it made sense; in practice, it rarely worked. Nevertheless, throughout 1969, linkage was one of the key concepts of the Nixon foreign policy.

"Negotiations" became another theme of the Nixon diplomacy. Nixon and Kissinger shared the view that force and diplomacy must go hand in hand, which meant that negotiation with adversaries was not incompatible with threats or the actual use of military might. Kissinger in particular was fascinated by the process of negotiations and proved to be an astonishingly successful negotiator in his own right. Soon after Nixon took office, negotiations on a wide range of issues—the Middle East, Vietnam, China, and strategic arms—were begun or accelerated.

The objective of the negotiations was to create, in the Nixon-Kissinger jargon, a "structure of peace," the main components of which would be U.S.-Soviet "détente," arms limitations, and eventually a normalization of U.S.-Chinese relations. All this was to be accomplished without detriment to traditional allies—the NATO partners and Japan—and without much regard for the third world, where détente would serve to limit the dangers to global peace inherent in local conflicts.

To pursue such an ambitious foreign policy at a time of great popular disenchantment, President Nixon sought to meet the demand that America no longer play the role of world policeman, while at the same time avoiding the extreme of isolationism. This delicately balanced posture of restrained internationalism came to be known as the Nixon Doctrine, one manifestation of which was Vietnamization—the gradual disengagement of American combat troops from Vietnam, coupled with high levels of aid to the Saigon regime and an active search for a political settlement.[13]

Nixon's great hope during his first term was that he would be able to recreate a domestic consensus on behalf of his foreign-policy goals. The style and timing of each major foreign-policy step were chosen with an eye toward domestic public opinion. Vietnamization and the end of the draft helped to ease the divisions created by the war, and the prospect of a peace agreement in Vietnam during 1972 greatly enhanced Nixon's popularity. The spectacular opening to China, carried out in total secrecy and with high drama, also strengthened the Nixon-Kissinger team. Finally, the Strategic Arms Limitation Talks (SALT) agreement of May 1972 seemed to hold out the promise of an end to the nuclear arms race.

Nixon seemed to worry about the explosive potential of the Arab-Israeli conflict—he repeatedly used the pre–World War I Balkans analogy. Tempering Nixon's willingness to tackle the Arab-Israeli conflict, however, was the poisoned domestic political climate created by the Vietnam War. And Middle East diplomacy held little prospect of restoring the shattered domestic consensus. On the contrary. A serious effort to resolve the differences between Israel and its Arab neighbors was bound to be controversial. In addition, the president's key advisers were not in agreement on how to proceed. Public opinion was very pro-Israeli, still seeing the Jewish state as a heroic David facing a pro-Soviet, aggressive Arab Goliath. Nor was there a compelling strategic reason for tackling the Arab-Israeli conflict, since the oil issue was generally not seen as related, the Arabs were not believed to have a serious military option, and American interests therefore did not seem to be immediately at risk. With these perceptions in mind, it seems, Nixon was only prepared to allow State to test the waters of Arab-Israeli diplomacy, but was reluctant to throw the full weight of his office behind an activist policy.

THE DEBATE OVER INTERESTS

Two sets of concerns dominated the thinking of policymakers in early 1969 as the administration undertook its first review of the situation in the Middle East. The president and Kissinger seemed to be chiefly worried by the global ramifications of the Arab-Israeli conflict. Nixon repeatedly used highly colored and explosive imagery in describing the area. Again and again the theme of confrontation between the superpowers was mentioned in discussions of the Middle East. This, it was said, was what made the Arab-Israeli conflict even more dangerous than Vietnam.[14]

The State Department professionals tended to agree that the situation in the Middle East was dangerous, but their perceptions were more affected by the prospective threats to American interests arising from trends within the area. At State, one heard of the "erosion" of American influence, the "deterioration" of the American position, the "radicalization" of the Arab world, and "polarization." The region was viewed in stark, sometimes simplistic terms: the United States, with Israel and the "moderate" Arabs, aligned against the Soviet Union and the "radical" Arabs. It was widely believed that the continuation of the Arab-Israeli conflict would work to the advantage of the Soviet Union, resulting in the isolation of the United States and Israel in a sea of radical, anti-American Arabs. The rise of the militant Palestinian fedayeen movement during 1968 was a harbinger of things to come: increased violence and terrorism, direct threats to American lives and interests, mounting instability, and eventually another war.[15]

The White House and the Departments of State and Defense were all concerned with one other issue involving the Middle East: the possibility that Israel would develop, or possibly already had developed, nuclear weapons. This fear brought together those who worried about regional trends and those who were preoccupied by global, strategic issues. No one knew quite what to do about the Israeli nuclear option, but it added to the sense that the Middle East was too dangerous to ignore.[16]

The combination of these preoccupations led to several related policy guidelines that shaped the American approach to the Middle East from early 1969 until August 1970. Most important was the broad consensus, minus Kissinger, that the United States should adopt an active diplomatic role in promoting a political settlement based on the principles embodied in UN Resolution 242. The efforts of the Johnson administration were judged as having been too passive, those of UN Ambassador Gunnar Jarring as too cautious. The United States, in concert with the other major powers, and in particular the Soviet Union, should therefore seek to engage the regional parties in a negotiating process, the first step of which would be a refinement of the principles of a settlement to be worked out in talks between the two superpowers. The hoped-for result would be considerably less than an imposed settlement, which the administration rejected, but would be something other than the directly negotiated peace agreement that the Israelis desired.[17]

The State Department had long advocated an "evenhanded" approach to the Arab-Israeli conflict. In essence, this meant adopting a posture that was neither overtly pro-Arab nor openly pro-Israeli. With respect to arms deliveries to Israel, the evenhanded approach urged restraint, and on territorial withdrawal it favored a clear statement opposing Israeli acquisition of territory from the 1967 war. As to the quality of the peace agreement, the standards to be applied to Arab commitments were not too rigorous. From the Israeli perspective, an "evenhanded" American policy was tantamount to being pro-Arab. When President-elect Nixon's special emissary to the Middle East, Governor William Scranton, used the word *evenhanded* in December 1968, it set off shock waves in Israel.

Fortunately for the Israelis, Kissinger was skeptical of the virtues of evenhandedness, and at an early date the Israelis began to bypass Rogers in favor of direct dealing with the White House. Kissinger, unlike Rogers and Sisco, believed a diplomatic stalemate in which Israel was kept strong would ultimately persuade the Arabs that it was pointless to rely on Soviet support. Then they would turn to the United States for assistance, the price for which would be a break with Moscow. The Arabs, in Kissinger's view, should not be given the impression they could count on both superpowers to pressure Israel to make concessions unless they were prepared for very far reaching concessions of their own. Kissinger had little patience with the view that the Arabs would show more moderation if the United States took some distance from Israeli positions and acted with restraint on arms supplies to the Jewish state.[18]

The basic difference between State and Kissinger could be summed up fairly easily. State saw tensions in the Middle East as growing from regional conditions that the Soviets could exploit for their own advantage. To reduce Soviet options, State officials argued, the United States should try to resolve the underlying disputes. Kissinger was less sanguine about the prospects for resolving the regional conflicts, and in any case he believed it was Soviet involvement in the disputes that made them particularly dangerous. From his balance-of-power perspective, the first order of business was to reduce the Soviet role. Nixon, interestingly, seemed to agree with both schools of thought, depending on circumstances.

POLICYMAKING

In January 1969 President Nixon expressed the view that the Middle East situation was potentially explosive. His thinking was best reflected in his answers to questions posed during a press conference on January 27, 1969, just one week after he took office:

What I want to do is to see to it that we have strategic arms talks in a way and at a time that will promote, if possible, progress on outstanding political problems at the same time—for example, on the problem of the Mideast and on other outstanding problems in which the United States and the Soviet Union, acting together, can serve the cause of peace. . . . I believe we need new initiatives and new leadership on the part of the United States in order to cool off the situation in the Mideast. I consider it a powder keg, very explosive. It needs to be defused. I am open to any suggestions that may cool it off and reduce the possibility of another explosion, because the next explosion in the Mideast, I think, could involve very well a confrontation between the nuclear powers, which we want to avoid.[19]

On February 1 the National Security Council met for an exhaustive review of Middle East policy. Three basic alternatives, each discussed at length in NSSM 2, were considered:

—Leave the search for a settlement of the Arab-Israeli conflict to the parties and to Ambassador Jarring.

—Pursue a more active U.S. policy, involving U.S.-USSR talks.

—Assume that no settlement is possible and concentrate efforts on objectives short of a settlement.

The second alternative was decided on, the third remaining available as a fallback position in the event of failure. The NSC discussions identified several principles that should guide U.S. policy.

—The parties to the dispute must participate in the negotiations at some point in the process. Although the United States would not hesitate to move somewhat ahead of Israel, any final agreement would be reached only with Israel's participation and consent.

—The objective of a settlement would be a binding agreement, not necessarily in the form of a peace treaty, but involving some form of contractual commitments. The administration was concerned about the imbalance in the concessions to be sought from each side. The Israelis would give up territory; the Arabs would give promises to respect Israel's sovereignty.

—Withdrawal of Israeli forces should take place back to the international frontier between Israel and Egypt, with a special arrangement for Gaza. There should be Israeli evacuation of the West Bank of Jordan, with only minor border changes.

—Some critical areas should be demilitarized.

—Jordan should have a civilian and religious role within a unified city of Jerusalem.

—There should be a settlement of the refugee problem.

Issues of a guarantee to Israel and assurances of arms were also discussed. Then the NSC considered two possible diplomatic strategies. First, the United States could unilaterally present a peace plan. This was rejected. Second, the United States could follow a step-by-step approach whereby specific elements of a settlement would be gradually injected into the negotiations. It was recognized that withdrawal and the nature of the peace agreement would be the most critical issues. Primacy would be given to developing common ground in the U.S.-Soviet talks, with the aim of producing a joint document that could then be approved by the four powers and given to Jarring to present to the local parties.[20]

On February 4 Nixon again met with the NSC to discuss the Middle East. This time he asked for a study that would describe a peace settlement, assess its acceptability to the parties, and discuss the role of outside guarantees. He also asked what the links would be between the two-power and four-power talks. Finally, he asked what the United States should plan to do if a general settlement was impossible. The following day Nixon announced that the United States was preparing a new initiative in the Middle East on a multilateral basis to head off a "major war." For the rest of the year U.S. policy adhered closely to the guidelines laid down in February. The eventual result was the Rogers Plan.

LAUNCHING THE ROGERS PLAN

Several simultaneous rounds of negotiations were soon under way. U.S.-Israeli meetings were frequent, as the administration tried to allay the apprehensions of the Israeli government, now headed by Prime Minister

Golda Meir.[21] Once the U.S.-Soviet talks began in earnest, Israel was initially kept closely informed of the progress in the talks, although by the fall this pattern of consultations had weakened. Finally, the four-power talks proceeded simultaneously with the U.S.-Soviet ones.

The U.S.-Soviet talks, conducted primarily by Sisco and Soviet Ambassador Anatoly Dobrynin, quickly took center stage. Between March 18 and April 22, they met nine times. The American objective in this round was to determine whether there was sufficient agreement on general principles to justify trying to reach a joint proposal. During this phase the United States spelled out its basic position on a settlement in a document presented to the participants in the four-power talks on March 24. The main points of this document were the following:

—Final borders would be agreed upon by the parties. Minor adjustments in the 1967 lines were possible.

—There would be no imposed settlement.

—The four powers would work closely with and through Ambassador Jarring.

—A final agreement would take the form of a contract signed by all parties.

—Peace would be achieved as part of a package settlement.[22]

The last point, on the need for a package settlement, was of fundamental importance. It meant that there would be no Israeli withdrawal until all elements of a peace agreement on all fronts had been achieved. This stood in stark contrast to the insistence of the Soviets and the Arabs that Israel should withdraw first, after which an end to belligerency and other issues could be discussed.

During March and April the situation in the Middle East began to deteriorate significantly. Fighting broke out along the Suez Canal; fedayeen attacks mounted in severity, as did Israeli retaliation; and in early April Nasser announced the abrogation of the cease-fire, initiating what came to be known as the war of attrition.[23] In Lebanon a state of emergency was declared in April after clashes with the fedayeen, and for months Lebanon was virtually without a government.

Against this background the pace of diplomacy quickened. The four powers—the United States, the Soviet Union, Great Britain, and France—held their first meeting on April 3. These talks continued at regular intervals into June. Meanwhile the United States began to talk directly with two of the Arab parties to the conflict, Jordan and Egypt.

King Hussein met with Nixon and Rogers on April 8. The administration was sympathetic to Jordan but realized that the king was unable to move on a settlement without Nasser. To help Jordan, it would also be necessary to help Egypt. Hussein did bring with him a concession from Nasser that might smooth the path of U.S.-Egyptian relations. The king publicly declared that he was authorized to state that, as part of a settlement, there would be freedom of navigation in the Suez Canal for all nations.[24]

Several days later Nixon met with a top aide of Nasser, Mahmoud Fawzi, who confirmed this point and added privately that Egypt would not feel constrained by Syria's opposition to a political settlement. In short, Egypt and Jordan indicated they were prepared for a settlement, even if Syria was not. Kissinger, however, was not persuaded by Fawzi that Egypt was prepared for much real flexibility.[25]

To assess the results of this first phase of Middle East talks, Nixon held a meeting of the National Security Council on April 25. The major question to be discussed was whether the United States should put forward more specific proposals for a settlement. Secretary Rogers took the position that the talks had not yet reached the "cutting edge." He noted that Nasser was an "enigma" and that the Israelis were showing a growing tendency to define security in terms of territory. It was decided that Sisco should resume his talks with Dobrynin, introducing more specific proposals as appropriate.[26]

Between May 6 and May 12 Sisco conveyed the main points of the United States proposal on an Egyptian-Israeli settlement to Ambassador Dobrynin. The Soviet position had evolved somewhat, the most important change being acceptance of the idea of a package settlement.[27] In the American view it was now up to the Soviet Union to bring pressure to bear on the Egyptians to accept these points. In return, the United States would be prepared to use its influence with Israel to gain Israeli adherence to the basic principles agreed upon by the superpowers.

A crucial debate within the American administration concerned the role of the Soviet Union. Some at State felt that the Soviet Union, for global-strategy reasons, would be prepared to cooperate with the United States in the Middle East, even if that might cause Moscow some strain in its relations with Nasser. In fact, it was privately hoped that the Soviets might weaken their position in Egypt by trying to force Nasser to accept the U.S.-Soviet proposals. Kissinger doubted that the Soviets would be prepared to sacrifice regional interests for the sake of improved U.S.-Soviet relations. He argued that the Soviet Union had worked hard to build a position of influence in the Middle East; to maintain that position, it depended chiefly on providing arms to key clients; and if peace was established, these arms would no longer be needed in large quantities. The Soviets therefore had an interest in preventing a real peace agreement, preferring instead a state of "controlled tension." From this perspective, the U.S.-Soviet talks had one purpose, as seen by Moscow and Cairo: to get the United States to pressure Israel to withdraw from Arab territory in return for only minimal Arab concessions. Nixon appeared to be suspicious of the Soviets but felt they should be tested.

An early indication of Soviet intentions was provided by Soviet Foreign Minister Gromyko's trip to Cairo from June 10 to 13. After high-level talks in Moscow, which included Ambassador Dobrynin, the Soviets on June 17 made a formal counterproposal to the U.S. position presented to them in May by Sisco. Although the Soviet position was still not entirely compatible with the U.S. proposal, there was agreement on the need for a lasting peace agreement and on a package settlement. In addition, the Soviets reported that they had persuaded Nasser to accept informal direct talks with the Israelis, patterned on the Rhodes armistice negotiations in 1949.

The Soviet proposal was sufficiently encouraging to prompt further discussions. From July 14 to 17 Sisco met in Moscow with Soviet leaders, and on July 15 he presented a document to them that embodied the earlier United States proposals, which had been modified to correspond to the Soviet points of June 17.[28]

With the completion of Sisco's talks in Moscow, the positions of the two superpowers were fairly well defined. Each pleaded its inability to move further in the absence of concessions from the other side. In particular, the Soviet Union urged the United States to be more explicit on the final border between Egypt and Israel. Sisco had said in Moscow that a more concrete American position might be possible on the final border if the Soviets could be more specific on Egyptian commitments to peace and on direct negotiations. In particular, the United States insisted that the state of war should end with the signing of an agreement, not with the completion of Israeli withdrawal, and also was adamant that peace was incompatible with continued fedayeen activity.

For the rest of the summer the positions of the superpowers remained essentially frozen,[29] but the situation in the Middle East did not. Fighting along the canal intensified; Israel informally approached the United States in July with a request for an additional 100 A-4 Skyhawks and 25 F-4

Phantoms to make up for the Mirages that France was refusing to sell.[30] Then, on September 1, one of the most conservative and pro-Western of the Arab governments, that of King Idris of Libya, was overthrown in a surprise coup d'état led by young Nasserist army officers. Coupled with the "radical" coup in Sudan the previous May, this seemed to confirm the fears of those who saw a trend toward extremism and violence in the Arab world in the absence of progress toward a peace agreement.

Early in September, the first F-4 Phantom jets (the furnishing of which President Johnson had agreed to in late 1968) reached Israel. They soon became a potent symbol to the Arabs of American support for Israel, and an intensive campaign began in the Arab world to prevent further such agreements.

On September 11 another NSC meeting on the Middle East was held. Rogers argued that the time had come for the United States to move to its fallback position on Israeli withdrawal to the Israeli-Egyptian international frontier. According to Kissinger, "The advocates of further concessions argued that time was working against us; the longer the deadlock lasted, the more our position in the Arab world would deteriorate. I stressed that the opposite was true. A continuing deadlock was in our interest; it would persuade Egypt to face the reality that Soviet tutelage and a radical foreign policy were obstacles to progress and that only the United States could bring about a settlement; it would demonstrate Soviet impotence and in time might impel a fundamental reconstruction of Arab, and especially of Egyptian, foreign policies." Nixon, who had already been warned of the "domestic buzz saw" that awaited him if he backed Rogers on the 1967 borders issue, sided with Kissinger. Thus Rogers was not given authority to reveal the fallback position in his upcoming talks with Gromyko.[31]

Between September 22 and 30 Rogers and Sisco met with Gromyko and Dobrynin in New York at the United Nations. President Nixon, in his speech to the UN General Assembly on September 18, had emphasized the need for "binding, irrevocable commitments" as part of a peace agreement in the Middle East. The question now was whether the Soviets would be able or willing to elicit such commitments from Egypt.

Meanwhile Nixon met with Prime Minister Golda Meir on September 25. Meir treated Nixon as if he were a great friend of the Jewish people, and in return he indicated considerable sympathy for Israeli concerns. Meir requested additional arms, 25 more F-4 Phantoms and 100 A-4 Skyhawks, as well as $200 million a year to help pay for them.

Nixon's response was somewhat elliptical, suggesting that he would trade "hardware for software," which seemed to mean that arms supplies would be linked to political concessions.[32]

During Meir's visit Nixon also agreed that a direct channel of communications between the two leaders should be established, bypassing the State Department. Nixon was fond of using such back channels, and soon Henry Kissinger and Israel's ambassador, Yitzhak Rabin, were linked by a private phone line. Rabin used this improved access to the White House to argue forcefully that Israel should intensify its bombardments deep inside Egypt. Even if the State Department might be urging restraint, Rabin could argue that his sources were egging Israel on.[33]

Seemingly unaffected by Meir's visit, the State Department continued to press forward with its plan for reaching a common position on principles with the Soviet Union. Gromyko reported some progress in his talks with the Egyptians. They would apparently agree to Rhodes-style talks. But then on October 10 Egypt denied that it had agreed to any such thing. Meanwhile attacks on United States policy in the Middle East were mounting, especially in Lebanon, where serious fighting was going on and Syria seemed to be on the verge of intervention.

In this confusing setting Rogers asked for authority to go forward with the fallback position in talks with the Soviets. Nixon agreed, and on October 28 Sisco handed Dobrynin the final paragraph of a proposed joint document containing the United States fallback position on Israeli withdrawal. (See appendix B.) But, according to Kissinger, the president characteristically sought "to hedge his bets by asking John Mitchell and Leonard Garment—counselor to the President and adviser on Jewish affairs—to let Jewish community leaders know his doubts about State's diplomacy. Nixon implied strongly to them that he would see to it that nothing came of the very initiatives he was authorizing."[34]

THE ROGERS PLAN AND ITS RECEPTION

The Rogers Plan, as it came to be known, consisted of a short preamble calling for the conclusion of a "final and reciprocally binding accord" between Egypt and Israel, to be negotiated under the auspices of UN Ambassador Jarring following procedures used at Rhodes in 1949, and to be based on the following ten points:

1. As part of a package settlement, Egypt and Israel would "determine a timetable and procedures for withdrawal of Israeli armed forces from UAR territory occupied during the conflict of 1967."

2. The state of war between Egypt and Israel would end, and a formal state of peace would be established. Both sides would undertake to prevent all forms of aggressive actions from their territory against the people and armed forces of the other.

3. Both sides would agree on the location of secure and recognized borders between them. The agreement would include the establishment of demilitarized zones, the taking of effective measures in the Sharm al-Shaykh area to guarantee freedom of navigation in the Strait of Tiran, and arrangements for security and the final disposition of Gaza. Within this framework, "the former international boundary between Egypt and the mandated territory of Palestine would become the secure and recognized boundary between Israel and the UAR."

4. The two sides would work out agreement on zones to be demilitarized, measures to guarantee freedom of navigation through the Strait of Tiran, and effective security measures for and final disposition of Gaza.

5. The two sides would agree that the Strait of Tiran is an international waterway, and the principle of free navigation would apply to all states, including Israel.

6. In exercising sovereignty over the Suez Canal, Egypt would affirm the right of ships of all nations, including Israel, to pass freely through the canal without discrimination or interference.

7. The two sides would agree to abide by the terms of a just settlement of the refugee problem as agreed upon in the final accord between Jordan and Israel.

8. Egypt and Israel would mutually agree to respect and acknowledge each other's sovereignty, territorial integrity, and right to live in peace within secure and recognized borders.

9. The final agreement would be recorded in a document signed by the two sides and deposited with the UN. The final agreement would provide that "a material breach of that accord by one of the parties shall entitle the other to invoke the breach as a ground for suspending its performance in whole or in part."

10. The two sides would agree to submit the final agreement to the UN Security Council for ratification.

On November 10 both the United States and the Soviet Union presented the text of the plan to Egypt. Several days later, the Egyptian foreign minister sent a noncommittal reply to Rogers, noting some positive elements in the proposals, but holding off on a final commitment until an "integrated formula" for a comprehensive settlement was put forward.

In brief, Egypt was not prepared to consider a bilateral deal with Israel even if it stood to recover all its territory.[35] After nearly a month with no further reply from Egypt and no official reaction from the Soviet Union, Secretary Rogers, on December 9, outlined the basic elements of the plan in a public speech.[36] The following day Israel rejected Rogers's proposals; the NSC met on the Middle East, against the background of warnings of worsening trends in the area conveyed the previous day to Nixon by a group of prominent businessmen and former officials, David Rockefeller, John McCloy, and Robert Anderson.

On December 18 the United States presented a parallel plan for a Jordan-Israel settlement to the four powers.[37] It was hoped that this would strengthen King Hussein at the Arab summit meeting that was to open in Rabat the following day. The plan contained many of the same points as the October 28 document, adding or modifying a few points to fit the special circumstances on the Jordanian front.[38] The permanent border, for example, would "approximate" the armistice demarcation line existing before the 1967 war but would allow for modifications based on "administrative or economic convenience." In addition, point four of the December 18 document stressed that Israel and Jordan would settle the problem of Jerusalem, recognizing that the city would be unified, with both countries sharing the civic and economic responsibilities of city government. Point eight provided guidelines for a settlement of the refugee problem that would allow for repatriation or resettlement with compensation. An annual quota of refugees to be repatriated would be agreed upon between the parties.[39] King Hussein was reported to be pleased with the American proposal.

On December 22 the Israeli cabinet issued a statement saying that "Israel will not be sacrificed by any power or inter-power policy and will reject any attempt to impose a forced solution on her. . . . The proposal submitted by the USA cannot but be interpreted by the Arab rulers as an attempt to appease them at the expense of Israel."[40] As Rogers was deploring the Israeli use of the word "appease" the following day, the Soviets delivered an official note rejecting the Rogers proposals virtually in their entirety.[41]

The Israeli and Soviet rejections of the Rogers Plan, and Egypt's nonacceptance, put a sudden end to the first Middle East initiative of the Nixon Administration. With it died the hope that "linkage" diplomacy would help provide the key to peace in that area. Not for the first time, a basic reassessment of policy toward the Arab-Israeli conflict was undertaken. And although the Rogers proposals remained the most explicit statement of a preferred American peace settlement, they ceased to be the operational basis for American policy toward the Arab-Israeli conflict. Somewhat ironically, however, the eventual peace agreement between Egypt and Israel in March 1979 bore a remarkable resemblance to the principles of the Rogers Plan.

REASSESSMENT

When foreign policies have fallen short of expectations or have spectacularly failed, previously held images that buttressed those policies may be rapidly revised. New "definitions of the situation" are likely to emerge in short order, reflecting both the "lessons learned" from the preceding phase of policy formulation and the assessment of the new situation to be dealt with.

The Rogers initiative of 1969 had clearly failed, at least for the time being. Apart from Jordan there were simply no takers, and the Israeli reaction in particular was extremely hostile. What had gone wrong? Most policymakers agreed in retrospect that it had been naive to assume that the United States would be able to separate the Soviet Union from Egypt during the process of negotiations. The justification for the two-power talks had been that the United States and the Soviet Union would find it easier to reach agreement on principles than Israel and Egypt, and that they could both use their influence constructively to moderate the positions of their "clients." The concept fit nicely with Nixon's emphasis on "linkage," "détente," and "negotiations."

Even if the Soviets could have been persuaded to sign on to the Rogers Plan, it is not at all obvious that Israel could have been budged. Kissinger was actively opposing the plan, and he seems to have been signaling Rabin that Washington would welcome a more aggressive Israeli military campaign against Nasser. Unless Nixon had been prepared to back Rogers fully, and he apparently was not, the Israelis would not conceivably comply. The Rogers-Kissinger feud, and Nixon's own ambivalence, meant that the Rogers Plan really never had a chance of succeeding.

Domestic politics in the United States played a role. Kissinger and Nixon respected the strength of Israel's support in Congress and in public opinion generally. Kissinger also found it misguided and possibly dangerous for the United States to try to improve its relations with adversaries—the Soviet Union and Egypt—by pressuring its own friend, Israel. While such things might be done in the interest of achieving a genuine peace agreement, they should not become part of the standard American negotiating repertoire. The Soviets and Arabs should instead learn that U.S. influence with Israel was conditional on their restraint and moderation.

The lessons drawn from the failure of the Rogers Plan of 1969 were fairly obvious by early 1970. First, since it was impossible to separate the Soviet Union from Egypt, Washington would henceforth deal directly with Nasser when necessary rather than through Moscow. Second, since American concessions had not been reciprocated, the next move would have to come from the Soviets or Egyptians. No further unilateral U.S. concessions would be made. The United States and Israel could afford to sit tight until the "other side" had completed its own reassessment and concluded that a resumption of serious negotiations was needed. Third, any future American initiative would be less legalistic in tone, less public, and perhaps less ambitious. The package-settlement approach, though appealing in theory, was simply too complicated. Failure on one issue would prevent progress anywhere. More modest initiatives would henceforth be considered.

Two developments threatened this new consensus almost as rapidly as it emerged. First, the fighting in the Middle East escalated sharply during the spring of 1970, particularly with the introduction of Soviet SAM-3 surface-to-air missiles in Egypt, Israeli deep-penetration bombing attacks near Cairo, the dispatch of ten thousand or more Soviet advisers to Egypt, and the appearance of Soviet combat pilots flying air cover over the Egyptian heartland.[42] Second, the domestic pressures on the Nixon administration to abandon the Rogers Plan and to accede to an Israeli request for 100 A-4 and 25 F-4 jets mounted rapidly. With congressional elections on the horizon, members of both the House and Senate became particularly vocal in support of Israel.

The administration now faced two urgent problems in the Arab-Israeli dispute. One was to take some type of political initiative to end the fighting and to begin talks on a settlement. The other was to respond to Israeli arms requests, especially as Soviet involvement in the conflict grew. A dilemma, however, was acutely perceived by State Department officials. To pursue a credible political initiative aimed at Nasser, the United States would have to appear to be evenhanded. This was particularly difficult at a time when American-made Phantom jets were bombing the outskirts of Cairo with impunity and the Israelis were virtually declaring that their goal was to topple the Nasser regime. At the same time the United States could not indefinitely stand by and watch Soviet arms and personnel flow into Egypt without some response. This need to respond had as much to do with global politics as with the Middle East. Kissinger was especially insistent on this latter point, and his influence with Nixon was on the rise. The somewhat schizophrenic nature of U.S. policy during the next seven months was rooted in this bureaucratic and conceptual dualism.

RESUMPTION OF DIPLOMACY AND ARMS FOR ISRAEL

The first signs of a new tone in American Middle East policy after the abortive Rogers effort came in January 1970. President Nixon, in several public statements, tried to mend the U.S.-Israeli relationship and warn the Soviet Union about the consequences of its uncooperative policy in the area. For example, on January 25 the president sent a message to an emergency meeting of the conference of presidents of American Jewish organizations in which he reaffirmed his support for Arab-Israeli negotiations and stated that the United States was carefully watching the military balance. Then, in a press conference on January 30, Nixon surprised his staff and the Israelis by stating that he would announce his decision on Israel's pending arms requests within thirty days. The issue of arms to Israel had become particularly acute in the aftermath of the French decision to sell Libya more than 100 Mirage jets, some of which had originally been earmarked for Israel.

While Nixon was seeking to mend fences with the Israelis, President Nasser was seeking to accelerate the flow of arms and aid from the Soviet Union. Early in January the Israelis, finally taking the advice of their ambassador in Washington, had begun an intensified bombing campaign in Egypt's heartland, ostensibly designed to force Nasser to divert some of his forces from the sensitive canal area but also aimed at exposing his weakness to his own people.[43] In response, Nasser decided to make a secret visit to the Soviet capital. According to Egyptian sources, Nasser pleaded not only for an effective missile defense against the Israeli Phantoms but also for Soviet personnel and pilots to ensure that the system should operate effectively while Egyptians were being trained for the new equipment.[44] The Soviet reply was affirmative, and by March large quantities of arms and advisers were arriving in Egypt. In mid-April the first Soviet pilots were observed flying combat sorties in response to Israeli raids.

The stepped-up Soviet role in the conflict did not come as a total surprise in Washington. In a very frank letter to President Nixon dated January 31, Premier Kosygin had stated:

There is danger that in the immediate future the military actions may become wide scale. . . . We consider it our duty, however, to draw your attention, Mr. President, to the highly risky consequences the course chosen by the Israeli leaders may have both from the point of view of the situation in the Middle East and international relations as a whole. . . . We would like to tell you in all frankness that if Israel continues its adventurism, to bomb the territory of the UAR and other Arab states the Soviet Union will be forced to see to it that the Arab states have means at their disposal with the help of which due rebuff to the arrogant aggressor could be made.[45]

Kissinger forwarded Kosygin's letter to Nixon, with the notation that this was the first Soviet threat to the Nixon administration. Kissinger recommended a tough reply, which was forthcoming on February 4.[46] President Nixon rejected the Soviet effort to place the blame for the fighting on Israel alone and called for the prompt restoration of the cease-fire and an understanding on limitations of arms shipments into the area. In concluding, the president noted:

It is a matter of regret that Soviet unresponsiveness to these proposals [of October 28 and December 18, 1969] is holding up this process [of negotiations]; a more constructive Soviet reply is required if progress toward a settlement is to be made.

We note your desire to work with us in bringing peace to this area. We do not believe peace can come if either side seeks unilateral advantage.[47]

This last point was stated even more forcefully in the president's "State of the World" message, released on February 18:

This Administration has shown its readiness to work with the Soviet Union for peace and to work alongside the Soviet Union in cooperation with nations in the area in pursuit of peace. But the United States would view any effort by the Soviet Union to seek predominance in the Middle East as a matter of grave concern. . . . Any effort by an outside power to exploit local conflict for its own advantage or to seek a special position of its own would be contrary to that goal [the freedom of other nations to determine their own futures].

For these reasons, this Administration has not only pressed the efforts to restore observance of the cease-fire and to help begin the process of negotiating a genuine peace. It has also urged an agreement to limit the shipment of arms to the Middle East as a step which could help stabilize the situation in the absence of a settlement. In the meantime, however, I now reaffirm our stated intention to maintain careful watch on the balance of military forces and to provide arms to friendly states as the need arises.[48]

Here are to be seen the strands of American policy over the next months: a warning to the Soviets; a call for restoration of the cease-fire and for the beginning of negotiations; and an ambiguous policy on arms for Israel, refusing a posture of unilateral restraint and promising to watch military developments closely. A distinctly Kissingerian tone could now be heard.

On balance, Nixon seemed to be leaning toward an early and positive decision on Israel's arms requests. The rest of the bureaucracy was generally opposed to the supply of more Phantom jets, arguing that Israeli military superiority was still unquestioned and that Soviet arms shipments were a response to Israel's reckless campaign of deep penetration bombing using the Phantoms.[49]

The president's thirty-day self-imposed deadline for making a decision on the F-4s came and went with no announcement. Several factors seem to have dictated continued restraint. First, and perhaps most important, was Nixon's displeasure at the way in which the American Jewish community had treated French President Georges Pompidou during his visit in late February.[50] According to many sources, the president was so incensed at the demonstrations and discourtesies during the Pompidou visit that he ordered that routine messages to pro-Israeli groups be suspended. Second, the four-power talks were resumed in late February and the Soviets hinted at a more flexible posture. In a secret meeting with Rogers on March 11, Ambassador Dobrynin stated that the Soviet Union had managed to obtain political concessions from Nasser in return for the new arms shipments that were just beginning to reach Egypt.[51] Third, the situation in Jordan was unstable, and a U.S. decision on arms to Israel might further weaken the king.

Just as Rogers was meeting with Dobrynin, Kissinger met with Rabin to signal the impending decision to hold Israel's request for aircraft in abeyance. At the same time he told Rabin that new supplies of aircraft would be forthcoming in due course, but that deliveries should not be accompanied by so much fanfare. Rabin then met with Nixon, who reiterated these points, and left Rabin with the impression that Israel should consider attacking the newly deployed SAM-3 missiles.[52]

Finally, on March 23 Secretary Rogers announced that the president had decided to hold Israel's request for 100 A-4s and 25 F-4s in abeyance pending further developments in the area. As a consolation, economic credits of $100 million were offered.[53]

AN APPROACH TO EGYPT

In an effort to build on the limited credibility with the Arabs generated by the decision on the Phantoms, the administration decided to send Joseph Sisco to Cairo for direct talks with Nasser. The Soviets had said that Nasser was prepared to make concessions. The Americans would try to find out for themselves. During his stay in Cairo from April 10 to 14, Sisco essentially invited Nasser to try dealing with the United States as an honest broker.[54] Although Nasser had little reason to hope for much from the United States, he was experiencing great losses in the continuing fighting with Israel, his dependence on the Soviet Union was growing, and perhaps a positive approach to the Americans would prevent new shipments of Phantoms to Israel. Nasser's reply to Sisco came in his May 1 speech in which he invited the United States to take a new political initiative.[55]

The Sisco visit and the Nasser speech marked the turning point of one aspect of American diplomacy and led the State Department during the following three months to pursue an intensive effort to restore the cease-fire. A parallel, partly related, strand of policy involved both arms to Israel and the growing Soviet involvement in Egypt. The White House assumed control of this area. Nixon had denied that arms supply would be used as a form of leverage over Israel, but in the ensuing months that fiction was dropped.

The last half of April was a very important period in the Middle East and for American foreign policy generally. Within the region, riots in Jordan prevented Sisco from visiting Amman, and King Hussein requested the replacement of the American ambassador there. In Egypt, Soviet pilots were first noted flying combat patrols on April 18. Several days later President Nixon began planning for a bold, and very controversial, military move into Cambodia. The operation began on April 30; violence flared on university campuses; and several of Kissinger's closest aides resigned their positions. The atmosphere in Washington was extraordinarily tense. In the midst of it all, Nixon, long preoccupied by other issues, finally ordered a full investigation of the expanded Soviet role in Egypt. A policy of restraint and dialogue would clearly be difficult to maintain much longer. Besides incurring hostility to his Southeast Asia policy, the president was earning little support for his policy in the Middle East.

On May 21 President Nixon met with Israeli Foreign Minister Abba Eban. The president assured him that the flow of military equipment to Israel would be quietly resumed, but he urged that no publicity be given to this. He gave no specific commitment on the A-4s and F-4s but made it clear that the jets that remained to be delivered from the December 1968 agreement would be delivered without conditions.[56] In return, Nixon asked for a public Israeli statement that would indicate a degree of flexibility on terms of a settlement. This was forthcoming on May 26, when Prime Minister Meir formally announced that Israel continued to accept UN Resolution 242 as the basis for a settlement and would agree to something like the Rhodes formula for talks.[57]

The next move came from the Soviet Union. On June 2 Dobrynin met with Rogers and Sisco. The Soviet Union, he claimed, had won two important concessions from Nasser. First, Egypt would agree to control fedayeen activities from Egyptian territory if a cease-fire went into effect. Second, Egypt would agree that the state of war would end with the signing of an agreement.

The American response was to ignore the Soviet bid for a joint initiative and to press forward instead with its own unilateral call for a cease-fire and renewed talks. The National Security Council met on June 10 and 18 to discuss the Middle East.[58] The president authorized Rogers in NSDM 62 to request the parties to agree to a cease-fire of at least three months' duration and renewed talks under Ambassador Jarring's auspices. This was done on June 19.[59] Rogers publicly revealed the initiative on June 25.

Israel's immediate reaction was to reject the appeal. Ambassador Rabin, however, refused to deliver the note of official rejection, and during the next month the White House devoted considerable energy to persuading the Israelis to accept the new initiatives.[60]

The first step in the campaign was to reassure the Israelis on continuing arms deliveries. This was done in a letter from Nixon to Golda Meir dated June 20. Next, Henry Kissinger was quoted on June 26 as saying: "We are trying to get a settlement in such a way that the moderate regimes are strengthened, and not the radical regimes. We are trying to expel the Soviet military presence, not so much the advisers, but the combat pilots and the combat personnel, before they become so firmly established."[61]

In an interview on television on July 1, President Nixon spoke at length on the Middle East. Referring to Egypt and Syria as Israel's "aggressive neighbors," the president went on to state:

I think the Middle East now is terribly dangerous. It is like the Balkans before World War I—where the two superpowers, the United States and the Soviet Union, could be drawn into a confrontation that neither of them wants because of the differences there. . . . Now, what should U.S. policy be? I will summarize it in a word. One, our interest is peace and the integrity of every country in the area.

Two, we recognize that Israel is not desirous of driving any of the other countries into the sea. The other countries do want to drive Israel into the sea.

Three, then, once the balance of power shifts where Israel is weaker than its neighbors, there will be a war. . . . We will do what is necessary to maintain Israel's strength vis-à-vis its neighbors, not because we want Israel to be in a position to wage war—that is not it—but because that is what will deter its neighbors from attacking it.

And then we get to the diplomacy. The diplomacy is terribly difficult, because Israel's neighbors, of course, have to recognize Israel's right to exist. Israel must withdraw to borders, borders that are defensible. And when we consider all these factors and then put into the equation the fact that the Russians seem to have an interest in moving into the Mediterranean, it shows you why this subject is so complex and so difficult.[62]

Several days later, on July 4, the president authorized the shipment of electronic-counter-measure (ECM) equipment to be used against the SAMs in the canal zone.[63] Although still holding back on new commitments on aircraft, the administration was now prepared to help Israel attack the SAMs with new sophisticated equipment. On July 10 the president also ordered that the remaining A-4s and F-4s under the existing contract be shipped to Israel at an accelerated pace.[64]

President Nasser had left for Moscow on June 29, primarily for a health cure. While there, he discussed the American proposal with the Soviet leaders and reportedly informed them that he intended to accept it.[65] At a minimum, it would provide him a breathing space to complete the construction of the "missile wall." Accordingly, shortly after his return from Moscow, on July 22, Nasser accepted unconditionally the Rogers initiative of June 19.[66] On July 26 Jordan also accepted.[67]

The United States now had to bring about a positive Israeli response or risk the collapse of its Middle East diplomacy. President Nixon wrote to Prime Minister Meir on July 23, urging that Israel accept the proposal and making several important commitments. First, the United States would not insist that Israel agree to the Arab definition of UN Resolution 242. Second, Israel would not be forced to accept a refugee settlement that would fundamentally alter the Jewish character of the state or jeopardize its security. Third, and most important at the moment for the Israelis, Israel would not be asked to withdraw any of its troops from the occupied areas "until a binding contractual peace agreement satisfactory to you has been achieved." This was merely the standard American position on the "package settlement," but the Israelis apparently saw it as a significant step away from the Rogers plan of 1969.[68] In addition, Nixon promised to continue the supply of arms to Israel.

In reply, Prime Minister Meir sought assurances that Israel would be allowed to purchase Shrike missiles and Phantom jets, that the Rogers Plan would be withdrawn, and that the United States would veto any anti-Israeli resolutions in the United Nations.[69] Israel received a commitment only on arms, but that was apparently enough for Meir to accept, with clear reservations, the American initiative on July 31.[70] The previous day Israeli pilots had downed four Soviet MiG-21s over Egypt.

The formal Israeli written reply was not forthcoming until August 6, and included some changes in the language that Jarring was authorized to use in announcing the cease-fire. The United States ignored the Israeli changes, to Prime Minister Meir's great displeasure, and on August 7 a three-month cease-fire, with a provision for a complete military standstill in a zone fifty kilometers wide on each side of the Suez Canal, went into effect. In the State Department the mood was one of elation. It was not to last for long.[71]

CONCLUSIONS

Between January 1969 and August 1970 the Middle East policy of the Nixon administration passed through two stages. During the first year an apparent consensus existed that the State Department should take the lead in negotiating with the Soviet Union to produce a set of principles that would spell out in some detail the terms of an Arab-Israeli settlement. As part of this policy the administration adopted a restrained position on new arms agreements with Israel.

Two potentially divergent concepts underlay this policy. The first saw the Middle East as primarily an issue in global politics, and was characteristic of Nixon and Kissinger. This view underscored the danger of superpower confrontation and the desirability of U.S.-Soviet talks. The second perspective stressed regional trends more than global "linkages." It emphasized that the American position in the Middle East was eroding and that radicalization of the area was inevitable in the absence of a peace agreement. So long as the Soviets seemed cooperative and the regional conflict remained within manageable limits, these two approaches were compatible with a single policy. Nixon orchestrated an uneasy truce between the State Department and Kissinger that resulted in the Rogers Plan of October 28 and December 18. But almost as soon as these documents had been presented, Nixon, prodded by Kissinger, undercut his own policy by signaling to the Israelis that they were not to be taken seriously.

The second stage of policy toward the Middle East began with the failure of the Rogers Plan and the escalation of Soviet involvement in Egypt early in 1970. The shift in policy was the result both of developments in the Middle East and the growing influence on Middle East policy of Henry Kissinger, who all along had been critical of Rogers's handling of Middle East diplomacy. The growing Soviet role made the possibility of direct superpower confrontation increasingly real. This was what the White House wanted to avoid. One way of meeting the Soviet shipment of arms to Egypt, and of demonstrating that lack of Soviet restraint in the Middle East would not pass unnoticed, was to provide arms to Israel. This decision was made in principle during the spring and was set in motion on a large scale during the remainder of the year.

The intensified fighting along the canal and the increasingly important role of the Palestinian fedayeen in Jordan confirmed the worst fears of the State Department specialists. In their view the best way to reverse the trends was with a new diplomatic initiative, this time less ambitious in scope than the Rogers Plan and less dependent on Soviet cooperation. A simple "stop shooting, start talking" formulation was therefore proposed directly to each party on June 19.

These two perspectives risked collision on one issue, namely, arms to Israel. New U.S.-Israeli arms agreements might lead Nasser to reject the American initiative and might provide the "radical" Arabs with strong arguments to use against the United States. Nixon recognized the danger and therefore dealt with the arms issue circumspectly.[72] Above all, he tried to ensure that arms for Israel should be coupled with Israeli acceptance of the new American initiative.

On August 7, as the cease-fire went into effect, it seemed as if both the State Department and the president could feel satisfied that their preferred policies had produced a successful outcome. Within days, however, the provisions of the cease-fire were being violated and a new crisis was in the making. The tenuous, delicate balance between the State

Department and Kissinger, who opposed the cease-fire initiative, was also shattered.[73] By the time the next crisis was over, Kissinger had won Nixon to his side, and those in the State Department who had urged evenhandedness were virtually banished from center stage. The Jordan crisis of September 1970 was thus a fitting culmination of the first two stages of the Nixon diplomacy in the Middle East.

CHAPTER FIVE

The Jordan Crisis, September 1970

As the guns along the Suez Canal fell silent on August 7, 1970, a new phase of the Arab-Israeli conflict opened. A few optimists held out the hope that talks might soon begin that would lead to a resolution of at least some of the issues stemming from the 1967 war. Nasser had hinted that he was prepared to consider a political settlement. King Hussein, despite the erosion of his authority within Jordan, could be expected to play his part. The United States seemed anxious that the Jarring mission be resumed.

The cease-fire, however, unleashed forces that quickly undermined the prospects for peace talks and instead led to a crisis of unprecedented danger for the Nixon administration. Regional in its origin, the Jordan crisis at its peak had much more to do with U.S.-Soviet relations than with the Arab-Israeli conflict or the Palestinians. At any rate, that was the view in Washington.

To understand this dramatic episode in American policy, one must look beyond the ostensible issues in dispute between Israel, Egypt, Jordan, and the Palestinians. As the Jordan crisis erupted in September 1970, Nixon was approaching an important moment in his presidency, the congressional elections of November. His popularity had been hurt by the worsening crisis in Southeast Asia during the spring. His foreign policy was still more rhetoric than realization. U.S. relations with the Soviet Union were strained, the Vietnam War was continuing to take American lives, the strategic arms race went on unchecked, and the Arab-Israeli conflict had reached an extremely critical point. The State Department had labored to bring about a cease-fire between Egypt and Israel, which had gone into effect, but, almost immediately, threatened to collapse.

During August and September Nixon and his national security adviser, Henry Kissinger, were increasingly preoccupied with the crisis in the Middle East. They held a particularly stark view of Soviet intentions, and as they began to reshape American policy in the midst of the Jordan civil war, the U.S.-Soviet perspective dominated their thinking. The result was a new definition of issues in the Middle East and a revised understanding of the political dynamics of the region, in which the U.S.-Israeli relationship came to be seen as the key to combating Soviet influence in the Arab world and attaining stability.

From the standpoint of the Nixon administration, the Jordan crisis was successfully handled: King Hussein remained in power; the militant fedayeen were crushed; U.S.-Israeli relations were strengthened; and the Soviet Union was forced to back down, reining in its Syrian clients under U.S.-Israeli pressure. Finally, Nasser's death, just as the crisis was ending, seemed to open the door to a more moderate Egyptian foreign policy. This image proved to be flawed in many respects, but for nearly three years it served as justification for an American policy aimed primarily at reducing Soviet influence in Egypt, mainly through a generous provision of U.S. arms to Israel.

PRELUDE TO CRISIS: THE AUGUST CEASE-FIRE CONTROVERSY

The achievement of the cease-fire on August 7 created a breach in U.S.-Israeli confidence that continued to widen in subsequent weeks. Before Prime Minister Golda Meir had time to recover from her anger at the way in which the United States had ignored Israel's efforts to qualify the terms of the cease-fire, a new issue of dispute had arisen. Israeli sources maintained that Egypt was not adhering to the standstill provisions of the cease-fire agreement. Missiles were being moved into the canal zone, new sites were being prepared, and missiles were being rotated from active sites to previously inactive ones.

Unfortunately no one in Washington had thought about the problem of how to verify compliance with the agreement. Normal American intelligence activities did eventually detect major changes, but the issue now was whether Egypt had moved new equipment into the canal zone immediately after the cease-fire had gone into effect. A baseline measure was needed to establish what was allowed and what was not. Israel was not, however, willing to authorize U-2 flights along the canal as the cease-fire came into effect.[1] Satellite photographs had been taken the previous week but could not serve as a point of comparison, because a very rapid buildup on both sides of the canal had gone on in the days just before the cease-fire. It was not until August 10 that a U-2 finally flew over the canal, providing a reference point for judging any subsequent changes in military deployments.

Nixon and Kissinger were angry at the State Department and the CIA for not anticipating the problem of determining violations. The Israelis were producing evidence of Egyptian movement of missiles. State was dismissing it as inconclusive and was urging the Israelis to stop making such a fuss and to get on with the talks sponsored by UN Ambassador Jarring.[2] Israel's credibility at the White House was by now greater than State's.

On August 14, before American intelligence had confirmed Egyptian violations, Nixon authorized a $7 million arms package for Israel, consisting of military equipment that could be used against the missile sites along the canal in the event the cease-fire broke down. Deputy Secretary of Defense David Packard met with Israeli Ambassador Yitzhak Rabin to try to work out an understanding on how the arms might be used and to ensure total secrecy. Nixon still did not want to provoke Nasser needlessly, but Israel would receive sophisticated electronic equipment, Shrike missiles, and cluster-bomb units (CBUs) that could be used to attack missile sites.

Gradually the United States was able to piece together a picture of what had happened along the canal after August 7. On August 19 State acknowledged there had been some forward deployment of Egyptian missiles, but that hard evidence of numbers and locations was still difficult to obtain. Three days later Egypt and the Soviet Union were informed that the United States had "incontrovertible evidence of clear-cut violations" of the standstill cease-fire agreement.[3] Egypt replied on August 24, claiming the right to rotate missiles within the zone and denying that any new missiles had been introduced. Finally, on September 3 the United States made a strong demarche to Egypt and the Soviet Union concerning the violations, presenting evidence that at least fourteen missile sites had been modified during August. There was little evidence of completely new sites—these were constructed later in September—but a number of technical violations had been confirmed: incomplete sites had been finished; dummy sites had been activated, and some live sites had been abandoned; and a few new missiles appeared in the canal zone.[4]

The military significance of the violations was difficult to assess, but the political consequences were very important. At a minimum, they showed bad faith on Nasser's part and added weight to Israeli demands for compensation through new American arms deliveries. In retrospect, it does appear as if Nasser had accepted the cease-fire mainly to be able to complete construction of his missile defenses. But Nixon and Kissinger read an even more sinister design into the violations: Egypt was not acting alone. Those were Soviet missiles that were being installed, with the help of Soviet technicians. Therefore the Soviet Union was clearly aiding and abetting Nasser in violating the cease-fire agreement. Beyond that, it was trying to sabotage the Rogers initiative, which had aimed at getting talks started to settle the conflict. The Soviets, so it seemed, were afraid that peace in the Middle East would hurt their position; hence they were doing all they could to sabotage it.

One might have wondered what obligation the Soviet Union had to respect the terms of an American-arranged cease-fire to which it had not been a party. The Soviet bid for a cooperative approach had been rebuffed in early June, and the United States had proceeded unilaterally. Nixon and Kissinger, however, were unhappy with the Soviets for a host of reasons—Southeast Asia, arms talks, the Middle East.[5] They felt the time had come to stand up to Moscow. Events in the Middle East were about to provide an unexpected opportunity for just that.

Perhaps the Soviets thought Nixon was too preoccupied with Vietnam to act elsewhere; perhaps they misread the public reaction against the Cambodian invasion as a lack of will to use power; perhaps they misunderstood American restraint in arming Israel. If that was how the Soviets were thinking, Nixon seemed to believe, they would have to be taught otherwise. Equally important, the Chinese, with whom Nixon hoped to open a new relationship, must recognize that the United States had the will and the capability to resist aggressive Soviet actions. Otherwise Mao would see little reason to compromise his ideological purity by tacit alignment with the United States against the Soviet Union. Only a strong America would be of interest to the Peking leadership.

Nixon was also aware that his domestic base of support would be affected by any signs of weakness toward the Soviet Union. If détente was seen as appeasement, Nixon believed his foreign policy would be in trouble. Munich had not been forgotten, nor had the cold war. The running quarrel with Israel over arms had already taken its toll. Nixon had been prepared to put up with that if peace talks could begin. Now, however, Israel was in a morally justified position, for Egypt had violated the cease-fire agreement, with apparent Soviet connivance. Public and congressional support for Israel was strong. Evidently a new policy on arms supply was needed.

Throughout his first year and a half in office, Nixon had exercised considerable restraint in responding to Israeli arms requests. But he had failed to convince the Soviet Union that it should observe comparable limits, as its behavior from January to August 1970 had unmistakably shown. Nor had American restraint served its purpose with Nasser. He, like the Soviets, seemed to be taking advantage of the cease-fire at Israel's expense. Consequently, on September 1, 1970, Nixon met with Kissinger, Secretary of State Rogers, and Assistant Secretary Sisco in San Clemente to review Middle East policy.[6] The decision was made to sell Israel at least eighteen F-4 Phantom jets. Egypt would be told of the sale, and it would be explained in the context of the violations of the cease-fire agreement. On September 3, Nasser was so informed. Meanwhile, the previous day the Senate had approved a military authorization bill with an amendment sponsored by Senator Henry Jackson, giving Nixon virtually unlimited authority to provide arms to Israel with U.S. financing.

On September 6 Israel announced it was unable to participate in the Jarring talks so long as the Egyptian violations of the standstill cease-fire had not been rectified. That same day the Popular Front for the Liberation of Palestine (PFLP) astonished the world by hijacking three international airplanes, two of which were flown to a desert airstrip in Jordan, where their passengers were held as hostages, while the other was flown to Cairo, where it was blown up minutes after the passengers disembarked.[7] Suddenly the Jarring talks and the cease-fire violations along the canal were overshadowed by a new situation, one that soon provided Nixon and Kissinger with an opportunity to confront the Soviet Union.

THE HIJACKINGS

When Egypt, Jordan, and Israel agreed to a U.S.-sponsored cease-fire in late July 1970, a danger signal went out to the Palestinian fedayeen. From February 1970 on, the fedayeen had succeeded in undercutting King Hussein's authority to the point of virtually becoming a state within a state. Now their position was endangered, as President Nasser, their most prestigious backer, was apparently joining Hussein in a political settlement that could only be at their expense. Leaders of the Palestine Liberation Organization energetically opposed the Rogers initiative, with the result that Nasser suspended their right to use Radio Cairo.

The fedayeen movement had reached a decisive crossroads in late August 1970, when it convened an emergency session of the National Council in Amman.[8] Some of the more radical groups called for the overthrow of the Hashemite monarchy, but Fatah, the mainstream movement, led by Yasir Arafat, contrived to temporize. Before any consensus could emerge, however, the maverick PFLP, led by George Habash, carried out the hijackings on September 6. On September 9 another plane was hijacked and flown to Dawson Field in the Jordanian desert.[9] Altogether, the PFLP held nearly five hundred hostages, many of whom were Americans.

The PFLP's announced objective was to force Israel to release fedayeen prisoners held in Israel. Beyond that, the PFLP sought to upstage other Palestinian groups by appearing more militant than they were. Most dangerous of all, the PFLP sought to provoke a confrontation between Hussein and the fedayeen movement, with Iraq and Syria throwing their weight behind the Palestinians. Iraq had nearly twenty thousand troops in Jordan, and the Syrian army was just across the border within an easy two-day march of Amman.

The United States had been concerned about Hussein's weakened position for some time. The situation in Lebanon was also worrisome. These two moderate Arab states might well be taken over by radicals, just as Nasser seemed ready to move toward a settlement with Israel. On June 17 a National Security Council meeting was held to discuss contingencies for U.S. military intervention if Lebanon or Jordan should be threatened. According to Kissinger, Nixon spoke to these possibilities: "Let us suppose late in the summer we get a request from Lebanon or Jordan for assistance. . . . There comes a time when the US is going to be tested as to its credibility in the area. The real question will be, will we act? Our action has to be considered in that light. We must be ready. . . . Is the question really a military one or is it our credibility as a power in that area?"[10]

Several days later the Washington Special Action Group (WSAG) met to plan for these Middle East contingencies. The conclusions were somber: without access to bases in the eastern Mediterranean, the United States would find it difficult to send a sizable ground force into the area. The Sixth Fleet could provide some air support if it was on station, but otherwise American military capabilities were not impressive. If a serious military option was required, Israel was far better placed to provide both ground forces and air cover, particularly on short notice, but that issue, of course, was politically sensitive.

No Arab regime would want to be rescued by Israel if there was any alternative. Hussein was a realist, however, and had gone so far as to query the United States early in August on the full range of available options, including Israeli intervention, if Iraqi troops were to move against him. At the end of the month, on August 31, the king informed the American embassy in Amman that he might soon have to take drastic measures against the fedayeen and hoped he could count on the United States.

When faced with the hijacking challenge, Hussein militarily played for time. His choices were not very attractive. If he did nothing, the Jordanian army might move on its own against the fedayeen, thus destroying his authority. If he acted, Syria or Iraq might intervene. Hussein knew his army could handle the fedayeen alone, but what about their friends? Hussein was therefore forced to look for possible support against outside intervention, and that meant the United States and Israel.

The initial American response to the hijackings was cautious. Rogers felt that nothing much could be done. Nixon, by contrast, wanted to use the crisis as a pretext to crush the fedayeen, and apparently went so far as to order that Palestinian strongholds be bombed. Secretary of Defense Melvin Laird reported that the weather was not suitable for such attacks, and Nixon did not raise the issue again. But at the outset of the crisis Nixon was much more prepared to use American force than to countenance Israeli intervention.[11] At a minimum, it might prove necessary to evacuate the several hundred Americans in Amman. Perhaps an opportunity to rescue the hostages would present itself. Looking a bit further ahead, Nixon could see the need for a strong show of American force in the eastern Mediterranean as a deterrent to Soviet, Syrian, or Iraqi moves.

The Egyptians and Soviets were acting circumspectly and were not openly supporting the fedayeen in Jordan. On September 9 Nasser had gone out of his way to inform the United States that he was still interested in the American peace initiative. If that was true, perhaps the crisis in Jordan could be contained and resolved without igniting a broader conflict. Nixon was determined, however, that the crisis should not be settled on terms set by the fedayeen. He would not pressure the Israelis to release prisoners as the price of recovering the hostages, and he urged the British to adopt the same tough attitude. This was Nixon at his law-and-order, no-capitulation-to-blackmail best. Kissinger agreed, insisting that the United States should look implacable. But Kissinger disagreed with Nixon over the advisability of using U.S. troops. If military action was needed to help King Hussein, he preferred that Israel take the lead.[12]

Determined to take a tough stand, Nixon ordered a series of steadily escalating series of military moves as deliberate signals of intent and to provide a modest intervention capability if needed. On September 10 the

82d Airborne Division at Fort Bragg, North Carolina, was placed on semialert; six C-130 transport planes were also flown from Europe to Incirlik air base in Turkey, where they could be available for evacuation of Americans from Jordan. The following day units of the Sixth Fleet began to leave port as part of what the White House termed "routine precautions in such a situation for evacuation purposes." Four more C-130s, escorted by twenty-five F-4 jets, were flown to Turkey. That same day the fedayeen blew up the aircraft and moved the remaining fifty-four hostages in their hands, thirty-four of whom were Americans, to an undisclosed location.[13]

On September 15 King Hussein told the British, who then contacted the United States, that he was forming a military government with the intention of moving against the fedayeen. He indicated that he might need to call on the United States and others for help. When the news reached Washington, Kissinger quickly convened a meeting of the WSAG at 10:30 p.m. Further military moves were ordered. The aircraft carrier *Saratoga* would proceed to the eastern Mediterranean, where it would join the *Independence* off the Lebanese coast; airborne units in West Germany would be placed on semialert; additional C-130s would fly to Turkey. Despite these preparations, it was decided that the United States would not unilaterally try to rescue the hostages, but the administration was determined to try to preserve King Hussein in power.[14]

CIVIL WAR IN JORDAN

With the outbreak of heavy fighting in Jordan between the army and the fedayeen on September 16 and 17, the United States suddenly faced a new set of dangers in the Middle East. At one extreme, the conflict in Jordan might ignite an Arab-Israeli war if Israel intervened directly. Egypt and the Soviet Union could then be drawn in, which might lead to a U.S.-Soviet confrontation, the fear that all along had haunted Nixon and Kissinger. Almost as dangerous would be Hussein's overthrow. A close friend of the United States would have been defeated by radical forces armed with Soviet weapons. Even if the Soviet Union was not directly involved, the symbolism of a fedayeen victory would work to Moscow's advantage.

Nixon clearly wanted Hussein to crush the fedayeen, but he also wanted the conflict contained within Jordan. The American role, as he and Kissinger saw it, was to encourage Hussein to act while restraining the Israelis from precipitate military moves. At the same time an American and Israeli show of force might help to deter the Syrians, Iraqis, and Soviets. The balance between restraint and belligerence would be difficult to establish; too much of either on the part of the United States or Israel could be counterproductive. Timing and a close monitoring of events on the ground were essential, and a high degree of coordination among Jordan, the United States, and Israel would be vital.

Nixon's first moves were to warn against outside intervention. At Kansas State University on September 16, he gave a tough law-and-order speech in which he denounced the fedayeen. He then flew to Chicago, where he met with Kissinger and Sisco for an update on the crisis. There were conflicting views in the intelligence community on the likelihood of Syrian or Iraqi intervention. On the whole, it was discounted as a possibility.

Nixon thought otherwise, however, and on September 17 he met twice with editors of Chicago newspapers to discuss the crisis in Jordan. The *Sun-Times* rushed into print that evening with a story summarizing Nixon's views. The United States was reportedly "prepared to intervene directly in the Jordanian war should Syria and Iraq enter the conflict and tip the military balance against Government forces loyal to Hussein."[15] Hussein's survival was judged by Nixon to be essential to the American peace-settlement effort. Israeli intervention against the fedayeen would be dangerous, and if Syria or Iraq were to enter the battle, the United States would have to intervene. Nixon reportedly also told the editors that it would not be such a bad thing if the Soviets believed he was capable of irrational or reckless action.[16] This was vintage Nixon—be tough; keep your opponents off balance; remain mysterious and unpredictable. With luck, no one would then test to see if you were bluffing.

Returning to Washington the evening of September 17, Nixon met with his advisers again. A third aircraft carrier, the *John F. Kennedy*, was ordered to move from the Atlantic into the Mediterranean, and the *Guam*, a helicopter carrier with fifteen hundred marines on board, was ordered to proceed as rapidly as possible from Norfolk to the Mediterranean. Nixon also discussed the meeting he was scheduled to have with Prime Minister Meir the following day. The time had clearly come to mend U.S.-Israeli relations, because the two countries might have to work closely during this crisis. Nixon therefore authorized $500 million in military aid for Israel and agreed to accelerate the delivery of eighteen F-4s.

Nixon and Meir met on September 18 for what the *New York Times* termed the most important talks between the United States and Israel in twenty-two years. Relations were judged to be at an "extraordinary low ebb" because of the quarrel over the cease-fire and restraint in providing arms.[17] The reality actually was less stark. Nixon's promise to give Israel's aid requests his "sympathetic attention" helped to set the stage for a remarkable improvement in the ties between the two countries during the next few days. In view of subsequent developments it seems odd that Nixon apparently did not discuss the possibility of intervention in the Jordan civil war with Meir. That was left to Rogers, Sisco, and Kissinger, for it still seemed a remote contingency. The king seemed to be gaining the upper hand in Jordan, and the Soviets were behaving themselves.

It was not until Saturday, September 19, that the first reports of a Syrian armored probe into Jordan reached Washington.[18] The Soviet Union was quick to warn against outside intervention in Jordan and joined President Nasser in a call for a cease-fire. The Soviet chargé in Washington, Yuli Vorontsov, informed the State Department that the Soviets were urging restraint on the Syrians and were themselves in no way involved in the attack. Kissinger relayed this news to Nixon at Camp David. Nixon was unimpressed and skeptical. The Soviets, after all, had denied complicity in the standstill cease-fire violations along the Suez Canal. And now their client, Syria, was sending tanks into Jordan. Could this really be done without the Soviets at least giving their tacit blessing? More likely, Nixon believed, the Soviets were egging the Syrians on.[19] Whatever the truth, U.S. diplomatic and military moves would thenceforth be aimed at getting the Soviets to pressure the Syrians to withdraw their forces.

CRISIS MANAGEMENT

It was not until Sunday, September 20, that the Syrian intervention became ominous. While Secretary of Defense Laird was denying any need for U.S. intervention, Nixon was preparing for precisely that contingency. This was his crisis, not Laird's or Rogers's. Only Kissinger would be fully involved with the president's decisions.

Kissinger recommended, and Nixon approved, an enhanced alert status for some military units in West Germany, and the Sixth Fleet was ordered to move farther east.[20] Besides these signals to the Soviet Union, Sisco conveyed a strong warning to Vorontsov in the afternoon, stressing that Syria's action "could lead to the broadening of the present conflict."[21] Rogers publicly denounced the Syrian "invasion."[22]

Besides these developments, U.S. diplomacy was engaged in two other vital tasks that day. First came King Hussein's urgent request through his trusted aide, Zaid Rifai, to the American ambassador for American help against the Syrians. The situation in Amman was under control, but in the north it was very threatening. Late in the evening in Jordan, King Hussein ordered Rifai to send U.S. Ambassador L. Dean Brown a request by radio for intervention by air and land from any quarter against the Syrian tanks.[23]

In Washington, the WSAG met at 7:00 p.m. to consider the king's extraordinary appeal. According to Kissinger, "A quick review of the pros and cons of American military intervention strengthened our conviction that our forces were best employed in holding the ring against Soviet interference with Israeli operations. To be effective unilaterally we would have to commit our entire strategic reserve; we would then be stretched to near the breaking point in two widely separated theaters and naked in the face of any new contingency. Our forces would have to go in without heavy equipment and with air support only from carriers."[24]

Nixon called Kissinger from the meeting at 7:50 p.m. and invited the other senior members of the WSAG to his office at 8:00 p.m. Shortly thereafter Kissinger's deputy, Alexander M. Haig, Jr., received a call from the British ambassador with the news that the king was now requesting immediate air strikes. He also informed the WSAG that Irbid had fallen to Syrian troops.[25] Responding to these developments, the WSAG recommended placing the airborne brigade in Germany and the 82d Airborne on a higher-alert status and flying a reconnaissance plane from a carrier to Tel Aviv to pick up targeting information and to signal that American military action might be nearing.[26]

At about 9:30 p.m. Kissinger, joined by Sisco, went to see Nixon, who happened to be at the bowling alley of the Old Executive Office Building. Nixon approved the WSAG recommendations and agreed it was important to establish contact with Ambassador Rabin.

Golda Meir and Rabin were in New York at that moment at a fund-raising dinner. At 10:00 p.m. Kissinger managed to reach Rabin by phone. He told Rabin that the king had asked for assistance, but the United States urgently needed intelligence on Syrian positions before it could respond. Could Israel fly reconnaissance as soon as the sun was up? Rabin asked if the U.S. favored an Israeli air strike. Kissinger said he first wanted to see the results of the reconnaissance. At this point, according to Kissinger, a new message arrived from King Hussein and he broke off the conversation.[27]

The king's new message spoke of a rapidly deteriorating situation and an urgent need for air strikes. Ground troops might also be needed. Kissinger spoke with Rogers, and both decided to recommend to Nixon that the United States should endorse an Israeli air strike. Sisco and Kissinger returned to the bowling alley to seek the president's approval, which was forthcoming. Kissinger again called Rabin, this time informing him that the United States would look favorably on an Israeli air attack if Israeli reconnaissance confirmed that Syria was in control of Irbid with large armored forces.[28] Before midnight Rabin called back with Golda Meir's response. Israel would fly reconnaissance at daybreak. Air operations might not be sufficient, but Israel would take no further action without consultations.

Monday, September 21, was indeed a critical day in the Middle East. King Hussein had called for help but had made it clear that Jordan must have the final say on the kind of intervention. He preferred that the United States or Great Britain be involved, not just the Israelis.

Early on September 21 Rabin contacted the White House to say that Israel did not believe air strikes alone would suffice. Ground action might also be needed. Kissinger called Nixon, and, after a short period of deliberation, Nixon dictated a message to Rabin. According to Kissinger, he said: "I have decided it. Don't ask anybody else. Tell him 'go.'"[29] Kissinger then consulted with Rogers and Laird, who had reservations. Nixon reluctantly agreed to convene a full meeting of the NSC at 8:45 a.m. Present were Laird, Rogers, Packard, Thomas Moorer (chairman of the joint chiefs), and Kissinger. Moorer was opposed to U.S. ground intervention because the capability simply was not there. Hence if ground action was needed, Israel would have to act. Intelligence estimates from Israel claimed that 250 to 300 Syrian tanks were in the Irbid area.[30] Nixon finally decided that Sisco should tell Rabin that the United States agreed to Israeli ground action in principle, subject to determining the king's view and prior consultation.[31]

In the course of the day, as the situation on the ground changed, the king frequently modified his initial request. During the morning Rifai had indicated that the king preferred air strikes alone but that ground intervention would be acceptable without further approval if communications broke down. Later that afternoon Rifai requested an immediate air strike to check the advancing Syrian tanks. In the evening Hussein shifted position once again, urging Israeli ground action into Syria but ruling out Israeli armored intervention in Jordan.

In view of the critical situation in Jordan and the apparent need for Israeli action, Kissinger was made responsible for providing Israel with answers to a list of questions about American policy in the case of wider hostilities. No further decisions seemed immediately necessary, since Israel was proceeding with its mobilization in any case and the battle would not be joined again in Jordan until the next day.

As events unfolded, the Israelis developed a plan for sending 200 Israeli tanks toward Irbid, combined with air strikes. Israel would guarantee that its forces would be withdrawn from Jordan once the military operation was over. Kissinger and Sisco relayed to Rabin the king's preference for Israeli ground action inside Syria, not Jordan. Such action was considerably more risky for the Israelis and might provoke an Egyptian military response along the canal, or even Soviet threats to intervene. Rabin therefore sought an American commitment to prevent Soviet intervention against Israel, as well as a promise of aid if Egypt attacked.

By the end of the day Rabin conveyed to Kissinger the cabinet's decision to intervene if Syrian tanks continued to advance on Tuesday. The Israeli air force would attack first, but if this was insufficient, a tank force would also be sent into Jordan, and perhaps also into Syria. Rabin insisted, however, on an American "umbrella," a presidential commitment to use the force necessary to prevent a Soviet attack on Israel, as well as a promise of arms. Nixon readily approved the request for arms, and considerable discussion of the "umbrella" assurances took place, without formal agreement ever being reached.[32]

The next day, Tuesday, September 22, was decisive. Israel, with U.S. encouragement but no binding agreement, was poised to act. Hussein, with the assurance that Israel and the United States were behind him, finally ordered his own small air force to attack the Syrian tanks around Irbid, which it did with satisfactory results.[33] By afternoon Syrian tanks were beginning to withdraw from Jordan. The need for Israeli intervention was less urgent. The king, speaking in code, informed Ambassador Brown that Israeli intervention was all right "up high" but should be directed elsewhere "down below."[34] An Israeli air strike would still be welcome, but land intervention should be only against Syria. Israel did not wish to undertake ground action in Syria, and by the end of the day the prospects for Israeli or American intervention had virtually passed.[35]

Kissinger and Nixon had met several times that day. They were acutely aware of how difficult it would be for the United States to intervene.[36] Even with access to British bases in Cyprus, only 50 sorties daily over Jordan could be flown. Aircraft from the Sixth Fleet would be able to carry out an additional 200 sorties a day, but even that could not compare with what the Israelis were capable of providing. With considerable relief, the president learned that Syrian tanks were beginning to withdraw. Just to make sure the Soviet Union did not change its position, Kissinger went out of his way that evening to tell Vorontsov at an Egyptian reception that it was up to the Soviets to rein in their friends. "You and your client started it, and you have to end it."[37] The State Department had announced earlier that day that the Soviets were claiming to be restraining the Syrians, but Kissinger seemed to feel that a few added tough words could do no harm.

By Wednesday the acute phase of the Jordan crisis had passed. Shortly after noon Nixon met with Rogers and Kissinger in the Oval Office. While discussing the crisis, they received the news that all Syrian tanks had left Jordan. A statement was soon released from the White House welcoming the Syrian withdrawal, and Sisco was asked to contact Rabin to obtain his assurance that Israel would make no military move.[38] The Jordanians had the situation under control and no longer wanted outside intervention. For the United States and Israel, the crisis was over. Nixon celebrated on Thursday by playing golf at Burning Tree Country Club with Rogers, Attorney General John N. Mitchell, and AFL-CIO president George Meany. The following day a cease-fire was announced in Jordan.

Nixon was proud of the way he had handled the Jordan crisis. He compared his restrained, yet forceful, use of military power with John F. Kennedy's behavior in the Cuban missile crisis of October 1962. Many of the participants praised Kissinger's management of the WSAG. On the whole, everyone from Nixon on down was pleased with the way the crisis had been handled. In something of a "victory lap," Nixon flew to Rome on September 26, and from there to the aircraft carrier *Saratoga*, where he spent the night of September 27.

Meanwhile President Nasser of Egypt was trying to arrange a stable cease-fire and a new modus vivendi between Jordan and the PLO. Nasser had differed with the fedayeen in their opposition to the Rogers initiative and in their desire to bring down King Hussein, but he did not want to see the PLO crushed by Hussein's troops. He therefore summoned Hussein, Arafat, and other Arab leaders to Cairo to work out an agreement that would govern the PLO presence in Jordan and prevent further clashes. The agreement was signed on September 27. The following day, while seeing off his last guests at the airport, President Nasser fell ill. He returned home, where, several hours later, he died of a heart attack. With Nasser's death, an era in Arab politics came to an end. By chance, it coincided with the beginning of a new U.S.-Israeli strategic relationship.

THE AFTERMATH

The outcome of the Jordan crisis was widely considered a successful result of American policy. Certainly Nixon and Kissinger portrayed it as such, and in terms of declared American objectives the claim seemed justified. King Hussein was securely in power. The fedayeen had been badly weakened, and the hostages had all been rescued. The Syrian military intervention had been turned back by Jordan without Israeli or American involvement. The Soviet Union had refrained from direct intervention once the United States made a strong show of force. And U.S.-Israeli relations were stronger than ever. The outcome of the crisis being consistent with U.S. goals, few bothered to consider the extent to which American or Israeli actions were responsible for these developments, nor were the premises of American policy closely examined. Apparently successful policies are spared the type of critical scrutiny reserved for failures.

Nixon and Kissinger, with considerable justification, were therefore able to take credit for successfully handling a major international crisis. Jordan was the first in a series of foreign-policy spectaculars that boosted Nixon's prestige and popularity and made Kissinger's name a household word. After Jordan came the opening to China, the Strategic Arms Limitation Talks agreement, and the Vietnam negotiations. Each of these achievements looks a bit tattered from the perspective of two decades, but at the time they contributed immensely to the reelection of Richard Nixon in November 1972. The theses of his foreign policy—negotiations, détente, a new structure of peace based on a multipolar power balance—all appeared to take on substance in the period after the Jordan crisis.

U.S.-Israeli relations, which had reached a low point in mid-1970, were quickly brought to an unprecedented high level by the Jordan crisis. There had been a long-standing debate within the bureaucracy concerning policy toward Israel. The conventional wisdom, especially in the State Department, was that American support for Israel was an impediment to U.S.-Arab relations. By granting economic and military aid to the enemy of the Arabs, the United States was providing the Soviet Union with an opportunity to extend its influence in the Middle East. Although few questioned that Israel's existence should be defended by the United States in an extreme case, many felt that an "evenhanded" policy, whereby the United States would not always align itself with Israel and would not become its primary arms supplier, was the best guarantee of U.S. interests in the region. In this view Israel was more of an embarrassment for U.S. policy than a strategic asset. Even if Israel was an impressive military power, that power could be used only to defend Israel, not to advance American interests elsewhere in the region.

Israelis have generally resented the idea that American support is rooted primarily in domestic politics or in some vaguely felt moral commitment. They reject the reasoning of the proponents of "evenhand-edness," who regard Israel as a burden on U.S. diplomacy in the Middle East. Particularly after the spectacular military victory of June 1967, Israelis began to argue that a strong Israel was in America's strategic interest.

The Israeli argument was less than fully convincing, especially to the seasoned Middle East specialists in the bureaucracy. Apart from appearing too self-serving, the argument did not fit the facts of the post–June 1967 situation. Soviet influence in the region did not decline; instead, it attained new levels, especially in Egypt, Syria, and Iraq. Radical forces in the Arab world gained strength, particularly with the rise of the fedayeen, the coup in Iraq in July 1968, and the overthrow of the conservative monarchy in Libya in September 1969. If King Faisal of Saudi Arabia was grateful to Israel for having checked Nasser's ambitions, he had a curious way of showing it. He was among the harshest critics of American support for Israel, arguing that such support played into the hands of radicals, communists, Zionists, and other dangerous elements. Even King Hussein, who, more than any other Arab leader, saw Israel as an important element in the regional balance of power, was angered by American aid to Israel and the continuing Israeli occupation of formerly Jordanian territory. He shared Faisal's view that Israel's 1967 military victory, and the subsequent American support for Israel, would polarize and radicalize the area. Only the Soviets and their friends would profit.

Nixon, however reluctantly, had been prepared to allow the State Department to pursue the logic of an evenhanded approach to the Arab-Israeli conflict up to a point, and this had led to the Rogers Plan and the August 1970 cease-fire. But both efforts had been flawed. The Soviet

Union had failed to cooperate; U.S.-Israeli relations had been badly strained, with little to show for it; and the Arabs had displayed little gratitude for U.S. restraint in providing arms to Israel.

As the Soviet dimensions of the Arab-Israeli conflict grew during the spring of 1970, Nixon began to accept Kissinger's argument that only a strong Israel could deal with the growing Soviet presence in Egypt. If the Soviet Union was allowed to succeed in helping Nasser recover Sinai by force of arms, Soviet aid would be sought throughout the region. Only by frustrating the Soviet-Egyptian scheme would American interests be protected. Arms to Israel would therefore serve an important global interest of the United States.

The August cease-fire violations created the necessary political climate for Nixon, encouraged by Kissinger, to turn to Israel as a strategic ally. The Soviets and Egyptians appeared to be double-dealing and were trying to exploit the American policy of restraint and to drive a wedge between Israel and the United States. Even without the Jordan crisis, Nixon would have agreed to new arms aid to Israel, but the crisis provided a convincing rationale for a policy based on arming Israel as a strategic asset for American policy in the Middle East. In an emergency Israeli forces had been prepared to protect King Hussein, a task that would have been much more difficult for U.S. forces.[39] By its mere presence, Israel had deterred the Syrian air force from entering the battle; Israeli armor massed in the Golan Heights must have helped convince the Syrians that they should withdraw. Then, too, by helping to force Syria to back down, Israel and the United States had further tarnished the Soviet image in the region while demonstrating that moderate Arab regimes could count on effective American support. The understandings, such as they were, worked out between Kissinger and Rabin on September 21, 1970, suggested the possibility of forging a far-reaching strategic relationship between the two countries.

For the next three years U.S.-Israeli relations flourished. Washington provided unusually high levels of aid. To both parties' satisfaction, the region remained comparatively calm, and Soviet influence seemed to be declining. When President Anwar al-Sadat suddenly expelled more than ten thousand Soviet military advisers from Egypt in July 1972, Nixon, Kissinger, Meir, and Rabin must all have congratulated themselves on the success of their joint policy.

The aftermath of the Jordan crisis did indeed constitute a momentary period of comparative stability. The cease-fire remained in force on all fronts. King Hussein successfully reestablished his authority in Jordan, from which the remnants of the fedayeen were expelled in July 1971. U.S.-Jordanian relations flourished, reaching substantial levels of economic and military aid. Jordan came to be treated as a regional partner of the United States. Jordan's special task on behalf of American interests, in King Hussein's view, would be to promote stability in the small oil-producing Arab states of the Gulf after the British departure at the end of 1971.[40] Nixon and Kissinger gave the king some encouragement and boosted aid to Jordan accordingly. In true Nixon-doctrine style, Israel, Jordan, and Iran were emerging in official Washington's view as regional peacekeepers. Aid and arms to these U.S. partners would serve as a substitute for a costly American military presence in the region or unpopular military intervention.

Elsewhere in the Middle East, post-Jordan-crisis trends also seemed favorable. In Syria the faction of the Baath party most closely associated with the intervention in Jordan was ousted by General Hafiz al-Asad in November 1970. Syria's new leaders were reportedly more moderate, or at least more cautious, than the former regime. Sadat was also viewed in Washington as a considerable improvement over Nasser. Sadat, at any rate, had less prestige in the Arab world than Nasser had possessed, and therefore less troublemaking potential. Perhaps he would turn to Egypt's domestic problems instead of promoting revolution elsewhere. This had long been the hope of American policymakers and had served as a major justification for aid programs to Egypt in the early 1960s.

In foreign policy Sadat was something of an enigma at first. His feelings toward the Soviet Union were unknown, but by the spring of 1971, after he successfully survived a coup attempt organized by Nasser's closest aides, Sadat's anti-Soviet colors became more evident. Even in Egypt, therefore, the trend seemed to be encouraging.

LESSONS LEARNED

The net effect of the regional developments growing out of the Jordan crisis was to breed a sense of complacency in Israel and the United States. The fears of radicalization, polarization, and confrontation that had haunted policymakers from 1967 to 1970 all but disappeared after September 1970. Now the region seemed to be relatively stable, and the key to this stability was a military balance that unquestionably favored Israel. The chief remaining threat came from the continuing Soviet military presence in Egypt and Syria. It thus became a prime objective of U.S.-Israeli policy to demonstrate to Sadat that the Soviet military presence in his country was an obstacle to his recovering Sinai. Soviet arms to Egypt would be matched by American arms to Israel, thus ruling out Sadat's military option. And so long as a Soviet military presence remained in Egypt, U.S. diplomacy would make only half-hearted attempts to promote a settlement.

The roots of this view, which dominated American policy during the next three years, can be traced to the Jordan crisis. Nixon and Kissinger had convinced themselves that Israel had played a vital role in helping to check the Soviet-inspired Syrian invasion of Jordan and might play a comparable role in thwarting Soviet designs in Egypt. Nixon and Kissinger, however, failed to grasp two critical dimensions of the Jordan crisis.

First, on the regional level, they misinterpreted the Syrian invasion, overemphasizing the Soviet role and minimizing the degree to which it grew out of internal Syrian politics. The difference was significant. If Syrian action was primarily rooted in domestic Syrian politics, a policy directed at the Soviet Union was unlikely to have much effect. Syrian withdrawal from Jordan may well have had little to do with Soviet pressure, and much more to do with the refusal of General Hafiz al-Asad to commit the Syrian air force to an adventure planned by his rival, Salah Jadid. Jordanian power, along with the obvious danger of Israeli intervention, was probably the key to the Syrian retreat, not Soviet demarches made in response to U.S. threats. In short, American policy in the crisis may well have had very little effect on the Syrian decision to withdraw its armor.

Second, Nixon and Kissinger exaggerated the global U.S.-Soviet dimension of the crisis. The Soviets had comparatively little at stake in Jordan. They were not on particularly good terms with the PLO, which was criticizing their primary client in the area, President Nasser. Syria was receiving military aid but was refusing to follow the Soviet political line on a settlement. Moreover, Syria was faction-ridden and unstable, was quarreling with Egypt and Iraq, and was essentially unpredictable. Once Syrian units did enter Jordan in the September crisis, the Soviets adopted a cautious policy. They made no threats. Instead, they warned against all outside intervention in Jordan, called for a cease-fire, and pointedly took credit subsequently for making demarches in Damascus to bring the fighting to an end.[41]

If the Soviet stand had been primarily a function of the strong position taken by the United States, and if Soviet pressures had significantly influenced Syria's behavior in the crisis, Nixon and Kissinger might have rightly concluded that the combination of U.S. and Israeli threats to act had produced the desired outcome. But no evidence can be found that such was the case. This is not to say that Nixon and Kissinger were wrong to make a strong show of force in the Jordan crisis. Among other things, it might have been a useful signal to the Soviets and the Chinese. The error was to conclude that the outcome of the crisis was mainly due to U.S. action. That was at least a debatable proposition, but instead it became something of an axiom in subsequent policy debates.

Although Nixon and Kissinger were wrong in the significance they attributed to American behavior in the Jordan crisis, this does not imply that the U.S. role was unimportant. On at least two counts the American contribution may well have been essential to the regional outcome. First, King Hussein needed encouragement to draw fully on his own military resources. He seemed to be afraid of committing his own air force without assurances that outside help would be available if he got into trouble. His willingness to order the successful counterattack on September 22, which removed the need for U.S. or Israeli action, may well have been a result of the assurances he received from the United States.

Second, the United States coordinated the Israeli response. Left to their own devices, Israeli leaders might have responded to the Jordan crisis differently. By working closely with the United States, Israel made its power available on terms King Hussein was able to accept. Because direct communication between Israel and Jordan did not exist during the crisis, serious miscalculations could have resulted. The United States was in close and continuous contact with both parties, however, and could urge restraint on Israel at the beginning and end of the crisis, while ensuring that Israel was prepared to act at the critical moment on September 22. To play this role effectively, the United States had to consider placing its own forces on the line as a possible backup to the Israeli operation.

Seen in this light, U.S. action in the Jordan crisis still appears relatively successful. Hussein took the necessary risks on September 22 because he knew that assistance would be available if needed. He thereby succeeded in removing the need for U.S. or Israeli intervention. The lesson of the crisis, from this perspective, was that American diplomacy, through a mixture of subtlety and restraint combined with visible force, had helped to create a situation in which Jordan was able to cope with its own problems. It had been a close call, however, involving a number of imponderables, such as factional balances in Syria and King Hussein's shifting moods. It would be hard to repeat the Jordan experience elsewhere, especially in situations in which U.S. and Israeli interests might not overlap so clearly with that of any other Arab regime. Even in this crisis the United States and Israel had not seen eye to eye. Rabin had characterized the American response to his request for an "umbrella" as reflecting a "predicament," perhaps alluding to the problem of any president promising to use force on behalf of a foreign power without congressional approval.[42]

What guidelines could this crisis provide for dealing with the serious problems of the Egyptian-Israeli conflict or with broader issues of the Soviet presence in the Middle East? What was the lesson regarding the role of American threats to use force in the crisis? Had they really been effective? Against whom? After all, the Syrian intervention came after Nixon's widely publicized threat on September 17 and after the visible movement of American military forces to the eastern Mediterranean. Was it possible that the Syrians had not taken the threats seriously, or that they came to their senses only when confronted with Soviet pressure and Israel's might? These were legitimate questions, well worth asking, but it was much easier for Nixon and Kissinger to see American power and diplomacy as responsible for the favorable outcome. Israel was regarded as the helpful junior partner in the successful management of a grave global test of superpower wills.

The result of these perceptions was a U.S. policy in subsequent years that was narrowly focused on Israel, Jordan, and the Soviet Union. The military balance was seen as the key to stability, if not to peace. Arms to Israel and Jordan were of higher priority than new peace initiatives. Little attention was paid to political developments in the region, to the mounting frustrations in Egypt and Syria and among the Palestinians, and to the growing activism of the Arabs, who had begun to recognize the potential power they possessed because of their petroleum resources.

In short, American policy became a captive of the perceived success in handling the Jordan crisis. The global dimension of the conflict was virtually all that Nixon and Kissinger seemed to care about. By ignoring regional trends, they misjudged the very forces that would lead within three years to a much more dangerous outbreak of war. During the interval the State Department launched several ineffectual diplomatic efforts, but Nixon and Kissinger, having taken charge of Middle East policy during the Jordan crisis, were reluctant to relinquish authority to Rogers and Sisco. The result was a series of half-hearted State Department initiatives, lacking White House support, that simply raised the level of Arab frustrations while reinforcing the sense of complacency felt in Israel and in Washington.

Several important opportunities to pursue a political settlement of the conflict may have been missed during this period. Caught in a perceptual trap largely of their own making, Nixon and Kissinger failed to notice them. The period of "standstill diplomacy" from 1970 to 1973 will not go down in the annals of American foreign policy as one of the more enlightened. In many ways the success in Jordan in 1970 resulted in a series of failures in the succeeding years, culminating in the October 1973 war.

CHAPTER SIX

Kissinger's Standstill Diplomacy, 1971–73

With the continuation of a cease-fire along the Suez Canal, the restoration of King Hussein's authority in Jordan, and the death of Egypt's president Gamal Abdel Nasser, the situation in the Middle East appeared to American policymakers to be less dangerous and more manageable than at any time since the 1967 war. The danger of U.S.-Soviet confrontation had passed. U.S. interests had survived intact through a difficult period, and less urgency was now attached to new American diplomatic initiatives.

Before the Jordan crisis the State Department had been primarily responsible for the formulation and conduct of policy toward the Arab-Israeli conflict. Thereafter Nixon and Kissinger were to play a more important role, chiefly through their emphasis on the Soviet dimension of the regional conflict and their desire for a close relationship with Israel. Over the next three years the White House refrained from day-to-day involvement in Middle East diplomacy but kept a careful eye on the State Department to ensure against excessive activism. Ultimately Nixon and Kissinger succeeded in undermining State Department initiatives and in establishing almost complete control over policy toward the Middle East.

The State Department was understandably loath to surrender this last remaining area of substantive responsibility. Instead, for nearly a year Secretary Rogers and Assistant Secretary Sisco tried to revive American diplomatic efforts. Initially they emphasized a resumption of talks through Ambassador Jarring. As that effort faltered in February 1971, they began to explore a conceptually different approach based on the idea of an "interim settlement" between Egypt and Israel. By August 1971, this approach had also failed. For the next two years the Arab-Israeli conflict was absent from the headlines, American diplomats remained uncharacteristically quiet and passive, and Arab frustrations mounted in direct proportion to the warmth of the U.S.-Israeli relationship. Even President Sadat's bold move in expelling more than ten thousand Soviet advisers from Egypt in July 1972 was not enough to lead to a serious reassessment of American policy. Instead, U.S. diplomacy continued to aim at what Kissinger was later to term the "complete frustration" of the Arabs, a policy that he later admitted was shortsighted and may have contributed to the October 1973 war.

The period from 1971 to 1973 thus seems to have been one of lost opportunities to prevent war and move toward a settlement. With the advantage of hindsight, one might say the type of agreement arrived at between Israel and Egypt in January 1974 could have been reached three years earlier at much less cost. But this conclusion may be wrong, for it fails to take into account other concerns weighing on policymakers at the time. The context of decisions must be kept in focus when one looks back at what might have been.

To understand this uninspiring chapter in American diplomacy between the Jordan crisis and the October 1973 war, one must recall the administration's intense preoccupation with other parts of the world. It was with relief that policymakers turned away from the Middle East to areas of higher priority. The Vietnam War was still raging, but in May 1971 Kissinger began a series of secret talks with top-level North Vietnamese representatives to try to reach a negotiated settlement. In parallel to these important talks, Nixon and Kissinger were planning a momentous opening toward Peking, symbolized by Kissinger's secret trip to China in July 1971. Finally, serious negotiations with the Soviet Union on limiting strategic armaments were under way.

Each of those three areas was so handled that in 1972, the presidential election year, Nixon would be able to point to visible achievements—visits to Peking and Moscow, and, it was hoped, an end to the war in Vietnam. The same election-year imperatives dictated a very low profile in the Middle East.[1] In the absence of any chance for a negotiated agreement there, Nixon focused instead on maintaining the military balance in Israel's favor, thereby preventing an unwelcome outbreak of fighting and no doubt earning the gratitude of Israel's many supporters in the United States.

In many ways the period from 1971 to 1973 is rich in lessons. It demonstrates the way in which Middle East issues can be influenced by global developments and by American domestic politics. Particularly in noncrisis periods U.S. foreign policy tends to be insensitive to regional developments, responding instead to strategic concepts, bureaucratic rivalries, and electoral necessity. The vacillation that so often seems to characterize American policy, especially in the Middle East, is likely to be especially intense at such times. The president is less involved than during crisis periods, and the bureaucracy is therefore left to devise policies that may ultimately fail for lack of presidential support.

Only one new policy concept concerning the Arab-Israeli conflict emerged during this period. Responding to Israeli and Egyptian suggestions, the United States backed away from the "package settlement" approach and began to emphasize the desirability of partial agreements unlinked to a final peace plan. A serious, but flawed, initiative was launched in the spring of 1971; several months later it came to an inglorious end. However, the concept of "interim steps" was eventually revived in a new setting by Henry Kissinger, the very person who opposed the 1971 effort. And it was he who made step-by-step diplomacy famous. By then, of course, Rogers was no longer secretary of state, and Sisco, the architect of the 1971 initiative, was serving as Kissinger's under secretary of state and chief adviser on Middle East policy.

THE JARRING TALKS AND U.S.-ISRAELI RELATIONS

During the post-Jordan crisis policy reviews on the Middle East, American officials considered several alternative approaches, including one dealing more directly with the Palestinians, before deciding to resume the interrupted Rogers initiative of the preceding June.[2] This time, however, the U.S.-Israeli relationship would remain close. Kissinger, in particular, felt that if Israel was ever going to make concessions, it would be from a position of strength and self-confidence, not under American pressure. Consequently a two-stage policy was adopted: first, an understanding would be reached with Israel on the terms of reference for the Jarring talks and on U.S. military assistance; second, Ambassador Jarring would be encouraged to take a more active role than previously in seeking agreement on basic principles of a peace agreement. The United States would support Jarring's efforts through bilateral talks with Israel, Egypt, and Jordan. The State Department was anxious for Jarring to try to establish the principle that Israel would withdraw from the occupied territories in return for Arab commitments to peace. That, after all, had been the essence of the original Rogers Plan.

The first step in the new American initiative was to bring Israel back into the Jarring talks and to extend the cease-fire beyond its expiration in early November. On October 15 Nixon approved an arms package of $90 million for Israel, consisting of antitank weapons, reconnaissance aircraft, and other minor items.[3] In addition, the administration decided to seek a $500 million supplemental appropriation for Israel in the current fiscal year to cover arms expenditures.[4] Israel was particularly anxious to receive a guarantee of the supply of high-performance aircraft in 1971 and had requested 54 F-4s and 120 A-4s. The Israelis were also beginning to press for long-term military agreements that would prevent the periodic supply disruptions and quarrels that had marked the previous two years.

Despite the American decision to send substantial quantities of arms to Israel, Egypt's new president, Anwar al-Sadat, agreed to a three-month extension of the cease-fire in early November. During this period he expected the Jarring talks to resume and to produce results. Egypt and the Soviet Union also began to show interest in outside guarantees as part of a peace settlement. If the United States adopted the idea, it might be prepared to pressure Israel to abandon Arab territory in return for guarantees from the major powers. In any event, this was an idea that might appeal to the Americans.[5]

Nixon's immediate problem, however, was to get the Israelis to return to the Jarring talks. The memory of the August cease-fire violations and the American vacillation was strong in Israel, and Prime Minister Meir decided to exact a high price for resuming the Jarring talks. Israeli Foreign Minister Eban informed Rogers on November 7 that Israel might return to the Jarring talks in the near future, but that it first needed assurances from the United States.

On December 1 Prime Minister Meir wrote to Nixon, asking for explicit commitments on aircraft deliveries after the end of the year; on freedom for Israel from American pressure in future negotiations; on support for Israel against Soviet intervention in the Middle East; and on the use of the U.S. veto against any anti-Israeli resolutions introduced at the United Nations.[6] Two days later Nixon replied with general reassurances and a strong bid to Israel to return to the Jarring talks. Israel would not be allowed, said Nixon, to be put at a diplomatic or military disadvantage if talks were resumed.

Meir pressed for further clarifications. In particular, she wanted the United States to drop its support for the idea of full withdrawal on the Egyptian front and from all but "insubstantial" portions of the other captured territories.[7] Defense Minister Moshe Dayan, who arrived in Washington for talks in mid-December, raised the issue of long-term military commitments. In return, he was told that the United States was prepared to participate in a multilateral UN-sponsored peace-keeping force as part of a settlement.[8]

This new twist in American policy was hardly what the Israelis wanted to hear. On December 17 Nixon replied to the Israeli prime minister's plea for further clarifications. The United States could not make any formal promise to use the veto at the UN, but it could offer more general assurances that Israel's security would not be endangered. The United States also promised to deliver twelve F-4s and twenty A-4s during the first six months of 1971. Not inclined to let the Americans off quite so inexpensively, the prime minister termed this a "step backward," one of the "greatest blows" from the United States. Soon her emotions calmed, however, and on December 28 she announced that Israel would return to the Jarring talks.

According to Meir, the United States had made commitments to preserve the balance of power in the Middle East. Israel would be allowed to negotiate freely, without fear that the United States would be a party to any UN effort to determine borders or the terms of a refugee settlement. The United States, she claimed, upheld the principle that Israel should have defensible borders, that Israel should be strong, that Israel should not be forced to withdraw to the June 4, 1967, lines, and that Israel would not be obliged to accept the Arab version of a refugee settlement. Furthermore, the conflict must be ended by a binding, contractual commitment to peace. Until that was achieved, not a single Israeli soldier would be expected to withdraw from the cease-fire lines. And finally, Jarring's terms of reference should not be altered.[9]

If indeed this represented United States policy, it was hard to see why Meir had been so upset at Nixon's December 17 letter. Perhaps she sensed the impending crisis over the Jarring mission and the American bureaucracy's reluctance to offer a blank check on arms. Perhaps she also realized that her insistence on no Israeli withdrawal without peace was being undermined by her own defense minister, who had begun to hint as early as November that it might be wise for Israel and Egypt to thin out their forces along the canal, perhaps even to withdraw them to a certain distance and to allow the canal to reopen.[10]

THE EGYPTIAN REACTION

While Nixon's exchanges with the Israelis were going on, he and Rogers had been in contact with Sadat as well. Sadat had sent Nixon a letter dated November 23, which reached him on December 14, indicating Egypt's interest in the Jarring talks. Nixon had replied orally through Mahmoud Fawzi on December 22, and Sadat sent word two days later through Donald Bergus, the American minister in Cairo, that he was genuinely interested in peace. Sadat, who had originally been viewed as something of a lightweight by Washington officials, was beginning to be taken more seriously.[11]

On January 5, 1971, Jarring met at the UN with representatives of Israel, Jordan, and Egypt. The next day he left for the Middle East. The Israelis presented him with a statement of their position, emphasizing the need for explicit and binding commitments to peace. Jarring conveyed this to the Egyptians, who replied with their own draft on January 15.[12] As might have been expected, Egypt stressed the need for Israeli withdrawal from all territory captured in 1967. Jarring redrafted the Egyptian document somewhat and presented it to the Israelis on January 18. The Israelis responded with a new draft on January 27.

At this point the United States began to urge Jarring to take a more aggressive approach, abandoning his role as message carrier and putting forward ideas of his own. The Israelis were opposed to such a procedure, but the State Department strongly favored it, particularly as time seemed to be running out. Sadat had agreed in November to a three-month renewal of the cease-fire, which therefore would expire on February 7.

Rogers had been in contact with the Egyptian foreign minister, Mahmoud Riad, earlier in the month. The Egyptians were clearly more interested in knowing what role the United States was prepared to play and what type of settlement it envisaged than they were in receiving Israeli proposals through Jarring. They had long believed that Israel was little more than an extension of the United States, so that if Washington favored full Israeli withdrawal, Israel would have to comply.

On January 27 Rogers sent Riad an oral message through Bergus. He appealed for an extension of the cease-fire, promising that Israel would submit new "substantive ideas" for a peace settlement immediately thereafter. Rogers confirmed that the views he had expressed in his December 9, 1969, speech were still valid and that the United States was prepared to make an "all out effort to help the parties reach a settlement this year." He took credit for having got Israel to drop the demand for face-to-face talks and denied that Israel had a veto over U.S. policy.[13]

With these assurances in hand, Sadat announced on February 4 that he would agree to a one-month extension of the cease-fire. Although he castigated the United States for its "full alignment with Israel," Sadat nonetheless presented a "new Egyptian initiative, compliance with which we shall consider as a true yardstick of the desire to implement the UN Security Council resolution." He went on to say:

We demand that during the period when we refrain from opening fire that a partial withdrawal of the Israeli forces on the east bank of the Suez Canal be achieved as the first stage of a timetable which will be prepared later to implement the other provisions of the Security Council resolution. If this is achieved within this period, we shall be prepared to begin immediately to clear the Suez Canal and reopen it to international navigation to serve the world economy. We believe that by this initiative, we shall be turning envoy Jarring's efforts from ambiguous words into definite measures.[14]

In fact, Sadat's initiative was soon to supersede Jarring's mission, but not before Jarring had made one last effort. On February 8 Jarring presented a memorandum to Egypt and Israel in which he asked both parties for "parallel and simultaneous commitments." Israel was asked to agree in principle to withdraw to the former international boundary between Egypt and the British mandate of Palestine, subject to practical security arrangements and freedom of navigation in the Suez Canal and the Strait of Tiran. Egypt was asked to enter into a peace agreement with Israel, including an end to belligerency, respect for Israel's independence and right to live in peace within secure and recognized boundaries, and noninterference in Israel's domestic affairs.

On February 15 Egypt replied, accepting all of Jarring's points and adding a number of others. Israel's reply was not forthcoming until February 26. Israel welcomed Egypt's unprecedented expression of readiness to enter into a peace agreement with Israel, but on the crucial issue of withdrawal the reply was blunt: "Israel will not withdraw to the pre-June 5, 1967, lines." Instead, Israel offered to negotiate without prior conditions. Egypt, however, viewed Israel's refusal to accept the principle of full withdrawal as an unacceptable prior condition. Under these circumstances the Jarring talks came to an abrupt end.[15]

THE INTERIM CANAL-AGREEMENT INITIATIVE

As Jarring was making his last effort to get the parties to agree to the outlines of an overall settlement, an alternative approach based on a partial agreement involving the Suez Canal was gaining increasing attention. Thus the collapse of the Jarring talks did not leave the diplomatic field empty. In fact, the idea of an "interim agreement," which had been in the wings for some time, was now to move to center stage.

Defense Minister Dayan had publicly spoken in November 1970 of the possibility of a mutual Egyptian and Israeli thinning out of forces along the Suez Canal. In Dayan's view such a step would help to stabilize the situation along the canal and reinforce the cease-fire then in effect. If the canal was open and the cities along its banks were rebuilt, Sadat could obviously not resume hostilities without paying a high cost. Besides, such a small step might relieve Israel from the continuing international pressure to accept the principle of full withdrawal from Arab territory.

Within Israel, Dayan's ideas received a mixed reaction. The prime minister seemed unenthusiastic, and others were overtly hostile. The concept apparently did have some appeal, however, to the Egyptian leadership. Shortly after the resumption of the Jarring initiative, a high-ranking Egyptian official approached an American diplomat in Cairo, on January 11, 1971, and expressed interest in Dayan's idea of a mutual thinning out of forces and a reopening of the canal. Several days later, Assistant Secretary Sisco informed Israeli Ambassador Rabin of this communication. Then, on February 4 Sadat publicly announced his initiative: in return for a partial Israeli withdrawal from the canal, Egypt would begin to clear and then reopen it. No mention was made of a mutual thinning out of forces, nor were specifics about the line of Israeli withdrawal mentioned.

The Israelis were immediately urged by Washington to take Sadat's proposal seriously. Egypt was pressing for a rapid reply. On February 9 Golda Meir stated that Israel was prepared to consider the idea of reopening the canal but that Israeli troops would not withdraw from the existing cease-fire lines until an overall settlement had been reached. In passing, she criticized the Americans for emphasizing international guarantees, which she implied might be substitutes for peace.[16] Three days later Israel asked the United States to convey a message to Egypt reiterating Israel's interest in discussing the reopening of the canal. This message was sent on February 14, along with an expression of hope that Egypt would respond positively to Jarring's initiative, which was done the following day.[17]

Nixon's own views, as articulated by Kissinger, were spelled out in his report to the Congress on U.S. foreign policy on February 25, 1971. Nixon termed the Middle East the most dangerous region in the world, chiefly because of the potential for superpower confrontation. After describing earlier American peace initiatives in 1969 and 1970, the report called for negotiations among the parties to determine the shape of peace. The United States would not impose a settlement. No specific mention was made of the interim canal-settlement idea. Instead, a lengthy analysis of the "great-power contest" ensued. In a direct warning to the Soviet Union, Nixon declared: "Any effort by any major power to secure a dominant position [in the Middle East] could exacerbate local disputes, affect Europe's security, and increase the danger to world peace. We seek no such position; we cannot allow others to establish one."[18]

In contrast to Sadat's insistence on a major U.S. initiative and a partial agreement between Egypt and Israel, Nixon placed greater emphasis on the U.S.-Soviet relationship in the area and the responsibility of the local parties to negotiate their own terms of settlement within a comprehensive framework. Sadat was not discouraged, however, and continued to try to draw the United States toward his own views, suggesting at one point that it was up to the United States to "squeeze Israel."[19]

After a secret two-day trip to Moscow on March 1 and 2, Sadat sent Nixon a long letter, on March 5. In it he set forward his reasons for not renewing the cease-fire upon its expiration two days later. More important, he appealed to Nixon to launch an initiative to bring about an interim agreement along the lines of his February 4 speech. Nixon took Sadat's bid seriously, and the State Department was instructed to begin work on the interim canal-settlement idea.

Israel was not particularly pleased to see the signs of American activism. The Nixon report to Congress, with its emphasis on the Soviet presence in the Middle East, had been welcomed, but now the State Department was showing signs of vacillation. Israeli leaders were distrustful of Rogers, suspecting that he would be prepared to pressure Israel for concessions as a way of conciliating the Arabs. Whether Nixon and Kissinger would support such a move was an open question. After the close working relationship established with the White House during the Jordan crisis, the Israelis had reason to hope that Rogers was not reflecting Nixon's true feelings.

As the American initiative began to get under way, the Israelis complained that arms agreements were being delayed as a form of pressure.[20] Reacting to questions about Israel's peace map, Prime Minister Meir publicly stated on March 13 that Israel must retain Sharm al-Shaykh and an access road to it, that Sinai must be demilitarized, that the border around Eilat must be changed, that the Egyptians must not return to Gaza, that the Golan Heights would remain under Israeli control, that Jerusalem must remain united, and that border changes on the West Bank would be necessary.[21] In talks with Foreign Minister Eban a few days later, Rogers urged Israel to rely on guarantees instead of territory for security.

As these exchanges suggest, it was difficult to keep the diplomacy focused on a limited, partial agreement involving the Suez Canal and a thinning out of forces. Both sides wanted to know the other's position on broader issues, and when those were raised the gap was enormous, especially on the issue of territory.

Nonetheless, on March 31 Nixon wrote to Sadat, welcoming the canal proposal. This message led to an intensified exchange of positions, with Sadat conveying to the American minister in Cairo, Donald Bergus, his opinion of the terms for a final settlement on April 1. His frame of reference was Meir's statement of March 13. Sadat would not accept the complete demilitarization of Sinai, nor could Israel remain at Sharm al-Shaykh. Limited demilitarized zones would be acceptable only if they were on both sides of the frontier.[22]

In an effort to get the talks back to the issue of the Suez Canal and a partial agreement, the United States encouraged the Israelis to set forth their position in writing. As an inducement, it was announced on April 19 that twelve more F-4s would be sent to Israel.[23] That same day Israel offered a proposal containing the following terms:

—After the reopening of the canal, Israeli ships and cargoes should be allowed through.

—A cease-fire of unlimited duration should be part of any future agreement.

—Israel would retain control of the Bar Lev line along the canal.

—Egypt would thin out its forces to the west of the canal.

—The line of withdrawal established in the interim agreement would not be considered a final border.

In addition, Israel asked for full U.S. support for its position and a reaffirmation of the assurances contained in Nixon's letters of July 23, 1970, and December 3, 1970. Two days later Nixon conveyed the desired assurances but declined to offer full support. The Egyptians were told that an Israeli proposal had been received, but its content was not immediately disclosed.

Reacting to press reports of the Israeli proposal, Sadat met with Bergus and Michael Sterner, the Egyptian-desk officer from the State Department, on April 23. Egyptian forces, he said, must be allowed to cross the canal; Egypt must control the strategically important Mitla and Giddi passes; demilitarized zones could be established; and Israel could retain Sharm al-Shaykh in the first stage, but within six months a full settlement must be reached. If Israel was not prepared to give up the passes, said Sadat, the United States should end its initiative.

Sadat's statement, if taken literally, would have brought the American effort to a halt. Israel was obviously not prepared to accept these terms. The White House drew the conclusion that there was little chance of agreement, but State was not prepared to give up so easily. Instead, hoping that Sadat would moderate his position, Rogers decided to travel to the Middle East, the first secretary of state since 1953 to visit Egypt and Israel.

By the time Rogers reached Cairo on May 4, Sadat's domestic political situation was clearly somewhat shaky. Two days earlier he had dismissed the powerful secretary general of the Arab Socialist Union, Ali Sabri. Since Sabri had a reputation for being pro-Soviet, his removal was welcomed by the Americans, and in this atmosphere the talks with Sadat went well. Sadat was polite, charming, and apparently willing to be flexible. Rogers reportedly praised his moderation and implied that the United States had nothing more to ask of him—or so Sadat later said.[24]

Rogers encountered more difficulty in Israel. The Israelis were cool to Rogers personally and suspected him of being pro-Arab. Nonetheless, the discussions were detailed and quickly hit upon the key issues. How would an interim agreement be linked to an overall peace settlement? Israel wanted no linkage, whereas Sadat wanted a timetable for full Israeli withdrawal, of which the interim agreement would merely be the first step. How long would the cease-fire last? Israel wanted an indefinite extension, whereas Egypt preferred a short renewal. How far would Israel withdraw from the canal? A few kilometers, or halfway or more across Sinai? How would the agreement be supervised? Would Egyptian troops be allowed across the canal? Would Israel's ships be allowed to use the canal after its opening? On each of these points the parties were far apart. Defense Minister Dayan sensed the danger of deadlock, and in talks with Sisco he outlined some modifications of the Israeli position. Israel would be prepared to accept Egyptian civilians and technicians on the east bank of the canal, but no military forces. Once the canal was reopened, Israel would agree to talk about the withdrawal of its forces.[25] Sisco was authorized to return to Egypt to discuss these ideas with Sadat and to report on the talks in Israel.

In Cairo, Sisco offered a number of ideas that he hoped might bridge the gap between the two parties.[26] Sadat indicated a willingness to consider only a limited Egyptian force on the canal's east bank and promised to send his trusted aide, Mahmoud Fawzi, to Washington with a reply to Sisco's other suggestions. A few days later, having just deposed some of his key ministers for having plotted against him,[27] Sadat asked for clarification on the points raised by Sisco. Was it correct to assume that the Israelis might consider a line of withdrawal east of the passes? Sisco replied on May 18 that such a line was not precluded, that there was some flexibility in the Israeli position.

Rogers and Sisco must have realized they were in a very delicate position. With the Egyptians, they were trying to present Israeli proposals as more forthcoming than they actually were. With the Israelis, the Egyptian statements were recast in the best possible light. But instead of succeeding in convincing either party of the other's good intentions, Rogers and Sisco seemed instead to lose credibility, especially with the Israelis. With the Egyptians it took a bit longer, but ultimately the sense of deception was equally great. At the White House, meanwhile, support for Rogers and Sisco was quickly fading.[28]

On May 20 Foreign Minister Riad met with Bergus to present Egypt's reply to Sisco's points of May 9. Bergus was sure the Egyptian statement was so negative in tone that the diplomatic effort would collapse. Riad was known to be opposed to an interim settlement in any event, but perhaps Sadat would agree to a softer statement of the Egyptian position.[29] Bergus returned to see Riad's deputy three days later with a redraft of the foreign minister's paper, which he offered as a suggestion of how Egypt could present its position more positively. He emphasized that he had done the rewriting on his own initiative and that his government had not been informed. At the top of the paper Riad's deputy wrote in Arabic that these were points suggested unofficially by Donald Bergus.

Meanwhile Sadat was trying to consolidate his tenuous hold on power in the aftermath of the internal shake-ups of May. The Soviet Union was uneasy because of the disappearance of some of its friends from key positions. On May 25 Soviet President Nikolai Podgorny arrived in Cairo with a draft treaty in hand for Sadat's signature. After two days of talks Sadat agreed, and on May 27 an Egyptian-Soviet treaty of friendship, to last for fifteen years, was signed.

Sadat hastened to inform the Americans that the treaty changed nothing, and to demonstrate his continuing interest in an interim agreement, he met with Bergus on May 30 to discuss Egypt's terms for a settlement. He still insisted on obtaining the passes and on sending tanks across the canal. Then, on June 4 Sadat handed Bergus a formal Egyptian proposal that included these and other points and that was virtually identical to the paper Bergus had prepared on May 23.

Sadat must have expected an early and positive reply to his proposal. After all, it was very close to Bergus's paper, and Sadat presumably thought Bergus must have been reflecting official American thinking. Bergus carried Sadat's June 4 document to Rogers immediately. But there was no reaction.[30] A month passed with no American reply. Rogers had asked Nixon if he could relaunch his initiative, but Nixon had demurred. There simply did not appear to be grounds for an agreement. A quarrel with Israel at this time would serve no purpose, and it could only hurt the administration. Moreover, this was a time when Nixon needed all the support he could muster. Unknown to the general public, Kissinger had begun to hold secret talks with the North Vietnamese in Paris, and Nixon wanted to concentrate on big issues like Vietnam. He had one other surprise in store as well. On July 9 Kissinger secretly flew to Peking from Pakistan, and this opening to China was made public a few days later. Compared with those dramatic developments, the Middle East was a tiresome distraction.

Meeting in San Clemente for a review of foreign policy after Kissinger's China trip, Nixon, Rogers, and Sisco discussed the Middle East. Sadat was apparently still interested in a limited agreement, but his patience was wearing thin. Nixon agreed that Sisco should travel to Israel to learn whether the Israelis would drop their objection to a token Egyptian force on the east bank of the canal. He pointedly refused, however, to promise that he would exert pressure on Israel if Sisco encountered difficulty. In brief, Sisco was on his own. Sisco's talks in Israel dragged on from the end of July through the first week of August.[31] Israel would not budge, and Sisco could do nothing but admit defeat. He did not even stop in Cairo, so that it was left to Bergus to brief Mohamed Heikal on the talks.

To say the least, the Egyptians were disappointed. At worst, the Americans had played Sadat for a fool. He had announced that 1971 would be a "year of decision," either war or peace.[32] He had made unprecedented concessions in February and had again tried to meet American expectations in June. He had risked his relations with the Soviet Union by moving against its supporters and by helping to crush a communist coup in Sudan in July. Not only had he failed to win the Americans to his side, but the Americans were considering new arms agreements with Israel. Frustrated and humiliated, Sadat decided to abandon the interim-settlement idea. The result was a two-year diplomatic stalemate.

KISSINGER TAKES CHARGE

The failure of the interim canal settlement effectively ended the predominance of Rogers and Sisco as Middle East policymakers. If there were to be any new American initiatives, Nixon and Kissinger would be in charge.[33]

Kissinger was critical of the way the State Department had handled the Middle East from the beginning. He had little admiration for Secretary Rogers and was unenthusiastic about the plan that bore his name. His attitude toward Sisco was more complex. He genuinely admired the assistant secretary's energy and intelligence but felt he was too much of an activist, a tactician more than a strategist, and more interested in procedure than in substance. Perhaps Sisco's worst fault, however, was that he did not defer sufficiently to Kissinger's authority.

With respect to the interim-settlement effort, Kissinger drew a number of lessons that later guided his own diplomacy after the October 1973 war. The United States, he thought, had become involved too quickly in the substance of the negotiations. Once that happened, the role of impartial negotiator was in jeopardy. Only when the parties were near agreement was it appropriate for the United States to make substantive recommendations. Kissinger also felt Rogers and Sisco had not been fully candid with Egypt and Israel. Although they had tried to soften the real positions of the two sides, they had succeeded only in raising false hopes, especially on the part of Sadat.

Kissinger strongly believed negotiations, to be successful, had to be carried out in secret. To do so was always difficult with both the Arabs and the Israelis, but Rogers and Sisco had deliberately conducted too much of the negotiations in the glare of publicity. And when secrecy was maintained, as during Rogers's talks in Cairo, it was the White House that was kept in the dark! Kissinger never knew exactly what Rogers told Sadat, nor did he know of the Bergus memorandum until it was publicly revealed at the end of June.[34]

The idea of an interim agreement unlinked to the final terms of settlement very much appealed to Kissinger. He was particularly anxious for such an accord if it would ensure the departure of the Soviet military advisers from Egypt. In practice, however, the interim-agreement approach had quickly drifted back to the package-settlement concept, with the canal pullback as only the initial stage of a comprehensive accord. Therefore Kissinger's initial interest in the approach began to fade by April, and by summer he was prepared to see it die an ignominious death, even at some risk to U.S.-Egyptian relations.

Kissinger also disagreed with the State Department's contention that Israel could be persuaded to moderate its negotiating stance if arms were withheld. Kissinger argued that to do so would simply make the Israelis feel more insecure and therefore intransigent. It would raise the hopes of the Arabs, particularly since Soviet arms were being delivered to Egypt and Syria in large quantities. Only if Israel felt strong would it be reasonable in negotiations, and only if the Arabs saw that Soviet arms did not hold the promise of a military solution would they turn to diplomacy in a serious way. Finally, Kissinger felt that the Israelis were on firm ground in refusing to make concessions to Egypt while the Soviet military presence there remained so large. Let Sadat expel the Soviets; then peace talks could begin.[35]

Kissinger's hope that the Soviet position in the Middle East might be undercut had been strengthened since the Jordan civil war. First, Sadat had moved against his allegedly pro-Soviet advisers in May; then Jordan had eliminated the remnants of the PLO remaining in the country. Even more important, a communist coup d'état in Sudan in July had been reversed by the combined intervention of Egypt and Libya.

Offsetting these desirable developments, however, was the Egyptian-Soviet treaty and an increase in the flow of Soviet arms to Egypt and Syria. Sadat had, on several occasions, stated that the Soviet advisers in his country would leave after the first stage of Israeli withdrawal, but until then he was anxious to keep his military ties intact. Kissinger now hoped to convince Sadat that the removal of the Soviet advisers would have to precede the first stage of withdrawal.

Sadat soon realized it was not worth dealing with Rogers and Sisco any longer. After the talks between Rogers and Riad in September 1971, Sadat thereafter communicated with Kissinger or Nixon through intermediaries, including his adviser on national security, Hafiz Ismail.[36] This link, which bypassed the State Department by relying on each country's intelligence channels, was rarely used in the following months, but it was available when needed.

The State Department nonetheless continued to try to promote an Egyptian-Israeli agreement. On October 14, 1971, Rogers spoke at the United Nations, outlining six areas of disagreement between the two parties that had emerged in the interim-canal-settlement talks. Now Rogers proposed that Egypt and Israel send high-ranking officials to the United States to engage in "proximity talks," with Sisco acting as mediator and "catalyst."[37] Sadat accepted, apparently still hoping for some progress before the end of the "year of decision."

Israel was less enthusiastic about proximity talks. Before returning to such a forum, Israel wanted a basic understanding with the United States on arms supply and on the U.S. and Soviet roles in future negotiations. On November 1, 1971, the United States and Israel signed a significant memorandum of understanding regarding American aid to Israel to enhance its military self-sufficiency.[38] Israel was planning to build a jet fighter modeled on the French Mirage. A complete set of blueprints for the plane had been smuggled out through Switzerland.[39] Israel could not produce the engine, however; hence the United States agreed in principle to provide the missing components.

Since midyear the United States had refrained from signing any new arms agreements with Israel. It had done so out of a conviction that the military balance remained in Israel's favor and in the hope of gaining leverage over Israeli policy. Moreover, the State Department did not want to undercut Sadat's position during the interim canal negotiations.

Prime Minister Meir visited Washington in early December 1971 to discuss a new arms agreement with Nixon. She argued that Israel needed to be assured of a continuing flow of aircraft and other equipment well into the 1970s. The Soviets had no hesitation about helping their friends. Why did the Americans insist on punishing Israel by withholding arms? That only increased Arab intransigence. A long-term agreement would convince the Soviets and the Arabs that they could not separate the United States from Israel and that a military solution was impossible, and such an agreement would allow Israel to negotiate from strength.

Nixon and Kissinger basically agreed with Meir's points.[40] A long-term agreement would also help to avoid periodic squabbles over new arms agreements. Each time a new arms package was requested, the United States and Israel argued over the terms and the timing. The Arabs saw the quarrels as encouraging signs, but then felt disillusioned when the United States eventually provided the arms. In an election year especially, Nixon had no desire to confront Israel over arms. Should a diplomatic initiative prove to be possible after the 1972 presidential elections, it would not be marred by arguments over a new arms agreement if a multiyear deal could be concluded in late 1971. Consequently, on

December 31 it was announced that the United States had agreed in principle to resume shipments of F-4s to Israel.

Equally important, Nixon and Meir reached an understanding on strategy and tactics for future peace efforts. They would abandon the search for an overall agreement for the time being. The focus now would be on an interim Egyptian-Israeli agreement. Sisco would try to arrange for "proximity talks" between the parties, but, in Kissinger's words, "the real negotiations would be carried out between Israeli Ambassador Rabin and me, and also between Dobrynin and me."[41]

Much of January 1972 was spent in discussing the terms of the new arms deal with the Israelis. And Sisco and Rabin met frequently to establish the ground rules for proximity talks. The result was another memorandum of understanding on February 2, 1972, whereby the United States agreed to sell Israel forty-two F-4s and eighty-two A-4s over the coming years. In the proximity talks the Soviet Union would play no substantive role. Most significant, the United States would take no initiative in the talks that had not first been fully discussed with the Israelis. If the memorandum was taken literally, the United States had tied itself almost completely to the Israeli position.[42] Four days later the Israeli cabinet agreed to the idea of proximity talks, but Egypt now refused, and no further diplomatic progress was made.

U.S.-Israeli relations, however, were stronger than ever. Throughout 1972 Nixon was able to portray his administration as a firm supporter of Israel. All the old disputes were forgotten, and Ambassador Rabin came very close to endorsing Nixon's bid for the presidency against the Democratic contender.

During 1972 U.S. Middle East policy consisted of little more than open support for Israel. The White House explicitly told the State Department not to consider any new initiatives until after the elections. Meanwhile Nixon set out to reap the rewards of Kissinger's negotiations with the Chinese and the Soviets. A successful foreign policy was clearly going to be a major theme in his reelection campaign.

In his survey of foreign policy presented to Congress on February 9, 1972, Nixon highlighted the Soviet role in the Middle East. He quoted himself to the effect that U.S.-Soviet interests were "very diametrically opposed" in the Middle East, except for the desire to avoid a confrontation.[43] He then reviewed earlier U.S. initiatives, emphasizing the obstacles to an Arab-Israeli agreement. The shortcomings of both the package-agreement and the interim-settlement approaches were candidly discussed, but the main theme of his remarks was the need for great power restraint:

The Soviet Union's effort to use the Arab-Israeli conflict to perpetuate and expand its own military position in Egypt has been a matter of concern to the United States. The U.S.S.R. has taken advantage of Egypt's increasing dependence on Soviet military supply to gain the use of naval and air facilities in Egypt. This has serious implications for the stability of the balance of power locally, regionally in the Eastern Mediterranean, and globally. The Atlantic Alliance cannot ignore the possible implications of this move for the stability of the East-West relationship. . . .

We hope the Soviet Union understands that it can serve this interest [of avoiding a major conflict in the Middle East] best by restraint in its arms supply, refraining from the use of this dispute to enhance its own military position, and encouraging the negotiation of a peace.

Aside from urging the parties to begin serious negotiations, Nixon made no suggestions on how the conflict might be resolved. He did, however, add: "Injecting the global strategic rivalry into the region is incompatible with Middle East peace and with detente in U.S.-Soviet relations."[44]

SUMMITRY

Toward the end of February 1972 President Nixon traveled to Peking for talks with Chairman Mao Tse-tung and Prime Minister Chou En-lai. The occasion was not only historic for U.S.-Chinese relations but also carried broader significance. Nixon and Kissinger were attempting to alter relations among the major powers in the interests of stability and the avoidance of nuclear war. They assumed the Soviet Union would remain the principal adversary of the United States and the greatest threat to U.S. interests. To help induce restraint on the part of the Soviet Union, the United States was prepared to develop ties with Moscow's main rival, the leadership in Peking. This was a classic stroke of balance-of-power politics, and if successful it would lend substance to the policy of détente that Nixon and Kissinger had widely promoted. Peking was thus an important way station on the road to Moscow, where Nixon was expected in May.

Between the Peking and Moscow summits, developments in Vietnam took an alarming turn for the worse. The North Vietnamese sent troops across the demilitarized zone on March 30, and for several weeks the communist forces made impressive gains. The United States responded with intensified bombing, and with a major concession to the North Vietnamese during Kissinger's talks in Moscow in late April.[45] On May 8 Nixon made a controversial decision to resume the heavy bombing of North Vietnam and to mine the harbor of Haiphong, hoping by those actions to cut the flow of arms to Hanoi. He realized this might bring the United States into open conflict with both the Soviet Union and China. Many of his advisers were sure that Brezhnev would feel compelled to cancel the upcoming summit conference. Nixon held firm, however, and the Soviets swallowed their pride and received Nixon in Moscow on May 22.

One of the great hopes of the Nixon-Kissinger foreign policy had been that détente between the superpowers would have benefits for American policy elsewhere. The summits seemed to confirm their belief that neither the Chinese nor the Soviets would allow developments in Vietnam to stand in the way of their interests in dealing with the United States. Perhaps Moscow could also be persuaded to subordinate its Middle East policies to the requirements of détente. In any event, Nixon and Kissinger were prepared to explore the possibility as one means of reducing the chances of superpower confrontation in the Middle East and, they hoped, of undercutting Soviet influence in Egypt.

In essence, this was a return to the linkage concept that had guided the Rogers-Sisco initiative of 1969, but now there was more to build on in the U.S.-Soviet relationship, particularly with the achievement of a treaty limiting strategic nuclear arms. Equally important, from Kissinger's point of view, was the fact that he, not Rogers or Sisco, would handle the talks with the Russians on the Middle East.

Kissinger's ostensible goal was to reach agreement with the Soviet leadership on a set of principles that could serve as a framework for an Arab-Israeli peace settlement. Next he would enlist their support for beginning a step-by-step negotiating process based on those principles, but leaving key issues such as final borders to be negotiated by the parties themselves.

Unbeknownst to the State Department, Kissinger and Foreign Minister Andrei Gromyko reached a tentative working agreement on eight principles. The two superpowers were in accord on the following points:

—The agreement should be comprehensive, but could be implemented in steps.

—The agreement should contain provisions for the withdrawal of Israeli forces from Arab territories occupied in 1967.

—Any border changes should result from voluntary agreement among the parties.

—Security arrangements could include demilitarized zones, UN forces at Sharm al-Shaykh, and international guarantees with the participation of the United States and the Soviet Union.

—The agreement should lead to an end of the state of belligerency and to the establishment of peace.

—Freedom of navigation through the Strait of Tiran and the Suez Canal should be assured. This would be consistent with Egyptian sovereignty over the canal.

—The agreement must include recognition of the independence and sovereignty of all states in the Middle East, including Israel.

—The Soviets maintained that the Palestinian refugee problem should be solved on a just basis in accordance with appropriate UN decisions.

—The United States maintained that completion of the agreement should involve negotiations between the parties.[46]

Although this tentative agreement remained secret, the United States and the Soviet Union did announce agreement on a set of basic principles.[47] The two superpowers committed themselves to conducting their relations on the basis of peaceful coexistence (article 1) and to "preventing situations capable of causing a dangerous exacerbation of their relations. . . . They will always exercise restraint in their mutual relations, and will be prepared to negotiate and settle differences by peaceful means" (article 2). "The U.S.A. and the U.S.S.R. have a special responsibility . . . to do everything in their power so that conflicts or situations will not arise which would serve to increase international tensions" (article 3).

In the joint communiqué issued on May 29, the United States and the Soviet Union reaffirmed their support of UN Resolution 242 and of the Jarring mission. A settlement of the Arab-Israeli conflict "would open prospects for the normalization of the Middle East situation and would permit, in particular, consideration of further steps to bring about a military relaxation in that area."[48]

Read in Cairo, the basic principles and the joint communiqué seemed to confirm Sadat's worst fears. Both the United States and the Soviet Union had agreed to freeze the Middle East situation for fear of damaging their own relations. Under the guise of détente, the United States had persuaded the Soviets to reduce their support for the Arabs. This would explain the Soviet reluctance to provide advanced weaponry and the delays in deliveries that had been irritating Sadat for months.

Sadat was well aware that the Americans viewed the Soviet presence in Egypt as an obstacle to a peace settlement. Rogers had raised the issue in May. Now, with the results of the summit meeting available, it seemed clear to Sadat that the Soviets were not prepared to press his case with the Americans. Not only was their presence in Egypt of concern to the Americans and the Israelis, but his own officers were complaining about it. Then, in June, Saudi Arabia's minister of defense, Prince Sultan, reported on his conversations with Nixon and Kissinger. Until the Soviet presence in Egypt was eliminated, the Americans would not press Israel for concessions.[49]

Which of these factors was most compelling to Sadat is unknown, but in early July he decided to act. On July 8 Sadat informed the Soviet ambassador that he was requesting the departure of most of the Soviet advisers and technicians in Egypt. Sadat publicly announced his decision on July 18. More than ten thousand Soviet personnel would leave Egypt, precisely as Kissinger and the Israelis had hoped.

REACTION TO THE EXPULSION OF SOVIET ADVISERS

If Sadat's primary motivation in announcing the expulsion of the Soviet advisers in Egypt was to open the way for an active U.S. diplomatic role, he had chosen a curious time for such a momentous step.[50] Nixon was in the midst of an election campaign and was not prepared to jeopardize his substantial lead over Senator George McGovern by embarking on a controversial policy in the Middle East. He and Kissinger, however, did recognize the importance of Sadat's move, and through the "back channel" they informed the Egyptian president that after the American elections were over, a new initiative would be launched. This time it would be under White House control.

A reelected president would presumably be immune to the normal pressures of domestic politics. Nixon's prestige was at its zenith, Kissinger's reputation was growing, and perhaps they could together fashion a settlement in the Middle East.

In midsummer 1972 few could have anticipated that Nixon's ability to conduct foreign policy, and eventually even his tenure in office, would be greatly affected by a seemingly minor incident on June 17. On that day five men had been apprehended inside the offices of the Democratic headquarters in the Watergate complex in Washington, D.C. Investigation of the break-in revealed that the burglars had curious connections with the Central Intelligence Agency and with the Committee to Reelect the

President. Perhaps some zealous Republicans had broken the law, but no one suspected that the president himself might be involved. On June 23, 1972, however, in a conversation with his chief of staff, H. R. Haldeman, Nixon became enmeshed in the Watergate affair by ordering the CIA to block the FBI's investigation of the incident for political reasons. The conversation was recorded on the president's secret taping system. Its disclosure a little more than two years later proved fatal to Nixon's struggle to survive Watergate. For the moment, however, Nixon and his aides had little reason to fear that the Watergate affair would not be contained.

On the eve of his reelection Nixon took pains to speak of his plans for the Middle East. "The Middle East will have a very high priority because while the Mideast has been, over the past couple of years, in a period of uneasy truce or armistice or whatever you want to call it, it can explode at any time."[51] The message to Sadat was intended to be that he should remain patient a bit longer. It would soon be his turn, once Vietnam was settled.

Nixon was reelected overwhelmingly on November 7, winning 60.8 percent of the popular vote and 97 percent of the electoral vote. But the "peace at hand" in Vietnam remained elusive. It was only after an intensive bombing campaign against North Vietnam in December that negotiations resumed. At long last, on January 13, 1973, the Paris talks were successfully concluded; on January 27 the final agreement was signed.

THE KISSINGER STRATEGY

With the end of the fighting in Vietnam, Kissinger was ready to turn his attention to the Middle East. He had previously paid little attention to briefing materials prepared for him on that region; now he requested studies, perused long memoranda, and began to develop a detailed strategy of his own.

Kissinger wanted to avoid endless debates over the meaning of Resolution 242, the Rogers Plan, and the Jarring memorandum. A legalistic approach was bound to bog down rapidly. The key demands of both parties were phrased in totally incompatible terms. The Israelis wanted peace and recognition; the Arabs wanted territory and justice. Rather than try for initial agreement on these ultimate goals, Kissinger hoped to move quickly to practical agreements, but he realized the importance of some formulation that would address the end result of the negotiating process. The Jarring formulation of "peace" for "withdrawal" did not appeal to him. Instead, he preferred the formulation recommended by his aides of establishing a balance between "sovereignty" and "security." The virtue of such a formula was that it opened the door to a wide range of negotiating outcomes. For example, it might be possible to recognize Egypt's sovereignty over Sinai at an early date, while establishing special security arrangements that would allow the Israelis to maintain a presence in key areas during a lengthy transitional period. If agreement could be reached on such a general formulation, then negotiations could begin on concrete issues, such as those identified during the interim-canal-settlement negotiations.

Kissinger had the chance to try out his ideas in February. King Hussein arrived in Washington for talks with Nixon and Kissinger on February 6. He had proposed the previous spring an unpopular plan to establish a United Arab Kingdom consisting of the East and West Banks of the Jordan, subject to approval in a referendum among the Palestinians. Little support had been found for the idea in the Arab world, and both Egypt and Syria had reacted hostilely. Nevertheless, Hussein was still interested in recovering the West Bank and was anxious, as always, for American help. In addition, he was in need of substantial increases in economic and military assistance. Nixon was prepared to accommodate him, for he liked and admired the king.

Still, little could be done to advance a settlement between Jordan and Israel without taking Egypt into account. Kissinger's next visitor, Sadat's national security adviser, Hafiz Ismail, was therefore unusually important. Ismail was the first high-level Egyptian official to meet with Nixon in some time. The visit had been arranged through the "back channel." The State Department was not informed until the last moment. Nixon met with Hafiz Ismail on February 23 and appeared relaxed and self-confident. He outlined a strategy for negotiating on two levels: one would be handled in secret by Kissinger, as with Vietnam; the other would be public and would involve the State Department.[52] Nixon also mentioned the sovereignty and security formula.

Ismail's real purpose in coming to Washington, however, was to confer with Kissinger. During the next two days Hafiz Ismail and his aides Ihab Wahba and Ahmed Maher met with Kissinger, who was accompanied by National Security Council staffers Peter Rodman and Harold Saunders, at a private estate in Connecticut.[53] Kissinger argued for the necessity of accepting the idea of a settlement being implemented over a prolonged period. He implied that Egyptian sovereignty over Sinai could be acknowledged at an early date but that special security arrangements might be required for a long time. Ismail seemed interested, and the talks seemed to go well. He indicated that a normalization of relations with Israel might eventually be possible and that Jordan might have a role to play in solving the Palestinian issue, but he was adamant about full Israeli withdrawal from Sinai and Golan, hinting at some flexibility in the West Bank.[54]

They then discussed in detail the obligations that Egypt and Israel would undertake as part of a peace agreement, the relationship between an Egyptian-Israeli agreement and resolution of the Palestine problem, and concrete security arrangements for Israel in Sinai. Unable to resolve all these issues, Kissinger and Ismail agreed to meet again at an early date. Kissinger was in no rush. He told Ismail that little could be accomplished before the Israeli elections, scheduled for late October 1973.

Three days later, on February 28, Golda Meir arrived in Washington to meet with Nixon and Kissinger and was told of the talks with Hussein and Ismail. As usual, she pressed the case for more military assistance to Israel. A decision on a new arms package was at that moment pending. In a meeting on March 1 Nixon urged her to be more forthcoming with ideas for an agreement on the Egyptian front. Pressed by Meir for new arms, Nixon agreed in principle to a new schedule of aircraft deliveries but sought to keep the agreement secret.[55]

As Hafiz Ismail was returning from his trip to Washington, an article appeared in the press saying that the president had decided on new arms aid to Israel. The timing of the article seemed designed to embarrass Ismail and raised serious doubts in Cairo about U.S. intentions. Kissinger, somewhat disingenuously, hastened to inform Ismail that the article was inaccurate. Shortly thereafter, however, an accurate account appeared in the press confirming that a decision on new arms had been made.[56]

The diplomatic effort launched in February had as its goal the establishment of a "negotiating framework" between Egypt and Israel. Kissinger saw this as being complemented by a U.S.-Soviet agreement on principles of a settlement, based on those tentatively drawn up in Moscow the previous May. He realized it would take time for all the pieces to fall into place.

During the spring, however, several events occurred that diverted the attention of the policymakers from the Egyptian-Israeli front. First was the assassination of the American ambassador in Khartoum, Cleo Noel, and his deputy, George Moore. The CIA had received intelligence that Black September, the terrorist wing of Fatah, was responsible and that Arafat might have ordered the killings.[57] In the wake of the Munich atrocity the previous September, when eleven Israeli athletes at the Olympic Games had been killed during a Palestinian terrorist attack, and the assassination in November 1971 of Jordan's prime minister Wasfi Tal by Black September, the Khartoum murders created an intense preoccupation with Palestinian terrorism. This was hardly an ideal moment to take initiatives aimed at improving U.S.-Arab relations.

A second preoccupation was the "energy crisis" that was increasingly apparent on the horizon. The price of oil had been rising rapidly since 1971. U.S. production was stagnating, U.S. refinery capacity was insufficient to meet the demand, and shortages of gasoline and fuel oil might be felt by the end of the year. The oil companies were nervous. The president had no policy except to appear to be in control while he cast about for someone to take charge. Visitors to Saudi Arabia began to report that King Faisal, for the first time, was speaking of using the oil weapon to bring pressure on the United States unless Israel was forced to withdraw from Arab territory.

Against this background, tensions in the Middle East mounted sharply in mid-April. Lebanon was thrown into a crisis by an Israeli raid into downtown Beirut that killed three top PLO leaders. More dangerous still, toward the end of the month Egyptian war preparations along the Suez Canal took on an air of determination.[58] Intelligence reports were also received that Syria had completed a detailed war plan and was prepared to attack Israel on short notice. Israel took the signs seriously and ordered a partial mobilization; by mid-May the crisis atmosphere had passed.

Meanwhile the smoldering Watergate issue had flared up. On March 21 a young lawyer working for the White House, John Dean, had informed Nixon of the extent of high-level involvement in the Watergate cover-up. He warned Nixon of a "cancer" growing on the presidency. Within weeks of this conversation Dean was telling his story to the FBI investigators dealing with Watergate. Evidence was rapidly accumulating that implicated the president's closest associates—John Mitchell, Haldeman, and John Ehrlichman. Increasingly, Nixon was obliged to devote his time and energies to the Watergate crisis. On April 30 he accepted the resignations of Haldeman and Ehrlichman. Of his closest advisers, only Kissinger now remained.

Kissinger tried to keep Middle East policy on the track charted in February, but because Nixon's authority was being undermined, it was increasingly difficult. On May 3 Nixon's fourth "State of the World" message was sent to Congress. It spelled out clearly the Kissinger strategy. In a section entitled "The Situation Today," Nixon argued for serious negotiations between the local parties, insisting that an imposed settlement would not last. Sovereignty and security were identified as key issues. Nixon continued to develop the theme of negotiations:

A step-by-step approach still seems most practical, but we fully recognize that one step by itself cannot bring peace. First, there is a relationship between any initial step toward peace and steps which are to follow toward a broader settlement. We are open-minded on how that relationship might be established in a negotiating process, and on what role the United States might play. But the relationship cannot be ignored. Second, all important aspects of the Arab-Israeli conflict must be addressed at some stage, including the legitimate interests of the Palestinians. Implementation can occur in stages, and it should not be precluded that some issues and disputes could be resolved on a priority basis. But a comprehensive settlement must cover all the parties and all the major issues.

The issues are formidable, interlinked, and laden with emotion. The solutions cannot be found in general principles alone, but must be embodied in concrete negotiated arrangements. The parties will not be tricked into compromise positions by artful procedures. But there is room for accommodation and an overwhelming necessity to seek it.[59]

Kissinger began to think of how he might induce the Soviet Union to cooperate with his efforts to begin a negotiating process. He wanted Moscow to endorse publicly a set of principles that would serve as guidelines for a settlement. Perhaps the Soviet Union would be more cooperative if it could be persuaded that the status quo was not working to its advantage in the Middle East. The expulsion of Soviet advisers from Egypt in 1972 had been a welcome development. Kissinger toyed with the idea of trying to weaken the Soviets in Iraq and South Yemen as well, perhaps with the help of Iran and Saudi Arabia. In his view such anti-Soviet moves in the Middle East would not be incompatible with his objective of enlisting Soviet support for negotiations, provided U.S. involvement remained secret.

On May 4 Kissinger arrived in Moscow to prepare for the second Nixon-Brezhnev summit meeting. While there, he received a new document from Gromyko that set forth nine principles of an Arab-Israeli settlement. Gromyko's document, unlike that of the previous May, called for complete Israeli withdrawal to the June 4, 1967, lines. It also referred to the "legitimate rights" of the Palestinians. One new note was included: failure by either party to implement any part of the agreement would give the other party the right to refuse to fulfill its own obligations. On the whole, Kissinger much preferred the May 1972 document.[60]

The State Department was kept in the dark concerning these discussions, which added greatly to Secretary Rogers's frustration. Kissinger's domination of U.S. foreign policy was increasingly apparent as Nixon became engulfed in the Watergate crisis. His position did not go unchallenged, however. On May 15, 1973, Rogers proposed a new American initiative for settling the Arab-Israeli conflict. He suggested an "exploratory" effort by the United States, which might help to stabilize the region even if it did not immediately produce results. He proposed a two-track approach, one public and one secret. The public effort would focus on a canal agreement, as in 1971. The secret effort would aim at direct Egyptian-Israeli talks on broader issues. To break the impasse encountered earlier, he recommended that the United States try to persuade the parties to agree that Resolution 242 neither endorsed nor precluded return to the pre-June 1967 lines. Kissinger was unenthusiastic, and at his suggestion Nixon gave Rogers no encouragement.

Rogers's exasperation was further increased when he learned by accident that Kissinger was planning to meet again with Hafiz Ismail. This time he insisted that one of his own representatives be present, and when Kissinger and Ismail met secretly outside of Paris on May 20, Alfred Atherton, the deputy assistant secretary of state for Near Eastern affairs, was part of the U.S. team.

Ismail was less interested in substance during these talks than he had been in February. He concentrated his questions instead on the role the United States intended to play. What kind of White House involvement could Egypt expect? Why was the United States continuing to arm Israel so lavishly? How could Egyptian sovereignty in Sinai be made real, not just a symbol? The unresolved issues from February were discussed, but inconclusively. Ismail insisted that a final peace between Egypt and Israel was contingent on a solution to the Palestinian problem.

Kissinger described to Ismail his strategy of trying for a U.S.-Soviet agreement on principles, to be followed by secret negotiations between the parties. Kissinger spoke with Ismail privately for a few minutes and felt he was making some progress. He then suggested that further talks would be desirable. Ismail promised an early reply, but when it came on

June 3, it was guarded and unenthusiastic. Perhaps the Egyptians were beginning to have their doubts about Nixon's ability to produce results, given his crumbling domestic base. In any event, the promising tone of the February talks was missing in May.[61]

BREZHNEV'S VISIT

If U.S.-Egyptian relations seemed to be stagnating, the same could not be said for U.S.-Soviet ties. Kissinger had been treated with great courtesy and attention in May, and now, in June, General Secretary Leonid Brezhnev arrived for his first visit to the United States. Talks on the Middle East were focused on the May 1972 document, with some additions from Gromyko's more recent draft. The Soviet language on full withdrawal and the "rights" of the Palestinians, however, was not accepted by the United States.

Nixon and Brezhnev, along with Kissinger and Gromyko and their staffs, discussed the Middle East at length. Brezhnev warned that the Egyptians and Syrians were intent on going to war and that the Soviet Union could not stop them. Only a new American initiative and, in particular, pressure on Israel to withdraw could prevent war.[62] The joint communiqué issued on June 25, 1973, gave little idea of the content of the talks. The Soviets even refused to allow Resolution 242 to be mentioned unless Jarring's February 1971 document was also included. The final language therefore merely stated: "Both parties agreed to continue to exert their efforts to promote the quickest possible settlement in the Middle East. This settlement should be in accordance with the interests of all states in the area, be consistent with their independence and sovereignty, and should take into account the legitimate interests of the Palestinian people."[63]

Following the June summit talks, U.S. Middle East policy entered the summer doldrums. Nothing much could be done until after the Israeli elections in any case, according to Kissinger. The Arabs were clearly frustrated—Sadat called the United States the "world's biggest bully" on July 23—and King Faisal was publicly linking oil and the Arab-Israeli conflict.[64] Sadat also seemed intent on forcing the United States into an anti-Arab posture by calling for a UN debate on the Middle East crisis and then pressing for a vote on a resolution strongly condemning Israel. For the fifth time in its history, the United States cast a veto. The Arab world reacted angrily. Kissinger wondered why Sadat was seeking a confrontation. Was he merely trying to compel the United States to take a more active role?

During the third week of July 1973, Kissinger devoted considerable time to the Middle East, particularly to the question of Soviet involvement. He was concerned that the State Department's penchant for solving conflicts made the United States "lean on" its friends. His preference was to build on those friendships to look after American interests in the region.

Kissinger, speaking to the press on background and to his staff, developed this perspective with regard to the Arab-Israeli conflict. He called the highly publicized American peace initiatives in the Middle East "disastrous." When the United States had gone public with its views, it had been attacked by Israel, the Israeli lobby, and the Arabs, and was thus caught in the middle. In his view the United States lacked the kind of leverage in the Middle East that it had in Vietnam. Before moving publicly with a new initiative, it should have one side lined up "so we can move against the other." In that way the United States would not be attacked by both sides. In addition, it could not dissociate itself too greatly from Israel without displaying dangerous signals to the Soviet Union.

He thought of the Arab negotiating position as "impossible." The Arabs called for total Israeli withdrawal in return for an end to belligerency; then, according to the Egyptians, Israel would have to negotiate with the Palestinians for a final peace. Egypt's position on the difference between the end of belligerency and a final peace was very vague. The United States could not simply tell Israel to withdraw and then to talk to the Palestinians. Furthermore, Egypt was not clear on whether King Hussein could speak for the Palestinians.

Kissinger argued that Israel could not be forced to accept an overall solution all at once. It would be necessary to segment the negotiations into pieces that Israel could manage, after which the negotiations should proceed step by step. Egypt, he felt, was playing into the hands of the Israelis because Israel was primarily interested in wasting time. On the other hand, if a negotiating process could begin, history could work on the side of a settlement.

Kissinger continued to try to separate sovereignty and security. He knew Sadat saw this distinction as phony, but it was better for Egypt's interests than previous positions. He also thought that for the United States to adopt a more balanced policy might be self-defeating. The Arabs wanted the United States to strike poses, but that would serve no useful purpose. Instead, Kissinger wanted to preserve American influence with Israel until the time when taking a separate position could produce tangible results. The United States sought a balanced policy, but it needed a "fulcrum to move the situation." It could not support the maximum Arab position in negotiations, but once negotiations did start, Israel would begin to move back and a process would be under way. In Kissinger's view it would be easier to dislodge the Israelis from almost anywhere else in Sinai than it would be from the cease-fire lines.

These thoughts well summarize Kissinger's views on the Arab-Israeli conflict as of mid-1973. The importance of the U.S.-Israeli relationship and his preoccupation with the Soviet Union stand out. The Jordan-crisis lessons were still alive nearly three years later.

On August 22 Nixon made a surprise announcement that he was nominating Henry Kissinger as secretary of state to replace William Rogers. Kissinger would keep his position as adviser to the president for national security affairs as well. No longer would Kissinger have to worry about the secretary of state undercutting his strategy.

Three days after becoming secretary of state, on September 25, Kissinger met with most of the Arab ambassadors to the UN. He tried to establish his credentials as a credible mediator, joking about his own Jewish background.[65] He promised to work for a settlement but warned the ambassadors not to expect miracles. He would only promise what he could deliver, but he would deliver all that he promised. This became a common refrain in Kissinger's talks with the Arabs.

Over the next two weeks Kissinger spoke several times with the Arab and Israeli foreign ministers attending the UN General Assembly in New York. He proposed, and they seemed to agree, that serious talks between Egypt and Israel, with the United States as mediator, should begin in November. On October 5 he met with Foreign Minister Zayyat of Egypt to confirm these arrangements. On the whole, he was satisfied with the results of his first foray as secretary of state into Middle East diplomacy.

The next day, Yom Kippur, Egypt and Syria launched a combined military offensive against Israeli forces in the Golan Heights and Sinai. Kissinger's policy lay in ruins, overtaken by a war that he had occasionally worried about but had not really foreseen. At the core of his misreading of Arab intentions was his belief that war would be prevented by maintaining the military balance in Israel's favor. This view, forged in the midst of the Jordan crisis, had been dangerously misleading.

CONCLUSIONS

The period between the Jordan crisis in September 1970 and the October 1973 war was deceptively calm in the Middle East. In the absence of acute crises, American policymakers paid comparatively little attention to the area. The basic frame of reference, set by Nixon and Kissinger, emphasized the U.S.-Soviet rivalry and the need to maintain the balance of power in Israel's favor. Periodically the State Department tried to launch a new initiative—the Jarring talks, the interim canal settlement, proximity talks—but the White House was only mildly supportive at best, and on occasion was distinctly negative. Bureaucratic rivalries became personalized in the Rogers-Kissinger quarrel. On the whole, Nixon sided with Kissinger.[66] As a result, United States policy during this period was particularly ineffective and inconsistent.

During the interim canal-settlement talks, it was especially flawed; the Rogers-Sisco mediation and the Bergus memorandum left a bitter aftertaste in Israel, Egypt, and the White House. During this noncrisis period domestic politics also began to intrude on policymaking in noticeable ways. Because of election-year imperatives in 1972, no initiatives were undertaken, even in response to Sadat's expulsion of the Soviet advisers. Then, in 1973, Watergate began to divert the attention of the president from the region to which he had promised to devote highest priority in his foreign policy.

As Kissinger began to focus on the Middle East, he toyed with the idea of seeking U.S.-Soviet agreement on principles as one strand of his policy, while also talking to Egypt and Israel about both interim steps and principles for an overall settlement. Curiously, each of these approaches had been tried by Rogers and had failed. Kissinger was no more successful, but his larger purpose, in any case, seems to have been to frustrate the Arabs so that they would break with their Soviet patron and turn to the United States for help. But when Sadat began to move in this direction in 1972, Kissinger did not take him very seriously.

The most impressive shift in policy during this period concerned U.S.-Israeli relations. Despite occasional disagreements over arms, the United States and Israel entered an unusually cooperative phase in their often troubled relationship. This phase was very much the result of the Jordan crisis and Kissinger's view of Israel as a strategic asset. In fiscal years 1968, 1969, and 1970 Israel had received from the United States military credits worth $25 million, $85 million, and $30 million, respectively.

After the Jordan crisis, in fiscal years 1971, 1972, and 1973, Israel received military credits of $545 million, $300 million, and $307.5 million, respectively—nearly a tenfold increase in aid.

Yet the military balance proved not to be the key to regional stability and the prevention of war. Nor did détente prevent the Soviet Union from continuing to arm Egypt, Syria, and Iraq despite the mounting signs of Arab intentions to resume hostilities. Nixon and Kissinger remained insensitive to the regional trends leading to war and ignored the growing importance of Arab oil as an element in the regional equation. The concepts guiding their policies were simply too broad to incorporate these developments; nor was Kissinger convinced of the need for a major American initiative in the Middle East.[67] It required the October war to change U.S. policy and to engage Nixon and Kissinger fully in the search for an Arab-Israeli settlement.

CHAPTER SEVEN

War and Reassessment, October 1973

The Arab-Israeli war of October 1973 had all the elements of a severe international crisis. It caught most of the world, including the United States and Israel, by surprise; it did not fit anyone's preconceptions of how a war in the Middle East was likely to develop; it threatened core values of the countries directly involved as well as those of outside powers; and it ended with a near-confrontation between the two nuclear superpowers, the United States and the Soviet Union.

Crises, by their nature, expose prevailing assumptions about reality in particularly acute ways. Faced with surprise, danger, and uncertainty, decisionmakers act from previously formulated conceptions of reality. When reality no longer conforms to these images, and policymakers are under great pressure of time and events, they are likely to restructure their perceptions with extraordinary speed. Impending failure or danger, much like the prospect of a hanging, clears the mind. Pieces of the puzzle are quickly rearranged, and new policies are tried. If the crisis is resolved successfully, the revised or restructured image is likely to endure for some time; lessons will be drawn; and a new policy framework will emerge to guide action until the next failure or crisis. The October war is therefore doubly important as an object of study, for it revealed the underlying assumptions of American policy toward the Arab-Israeli conflict from 1970 to 1973 and produced a major revision of those assumptions within a very short period.

WHY THE SURPRISE?

Shortly after 6:00 a.m. Washington time on October 6, 1973, the White House situation room received a flash cable from the American embassy in Tel Aviv. Israel finally had conclusive evidence that the Egyptians and Syrians planned to attack by 6:00 p.m. Middle East time (noon in Washington). Prime Minister Golda Meir assured the United States that Israel did not intend to preempt and asked that American efforts be directed at preventing war. Kissinger received the message while in New

York; Nixon was in Key Biscayne, Florida, worrying about recent evidence of corruption by Vice President Spiro Agnew. Nixon was not immediately informed of the alarming new message. From the outset, this was to be Kissinger's crisis, not his.

In the less than two hours that remained before the war began, Kissinger took charge, calling the Israelis to warn against preemption, urging the Soviets to use their influence to prevent war, telephoning the Egyptian ambassador to the UN with the Israeli message that Israel would not preempt, and sending messages to King Hussein and King Faisal to enlist their help on the side of moderation. Kissinger's efforts were futile, and the first word of hostilities was received shortly after 8:00 a.m.

Why was Washington caught off balance? Surely there was ample evidence that Egypt and Syria were frustrated over the status quo, that they had sizable military capabilities, and that they intended to resort to force at some time to recover their territories lost in 1967.[1] Sadat had publicly stated on several occasions his intention to go to war, most explicitly in April 1973.[2] During the spring Egyptian military maneuvers had been unusually realistic and had prompted a genuine war scare. State Department intelligence analysts, reflecting on the spring crisis, had predicted on May 31 that the chance of Sadat's going to war by fall was "better than even" in the absence of a credible political initiative toward a settlement.[3] General Secretary Brezhnev, in his talks with President Nixon in San Clemente in June, had warned that the Arabs were planning for war and that this time they were determined. Only American pressure on Israel to make concessions would prevent hostilities.

Kissinger had been sufficiently alarmed by these signs of tension in the Middle East to ask that a new contingency plan on the Arab-Israeli conflict be drafted. What would happen if there was another war? What options would be available to the United States? The bureaucracy abhors contingency plans, so the task fell to a junior State Department official who thought the whole exercise was a waste of time. The Israelis were so powerful that the Arabs would never dare attack. When war broke out several months later, the contingency plan lay half-finished in his file drawer.

By fall several new signs of danger were available to anyone who cared to watch. Soviet military shipments to Egypt and Syria, especially to the latter, were going on at a high level. In mid-September Egypt, Syria, and Jordan patched up their differences, just as tension flared on the

Syrian-Israeli front.[4] Shortly thereafter Syria began to redeploy some of its forces from the Jordanian border to Golan and moved large numbers of surface-to-air missiles into the region between Damascus and the Israeli front. These movements were known in Washington and were interpreted as a reaction to the September 13 air battle in which Israel had shot down twelve Syrian planes and to the easing of tensions with Jordan. At about the same time Egypt began its fall maneuvers. On September 26 Kissinger was awakened with news that Egyptian forces had gone on a high stage of alert. In response, U.S. intelligence-collection activities in the Middle East were increased, and Kissinger requested that the CIA and the Bureau of Intelligence and Research (INR) prepare an estimate of the likelihood of an Arab-Israeli war. The flow of information was staggering, but it was also inconsistent. Along with one "reliable" report that Egypt and Syria were planning a combined military offensive in the near future came dozens of equally reliable reports painting a very different picture.

On October 5 a new element entered the equation. Soviet civilians were reportedly being evacuated from Syria and Egypt. Did the Soviets know something of which the Americans were ignorant? Or was the evacuation, as in July 1972, a sign of a crisis in Arab-Soviet relations?[5] Neither interpretation could be confirmed initially, but the CIA daily report on October 6 tentatively concluded that the latter explanation seemed more plausible, inasmuch as there were no clear signs of impending hostilities.[6]

Why was the American intelligence community wrong? Why was Kissinger caught by surprise?[7] Where were all the Middle East "experts"? Two basic conceptual biases led to the misperception of Egyptian-Syrian intentions. First, it was widely assumed that the "military balance" was the key to whether there would be another war in the Middle East. This had been a basic element in American policy since 1967. However strongly the Arabs might feel about the need to regain their territory, they would not go to war if they faced certain defeat. In view of Israel's qualitative advantages in the military realm, and the substantial flow of American arms after 1970, it would be an act of folly for the Arabs to initiate a war. Nor was it expected that Israel would feel the need to preempt.

A deliberate, rationally planned war was simply implausible in the light of military realities. An unintended war, caused by each side's reacting to defensive moves of the other, seemed more likely, but it would be difficult to anticipate or predict.[8] Finally, war as an irrational act might occur, but again could not be predicted with accuracy.

Second, war seemed to make sense for the Arabs only if a political alternative for recovering their territory was precluded. Although most of the U.S. bureaucracy remained uninformed, top officials were aware that Kissinger, in his talks with Israelis and Egyptians at the UN, had arranged for preliminary talks on a settlement to begin in November, after the Israeli elections. The continuation of Israeli military superiority and the option of a political alternative made an Arab-initiated war implausible. The maneuvers, threats, and warnings could all be explained away as part of a Soviet-Arab campaign to force the United States to lean on Israel to make concessions.

Perhaps as important as these conceptual errors was a sense that Israel had the greatest incentive and the best capabilities for determining whether war was likely or not.[9] After all, Israel, not the United States, would be the target of any Arab military threat, and Israeli intelligence had an excellent reputation, drawing on sources unavailable to the United States; therefore, if the Israelis were not too worried, why should Americans be? Repeated checks with Israeli sources showed a fairly relaxed attitude. Even on October 5, when Israel was close to putting the pieces together accurately, a message to Kissinger from Golda Meir included the assessment that neither Egypt nor Syria was planning to go to war. But just in case the Arabs feared Israel's intentions, Meir asked Kissinger to reassure them that Israel had no plans to attack.[10]

Despite all the technically accurate information available in Washington about Arab war preparations, Egypt and Syria did manage to observe high standards of secrecy and deception. Well-placed Israeli intelligence agents in Egypt had been captured early in 1973.[11] Presidents Anwar Sadat and Hafiz al-Asad confided in almost no one concerning the precise moment of the attack. Communications security in the days preceding the attack was unusually good, and deliberate deception tactics were used successfully. Even so, Israel had nearly ten hours' warning.[12] But there was not enough time to take any steps to prevent war, and very little could even be done to limit the damage of the initial Arab attack.

Some have argued that if Israel had launched a preemptive air strike, the course of the war would have been significantly different. And in some quarters the United States has been blamed for preventing Israel from preempting. It is true that Kissinger and Nixon had consistently warned Israel that it must not be responsible for initiating a Middle East war. Kissinger repeated this admonition immediately before the outbreak of hostilities, but by then Prime Minister Meir had already said that Israel would not preempt. The Israeli decision was not made in Washington, at least not on October 6.

For several hours after the outbreak of war, Washington did not know whether the Israelis or the Arabs had fired the first shots. During the rump session of the Washington Special Action Group (WSAG), convened at 9:00 a.m., the prevailing view was that Israel had probably struck first.[13] CIA Director William Colby judged that, in any event, neither side had premeditated military action, but rather that the war was the result of mutual fears of actions and reactions that had escalated to hostilities.[14] The United States, it was felt, should not make accusations against either side. A multiplicity of interests was at stake—U.S.-Soviet détente, U.S.-Israeli relations, American credibility with the Arabs, and the weakened authority of the president. The initial American reaction was therefore cautious.

It soon became clear that the Egyptians and Syrians had indeed begun the hostilities, but at no point during the next three weeks did any United States official make this an issue. The public record will be searched in vain for references to Arab "aggression."[15] Unlike President Johnson, who held Nasser responsible for the 1967 war despite Israel's opening fire on June 5, Nixon and Kissinger ignored the issue of who was at fault. Among the reasons for this "evenhanded" perspective was the feeling that U.S.-Arab relations were growing in importance because of oil and this was no time for a confrontation; that an Arab attack on Israeli forces in occupied Arab territory was not the same as an attack across recognized borders; and that the status quo prevailing before the war had, in fact, given the Arabs ample incentive to try to break the "no war, no peace" stalemate by engineering an international crisis. For several days it was widely considered that the Arab action had been foolish, but not that it had been immoral.

Toward the end of the first day of fighting, a second WSAG meeting was convened, this time under Kissinger's chairmanship. For all practical purposes, he, usually in consultation with Nixon directly or through Chief of Staff Alexander Haig, made policy during the next several weeks, with occasional inputs from Defense Secretary James Schlesinger. Kissinger's initial views are therefore of particular interest.

When Kissinger entered the situation room at 7:22 p.m., one cabinet member was calmly reading the comic strips in the local newspaper.

Other WSAG participants were bantering lightly about the crisis. With Kissinger's arrival the serious discussion began. He reported that he had just been on the telephone to Nixon, to the Soviet ambassador, Anatoly Dobrynin, and to the Israeli foreign minister, Abba Eban.[16] The president wanted the Sixth Fleet moved east and held near Crete as a visible sign of American power. One aircraft carrier was ordered to leave port in Athens; other moves would be considered later.

Kissinger was concerned about the Soviet Union. If the Arabs suffered a real debacle, he thought, the Soviets would have a hard time staying out of the fighting. U.S. military moves should be restrained so as not to give the wrong impressions to the Soviet Union. Reminded that future American military steps might require the use of the Azores base, Kissinger quipped that the Portuguese would be happy to grant permission, because he had just refused to see their foreign minister in New York!

Discussion ensued on the diplomatic contacts taken to date. In the UN the United States would try to work with the Soviet Union to reestablish the cease-fire on the basis of the status quo ante. Kissinger, expecting a reprise of June 1967, said the Arabs, in their "demented state," currently opposed that position, but they would beg for it once the Israeli counteroffensive got under way. The U.S. strategy would be to prevent the diplomatic debate from going to the UN General Assembly, where an automatic pro-Arab majority would be available. The Soviets, it was acknowledged, would have a problem accepting a cease-fire based on the status quo ante, for it would mean Arab forces would have to withdraw from Arab territory. A Soviet response would nonetheless be forthcoming the next day.

Israel would undoubtedly reject any cease-fire not based on a return to the status quo ante. Nixon did not want a situation in which Israel, the victim of the attack, would be condemned for rejecting a cease-fire appeal. The U.S. goal was to adopt a position that would remain consistent throughout the crisis. The war would quickly shift in Israel's favor, and what appeared to be a pro-Israel position of a cease-fire on the post-1967 lines would soon look pro-Arab. If Israel went beyond the previous lines, the United States would oppose that, thereby regaining some credit with the Arabs. Consequently the United States would propose a cease-fire status quo ante but would not push hard for it until the military realities made both parties want to accept it.

Everyone felt the crisis would be crucial for U.S.-Soviet relations. If collaboration worked, détente would take on real meaning; if it failed,

the Soviets could "kiss MFN [most favored nation] goodbye."[17] Although
the Soviets might have been duplicitous in helping the Arabs plan the
war, some still held the hope of working with Moscow to end it. U.S.-
Israeli relations were also on many minds. By sticking close to the Israelis
during the war, the United States should be able to enhance the credibility
of a future guarantee as part of a peace settlement. Eventually American
and Israeli positions on a settlement would diverge, and the only way to
get the Israelis to withdraw from Arab territory would be to offer some
kind of formal U.S. guarantee. The president felt strongly about this
issue. The Israelis must see the United States as a reliable partner during
the crisis for the sake of postwar diplomacy. Arms and oil were briefly
mentioned. Kissinger concluded with the thought that the worst outcome
for the United States would be to appear crippled by the domestic
crisis over Watergate. Kissinger then left for an evening meeting with
Ambassador Dobrynin.

A basic strategy was already set. The United States, expecting a short
war in which Israel would quickly prevail, hoped to be in a strong
position vis-à-vis Israel and the Soviets for postwar diplomatic moves. In
addition, Kissinger wanted to avoid a confrontation with the Arabs. For
the moment, the United States would adopt a low profile, developing a
position on a cease-fire that would soon be seen as balanced. The viability
of this policy depended on a quick Israeli reversal of the military situation
and Soviet restraint. For the next two days these conditions seemed to
hold.

On Sunday, October 7, Kissinger kept in close touch with the Soviets,
Egyptians, and Israelis. Nixon sent Brezhnev a letter urging mutual
restraint and calling for a meeting of the Security Council. Brezhnev's
reply was conciliatory and encouraging.[18] Together with the movement
of Soviet ships away from the zone of combat, this was a promising sign.

Supplementing Kissinger's talks with Foreign Minister Zayyat, the
Egyptians began to send messages through the back channel that had
been established in 1972. Although rejecting the idea of a cease-fire that
was not linked to Israeli withdrawal to the pre-1967 lines, Sadat,
communicating through his adviser, Hafiz Ismail, made it clear he did
not want a confrontation with the United States.[19]

The Israelis were in a grim mood, but in communications with the
United States they still appeared confident of success. Anticipating Israeli
requests for arms, Kissinger made arrangements for El Al aircraft to pick

up some items—ammunition, high technology products, and Sidewinder missiles—at a naval base in Virginia. Ambassador Simcha Dinitz, just arrived from Israel, met with Kissinger in the evening and, as expected, presented a list of arms that Israel needed, but the sense of urgency was not particularly great, or at least so it seemed to Kissinger and Schlesinger.[20] A modest resupply effort soon began, but Kissinger was still hoping to keep any visible involvement with Israel's war effort at a minimum.

By the time the WSAG met shortly after 6:00 p.m. on October 7,[21] the best estimate of the CIA was that Israel would regain the initiative the following day and would go on to win the war by the end of the week. Initial concentration would be on the Syrian front, then on the Egyptian front. Kissinger voiced his perplexity about why the Arabs, if their situation was really so precarious, were refusing a cease-fire that would protect their initial gains.[22] Schlesinger felt they were being illogical; Kissinger replied that the Egyptian strategy would be to cross the canal and then sit tight. The Arabs, he thought, had attacked to upset the status quo, because they feared there would be no diplomatic movement unless there was a crisis.

After a brief discussion of oil, the possible evacuation of American citizens from Libya[23] and other Arab countries, and the Israeli request for arms, the meeting ended. Kissinger said he would ask the president, who was arriving at 10:00 p.m. from Florida, about further American military moves and Israeli requests for arms. For the moment, he felt, the United States was in a good position to come out of the crisis with its essential interests intact.

The following day, October 8, the UN Security Council was convened. John Scali, the American representative, mentioned in his speech that a cease-fire based on the status quo ante would be the "least damaging" solution to the crisis, but he did not formally propose a resolution for a vote.[24]

Israel was now beginning to encounter military difficulties on both fronts. In Golan the Syrian air-defense system was taking a high toll of Israeli Skyhawks and Phantoms. In Sinai an Israeli effort to break through Egyptian lines with armor had been thwarted. Demands for resupply of equipment from the United States mounted. Dinitz spoke to Kissinger several times and was told that Israeli losses would be replaced. When Dinitz complained about the slow American response, Kissinger blamed it on the Defense Department, a ploy he used repeatedly with the Israeli ambassador over the next several days.[25] In fact, the U.S. position was still based on the expectation of an early end to the fighting and a desire to maintain a low profile. The arms issue was therefore handled discreetly.

The WSAG met again at 5:30 p.m. on Monday, October 8, to review the day's events.[26] The CIA reported that Israel was making rapid progress and had virtually retaken the Golan Heights. One member offered the opinion that if the Soviets did not resupply the Arabs, perhaps the Americans should not resupply Israel. Kissinger again expressed puzzlement over why the Arabs were refusing a cease-fire. The Soviets, by contrast, were being very conciliatory. With their help, it was felt, a cease-fire could be achieved by Wednesday night. The Soviets would respond on Tuesday. Even if Israel crossed the canal, the United States would be in a good position by sticking to a call for a cease-fire based on the status quo ante. Military realities would shortly make the American proposal acceptable to Egypt, Syria, and the Soviet Union. When the meeting ended at 6:30 p.m., Kissinger immediately went to his White House office to confer with Dinitz. He then delivered a previously scheduled speech to the Pacem in Terris conference in Washington in which he alluded to the Middle East and the need for Soviet restraint there if détente was to survive.[27]

The basic U.S. policy, rooted in the initial assumptions of a short war with an Israeli victory, was still on the tracks, but it would not be for much longer. In the jargon of Washington it was about to be "overtaken by events."

THE CRISIS DEEPENS

From the perspective of Washington the war entered a new and acute phase on October 9. Reality was refusing to conform to the comparatively optimistic forecast upon which initial U.S. policy had been based. Between October 9 and October 12 the possibility of a swift and conclusive Israeli military victory on both fronts faded; Soviet restraint began to erode; and pressure began to build for an urgent military resupply of Israeli forces. The American response was to modify gradually two aspects of policy: the call for a cease-fire based on the status quo ante was replaced by an exploration of the idea of a cease-fire in place; and arms for Israel began to flow in modest quantities, not only aboard El Al aircraft, but increasingly with direct American involvement.

In one of the most controversial decisions of the war, Nixon and

Kissinger held back on a full-scale commitment of American resources to the resupply effort until the fate of the cease-fire-in-place initiative was clear and the scope of the Soviet resupply effort made further delay politically difficult. Under pressure on the ground, short of supplies, and without a guarantee of a full-scale American airlift of arms, the Israeli government reluctantly accepted a cease-fire in place on October 12. But early on October 13 President Sadat refused the cease-fire proposal, which led to a dramatic change in American policy.

This second stage of the crisis opened on Tuesday morning, October 9, with an urgent Israeli appeal for arms.[28] Dinitz informed Kissinger of heavy Israeli losses, especially of aircraft on the Syrian front, as well as some 500 tanks, mostly on the Egyptian front. At the end of the meeting Dinitz asked to talk with Kissinger alone to convey a request from Meir for a secret visit to Washington to plead the case for arms with Nixon. Kissinger refused to consider the proposal, later claiming that it reflected "hysteria or blackmail."[29]

Shortly thereafter Kissinger convened the WSAG principals for two emergency sessions before noon. Only Schlesinger, Thomas Moorer (chairman of the Joint Chiefs), Kenneth Rush (deputy secretary of state), William Colby (CIA director), and Brent Scowcroft (deputy national security adviser) met with Kissinger to consider the new Israeli request. To date, this was the most difficult moment of the war. The two recommendations that emerged from these sessions were presented to Nixon by Kissinger at 4:45 p.m. First, some arms must begin to reach Israel quickly, without violating the principle of maintaining a low American profile in the conflict. Second, over the next several days a new formula for a cease-fire would be explored. Nixon, deeply distracted by the impending resignation of his vice-president, agreed to meet most of Israel's requests.[30]

While these deliberations were going on, word began to reach Washington that Israel had launched a major counteroffensive on the Syrian front. On the ground, Israeli troops had recovered virtually all the territory lost during the first three days of fighting and in some areas were pushing beyond the former cease-fire line. Nonetheless, the fighting was still difficult. The Syrians were not breaking, and Iraqi reinforcements were on their way. In the air, the Israelis, thwarted in their efforts to use the air force for close support of ground troops, initiated a campaign of strategic bombing deep within Syria. The oil refinery at Homs was attacked; the defense ministry and air-force staff headquarters in Damascus were bombed; and, by mistake, the Soviet cultural center in Damascus was hit, causing at least one Soviet fatality.

As the Syrian front began to weaken, King Hussein of Jordan came under great pressure to enter the war, if not by opening a new front, then at least by sending some of his troops to Syria. Israel conveyed an extremely harsh message to Hussein on October 9, warning of the consequences of opening a front along the Jordan River. Kissinger also urged Hussein to stay out of the fighting, stressing that a diplomatic effort was under way that, it was hoped, would succeed in ending the war within a few days.

This diplomatic effort consisted of sounding out the Egyptians, Soviets, and Israelis on the possibility of a cease-fire in place. Dinitz was the first to convey his government's refusal, emphasizing the need for any cease-fire to be tied to the restoration of the status quo ante.[31] Egypt's position was equally negative. Any cease-fire must be directly linked to a concrete plan calling for full Israeli withdrawal from all territories captured in 1967. Kissinger had raised the issue of a cease-fire in place through his back channel to Hafiz Ismail on October 9, stressing that Egypt had "made its point." Ismail's reply, reportedly drafted by Sadat, reached him the following day:[32]

—There should be a cease-fire followed by a withdrawal within a specified period, under UN supervision, of all Israeli forces to the pre–June 5, 1967, lines.

—Freedom of navigation in the Strait of Tiran should be guaranteed by a UN presence at Sharm al-Shaykh for a specified period.

—Following the complete withdrawal of Israeli forces, the state of belligerency with Israel would be ended.

—Following the withdrawal of Israeli troops from Gaza, the area would be placed under UN supervision pending its self-determination.

—Within a specified period after the ending of the state of belligerency, a peace conference would be convened under UN auspices, to be attended by all interested parties, including the Palestinians, and all members of the Security Council. The conference would deal with all questions of sovereignty, security, and freedom of navigation.

Egypt also promised that once Israeli evacuation began, diplomatic relations with the United States would be resumed, and work on clearing the Suez Canal would start.

This proposal was hardly the simple cease-fire in place that Nixon and

Kissinger now envisaged. Under no circumstances were they prepared to link a cease-fire to the terms of a final settlement. Not only would the Israelis adamantly refuse such a linkage, but it also was entirely contrary to Nixon's and Kissinger's negotiating strategy. Sadat was aiming far too high. Either the Soviets or Israeli military successes would have to bring him to a more realistic sense of what was possible.

Fortunately for Kissinger's strategy, the Soviets now seemed to be supporting the idea of a cease-fire in place, and indicated in a message on October 10 that Egypt would most likely go along. The Soviets thought that both great powers should abstain on any Security Council Resolution calling for a cease-fire. Kissinger claims that his initial reaction was negative because he felt Israel needed more time to change things on the battlefield. In an effort to stall, he accepted the Soviet proposal "in principle" but urged the Soviets not to take any immediate action at the United Nations.[33]

THE CEASE-FIRE INITIATIVE

Offsetting this conciliatory gesture, however, was the first evidence that the Soviets were beginning an airlift of arms to the Middle East. On October 10 twenty-one AN-12s flew to Damascus with more than 200 tons of military equipment.[34] Late that day Washington learned that seven Soviet airborne divisions had been placed on a high state of alert. Obviously the Soviets were worried about the deteriorating situation on the Syrian front. Whether their solution to the danger posed to their interests would emphasize diplomacy or force was at the moment an unanswered question. Elements of both courses of action were visible.

Meanwhile the U.S. resupply of Israel was beginning on a modest scale. On October 9 Dinitz had been informed that a number of F-4 Phantoms would soon be on their way. In addition, El Al planes were being allowed to pick up preassembled cargoes at Oceana Naval Station near Norfolk, Virginia. The first of these resupplies had reached Israel by October 10, the same day on which the first Soviet resupplies by air reached Damascus.

The intensity of the fighting was such, however, that Israeli requests for arms could not be met simply by El Al flights. Consistent with the principle of avoiding direct official American involvement in the transport of arms to Israel, Kissinger and Schlesinger began on October 10 to explore the possibility of chartering civilian transports for that purpose. Ten to twenty flights a day were envisaged. That same day Kissinger spoke with Dinitz several times about arms, a possible Jordanian movement of troops to Syria, and Moscow's renewed interest in a cease-fire in place. Dinitz relayed the Soviet position to the prime minister, who still refused to consider it.[35]

At this point the American and Israeli positions began to diverge. The United States wanted an early cease-fire, at least within the next two days. Israel wanted arms in sufficient quantity to ensure a military victory. Over the next forty-eight hours the United States seemed to move slowly on sending arms to Israel, either, as Kissinger maintains, because of bureaucratic confusion, or, as others believe, as a form of pressure to induce the Israelis to accept a cease-fire in place and in the conviction that the fighting was nearly over in any case.

President Nixon, in one of his rare public remarks about the crisis while it was under way, summed up the American position on October 10 as follows: "The United States is trying its best to play a mediating role and bring the fighting to an end and then, beyond that, to help to build not just a temporary, but a lasting peace for the people in that very troubled section of the world."[36]

October 11 was a day of regrouping and consolidation. Nothing extraordinary happened on the battlefield or in Washington. Israel began to transfer troops from the Syrian to the Egyptian front in order to push Egyptian forces back to the canal. U.S. diplomacy aimed at restraining King Hussein, now under pressure from Asad, Sadat, and Faisal, from joining the war, and at reassuring the Israelis that the charter flights and F-4s would soon be on their way. Israel's refusal to consider a cease-fire in place was now beginning to weaken somewhat. Having made new gains on the Syrian front, Israel was prepared to consider a cease-fire coupled with a subsequent exchange of Israeli control over captured Syrian territory for a restoration of Israeli positions in Sinai.[37] Syria might see some merit in this plan, but Sadat would not; hence the United States continued to press for a simple cease-fire in place. On October 12 it seemed within grasp.

The day began with Israeli queries about the charter flights that had been promised but that had not yet begun. In an effort to retain credibility with the Israelis, Kissinger tried to accelerate the process. A message was sent at 11:09 a.m. to the Portuguese requesting the use of Lajes airbase in the Azores for chartered civilian aircraft flying military consumables to Israel. Ten to twenty flights, chartered by the Defense Department, would pass through Lajes each day. The flights were to begin that same evening. The Portuguese, no doubt resenting the fact that the United States seemed to take their acceptance for granted, delayed their response.

Meanwhile the Defense Department, having failed to arrange the charter of civilian transport, was exploring the possibility of using American military transports to carry equipment to Lajes, where it would then be transferred to Israeli transports. The United States was still reluctant to have its own military aircraft fly into Tel Aviv. Nixon, concerned with delays on resupplying the Israeli military, called Schlesinger in the afternoon to urge him to accelerate the effort, including the use of American military aircraft if necessary.[38]

According to Kissinger, during the morning he was informed that Israel was prepared to accept a cease-fire in place.[39] Apparently Golda Meir, in consultation with her top military leaders, but without a formal cabinet vote, had made the decision out of concern about both the costs of continued fighting and the pressure generated by the delay in the resupply effort.[40]

At a press conference called at 11:00 a.m., Kissinger tried to clarify the various, sometimes conflicting, strands of American policy as of October 12:

After hostilities broke out, the United States set itself two principal objectives. One, to end the hostilities as quickly as possible. Secondly, to end the hostilities in such a manner that they [sic] would contribute to the maximum extent possible to the promotion of a more permanent, more lasting solution in the Middle East. . . . We have not gratuitously sought opportunities for confrontations in public forums which might harden dividing lines. . . . [T]he Middle East may become in time what the Balkans were in Europe before 1914, that is to say, an area where local rivalries . . . have their own momentum that will draw in the great nuclear powers into a confrontation.

Kissinger went on to "urge, all the parties in the conduct of their diplomacy now to keep in mind that whatever momentary advantages might be achieved in this or that forum, our principal objective should be to maintain relationships that can move both the area and the world towards a more lasting peace."

Kissinger then referred to the "traditional friendship" of the United States for Israel and to the continuing military relationship with that country. He termed the Soviet airlift "moderate," "more than light. It's a fairly substantial airlift." Then, in something of a forewarning to the Arabs of the impending United States role in aiding Israel militarily, Kissinger stated: "We have made a very serious effort, in this crisis, to take seriously into account Arab concerns and Arab views. On the other hand, we have to pursue what we consider to be the right course; we will take the consequences in pursuing what we consider to be the right course."[41]

Kissinger was apprehensive that, in the absence of a rapid end to the war, the United States would have to increase the visibility of its role in rearming Israel; then the Arabs might react by embargoing oil and attacking American interests throughout the region. There was all the more reason, therefore, for one additional try at a cease-fire.

Prime Minister Meir's acceptance of the idea of a cease-fire in place was followed by a message from Dinitz that Israel would not object if the cease-fire idea was put to the UN immediately. Later in the evening of October 12 Dinitz came to the White House with an urgent personal appeal from Meir to President Nixon to order an immediate resupply of arms to Israel. She went so far as to raise the specter of an Israeli military defeat.[42]

Meanwhile the cease-fire initiative was running into trouble. Kissinger had urged the British to introduce the idea in the UN on October 13. During the evening of October 12 the British told Kissinger they would only introduce a resolution the following day if they were sure it would be accepted by the parties. From their information, they doubted that this would be the case. Kissinger assured them that they should proceed. But late in the morning of October 13 the British informed Kissinger that they had concluded that a cease-fire in place was a mirage. Britain insisted on getting Sadat's prior acquiescence. Meanwhile Kissinger began to explore the possibility that Australia might introduce a cease-fire resolution. But, inexplicably, the Soviets were cool to the idea. Finally, at 3:35 p.m. the British told Kissinger that Sadat rejected any variation of a cease-fire. The initiative had reached a dead end.[43]

THE AIRLIFT

President Nixon's role in shaping American policy during the October war is difficult to assess accurately. He was obviously preoccupied by his own domestic political difficulties and with the resignation in disgrace of his hand-picked vice-president, Spiro Agnew, on October 10. The president showed little interest in the details of policy, leaving the task of day-to-day diplomacy to Kissinger. Nixon did make key decisions, however, and it was his authority that could be invoked to influence other governments.

Early in the morning of October 13 Schlesinger became convinced that the only effective way to get arms to Israel would be in American military planes. Kissinger and Haig were opposed, still preferring to keep a low profile.[44] On the morning of October 13, having been briefed on Meir's urgent appeal for help and Schlesinger's recommendation, and without any positive indication that a cease-fire agreement was in sight, President Nixon took the responsibility of ordering a full-scale airlift of military equipment to Israel.[45]

The Portuguese, who had still not granted the United States permission to use Lajes, received a harsh note from Nixon, dispatched from Washington at 8:00 a.m. At this point, consideration was still being given to the plan to fly equipment to the Azores, where it would be picked up by the Israelis. Portuguese permission was finally received at 3:40 p.m.

Besides Nixon's decision to mount an American airlift, an SR-71 reconnaissance plane was ordered to photograph the battle area to provide an independent basis for judging losses on both sides. The continuation of the Soviet airlift, Israel's apparent trouble on the battlefield, and the collapse of the cease-fire effort were creating a concern in Washington that the war might now drag on. Good battlefield intelligence was needed. This was the first such flight during the hostilities.[46]

The main considerations underlying this stage of the Nixon-Kissinger strategy were to convince Sadat that a prolonged war of attrition, fueled by Soviet arms, would not succeed and to demonstrate to the Kremlin that the United States was capable of matching Soviet military deliveries to the Middle East. Above all, for the sake of the future American position globally and in the region, Soviet arms must not be allowed to dictate the outcome of the fighting. This did not mean that the United States now favored a total Israeli military victory, but it did mean that Israeli success on the battlefield had become an important factor in persuading the Arabs and the Soviets to bring the fighting to an end.[47]

Nixon and Kissinger were aware of the likelihood of adverse Arab reaction to the airlift of arms to Israel. Up to this point in the crisis there had been no confrontation between the United States and the Arab world. The "oil weapon" had not yet been brandished, as many had feared; American lives were not endangered in any Arab country, including Libya, which had been a source of early concern; no Arab country had broken diplomatic relations; and Sadat was in continuing contact with Nixon through the back channel. U.S. influence with King Hussein had helped keep Jordan out of the war, although a token Jordanian force was now being sent to Syria. All this might change as a result of the airlift, but Nixon and Kissinger were prepared to take the risk. The airlift, they would argue, was a response to prior Soviet intervention on the Arab side. Global political realities dictated that the United States respond. This was not an anti-Arab move, for it was not designed to ensure Israeli supremacy over the Arabs or to rob the Arabs of their recaptured dignity. Rather, it was a simple fact of international political life. In any event, the United States would use its influence with Israel, gained through the provision of arms, on behalf of an equitable peace settlement. This, at least, was how Nixon and Kissinger would explain the policy to the Arabs[48] and to the U.S. bureaucracy. In Washington there was little dissent, even from allegedly pro-Arab elements.

By 12:30 p.m. Washington time, on October 14 (6:30 p.m. in Israel), the first giant C-5 transport plane arrived at Lod airport. An air bridge capable of delivering nearly 1,000 tons a day was now in operation, consisting of four to five flights of C-5s and twelve to fifteen flights of C-141s. El Al planes also continued to carry military supplies to Israel. In addition, twelve C-130 transports were flown to Israel and were turned over to the Israeli air force.[49]

When it became clear that Sadat would reject a cease-fire, Kissinger had proposed going all-out with the American airlift of arms to Israel. No longer would the United States try to minimize its visibility by seeking charters. With the airlift in full swing, Washington was prepared to wait until the new realities on the battlefield led to a change of Egyptian and Soviet calculations.

In the meantime the United States began to plan for an anticipated Arab oil embargo. Only 12 percent of U.S. oil consumption, or 5 percent of total energy, consisted of crude oil and refined products received directly or indirectly from the Arab world. Through reduction of demand for oil and some redirection of imports, the overall impact of a selective Arab oil embargo against the United States would hardly be felt. If, however, an embargo was combined with severe cutbacks in production, then not only the United States but also Europe and Japan would feel the pinch. Consequently plans for the sharing of oil among allies, as well as a domestic energy plan, were required. At a minimum, the Middle East crisis might provide an incentive for Congress and public opinion to support a major energy project. Former governor John Love, energy coordinator for Nixon, his aide Charles Di Bona, and Deputy Secretary of the Treasury William Simon were given primary responsibility for working out a plan in the event of an embargo.

By the time the first C-5 had set down in Israel on the afternoon of October 14, the decisive battle of the war on the Egyptian front had been fought and won by Israel. An Egyptian offensive toward the Mitla and Giddi passes had failed, at a cost to Egypt of more than 200 tanks. It had been for the sake of this battle that Sadat had rejected the cease-fire in place offered by the British ambassador the previous day.[50] Now, with this victory behind them, the Israelis showed little interest in the cease-fire they had been prepared to accept two days earlier.[51] Instead, Israel, assured of continuing American supplies, decided to undertake a risky military operation to cross the Suez Canal. If successful, this action might result in the destruction of Egyptian missile fields, thereby exposing Egyptian ground troops to bombing by the Israeli air force. Also, Egyptian forces in Sinai ran the risk of being cut off from their lines of communication and surrounded by the Israelis. A critical moment was approaching. The Israeli operation was scheduled for the night of October 15–16.

Kissinger convened morning sessions of the WSAG on both October 14 and October 15. Besides discussing oil, the group assessed the evolving military and diplomatic situation. By October 15 the American airlift to Israel had been publicly acknowledged and widely reported. Kissinger was surprised at the moderation of the Arab response. Although he did not expect the Arab oil ministers' meeting in Kuwait the following day to cut off oil to the United States, he did feel that a plan for counterpressure on the Arabs was necessary if they did. An administration already weakened by its domestic political problems could not afford to appear susceptible to "blackmail" by Arab oil producers.

On the Soviet role in the conflict, Kissinger still reflected a certain ambivalence. The noted Washington columnist Joseph Alsop had published an article on the morning of October 15 accusing the Soviets of collusion in and extensive foreknowledge of the Arab war effort. Kissinger was suspicious, but at the same time he felt the Soviets were still interested in a diplomatic settlement. Perhaps because of the American airlift, or perhaps because of the outcome of the October 14 battle in Sinai, the Soviets early on October 15 had indicated that they were again actively trying to persuade the Arabs to accept a cease-fire. Premier Kosygin, the secretary was told, would go to Cairo the next day.

Kissinger planned to see Egyptian Foreign Minister Zayyat on October

16, and President Nixon would meet with four Arab foreign ministers on October 17. Diplomatic channels would thus remain open with both the Arabs and the Soviets despite the growing superpower involvement in the conflict.[52]

THE TIDE BEGINS TO TURN

October 16 was a crucial day for the war and the diplomacy. Both President Sadat and Prime Minister Meir gave important public speeches outlining their policies. Israeli forces had managed to cross the Suez Canal in small numbers and were moving into the missile fields, causing havoc among the Egyptian forces. Kosygin was en route to Cairo to try to persuade Sadat to stop fighting, and Kissinger had reason to feel that the U.S. strategy was working well. Sadat's speech was fairly moderate in tone and contained an "open message" to Nixon on Egypt's peace terms. Kosygin's mission had been foreshadowed in Soviet communications during the previous day. As yet, no Arab embargo of oil had been announced. And the Israeli military successes, although not specifically designed or intended by Washington, were consistent with Kissinger's view that Sadat had to be persuaded by battlefield developments to accept a cease-fire. It was of prime importance that the fighting should be ended at the moment when all parties could still emerge from the conflict with their vital interests and self-esteem intact.

At the WSAG meeting on Tuesday morning, October 16, Kissinger further elaborated on the objectives of the airlift. He minimized its importance in the context of the Arab-Israeli conflict. Rather, he stressed, the Soviets must see that the United States could deliver more than they could. Each day until a cease-fire the United States should send by air 25 percent more equipment than the Soviets did. The Soviets should be "run into the ground," "forced down." American arms in Israeli hands would outmatch Soviet arms in Arab hands.

As Kissinger was expounding on the U.S.-Soviet aspects of the crisis, the door to the situation room opened and a message was passed in. The time was 10:55 a.m. General Scowcroft read the message and passed it to Kissinger, who broke into an embarrassed laugh and then a proud grin. He had just received word that he would share the Nobel peace prize with North Vietnam's Le Duc Tho, his negotiating partner during the Paris talks.

Turning its attention again to the Middle East, the WSAG addressed the question of aid to Israel to finance the arms being sent. To some, it was time to get maximum credit with Israel, because during the subsequent diplomatic effort the U.S. and Israeli positions were bound to diverge. Kissinger therefore argued for a very large aid bill for Israel—as much as $3 billion—as well as another $500 million for Cambodia and other countries, thrown in for good measure. In his view the United States had already paid its price with the Arabs, and a massive aid bill for Israel would do little further damage.

By noon he may have had some second thoughts upon receiving a letter from King Faisal in response to his message on the airlift to Israel. The king was "pained" by the American action. The United States should stop sending arms and should call on Israel to withdraw. Otherwise U.S.-Saudi relations could become "lukewarm." (Nonetheless, the aid bill went forward, and on October 19 President Nixon formally requested $2.2 billion in aid for Israel. The following day King Faisal announced an embargo of oil to the United States as well as substantial production cuts. In retrospect Kissinger wondered whether he had pushed too hard on the Arabs with the $2.2 billion aid request just as the military situation was turning to Israel's advantage.)

The following day, October 17, was largely devoted to talks with the foreign ministers of Morocco, Algeria, Saudi Arabia, and Kuwait. Shortly after 10:00 a.m. Kissinger met with the four ministers in his White House office.[53] He listened while the Saudi foreign minister spelled out the Arabs' concerns: an immediate settlement of the conflict based on complete Israeli withdrawal from Arab territory seized in 1967 and restoration of Palestinian rights in accordance with UN Resolution 242. Kissinger then explained that the basic American policy was now to end the current fighting and to prevent its spread. After the war the United States would engage in a diplomatic effort for a just and lasting peace. U.S.-Arab relations should therefore remain as strong as possible. The Arabs had created a new reality in the Middle East, and the time had come for a diplomatic effort. The United States had initially expected the Arabs to be defeated, which was why the October 6 lines had been proposed for a cease-fire. Now a cease-fire would have to take into account new realities, but it would be a mistake to try to link a cease-fire to a total settlement. A better strategy would be to get a cease-fire quickly and then to launch a diplomatic effort. The guarantee that such an effort would be made resided in Arab strength. The United States had more influence with Israel, the Arab military and diplomatic positions had improved, and the time was therefore ripe for diplomacy. The United

States would not promise to do what it could not accomplish, but it would do everything it promised.

Kissinger concluded by remarking that he did not like big plans, but preferred quiet diplomacy. He recounted how his talks with the Chinese had progressed and urged the same step-by-step procedure on the Arabs. He warned that the Middle East should not become involved in the U.S.-Soviet global rivalry. Then he excused himself, remarking lightly that he was not used to dealing with "moderate Arabs" and that he needed to talk to the president for a few minutes before their appointment in the Oval Office.

At 11:10 a.m. President Nixon began his talks with the four Arab foreign ministers. Omar Saqqaf, the Saudi representative, again presented their collective position, emphasizing the American responsibility to force Israel to withdraw to the 1967 lines. He evoked the long history of Arab friendship for the United States and appealed to it to uphold the principle of the territorial integrity of all states in the area. Nixon replied by referring to his visits to the Middle East, his meetings with various Arab leaders, and his desire to travel again to the area once a peace settlement had been achieved. Echoing Kissinger's themes, he said the United States was now working for a cease-fire, after which it would engage in active diplomacy. He denied that domestic politics would influence U.S. Middle East policy and urged the Arabs to trust Kissinger despite his Jewish background. He concluded by promising to work for the "implementation of Resolution 242" after a cease-fire, but emphasized that he could not promise that Israel would withdraw to the 1967 lines.

After the talks Saqqaf spoke briefly with the president alone, and then proceeded to the Rose Garden to tell the press that the talks had been constructive and friendly. Kissinger then returned to the State Department with the ministers for further talks in the early afternoon.

On the whole Kissinger felt the meetings had gone well. At the afternoon WSAG meeting he stated that he no longer expected the Arabs to cut off oil to the United States. Ironically, just as he was drawing this optimistic conclusion, the Arab oil ministers meeting in Kuwait were announcing that oil production would be cut by 5 percent each month until Israel had withdrawn from all Arab territories. Three days later King Faisal pushed even further, calling for a 10 percent cut immediately and an embargo of shipments of oil to the United States and the Netherlands.

On the diplomatic front the only sign of progress from the Kosygin visit to Cairo was a Soviet request for the U.S. view of a cease-fire in place linked to Resolution 242.[54] The American response was positive, but asked for a concrete proposal. The Soviet position was conveyed to Ambassador Dinitz, who passed it to Israel, where Golda Meir found it unacceptable. Rather than link a cease-fire in place to Resolution 242, the Israelis favored a link to direct negotiations between the parties.[55] The next day brought little change. Sadat was still not ready to stop.

As Kissinger had expected, the diplomacy opened up on October 19, shortly after Kosygin's return to Moscow from Cairo.[56] During the morning a message from Brezhnev reached the White House requesting urgent consultations on the Middle East crisis. Kissinger should come to Moscow "in an urgent manner." Time was of the essence.[57] Kissinger now felt that a cease-fire could be achieved quickly. In talks with Dinitz he implied that by agreeing to go to Moscow, he would be able to gain Israel a few more days to complete its military operations.[58] Dinitz emphasized the need for a link between a cease-fire and negotiations.[59]

Later that afternoon the administration sent Congress its $2.2 billion aid request, which stated that the United States was trying to reach "a very swift and honorable conclusion, measured in days, not weeks." Then, shortly after midnight, having dined with the Chinese representative in Washington, Kissinger left for Moscow.[60] Before his departure he congratulated the WSAG members on "the best-run crisis ever."

THE MOSCOW TALKS

Whatever he had told Dinitz, Kissinger primarily went to Moscow not to gain time for Israel's battlefield success but to obtain Soviet and Arab agreement to a cease-fire resolution that could serve as the basis for a subsequent diplomatic effort. If the Soviet and Arab position remained locked into an unacceptable formulation, then Kissinger was prepared to wait, assuming that Israeli advances on the west bank of the canal would eventually bring about a change. On the other hand, if Brezhnev and Sadat were prepared for a simple cease-fire, then Kissinger would press for a quick end to hostilities. He had no interest in seeing Sadat humiliated, especially in view of the encouraging tone of U.S.-Egyptian exchanges over the past two weeks. Nor did he want to force the Soviets to choose between standing aside to watch their clients be defeated by Israel with American arms and intervening militarily on the Arab side, with the attendant risks of nuclear confrontation.

The trick would be to get a cease-fire at just the right moment. Until then, Israel should continue to advance on the ground, but, Kissinger felt, Israel must be prepared to stop once the superpowers reached agreement on a cease-fire. After all, the stakes were no longer confined to the Middle East; they were also global. If necessary, Kissinger was prepared to lean hard on the Israelis.

During his flight to Moscow Kissinger received two important messages. One informed him of the Saudi decision to embargo oil shipments to the United States. Another, from Nixon, was a message for Brezhnev in which Nixon made it clear that Kissinger had full authority to negotiate. Kissinger claims that he resented this unusual procedure, since it deprived him of the tactic of saying that he would have to refer to Washington for final decisions.[61] At the time Kissinger was unaware of the depth of the domestic crisis surrounding Nixon. The appeals court had ruled against Nixon on his bid to withhold nine Watergate tapes. The special prosecutor, Archibald Cox, was requesting tapes that Nixon did not want released, so he decided to fire Cox. However, Attorney General Elliot Richardson and his deputy, William Ruckelshaus, refused to carry out Nixon's orders to dismiss Cox, preferring instead to resign. All these events culminated in the "Saturday night massacre," just as Kissinger's first talks with Brezhnev were getting under way in the Kremlin.[62] Little wonder that Nixon had decided to leave the cease-fire negotiations to Kissinger.[63]

The crucial U.S.-Soviet talks began in Moscow on October 21 at about 11:00 a.m. and lasted only four hours. The Soviets, who had initially tried to link a cease-fire to some type of call for Israeli withdrawal from all Arab territory and to guarantees by the superpowers, were swift to change their negotiating position. Time was at a premium, and their client's position was in jeopardy. Ultimately Brezhnev agreed to a simple cease-fire in place, together with a call for the implementation of Security Council Resolution 242, and, at American insistence, also agreed to negotiations between the parties under appropriate auspices.[64] In addition, both sides agreed that they would serve as cochairmen of an eventual peace conference and that prisoners should be immediately exchanged by the parties after the cease-fire.

By noon, Washington time, on October 21 the United States and the Soviet Union had agreed upon the text of a cease-fire resolution. It was now up to Kissinger to persuade Israel to accept it. In mid-afternoon Alexander Haig, now serving as Nixon's chief of staff, telephoned Ambassador Dinitz with the proposed text of the resolution. Dinitz was told that time was short and that no changes could be made. The Security

Council would meet that evening. Dinitz was given a message from President Nixon to Prime Minister Meir asking that she immediately agree to the resolution. Arms would continue to flow to Israel. Dinitz immediately called Meir with the text of the resolution and Nixon's message. She was irritated that she had not been consulted in advance and was now being confronted with a fait accompli. At about 8:00 p.m., Washington time, Meir reportedly tried calling Nixon direct to seek a delay in the cease-fire, but she did not get through to him.[65] At 9:00 p.m., shortly before the UN Security Council was to convene, the Israeli cabinet decided to accept the cease-fire resolution. In her message informing Nixon of Israel's decision, Meir requested that Kissinger stop in Tel Aviv on his return from Moscow for consultations.

At 10:00 p.m. the Security Council met. Two hours and fifty minutes later, at 12:50 a.m. October 22, it adopted Resolution 338 (see appendix A). Within twelve hours the fighting was to stop on all fronts.

Kissinger left Moscow on the morning of October 22 for Tel Aviv,[66] where he arrived at 12:45 p.m., Middle East time (6:45 a.m., Washington time). The cease-fire was still not in effect, but in his talks with Meir, Kissinger was insistent that Israel move into defensive positions and not violate the cease-fire. He later claimed that he was very tough with the Israelis on this point, and that Prime Minister Meir, Defense Minister Dayan, and Foreign Minister Eban, if not the Israeli military, agreed that Israel had nothing further to gain from fighting.[67] Kissinger emphasized that the resolution called for the first time for negotiations between Israel and the Arabs. He also assured Meir that there were no secret U.S.-Soviet understandings. Resolution 242 remained as ambiguous as ever as a guideline for the subsequent diplomacy. Israel's bargaining position was not being undercut in advance. Arms would continue to be sent. Kissinger left Israel five hours after his arrival with a feeling that Israel would abide by the cease-fire.[68] One hour after his departure, at 6:50 p.m., Middle East time, the guns fell silent, but not for long.

TOWARD CONFRONTATION

With the achievement of the cease-fire on October 22, Nixon and Kissinger had reason to feel satisfied. A long and dangerous crisis had been brought to an end without a U.S.-Soviet military confrontation. The parties to the conflict had each made some gains to offset their heavy losses, so perhaps the prospects for peace negotiations would be good. Even the oil embargo seemed manageable, if irritating.

Soon after he reached his office on Tuesday morning, October 23, Kissinger was contacted by the Soviets with charges that Israel was violating the cease-fire.[69] Kissinger was worried. He had sensed the bitterness among the Israeli military at being deprived of victory. He had assured the Soviets that Israel would respect the cease-fire; hence when he called Dinitz to report the Soviet charges, he made it clear that Israel should not try to destroy the nearly surrounded Egyptian Third Army Corps.

From the onset of the crisis Kissinger had realized that American credibility with the Arabs might ultimately be tested in circumstances like these. If the United States were now to stand idly by and watch the Third Army Corps be destroyed with newly delivered American weapons, Kissinger's future role as peacemaker would be gravely jeopardized. It did not now matter which side was technically responsible for firing the first shot after the cease-fire was to have gone into effect. What was clear was that Israeli forces were advancing beyond the October 22 cease-fire lines. Despite his concern, however, Kissinger was not yet unduly alarmed.

During the afternoon of October 23 the UN Security Council passed Resolution 339, calling for immediate cessation of hostilities, a return to positions occupied on October 22 when the cease-fire went into effect, and the dispatch of UN observers to supervise the cease-fire on the Egyptian-Israeli front. Syria had still not accepted the cease-fire but finally did so later that evening.

Wednesday, October 24, began for Kissinger with a series of exchanges with the Egyptians, Israelis, and Soviets. Sadat was now in frequent communication with Nixon, even on small matters.[70] He asked for the president's help in getting the Israelis to allow medical and food supplies through to the nearly entrapped Third Army Corps. He requested that a U.S. military attaché from Tel Aviv proceed to the front lines to verify Israel's observance of the cease-fire. Kissinger was prepared to cooperate. He called Dinitz and requested that Israel respect the cease-fire and allow supplies through to the Third Army Corps.[71]

At 10:20 a.m. Kissinger met with the WSAG. He expressed his feeling that the United States was now in the "catbird seat. Everyone is looking to us." But he would not act under the threat of the Arab oil embargo. Egypt, he thought, understood this point and would be helpful. The next phase would involve direct Arab-Israeli negotiations under U.S.-Soviet auspices.

In mid-afternoon word reached Washington that President Sadat had publicly appealed to the United States and the Soviet Union to send forces to the Middle East to oversee the cease-fire. The White House immediately issued a statement rejecting the idea of forces from the superpowers being sent to the area. Shortly thereafter Kissinger met with Dobrynin at the State Department to discuss the convening of a peace conference. They agreed on Geneva as the site and considered other procedural matters. Dobrynin denied that the Soviets were interested in sending a joint U.S.-Soviet force to the Middle East in response to Sadat's appeal. The meeting ended on a cordial note, and there was no hint of impending crisis.[72]

Three hours later, at 7:05 p.m., Dobrynin called Kissinger to tell him that the Soviets would support the idea of a joint U.S.-Soviet peacekeeping force if the nonaligned members of the UN were to call for one, and shortly thereafter called again to say the Soviets were considering introducing such a resolution. These messages caused deep concern in Washington. Then, at 9:35 p.m. Dobrynin called Kissinger with a "very urgent" message from Brezhnev to Nixon. He slowly read the text over the telephone. It began by noting that Israel was continuing to violate the cease-fire, thus posing a challenge to both the United States and the Soviet Union. Brezhnev stressed the need to "implement" the cease-fire resolution and "invited" the United States to join Moscow "to compel observance of the cease-fire without delay." Then came the threat: "I will say it straight that if you find it impossible to act jointly with us in this matter, we should be faced with the necessity urgently to consider the question of taking appropriate steps unilaterally. We cannot allow arbitrariness on the part of Israel."[73] Kissinger quickly relayed the message to Haig for Nixon. The president's records show that he spoke to Haig for about twenty minutes around 10:30 p.m. That was his only communication with his advisers until the next morning. Nixon reportedly empowered Kissinger to take any necessary action, including calling a military alert.[74] Kissinger then convened an ad hoc session of the National Security Council, which at that point consisted only of himself and the secretary of defense as ex-officio members. In addition, Colby, Moorer, Haig, Scowcroft, and Jonathan Howe, Kissinger's military assistant, participated in the deliberations.

Unquestionably the situation was dangerous. No one knew what the Soviet Union intended to do, but Brezhnev's note unmistakably conveyed his determination not to let Israel destroy the Egyptian Third Army

Corps. Kissinger understood the difficulty of the situation for the Soviets and the pressures they would be under to act. Their prestige as a superpower was on the line. This was something with which Kissinger could empathize. But did the Soviets have the capability to intervene, whatever their intentions? The answer seemed definitely to be yes. The transport aircraft that had been flying arms to the Middle East had all returned to the Soviet Union and could be used as troop carriers. At least seven airborne divisions were on a high state of alert.[75] Two amphibious landing craft were in the eastern Mediterranean with the Soviet squadron.

Even though a massive Soviet intervention was still hard to imagine, even with this combination of motives and capabilities, Moscow might yet resort to impressive displays of military power that could have explosive political, and perhaps even military, consequences. For example, a small "peacekeeping" contingent might be sent to deliver supplies to the entrapped Third Army Corps. Would the Israelis fire on Soviet forces in such circumstances? If so, the Soviets might feel compelled to react on a larger scale. If not, Soviet prestige would have gained a significant boost, precisely at a critical moment in U.S.-Arab relations.

Kissinger and the other participants in the NSC meeting reached two conclusions. The Soviets, who had seemingly not taken seriously U.S. warnings about the introduction of their forces into the area, must be under no illusion that the United States did not have the will and the ability to react to any move they might make. To underline this ability, U.S. military forces would be placed on a Def Con 3 alert, which meant that leaves would be canceled and an enhanced state of readiness would be observed. The Strategic Air Command would be on a higher state of alert than the normal Def Con 4. No change would be needed for the Sixth Fleet, which was already on a stage 3 alert. Although considerably short of a decision to go on a war footing, these visible moves should convey to the Soviets the American determination to act if necessary. If the crisis was quickly resolved, it would be easy to change the alert status.[76]

As had been true earlier in the crisis, Kissinger was concerned that the Watergate scandal not appear to impede the conduct of American foreign policy. Intentional overreaction would be better than underreaction. To underscore the meaning of the alert, Kissinger sent a message to Brezhnev in Nixon's name saying that the sending of Soviet troops to the Middle East would be considered a violation of article 2 of the agreement on the prevention of nuclear war of June 22, 1973.

Before the Soviet threat of intervention, Kissinger and his colleagues had felt that Israel must stop its advances on the Egyptian front. The Israelis had been told in no uncertain terms that the United States would not permit the destruction of the Third Army Corps.[77] But the Soviet threat introduced a new element, and apparently Kissinger signaled to the Israelis that they should be prepared to move against the Third Army if Soviet troops tried to intervene.[78]

Around midnight the first orders for the alert were issued, and at 1:30 a.m. on October 25 its scope was widened. Nixon had not participated in the deliberations of the NSC, but he had reportedly given his approval for the alert in advance.[79] Now the United States would await the Soviet reaction.

During the morning of October 25, while most Americans were first learning of the alert and wondering about its meaning, Kissinger met with Nixon for a long talk.[80] Several new bits of information were now available. Further messages had been received from Sadat, denying that Egypt was violating the cease-fire and emphasizing again that U.S. and Soviet forces were needed to enforce the cease-fire. Moreover, several ships from the Soviet squadron, including the amphibious landing craft, were steaming toward Egypt. A fragmentary piece of intelligence had been received referring to the imminent arrival of Soviet troops in Cairo. In fact, these proved to be the seventy observers and their interpreters that the Soviets did send to Cairo, but at the time the number was unknown. All in all, the Soviets seemed to be moving toward a confrontation, and the Egyptians seemed to be encouraging it. The president ordered Kissinger to develop a plan for sending U.S. troops to the Middle East in case the Soviets did intervene. Doing so would, at a minimum, provide some leverage to get the Soviet troops out of the region after the crisis subsided. Nixon also told Kissinger to hold a press conference explaining the U.S. moves.

At 10:15 a.m. Kissinger convened the WSAG once again and explained the steps leading to the crisis and the president's latest instructions. Kissinger was worried by the behavior of the Soviets, who did not seem interested in finding a solution and were instead exploiting the situation. Schlesinger suggested that they might be genuinely fearful of a collapse on the Egyptian front and might even suspect American duplicity in urging the Israelis on. The meeting ended at 10:50, with Kissinger requesting a contingency plan for sending U.S. forces to the Middle East, including Arab countries if possible.

Shortly after noon Kissinger appeared before the press in the State Department auditorium. In a somber but restrained tone he described the various stages of the crisis and the evolution of U.S. policy. It was a brilliant performance, one of his most impressive.

After reviewing the diplomatic efforts of the first two weeks of the crisis, he spoke of the cease-fire and the alert. In the president's name he reiterated U.S. opposition to the sending of U.S.-Soviet forces to the Middle East. He was even more strongly opposed to a unilateral Soviet move into the area. He then reviewed the prospects for a peace settlement, which he termed "quite promising," and had conciliatory words for Israel, the Arabs, and even the Soviets. Afterward he took questions.

In response to several questions about U.S.-Soviet détente, Kissinger emphasized the complex adversarial nature of the relationship, but he refused to condemn the Soviets for violating the spirit of détente. Asked whether the alert had been called because of the American domestic crisis, Kissinger, more in sorrow than in anger, dismissed the idea, although he went on to say that the Soviets might have acted as boldly as they did because of the weakened position of the American president. "One cannot have crises of authority in a society for a period of months without paying a price somewhere along the line."

In his concluding remarks Kissinger spelled out the principles of a new American policy toward the Arab-Israeli conflict:

Our position is that . . . the conditions that produced this war were clearly intolerable to the Arab nations and that in the process of negotiations it will be necessary to make substantial concessions.

The problem will be to relate the Arab concern for the sovereignty over the territories to the Israeli concern for secure boundaries.

We believe that the process of negotiations between the parties is an essential component of this. And as the President has stated to the four Arab Foreign Ministers, and as we have stated repeatedly, we will make a major effort to bring about a solution that is considered just by all parties. But I think no purpose would be served by my trying to delimit the exact nature of all of these provisions.[81]

One hour later the UN Security Council passed Resolution 340, calling for an immediate and complete cease-fire, return to the October 22 lines, dispatch of an augmented UN observer force, creation of a UN Emergency Force composed of nonpermanent members of the Security Council, and implementation of Resolution 338. This time the cease-fire did take hold, and the fourth Arab-Israeli war finally ended. A new chapter in American diplomacy was about to open, with Kissinger as the star performer.

CONCLUSIONS

American policy toward the Arab-Israeli conflict was fundamentally affected by the events of the October 1973 war. Before the outbreak of hostilities it was widely believed in Washington that stability in the Middle East was ensured by Israeli military predominance; that Arab oil could not be effectively used to pressure the West; that Sadat was not seriously interested in a peace settlement with Israel; and that Soviet influence in the region had reached its limit. The situation in the area caused concern, but not anxiety. Diplomatic initiatives were contemplated, but not with a sense of urgency or with expectations of success.

It would be wrong to maintain that the United States shifted from a pro-Israeli to a pro-Arab policy as a result of the October war. The changes that did occur were more nuanced and multidimensional than the simple Arab-versus-Israel dichotomy suggests. The war did, however, challenge several basic assumptions of U.S. policymakers that had been central to prewar policy.

First, Israeli military power had not ensured stability, as had been expected after 1967. That "lesson," reinforced in the September 1970 crisis, was shattered on October 6. This did not mean, of course, that the military balance was seen as having no importance. The latter stages of the war clearly showed that military power counted for a great deal. Israeli strength alone, however, would not lead to a political settlement, as Johnson in 1967 had hoped it would.

Second, the October war undermined the belief that U.S.-Soviet détente would serve to minimize the danger of regional conflicts. Although Nixon, Kissinger, and Schlesinger all emphasized that détente had been helpful in resolving the crisis, they were acutely aware that the two superpowers had not been able to remain aloof from the Middle East conflict. Each side was too deeply committed to allow its friends to be sacrificed for the spirit of détente. Concrete local interests won out over global abstractions when put to the test. This meant not that détente was illusory or dangerous but rather that it was limited in scope. Superpower confrontation was still a possibility in the era of détente and negotiations, and this, above all, preoccupied the senior decisionmakers. The events of October 24–25 confirmed their worst fears.

Third, the war challenged the prevailing attitude of policymakers toward the Arab world. Despite the remarkable Israeli military achievements on both fronts, the Egyptians and Syrians had apparently fought quite well. They had also achieved surprise in the initial attack. Moreover, the degree of Arab solidarity was impressive; the use of the oil weapon was well coordinated with the diplomatic and military moves; and the tone of restraint in private and public communications was a welcome contrast to that of 1967. Sadat, in particular, was emphatic in his desire to work with Nixon and Kissinger for a post-hostilities diplomatic settlement. This was a very important new element in the picture.

Fourth, American officials, and Kissinger in particular, found themselves having to learn about petroleum economics as a part of international strategy. Kissinger had paid almost no attention to oil issues before the October crisis. He and others had a hard time distinguishing between the effects of the embargo, which was highly visible but not very important, and the curtailment of production, which sparked the dramatic price increases. Had Nixon and Kissinger been more sensitive to these issues, they might have been more discreet in their handling of the $2.2 billion aid package to Israel, announcing it after the war was over rather than in the midst of the battle. In any event, much of the subsequent diplomacy surrounding the Arab-Israeli conflict was played out under the shadow of the Arab oil weapon, which not only added a sense of urgency but also raised the specter of blackmail.

These changes in widely held beliefs did not all take place at once. Some came more readily than others. In particular, the reassessment of Egyptian policy began within three days after the outbreak of war. The initial call for a cease-fire based on the status quo ante, and the restraint in rearming Israel, were products of pre-war views—namely, that Israel would win a quick and fairly easy victory over incompetent Arab armies. Between October 9 and 13 these perceptions underwent steady modification, culminating in a revised position on both a cease-fire and arms for Israel. The new policies, which contributed to the cease-fire on October 22, resulted from a reordering of a few elements in the views of the decisionmakers, rather than from an entirely new appreciation of the situation. The Israelis were encountering more difficulties than anticipated; the Arabs were both more effective at arms and more skillful at diplomacy. These incremental changes in perception, combined with the reality of a prolonged and dangerous war, produced a shift in American policy that was both quantitative and qualitative.

The United States would henceforth devote much more attention to the Middle East. It would be a top-priority concern for Nixon and Kissinger. Moreover, the United States would consciously try to improve its relations with the principal Arab countries, especially Egypt. This effort would be a primary element in the new American diplomatic strategy, an element that had been conspicuously lacking before October 1973. Nixon and Kissinger felt they could court the Arabs without sacrificing the U.S.-Israeli relationship. In fact, as they saw it, it was the strength of the U.S.-Israeli tie, with the obvious influence this gave Washington over Israeli policy, that would impress the Arabs and convince them that the United States held most of the diplomatic cards once the fighting was over. The Soviets could provide arms; the United States could help regain territory, provided the Arabs were prepared to make appropriate concessions of their own in the context of peace negotiations.

The shift in policy brought about by the October war was at least as important as that produced by the Jordan crisis of 1970. The result of the earlier crisis had been an inactive, status quo–oriented policy; the result of the October 1973 crisis was a much more active approach aimed at bringing about substantial change. For the first time the United States committed its top diplomatic resources to a sustained search for a settlement of the Arab-Israeli conflict.

In view of the importance of the policy change during October 1973, one is tempted to seek explanations in domestic or bureaucratic politics, or in the psychological makeup of the individuals involved. After all, Watergate and the energy crisis were persistent themes throughout the crisis. And both Nixon and Kissinger had strong and unusual personalities.

Domestic politics is often linked in complex ways to foreign policy, and Nixon and Kissinger certainly took it into account as they considered policy choices. The key decisions of the crisis, however—the cease-fire proposals, the airlift to Israel, and the alert—were not responses to domestic politics. Pro-Israeli groups were not responsible for the decision to rearm Israel, largely because Kissinger skillfully persuaded the Israeli ambassador not to "unleash" Israel's supporters. Pro-Arab groups and oil companies played no role in Nixon's decision to press Israel to accept a cease-fire on October 12 or to save the Third Army Corps. Nor does Watergate explain the military alert of October 24–25.

Crisis periods, especially, tend to isolate policymakers from domestic pressures. Decisions are often made rapidly, before public opinion can be mobilized. Information is closely held, depriving interest groups of the means for effective action. The stakes are high, and the public tends to be deferential to presidential authority, even when that authority has been weakened, as Nixon's had been.

One theme did recur in Kissinger's comments: the rest of the world must not draw the conclusion that the Watergate crisis had weakened the president's ability to conduct foreign policy. The size of the U.S. airlift to Israel, once begun, the magnitude of the aid bill for arms to Israel, and the scope of the American military alert may have been partly related to this desire to appear strong and decisive. In each case, however, the basic decision was not rooted in the fear that Watergate had led other nations to underestimate the United States. Rather, the decisions were responses to external events that seemed to require urgent action. With or without the Watergate affair, the same course almost certainly would have been taken.

Other explanations of U.S. policy during the war have emphasized bureaucratic or personality factors. In some accounts Schlesinger and Deputy Defense Secretary William Clements are portrayed as opposing the airlift to Israel; in others, Kissinger is painted as responsible.[82] The reasons given may be institutional—military men resented seeing arms taken from active U.S. units and sent to Israel; they may be linked to economic interests—Clements had ties to the oil industry; or they may be traced to personality—Kissinger and Nixon had deluded themselves with the success of détente and therefore failed to appreciate the ways in which the Soviets were manipulating the situation to their advantage.

Those perspectives, however, do not account for the fact that individuals from widely different backgrounds agreed on each of the major decisions. Whatever their subsequent relationship, Kissinger and Schlesinger did not argue over basic policy in the October war. Whatever his personal feelings toward Israel, Clements helped organize a remarkably efficient airlift to Israel once the orders were given. Bureaucratic politics was barely in evidence, so tight was Kissinger's control over the policymaking machinery. Nor did the policy changes result from the replacement of individuals with one set of views by those of contrasting persuasions. The same officials were in place, with about the same relative power, before and after the war. The difference was that they now saw the situation differently.

The key to the consensus among top officials was the ability of Kissinger to draw on President Nixon's authority. On occasion Nixon directly gave orders, but even when he was not present, Kissinger was clearly speaking in his name. In the principal decisions the president was involved, although sometimes rather remotely. When Kissinger would say, "The president wants" or "The president has ordered," few of the other key officials were inclined to argue. Moreover, only Kissinger—and Haig, who often relayed Kissinger's views to the president and then reported back to his former boss—had direct, continuing access to the president.[83]

American policy during the October 1973 war demonstrated once again the centrality of the authority of the president in the conduct of foreign policy, particularly in crises. In this case, Kissinger must be considered an extension of the president, for he was given an unusual margin of responsibility. It was his tie to Nixon, however, not his position as secretary of state, that ensured the acceptance of his formulations. Perhaps if the policies had been less nuanced, less complex, there might have been some overt dissension within the bureaucracy. The Nixon-Kissinger policy, however, could be seen as pro-Israel, pro-Arab, pro-détente, or anti-Soviet, depending on what one was looking for. Those who disagreed with one element of policy were likely to support other aspects. This complexity left Kissinger in a commanding position.

As the crisis came to an end, the Middle East undoubtedly had top priority in American foreign policy. American relations with allies had been damaged by the crisis; détente was under attack; the energy crisis was likely to become more acute. Progress toward an Arab Israeli settlement would not necessarily solve these problems, but failure to defuse the Middle East situation could only complicate them. Perhaps equally important, for the first time Nixon and Kissinger sensed the opportunity to make progress toward a settlement. The Arabs were looking to Washington now, not to Moscow. The Israelis were heavily dependent on American arms and financial support, which could be translated into influence in the proper diplomatic setting. Public opinion would be supportive of a major U.S. initiative provided it did not become anti-Israeli or appear to be responsive to the Arab oil embargo.

By the time the cease-fire had gone into effect, the United States was already preparing for a new diplomatic effort. It would not be like the Rogers Plan, formal, legalistic, and worked out in U.S.-Soviet negotiations. Instead, the Soviets would be kept out of the substance of the negotiations. Their record during the war had not inspired confidence that they were prepared to play an evenhanded role in settling the conflict. Nor did Sadat seem to want them involved. Furthermore, no American plan would be presented to the parties. Instead, the United States would try to play the role of mediator, eliciting propositions from the parties, trying then to modify them, and eventually pressing for a compromise. The process would move slowly, beginning with concrete issues of particular urgency and proceeding later to more fundamental problems, such as the nature of a final peace settlement. Above all, each step must remain independent of the next; otherwise the process would never get under way, as the United States had discovered in the interim-settlement effort of 1971.

As the war came to a close, Kissinger had already decided on his new strategy—step-by-step diplomacy. Now he merely needed to persuade Israel, the Arabs, the Soviets, Congress, and the American public to give him a chance to prove his success where others had failed. For the next six months Kissinger was accorded the opportunity to demonstrate both the strengths and limitations of his conception of how to solve the Arab-Israeli conflict.

CHAPTER EIGHT

Step by Step: Kissinger and the Disengagement Agreements, 1974

The eight months that followed the October 1973 war witnessed an un-precedented American involvement in the search for a settlement of the Arab-Israeli conflict. Henry Kissinger, before becoming secretary of state, had devoted little energy to the seemingly intractable issues dividing Israel and its Arab neighbors. Nor had he progressed far in his understanding of the "energy crisis" and the part played by Middle East oil in the international economy. Only the danger of confrontation between the superpowers growing out of tensions in the Middle East seemed capable of arousing in him a sustained interest in the affairs of the region. Now with the October war a vivid example of the volatility of the Arab-Israeli conflict, Kissinger, with Nixon's full backing, set out to become the peacemaker, orchestrator, mediator, and catalyst in a new diplomatic initiative that would take him repeatedly to countries he had never before visited to deal with statesmen he had previously not taken seriously.

Although President Nixon was eager for the United States to play an active part in resolving the Arab-Israeli conflict, he was also increasingly preoccupied with his crumbling domestic base of support as the Watergate scandal continued to unfold.[1] Kissinger was therefore allowed extraordi-nary latitude in shaping the details of American diplomacy, calling on Nixon to invoke presidential authority as necessary, keeping the president informed at each stage, and on occasion ignoring his directions.

Above all, Nixon wanted results. Internationally, he worried about the consequences of other nations concluding that the American domestic crisis had weakened the president's ability to act in foreign affairs. Domestically, he hoped that foreign-policy successes would help him through the crisis of confidence in his judgment and leadership stemming from his handling of Watergate.

SHAPING AN AMERICAN STRATEGY

During the October 1973 hostilities Kissinger and Nixon had both promised an active American diplomatic initiative aimed at "implementing

Resolution 242" after the war ended, but they steadfastly refused to promise any specific results, despite Sadat's pleas. The United States, they repeated, was committed to a process, not an outcome. The administration could guarantee that it would make a major effort, but it could not guarantee that Israel would withdraw from all Arab territory or that Palestinian rights would be restored. To do so would be to invite severe domestic criticism and to raise Arab hopes to an unrealistic level. Kissinger frequently mentioned that he feared the Arabs' "romanticism," their impatience, their desire for quick results.[2]

These initial perceptions, shaped by the October war, became the foundations of postwar policy. With the achievement of the shaky cease-fire of October 25, Nixon and Kissinger began to define what the contours of that policy would be. Two key elements quickly emerged. First, the United States would play an active role in trying to resolve the Arab-Israeli conflict. Unlike Johnson after 1967, and they themselves after 1970, Nixon and Kissinger now felt the situation in the Middle East was too threatening to American interests to be ignored; perhaps even more important, an opportunity for a successful American initiative existed.[3]

As Kissinger had sensed during the war, everyone was looking to the United States. He held the cards, or at least so the principal actors believed, which was what mattered. The Israelis, more isolated internationally than ever before, were in the awkward position of being heavily dependent on Washington for arms, economic aid, and diplomatic support. The Arabs, realizing the potential for U.S. influence with Israel, were anxious to turn that potential to their own advantage. As Kissinger and others had hinted, the Soviets could provide arms to the Arabs, but only the United States could produce Israeli territorial concessions through negotiations.[4]

Second, the new American strategy would try to avoid linking initial diplomatic steps with the nature of a final peace agreement. Kissinger had disliked the Rogers Plan of 1969 and was not even particularly keen on UN Resolution 242. Such public statements of principles might provide psychic gratification to one side or the other, but in his view they did little to advance the diplomatic process. Instead they allowed each side to focus on what it rejected in the abstract plan instead of concentrating on tangible issues in the present. If an active U.S. role in the diplomacy was meant as a signal to the Arabs of a more balanced American policy, Washington's refusal to link first steps with final outcomes was meant to reassure Israel that a settlement would not be imposed against its will.

To sustain an active and effective U.S. role in the evolving diplomacy of the Arab-Israeli conflict, Kissinger felt it necessary to mitigate the international pressures created by the October 1973 war. The Arab offensive had succeeded in mobilizing European, Japanese, and third world support for a rapid settlement on essentially Arab terms. The UN could be counted on to support Egypt, Syria, and the Palestinians. The Soviets were committed to the Arab position, even at some risk to détente and U.S.-Soviet relations. The Arab oil embargo was an added source of tension, as was the continuing danger that the cease-fire would break down.

Although he admired the way in which Sadat had succeeded in marshaling his forces, Kissinger was not prepared to act under these combined pressures. He would therefore try to persuade the American allies to leave him a free hand; he would isolate the Soviets from the substance of the negotiations; he would endeavor to get the oil embargo lifted; he would build support for "moderate" Arab positions at the expense of "radical" ones; he would try to avoid a public quarrel with Israel that might have serious domestic repercussions; and he would attempt to win over the U.S. Congress and press to support his role in the diplomacy. Much of Kissinger's tactical maneuvering in succeeding months was aimed at ensuring that the United States could act free of the multiple pressures, domestic and international, generated by the October war. On the whole, he was remarkably successful.

Kissinger felt previous administrations had erred in viewing their choices as being pro-Israel or pro-Arab. In his view it was precisely the special American relationship with Israel that obliged the Arabs to deal with the United States in the diplomatic arena. Power, not sentiment, was what counted. The difficulty, of course, was that to keep the Arabs looking toward the United States, the diplomatic process had to hold out more hope to them than would another round of war. If war was seen as the answer, the Soviet Union could always provide more than the United States. Consequently, progress toward a settlement was an absolute prerequisite for maintaining the confidence of the Arabs. At a minimum, this meant the return of territory, and eventually some move in the direction of addressing Palestinian grievances. For the United States, it meant that Israel would have to make concessions to keep the diplomacy alive. Where possible, the United States might try to extract comparable Arab concessions, but given the kind of issues, to do so would be difficult. An additional dimension of U.S. diplomacy would therefore be offers of aid to Israel—with the implied threat of withholding it if circumstances so dictated—and promises of assistance to Egypt, Syria, and Jordan to strengthen bilateral relations through other means than delivering Israeli concessions.

U.S.-Egyptian relations were seen as the linchpin of the new American policy in the Arab world, with Jordan and Saudi Arabia playing key supportive roles in favor of Arab "moderation."[5] Only gradually did Kissinger come to perceive Syria's importance; he was even more reluctant to acknowledge the Palestinians as participants in the settlement process. For the moment the new U.S.-Egyptian relationship, already in evidence during the war, was to receive most of Nixon's and Kissinger's attention.

The role of the Soviet Union in the Middle East had long preoccupied Nixon and Kissinger. Having at one time overrated Soviet influence in the Arab world, they were now inclined to minimize the Soviet role in the settlement process. Soviet behavior in the October war, though not viewed as totally contrary to the spirit of détente, was nonetheless not encouraging.[6] Nor had previous U.S.-Soviet efforts to reach agreement on the terms of settlement been successful. The two superpowers not only had different interests in the region but also had a different concept of what a peace settlement should entail. Perhaps most important of all, the key participants in the regional conflict were not anxious to see the Soviets deeply involved in the diplomacy. Certainly the Israelis were unenthusiastic, given Soviet hostility and the lack of diplomatic relations. Jordan was still prepared to work with the United States instead of with the Soviet Union. Sadat was also ready to play his American card, and Soviet-Egyptian relations suffered as a result. Even President Asad of Syria showed a willingness to let Kissinger try his hand, although his skepticism was considerably greater than Sadat's. Finally, there was enough of the cold warrior left in both Nixon and Kissinger to produce a sense of real pleasure in demonstrating the limits of Soviet influence in the Middle East.[7]

To maintain an effective American role in the resolution of the Arab-Israeli dispute, domestic public opinion would have to be mobilized. Most Americans were sympathetic to Israel, a sentiment that was particularly strong in Congress and in the press.[8] The Arab oil embargo was doing little to change this feeling; in fact, it seemed more likely that an anti-Arab backlash might result, making it difficult to pursue the policy of building the new ties to the Arab world that were central to the Nixon-Kissinger strategy. American policy could not appear to be dictated by Arab oil pressures. Domestically and internationally, that would be an untenable posture for the administration. Consequently the new diplomatic initiatives would have to be explained to the American public and to Congress in terms of the overall objective of seeking peace in the Middle East, of strengthening United States ties with the Arab world without sacrificing Israel, and of minimizing the ability of the Soviets to threaten Western interests, including oil. Broad support for these objectives could be expected, especially if aid to Israel continued to flow at high levels and if the oil embargo was lifted.

If an active United States diplomatic role in the search for an Arab-Israeli settlement was the first principle of the new American policy, the second was the pursuit of a settlement through a step-by-step process.[9] This method soon came to be the hallmark of the Kissinger diplomacy. Kissinger's negotiating experiences with the Chinese, the Vietnamese, and the Soviets had convinced him that the process of negotiation had a dynamic of its own.[10] It was important to create the proper balance of incentives first, and then to reach limited results at an early stage without making commitments to the final goal; eventually, when a mutuality of interests had emerged, more substantial areas of agreement would be possible. Kissinger was skeptical of the American penchant for the "quick fix," the technical solution to a political problem, of negotiations carried on in the blaze of publicity, of bureaucratic compromises, and of good will as a substitute for tangible concessions. Although he would later be charged with some of these mistakes in his own conduct of diplomacy, he was at least conscious of these pitfalls, the weakness of his own role as mediator, and the sizable gap that separated the parties. Unlike other negotiations he had engaged in, the Arab-Israeli arena was one in which the United States faced the challenge of persuading adversaries to make commitments to one another. It was not enough for the United States to develop its own policies; the key to success would be to induce the parties to modify their irreconcilable positions.

Timing would be an important element of the Kissinger step-by-step diplomacy. He envisaged negotiations probably going on for several years. The Arabs were pressing for immediate Israeli withdrawal; the Israelis were pleading for time. Kissinger was anxious to pace the negotiations so that some results could be produced at an early date, while still allowing time for all parties to adjust to a gradual, phased approach to a settlement. Most immediately, the Israelis had a national election scheduled for the end of December, and until then no serious negotiations could be expected. Somehow the Arabs would have to be persuaded to wait until early 1974 for the first Israeli withdrawals.

In the meantime it would be important to establish a negotiating framework, a forum that would provide the symbolic umbrella under which various diplomatic moves might be made. This forum would be a multilateral conference, with U.S. and Soviet participation, to be held at Geneva under UN auspices. Its primary value would be to legitimize the settlement process, give the Soviets enough of a sense of participation to prevent them from disrupting the peace effort, and provide a setting where agreements could be ratified, talks could be held, and delegations could meet. Kissinger fully expected, however, that progress toward agreements would not be made in such a cumbersome forum.

Instead of counting heavily on Geneva, Kissinger planned to deal with concrete issues through bilateral channels. Most urgent were the problems on the Egyptian-Israeli front. There the armies were entangled in a dangerous fashion, constantly tempting one side or the other to resume hostilities. The Egyptian Third Army Corps was nearly cut off from supplies, a situation that was intolerable for Sadat to accept. International pressure was building for Israel to pull back to the October 22 lines, which would release the Third Army. Prisoners of war had to be exchanged, an issue of very great sensitivity to the Israelis. The Egyptian semiblockade of Bab al-Mandab at the southern entrance of the Red Sea was preventing the movement of Israeli shipping to and from Aqaba. Taken together, these issues might be negotiated in a first step that would stabilize the cease-fire through a "disengagement" of military forces.

The conceptual underpinnings of the new American policy in the Middle East, initially forged in the midst of the October war, were quickly established. Nixon and Kissinger, with virtually no opposition from the bureaucracy, were committing the United States to an unprecedented active role in mediating the Arab-Israeli conflict, to a step-by-step diplomatic process, and to a disengagement of Egyptian-Israeli military forces at an early date.

SETTING THE STAGE

One result of the improved relationship between Cairo and Washington was President Sadat's frequent and urgent appeals to the United States to help the entrapped Third Army Corps. The Israelis, by contrast, were determined to use pressure on the corps to obtain the release of prisoners of war and the end of the naval blockade at Bab al-Mandab. The stalemate threatened to destroy the precarious cease-fire. Kissinger therefore quickly set two urgent goals: first, to stabilize the cease-fire; second, to bring about a separation of military forces. By October 27 the State Department was able to announce that Egyptian and Israeli representatives had agreed to meet to implement the cease-fire agreement. Even before the talks began on October 30, temporary arrangements had been made for the nonmilitary resupply of the Third Army Corps.

The Egyptian and Israeli positions on the terms of a cease-fire and on a military disengagement proved to be far apart. Ismail Fahmy, Egypt's new foreign minister, met with Kissinger on October 29.[11] Two days later he again met Kissinger, as well as President Nixon. Besides discussing the secretary's forthcoming trip to Egypt, Fahmy was authorized to present an eleven-point proposal. Most urgently, Egypt insisted that Israel withdraw unconditionally to the October 22 lines, as called for in UN Resolutions 339 and 340. Once that was done, Egypt would agree to release all prisoners of war. Then Israel should withdraw to a line inside Sinai that would lie east of the passes, and Egyptian forces would remain in place. UN forces would man a zone between Egyptian and Israeli forces. The blockade of Bab al-Mandab would be lifted once Israeli forces began to withdraw toward the disengagement zone, and the clearing of the Suez Canal would begin after this stage was completed. Within an agreed time period Israel would withdraw in one more step to the international frontier, at which point the state of belligerency would end. Similar steps should be planned for Syria, and a peace conference should be convened during the implementation of the disengagement phase. Finally, U.S.-Egyptian diplomatic relations would be restored at an early date.

Kissinger told Fahmy that the plan contained constructive ideas but that it seemed too ambitious at that stage. In discussions during the next two days, Kissinger raised the issue of the October 22 lines, emphasizing that it would be difficult to persuade Israel to withdraw to them and that a broader step as part of the disengagement of forces would make the October 22 lines irrelevant in any case.[12] Reflecting the new tone in U.S.-Egyptian relations, President Sadat, in a speech delivered on October 31, termed the American role "constructive."

Kissinger and Nixon then talked with Prime Minister Meir, who arrived in Washington on October 31. Kissinger met with her on the morning of November 1.[13] She was particularly concerned about the fate of Israeli prisoners in Egypt. Continued resupply of the Third Army

Corps, she argued, was conditional upon the return of wounded prisoners of war (POWs), a complete list of all prisoners, and Red Cross visits to them. Israel would agree to a permanent nonmilitary supply of the Third Army Corps once the prisoners were returned and the naval blockade was lifted. Only then would Israel agree to talk to Egypt about the October 22 lines. Kissinger was authorized to convey these terms to Sadat, with the understanding that the United States would not take a position on the location of the October 22 lines and would not pressure Israel on this issue, leaving it instead to negotiations between the two parties.

Shortly after noon, President Nixon met with Prime Minister Meir. Nixon offered the opinion that Sadat really wanted peace and then laid out the American strategy for the months ahead. He would try to break up the problems so they could be dealt with step by step. The United States would stand up to the Soviets, as it had done in the October war. It would try to improve its relations with Egypt and Syria, which would also help Israel. Nixon's goal would be to ensure "secure borders" for Israel. Meir was undemonstrative, emphasizing only that Israel did not want to be pressed on the October 22 lines. That evening Kissinger dined with Meir and a few others. The atmosphere was chilly, if not hostile. The Israeli prime minister barely spoke to Kissinger, and when she did, her tone was reserved. There was no expression of gratitude for U.S. aid, only anger at being deprived of victory by "friends." No toasts were drunk.

The following morning Kissinger convened a meeting of the WSAG. Still incensed over the previous day's talks with the Israelis, he implied that Israeli leaders had deliberately misled him on several occasions during the war. Now, Kissinger said, U.S. foreign policy would be determined by the United States, not Israel. By working for a moderate peace proposal, the United States would reduce Soviet influence and end the oil embargo. If this effort failed, the Arabs would be driven back to the Soviets, the oil crisis would worsen, and the United States and Israel would be isolated internationally. The Arabs must see that they would be better off dealing with the United States than with the Soviet Union. Kissinger expressed the view that Egypt's position on accepting a nonmilitary resupply of the Third Army Corps and an exchange of POWs once Israel returned to the October 22 lines was reasonable. If necessary, Israel would be forced to accept it. Eventually the tone of the discussion moderated, but Kissinger's anger at Israeli intransigence was genuine and would be displayed repeatedly in succeeding months.[14]

KILOMETER 101

With these initial talks behind him, Kissinger set off for the Middle East on November 5. His first stop, which also marked his first visit to an Arab country, was in Morocco, partly to symbolize the long tradition of friendly U.S.-Arab relations, and partly to open channels through King Hassan to Syria and the Palestinians.[15] Cairo, not Rabat, however, was the real goal of Kissinger's travels. There, on November 7, he met President Sadat for the first time. In private talks that day Kissinger began to develop a genuine admiration for the Egyptian leader.[16] The turning point came in discussing the issue of the October 22 lines. Kissinger was in an awkward position, for he knew the Israelis could not easily be pressured and yet he felt Sadat was right that Israeli forces should not be allowed to keep the Third Army Corps at their mercy. By the time Kissinger arrived in Cairo, the Israeli cabinet had approved the positions presented to Kissinger by Prime Minister Meir on November 3. He was thus able to tell Sadat that Israel would respect the cease-fire; that nonmilitary resupply of the Third Army Corps would be allowed, with UN and Israeli inspection of convoys; and that the town of Suez would receive food, water, and medicine. Concurrently with the agreement on nonmilitary supplies, POWs should be exchanged and the naval blockade lifted, and the October 22 lines could be discussed in the framework of the disengagement of forces. Israel had also said that in exchange for the POWs in Syria, Syrian civilians could return to areas controlled by Israel and two outposts on Mt. Hermon could be transferred to the United Nations.

Sadat was prepared to accept most of these points, although he was still anxious for Israel to pull back to the October 22 lines. Kissinger replied that if Egypt insisted, he would agree to try to persuade the Israelis. But he offered his opinion that it might be just as easy, although it might take more time, to work out a substantial disengagement of forces that would bypass the issue of the October 22 lines. Meanwhile arrangements could be made to resupply the Third Army Corps. To Kissinger's surprise Sadat agreed with this line of argument. He urged Kissinger to strive to obtain rapid agreement on the Israeli points. At the conclusion of the talks they agreed that diplomatic relations between Egypt and the United States would be restored "in principle" immediately.[17]

Kissinger promptly decided to send two of his aides, Joseph Sisco and Harold Saunders, to Israel to work out the details of an accord. Upon learning that Sadat had agreed to drop the issue of the October 22 lines, the prime minister termed this a "fantastic achievement," but she quickly found fault with the Egyptian position. Sadat did not want Israel to control the road used to supply the Third Army Corps, nor was he prepared to acknowledge publicly that Egypt would lift the naval blockade. After several rounds of discussion on these two points, Israel agreed to accept United States assurances that the blockade would be ended. On November 9 agreement on a cease-fire plan and the exchange of POWs was announced, and two days later a six-point agreement modeled on the original Israeli proposal was signed by Israeli and Egyptian military representatives at a point along the Cairo to Suez road known as Kilometer 101.[18] The settlement process was off to a start, albeit a shaky one.

Meanwhile Kissinger flew to Jordan to talk with King Hussein, and encouraged the king to participate in the peace negotiations. Without making firm commitments, he expressed sympathy with the king's opposition to a West Bank Palestinian state dominated by the Palestine Liberation Organization. For the moment, however, Kissinger was still concentrating on the Egyptian-Israeli front. Jordan and the Palestinians would be left for later.

In Saudi Arabia Kissinger appealed to King Faisal for support of his diplomatic effort, referring to the oil embargo as an obstacle to the American efforts.[19] He argued the logic of the step-by-step approach and appealed to Faisal for help in opening channels of communication with the Syrians.[20] Faisal gave Kissinger his standard rendition of the Zionist-communist conspiracy but also promised some help, including an easing of the oil embargo once progress began on Israeli withdrawal.[21]

On balance, Kissinger felt pleased with the results of his first trip. He had established a personal relationship with Sadat, and U.S.-Egyptian relations seemed off to a good start. The cease-fire had been stabilized. An important agreement had been signed by Israel and Egypt, with American help. Faisal had promised to relax the oil embargo. Now it was necessary to develop the broad negotiating framework at Geneva as a prelude to disengagement talks. Kissinger was in no rush, being still committed to a gradual pace under close U.S. control.

THE GENEVA CONFERENCE

The first Egyptian and Israeli prisoners were exchanged on November 15. The next day General Aharon Yariv of Israel and General Abd al-Ghany Gamasy of Egypt began talks at Kilometer 101 aimed at implementing the six-point agreement, particularly its second point, concerning "return to October 22 lines in the framework of agreement on the disengagement and separation of forces." On November 18 Kissinger reminded Foreign Minister Fahmy that disengagement should be the first order of business at the upcoming Geneva peace conference, but it could not become a precondition for the convening of the conference. Nor could the issue of Palestinian participation in the peace conference be settled at this stage. Only at the peace conference would the United States be able to use its full influence. In short, Kissinger was trying to build up Geneva as an important step in the process of negotiations and to keep the U.S. role central to substantive progress.

Meanwhile Israeli and Egyptian positions were being discussed at Kilometer 101. Israel initially proposed that both sides should pull back from territory gained in the October war and that UN forces should take over those areas. The Egyptian reply was to insist that Egyptian forces would stay in place and that Israeli forces should withdraw to a line running from Al-Arish to Ras Muhammad in the southern tip of Sinai. Gamasy then proposed Israeli withdrawal in a more modest disengagement phase to the vicinity of the Mitla and Giddi passes, with designated zones for both the Egyptian and the Israeli main forces, lightly armed forces, and a UN buffer between them. On November 22 General Yariv replied that Israel would withdraw from the west bank of the canal provided Egyptian forces on the east bank were thinned out.[22]

Negotiations continued for several days, with Israel offering deeper withdrawals in return for a substantial reduction of Egyptian armored strength. On November 26 Yariv suggested that Israel would even withdraw east of the passes if Egypt would reduce its level of armor in Sinai to token strength. Egypt showed interest in the proposal but insisted on mutual force reductions; then on November 29 Gamasy discovered that Yariv had gone back to his original proposal that both sides should withdraw from territory gained in the war. This reversal of position angered the Egyptians and led to the breakdown of the talks.

Kissinger has been charged with responsibility for aborting this promising experiment in direct Egyptian-Israeli negotiations.[23] There is some truth in the charge. Kissinger felt the talks were proceeding too rapidly. He was beginning to think of the Syrian front, and feared that if Egypt and Israel reached a disengagement agreement before Geneva, Asad would insist on the same, which might mean an indefinite delay in convening the Geneva conference. Then, too, Kissinger wanted to demonstrate that a U.S. role was essential for sustained diplomatic progress. Perhaps Egypt and Israel could reach agreement without his help, but would the same be true when it came to Syria, the Palestinians, or even a second Egyptian step? He doubted it. If the oil embargo was to be lifted, which Nixon was very keen on, that would also be in return for American success in promoting agreement.[24] And if Soviet prestige was to remain low, the United States must remain in control of the negotiations. Kissinger therefore advised the Israelis to slow down at Kilometer 101 and to withhold their position on disengagement until Geneva. To some observers, the suggestion seemed cynical, but it fitted into Kissinger's broader diplomatic scheme. And it should be added that Israel did not resist this piece of advice, as it so often did on other occasions. In retrospect, it appears as if General Yariv was considerably ahead of the Israeli cabinet in his willingness to offer concessions in the disengagement stage.[25]

Kissinger now turned his attention to organizing the Geneva conference.[26] On December 6 he announced it was "extremely probable" that a conference would be convened at Geneva on December 18. But who would attend? Egypt would go, and Sadat had implied that Syria would go as well.[27] Jordan could be counted on, but since the Arab summit meeting in Algiers the previous month the PLO had been recognized by all Arab countries except Jordan as the sole legitimate representative of the Palestinian people. If the PLO attended the Geneva conference, Israel would not, nor would Israel sit with Syria unless a list of Israeli prisoners held in Syria was forthcoming.

To help overcome Israeli reluctance to attend the conference, Kissinger talked to Defense Minister Dayan in Washington on December 7. Dayan presented a long list of arms requests, and Kissinger implied that the United States would give it favorable consideration. In return, Dayan said disengagement need not await Israeli elections. He proposed a disengagement based on Israeli withdrawal to a line west of the passes, combined with substantial demilitarization of forward areas and an Egyptian commitment to reopen the Suez Canal. Once again, however,

Kissinger urged the Israelis not to move too quickly in negotiations. Israel should not look weak. The Arabs should believe it was difficult for the United States to influence Israel; otherwise their expectations would soar.

Kissinger set off on his second trip to the Middle East on December 12, stopping in London en route to deliver an important speech.[28] He proceeded to Algiers for talks with President Houari Boumedienne and was successful in gaining his support for the Geneva conference. Boumedienne would thereafter be kept well informed on the peace negotiations, for Kissinger believed Algeria's endorsement of his strategy would make it easier for both Sadat and Asad to resist radical Arab pressures.

During the next several days Kissinger traveled to Cairo, Riyadh, Damascus, and Tel Aviv. Only the talks with Sadat were devoid of difficulty. Sadat had already accepted a short delay in opening the Geneva conference, and he now agreed to postpone the substantive phase of disengagement negotiations until mid-January, after the Israeli elections.[29] With King Faisal the next day, December 14, Kissinger won Saudi endorsement for Sadat's approach and a promise that the oil embargo would be ended and production restored once agreement had been reached on the first stage of a settlement.

While Kissinger was lining up support for Geneva among key Arab countries, Israel was making its participation in a peace conference conditional on a number of important points. Israel opposed a strong role for the UN secretary general, it refused to discuss the issue of eventual Palestinian participation at the conference, as Sadat had proposed, and Israel's representatives would not sit in the same room with the Syrians until Syria complied with Israeli demands for a list of POWs and Red Cross visits to them. It began to appear that Israel might boycott Geneva.

At this point Nixon and Kissinger began to exert heavy pressure on Israel. At 6:45 p.m. on December 13 in Washington, Israeli Minister Mordechai Shalev was handed a letter from Nixon to Meir. She had objected to the draft of a joint U.S.-USSR letter to the UN secretary general on convening the Geneva conference. Nixon said he was disturbed by her attitude and denied that the UN secretary general would have more than a symbolic role. Regarding the Palestinians, Nixon argued that the mention of Palestinian participation in the conference did not prejudice the outcome and that, in any case, the participation of additional members of the conference would require the agreement of all the initial participants. In short, Israel would not be forced to negotiate with the

Palestinians. Nixon concluded his letter by warning the prime minister that the United States would not understand Israel's refusal to attend the conference and that he would no longer be able to justify support for Israel if Israel did not send its representatives to Geneva.[30]

The next day, on learning that the Israeli cabinet had not been able to reach a decision on attending Geneva, Nixon sent another message. The United States was prepared to delay the conference to December 21. Nixon referred to Israel's long-standing goal of negotiations with the Arabs, terming it inconceivable that Israel would not now take this step. In any event, the president had ordered Kissinger to attend the opening session of the Geneva conference whether Israel was present or not.[31]

While an effort was being made to obtain Israeli agreement to the Geneva conference through a combination of pressures and promises,[32] Kissinger set off for his first meeting with Syria's president, Hafiz al-Asad.[33] Kissinger found Asad to be intelligent, tough, personable, and possessed of a sense of humor. He was also the least conciliatory of all the Arab leaders Kissinger had met to date. Asad implied that he did not object to the convening of the Geneva conference on December 21 but that Syria would not attend unless a disengagement-of-forces agreement was reached first. And disengagement, he thought, should involve the entire Golan Heights. Nor was he prepared to yield to Kissinger's pleas to turn over a list of Israeli POWs. After six and one-half hours of talks with Asad, Kissinger left for Israel empty-handed.[34]

During the next two days, December 16 and 17, Kissinger used all his persuasive abilities to convince the Israelis they should attend the Geneva conference. He met with Golda Meir alone and with members of her cabinet, painting for them a grim picture of the consequences of a breakdown in the diplomatic process. Much more than the Middle East was at stake. Global stability, international economic order, the coherence of the NATO alliance, and virtually every other major issue in world politics was linked to Israel's decision. During a private dinner with most of the Israeli cabinet at Foreign Minister Eban's house on December 16, Kissinger was at his most persuasive.[35] The Israelis held out for one more change in the letter of invitation—no mention of the Palestinians by name—and, subject to that condition, the cabinet met late at night to approve of Israel's attending the Geneva conference on December 21.

Kissinger now made one last try to obtain Syrian attendance. In return for a list of POWs, Israel would allow Syrian villagers to return to their homes in Israeli-controlled areas. Egypt's foreign minister, Fahmy, discussed the proposal with Asad at Kissinger's request, and the American ambassador in Beirut traveled to Damascus to take up the matter again with the Syrian leader. On December 18 Kissinger received Asad's reply, to the effect that Syria would not attend this phase of the Geneva talks but might participate later.[36]

On December 21 the Geneva conference finally convened under the auspices of the UN secretary general, with the United States and the Soviet Union as cochairmen, and with the foreign ministers of Egypt, Jordan, and Israel in attendance. A table with Syria's nameplate on it remained unoccupied. Each foreign minister spoke, but largely for the public back home, not for one another. Kissinger tried to articulate his step-by-step strategy, stating that the goal of the conference was peace but that the urgent need was to strengthen the cease-fire by accomplishing a disengagement of forces as the "essential first step" on the path of implementing UN Resolution 242.

With these formal remarks the Geneva conference recessed, not to be convened in plenary session again for an indefinite period. A symbol now existed, however, a useful fiction perhaps, and a forum where working groups might discuss aspects of a settlement was available if needed. The endeavor had not all been in vain, but one might wonder if the results were commensurate with the effort.

EGYPTIAN-ISRAELI DISENGAGEMENT

Having successfully convened the Geneva conference, Kissinger now faced the challenge of producing early results on the Egyptian-Israeli front. Several related problems stood in his way. The Syrians were on a high level of military alert in late December, and a resumption of fighting seemed possible. The oil embargo was continuing, and, equally important, the Organization of Petroleum Exporting Countries (OPEC) had decided to double oil prices on December 23. The fact that the shah of Iran played the leading role in the price rise did not make it any more palatable. More than ever, the energy crisis hung over the Arab-Israeli negotiations.

Apart from difficulties with Syria and the frustration of the continuing oil embargo, Kissinger had to confront again the fact that the positions of Egypt and Israel on disengagement were still far apart. In Israel on December 17 he had discussed disengagement with Meir and her top aides. The Israeli position was that a small Egyptian force would be allowed to remain on the east bank of the canal up to a distance of ten kilometers. A lightly armed Israeli force would control the main north-south road beyond the Egyptian forces, and the Israeli main forces would be stationed east of the Mitla and Giddi passes, beyond Egyptian artillery range. Israel would not yield the passes in the disengagement phase. On other points there was less Israeli consensus. Some cabinet members felt Egypt should end the state of belligerency in return for the pullback of Israeli forces and should allow free passage for Israeli ships in the Suez Canal and at Bab al-Mandab. Some limits on Egyptian forces on both banks of the Suez Canal were also desired. Egypt should begin work on reopening the canal and rebuilding cities along it as a sign of peaceful intentions.

Egypt's position, as conveyed to Kissinger during his pre-Geneva talks in Cairo, began with the proposition that neither Egypt nor Israel should gain military advantage in the disengagement phase. In other words, any force limits would have to be mutual, as Gamasy had insisted at Kilometer 101 in November. Egypt would keep its forces east of the canal on existing lines in numbers not to exceed two divisions, a reduction of three divisions from current levels. No heavy artillery and no surface-to-air missiles would be placed across the canal. Israel would retain control of the eastern ends of the passes. A demilitarized zone would be established between the Egyptian and Israeli lines, to be patrolled by UN troops. Egypt would begin work on clearing the canal and would rebuild the cities once Israeli troops had withdrawn. Israeli cargoes would be allowed to pass through the canal after it reopened.

Two gaps separated the Egyptian and Israeli positions. Egypt wanted Israeli forces to withdraw east of the passes; Israel refused. Israel wanted only a token Egyptian force on the east bank; Sadat was thinking of two infantry divisions with 100 tanks each. It would be difficult for him publicly to accept substantial force limitations in territory returned to his control. Nonetheless, the conceptual underpinnings of the two sides' positions were not very far apart, and agreement seemed possible.

Israeli elections for the Knesset were held on December 31. The opposition to Prime Minister Meir's Labor Alignment coalition gained some strength, but not to the point of making a new cabinet and prime minister necessary. For the next six months, despite her own loss of popularity and the public disenchantment with her defense minister, Moshe Dayan, Meir carried the heavy burdens of government, fighting hard against American and domestic pressures in order to win agreements that protected Israel's vital interests. Kissinger found her to be tough and often emotional, and their talks were at times stormy, but the two nevertheless developed a genuine respect for each other during the difficult disengagement negotiations.

With Israeli elections out of the way, Dayan was sent to Washington for talks with Kissinger on January 4 and 5. He presented a five-zone concept for disengagement, in which each party would have two limited-force zones, separated by a UN buffer. He also specified the type of force limitations Israel could accept. Basically, each side's forces should be beyond the artillery range of the other side, and surface-to-air missiles should not be able to reach the other's aircraft. Also, the number of tanks in the limited zones should be kept very small.

During their talks Dayan urged Kissinger to return to the Middle East to aid in reaching an agreement. This idea proved to be acceptable to Sadat, and Kissinger left late on January 10. Kissinger originally expected to help establish the framework for an agreement, the details of which would be worked out by the parties at Geneva, but Sadat was anxious for results and asked Kissinger to stay in the region until an agreement was reached. Kissinger thus embarked on his first exercise in "shuttle diplomacy," flying between Egypt and Israel with proposals.

On January 13 the Israelis handed Kissinger a map of the proposed disengagement line and authorized him to show it to Sadat, which he did the next day. Sadat had already accepted, in his first talk with Kissinger, the idea of force limitations in three zones, and had promised to work for the end of the oil embargo once an agreement was reached. Now he also said he would accept Israeli forces west of the passes, but he had trouble with the extent of force limits.[37] To overcome Sadat's reservations, Kissinger suggested that the United States might take the responsibility for proposing the limitations on forces. Perhaps it would be easier for Sadat to accept an American plan than an Israeli one. And instead of publicly announcing the limits in the formal documents, these could be defined in letters exchanged by Sadat and Nixon. In addition, Sadat's private assurances on Israeli cargoes transiting the canal could be handled in a secret memo of understanding. Sadat agreed.

In Israel the next day, January 15, Prime Minister Meir dropped the demand for an end of belligerency as part of the disengagement agreement. A few changes in force levels and the line of disengagement were made, wherein Dayan played an especially constructive role. With a new map in hand Kissinger returned to Aswan to see Sadat on January 16, and Sadat agreed to scale down the Egyptian presence on the east bank to eight battalions and thirty tanks.[38] Kissinger then went back to Israel, and the next day, at 3:00 p.m., President Nixon announced that the two parties had reached an agreement on the disengagement of their military forces. The following day the chiefs of staff of Israel and Egypt signed the agreement at Kilometer 101.[39]

As part of the agreement, Israel and the United States signed a detailed ten-point memorandum of understanding.[40] The United States conveyed several Egyptian statements of intention concerning the Suez Canal and the demobilization of its armed forces. The United States promised that the completion of the disengagement agreement would take precedence over new steps at Geneva; that UN troops would not be withdrawn without the consent of both sides; that the United States regarded Bab al-Mandab as an international waterway; and that the United States would try to be responsive to Israel's defense needs on a continuing and long-term basis.

In letters exchanged with both Sadat and Meir, Nixon detailed the force limitations agreed upon. In the limited zones there would be no more than eight reinforced battalions with thirty tanks; no artillery above 122 mm would be allowed, and only six batteries of these weapons were permitted.[41] No weapons capable of interfering with reconnaissance flights over one's own zone were permitted; a maximum troop strength of seven thousand in the limited zone was set; and up to a distance of thirty kilometers from the Egyptian and Israeli lines, no weapons capable of reaching the other side would be allowed, nor would any surface-to-air missiles. Arrangements were specified whereby the United States would perform reconnaissance flights at regular intervals to monitor the agreement, and the results were to be made available to both sides.[42] Finally, a timetable for implementing the agreement was made part of the public text, and Sadat received a special guarantee from Nixon that the United States would use its influence to bring about the full implementation of Resolution 242.

With the signing of the disengagement agreement on January 18, Nixon and Kissinger had entered into important and unprecedented commitments for the United States. American prestige in the Arab world was on the rise, and more than ever the United States seemed to hold the key cards. The Israelis might complain of excessive pressure, but the agreement was not bad for Israel and U.S. aid was still flowing in large quantities. A mood of optimism, a rare occurrence, could be sensed in much of the Middle East.

INTERLUDE BETWEEN DISENGAGEMENTS

Kissinger's next task was to preserve this mood by translating it into new agreements that would help develop momentum toward a settlement. To do so, he set off immediately from Aswan for talks with King Hussein and President Asad. Meanwhile President Sadat, as promised, flew to Saudi Arabia to try to persuade King Faisal to take the lead in lifting the oil embargo against the United States, an act that Kissinger had termed "increasingly less appropriate" earlier in the month.[43]

Agreement on the Egyptian-Israeli front did little to dampen expectations or ease tensions elsewhere in the Middle East. Now Syria, Jordan, and perhaps even the PLO were ready to get in on the act. Israel, however, was hardly anxious to face a new set of negotiations, fearing that once more American pressure would be brought to bear to extract territorial concessions as the price of keeping diplomacy alive. Much as improved U.S.-Arab relations might be desirable in the abstract, Prime Minister Meir feared they would be purchased in Israeli coin. Timing of a second step was therefore bound to be a problem. Kissinger decided to use the unavoidable interval to consolidate the gains of the first round and to lay the basis for a next step between Syria and Israel.

Before returning to Washington after the signing of the Egyptian-Israeli disengagement agreement, Kissinger flew to Jordan for talks with Hussein. This was basically a holding action, since no movement on the Jordanian front was likely until after Syrian-Israeli disengagement. Kissinger told the king that Israel opposed the idea of territorial withdrawal from the Jordan River, preferring to allow Hussein to assume gradual administrative responsibility on the West Bank without immediate Israeli withdrawal. Kissinger posed the issue as one of reinstating the king's authority on the West Bank. Israel would deal either with Jordan now or with Arafat later. Despite Kissinger's efforts to convince Hussein of the merits of "administrative disengagement," the king insisted on recovering some territory, delineated clearly on a large map given to the American party before its departure. The Jordanian plan would have Israel withdraw to a line parallel to the Jordan River at a distance of approximately eight to ten kilometers.[44] Given the Israeli insistence on keeping control of the Jordan Valley, this plan seemed like a nonstarter, but at least an exchange of positions had begun. At this point Kissinger was not thinking so much of an early agreement as he was trying to devise a strategy for keeping the more radical PLO out of the picture for a bit longer. He would have problems enough in dealing with Asad, as he discovered the next day in Damascus.

In talks with President Asad on January 20, Kissinger managed to obtain a new Syrian disengagement proposal. In December Asad had spoken of Israeli withdrawal from all of the Golan Heights as part of a disengagement agreement. Now Syria was holding out for half of the territory conquered by Israel in 1967, as well as all of that gained in 1973, in a disengagement agreement. Asad also clung tenaciously to his one bargaining card—the Israeli prisoners. Kissinger left Damascus with the feeling that Asad did want an agreement and with a map showing two straight lines running north-south through the Golan Heights. These, presumably, would be the disengagement lines under the Syrian proposal.[45] Later that day Kissinger flew to Israel to brief the Israeli leadership on Asad's thinking, and then returned to Washington to explain the details of the Egyptian-Israeli agreement to a generally supportive Congress and public.

Kissinger next began to try to end the oil embargo, while simultaneously laying the groundwork for a Syrian-Israeli agreement. Nixon was anxious to be able to announce the end of the embargo in his State of the Union message to Congress at the end of the month, and the Egyptians and Saudis were bombarded with messages to that effect.[46] Kissinger also began to try out an idea he had tentatively discussed during his recent trip to Syria and Israel. If Syria would give the United States a list of Israeli POWs, Israel would agree to make a concrete proposal on disengagement. This vague procedure was conveyed to Sadat for his information and approval. Several days later, on February 3, King Faisal, who had just conferred with President Asad in Saudi Arabia, informed President Nixon that the oil embargo could not be lifted until a disengagement agreement had been reached on the Syrian-Israeli front. Nixon replied on February 6, saying that unless the embargo was lifted, the United States would not be able to continue its diplomatic efforts.

Nonetheless, the United States did propose a five-point plan to Asad on February 5. Syria would tell the United States the number of Israeli POWs, and the information would then be conveyed to Israel. Syria would give a list of POWs to the United States Interests Section in Damascus, and in exchange for the list Israel would make a concrete proposal. After Red Cross visits with the Israeli prisoners in Syria, Kissinger would transmit the Israeli proposal to Asad and would invite an Israeli delegation to Washington for further talks. Negotiations would then begin at Geneva in the context of the already existing Egyptian-Israeli military working group. On February 9 Asad accepted this procedure.

The following week Presidents Asad, Sadat, and Boumedienne, and King Faisal, met in Algiers for two days. They agreed not to lift the embargo until further progress toward Syrian-Israeli agreement had been made, and Foreign Ministers Fahmy and Saqqaf were sent to Washington to inform Kissinger. Nixon and Kissinger were angry but realized they could not go through with their threat to withdraw from the diplomacy. That would clearly link American policy to the oil embargo, and Kissinger was anxious to convince Asad and the American public that U.S. action in the Middle East was not primarily a function of oil interests. If the United States had reasons of its own to want peace in the Middle East, it would continue its efforts despite the embargo. On February 18 Nixon and Kissinger decided to drop the issue of the embargo for the time being. The next day Nixon announced that Kissinger would make another visit to the area, and on February 25 Kissinger departed on his fourth trip in as many months.

SHUTTLE DIPLOMACY

Kissinger met with Asad for four hours on the night of February 26 and again on the following morning. The discussions were complex but basically friendly, Asad showing flexibility on procedural issues and toughness on substance. As previously agreed, Kissinger was authorized to transmit to the Israelis the list of POWs, which he had actually been given before he left Washington.[47] Red Cross visits would begin, and Israel would be expected to make a concrete proposal on disengagement. Asad made it clear that if Israel offered nothing more than a pullback to the post-1967 cease-fire lines, he would break off the talks. Kissinger was inclined to think he was serious and so told the Israelis during his stop on February 27. He then left the Israelis to develop their proposal over the next twenty-four hours before his return visit.

Meanwhile Kissinger flew to Egypt for talks with Sadat. U.S.-Egyptian ties were developing well and rapidly, and full diplomatic relations were restored on February 28. Sadat extended an invitation to Nixon to visit Egypt. Bilateral issues, including aid and the long-term prospects for U.S. arms sales to Egypt, financed by Saudi Arabia, were also discussed. By that time Kissinger was relying heavily on Sadat's advice on how to deal with other Arab leaders. The Libyans wanted to purchase American radar. What was Sadat's opinion? Asad was insisting on Israeli withdrawal beyond the 1967 cease-fire lines. What were Sadat's views? When would the oil embargo be lifted? How could Soviet influence in Iraq be weakened? Kissinger and Sadat began to develop what amounted to a joint strategy in the Middle East.

As for the specific problem of disengagement on the Syrian front, Sadat argued for a line just west of the town of Quneitra. He offered to send his chief of staff to Syria before Kissinger's next visit, to press for an agreement based on such a line. If Asad refused, Sadat would nonetheless support it publicly and would continue to try to build Arab backing for a moderate disengagement agreement between Syria and Israel. Kissinger was pleased with his talks with Sadat and began to count heavily on Egypt's leadership in the Arab world. Having once erred by underestimating Sadat and Egypt, Kissinger now seemed on the verge of making the opposite mistake.

From Egypt Kissinger flew to Israel, where he received the Israeli proposal. Basically the Israeli plan was for disengagement to be modeled on the Egyptian-Israeli agreement of January, with three zones—one Israeli, one UN, and one Syrian—all within the territory captured by Israel in October 1973. Not only would Quneitra remain entirely under Israeli control, but also Israeli forces would remain well beyond the October 6 lines.

Kissinger feared that Asad would reject the proposal and that the talks would end then and there. Therefore, when in Damascus on the evening of March 1, Kissinger did not give Asad the details of the Israeli plan. Instead he concentrated on the concept of limited-force zones and a UN buffer. He also pinned down Syrian agreement to send a representative to Washington for talks later in the month, following a similar visit by an Israeli official. Kissinger left Damascus with little in the way of substantive progress, but did reach agreement on a further exchange of views over the next several weeks. Asad, not to be outdone by the more effusive Sadat, had embraced the secretary in Arab fashion for the first time. An improbable but genuine personal relationship was beginning to develop between these two very different men.

Kissinger's next stop was Saudi Arabia, his goal there being to urge again the removal of the oil embargo and to solicit support for a Syrian-Israeli disengagement. The secretary also discussed with the Saudis ways of strengthening bilateral economic and security relations. The idea of creating several joint commissions was put forward and eventually was implemented, symbolizing in a tangible way Kissinger's desire to use American technology and arms as complementary to his diplomatic efforts, with the aim of building a strong U.S. presence in key Arab countries.

On March 2 and 3 Kissinger met with King Hussein for lengthy strategy talks. Hussein was growing impatient. The Arab leaders who had met in Algiers in February had agreed on the need to create a Palestinian state headed by PLO leader Yasir Arafat. Pressures were building for the creation of a Palestinian government-in-exile. Hussein asked whether the United States would recognize such a government. Kissinger denied any such intention. The king went on to stress his need for a good agreement with Israel to justify his participation in future negotiations. Ultimately, he said, he would have to obtain all the West Bank of the Jordan and Arab Jerusalem. Anything less would expose him to charges of being a traitor. If Israel was not prepared to go that far, then perhaps Jordan should step aside and let the PLO try to negotiate a better deal than he was able to get. It would, of course, fail, which might bring the Israelis and Palestinians back to reason and open new possibilities for Jordan.

Kissinger urged the king to give the Israelis another chance to come up with a more meaningful proposal than "administrative disengagement." Meanwhile both Jordan and the United States should work to forestall the creation of a Palestinian government-in-exile. Hussein would be visiting Washington shortly; hence further talks would take place soon. Meanwhile Kissinger would contact Sadat on the Palestinian issue, and Jordan should try to learn whether Israel was prepared to make a serious offer. If not, Jordan should threaten to pull out of the negotiations.

As Kissinger flew back to Washington on March 4, the Egyptian-Israeli disengagement agreement was completed, with all parties in their new positions. Simultaneously, tensions increased on the Syrian front as Asad began to raise the danger of renewed hostilities. In the course of the next two months, negotiations on Syrian-Israeli disengagement were to be accompanied by heavy shelling and many casualties on the Syrian front. Asad was clearly going to be more difficult to deal with than Sadat had been, nor were the Israelis in a particularly conciliatory frame of mind.

Upon his return to Washington Kissinger consulted with Nixon on the results of his trip. By that time the president was deeply preoccupied with his Watergate defense. His closest aides had been indicted by a grand jury on March 1 for perjury, obstruction of justice, and illegal payments to suppress evidence. Tapes had come to light that seemed to suggest that Nixon himself had been involved in the payment of hush money to one of the Watergate burglars. Demands for the full transcripts of the tapes of presidential conversations were being made. With all these worries Nixon turned to foreign policy as a form of release and escape, but only to deal with the large issues. Details were still left to Kissinger.

One question requiring presidential decision concerned the terms on which Israel would receive the $2.2 billion in emergency assistance to cover the purchase of military equipment. Nixon was not averse to pressuring Israel; he was unhappy with the recent Israeli proposal on disengagement. He and Kissinger therefore agreed that for the moment all $2.2 billion would be extended as credit. The president would have the option until July 1 of waiving repayment of as much as $1.5 billion. If Israel was forthcoming, it could expect favorable presidential action. Meanwhile an aid package was being put together for fiscal year 1975 which would, for the first time in years, contain a substantial sum, $250 million, for Egypt, and an unprecedented $207.5 million for Jordan.[48] Only $350 million would be requested for Israel, in the knowledge that Congress would increase that sum significantly in any event. Aid was clearly going to be an important adjunct of the Nixon-Kissinger diplomacy.

Kissinger recognized that it would be difficult to reach an agreement between Israel and Syria on disengagement. The United States alone might be able to persuade Israel to make the necessary concessions, using a combination of pressure and positive inducements, but how could Syria be brought to a more workable position? Could Sadat and other Arab leaders play a role? What about the Soviets, who seemed so anxious to be involved in the negotiations? Would Asad be influenced by the offer of American aid? Kissinger needed time to explore each of these possibilities and to let each of the parties reconsider its opening stance on disengagement.

The first order of business was to end the oil embargo. Nixon referred to this again in a press conference on March 6. The Arab oil producers would soon be meeting in Tripoli. If the embargo was not then lifted, the American diplomatic effort would be undermined. After some delays most Arab oil producers announced on March 18 that the embargo against the United States was ended, at least provisionally. Privately, Faisal stressed the importance of achieving a Syrian-Israeli disengagement agreement within two months to avoid the reimposition of the embargo. Already Arab oil production was inching back up to pre-war levels, after a reduction of some 15 percent in December and January. OPEC had imposed a new price of about $10 per barrel, a quadrupling of pre-war levels, but further increases were no longer likely once production returned to normal levels.

Syria had opposed the lifting of the embargo. Kissinger was now anxious to bring inter-Arab pressure to bear on Asad to accept a disengagement agreement. Egypt, Saudi Arabia, and Algeria could all play a role. If Syria refused a reasonable offer, Kissinger wanted to make sure that Asad would be isolated rather than supported by a bloc of rejectionists. Only Iraq might be able to strengthen Asad's resolve to resist making concessions. Iraqi forces could help reinforce the Syrian front, as they had done in October. If fighting resumed, Asad might be obliged to turn to Iraq and the Soviets for more military help. But Iraq was becoming preoccupied with its border with Iran, where serious clashes had occurred in February, and with the Kurds, who had entered into armed opposition to the Baghdad regime in late February. Egypt, Israel, Iran, and the United States all played a part in orchestrating this operation to ensure that Iraq would not be able to go to Syria's help.

Kissinger now needed a reasonable Israeli offer to lure Asad toward an agreement. On March 15 and 19 Kissinger met with Foreign Minister Eban. He explained his strategy of trying to isolate Syria from the radical Arabs and stressed the need for continued movement in the diplomatic arena. Israel would have to pull back to the October 6 lines, if not farther, and would have to give up Quneitra. Israel should not, however, be expected to abandon any settlements on the Golan Heights at this stage. Dayan should bring an Israeli proposal based on this thinking when he visited Washington later in the month.

On March 24 Kissinger set off for the Soviet Union, where, among other things, he would try to keep the Soviets from obstructing his efforts at disengagement on the Syrian-Israeli front. During a three and one-half hour meeting on March 26, described as the "toughest and most unpleasant" he had ever had with Brezhnev and his top aides, Kissinger resisted Soviet pressure to return the negotiations to Geneva. General Secretary Brezhnev hotly accused Kissinger of violating agreements that the talks would be held under joint U.S.-USSR auspices, and referred to assurances given to Foreign Minister Gromyko in February that the negotiations would be conducted at Geneva. Kissinger defended his actions as being taken at the request of the regional parties. In any case, they were only paving the way for talks on a final settlement that would be held at Geneva.

Brezhnev referred to the good relations existing between Iraq and the Soviet Union, and also mentioned Asad's forthcoming visit to Moscow, observing that he would surely ask for more arms. Kissinger replied that he was sure Asad would ask the Soviet Union for arms, because he had just made such a request of the United States. Brezhnev noted that he was withholding arms from Egypt, and then returned to the discussion of Syria, asking Kissinger why the United States did not give Asad arms. Kissinger replied with a straight face that he did not want to fuel the arms race! Obviously irritated at the growing American involvement in the Arab world, Brezhnev accurately accused Kissinger of trying to keep the Soviet Union out of the substance of the negotiations. He argued that Syria wanted the Soviets to be present.

Kissinger quickly checked with Asad on whether he did in fact want the Soviets involved at this stage. Asad obliquely replied that the agreed procedure was for Dayan to go to Washington, followed by a Syrian representative. Then Kissinger would return to the Middle East, after which a military working group could conclude the details of an agreement in Geneva with the Soviets present.

Shortly after his return from Moscow, the secretary of state met with Dayan in Washington on March 29.[49] Dayan brought a large arms request—for 1,000 tanks, 4,000 armored personnel carriers, and much more—as well as an Israeli proposal for a disengagement line that would run east of the October 6 line. Israeli forces would emphatically remain in Quneitra. Kissinger was irritated by the Israeli proposal, whose only value, in his view, was the concept of a buffer zone flanked by two limited-force zones to the east and west. Kissinger warned the Israelis that Asad would not accept the line and termed their proposal inadequate, but he repeated that Israel should not give up any settlements at this stage. Against the background of intensified fighting on the Syrian-Israeli front, Brigadier General Hikmat Shihabi of Syria flew to Washington for talks with Kissinger on April 13. Shihabi brought with him a revised map showing a disengagement line running west of Quneitra. Though far from being Dayan's proposal, it was an improvement over the Syrian position of January. Kissinger showed Shihabi the line proposed by Dayan, terming it unacceptable but emphasizing the desirability of the three-zone concept. The secretary implied that he would try to persuade the Israelis to go back to the October 6 line and to leave Quneitra, but that would be the most that Syria could hope for at this stage. Two days later Kissinger passed the Syrian map to Israeli Ambassador Dinitz.

While Kissinger was trying to induce Israel and Syria to modify their respective proposals, Sadat spent the month of April in a strident press campaign against the Soviet Union. He publicly mentioned that he had nearly canceled the treaty between the two countries. On April 18 he declared his intention of ending his exclusive dependency on the Soviets for arms and said he would seek arms in the West, including the United States. His foreign minister, Ismail Fahmy, was at that moment talking to Nixon and Kissinger in Washington, presumably on the same topic. Surprisingly, a long-time ardent supporter of Israel, columnist Joseph Alsop, responded to Sadat's bid by calling on April 26 for an American policy of becoming the main arms supplier of Egypt. Such a policy would confirm the "complete reversal of alliances that President Sadat has been publicly talking about" and would constitute "the most dazzling feat of diplomacy in the 20th century."[50]

This tone in Sadat's speeches and in Alsop's column could scarcely be expected to put the Soviets in a conciliatory mood. Kissinger did, however, meet with Gromyko several times during April and seemed to succeed in at least neutralizing Soviet opposition to his diplomatic efforts with Syria and Israel. Having achieved enough during March and April to justify another round of shuttle diplomacy, Kissinger departed for the Middle East on April 28. Little did he realize at the time how long and difficult the negotiations would be.

SYRIAN-ISRAELI DISENGAGEMENT

It was clear to Kissinger and his colleagues that a disengagement agreement between Syria and Israel would be much more difficult to attain than the one between Egypt and Israel. In the latter case, both sides wanted an agreement and had come close to an accord on basic issues before Kissinger began his shuttle. In the Syrian-Israeli case, the positions of the two parties were far apart, the incentives for an agreement were lacking, and the objective situation on the ground lent itself less well to an agreement than did the situation in Sinai. Moreover, both Syria and Israel were governed by somewhat shaky coalitions. Neither could afford to appear soft in the negotiations.

If the local parties had less interest in an agreement, the United States had more of a stake than before. Among other things, it must protect the

Egyptian-Israeli agreement, and beyond that, the flourishing U.S.-
Egyptian relationship. If Syria refused to reach a comparable disengagement agreement, Sadat's position would be threatened in the Arab
world, and a radical, rejectionist bloc might gain influence. War might
resume on the Syrian front, and Egypt might well be pulled in. Apart
from the intrinsic danger of another war, that situation would provide
the Soviet Union with new opportunities for reasserting its presence in
the region. Finally, without an agreement there might be another
troublesome oil embargo.

Kissinger realized he would have great problems with the Syrians and
the Israelis. To deal with the former, he counted on building strong Arab
support for his efforts. With the Israelis, he would, as usual, have to
combine carrot and stick. Before Kissinger's departure for the Middle
East, Nixon had waived repayment on $1 billion of the $2.2 billion in
aid to cover arms purchases. In normal times that might have won
Kissinger a cordial reception in Israel, but these were not normal times.
Besides, the United States had just voted in the UN to condemn Israel
for a retaliatory raid in southern Lebanon. Whatever credit Kissinger
may once have had with the Israelis was rapidly being dissipated. Nixon's
authority would have to be invoked when the going got rough, but that
authority was itself in question. The day after Kissinger's departure
Nixon released edited texts of a large number of taped conversations
concerning Watergate. They did not make for edifying reading. Slowly
but surely the judicial process seemed to be leading to Richard Nixon's
impeachment. For this very reason Nixon seemed extremely anxious for
Kissinger to succeed in his mission. During the ensuing weeks a severely
weakened president repeatedly threw his weight behind his secretary of
state, in what proved to be some of the bluntest exchanges with the
Israeli leadership ever to take place.

Kissinger's itinerary took him first to Geneva, for talks with Gromyko,
and then to Algeria and Egypt. Boumedienne and Sadat were key Arab
leaders, whose support Kissinger sought. The Algerians had close relations
with the Syrians and had good credentials as revolutionaries.[51] No one
would accuse them of being stooges of the Americans. In Alexandria, the
next day, Kissinger received Sadat's blessings and a prediction that "my
friend, Dr. Henry" would succeed in his mission. With that, Kissinger
braced himself for the arduous business of talking with the Israelis and
Syrians.

Kissinger felt that Israel would have to make concessions on the line of disengagement and that the Syrians, who rejected any force limitations other than a narrow buffer zone, would have to back down as well. First he would try to win consensus on an acceptable line. Then, it might be hoped, the other elements of agreement would begin to fall into place.

His talks in Israel on May 2 did nothing to make Kissinger optimistic. The Israelis were angry at the United States for its UN vote and were obdurate about any alteration of the position Dayan had presented in late March. Why should Asad be rewarded for having gone to war against Israel and lost? Why now should he get a better offer than the more reasonable Sadat? Was it good for U.S. interests to appease the most militant of the Arabs? What would the world think if Israel and the United States submitted to such blackmail? And so the arguments went, until in despair Kissinger turned to Nixon for help. A letter from Nixon to Meir on May 4 warned her not to allow Israeli actions to jeopardize the favorable trends in the area. Otherwise the United States, out of friendship for Israel and a sense of responsibility, would have to reexamine the relationship between the two countries.

In Damascus the next day, Kissinger avoided precise discussion of the Israeli line of disengagement. Instead he emphasized to Asad the weakness of Prime Minister Meir's domestic position and the linkages between Israeli domestic politics and its foreign policy. He raised the issue of U.S. aid to help Syria with reconstruction. Asad remained adamant that the disengagement line would have to be west of the October 6 line but seemed to show flexibility on other issues, such as force limitations. The following day, however, he repeated to Kissinger his "nonapproval" of the idea of limited-force zones. Kissinger, for his part, then tried to encourage Egyptian, Algerian, and Saudi pressure on Asad to moderate his views.[52]

In the course of the next several days, Israel began to modify its proposal on the disengagement line.[53] Part of Quneitra would now be returned to Syria, but the western part of the city must remain under Israeli control. Kissinger told the Israelis that Asad would not accept such an arrangement. On May 7 Kissinger flew to Cyprus to brief Gromyko on the talks and found that the Soviets were prepared to remain neutral.[54]

Despite some progress in Israel on May 6 and 7, Kissinger was not optimistic. In Damascus on May 8 he disclosed some of Israel's concessions to Asad, but he withheld others so that he would have something to show on later trips. The tactic was risky, but Kissinger felt he had to avoid whetting Asad's already substantial appetite for Israeli concessions, while at the same time being able to show continued progress.[55] In any event, on May 8 Asad began to talk seriously about a line in the vicinity of that proposed by Israel.[56] Quneitra and the three surrounding hills now loomed as the main obstacle.

Kissinger continued to seek Egyptian, Algerian, and Saudi help. He kept the leaders well informed on the negotiations and asked for their support. At the same time he tried to persuade the Israelis to make more concessions, but to little avail. On May 9 he reported to President Nixon that he was organizing forces for what he expected to be his "climactic meeting" with President Asad on May 11.

Instead of the hoped-for breakthrough, Kissinger encountered a stalemate. Asad insisted on all of Quneitra as well as the three surrounding hills. Israel would simply not yield on the hills, the "Himalayas of General Gur," as Kissinger termed them. On May 13, however, he did get Israeli agreement to a Syrian civilian presence in all of Quneitra, along with two other minor concessions.[57] He decided on one last trip to Damascus on May 14; then he would return to Washington. In Damascus he found that Asad was not satisfied with the last Israeli proposal, insisting that the line must lie along the peak of the hills and that UN troops, not Israelis, must occupy the peaks. By now the bargaining concerned a few hundred meters, but neither side seemed prepared to yield.[58]

At this point President Nixon weighed in with Kissinger, urging him to continue to work for an agreement and promising him his full support. If Israel was intransigent, Nixon was prepared to go very far if necessary. On May 14 he asked for a list of all military and economic aid promised to Israel, as well as the total of tax-free private contributions to Israel.[59] He also asked for ideas on aid to Syria as a possible incentive.

This was what the Israelis had long feared—pressure on them and offers of aid to the Arabs. In this instance, however, Nixon did not cut aid to Israel. Instead the negotiations inched forward, as Kissinger shuttled back and forth. Encouraged by some members of the Israeli cabinet, Kissinger decided on May 15 to begin to introduce his own ideas in talks with Asad and the Israelis. As he had done in January once the gap had been narrowed, he would try to find a compromise that left each side's basic interests intact. Perhaps the Syrians would find his ideas easier to accept than Israel's.

On May 16 Kissinger succeeded in inducing the Israelis to pull back to the base of the hills. He immediately flew to Damascus to try out ideas of his own.[60] The next day he reported to Nixon that he was close to an agreement on a disengagement line. In Damascus on May 18, however, it seemed as if the remaining gap could not be bridged. Kissinger decided to leave, began drafting a departure statement, and had his luggage sent to the plane. At the last moment Asad dropped his insistence on controlling the hills west of Quneitra and urged Kissinger to keep trying for an agreement. Israel could keep the hills if Kissinger would guarantee that no heavy weapons capable of firing into Quneitra would be placed there. On May 19 Kissinger was able to obtain Israel's assent to Asad's request, and on May 20 he returned to Damascus with a map of the agreed line.

With agreement on the line of disengagement virtually assured, the problem arose of force limitations and the size of the restricted armaments zones.[61] In addition, Asad wanted Israel to give up all the positions on Mt. Hermon. Syria also wanted only a small UN force in the buffer zone, whereas Israel preferred at least 2,000 to 3,000 UN troops. After two more days of haggling over these issues, on May 22 Kissinger began to lose heart. Once again he drafted a departure statement and planned to leave the next day. Egypt, however, had sent General Gamasy to Syria, and by the time of Kissinger's next visit to Damascus, on May 23, Asad had changed his position to accept a large UN force and a wider buffer zone of ten kilometers and limited-force zones of fifteen kilometers. He was still insisting, nevertheless, on fairly sizable armaments in the limited zones, while accepting the concept developed on the Egyptian front of keeping surface-to-air missiles and heavy artillery out of range of the other side's lines. Kissinger returned on May 24 to Israel, where he faced demands that Asad commit himself to preventing terrorist attacks from his side of the lines. Israel also asked for a U.S. commitment that the UN force would not be withdrawn without the consent of both parties to the agreement. Israel also wanted reassurances on long-term military supplies. From this point on, Prime Minister Meir and Defense Minister Dayan were extremely helpful and flexible in working out the final details of an agreement.

On May 26 the drafting of the final documents began. To Kissinger's consternation, issues that he thought had been settled were now reopened by Asad. Once more it seemed as if the talks would collapse.[62] On May 27 Asad backed down and after ten hours of talks, Kissinger agreed to make one more trip to Israel to work out compromises on several more points. Then, on May 28, in four hours of private conversation, Asad gave Kissinger his oral commitment that he would not allow the Syrian side of the disengagement line to become a source of terrorist attacks against Israel. With that concession in hand, Kissinger flew to Israel, and on May 29 the announcement was made that Syria and Israel had reached agreement on the terms of a disengagement agreement. Two days later Syrian and Israeli military representatives signed the necessary documents in Geneva.[63]

The agreement consisted of a public document, a map, a protocol on the status of the UN forces, and several secret letters between the United States and the two parties detailing the understandings on force levels and other issues.[64] The force-limitation agreement specified a UN buffer zone paralleling the post-1967 line and including the city of Quneitra. In zones of ten kilometers east and west of the buffer zone, each party could station two brigades, with no more than 6,000 men, 75 tanks, and 36 short-range (122 mm) artillery pieces. In adjacent zones of ten kilometers, no artillery with a range of more than twenty kilometers, and no more than 162 artillery pieces, would be allowed. No surface-to-air missiles could be closer than twenty-five kilometers to the front lines. UN Disengagement Observer Forces (UNDOF) would have the right to inspect these zones, and U.S. aircraft would carry out reconnaissance flights as in the January Egyptian-Israeli accord. Agreement was reached on the exchange of prisoners, and both sides declared that disengagement was only a step toward a just and durable peace based on UN Resolution 338.

Nixon wrote to Asad on May 29 to confirm that Israel would observe the cease-fire on the hills around Quneitra, that no Israeli forces or weapons would be stationed on the eastern slopes of the hills, and that no weapons would be placed on the hills that would be capable of firing into Quneitra. Nixon also informed the Israelis that the last paragraph of the public agreement was to be interpreted to mean that guerrilla raids were contrary to the cease-fire and that the United States recognized Israel's right of self-defense in the event of violations. As usual, the Israelis also insisted on a memorandum of understanding dealing with such contingencies as a breakdown in the cease-fire at Syria's initiative and on the pacing of the negotiations. To the Syrians, the United States committed itself to work for the full implementation of UN Resolution 338.

With the signing of the agreement between Syria and Israel, together with all the side agreements conveyed through the United States, Kissinger and Nixon could point to another outstanding achievement in their Middle East diplomacy. By itself, the step was modest, but in light of the recent history of Syrian-Israeli relations it was substantial indeed. The lingering question, of course, was whether it was a step toward a more comprehensive peace agreement, or whether it would prove to be merely a pause before another round of fighting at a later date. Was Kissinger determined to continue his efforts, or, after spending one month of murderously difficult negotiations for limited results, would he conclude that no further progress was possible? Would "step-by-step" remain his preferred tactic, and if so, where would the next step be? All these questions would have to be dealt with in the near future, but first President Nixon wanted to reap the rewards of Kissinger's efforts by staging a whirlwind tour of the Middle East. The adulation of the Egyptian crowds might take his mind off Watergate.

NIXON TO THE MIDDLE EAST

President Nixon's trip to the Middle East was an odd affair.[65] Inevitably he was accompanied by an enormous retinue of aides, security men, and journalists. Every detail of the visit had been worked out by advance men. The local governments were nearly overwhelmed by the onslaught of American technicians, public-relations experts, TV crews, and assorted hangers-on.

Nixon himself was not in good health, his leg being inflamed and sore from a mild attack of phlebitis. Presumably his emotional state was less than serene as well. He reportedly spent his free time listening to the possibly incriminating Watergate tapes. The House Judiciary Committee was holding hearings on whether there was sufficient evidence to warrant his impeachment. Subpoenas for evidence had been issued, Nixon had refused to comply, and the Supreme Court would have to decide the matter.

Even Kissinger was under attack, not for his Middle East efforts, for which he had won overwhelming praise, but for his alleged role in ordering the wiretapping of members of his own staff in 1969. In Salzburg on June 11, the first stop of the presidential party, Kissinger had emotionally denied any wrongdoing and had threatened to resign if his name was not cleared. The one man who could instantly have cleared his name by assuming responsibility for the wiretapping, President Nixon, remained silent.

For the next several days Kissinger seemed to sulk in the background as Nixon received an incredibly enthusiastic reception in Cairo and Alexandria. Sadat went to great lengths to emphasize the new chapter in U.S.-Egyptian relations that he had helped to open. In public the two men were friendly, and the immense crowds almost succeeded in raising Nixon's flagging spirits. After all, it was the first official visit of an American president to Egypt, and Nixon liked firsts. Moreover, he could be proud of the results of his foreign policy. He saw himself as a man working for peace against adversaries at home and abroad, and as someone misunderstood by those who were seeking to bring him down. A touch of the martyr in Nixon showed through as he disobeyed his doctor's orders and needlessly tired himself to remain on display before the cheering Egyptian crowds.

In private Nixon was uncommunicative. Conversations were stilted and marked by frequent pauses.[66] He did, however, make promises of future American assistance. Egypt would be allowed to purchase a nuclear reactor for energy production,[67] and economic aid would continue; Nixon even turned over his personal helicopter to Sadat. In the diplomatic arena Nixon promised he would work for the restoration of the international frontier as Egypt's border in a final settlement, a position that had not been taken since the ill-fated Rogers Plan in 1969. The president also agreed that the Palestinians should be brought into the negotiations at an early date. Sadat suggested that the United States should secretly talk to the PLO leaders, and Nixon seemed receptive, if noncommittal. The talks concluded with the issuance of a joint statement of principles.

Nixon then flew to Saudi Arabia for two days of talks on June 14 and 15. Here the focus was primarily on strengthening bilateral relations and on oil. He next went on to Damascus, for a somewhat restrained reception and cordial talks with President Asad. Full diplomatic relations were restored on June 16. Nixon and Asad also discussed next steps in the peacemaking process. The president said that the Geneva conference should be reconvened in September. Then to an astonished and delighted Asad, he explained that the purpose of step-by-step diplomacy was to persuade the Israelis to pull back gradually on the Syrian front until they reached the edge of the Golan Heights, tumbled over, and returned to the old borders.[68] The imagery was fanciful, but the Syrians took it as a commitment to work for full Israeli withdrawal. As he left Damascus, Nixon drafted a long list of possible aid projects that might be offered to Syria. He feared that Asad might require substantial inducements to remain on good behavior.

The president was more at home on his next stop, Israel, than earlier. His counterpart, however, was no longer the worthy friend and adversary of former crises, Golda Meir, but rather Yitzhak Rabin, the new prime minister of Israel and something of an unknown quantity, despite his years in Washington as ambassador. The Israelis, who had not been informed in advance, were less than pleased with the American offer of nuclear reactors to Egypt, and to soothe them, Nixon made them the same offer. He also talked at some length about the importance of dealing quickly with King Hussein on the fate of the West Bank. Better Hussein now, he observed, than Arafat later.[69] When discussing terrorism with the Israelis, Nixon startled his hosts by leaping from his seat and declaring there was only one way to deal with terrorists. Then, Chicago-gangland style, he fired an imaginary submachine gun at the assembled cabinet members. Strange behavior, strange president. Best friend or dangerous enemy of Israel? It was hard to tell.

Nixon concluded his swing through the Middle East by visiting Jordan.[70] Determined to proceed with talks concerning disengagement on the Jordan-Israel front, Nixon invited Hussein to Washington in late July.

On June 19 the president returned to Washington. Three days later, the Judiciary Committee completed its hearings, which had been watched by a fascinated television audience while Nixon was winging his way through the Middle East. On June 24 the committee issued four more subpoenas to Nixon. The next day he left for Moscow. Affairs of state continued to provide him with some relief from Watergate, and he could be sure that the Soviet leaders would not take seriously the charges against him of obstructing justice and misusing the office.

THE FINAL DAYS

Back in Washington, Nixon agreed on the last day of the fiscal year to waive Israel's repayment of $500 million in credit for arms, a bit more carrot in anticipation of negotiations between Jordan and Israel. Throughout July Nixon and Kissinger kept up the pressure for an agreement.[71] Sadat was prepared to reverse his previous stand and endorse King Hussein as the spokesman for the Palestinians living in the Hashemite Kingdom of Jordan.[72] The Israeli cabinet, which had been toying with a formula providing for Israel to talk with the PLO if the PLO ended acts of terrorism and accepted Israel's existence, quickly reversed itself and went back to the position that Jordan was the spokesman for the

Palestinians.[73] On July 21, however, the cabinet rejected the concept of disengagement along the Jordan River, and in talks with Foreign Minister Yigal Allon the next week Kissinger was unable to persuade the Israelis to change their position.[74]

American involvement in the search for an agreement between Jordan and Israel was temporarily deflected by another Middle East crisis, this one in Cyprus. For several weeks Kissinger and his top aides were engaged in trying to prevent Greece and Turkey, two NATO allies, from going to war. The Arab-Israeli conflict, for the first time in months, was eclipsed by a crisis elsewhere in the world.[75]

But the gravest crisis, in certain respects, was in Washington. On July 24 the Supreme Court unanimously ruled that Nixon must turn over the records of sixty-four subpoenaed tapes. Three days later the House Judiciary Committee began voting the first of three articles of impeachment. Nixon seemed committed to fighting to the last moment to save his presidency and his reputation, but on August 5 the final bit of evidence that alienated even his most ardent supporters was made public. In a taped conversation on June 23, 1972, shortly after the Watergate break-in, Nixon was clearly heard ordering that the CIA be used to prevent the FBI investigation into the case. Two days later the president reluctantly reached the conclusion that he would have to resign, a decision he announced at 9:00 p.m. on August 8. At noon on August 9, Richard Nixon ceased to be president. His successor, Gerald Ford, was sworn into office as the country's first nonelected president. He quickly assured a troubled nation that Secretary of State Henry Kissinger would remain in the cabinet to conduct the foreign policy of the country. It would be some time before Middle East affairs would become the new president's strong suit. And Kissinger himself would have other preoccupations in the weeks ahead. Step-by-step diplomacy seemed to have reached an end, at least for the moment.

CONCLUSIONS

It is impossible to know with certainty whether American policy toward the Middle East after October 1973 would have been substantially different without the deleterious effects of the Watergate scandal. On the whole, the answer seems to be no. The policy that grew out of the October crisis had little to do with Watergate. It was aimed at ending the multiple pressures generated by the war and bringing the United States to a position of influence over the peacemaking process between

Israel and its Arab neighbors. The level of commitment and the amount of energy expended in pursuit of this policy could not have been greater. Nor does it appear as if the pace of diplomacy could have been quickened, or that more substantial agreements might have been reached. After all, the Israelis, Egyptians, and Syrians were operating under severe constraints. Even the modest disengagement agreements strained their political systems almost to the breaking point.

Kissinger has been criticized for specific decisions that he took during the negotiations, such as discouraging the Israelis and Egyptians from reaching agreement at Kilometer 101 in November. He has been accused of exerting too much pressure on Israel, of being less than straightforward in his dealings with the parties, and of being more of a tactician than a strategist. Yet his critics have rarely presented a viable alternative to his gradualist, step-by-step diplomacy, and few would argue that more could have been achieved in the first seven months after the October war.

Serious doubts do arise, however, about whether Kissinger conceived of his diplomacy as a step toward a comprehensive political settlement or whether, pessimist that he often was accused of being, he saw his efforts as aimed at buying time and reducing pressures on the United States and Israel. To the Arabs Kissinger consistently stressed the former goal, while reassuring the Israelis with the latter.

If step-by-step diplomacy as carried out by Kissinger is to be judged on its own merits, it rates high as a tactic but fails to convey any sense of long-term purpose. To gain or lose a few kilometers of Sinai or Golan was surely not worth repeated crises of confidence with Israel and substantial offers of aid to all parties. Kissinger's justification for his efforts was that without the disengagement agreements there would be another war, accompanied by another oil embargo and by a resurgence of Soviet influence in the Arab world. To prevent these upheavals was ample justification for his endless travels and his deep involvement in the disengagement negotiations.

Kissinger knew what he wanted to avoid better than he knew what positive goals he might be able to achieve. The October war was his immediate point of reference. The simple lesson from that crisis was that the status quo in the Middle East was volatile and dangerous, and could disintegrate, with serious consequences for American global and regional interests. Consequently the status quo had to be stabilized through a combination of diplomacy and arms shipments. A political process must begin that would offer the Arabs an alternative to war, but it must be carried on at a pace the Israelis could accept. This was the extent of Nixon's and Kissinger's initial conceptualization. There was no overall American peace plan—that had been tried in 1969 and had failed.

Without a convincing picture, however, of where step-by-step diplomacy was heading, would the parties to the negotiations ever be able to address the core issues of peace, security, and the Palestinians? And would the United States indefinitely be able to remain uncommitted to outcomes? The answer was unmistakably no, and by mid-1974 Nixon found himself making private commitments to Sadat, Asad, Rabin, and Hussein on where American diplomacy was heading.

With strong presidential leadership, step-by-step diplomacy might have turned into a search for a broader settlement, including Jordan and the Palestinians. Instead the United States was involved in an unprecedented crisis of authority, and Nixon's successor was unlikely to convey a clear sense of purpose in foreign policy. Step-by-step diplomacy therefore remained a tactic for buying more time, a tactic cut off from a larger political concept of peace in the Middle East. Unable to move beyond step-by-step diplomacy, yet fearing the loss of momentum if no results were achieved, Kissinger was obliged to continue the search for partial solutions, either on the Jordanian or the Egyptian front, whichever seemed more feasible. The chance for a more ambitious policy was lost when Nixon was forced to resign, and considerable time would have to pass before a strong American initiative in the Middle East would be resumed.[76]

PART THREE

The Ford Presidency

CHAPTER NINE

Beyond Disengagement?
Ford and Kissinger, 1975

Gerald Ford was an unlikely president. He had not sought the office. As a long-time member of the House of Representatives, his political ambition had been to become Speaker of the House—until Richard Nixon selected him as vice-president in October 1973. Less than a year later, in early August 1974, the final act of the Watergate scandal brought Ford to the White House.

There is a strong presumption in American politics that it does matter who occupies the Oval Office. Immense sums are spent on presidential election campaigns. And in no other area is presidential discretion thought to be so great as in foreign policy, or at least so it seemed in the pre-Vietnam, pre-Watergate era.

This president, however, was different from his predecessors. He had not been elected. His initial popularity stemmed from his apparent honesty and openness, not from confidence in his ability or leadership, and even that popularity began to wane after he pardoned Richard Nixon. Foreign policy was obviously not his field of expertise, and it seemed likely that he would defer to his prestigious secretary of state and national security affairs adviser, Henry Kissinger. But could Kissinger be as effective as he had been in the past without a strong president to back his initiatives? Although Kissinger may have harbored misgivings about Nixon, he had admired Nixon's decisiveness and his willingness to take risks. Would Ford have the same attributes?

Little was known of Ford's views on foreign policy generally. As a congressman he had supported a strong defense and had backed Nixon in his Southeast Asian policy. He was known to be a good friend of Israel, but otherwise his ideas on the Middle East were uncertain. It would probably be some time before a distinctive Ford foreign policy would take shape. For the moment, Kissinger would remain in charge.[1]

Kissinger had adopted step-by-step diplomacy as the means to deal with the problems created by the October 1973 war and to establish the United States as the key diplomatic broker between Israel and the Arabs.

Despite some reservations, Egypt, Syria, and Israel had all gone along with Kissinger's approach, and he had even been able to enlist the support, or tacit agreement, of Saudi Arabia, Algeria, and Jordan. By mid-1974 two disengagement agreements stood as testimony to the success of Kissinger's efforts. But the issues between Israel and its Arab neighbors went well beyond the disengagement of military forces, and subsequent diplomatic moves would have to address many more complex political issues than those considered in the first round of step-by-step diplomacy.

Kissinger may well have had his doubts about the wisdom of continuing to seek political agreements on each Arab front separately. But what were the alternatives? A global negotiation at Geneva was sure to fail unless carefully prepared in advance. The Israelis were wary of Geneva, and Kissinger himself was opposed to bringing the Soviet Union back into the peacemaking moves. A U.S.-Soviet imposed settlement would require both a higher degree of superpower agreement than existed and a strong American president. A suspension of U.S. diplomacy was a possibility, but it ran the risk of weakening the "moderate" Arab coalition Kissinger had been trying to encourage.

By a process of elimination Kissinger came back to step-by-step diplomacy, with all of its obvious limitations, as the best means to keep the peace process alive. But where to begin? The answer, never fully thought through, was the Jordan-Israel front. The unstated belief was that it was worth trying to bring Jordan into the diplomacy as a way of undercutting the more radical PLO. Kissinger would also continue to press for a second step between Egypt and Israel.[2]

A JORDANIAN-ISRAELI SETTLEMENT?

Negotiations on the Jordanian-Israeli front presented Kissinger with unprecedented problems. "Disengagement" was hardly an appropriate concept here, since there had been no military engagement between the two countries in the October war. Rather than separate military forces along cease-fire lines, Kissinger would have to deal with sensitive political issues such as sovereignty and the status of the Palestinians. Despite the tacit cooperation that existed on some levels between Jordan and Israel, the prospects for reaching agreement were unusually dim, largely because of domestic Israeli politics and inter-Arab pressures on King Hussein. Israel was now led by an untried and untested leader, Prime Minister Yitzhak Rabin. On foreign-policy matters he was obliged to work closely with his popular defense minister, Shimon Peres, and his foreign minister,

Yigal Allon. Unfortunately for Rabin these two key figures in his cabinet did not often see eye to eye. The only consensus Rabin was able to develop regarding the West Bank was essentially negative: he would call elections before agreeing to anything affecting the former Jordanian territory.

The pressures on Hussein were equally confining, but less focused. His own sense of responsibility, and his understandable fear of being accused of selling out to the Israelis, led him to insist on negotiating terms that he could defend before other Arabs and before the Palestinians. Despite Hussein's own "moderate" inclinations, and his genuine acceptance of Israel's right to exist, he was not in a position to capitulate to Israeli demands. He needed to prove to his people and to the Arab world that he, like Presidents Asad and Sadat, could recover Arab territory held by Israel. Above all, he could not accede to the Israeli position of administering the populated areas of the West Bank while Israel retained military control of the area.

Kissinger recognized the danger that negotiations might fail on the Jordan-Israel front. If they did, the momentum he had hoped to develop through step-by-step diplomacy might be dissipated, precious time might be lost, and Kissinger's own reputation might suffer. An alternative strategy did exist; namely, to concentrate on another quick step on the Egyptian-Israeli front and then to move on to more comprehensive negotiations at Geneva during 1975. Kissinger wavered, but finally opted for a half-hearted attempt at a Jordanian-Israeli agreement.

Within days of becoming president, Ford was conferring with Middle East diplomats and leaders, while Kissinger tried to bring him up to date on the intricacies of the Arab-Israeli negotiations. First to arrive for talks with Ford was Egyptian Foreign Minister Fahmy.[3] A few days later King Hussein met with Ford, Kissinger, and Secretary of Defense James Schlesinger. The king was told that the United States would accord priority to the search for a Jordanian-Israeli agreement, while also exploring possibilities for another step in Sinai. Next Syrian Foreign Minister Abd al-Halim Khaddam arrived to see Kissinger, on August 22. Not to be outdone, Prime Minister Rabin came to Washington on September 10 for discussions with the new president. Rabin made it clear he favored another interim step with Egypt, not one with Jordan.

The upshot of all these preliminary consultations was another Kissinger trip to the Middle East. Israel was still reluctant to pull back from the Jordan River, and Hussein would accept nothing else.[4] The alternative of Israeli withdrawal from the town of Jericho, and perhaps even from the important Nablus area, had been suggested, but neither side was enthusiastic. Kissinger therefore began his travels with little chance of success. In talks with Sadat he tried to press for Egyptian support of Jordan at the forthcoming Arab summit conference in Rabat. That support had slipped somewhat during September, and the dynamics of inter-Arab politics might well produce a ringing endorsement of the PLO, to the exclusion of Jordan, which Kissinger wanted to prevent. As bait he discussed with Sadat the outlines of another agreement between Egypt and Israel. Sadat's position was firm: in a second step he must recover the Mitla and Giddi passes and the oil field at Abu Rudeis. Nothing less would justify the risks for Egypt of entering into a second agreement with Israel.

In Amman Kissinger and Hussein reviewed the bleak prospects for an agreement and discussed the possibility that at Rabat the PLO would be endorsed as the sole negotiator for the West Bank and as the only spokesman for the Palestinians. If that happened, the king would withdraw from the negotiations entirely. Many Jordanians would be delighted to wash their hands of the whole Palestinian problem. It would be far better to concentrate on developing the East Bank and on building ties to Syria and Saudi Arabia than to run the risk of isolation and violent opposition that might result if the king signed an unpopular agreement with Israel. For the time being Hussein and Kissinger agreed to await the outcome of the Arab summit in Rabat. With support from Sadat, Kissinger felt sure that Hussein would emerge with a mandate to negotiate for the West Bank.

To Kissinger's considerable annoyance and dismay, the Arab heads of state who assembled in Rabat during the last week of October did not behave as he anticipated. On October 28 the conference unanimously endorsed the PLO as the sole legitimate representative of the Palestinian people. Hussein had no more right in the eyes of the Arab world to negotiate for the West Bank than any other Arab leader. Faced with such an overwhelming consensus, even Hussein had accepted the final resolution. Sadat had tried to bring about a more ambiguous outcome but had failed. Saudi Arabia, ostensibly a moderate Arab state, and Syria had been among the most vocal champions of the PLO.

The Rabat summit, followed shortly by the appearance of PLO Executive Committee Chairman Yasir Arafat at the United Nations on November 13, suddenly propelled the Palestinians to the front and center of the Arab-Israeli conflict. Kissinger was unprepared for this turn of events. He had hoped to put off the Palestinian issue until later, while trying to strengthen King Hussein at the expense of the PLO. He had expected Egypt, Saudi Arabia, and perhaps even Syria to recognize the practical necessity of keeping Jordan in the negotiations. Now his carefully constructed policy had been derailed. American public opinion, which had strongly supported his efforts until then, began to express skepticism of step-by-step diplomacy, as well as firm opposition to pressure on Israel to deal with the PLO. Some felt that Rabat symbolized the failure of Kissinger's diplomacy, that Egypt and Syria were now preparing to back Arafat in his demands for dismantling the Zionist state, and that the proper response of American policy was to throw all its weight behind Israel, while invoking any sanctions available against the Arabs.[5]

In fact, the Rabat action was much less decisive than it appeared at the time, but it did cause problems for Kissinger. To salvage his policy and his reputation, he needed another success. Because it could not be on the Jordan front, it would have to be in Sinai. Egypt, however, was not the strong leader of the Arab world that it had been under Nasser—the Rabat meeting had shown that to be true—and would have to move carefully in any next step. At the same time Israel was hardly in the mood to make concessions, nor did the new government seem to have any clear diplomatic strategy. Golda Meir may have been tough and difficult to deal with, but at least she was in control of the government. It was less clear that Rabin could guide the divided country through a complex set of negotiations, particularly with his defense minister, Shimon Peres, eager to take his place if he should falter. To reach any agreement would definitely take time. Meanwhile other Middle East issues demanded attention.

OIL PRICES AS AN ISSUE

Issues have a curious way of coming and going in American politics, and that is especially true of complex problems such as the energy crisis. Few people understand the economics and politics of oil and energy, or the nature of the international petroleum market.

The Arab oil embargo was at least a concrete act that could be isolated from other issues and dealt with accordingly. It had a clear beginning and end. Yet the crisis did not seem to go away when the embargo was lifted in March 1974. In fact, it seemed as if the embargo per se had not really had much impact on the U.S. economy. But then what about the price of oil?

Oil prices became a major issue in the latter part of 1974, when the price of Persian Gulf oil reached almost $10 a barrel. At that price the United States would be spending approximately $20 billion a year on petroleum imports. Even if the United States could afford such a drain on its economy, Europe and Japan might not be able to handle the cost. The sheer magnitude of the financial transactions between oil importers and exporters might overwhelm the international financial system.

New terms like *petrodollars* and *recycling* began to appear. The rush to sell goods to Saudi Arabia, Iran, Iraq, and other oil-rich countries was on. Despite pious calls for cooperation among oil consumers and between consumers and producers, the reality was one of fierce competition. How long could that situation go on?

Kissinger began to worry about the international economic repercussions of the high price of oil sometime in the fall of 1974. The continued sluggishness of the Western economies, combined with high rates of inflation and unemployment, were apparently linked to oil prices. American public opinion tended to blame the Arabs for these economic ills, failing to note that other OPEC members, such as Iran and Venezuela, were more militant on prices than Saudi Arabia was. The net effect of this shift in mood was to make it even more difficult for Kissinger and Ford to pursue a diplomatic strategy aimed at promoting an Arab-Israeli settlement. After all, why do favors for the Arabs when they were threatening to bring down the economies of the Western democracies by their irresponsible behavior?

Kissinger made several efforts to try to persuade the Saudis and the Iranians to take the lead in lowering oil prices. At the same time the United States worked out an agreement with the OECD (Organization for Economic Cooperation and Development) countries of Europe and Japan for the sharing of oil in an emergency.[6] In addition, a producer-consumer dialogue was begun. Behind these efforts was the realization that in the event of another war between Israel and the Arabs, another embargo might occur, followed by oil-price increases. No one was quite sure, but it seemed plausible that progress toward a settlement of the Arab-Israeli conflict would remove the incentive for Arab oil producers to manipulate supplies and prices as a means of pressuring the United States.[7] Meanwhile the public concern over oil prices and possible embargoes was weakening the support for Kissinger's diplomacy, and an alternative strategy of counterpressure against the Arabs, including the use of force, began to receive a hearing.[8] A number of rather lurid pictures of impending financial chaos were painted. If OPEC did not collapse, the economies of the industrialized west were bound to do so. Neither, of course, happened, but throughout the next phase of Kissinger's diplomacy, petroleum and its financial ramifications were very much part of public and official preoccupation. Only gradually did the intense concern over the issue wane, as prices stabilized at a high level, adjustments were painfully made, and economic recovery began in the latter part of 1975.[9] By 1976 the issue had all but disappeared as a topic of public debate.

A SECOND EGYPTIAN-ISRAELI STEP

Kissinger's technique for arranging limited agreements between Israel and the Arabs was by now well developed. It began by eliciting proposals from each side, getting preliminary reactions, identifying obstacles, and then starting the diplomatic process that would eventually bridge the substantive gaps. This process would include a heavy dose of reason and persuasion, as Kissinger would explain the dire international consequences of failure to reach an agreement; it also involved marshaling forces that might influence the parties, such as other Arab countries or the U.S. Congress. Then Kissinger would commit his own prestige to bringing about an agreement, shuttling back and forth between the two sides. At this last stage Kissinger was likely to involve the president if additional pressure on Israel or commitments on future aid were needed.

Even before the Rabat meeting, Kissinger had obtained a fairly good idea of the Egyptian and Israeli objectives in a second step. Egypt wanted Israel to withdraw beyond the strategically important Mitla and Giddi passes and to relinquish control over the Abu Rudeis and Ras Sudr oil fields, which were providing Israel with about 50 percent of its total oil needs. Sadat wanted this step to be treated as another military disengagement, with only minimal political overtones. He felt he could not afford to be seen in the Arab world as having withdrawn from the conflict with Israel.

Israel's objectives in a second agreement with Egypt were quite different. Israel hoped to split Egypt from Syria and thus reduce the prospects of a combined Arab offensive such as had occurred in October 1973. To do so would require that Egypt make substantial political concessions as the price of further Israeli withdrawals. Israel would demand that Egypt renounce the state of belligerency, that the new agreement be of long duration, and that Israeli withdrawal would not include the passes or the oil fields.

During November and December 1974 Kissinger was able to clarify each side's position. He was convinced that Sadat would settle for nothing less than Mitla, Giddi, and the oil fields and that he would not formally renounce the state of belligerency. He so informed the Israelis, urging them to concentrate instead on the "functional equivalents" of nonbelligerency, such as the end of the economic boycott.

As Egypt and Israel began to show readiness for a second agreement, two potentially dangerous sources of opposition appeared. The Syrians were well aware that Israel was trying to isolate Egypt, which would then leave Syria alone to confront the militarily superior Israeli forces. Asad was therefore opposed to a second step on the Egyptian front. To underscore his attitude, Asad ordered his armed forces on high alert in mid-November, just on the eve of the renewal of the mandate of the UN forces. The crisis subsided, but not before Asad had made his point.

The second source of opposition to Kissinger's strategy was the Soviet Union. By now the Soviets saw clearly that one of Kissinger's primary goals was to weaken Soviet influence in the Middle East, especially in Egypt. President Ford and General Secretary Brezhnev met in Vladivostok on November 23–24, 1974, primarily to discuss a second strategic-arms agreement but also to consider the Middle East. The two sides remained far apart, the Soviets insisting on reconvening the Geneva conference and Ford favoring a continuation of step-by-step diplomacy, at the request, of course, of Egypt and Israel.[10] On the whole, U.S.-Soviet relations were cooling, as would become clear on January 14, 1975, when the Soviet Union rejected the offer of most-favored-nation trading status on terms that would have required a liberalization of emigration for Soviet Jews.

Meanwhile, despite Syrian and Soviet opposition, Kissinger pressed forward, his task complicated by the curious unfolding of the Israeli negotiating position. On December 3, 1974, in an interview with the newspaper *Haaretz*, Prime Minister Rabin openly stated that Israel's goal was to separate Egypt from Syria and delay negotiations until after the U.S. elections in 1976. Because of the oil crisis, Rabin said, there would be seven years during which Israel would be subjected to heavy pressures for concessions, but by the early 1980s alternatives to petroleum would have been found, thus weakening the power of the Arab world. Rabin added that it was unrealistic to expect Egypt to offer nonbelligerency at this stage of the negotiations.[11]

A few days after the Rabin interview, Foreign Minister Allon arrived in Washington for talks with Kissinger. For several hours on December 9 they discussed a ten-point proposal Allon had brought with him.[12] The points included an end to the state of belligerency, the demilitarization of evacuated territory, an end to economic and propaganda warfare by Egypt against Israel, a duration of twelve years for the agreement, and a number of other demands similar to those written into the January disengagement accord. In return for these demands, Israel would withdraw thirty to fifty kilometers, but would remain in control of the passes and oil fields.

Kissinger and Ford were unimpressed by Israel's offer. Allon hinted that it was only a bargaining position and might be changed. For example, the duration of the agreement could be five years instead of twelve. Kissinger's main problem with the Israeli proposal, however, was the demand for nonbelligerency, which Rabin himself had termed unrealistic, and the refusal to cede on the passes and oil fields. The Israeli points were nonetheless transmitted to Sadat, and Sadat's expected rejection was duly received. Kissinger then asked the Israelis to make a new proposal.

As frequently happens in Arab-Israeli affairs, external events impinge on the local parties in unanticipated ways. In late December an important development took place in Soviet-Egyptian relations. After a short visit to Moscow by Egypt's foreign minister and its chief of staff, it was announced on December 30 that the expected visit by Brezhnev to Cairo had been canceled. Kissinger had been planning to await the results of the Brezhnev visit before pressing ahead with his own strategy. Now it seemed as if Egyptian-Soviet relations were indeed very poor; more than ever, Sadat needed to demonstrate that his turning to the United States had not been foolish. Without Soviet arms he would not easily be able to make war, but with American support he might recover his territory anyway and get on with the urgent task of developing the Egyptian economy.

When Allon arrived in the United States for another round of discussions with Kissinger, he acknowledged that the cancellation of the Brezhnev visit had created a new situation, but during his talks with Ford and Kissinger on January 15–16, 1975, he had nothing new to offer except an invitation to Kissinger to return to the area. Kissinger repeated his warning to Allon that an agreement could not be reached on the basis of the Israeli proposal.[13] He would nonetheless make another trip to see if the gap could be narrowed. After an exploratory round of talks in

February, he would return in March to complete the negotiations, but Israel would have to drop the demand for nonbelligerency and be more forthcoming over territory.

Before Kissinger's departure Sadat publicly endorsed his efforts, adding that the United States now held virtually all the trump cards.[14] These words were precisely what Kissinger wanted to hear from Sadat. From the Syrians and the Soviets, however, he was continuing to encounter resistance to his efforts. As Sadat seemed to move forward toward another agreement, Syria began to band together with Jordan and the Palestinians in opposing him, with growing support from the Soviet Union.[15]

Even though Syria and the Soviet Union were aligning against Sadat, Israel at least seemed to be softening somewhat in its demands. On February 7 Rabin gave an interview to John Lindsay, former mayor of New York, in which he stated that "in exchange for an Egyptian commitment not to go to war, not to depend on threats of use of force, and an effort to reach true peace, the Egyptians could get even the passes and the oil fields."[16] Kissinger was appalled at Rabin's carelessness in revealing Israel's position in such a forum—he would no doubt have preferred to appear responsible for achieving such an Israeli concession—but at least the chance for an agreement now seemed brighter. On this somewhat optimistic note, Kissinger left for the Middle East on February 9.

Kissinger's February trip was admittedly exploratory. He did not expect to reach agreement, but he did hope that Egypt and Israel would each recognize the constraints the other was operating under and modify some elements of their proposals. Instead he found little new. The Israelis seemed to ease up a bit on the issue of nonbelligerency, and Sadat indicated a willingness to end some hostile actions against Israel, but a substantial gap remained. Nor did Kissinger succeed in persuading the Syrians to drop their opposition to a second step in Sinai.[17] The only positive note of the trip came from Kissinger's talks with the shah of Iran in Zurich on February 18, when the shah said he would be prepared to provide Israel with oil if it gave up Abu Rudeis and Ras Sudr.

For the next several weeks Kissinger continued to urge the parties to moderate their positions, for he wanted an agreement, and soon. But he did not want to embark on a third "shuttle" until he was virtually certain of success. Assuming that the parties now understood the minimum terms required for a successful negotiation, Kissinger left for the Middle East once again, arriving in Egypt on March 8.

Kissinger's task was complicated by a number of domestic and international developments. Both he and Ford were experiencing a decline in their popularity. Congress was becoming more assertive in its demands to guide foreign policy. Indochina was progressively coming under communist domination. A leftist coup in Portugal had created a potentially dangerous situation in the western Mediterranean. U.S.-Turkish relations were at a low point because of a congressional ban on arms to Turkey. Only on the Egyptian-Israeli front was there the chance of another Kissinger spectacular. The Israelis seemed apprehensive that Kissinger was a bit too anxious for success. They, after all, would be asked to make the major concessions, and that was more than Rabin's weak government was anxious to do.

Kissinger did succeed in obtaining new Egyptian proposals during the March shuttle. Sadat was prepared to say the following: the conflict with Israel would not be solved by military means; Egypt would not resort to force; it would observe the cease-fire and would prevent all military and paramilitary forces from operating against Israel from Egyptian territory; a new agreement would remain in effect until superseded by another agreement; hostile propaganda against Israel in Egyptian-controlled media would be reduced; and the economic boycott would be selectively eased.[18]

Israel's position, as first conveyed informally by Rabin to Kissinger on the evening of March 9, consisted of seven points entitled "Proposal on Main Elements of Agreement between Israel and Egypt." Israel sought a separate agreement with Egypt that would not depend on agreements with other Arab parties. The agreement must be a step toward peace in some practical aspects, such as the free passage of Israeli cargoes through the Suez Canal, the end of the economic boycott, and the free movement of persons between Egypt and Israel. Egypt must agree to the end of the use of force through a "renunciation of belligerency clearly and in its appropriate legal wording." A real buffer zone must be created between the military forces of both sides. Some solution must be found for the "dilemma of vagueness" about the duration of the agreement. An understanding must be reached on the relationship between an interim agreement in Sinai and what might happen later at Geneva. Finally, Israel would agree to discuss the question of the line of withdrawal only after Egypt had responded to the first six points.[19]

Kissinger was dismayed that Israel was still holding out for nonbelligerency. Sadat was prepared to meet some of Israel's demands but insisted on knowing whether Israel would remain in the passes. He also flatly refused to agree to nonbelligerency, though he would consider a formula based on the "nonuse of force." After several days of shuttling, Kissinger managed to persuade the Israelis to accept the nonuse-of-force formulation, but Rabin and his negotiating team were adamant that Israel would not withdraw from the passes for anything less than nonbelligerency. At best they might consider pulling back to a line halfway through the passes, but at no point in the negotiations did the Israelis provide Kissinger with a map showing a line they would accept. Complicating the bargaining further was Israel's insistence on maintaining control over an electronic intelligence station at Umm Khisheiba at the western end of the Giddi pass. Sadat would not agree to Israel's keeping the station, even if it was formally placed in the UN zone. Consequently the negotiations deadlocked on the issues of nonbelligerency and its functional equivalents, on the extent of Israeli withdrawal in the passes and the oil fields, and on the status of the Umm Khisheiba facility.

After ten days of shuttling between Egypt and Israel, with side trips to Syria, Jordan, and Saudi Arabia, Kissinger was still not able to get the Israelis out of the passes. Israel agreed to cede the oil fields but refused to give Egypt control over a road connecting the fields to the Egyptian zone. On Friday, March 21, Kissinger arrived in Israel with Sadat's final word: Israel could not keep the intelligence station, and the mandate of the UN forces would be renewed only for a second year. Without further Egyptian concessions the Israelis would not budge. Even a tough letter from President Ford, which reached Israel on March 21, was unable to change the situation.[20] It may, in fact, have stiffened Israel's will to resist. In any event, the cabinet met Friday night and rejected virtually all Sadat's demands. Kissinger conveyed Israel's rejection to Egypt and awaited Sadat's reply. Meanwhile he spent the day of March 22 touring the historic site of Masada, where, nearly two thousand years earlier, Jews had taken their own lives rather than surrender to the Romans. The symbolism of Masada hung over the talks later that evening when Kissinger met with Rabin and other top Israeli officials. Kissinger was deeply concerned. According to the notes of his remarks, he stated:

The Arab leaders who banked on the United States will be discredited. . . . Step-by-step has been throttled, first for Jordan, then for Egypt. We're losing control. We'll now see the Arabs working on a united front. There will be more emphasis on the Palestinians, and there will be a linkage between moves in the Sinai and on Golan. The Soviets will step back onto the stage. The United States is losing control over events. . . . Our past strategy was worked out carefully, and now we don't know what to do. There will be pressures to drive a wedge between Israel and the United States, not because we want that but because it will be the dynamics of the situation. Let's not kid ourselves. We've failed. . . .

An agreement would have enabled the United States to remain in control of the diplomatic process. Compared to that, the location of the line eight kilometers one way or the other frankly does not seem very important. And you got all the military elements of nonbelligerency. You got the 'nonuse of force.' . . .

This is a real tragedy. . . . We've attempted to reconcile our support for you with our other interests in the Middle East, so that you wouldn't have to make your decisions all at once. . . . Our strategy was to save you from dealing with all those pressures all at once. . . . If we wanted the 1967 borders, we could do it with all of world opinion and considerable domestic opinion behind us. The strategy was designed to protect you from this. We've avoided drawing up an overall plan for a global settlement. . . . I see pressure building up to force you back to the 1967 borders—compared to that, ten kilometers is trivial. I'm not angry at you, and I'm not asking you to change your position. It's tragic to see people dooming themselves to a course of unbelievable peril.[21]

This was vintage Kissinger. He could have made virtually the same remarks at any point from October 1973 on. The emphasis on U.S. control of the diplomacy, on breaking issues into manageable parts, and on avoiding an overall peace plan were all basic elements of the strategy developed in the midst of the October war. Now that strategy seemed to have failed. The next day Kissinger left Israel, having announced that his negotiating effort was being suspended.[22] After Kissinger returned to Washington on March 24, President Ford ominously announced that there would now be a reassessment of U.S. policy toward the Middle East.[23]

REASSESSMENT

Kissinger's disappointment with the Israelis for thwarting his efforts to arrange a second agreement in Sinai was genuine. He felt the Israeli leadership was shortsighted, incompetent, and weak. In his view Israel had no foreign policy, only a domestic political system that produced deadlock and stalemate. A David Ben-Gurion or a Golda Meir might be able to lead Israel, but not the Rabin-Peres-Allon triumvirate, in which each man pulled in a different direction. In his less guarded moments Kissinger suggested that the Israelis were trying to bring him down. Reassessment, however justified, became in part an instrument for Kissinger to vent his exasperation with Israel.

President Ford, whatever his sentimental attachment to Israel might have been in the past, was also irritated at Israel, and publicly blamed

Rabin for his lack of flexibility.[24] He lent his weight to a serious reassessment of policy during which new military and economic agreements with Israel were suspended. Like each of his predecessors, Ford found that his sympathies for Israel and his perception of American global and regional interests did not always mesh. When the two seemed to come into conflict, Ford was as capable as Nixon of putting pressure on Israel for concessions. The test, however, would be whether pressure could produce the desired results—and whether Israeli counterpressure might not raise the cost of the effort.

Israel, after all, was not without influential friends and supporters in the United States, nor did it lack effective spokespersons who could defend it before the American public against the charge of inflexibility. If the administration insisted on withholding needed aid, Israel could appeal to Congress to support its requests. The Israeli case did seem plausible: in return for making important economic and territorial concessions, Israel was merely asking that Egypt renounce belligerency. Why was that unreasonable or inflexible? Should Israel risk its security for anything less?

Kissinger's case against Israel was less convincing to many Americans. He claimed that the Israeli leaders had misled him into undertaking the shuttle when they knew that nonbelligerency could not be achieved, and yet they continued to insist on it. Israel had refused to make the minimal territorial concessions in the passes and around the oil fields. Kissinger argued that an agreement was necessary to preserve the delicate balances he had brought into being after the October 1973 war. On occasion, he implied that the alternative to an agreement might be war and another Arab oil embargo.

During the nearly three months of reassessment that followed the collapse of the Egyptian-Israeli talks on March 22, American foreign policy witnessed the final denouement of the Southeast Asia conflict and the beginning of a tragic civil war in Lebanon. In both cases the United States seemed powerless to act constructively. The Cambodian capital of Phnom Penh fell to communist forces on April 17. Shortly thereafter, on April 29, Saigon also came under communist control. So much for the peace with honor in Indochina that Nixon and Kissinger had proudly proclaimed in January 1973. Events in the Middle East, too, did not hold out the hope of peace. On March 25 one of the mainstays of American policy in the area, King Faisal of Saudi Arabia, was assassinated. A period of uncertainty began. Was Saudi Arabia on the verge of revolution?

Would the new rulers continue the same foreign policy of friendship for the United States and support for Sadat? It would be some time before anyone would know. Meanwhile the always tense situation in Lebanon was about to explode. On April 13 right-wing Christian gunmen had opened fire on a busload of Palestinians, killing twenty-two of them. Not long afterward a vicious cycle of reprisals and counterreprisals was under way.

Against this disquieting background Kissinger carried out the promised policy reassessment. On April 1 he met with a group of prominent men from the foreign-policy establishment—Dean Rusk, McGeorge Bundy, George Ball, Douglas Dillon, Cyrus Vance, George Shultz, Robert McNamara, David Bruce, Peter Peterson, John McCloy, William Scranton, and Averell Harriman. Some of the group, such as Ball, had been openly critical of Kissinger's step-by-step policy and Israel. Ball favored a more comprehensive agreement in which the United States and the Soviet Union would work out the guidelines for a settlement, which would then be negotiated by all the parties at Geneva. He had criticized Kissinger for ignoring the Soviets and trying to divide the Arabs. He did not shy away from the notion of an imposed settlement.[25] Others at the meeting also favored a return to the Geneva conference and a major effort to work out an American peace plan.

Over the next several weeks Kissinger heard essentially the same recommendations from his closest aides, from eminent academics, and from American ambassadors to the key Middle East countries.[26] The time for step-by-step diplomacy was past. A more ambitious strategy was needed. The Palestinians could no longer be ignored. The Soviets would have to be brought into the negotiations. It all sounded reasonable in the abstract, but Kissinger was haunted by the fear that this approach, too, would fail. No one could detail the steps that would be required to ensure success. And it would be costly in domestic political terms, since it would surely require heavy and sustained pressure on Israel. Ford and Kissinger were not at all certain they wanted to take on that battle unless the results were sure to warrant the effort.

By the third week of April reassessment had produced three basic options for the president. The first, supported by many in and outside the government, was a return to Geneva with a detailed American peace plan. The United States would call for Israeli withdrawal, while offering strong guarantees of Israel's security. The Soviets would be invited to cooperate. A second option would aim for a virtually complete settlement, especially on the Egyptian-Israeli front, but would fall short of calling for full withdrawal and final peace. The third option was to resume step-by-step diplomacy where it had left off in March.[27] Ford referred publicly to these three options in a general way on April 21.[28]

For several weeks it seemed as if a new American approach to peace in the Middle East might emerge, but gradually the realization set in that nothing of the sort could be expected. Kissinger's consultations with Allon, King Hussein, and the Soviets had not given him any reason to be optimistic about a new policy. American public support for a global initiative was not strong, and Congress was beginning to respond to arguments that Kissinger was exerting too much pressure on Israel. On May 21 seventy-six senators sent a letter to President Ford, urging him to be "responsive to Israel's economic and military needs." This was a clear sign that continued pressure on Israel would be politically counterproductive. Ford and Kissinger realized that the only viable strategy, in light of these realities, was to resume step-by-step diplomacy.[29] Ford himself would participate in talks with Sadat and Rabin to explore the prospects for an agreement. Sadat helped to improve the atmosphere by unexpectedly announcing that the Suez Canal would be reopened on June 5 and that the mandate of the United Nations Emergency Force would be extended. The Egyptian president still seemed to want to reach an agreement.

On June 1–2 President Ford and Sadat met for the first time, in Salzburg. The two men got on well together, feeling relaxed in each other's company and finding it easy to talk. Sadat appealed for a public statement from Ford that Israel should withdraw to the 1967 lines, but Ford demurred, reportedly repeating instead Nixon's private commitment of the previous year to work for that goal.[30] Ford then sounded out Sadat on his willingness to try again for a limited agreement in Sinai. Sadat was favorably disposed, but his terms were still those of the previous spring: Israel must leave the passes and the oil fields and must not demand nonbelligerency. Sadat was still opposed to the idea of the Israelis' keeping the intelligence-gathering facility at Umm Khisheiba, but he did say he might accept an American presence there.[31] The idea of an American military contingent in the buffer zone had been raised earlier in the spring, but Kissinger had been unenthusiastic. The more modest concept of an American civilian presence, however, soon began to emerge as the solution to one of the problems in the negotiations.[32]

SINAI II

By the time Prime Minister Rabin reached Washington for talks with President Ford and Secretary Kissinger on June 11–12, the decision to continue with step-by-step diplomacy had basically been made. The alternative of Geneva, of a U.S.-Soviet imposed settlement, or of a withdrawal from the peacemaking effort had all been rejected. Ford and Kissinger felt the situation in the Middle East required continued diplomatic progress; as had been shown early in 1974, that could best be done through U.S. mediation. If progress toward a settlement was not made during the next few months, the United States might not be able to launch a new initiative until 1977. After all, 1976 was an American election year, and Middle East politics could hardly hope to compete for attention with a presidential campaign.

Ford, now very much involved in the conduct of Arab-Israeli diplomacy, asked Rabin to be more forthcoming in the negotiations and pressed for a new Israeli line of withdrawal to the eastern ends of the passes. Rabin was anxious to end the painful and costly confrontation with the United States. His refusal of Kissinger's demands in March had greatly contributed to his prestige within Israel. Now he might be able to negotiate with more confidence. A new line therefore was drawn to demonstrate Israel's good will, and this was seen as a modest step in the right direction. Ford reciprocated by promising that after the next interim agreement between Egypt and Israel, "the overall settlement can be pursued in a systematic and deliberate way and does not require the U.S. to put forward an overall proposal of its own in such circumstances. Should the U.S. desire in the future to put forward proposals of its own, it will make every effort to coordinate with Israel its proposals with a view to refraining from putting forth proposals that Israel would consider unsatisfactory."[33]

Despite these assurances from Ford, Rabin was unable to win cabinet authorization to make further concessions. A week later he was obliged to return to Israel's previous offer of withdrawal halfway through the passes.[34] Once again Ford and Kissinger were angry at Rabin for his apparent inflexibility and his awkwardness.

During the next six weeks Kissinger remained in Washington while Israeli and Egyptian positions were refined and transmitted through him to the other side. Israel's ambassador in Washington, Simcha Dinitz, was his channel to the Israeli government, and the American ambassador to Egypt, Hermann F. Eilts, shuttled back and forth between Cairo and Washington with messages and clarifications.

Sometime in the last half of June the Israeli leaders apparently decided it would be impossible to obtain the desired political concessions from Sadat and undesirable to resist the United States indefinitely. If Egypt would not make peace, then at least Israel could bargain with the United States on issues involving Israeli security. If the Americans wanted an agreement so badly, they could pay for it. Israel would agree to withdraw to the eastern slopes of the passes but would maintain control over the high ground above the passes. At the urging of Defense Minister Peres, Israel also sought to make the buffer zone between the two sides into a genuine barrier to military surprise attack by stationing American civilians there to monitor early-warning stations. The Americans could also serve as a cover for continued Israeli use of the intelligence facility. If Sadat objected, the Americans could offer to build a comparable facility for him as well.

Sadat was also prepared to be somewhat more forthcoming. He would agree to three annual renewals of the mandate of the UN forces and to the continued Israeli use of the intelligence facility, provided he was given one facing the Israeli lines. He accepted the idea of easing the boycott of some companies dealing with Israel and promised to tone down anti-Israeli propaganda. And finally, he would be willing to have most of the terms of the agreement published.

It remained for the United States and Israel to work out their own understanding of the American commitments necessary to gain Israel's consent to a new agreement. Early in July Dinitz met with Kissinger in the Virgin Islands to present the full package of Israeli proposals and requests.[35] In addition to a promise of about $2 billion in aid, the United States agreed to drop the idea of an interim step on the Jordan-Israel front and to accept that only "cosmetic" changes could be expected on the Golan Heights in another step. Israel also wanted a clear commitment that the United States would prevent Soviet military intervention in the Middle East.[36]

During the next several weeks further discussion of these and other points took place.[37] By the time Kissinger left for Israel on August 20, an agreement was within reach. Only the exact location of the Israeli line, the levels of U.S. aid, and the technical aspects of the American civilian presence in the passes remained to be negotiated.

Kissinger was received in Israel with unprecedented hostility, mainly from the right-wing opposition parties, and demonstrators accosted him at each stop. Nevertheless, his discussions with the leadership progressed. This time Rabin wanted an agreement. Kissinger continued to harbor misgivings about the American presence in Sinai, which by now was an essential ingredient of the Israeli package, but he was prepared to go along with the idea. Sadat was willing to accept this condition, but some quibbling still went on over the exact location of the line.[38]

By August 25 Kissinger was working with the Israelis on the language of a draft agreement. Gradually Israel began to soften its position on the line of withdrawal, finally agreeing to give Kissinger a map for Sadat's consideration late in the second week of talks. Squabbling over withdrawal in the Giddi pass continued, as well as over the oil fields. Only at the very last minute did Israel agree to complete withdrawal from Giddi. Very detailed discussions on force limits and on the American presence were also required. Then, in a nonstop session in Jerusalem lasting from 9:30 p.m. August 31 to 6:00 a.m. the following day, the United States and Israel worked out the fine points of their bilateral military relationship, assurances on Israel's supply of oil, and an understanding on the need for consultations in the event of Soviet military intervention in the Middle East. Israel was disappointed with the weak language on Soviet intervention but otherwise could point to a very impressive list of American commitments. Later that afternoon both Egypt and Israel initialed the text of the agreement. It was formally signed in Geneva on September 4, 1975.

Unlike the January 1974 accord, Sinai II was greeted with a sigh of relief, but with little real enthusiasm by the parties to the negotiations. Within both Israel and the Arab world, many were violently opposed to the agreement, although for entirely different reasons.

The agreement itself was modeled in part on the previous disengagement pacts.[39] The two parties committed themselves to resolve the conflict between them by peaceful means and not to resort to the threat or the use of force against each other. The UN force would continue its function, and the lines for each side's military deployments were designated on a map. Egypt agreed to allow nonmilitary cargoes destined for or coming from Israel to pass through the Suez Canal, which had been reopened to traffic the previous June. The agreement would remain in force until superseded by a new agreement.

Attached to the agreement was a detailed annex dealing with military deployments and aerial surveillance. At Sadat's insistence the forces allowed in the limited zone under the agreement were slightly larger than those permitted in January 1974: up to 8,000 men in eight battalions, with 75 tanks and 72 short-range artillery pieces. Neither party, however, was permitted to locate any weapons in areas from which they could reach each other's lines.

The arrangements for U.S. manning and supervision of the early-warning systems in the buffer zones were also spelled out in detail. Israel and Egypt would be allowed to have up to 250 technical and administrative personnel at their respective surveillance stations. U.S. civilians would operate three other smaller watch stations and would establish three unmanned sensor fields as well. Israel's willingness to implement the terms of the agreement was contingent on U.S. congressional approval of the U.S. role in Sinai. The United States also signed five secret agreements, four with Israel and one with Egypt. A sixteen-point U.S.-Israeli memorandum of understanding dealt with military assistance, oil supply, economic aid, and several political points. The United States and Israel agreed that the next step with Egypt should be a final peace agreement. The same should be true on the Jordan front. The United States also agreed to consult promptly with Israel in the event of any threat to Israel from a "world power," namely, the Soviet Union. In an addendum on arms the United States gave a vague commitment to provide a "positive response" to Israeli requests for F-16 aircraft and the Pershing missile with a conventional warhead.[40] In effect, the freeze on new arms agreements, which had begun the previous April, was ended.

A special memo dealing with Geneva was signed, which spelled out the policy of the United States with respect to the Palestinians: no recognition of and no negotiation with the PLO until it recognizes Israel's right to exist and accepts UN Resolutions 242 and 338.[41] The United States would also carefully coordinate its strategy at Geneva with Israel and agree to keep the negotiations on a bilateral basis. In addition, Ford wrote a letter to Rabin stating: "The U.S. has not developed a final position on the borders [between Israel and Syria]. Should it do so it will give great weight to Israel's position that any peace agreement with Syria must be predicated on Israel remaining on the Golan Heights. My view in this regard was stated in our conversation of September 13, 1974."[42]

As for Egypt, the United States merely committed itself to try to bring about further negotiations between Syria and Israel, to provide assistance for the Egyptian early-warning system in the buffer zone, and to consult with Egypt on any Israeli violations of the agreement.

REACTIONS TO SINAI II

In his more optimistic moments Kissinger had justified step-by-step diplomacy as a process by which parties to a negotiation would gain confidence, become committed to achieving results, and be carried along by the momentum of peacemaking to resolve issues that had previously seemed intractable. But Sinai II came closer to confirming his more somber vision of the Arab-Israeli conflict. The issues were so complex, the emotions so deeply involved, that peace between the two sides was unattainable in this generation. Although some agreements might be reached, they would be modest and imperfect at best. The diplomat aspiring to mediate between Israel and the Arabs would have to be content with small achievements. These, at least, were better than nothing. The stabilization of the region, the reduction of the chances of war, and the end of the oil embargo were far preferable to renewed hostilities and superpower confrontation. Egypt, in any case, seemed firmly committed to a moderate course.

Kissinger had not consciously sought to provoke dissension among the Arabs. On the contrary, he was deeply concerned that Saudi Arabia continue to back Sadat's policies. He also recognized that Syria played a vital role in inter-Arab politics, and he genuinely wanted to draw Syria toward a moderate settlement with Israel.[43] The objective situation, however, thwarted his efforts. Golan was not Sinai, and a second step there would be difficult to manage unless Israel was prepared to give up the settlements beyond the post-1967 cease-fire lines. Israel had just demonstrated a remarkable capacity to hold out against American pressures and to exact a high price for eventual compliance. Was it worth the effort for a few kilometers on Golan? Sadat had very much wanted a second agreement, whereas Asad, by contrast, was lukewarm to the idea. He did not entirely reject the concept of a second step, but he made it clear that he was not prepared to pay much of a price for it. Instead Asad began to attack Sadat for having forsaken the struggle against Israel and to press for international recognition of the PLO. Inter-Arab politics had a dynamic of its own that was unleashed by Sinai II. Short of abandoning step-by-step diplomacy, it is not clear what Kissinger could have done to keep Egypt and Syria from drifting apart.

Kissinger's most serious effort to demonstrate his continuing willingness to work for a comprehensive peace agreement came before Syria's renewal of the UN disengagement observation force in late November 1975. On November 10, 1975, the UN General Assembly had passed a resolution defining Zionism as "a form of racism or racial discrimination." The United States had voted against the resolution, and the U.S. ambassador to the UN, Daniel Patrick Moynihan, had stated that "the United States . . . does not acknowledge, it will not abide by, it will never acquiesce in this infamous act." American public reaction had been strongly supportive of Moynihan's tough words. Many expressed their contempt for those nations who had presumably succumbed to Arab oil blackmail. In this atmosphere it was particularly remarkable that on November 12 the deputy assistant secretary of state for Near Eastern affairs, Harold H. Saunders, appeared before a House of Representatives subcommittee to make a policy statement on the Palestinians.

The Saunders document, as it came to be called, infuriated the Israelis and encouraged the Arabs. It spoke of the Palestinian dimension of the Arab-Israeli conflict as being, in many ways, the "heart of that conflict." Saunders went on to state that "the legitimate interests of the Palestinian Arabs must be taken into account in the negotiation of an Arab-Israeli peace." It was a question of how, not whether.[44] Although there was little new in the statement, its timing was significant. It was meant to symbolize a continuing willingness on the part of the administration to work for a peace settlement. Kissinger had gone over the draft carefully, had checked the wording, and had reportedly cleared it with President Ford. When confronted with Israel's hostile reaction, however, he dismissed the Saunders statement as an academic exercise. Nonetheless, the United States seemed to take a somewhat more flexible position than in the past when the issue of PLO participation in the UN debate scheduled for January 1976 came up. Briefly, Arab hopes were raised, but they were to be disappointed. Behind the symbolic shift in American policy there was no real substance.

Public opposition to dealing with the PLO was only one aspect of a broader disenchantment with Kissinger's foreign policy. Détente, once the hallmark of the Nixon-Kissinger policy, was increasingly being attacked, not only by such inveterate cold warriors as Henry Jackson but also by former defense secretary James Schlesinger and by Moynihan, once he had ceased to be the UN ambassador.[45] Furthermore, the Nobel-prize–winning Russian author who had been forced into exile by the Soviet government, Alexander Solzhenitsyn, was drawing considerable attention by his gloomy warnings about the dangers of détente with the Soviet Union. All these opponents of détente proved to be ardent supporters of Israel: Israel was anti-Soviet; Israel was in the forefront of defending the human rights of Soviet Jews; Israel was democratic. American pressure on Israel for the sake of détente or Arab oil was especially to be deplored, in the eyes of these critics.

Congress, for its part, was not very pleased with Sinai II as an example of Kissinger's diplomatic prowess. At a minimum, U.S. aid to the Middle East in fiscal year 1976 would exceed $3 billion, $2.25 billion of which would go to Israel, thereby cutting deeply into aid funds available for the rest of the world.[46] Moreover, Congress initially balked at the idea of sending American civilians to monitor the buffer zone between Egypt and Israel. The Vietnam analogy was raised, although it was not sufficiently compelling to cause Congress to reject the idea. Then, too, even the most ardent supporters of Israel were dismayed to find Pershing missiles among the military items requested by Israel. It seemed doubtful that Congress would authorize the sale of Pershings to Israel, and in December 1975 Israel withdrew its request, at least for the time being.

As the election year 1976 began, it became apparent that President Ford would be preoccupied with domestic politics. His position within his own party was precarious, and it was not certain that he would even be nominated at the Republican convention in August. Ronald Reagan, former governor of California, was mounting a strong challenge, with the support of the most conservative elements in the party. Kissinger and his foreign policy were emerging as a campaign issue for the Reagan Republicans as well as for the Democrats. And although the Middle East was not initially one of the issues in the campaign, the criticisms aimed at Ford and Kissinger did drive them to a tougher stance toward the Soviet Union, as symbolized by American policy in Angola, and precluded an ambitious new initiative in the Arab-Israeli arena.

Despite these election-year pressures, however, President Ford persevered in the attempt to improve U.S.-Egyptian relations. In October 1975 Sadat had been the first Egyptian president to pay an official visit to the United States. During that visit Sadat had appealed for American economic and even military assistance. A complex debate between Congress and the administration ensued, with Ford reducing requested aid for Israel in fiscal year 1977 from $2.25 billion to $1.8 billion and simultaneously urging Congress to consider the approval of a limited sale of six C-130 transport planes to Egypt.

Congress not only favored higher levels of aid to Israel but also felt that Israel should receive a supplemental grant to cover the "transitional quarter" from July 1976 to October 1, 1976, the beginning of the new fiscal year. In one of the rare instances of public disagreement between Ford and Kissinger, Ford opposed on budgetary grounds additional aid to Israel for the transitional quarter, whereas Kissinger said the administration would not mind if Congress chose to vote an additional $500 million.

The consideration of arms for Egypt took a new turn in mid-March 1976, when President Sadat announced the abrogation of the fifteen-year treaty of friendship and cooperation with the Soviet Union. Against the background of the news that Israel, according to CIA analysts, possessed from ten to twenty operational atomic weapons,[47] opposition to the sale to Egypt faded, although Congress preferred that it be handled purely as a commercial transaction. Eventually Egypt got the planes, worth about $50 million, and Israel received the supplementary aid, worth many times more.

Ford's willingness to take a hard line on aid to Israel and to oppose in the United Nations the Israeli policy on settlements in the occupied territories lasted through the first part of the election campaign. By the fall, however, when Governor Jimmy Carter of Georgia, the Democratic candidate, was enjoying a huge lead in the polls, the president began to play up his credentials as a strong supporter of Israel. In the last month of the campaign the Middle East became a topic of occasional debate, wherein Carter and Ford tried to outdo each other as the better friend of Israel, and Carter in particular hinted at very severe action against any future Arab oil embargo.

Carter's narrow victory over Ford on November 2, 1976, settled the issue of who would be the next president, but neither the Israelis nor the Arabs had any clear idea of what the next president's policies would be. Both expected new initiatives, and both were apprehensive.

THE LEBANON CRISIS

Throughout the early part of 1976, as the Americans turned their attention inward, inter-Arab relations continued to deteriorate in the absence of progress toward a settlement. Egypt was trying to emerge from the isolation produced by Sinai II, but only Saudi Arabia offered support. Syria and Jordan were moving together, and the Palestinians were still denouncing Sadat as a traitor to the cause.

In January 1976 the ongoing crisis in Lebanon grew more acute as hundreds of casualties were registered every day. Conspiratorial interpretations of the events in Lebanon abounded, producing a particularly suspicious and mistrustful mood in the Arab world. The only party that seemed to be profiting from the Lebanon crisis, in the eyes of many Arabs, was Israel. Some would also add the United States and Egypt. Lebanon was deflecting attention from Sinai II and was ensuring that combined Arab pressure could not be brought to bear on Israel or the United States. In addition, the right-wing Christian groups in Lebanon, armed and supported by the West and even Israel, were inexplicably pressing their attacks against the Lebanese left, and the Palestinians in particular. Some saw these attacks as part of a master plan, orchestrated in Washington, to destroy the PLO. Then Egypt, Syria, and Jordan could make peace with Israel under U.S. auspices.

Syria's objective in Lebanon appeared to be to bring the fighting to an early end. Initially Syria allowed several battalions of the Palestine Liberation Army to enter Lebanon. The tide of the battle seemed to turn in ensuing months, to the point where the left, headed by Kamal Jumblatt, spoke of an impending military victory over the right. This possibility concerned the United States, because a leftist Lebanon might allow Palestinian guerrilla attacks against Israel, which could eventually lead to war. Syria, and perhaps even Egypt, would be drawn in. During this period, then, the United States played a very active role in urging restraint on Israel and Syria.[48] Above all, the United States feared that large-scale Syrian intervention on the side of the Palestinians would provoke an Israeli military reaction, thus threatening to upset the fragile stability of the agreements so laboriously negotiated by Kissinger.

The warnings to Syria may have struck home. Asad was perfectly aware that a leftist- or Palestinian-dominated Lebanon would cause him problems. It might invite Israeli attacks, drawing Syria into premature military action against Israel. Or it might align itself with Syria's bitter rival, Iraq. What Asad most wanted was a Lebanon responsive to Syria's leadership, but as the fighting went on it became clear that the left and Palestinians were not about to take orders from Damascus. The American assessment of Syria's interests in Lebanon began to change, and by May the United States, with the encouragement of Jordan's King Hussein, was saying that a limited Syrian military intervention in Lebanon might help to stabilize the situation and restore security. Inasmuch as the United States, and presumably Israel as well, no longer opposed a Syrian move, Asad ordered his armed forces into Syria on a large scale in early June to protect the embattled Christians and rightists against the left and the Palestinians.

Soon most of Lebanon was under Syrian control, but the fighting raged on, especially in Beirut. Syria's intervention in Lebanon was roundly condemned by other Arab states, especially Egypt, which joined forces with Iraq, Libya, and the PLO to thwart the Syrian moves. New conspiracy theories began to emerge, linking Syria's action to Kissinger's diabolical policies: Syria would crush the PLO and would be rewarded by the return of the Golan Heights. Jordan would recover the West Bank. A Pax Americana would then descend over the area. Radical forces and Soviet influence would be banished. Saudi oil money would finance the flow of American technology.

The only flaw in the theories was that they bore little resemblance to reality. American officials, rather than having a grand policy for dealing with the Lebanon crisis or the Palestinians, were confused and perplexed by the internecine war in Lebanon. Kissinger dealt with the crisis chiefly as an extension of the Arab-Israeli conflict; hence the warnings to both Israel and Syria not to intervene during the spring of 1976. The conflict had a logic of its own, however, as did Syrian policy, once the commitment to Lebanon was made early in 1976. Asad was not playing the American or Israeli game in Lebanon, whatever the superficial appearances. Kissinger and Ford, quite simply, had no game in mind, other than to prevent a full-scale Arab-Israeli war. Apart from urging the evacuation of Americans in Lebanon, the United States did little.[49]

The fighting in Lebanon continued into the fall, and the Christians consolidated their control over a small coastal strip between Beirut and Tripoli. For all intents and purposes this became an autonomous region with its own government and armed forces. Even the newly elected president, Elias Sarkis, had little sway over the Christians. Syria helped them by removing the Palestinians from the mountainous areas to the east of the Christian-held areas, gradually and methodically pushing them toward their stronghold around the port of Sidon. The Palestinians, with help from the Iraqis, Libyans, and Egyptians, fought against great odds but could not withstand the Syrian offensive.

At the moment of impending Syrian victory, Saudi Arabia flexed its diplomatic and financial muscles, summoning President Asad and Sadat, along with PLO Chairman Arafat, to Riyadh in late October 1976 for an urgent conference to end the bloodshed in Lebanon. Asad conducted himself with considerable sophistication, seeking a reconciliation with Sadat in return for Egypt's endorsement of Syria's predominant role in Lebanon. Within hours the course of events in the Arab world reversed direction. A hastily convened Arab summit meeting in Cairo a few days later ratified the agreements reached in Riyadh, the key element of which was the creation of an Arab peacekeeping force, consisting mainly of Syrians, which would restore law and order in Lebanon. The PLO, reading the new Arab consensus correctly, concluded that it had no alternative but to acquiesce. By November most of Lebanon was under effective Syrian control, and the eighteen-month-long civil war seemed to be at least at a temporary end. Only in southern Lebanon, where Syrian troops were constrained by Israeli threats, was the situation still explosive, but even there neither Syria nor Israel seemed to be anxious for a confrontation.

The Arab coalition, which had fallen apart over Sinai II, now seemed to be resurrecting itself. With Saudi encouragement, Egypt and Syria were back on speaking terms, Jordan maintained good relations with Syria, and the PLO, chastened by its severe setbacks in Lebanon, gave off signals that some interpreted as a willingness to pursue more moderate policies in the future. Perhaps not coincidentally, the Arabs seemed to be putting their own house at least partly in order to be better able to confront the new American president with a coherent position. The divisions that had so crippled them throughout the American election year were apparently forgotten, although in other times and in other circumstances they would almost certainly come to the surface again. For the moment, however, the renewed sense of Arab solidarity could be a valuable asset in a new round of diplomacy, just as it could raise the risks of war if diplomacy failed.

THE KISSINGER LEGACY

Henry Kissinger's impact on American foreign policy will be debated endlessly. Of the accomplishments credited to him, few were not also in part the product of circumstances or the actions of others. But Kissinger will undoubtedly be regarded as one of the most powerful and most successful of American statesmen in the post–World War II era. How he managed to achieve such prominence is a story in its own right, revealing

Kissinger's remarkable talents as a bureaucratic maneuverer and politician. His more enduring legacy, however, will be his policies and the concepts behind them.

After several false starts Kissinger finally developed a coherent approach to the Arab-Israeli conflict after the October 1973 war. He started from the premise that the United States need not choose between a pro-Arab or pro-Israeli policy. In fact, it was the American special relationship to Israel that compelled the Arabs to deal with Washington instead of Moscow when it came to diplomacy. Consequently, if an alternative to war could be offered to the Arabs, their interests, quite apart from their sentiments, would lead them to deal with the United States. A credible diplomatic process was therefore essential to the weakening of Soviet influence in the Middle East. This view, once stated, seems unexceptional, perhaps obvious; even so, it was often ignored, on occasion by Kissinger himself.

Kissinger's second contribution to American diplomacy in the Middle East was the development of specific negotiating techniques designed to produce limited agreements between Arabs and Israelis. If Kissinger's grand strategy often seemed fairly conventional, his tactical skills as a negotiator and mediator were unsurpassed. Here his originality, his sense of timing, his intelligence, and even his personality served him especially well.

Kissinger demonstrated that, in practice, successful negotiations require an ability to break issues into manageable pieces that can then be imaginatively recombined into viable agreements. Mastery of detail is essential to success, as is a sense of context and nuance. A sustained, high-level effort, fully supported by the president, is the only American approach to negotiations likely to produce results. Kissinger showed that such an effort could succeed, as well as how difficult it could be.

Finally, Kissinger translated into practice his belief that power and diplomacy must always go hand in hand. The United States can never rely solely on force or on negotiations in the Middle East. The test of statesmanship is to find the critical balance of the two. Arms supplies to the Israelis or the Arabs must be viewed as part of the diplomatic process, not as a technical military issue. Whatever troubles Kissinger may have had in practice with this principle, he clearly saw that political considerations outweighed narrowly military ones in decisions of this sort.

Kissinger's successors no doubt pondered the value of these views and reflected on both the strength and the limits of the Kissinger approach.

Kissinger was unable to decide how to deal with the Soviets in the Middle East. He wavered between exaggerating their role and then minimizing it. Similarly, his views on a comprehensive approach to negotiations seemed to fluctuate between a recognition that some kind of framework was essential and a belief that each step could and should be taken in isolation from the others. Behind this ambiguity seems to have been a doubt whether peace between Arabs and Israelis could really be established in his lifetime. At times he acted as if he believed it could be, whereas on other occasions he seemed to be prepared to settle for a stable status quo.

Lastly, Kissinger had a blind spot toward the Palestinian issue. He knew that at some point the problem would have to be confronted. He even appeared to be tempted by the idea of dealing directly with the PLO leadership. But he geared much of his diplomacy to trying to circumvent this crucial issue, to putting off the moment of truth, and to weakening the appeal of the Palestinian movement, all the while hoping that some alternative would appear. Perhaps with time, with better luck, and with a strong president behind him, Kissinger would have helped find acceptable solutions to all these unanswered problems. But Ford's defeat brought Kissinger's public career to an end and left to the Carter administration the unenviable task of shaping an American policy toward the Arab-Israeli conflict.

PART FOUR

The Carter Presidency

CHAPTER TEN

Ambition and Realism: Carter and Camp David, 1977–78

Jimmy Carter came to the presidency with remarkably little experience in foreign affairs. He had served one term as governor of Georgia, and had earned a reputation for his strong commitment to civil rights. But as far as the Middle East was concerned, he had no known record apart from a few comments made during the campaign that offered little guide to what his policies might be.

If Carter's specific views on Arab-Israeli issues were difficult to anticipate, he had displayed certain habits of mind that might be revealing of his basic approach. Trained as an engineer, Carter seemed to believe complex problems could best be tackled by careful study, detailed planning, and comprehensive designs. To say the least, he was a problem solver more than a grand strategist.

Carter also seemed to have an optimistic streak that led him to believe problems could be resolved if leaders would simply reason together and listen to the aspirations of their people. Here he may have been consciously influenced by his experience with the civil rights movement and by his personal beliefs as a born-again Christian. None of these attributes ensured that Carter would take a strong interest in the Arab-Israeli conflict, but they did suggest that he would not be deterred from doing so by the difficulty or complexity of the issue. He might even sense a challenge in tackling a problem that had for so long defied solution.

Much would depend on his foreign-policy team, and there the evidence suggested that he would rely on mainstream figures from the Democratic party establishment. For secretary of state he selected Cyrus R. Vance, a seasoned negotiator, international lawyer, and the deputy secretary of defense during the 1967 Arab-Israeli war. Vance's views on Middle East issues were not widely known, but his would be a voice for continuity, negotiations, and steady, quiet diplomacy.

As national security adviser, Carter selected the Polish-born academic Zbigniew Brzezinski. Unlike Vance, Brzezinski had left traces, primarily in the form of numerous articles and books, mostly on Soviet-related topics but a few on the Middle East as well. Brzezinski was an activist who believed in competing for influence with the Soviets, and who saw the Arab-Israeli conflict as a source of instability and radicalism in a sensitive geostrategic region. He had publicly endorsed the idea of a Palestinian state in the West Bank and Gaza and was one of the signatories of the controversial Brookings Report.[1] Brzezinski, who clearly hoped to achieve the stature of his predecessor and academic rival, Henry Kissinger, seemed determined to put the Arab-Israeli conflict near the top of the new administration's agenda.

While other players in the policy game moved in and out of the inner circle, Carter, Vance, and Brzezinski were the key decisionmakers. On defense matters Secretary of Defense Harold Brown carried great weight and exhibited a sharp intellect, but he was not particularly forceful in pushing his views on most policy issues outside his immediate area of responsibility. Vice President Walter Mondale had close ties to the Jewish community, and he was particularly attuned to any step that would produce a negative reaction there or in Congress. From time to time he would intervene strongly in internal deliberations, but he did not have an important role in policy formulation. Nor did the "Georgia mafia" of Hamilton Jordan, Stuart Eizenstat, Jody Powell, and Robert Lipshutz have much influence, although Jordan, who eventually became chief of staff, was a shrewd tactician and had unimpeded access to Carter. He and Mondale were attentive to the domestic fallout from Carter's Middle East policy, but they were not architects as much as they were damage controllers.[2]

THE INITIAL ASSESSMENT

Within days of reaching Washington, President Carter's foreign policy team was beginning to discuss how and whether to launch a new Middle East peace initiative. Both Secretary Vance and National Security Adviser Zbigniew Brzezinski were on record with the president as favoring a strong U.S. role in Middle East peace negotiations. Their assessment, and that of most Middle East specialists at the State Department, was that early 1977 was a good moment for the United States to exercise leadership in a new round of negotiations. The key Arab states seemed to be ready for serious talks, and a degree of consensus appeared to have been forged through Saudi mediation in the fall of 1976. The conflict in Lebanon had subsided, and the oil situation had begun to stabilize. Egypt's president, Anwar Sadat, who enjoyed great prestige in Washington, was urging the new administration to take advantage of this moment of moderation in the Arab world, a message seconded by the Saudis.

Israel also seemed to expect the United States to return to the diplomatic arena after the enforced absence of the election year. The cabinet of Prime Minister Yitzhak Rabin was to face elections in the spring, and was on the defensive to an unprecedented degree. But Washington officials felt that preliminary talks could be conducted before Israelis went to the polls, and even if they were not, that any new government would be built around the Labor alignment that had ruled Israel since its birth. And Labor was a known element, likely to adopt a tough stance in negotiations but ultimately prepared to bargain and to coordinate policies with Washington. Three disengagement agreements had been hammered out with Labor governments, and American negotiators had come to respect the skills of leaders like Golda Meir, Yitzhak Rabin, Moshe Dayan, and Shimon Peres.

If political realities in the Arab world and in Israel were seen as conducive to a new round of diplomacy, the shadow of the October 1973 war served as a constant reminder of the dangers of a collapse in the peace process. Barely three years had passed since that round of hostilities, and the memories of the near-confrontation between the United States and the Soviet Union, the nuclear alert, and the oil crisis were still very much in mind. Rarely mentioned but also present was the recognition that full-scale war in the Middle East could some day involve the use of nuclear weapons. This possibility made the region exceptionally dangerous and added a strong impulse to peacemaking efforts.

Having made this initial assessment, the Carter administration spent little time on whether to accord the Arab-Israeli conflict high priority. Most of the early discussion centered on means. It was widely believed that Henry Kissinger's technique of shuttle diplomacy to achieve limited agreements had run its course with Sinai II. The United States had paid a high price for a partial Israeli withdrawal that had not opened the way for any further such agreements. Neither Syria nor Jordan was prepared to follow Sadat's lead, and even Sadat was insisting that the next step should move toward an overall settlement. And the Israelis were also disinclined to be edged back from their strategically solid positions in Sinai for less than a peace agreement and direct negotiations with Egypt.

At a meeting on February 4, 1977, the Policy Review Committee of the National Security Council agreed to recommend to the president that the Middle East should be dealt with as a matter of urgent priority and that Secretary Vance should go to the area immediately to begin discussions on procedures and substance. The president's key advisers felt the United States should promote an agreement on broad principles and then seek their staged implementation. From the Arab side the administration should seek a clear definition of peace, and from the Israelis it should try to get an understanding that security could be achieved without significant territorial adjustments in the 1967 lines. At this stage in the internal discussions, there was no sense of urgency about going to Geneva for a formal conference, and the emphasis was on pre-Geneva talks to prepare for more formal negotiations at a later date. It was also agreed at the meeting that the Soviets should be kept informed of the progress of U.S. conversations with the parties but should not be involved in the negotiations at this stage.[3]

The president approved of these suggestions and noted that his own meetings with Middle East leaders over the coming few months could help lay some of the substantive groundwork before direct talks among the parties began. Already in these discussions among the president and his advisers, however, one could detect a nuance of difference between those who were more inclined to see Geneva as a desirable goal in itself, who felt cooperation with the Soviets was to some degree inevitable, and those who were more skeptical of both Geneva and Moscow. Interestingly, no one raised the argument that early U.S. initiatives might prove to be destabilizing in Israel, or might raise Arab expectations to unrealistic levels.

In mid-February Vance was already in the Middle East sounding out each of the leaders on how he saw the situation, while making it clear that the United States also had some ideas of its own. Rabin, Sadat, King Hussein of Jordan, and Saudi Crown Prince Fahd were all invited to come to Washington to meet the new president, and the idea of a meeting between Carter and President Asad of Syria was also raised.

A formal meeting of the National Security Council was held after Vance's return on February 23. He reported that all the parties with whom he had consulted professed to be ready for a peace agreement. They all agreed to go to a Geneva conference in September and to discuss substance prior to those talks. All concurred that the three main issues on the agenda were the nature of peace, withdrawal, and the Palestinian question. The most difficult procedural issue was how to include representatives of the Palestinians in the negotiations. Vance seemed to believe that the Arabs might form a single delegation at Geneva, which could include members of the PLO. He had told the Arab leaders it was up to them to produce an acceptable position on this question before Geneva. Sadat had urged the United States to include the PLO, but had also raised the possibility of representing them through some other means, such as a representative of the Arab League.[4]

In talks with Israeli leaders during his first trip, Secretary Vance had been told that no Israeli government would agree to talk to the PLO so long as it remained committed to the destruction of Israel. Vance had asked Foreign Minister Yigal Allon if it would make any difference if the PLO were to accept UN Resolution 242 and Israel's right to exist as a state. He replied that a PLO which accepted Israel's existence would no longer be the PLO, and Israel's attitude would be different.[5] This answer encouraged the United States to look into the possibility that the PLO might change its formal position on 242. The Egyptians and Saudis both promised to use their influence, and the Egyptians went so far as to say that they would urge the PLO to change its covenant, which called for Israel's destruction.

The next phase of the U.S. strategy included a highly public use of presidential power to try to break the logjam on several substantive issues. Carter and his advisers had little patience with some of the conventional wisdom on how the American role should be played. He had little sympathy for the Arab refusal to make peace with Israel, or to even use the word *peace*; and he strongly believed Israel would in some way have to come to terms with the Palestinians, and probably with the PLO, names he used almost interchangeably in his early months in office. And though he was very sympathetic to Israel's security concerns, he did not feel that territorial aggrandizement was the key to that security.

Carter was willing, even anxious, to speak out in public on all these issues, and to discuss them in private. One of his criticisms of the Kissinger style had been the emphasis on secrecy, which kept the American public in the dark about major foreign problems. Carter's inclination was to talk openly about the foreign-policy initiatives he was considering. At times this openness jangled the nerves of more traditional diplomats, and of foreign leaders, but Carter often seemed to be trying to do so deliberately. He appeared to feel he had a limited period in which to make his mark on Middle East policy and that controversial issues should be tackled early in the administration. This viewpoint led to a profusion of comprehensive plans to settle all sorts of problems, including the Middle East. On occasion, the president spoke with an awareness of the political cycle, the need to stake out strong positions during the early honeymoon phase of the administration, knowing perhaps that he would be obliged to settle for less in the end, but also hoping for a breakthrough here or there.

On March 7–8, 1977, Carter met with Prime Minister Rabin at the White House for very serious substantive discussions. The personal chemistry between the two was not particularly good, but the record of the talks shows that both leaders conducted thoughtful explorations of what might come out of the forthcoming negotiations. In retrospect, these talks stand out as one of the best substantive discussions Carter had with any Middle East leader. Shortly after the talks, however, a misunderstanding arose. Rabin publicly claimed that Carter had supported the Israeli idea of "defensible borders." Carter did not want to leave the false impression that he had offered Rabin a blank check, so the White House issued a clarification. This episode left the false impression that a crisis had broken out in U.S.-Israeli relations, a notion that may have contributed to Labor's defeat at the polls two months later.[6]

Almost immediately after meeting with Rabin, and in part to counter some of the Israeli leaks about what had been discussed, Carter publicly spelled out the three basic principles, as he saw them, of a comprehensive Middle East peace. These entailed the need for concrete manifestations of peace and normal relations, such as trade and the exchange of diplomats; the need for security arrangements for all parties, but without prejudice to the establishments of recognized borders along the 1967 lines; and the need for a solution to the Palestinian problem, which had a political as well as a humanitarian dimension. A few days later, on March 16, in Clinton, Massachusetts, Carter reiterated these points, using for the first time the formulation of a "Palestinian homeland."[7] Needless to say, the Israelis were stunned and apprehensive, and the Arabs were generally encouraged.

Although the Palestinian homeland became the focus of much of the public debate, Carter's two central assumptions, which deserved careful scrutiny, were his belief that a peace settlement must evolve from prior agreement on basic principles—the comprehensive framework—rather than through piecemeal bargaining over discrete issues, and his conviction that Israel could achieve security (as well as peace and recognition) within the geographic confines of 1967, with only minor adjustments. This latter point was based on the belief that no Arab leader would ever agree to recognize Israel unless most of the territory captured in 1967 was returned, and that ultimately Israel's security would be as much a function of the quality of political relationships with its neighbors as of its military might. The final judgment lying behind Carter's public statements was that Egypt, the Arab country most willing to make peace with Israel, would not do so unless some broader peace process was under way. Sadat himself was the most insistent in arguing this point.

Over the next three months Carter met with Sadat, Hussein, Fahd, and Asad. In each meeting the substantive trinity of peace, borders-security, and the Palestinian question was discussed in some depth, along with procedural questions on how to get the Palestinians represented in the upcoming negotiations. The most encouraging sign during this phase was Sadat's willingness to accept the idea that peace would entail normal relations with Israel, including the exchange of diplomats and full recognition.[8] But also, the Israeli government, while insisting that it would never accept an independent Palestinian state on the West Bank, was prepared to discuss withdrawal and was open to the idea that security would not necessarily require significant border changes beyond the 1967 lines. In addition, Rabin, Allon, and Peres all talked of the need to solve the Palestinian problem if there was to be peace in the region. And the Arab leaders were confidently predicting that the PLO would consider softening its position on the recognition of Israel.

By midyear, then, the Carter administration was well launched with its peace initiative, and the results were fairly encouraging. It is fair to say, however, that the president often felt frustrated with the seeming intractability of the issues, with the complexity of the problem, with the domestic political sensitivities aroused by his public comments, and by the sheer amount of time required to move the process forward.

Then, on June 21, 1977, the unexpected happened. Menachem Begin, whose Likud bloc had won the Knesset elections the previous month, became prime minister of Israel. Begin was an unknown figure in Washington. Insofar as administration officials knew his views, they were aware that he opposed Labor's approach to "territorial compromise" with Jordan as a means of dealing with the West Bank and the Palestinian question. Begin was known to favor an expansion of Israeli settlements, and one of his first acts that irritated the Carter administration was his visit to Elon Moreh, where he announced he would support many more such settlements. These two issues—Begin's unwillingness to accept the principle of withdrawal from the West Bank under any circumstances, and his commitment to settlements—became the main sources of conflict between the United States and Israel over the next two years.[9]

POLICY REAPPRAISAL

Somewhat surprisingly, Carter's first meeting with Begin was much more cordial than the one with Rabin. Carter apparently believed Begin would become more rigid if pressured, and some of his advisers were convinced that Begin would respond best to a respectful, polite initial encounter. The personal chemistry between the two men was hardly warm, but the talks were conducted in a friendly manner.

Although Begin came prepared with procedural proposals for negotiations with the Arabs, he showed no sign of wanting to discuss substance with the United States. This, in fact, was one of the initial differences between Begin and Rabin: Begin argued that the United States should not be involved in the substance of Arab-Israeli talks but should limit its role to getting the parties together. He obviously feared that the U.S. stand on many issues would be closer to the Arab position, and therefore he wanted as little substantive role for Washington as possible. Previous Israeli governments had, by contrast, insisted on close consultation with the Americans as a way of preventing unilateral moves that might undercut Israel's bargaining position. Begin seemed to be saying that Israel did not feel the need to consult, and at the same time asked that the United States refrain from putting forward any ideas of its own on substance.

Unfortunately for Begin, the United States was already rather far down the road of trying to devise draft principles that should be agreed on before a Geneva conference. In discussions held within the administration early in July, five principles had been agreed on, and during Begin's visit these were discussed. The first point set the goal of comprehensive peace; the second reiterated the relevance of UN Resolutions 242 and 338 as the bases of negotiations; the third defined the goal of peace as involving normal relations, not just an end of belligerency; the fourth dealt with the question of borders and withdrawal in stages; and the fifth point concerned the Palestinians and their rights, including means "to permit self-determination by the Palestinians in deciding on their future status."

Vance, and then Carter, reviewed these points with Begin on July 19–20 and found, not surprisingly, that Begin entirely rejected the fifth point on the Palestinians, and was insistent that on point four the United

States should not say in public or private that it favored withdrawal to the 1967 lines with only minor modifications. During an evening session alone with Begin, Carter agreed not to mention the 1967 lines with minor modifications in public, and in return he asked Begin to show restraint on settlements. This compromise was part of an effort to calm the heated atmosphere prior to Geneva, but it also reflected a slight shift toward accepting the idea that little real progress could now be made until the parties began to talk to one another. Procedural issues began to assume greater importance, and prior agreement on key principles before Geneva came to be seen as unlikely, given the enormous gap between Begin and even the most moderate Arab leaders.[10]

Secretary Vance, who began to focus on the question of how the PLO might be represented at Geneva, found himself leaning increasingly toward the idea of a single Arab delegation that would include Palestinians. Israel had made it clear it would not deal directly with the PLO as a separate delegation but would not object to Palestinians within the Jordanian delegation. Jordan, however, had no intention of representing the Palestinians and preferred the Syrian idea of a common Arab negotiating front, primarily as a way of preventing unilateral moves by Sadat. Egypt favored a PLO delegation but had shown a willingness to consider other formulations as well. During much of July, August, and September this issue was a major topic of discussion, and some progress seemed possible.

Meanwhile Vance had been toying with ideas on how to deal with the West Bank in a somewhat different context than in the other occupied territories. He was intrigued first by the idea of a referendum among the inhabitants of the West Bank to get their views into the negotiating process. Later he fastened on the idea of a "trusteeship" for the area for a transitional period, and several studies were done to assess the practicality of this notion.

In early August 1977 Vance left on a very important trip to the Middle East. With him he took a revised set of the five principles to discuss with leaders in Egypt, Israel, Syria, Jordan, Saudi Arabia, and Lebanon. He also had with him four possible ways for the Palestinians to be included in the Geneva negotiations, and he was prepared to try out his new idea of a trusteeship as well.

During Vance's talks in Egypt, Sadat showed considerable anxiety about the shift toward procedural discussions and away from the idea of prior agreement on principles before Geneva. In his view Geneva should be used for signing a pre-agreed document, little more. Sadat had little patience with the idea of negotiating with Israel, preferring that the United States present a plan, to which all the parties could react. To encourage this line of thought, Sadat presented a highly secret document to Vance in Alexandria.[11] It was the draft of a peace treaty that Sadat said he would be prepared to sign, but he did not want any of the other parties to know it existed. Instead he urged Vance to ask the Israelis to put forward a draft treaty of their own; then Vance could unveil the Egyptian draft, which would lead to an eventual U.S. compromise proposal. In a tactic that he was to use repeatedly, Sadat took the Egyptian draft and wrote in the margins in his own handwriting the further concessions he would be prepared to make. These notations were intended, presumably, to convince Vance that Sadat would be flexible on most substantive points, though not on "land and sovereignty," as the Egyptian president repeatedly said.[12]

During the talks with the Egyptians, Vance was also encouraged to believe the PLO was about to change its position on UN Resolution 242. To add an incentive, Vance recommended that President Carter publicly repeat that the United States would be willing to enter into high-level talks with the PLO if the PLO accepted 242, even with a statement of reservation. Carter did so a few days later from Plains, Georgia, while Vance was in Saudi Arabia, all of which ensured that Vance's arrival in Israel was less than warm.[13] At a dinner in the secretary's honor Begin gave a long, and in the view of most of the Americans present, very offensive speech, implying that anyone thinking of talking to the PLO should be compared with those who had sought to appease Hitler before World War II. Begin's reputation for verbal excess and extremism gained considerable credibility during Vance's trip, and little remained of what Begin wistfully later called the good feelings of July 1977. The Israelis did agree, however, to provide the United States with a draft peace treaty, and arrangements were made for further meetings between Vance and the various foreign ministers in New York in conjunction with the UN General Assembly.

September 1977 proved to be an eventful month in the evolution of Carter's Middle East strategy. American efforts were concentrated on four parallel, potentially even conflicting, goals. First was the attempt to get each of the parties to provide a written draft of a peace treaty. Israel complied, with a lengthy and legalistic document that left the delicate question of the border and the status of settlements in Sinai obscure.

Jordan and even Syria eventually submitted a list of principles that should govern any peace agreement. Although the drafts per se were far from what was needed, they did provide Vance with some building blocks from which to fashion an American compromise proposal, and they had the positive effect of getting the parties to think of committing themselves to concrete positions on paper.

The second strand of policy, largely working through the Syrians, but also pursued in other channels, was an attempt to find a solution to the question of how the Palestinians would be represented in upcoming negotiations at Geneva. Agreement was reached on how the PLO might express its reservation to UN Resolution 242, but the conditions demanded by the PLO for an overt acceptance of 242 were beyond what Washington was prepared to promise.[14] Nonetheless, by early October Sadat had informed Carter that the PLO would agree to be represented in a unified Arab delegation by a Palestinian who was not a PLO official. Since everyone had by then accepted the idea of a unified Arab delegation that would include Palestinians, this issue seemed to be nearly resolved.[15]

The third focus of U.S. efforts was to try to develop some understanding among the negotiating parties about the procedures of the Geneva talks. Sadat was still insistent that Geneva must be "well prepared" in advance; otherwise it could bog down and turn into a hopeless stalemate. He remained wedded to the Kissinger model of highly secret talks at the level of head of government, which would then be finalized and legitimized in a public forum like Geneva. If the actual negotiating was to be done in a semipublic forum like Geneva, he seemed to fear that the other Arabs would try to restrict his freedom to maneuver, and that the United States would be subject to the ever-present pro-Israeli pressures generated by American public opinion and Congress. Israel tended to share this suspicion of Geneva, and Foreign Minister Moshe Dayan warned that a unified Arab delegation was a formula for stalemate. Syria, and to a lesser extent Jordan, favored a single delegation as a way of preventing the much-feared separate Egyptian-Israeli agreement they had come to expect after Sinai II.

The American compromise proposal, largely crafted by Vance, was to get everyone to accept the idea of a unified Arab delegation. The main purpose, in his mind, was to bring the Palestinians into the peace process by that means. After a formalistic opening of the Geneva conference at which the Arab side would appear to be a single delegation, talks would break up into subcommittees, which would essentially be bilateral, except for the discussion of the West Bank and Gaza, in which Egypt and Jordan would join the Palestinians. The American side, mistakenly, did not realize the Syrians would object to being left out of the talks on the Palestinian issue. The main problem seemed to be to get Israel to agree that the Palestinians could be at the talks in their own right, not just as members of the Jordanian or Egyptian delegations.

The fourth, and probably least carefully thought out, part of the U.S. strategy was aimed at the Soviet Union. As Geneva became more of a real concept, rather than just a symbolic umbrella for a whole series of contacts and talks, the United States had to address the question of the role to be played by the other cochairman. A number of procedures had already been worked out in December 1973, when the Geneva conference had convened in plenary session for the first and last time. To the extent possible, it was useful to adhere to those precedents. But the Soviets were clearly seeking more of a role, and in mid-September they presented a draft of a joint statement to Secretary Vance. For a Soviet document it was remarkably balanced. It did not include calls for a Palestinian state or participation by the PLO. It paid due regard to the need for security and normal peaceful relations among the states of the area. Most of the language was from UN Resolution 242. Practically the only formulation the United States had not itself used was a reference to Palestinian rights, which went a step beyond the standard American reference to Palestinian interests.

The task of trying to work out an agreed text was turned over to Ambassador Alfred L. Atherton, Jr., who was advising Vance on Arab-Israeli peacemaking, and a Soviet diplomat, Mikhail Sytenko. With little effort, these two professionals produced a generally acceptable text. The question that was hardly discussed was how and when to issue this joint statement so as to advance the other efforts that were under way. At the time it was thought that a strong statement by the Soviets in conjunction with the Americans might put some pressure on Syria and the PLO to cease their haggling over procedural matters and to agree to enter negotiations on the basis of a joint invitation from the superpowers. Little thought was given to Israel's reaction, or to the need to prepare public opinion in the United States. The Israelis were shown a draft in late September, and Dayan's initial reaction was restrained.

Among the potentially controversial elements in the draft were an explicit call for reconvening the Geneva conference by the end of the year; the fact that the Soviet Union would be cochairman; the lack of explicit reference to UN Resolution 242; and a formulation the United States had not previously used referring to Palestinian *rights*. Largely because of these references the Israelis were uncomfortable with the document. But the Carter administration had not picked up any warning signals from Dayan. Thus, when the U.S.-Soviet communiqué was issued on October 1, 1977, few on the American side anticipated the storm of adverse reaction from Israel and Israel's supporters in the United States.[16] (See appendix D for the text.)

While American efforts were aimed in these various directions, Egypt and Israel were embarking on a round of secret diplomacy. At Sadat's initiative a meeting was held between Dayan and an aide to Sadat, Hassan Touhamy, in Morocco in mid-September.[17] Similar contacts had been held over the years, including that month, between Israeli and Arab leaders, so even when the United States learned of this meeting after the fact, it was not viewed as a vote of no confidence in the ongoing U.S. strategy. In retrospect, one can see that Sadat was beginning to hedge his bets for fear that Geneva would become a straitjacket for his free-wheeling style of diplomacy. It is fair to say that the American side consistently underestimated the degree of distrust between Sadat and Asad, and also tended to take Sadat at his word when he repeatedly said he could never afford to make a separate peace with Israel.

Not surprisingly, with so many initiatives under way during September, something was bound to come unstuck. The proximate cause of the explosion was the U.S.-Soviet communiqué and the firestorm of negative American and Israeli reaction it provoked. Much of the pent-up anxiety and frustration with Carter's Middle East policy now spilled over, finding willing allies in the neoconservative, pro-Israeli, anti-Soviet circles. What was in fact a political error, showing considerable amateurishness, was portrayed as a move of vast significance that would reestablish the Soviets as a major power in the Middle East. To read the text of the communiqué several years later is to wonder what all the fuss was about. The words themselves are innocuous, and even Begin used the phrase "Palestinian rights" at Camp David. Nonetheless, the political reality of early October 1977 was that Carter was under great pressure from the friends of Israel, and the Israelis played on his discomfort with extraordinary skill.

Many analysts believe Sadat went to Jerusalem in November 1977 to escape the dead end of a U.S.-Soviet sponsored Geneva conference. They often emphasize his desire to keep the Soviets out of the diplomatic arena. But the available evidence, including Sadat's own account, does not support this widely held belief.[18] When first informed of the U.S.-Soviet joint communiqué, Sadat termed it a "brilliant maneuver," since he, like some U.S. officials, thought it would soften up the Syrians.[19] In any case, he had ensured against Geneva becoming an Arab-Soviet trap by opening his own direct channel to the Israelis, and from that contact he seemed to be assured that whenever he was ready to sign a separate peace with Israel he would recover most of Sinai. In early October Sadat was still testing to see how much more he could get with U.S. help. It was not the U.S.-Soviet communiqué that disillusioned him; it was Carter's apparent inability to stand up to Israeli pressure, coupled with evidence that Carter was tired of spending so much time on an apparently intractable problem, that seems to have convinced Sadat to strike out on his own.

If this interpretation is correct, then the crucial step along the way was the meeting between Carter and Dayan in New York on October 4, 1977.[20] Dayan began by asking if Israel was expected to accept the U.S.-Soviet communiqué as the price of going to Geneva. He termed the agreement totally unacceptable to Israel but said Israel would still go to Geneva on the basis of 242. Carter said Israel did not have to accept the communiqué. Then Dayan upped the ante by asking Carter to reaffirm publicly all past U.S. commitments to Israel as a way of calming the crisis atmosphere set off in Israel by the communiqué. He said that if Carter did not do so, Israel might feel obliged to publish these agreements. He also asked for a statement that the United States would not use pressure on Israel to accept a Palestinian state. When Carter said he did not intend to use pressure but did not want to make any such statement, Dayan said he would therefore be obliged to say that he had asked and Carter had refused. Having issued these barely veiled threats, Dayan proceeded to deal in a businesslike way with Secretary Vance on the question of Palestinian representation, going further toward the U.S. position than Begin had probably authorized, and thus winning back for himself the reputation of being the most pragmatic and reasonable of the members of the Israeli cabinet.[21] After a formula for including Palestinians at Geneva was worked out fairly smoothly, Carter returned to the discussion.

Dayan made a strong pitch for American support for a separate Egyptian-Israeli agreement. In Dayan's words, "the future is with Egypt. If you take one wheel off a car, it won't drive. If Egypt is out of the conflict, there will be no more war." The discussion then turned to politics, and Dayan said he could help Carter quiet the fears of American

Jews if Dayan could announce an agreement on Geneva between the United States and Israel. "But if we say we have to deal with the PLO or a Palestinian state, and this is bad for Israel, then there will be screaming here and in Israel. We need an agreed formula so I can say there is agreement, not confrontation, to Israel and American Jews." Secretary Vance was clearly very nervous about the image of a joint U.S.-Israeli position and suggested that both parties should state their own positions separately. Dayan objected, saying that something should be announced at the end of the meeting, or it would be very bad. President Carter then agreed that the two sides should try to issue a common statement dealing with Geneva and explaining that the U.S.-Soviet communiqué was not a precondition for Israel's participation at Geneva. After several more hours of drafting, Dayan and Vance appeared in the early morning hours of October 5 to reveal the U.S.-Israeli "working paper," as it became known.[22] To the Arabs, including the Egyptians, this document appeared to be a major retreat from the U.S.-Soviet communiqué, as well as evidence of the considerable power Israel could wield because of its strong base of support in Congress and U.S. public opinion.

In brief, the whole episode left Carter exhausted and somewhat cautious, the Israelis both distrustful and aware of their power, and the Arabs confused and alarmed at the spectacle of the United States appearing to retreat under pressure on the eve of the Geneva conference. In retrospect, it is easy to see the significant role played by the careless handling of the U.S.-Soviet communiqué. Most of the American officials involved subsequently acknowledged that they should have been more attentive to the negative political fallout from such a joint move with the Soviets. The simple truth is that not much thought was given to the matter because so many other important developments were occurring in the Middle East arena by late September.

The next step along the way in Sadat's decision to go to Jerusalem came later in October. By then the procedural tangles of forming a unified Arab delegation had produced a near deadlock between Syria and Egypt. Progress in resolving the impasse was glacial, and Carter seemed to feel that time was running out. He repeatedly said that he and Secretary Vance had other pressing matters to attend to and could not spend all their time on the Middle East, especially when the problems were among the Arab parties themselves. In this spirit, one Friday morning toward the end of October, Carter decided to send a very personal appeal to

Sadat in the form of a handwritten note to be delivered directly to the Egyptian president. In it he reminded Sadat of their mutual pledge in April to do all they could for peace. Carter came close to saying that he had little more to offer, and that the time had come for a bold move from Sadat. No specifics were mentioned, but the point was clear: if further progress was to be made, Sadat would have to take the initiative.[23]

Within a week the response came, first in the form of a handwritten note from Sadat, and more formally and with more details as a cable from Cairo. Sadat's idea was to convene a super-Geneva conference in east Jerusalem, to be attended by the heads of state of all the permanent members of the Security Council, as well as by the leaders of Egypt, Syria, Jordan, Israel, and the PLO. It all seemed a bit grand and implausible, and Carter's response was cool.[24] By his own account Sadat began to think of a solo venture to Jerusalem to break the deadlock. But this time he did not bother to tell President Carter. Thus, on November 9, when Sadat publicly revealed his intention to go to Israel, Washington was caught by surprise, just as it had been by Begin's election. And once again the United States was obliged to adjust its strategy because of events in the Middle East that had proved to be beyond its control.

AFTER JERUSALEM

The initial reaction to Sadat's trip to Jerusalem in official Washington was one of admiration for the personal courage required, and some puzzlement over what Sadat had in mind for an encore. He had often said that 99 percent of the cards were in American hands, but now he seemed to be ready to play his own cards without much help from Carter. No one in Washington proposed that the United States should try to thwart his moves, but there was some concern that negative Arab reactions, coupled with Begin's essential rigidity on the Palestinian issue, would cause the initiative to fall far short of the psychological breakthrough that Sadat sought. Consequently, sooner rather than later the problem would end up back in the American lap. In any case, Sadat's move would not be helped by its appearing to have been made in the United States. These considerations, coupled perhaps with some envy on the part of the politically minded members of the administration for a media-catching move they would have liked to have thought of themselves, led to a fairly reserved public posture, which was strongly criticized at the time by the friends of Israel.[25]

It took some weeks for American officials to correctly assess Sadat's reasons for going to Jerusalem. The depth of animosity between Egypt and Syria had not been recognized, but Sadat's contemptuous comments toward Asad and other Arab leaders after his trip to Israel suggested that he was determined to go it alone for the time being. When asked whether the United States could do anything helpful in Damascus to temper opposition to his moves, Sadat replied that the United States could inform Asad that Egypt was the center of the Arab world.[26]

By early December the internal consensus in the administration was that Sadat's initiative should be supported strongly but that the United States should continue to use its influence to try to get as broad agreement as possible. The administration still felt that Sadat would, in the end, not make a separate peace with Israel and that at least some measure of agreement on the Palestinian question would have to serve as a cover for any Egyptian-Israeli deal. Syria would henceforth be ignored for most practical purposes, as would the PLO, but American policy would continue to focus on some form of West Bank–Gaza accord. During the second week of December, Secretary Vance went to the Middle East to consult with the various governments and to begin the process of redefining American strategy.

Just after Vance's return from the area, Begin invited himself to Washington to see President Carter. Vance had seen the prime minister only a few days before, and Begin had not put forward any new ideas, but now he said he had important proposals to discuss with the president before going to a scheduled meeting with Sadat in Ismailia on Christmas day. Some in Washington were suspicious that Begin's purpose was to try to elicit an American endorsement of his ideas before they were shown to Sadat.

Carter's talks with Begin on December 16–17 confirmed the American suspicion. Begin practically pleaded with the president to say that his proposals were a fair basis for negotiation. In fact, Carter did tell him his Sinai proposal looked promising, adding the caveat that there might be points in it that he did not fully understand yet. (This comment became a source of discord later when the Israelis claimed that Carter had approved of the Sinai proposal, knowing it included a provision that Israeli settlements would not be removed.)

If Begin's Sinai proposal was genuinely seen in positive terms, the same could not be said for his "home rule" proposal for "Judea, Samaria and the Gaza District."[27] In lengthy discussions with Begin, the president, the vice-president, Vance, and Brzezinski all tried to encourage Begin to modify his plan. Several points stood out. The home rule proposal was intended as a permanent arrangement, not as a transition to the return of the territory to Arab political control once a peace agreement had been reached. The plan also contained the type of detail that would be bound to irritate Sadat, and Begin was urged to present a simpler set of principles, perhaps only orally. But Begin seemed to be proud of his creation and rather arrogantly told the American side that he did not need their advice on how to negotiate with Sadat. Begin was so eager to win U.S. endorsement, however, that he did imply he would make some improvements in the plan after consulting with his cabinet. With that, he promptly went public with a statement that came very close to saying the president had approved of his plan, which required a clarification from the American side to the effect that the plan was a positive step in the direction of negotiations.

Some in the administration saw merit in Begin's proposal, in part because they thought he could be tricked into turning it into a proposal for only a transitional period.[28] They saw as positive elements Begin's willingness to leave Israel's claim to sovereignty over the West Bank and Gaza in abeyance for five years; his acceptance of the idea that a special administrative regime would go into effect in all the territory of the West Bank and Gaza; and his suggestions about equality of rights and obligations for Arabs and Israelis. (Some of the most attractive points were dropped a few days later from the proposal that was actually presented to Sadat, which left the American negotiators feeling that Begin had used the meeting with Carter just as they had expected and that their entreaties for greater moderation and flexibility had fallen on deaf ears.)[29]

Indicative of the gap between the Egyptian and Israeli positions was the difference in Begin's and Sadat's accounts of their meeting in Ismailia. According to the Israeli version, Sadat was on the verge of accepting the Israeli proposals and issuing a common declaration of principles, but was persuaded not to do so by his hard-line advisers from the Foreign Ministry. Sadat's account, by contrast, said that Begin had not grasped the importance of his Jerusalem visit and that the Israelis were trying to haggle and tread on sovereignty. He was quite caustic in his remarks, suggesting there was little point in going on with direct negotiations.

Carter and Vance, who had anticipated that further U.S. help would be needed to keep the negotiations alive, believed a continuing negotiating process was essential if the United States was to use its influence. Consequently a meeting of the so-called political committee was arranged in January at the level of foreign ministers. For Egypt this meant that Muhammad Ibrahim Kamel, Sadat's new foreign minister, would make his first visit to Jerusalem, something he obviously did not welcome. In fact, the talks seemed to proceed fairly well on the technical level, with the objective of drafting a declaration of principles. (By now the United States was pushing the Aswan formula calling for "the right of the Palestinians to participate in the determination of their own future.") For reasons still not entirely clear, but perhaps reflecting Kamel's anger at a toast delivered by Begin at a dinner the first night, Sadat suddenly called his delegation home. Vance, who had seen many negotiations go through such moments, termed it "a bump in the road" and returned to Washington to help forge a new approach in light of events that once again seemed to have taken a somewhat alarming turn.

U.S.-EGYPTIAN COORDINATION

Discussions within the American negotiating team in January led to a strategy of trying to change two key elements in Begin's position: to achieve a freeze on the construction of new settlements in the occupied territories, an issue of special concern after Begin blatantly allowed new settlements to be started in Sinai within days of his talks in Ismailia with Sadat; and to convince Begin to return to the previous Israeli formula for the West Bank and Gaza by offering to withdraw, at least partially, as the quid pro quo for peace and recognition. This latter point was put in terms of Begin's unwillingness to accept the fact that the withdrawal provision of UN Resolution 242 applied to the West Bank and Gaza. The Labor party in formally accepting 242 in mid-1970 had interpreted the resolution as requiring "peace for withdrawal" on all fronts, and because of this Begin had left the national unity government that existed at the time.[30]

The Americans thought that the two issues of settlements and withdrawal were intrinsically important if there was to be any chance of a negotiated peace, and that on these issues Begin was vulnerable at home and in the American Jewish community. They therefore decided to mount a campaign of public pressure against Begin on these two points, and to that end they prepared a very comprehensive "white paper," which showed conclusively that Begin did not accept 242 in the same terms as previous Israeli governments had. The document was never released, but it was used for judicious leaking to the press. On settlements, the administration in public and private tried to get a settlements freeze, and indeed the record of 1978 shows very few new settlements being established that year, even though Begin never formally agreed to a freeze until the Camp David talks.

The Carter administration felt it was on sure ground on the two issues of settlements and withdrawal, provided the United States remained clearly committed to Israel's security and supported the Israeli idea that peace should entail normal relations. But Carter felt that Sadat should help the campaign to pressure Israel and worried that Sadat's decision to pull out of the political talks in Jerusalem would weaken the case against Begin. Consequently Carter decided to invite the Egyptian president to Washington in February for a serious review of strategy.

One idea discussed before Sadat's arrival was to try to work out with the Egyptians a series of coordinated moves that would maximize the pressure on Begin. The risk of appearing to collude with the Egyptians was obvious, but Sadat's reputation for making sudden and sometimes unhelpful moves was very much on the Americans' minds. It was also thought that Sadat would be delighted at the prospect of playing a somewhat Machiavellian game aimed at Begin.

A second American effort in early 1978 was to redraft Begin's autonomy proposal into a number of general principles that might be agreed upon between Egypt and Israel as a formula for a transitional period of three to five years. By the time of Sadat's arrival at Camp David in the first week of February 1978, a nine-point document had been developed.[31]

Sadat and Carter spent the weekend at Camp David alone. The weather was cold and there was snow on the ground. Sadat was not in good health and clearly disliked the setting, so far from his normal winter refuge of Aswan. By the time the sessions with advisers began, Sadat had convinced Carter that his initiative had nearly reached an end and that he saw no point in going on. Sadat, it must be remembered, was a consummate actor, and some of his posture was no doubt theater, but some was also real. After a lengthy exposé by Carter of all the problems, during which Sadat looked despondent, the president asked his pipe-smoking guest if he had any comment to make. Sadat puffed on his pipe, looked grave, and finally said he had only one question to ask: would there be an American proposal? The answer from Carter was yes, and much of the rest of the day was spent developing an agreed strategy that would culminate in a U.S. proposal.

The Americans insisted that Sadat must first return to the negotiating table and reiterate his commitment to the peace process. Then Begin would be invited to Washington, and Carter would privately press hard on the issues of settlements and Resolution 242, issues that the Egyptians would also stress. The United States would also present the nine-point plan as a basis for a possible joint declaration. Part of the strategy also meant getting a formal Egyptian counterproposal to Begin's home rule plan before an American proposal would be put forward. Sadat was urged to make his initial proposal fairly tough, even at the risk of creating a crisis in the negotiations, so that the United States could be in a position of arguing with both Israel and Egypt over aspects of their proposals. To be in that position would help protect Carter's flank at home, since one-sided pressure on Israel could not easily be sustained. The key point in this strategy was that Sadat would, at the appropriate point in the crisis, moderate his position and accept American compromise proposals, making it possible for U.S. pressure then to turn on Israel. The strategy was complex, a bit devious, and only partly internalized by the American and Egyptian officials who were supposed to carry it out. But Sadat loved it. His long-sought goal of forging a joint U.S.-Egyptian strategy seemed to be at hand.[32]

What happened to the Sadat-Carter accord of February 1978? First, the agreed-upon calendar, which envisaged an American proposal by midyear, was thrown off by the decision to seek congressional approval for the sale of advanced aircraft to Saudi Arabia, Egypt, and Israel. The F-15s for Saudi Arabia proved to be very controversial, and the administration had to spend large amounts of time and political capital to get the sale through. This issue arose right at the moment that the first stage of the joint U.S.-Egyptian strategy should have been taking shape. Second, Sadat was a bit shaky in carrying out his side of the bargain. He tended to ignore the themes of 242 and Israeli settlements in his public statements, making it appear that Carter was being more pro-Arab than Sadat himself. In addition, when he finally did send the United States a proposal, it was very general and did not really serve as a counter to Begin's autonomy plan. Third, Vance decided to ask the Israelis to clarify their views on what would happen at the end of the five-year period of autonomy, and the Israelis took a long time to answer. When they did so, they basically confirmed what was already known of Begin's annexationist intentions.

By midsummer neither Carter nor Vance seemed to feel that the more manipulative aspects of the strategy discussed with Sadat could be made to work, although both remained wedded to the idea that a U.S. proposal should be developed. But no one seemed to relish the idea of a showdown with Begin, except perhaps for Brzezinski, who felt Begin was manipulating the United States and needed to be reminded that Washington was capable of pursuing its national interests in a vigorous way and would not always succumb to domestic pressures.

While the American side was edging away from a joint U.S.-Egyptian strategy by mid-1978, Sadat seemed to be operating on the assumption that the general outline of what had been discussed at Camp David was still valid. Thus he periodically adopted extreme positions in public, threatened to call off talks with Israel, talked ominously of October 1978 as the expiration date of the Sinai II agreement (not true), and generally seemed to be trying to engineer an Egyptian-Israeli crisis into which Carter could step with a compromise proposal. Though prepared to go along with the stage setting insisted upon by the Americans, such as the Leeds Castle talks at the level of foreign minister in July, Sadat was clearly getting impatient for the showdown with Begin.

Through the spring and summer of 1978 little substantive progress was made in an endless series of contacts with Egyptian and Israeli leaders. Carter was impatient with the slow pace of diplomacy and seemed to feel a desire to get more directly into the act. During much of July a highly secret planning group began to develop a U.S. proposal under Vance's supervision, and the president followed the progress with interest. On July 20 he discussed with his advisers an idea he had been toying with for some time—a summit meeting at Camp David with both Begin and Sadat.[33] Carter seemed to view a summit as the only way to force decisions to a head, and he doubtless counted on his own role as mediator to bridge the still very large gaps. His view of a summit was psychological and political: once the leaders were committed, they could not afford to fail, and he counted on the special atmosphere of Camp David, away from the press and the burdens of everyday governing, to help produce a positive result. The rest of the foreign-policy team was somewhat more wary of the summit idea, tending to focus on the need for very careful substantive preparations. In early August Vance went to the Middle East to invite Begin and Sadat to Camp David in early September. Both accepted readily, and no doubt Sadat saw this event as the much-awaited moment of truth when he and Carter would corner Begin.

THE CAMP DAVID SUMMIT

Carter, Sadat, and Begin, along with their top advisers, isolated themselves at the president's mountaintop retreat, Camp David, from September 5 to September 17. Little information reached the outside world of these deliberations at the time, so many were surprised at the news on the last day that agreement had been reached on two frameworks for negotiations. The first dealt with the principles of an Egyptian-Israeli agreement; the second, more complex and less precise, consisted of a formula for an interim period of self-government for Palestinians living in the West Bank and Gaza. The outcome was not quite what anyone had expected at the beginning of the historic summit.

Carter prepared himself meticulously for the talks. His briefing book contained an analytical paper entitled "The Pivotal Issue," which focused on the question of "linkage" between agreements on Sinai and on the West Bank.[34] The point was made that Begin would seek to ensure that any agreement he might reach with Sadat concerning Egyptian-Israeli relations should in no way be dependent on resolving the Palestinian question. Sadat, by contrast, would want some relationship between the two so as to protect himself from the charge that he had abandoned the Palestinians and had accepted a separate peace with Israel. The problem for Carter would be to see if an agreement could be reached at the summit that would make it possible to use the incentive of reaching peace with Egypt to moderate Begin's position on the Palestinian question, without at the same time making Egyptian-Israeli relations entirely subject to whether a solution could be found to the most difficult part of the Arab-Israeli conflict.

The American delegation had identified several specific issues that were likely to be obstacles to a successful agreement at Camp David. First was Begin's unwillingness to accept that the principle of withdrawal from occupied territory, as called for in Resolution 242, should apply to the West Bank and Gaza at the end of a transitional period. Second was the problem of Israeli settlements in Sinai and in the West Bank. Third was the question of how to associate Jordan and the Palestinians with subsequent rounds of negotiations.

The American team felt it was pointless at Camp David to try to resolve the questions of the border between Israel and a Palestinian-Jordanian entity.[35] Not only would Begin be at his most intransigent, but also the Arab parties most directly concerned would not be present. Similarly the Americans felt the question of sovereignty over the West Bank and Gaza, as well as the status of Jerusalem, should be deferred. Instead they thought that Egypt and Israel could make some headway on outlining a transitional regime for the West Bank, building on Dayan's idea of dismantling the military occupation and replacing it with an elected Palestinian body with broad responsibility for day-to-day affairs, perhaps including control over state lands (which would have effectively foreclosed the possibility of extensive new Israeli settlement activity during the transitional period).

No one on the American side anticipated insurmountable problems in reaching a general agreement on principles regarding Sinai. Israel was expected to leave the settlements and the airfields, provided firm security arrangements could be worked out. Sadat was taken seriously when he said that he could not bargain over land or sovereignty, but that everything else could be negotiated.

These assessments led the American team to think in terms of seeking agreement between Begin and Sadat on general principles regarding both Sinai and the West Bank and Gaza. Begin would have to cede on the applicability of 242 to the West Bank and Gaza in any final settlement, and to a freeze on settlement activity, in return for which he could expect Sadat to be forthcoming on Israeli security requirements in Sinai and the West Bank, and to accept a very loose linkage between negotiations on the two fronts. In Vance's view an agreement of this sort would serve to guide the efforts of the foreign ministers as they sought to translate the principles agreed upon by the political leaders into a concrete document leading to an Egyptian-Israeli peace treaty and to a formula for Palestinian self-government for a transitional period.

President Carter's initial reaction to the advice of his team was that it should have aimed higher.[36] Rather than just seek agreement on principles concerning an overall settlement, he wanted to work out the details of an Egyptian-Israeli peace treaty, including specific security arrangements. At Camp David this became his special project, and the first draft of the Egyptian-Israeli accord was done in his hand.[37] Carter, it is fair to say, was less concerned with the so-called linkage problem than were other members of the American team, and he was also more optimistic about the chances of reaching a satisfactory agreement through direct talks with Begin and Sadat.

Those who were somewhat more pessimistic about the prospects of bridging the very large gaps between the two parties were also more inclined to see the Camp David talks as part of an ongoing process. From this perspective, even if the talks fell short of full agreement, negotiations would continue, with the issues, it was hoped, more narrowly focused than before. This somewhat apolitical view stood in sharp contrast to the position taken by the president's domestic affairs advisers, who felt Carter needed to leave Camp David with an apparent success.

Carter's views proved to be partly correct and partly wrong. He was right in sensing that the best avenue for real progress lay in getting a detailed understanding between Begin and Sadat on Sinai and on the basic elements of an Egyptian-Israeli peace treaty. Begin skillfully withheld his final concessions on removal from Sinai of Israeli settlements and return of three airfields to Egypt until the very end, but from the outset it was clear that an agreement was possible. Carter was wrong, however, in believing that the talks could be concluded quickly and that the three leaders could work well together to solve problems. After only two sessions with both Begin and Sadat in the same room, the president realized it would be better to keep them apart.[38]

Sadat arrived at Camp David ready for a fight with Begin. To ensure that it would happen, he presented to Carter and Begin an Egyptian draft of a fairly tough agreement. Begin reacted sharply, and the Israelis began to write a counterdraft. At the same time, however, Sadat privately told Carter that he was prepared to be flexible on most points, except for land and sovereignty, but that Carter should put forward proposals for both delegations to react to.[39] On the Israeli side, Attorney General Aharon Barak had also reached the conclusion that the time had come for the United States to put forward proposals of its own, and that Begin and Sadat should be kept apart. Thus, by the first weekend, the American team began to polish the first of many negotiating drafts.

Over the next ten days a pattern developed whereby the U.S. delegation, and often just the president and Secretary Vance, would meet separately with the Israeli and Egyptian leaders. They would work from nonbinding written drafts, each time trying to elicit concrete reactions to proposals. These would then be discussed within the American team, and a new draft would be produced, often only marginally different than the previous one. By this means the main issues of disagreement surfaced quickly.

On Sinai there were essentially two problems: settlements and airfields. Both were resolved satisfactorily toward the end of the talks, with Begin reserving his position on settlements by saying the issue would have to be put to a vote of the Knesset. Predictably, the final status of the West Bank and Gaza and the question of linkage were the main stumbling blocks. In addition, the Egyptians insisted on including language from Resolution 242 on the nonacquisition of territory by war. The Israelis refused, even though the language was found in 242, which Begin professed to accept. The not-very-elegant solution was to append the full text of 242 to the Camp David Accords, but not to single out that phrase in the text. For Begin this was a minor victory, typical of his tenacious concern for words and principles, and also indicative of Sadat's comparative indifference to precise language.

Two central issues seemed likely to prevent agreement as the days wore on. First was the bedeviling question of what would happen on the West Bank and Gaza after a five-year transitional period. The Egyptians, supported by the Americans, wanted to make it clear that a final agreement would be negotiated during the transitional period which would resolve the questions of borders, sovereignty, security, and recognition according to the same principles of 242 that would govern agreements on other fronts, such as Sinai. In other words, the "peace for withdrawal" formula would remain intact even if the details might be worked out somewhat differently and over a longer period. Begin would have none of it, but instead of fighting the issue head on, he preferred to focus on other matters until the very last days of the negotiations.

Begin, more than any of the other negotiators, seemed to have a feel for the strategic use of time, taking the negotiations to the brink of collapse over secondary issues to avoid being pressed on key problems. Sadat, by contrast, simply refused to negotiate at all over those matters of deepest concern to him—Egyptian land and sovereignty—while leaving to his aides the unhappy task of trying to stand up to Begin on the Palestinian issue. Carter, who often grew impatient with Sadat's subordinates, frequently went directly to Sadat to get them overruled, something that did not recommend itself on the Israeli side, since there it was Dayan, Defense Minister Ezer Weizman, and Barak who showed flexibility, while Begin was the hard-liner (a much stronger negotiating position to be in, as the results showed).[40] Begin's position was also strengthened by his willingness to accept a failure in the talks. Both Sadat and Carter were more committed to a positive outcome, and Begin could therefore credibly use the threat of walking out, as he did, to extract some concessions.

The second difficult issue was the question of settlements: the American and Egyptian teams wanted to get a freeze on them during the negotiations over Palestinian self-government. Again, Begin deferred the discussion of this issue until near the end of the talks.

September 16, a Saturday, proved to be the crucial day for addressing the hard issues involving the West Bank and Gaza.[41] Up until that time all of the American drafts contained language on the applicability of 242, including the principle of withdrawal, to the final negotiation on the West Bank and Gaza. And a paragraph calling for a freeze on settlements had always been included. That morning Dayan and Barak met with Vance. The Israelis explained why Begin would never accept the language on 242 and withdrawal. Barak added that he felt a solution could be found, but only if they were all prepared to continue negotiating for another week or so. Prophetically, he said that if agreement had to be reached that day, all they could hope to do was to paper over some very major problems that would come back to haunt them.

Apart from Barak and a few others, however, no one had the stomach for another week in the claustrophobic environment of Camp David. As a result, in the course of the day on Saturday, the American draft was fundamentally changed. The elements of 242, including withdrawal, which had previously been spelled out, were deleted. The language was changed to make it clear that the negotiations, but not necessarily the results of the negotiations, would be based on the principles of 242. And the negotiations about the West Bank and Gaza were artfully obfuscated by creating two tracks, one involving peace-treaty negotiations between Israel and Jordan, and the other involving talks between Israel and representatives of the Palestinians about the West Bank and Gaza.

Israel had no objection to saying that 242 should be the basis for negotiations with Jordan. In Begin's view Jordan had no right to the West Bank, and saying that did not imply a commitment to the "peace for withdrawal" formula. In the Israeli view, 242 did not apply to the talks on the final status of the West Bank and Gaza. A careful reader of paragraph 1(c) of the "Framework for Peace in the Middle East" signed on September 17, 1978, will see language about "two separate but related committees," and "the negotiations shall be based on all the provisions and principles of UN Security Council Resolution 242." It may take a lawyer to explain how, but Begin successfully protected his position of principle that 242 did not apply to the negotiations over the West Bank's future; the Americans accepted the ambiguity; and Sadat may well have wondered what all the verbal gymnastics were about. In any case, Begin won this round as well.

Later on Saturday evening Carter and Vance thought they had finally won a round with Begin. At a late-night session Carter insisted that Begin agree to a freeze on settlement activity in the West Bank and Gaza for the duration of the negotiations over autonomy. Carter agreed to delete the paragraph in the draft text and to substitute a letter from Begin to him, and he dropped his insistence that existing settlements should not be thickened. But he clearly thought a commitment had been made not to construct new settlements during the autonomy talks. Vance also understood Begin to have made such a promise, although he was concerned about Begin's hesitation to accept an open-ended commitment to a freeze.[42]

In any event, the issue should have been settled on Sunday morning, when Begin sent a draft letter on the topic to Carter. By this time Sadat had already been informed that Begin had agreed to a freeze on settlements. But the actual letter did not conform to Carter's understanding, and, without speaking directly to Begin, Carter sent it back. Begin had promised to freeze settlements for three months, a time period he had mentioned the previous evening. Now, however, Begin was linking the freeze to the duration of the Egyptian-Israeli negotiations, not to the autonomy talks, which was an entirely inappropriate and unprecedented step. Alarm bells should have gone off, but so many other issues were on the agenda that day, especially a diversionary argument over Jerusalem which erupted in the afternoon, that both Carter and Vance continued to act as if there had merely been a misunderstanding that would be cleared up as soon as Begin sent back a new draft.

The final version of the letter did not arrive until after the Camp David Accords had been signed, and in it Begin held stubbornly to his position that the freeze would last only through the three-month period of the Egyptian-Israeli talks. Another round went to Begin, and on a position of considerable importance to the skeptical Arab audience that was waiting to see what, if anything, would be offered to the Palestinians as a result of the Egyptian-Israeli separate peace apparently in the making. Carter never got over the feeling that Begin had misled him, and this episode caused deep mutual distrust between the two leaders.

Late in the afternoon of September 17 Sadat and Carter met for the last time to discuss the agreement that was nearing completion. Sadat was reserved, and his mood was not one of pleasure at a job well done. The American team also realized that many problems lay ahead, but in the end it had made the political decision to get the best agreement then available, while hoping that the next stage of talks would fill in some of the gaps and clarify areas of ambiguity. And it is also true that the key players on the American side tended to think the Camp David Accords would eventually win Saudi and Jordanian support. To a large extent this was wishful thinking, and in part it reflected a tendency to take the Saudis too literally when they mumbled positive generalities to visiting Americans.

CONCLUSIONS

During the lengthy talks that preceded Camp David and at Camp David itself, U.S. policy constantly had to adjust to two realities: events in the Middle East cannot be easily controlled or influenced, so developments there frequently caught the Americans by surprise and obliged them to revise their strategies; and domestic American political realities intrude with particular force on the decisionmaking process regarding the Middle East. A president must simultaneously adjust his plans to the unpredictable twists and turns of Middle East politics and keep an eye on his domestic political base. What seems possible and desirable in the first year of a president's term is likely to be seen as hopelessly ambitious by the third year.

The result of these Middle East and domestic pressures is to move American policy away from grand designs with strong ideological content toward a less controversial, and less ambitious, middle ground that can win bipartisan public support as well as acceptance by Arabs and Israelis. To do so, of course, is not always possible, as much as it might be politically desirable, so American policy toward the Middle East rarely manages to satisfy everyone that has an interest in shaping it. Presidents seem to tire of all the controversy generated by Middle East problems, and the intractability of the issues is a source of much frustration.

The Camp David Accords amply demonstrate the limits of what in fact can be achieved, even with a massive commitment of effort. But they are also a reminder that diplomacy can produce results, if the will, the energy, and the creativity are there. The historical verdict on Camp David cannot be fully rendered, although with each passing year it seems to be more widely accepted as part of the new reality of the Middle East. By any standard, however, this remarkable adventure in summit diplomacy achieved more than most of its detractors have been willing to acknowledge, and less than its most ardent proponents have claimed.

CHAPTER ELEVEN

Descent from the Summit: To Link or Not to Link?

The two agreements reached at Camp David marked an important watershed in the peace negotiations, but much remained to be done before peace would actually be achieved. Many of the blanks in the Camp David Accords had to be filled in, and many of the ambiguities had to be resolved one way or another. Along the way there would be pauses, detours, some backtracking, and many dead ends. Egypt and Israel would finally reach their goal of a formal peace treaty, but the broader objective of finding a peaceful resolution to the Palestinian question remained elusive.

The phase of detailed drafting was now to begin, a seemingly technical task, but in fact a complex process during which major political battles were still fought and attempts to revise the basic framework of negotiations were still made. Although the technicians were sitting at the table drafting documents, the political leaders were still deeply involved.

Menachem Begin, Anwar Sadat, and Jimmy Carter each devised strategies for this phase of negotiations, but the special circumstances of the summit could not be recreated. Isolating the leaders from the press and their own public opinion had no doubt been a prime factor in reaching the two framework agreements. Now, however, each leader would have to return to the real world in which domestic constituencies would have their say.

As each of the Camp David participants felt compelled to justify what he had done at the summit, the gap separating them began to widen again. By the time of the self-imposed target of three months for negotiating the peace treaty between Egypt and Israel, the talks had come to a halt.

POST-SUMMIT STRATEGIES

Carter left Camp David with a feeling of real satisfaction. The reaction in Congress, the press, and the public at large to the news of an agreement between Begin and Sadat was overwhelmingly positive. Carter received much of the credit, and his political fortunes seemed to improve significantly as a result.

To sustain this political boost, however, Carter needed to make sure that the Camp David frameworks did not remain dead letters. Time was of the essence in reaching a formal peace treaty. Among other considerations, midterm congressional elections were scheduled for early November, and it would probably help Democratic candidates, and therefore Carter, if a peace treaty could be signed by then.

Although Carter was no doubt pleased by the domestic American reaction, he was worried by the early signs of disenchantment in the Arab world. He had implied to Sadat that he would make a serious effort to win support from Jordan and Saudi Arabia, and in his more careless moments he had said that anything he and Sadat agreed to would have to be accepted by King Hussein and the Saudis. But Hussein was wary of the accords reached at Camp David and refused to meet with Sadat on the Egyptian president's return trip to Cairo.

Carter's clear priority after Camp David was to conclude the treaty negotiations as quickly as possible, literally within days. As usual, the president tended to see the remaining issues as technical and therefore susceptible to rapid resolution. The deeper political problems faced by both Begin and Sadat were harder for him to fathom. Carter found it difficult to accept the fact that neither shared his own sense of urgency.

Not only did Begin not share Carter's feeling that time was of the essence, but he also wanted to slow down the pace of negotiations for fear that too much pressure would otherwise be put on Israel. Whenever Carter showed himself too eager for quick results, Begin seemed to dig in his heels to resist demands for Israeli concessions. He was particularly recalcitrant about the settlements in the West Bank and Gaza. As hard as Carter might press to resolve this issue, Begin simply said no to the idea of a prolonged freeze on new settlements. And that was that.

If Begin was attentive to the rhythms of American politics, and surely he was, he must have realized it would be increasingly difficult for Carter to play a strong role in the negotiations as 1979 unfolded. At some point the preelection atmosphere would take hold, and Carter would have to turn to shoring up his political position. He would not then want to engage in confrontations with Israel. Begin was well aware that Carter tended to side with Sadat on the Palestinian question and that the negotiations over the West Bank and Gaza would be extremely difficult.

It would be far better, then, not to begin talks on autonomy until sometime well into 1979, when Carter would have other preoccupations.

In many ways Sadat was in a weaker position than Begin, which inevitably influenced the outcome of the negotiations. If the talks now broke down, Israel would stay put in Sinai. Sadat would have nothing to show for his "historic initiative." And his hope for American economic, military, and technological assistance would fade if the peace negotiations collapsed because of his actions. Carter had already warned him of that at Camp David. Sadat worried less about time than Carter, but he too must have understood that Carter's role would have to change as the election year of 1980 approached.[1] Sadat also knew, however, that any show by him of impatience or eagerness to conclude the negotiations would be used by Begin to try to extract further concessions.

From the perspectives of Carter, Sadat, and Begin, the post-summit phase of negotiations was bound to be difficult. The unique circumstances of the thirteen days at Camp David had facilitated reaching agreement, but now most of the pressures were working in the opposite direction. It was not a propitious atmosphere in which to resume the talks.

PREPARING FOR THE NEXT ROUND

Carter was not content to sit and wait for the results of the Knesset vote on the Camp David Accords, scheduled for two weeks later. There was one item of unfinished business. On Monday, September 18, 1978, Begin had sent Carter the promised letter on the settlements in the West Bank and Gaza. The text was identical to the one Carter had rejected the previous day. Referring to his notes of the Saturday night conversation, Carter wrote down what he thought had been agreed to and had Assistant Secretary of State Harold Saunders deliver his version to the Israelis, along with the original of Begin's letter, which Carter refused to accept.

For several days American and Israel officials tried, without success, to find language that might resolve the difference. Sadat did not help matters when he said to the press on September 19 that he understood there would be a freeze for three months and that Israel had also agreed not to expand settlements during this period.[2]

Carter continued to look for ways to push Begin into agreeing to a freeze on settlements for the duration of the negotiations on self-government for the Palestinians. At one point Carter decided that until he had received the letter he sought on settlements, he would not send a letter to Begin promising to help build two airfields in the Negev. On

September 22 he signed a letter to Begin spelling out once more what he thought had been agreed on, pointedly noting that he had so informed Sadat on September 17. But the letter was never sent. A few days later, however, he dispatched an oral message to Begin, repeating his view on what had been agreed on and warning that "the settlements could become a serious obstacle to peace. Construction of new settlements during the negotiations could have a most serious consequence for the successful fulfillment of the agreement."

When Begin met with the American ambassador to Israel, Samuel W. Lewis, on September 27, 1978, he provided the text of Attorney General Barak's notes from the meeting on the night of September 16. According to Begin, the notes proved that he had not agreed to the freeze Carter had requested. He had agreed only to consider it. He went on to say he would never agree to give Arabs a veto over where Israelis could settle. In his view Jews had as much right to settle in Hebron as in Tel Aviv. That was precisely the crux of the disagreement.

Neither Carter nor Begin would budge, but soon Carter turned to other matters. To the many bystanders who were waiting to see the outcome of this dispute, round one seemed to go to Begin—not an encouraging sign for Sadat or King Hussein.

While Carter was trying to untangle the controversy over settlements, Secretary of State Cyrus Vance was traveling in the Middle East. His goal was to try to win Jordanian and Saudi support for the Camp David Accords. What he found instead was deep skepticism, coated only with a formal politeness that some Americans interpreted as an expression of hope that the next round of negotiations would succeed.[3]

Carter and Vance both felt that some of Begin's public interpretations of the Camp David Accords were making it difficult for King Hussein and the Saudis not to reject them.[4] The Americans were also frustrated by Sadat's seeming unwillingness to communicate with either the Jordanians or the Saudis.[5]

Despite all these problems, Carter remained somewhat optimistic that Jordan would join the negotiations.[6] Vance was more skeptical, especially after his visits to Amman and Riyadh. King Hussein had raised many questions, and Vance knew it would be difficult to overcome his doubts. In an attempt to do so, however, Vance did agree to give the king written answers to questions he might have about the accords.

Meanwhile through intelligence channels the PLO was making queries to Washington about the meaning of the agreements. Arafat was skeptical, but he showed a serious interest in finding out if there might be more to Camp David than met the eye. Although the Americans had no reason for optimism, they could see that an Arab consensus had not yet formed. If the Arabs took Begin's interpretations, or Sadat's contemptuous expressions, as the final words on the matter, the case would be closed. But the Americans hoped they might succeed in giving a more open-ended interpretation to the framework dealing with the Palestinians and thus prevent a strongly negative Arab reaction. They therefore decided to use the questions from King Hussein as the means for offering a liberal American interpretation of Camp David.

Not everyone in the administration was pleased with the idea of responding in writing to King Hussein. Vice President Mondale, for example, thought it was undignified for the United States to submit to this sort of interrogation. But Vance had given the king his word, and Carter decided to provide written answers. As soon as the fourteen questions arrived on September 29, the bureaucracy began to churn out answers. Most of them consisted of repeating well-known American positions, but in some cases they involved interpretations of Camp David. For example, the United States went on record as favoring the inclusion of the Palestinians in East Jerusalem in the election for the self-governing authority. And in an early draft the Americans had taken the position that sovereignty in the West Bank and Gaza resided with the people who lived there. When Mondale saw the draft, he strongly opposed such a formulation, and it was removed from the final version signed by Carter.[7] (See appendix F for the text.)

While the Americans were working to convince other Arabs to be open minded about Camp David, the Israeli Knesset met on September 27, 1978, to vote on the Camp David Accords, including the provision for withdrawing settlements from Sinai. After lengthy arguments, the vote was 84 in favor and 19 opposed, with 17 abstentions.

Carter phoned Begin the next day to congratulate him on the outcome of the Knesset debate. He also mentioned his hope that the "difference of opinion" between them over settlements in the West Bank and Gaza would soon be resolved. Begin said he had already sent the president a letter on the topic. Carter repeated that he was determined to solve this problem and that he and Begin should try to minimize their differences. He added that he would like to see a Sinai agreement within days. Begin said it should be possible if everyone agreed to use the standard form of a peace treaty and just fill in the blanks with appropriate details.

Carter then called Sadat, and the two agreed that negotiations on the peace treaty could begin in mid-October. With these conversations Carter seems to have given up the idea of trying to force Begin to change his position on West Bank and Gaza settlements. By continuing to dwell on that topic, Carter would risk the Sinai agreement he so badly wanted. He would also be reminding the other Arabs of one of the flaws in the Camp David framework. Instead, he apparently decided to end the public debate over the issue. For three months, in any case, there would be no more Israeli settlements, and during that period Carter hoped that a solution might be found. So that same day, September 28, he authorized Secretary of Defense Harold Brown to sign a letter to Israeli Defense Minister Ezer Weizman promising American support in building two airfields in the Negev.

On September 29, 1978, Secretary Vance spoke before the UN General Assembly. He had urged Carter to allow him to say something on the Palestinian question that might change the negative atmosphere growing in the Arab world. Carter agreed, and Vance included the following phrase in his text: "As the President said, our historic position on settlements in occupied territory has remained constant. As he further said, no peace agreement will be either just or secure if it does not resolve the problem of the Palestinians in the broadest sense. We believe that the Palestinian people must be assured that they and their descendants can live with dignity and freedom and have the opportunity for economic fulfillment and for political expression. The Camp David Accords state that the negotiated solution must recognize the legitimate rights of the Palestinian people."[8]

THE BLAIR HOUSE TALKS

To prepare for the next phase of negotiations, the American team had drawn up a draft of an Egyptian-Israeli peace treaty. Vance wanted to use the same procedure that had proved successful at Camp David. Each side would be asked to comment on the American draft, but changes in the text would be made only by the American side after consulting with the others. The device of a "single negotiating text" was one of the methodological devices the Americans had found useful, and both the Egyptians and Israelis had come to accept it.

Carter reviewed the draft treaty on October 9. His only comment was that Israel should withdraw fully from Sinai in two, not three, years. The draft treaty was a fairly simple document. It formally ended the state of war and established a relationship of peace. Israel would withdraw to the international border according to details to be worked out by the parties. On the completion of an interim phase of withdrawal, diplomatic relations would be established. The border between the two countries was defined as the former international boundary between Egypt and mandated Palestine. Article 3 of the treaty called for normal peaceful relations, the details of which were to be spelled out in an annex. Article 4 called for security arrangements in Sinai and along the border. Article 5 dealt with freedom of navigation. And article 6 spelled out the relation between this treaty and other international obligations of the parties.

From the beginning the Americans realized that several issues would be contentious. For Israel, there was the question of the timing of withdrawal. Israel's fear was that Egypt might get most or all of its territory back before entering into any form of peaceful relations with Israel. For the Israeli public, all the concessions would then seem to be coming from the Israel side. Israel therefore insisted that Egypt should establish diplomatic relations before final withdrawal and that some aspects of normal relations should begin at an early date. For Egypt, this timing posed a problem. Sadat wanted to withhold the exchange of ambassadors until Israel had at least carried out the provisions of the Camp David Accords that called for elections for the Palestinians in the West Bank and Gaza to establish their own self-governing authority. This was the famous issue of linkage, which here boiled down to when Egypt would send its ambassador to Israel. Since that was a matter of great importance to Begin, it acquired significance for Sadat as well. A test of wills quickly developed over the issue.

A second issue of likely contention was the so-called priority of obligations. Israel wanted the treaty to contain a clear statement that it superseded other Egyptian commitments, such as Egypt's many mutual defense pacts with Arab countries. Sadat found it intolerable to say in public that commitments to Israel counted for more than commitments to Arab states. For example, if Israel carried out aggression against an Arab state allied to Egypt, Sadat did not feel it would be a violation of the treaty if he went to the aid of that state. In reality, of course, whatever was written on paper would not guarantee what would happen in some future conflict, but these were issues of high symbolic importance for each party, and each was trying to make its position clear to the United States in the event of future disputes. Much more was to be heard about the priority of obligations. Vance, the experienced international lawyer, realized from the outset that this issue would be a sticking point.

Perhaps most difficult was the question of how the two parties would express their continuing determination to work for a solution to the Palestinian question after they had signed the treaty. Begin wanted only a vague commitment to negotiate, whereas Sadat insisted on deadlines and specific commitments that would demonstrate that Egypt had not concluded a "separate peace." Here again was the linkage issue in its pure form.

Besides these difficult conceptual problems, there were also some complicated details. Israel wanted to retain access to Sinai oil, and wanted some form of guarantee from the United States if Egypt later refused to supply the oil. Some of the specific issues involving security arrangements in Sinai might also prove difficult, even though the military men on both sides had a good record of finding concrete compromise solutions.

This phase of the negotiations differed from Camp David not only in content but also in format and personnel. On the American side, Carter was less involved. He felt he had spent too much time on the Middle East and that he now had to turn his attention to other issues. Normalization of relations with China and the conclusion of SALT II with the Soviet Union were high on his foreign-policy agenda. Vance was designated as the principal negotiator on the American side, though he too had other responsibilities. He hoped to delegate much of the day-to-day work to Alfred Atherton, the U.S. ambassador for the peace talks.

The Egyptian team was also somewhat different. In the past Carter had relied heavily on his ability to deal directly with Sadat over the heads of the Egyptian delegation. Now that the time had come to put words to paper in a peace treaty, the Egyptian lawyers would have their chance again to push Sadat toward harder positions. Muhammad Ibrahim Kamel had resigned, and then without much explanation Sadat had also replaced Minister of Defense Abd al-Ghany Gamasy. The new minister of foreign affairs and head of the Egyptian delegation was Kamal Hassan Ali, who was assisted in the negotiations by Boutros Boutros Ghali and Usama al-Baz, both veterans of Camp David. Sadat also soon named a new prime minister, Mustafa Khalil, who had played no previous part in the negotiations.

The Israeli participants were more familiar, most of them having been at Camp David. Foreign Minister Dayan and Defense Minister Weizman led the negotiating team to Washington, accompanied by Attorney General Barak and Meir Rosenne, a legal adviser to the foreign minister. Begin refused to delegate much authority to the team, however, and the Israeli cabinet as a whole wanted to be kept abreast of most of the details of the talks. As a result, the comparative moderation of the negotiating team meant little.

The delegations arrived in Washington in the second week of October, and the first sessions were scheduled for October 12. Carter met with both the Israelis and Egyptians before the formal resumption of the talks in order to urge both sides to move toward agreement quickly. In his talks with the Egyptians on October 11, Carter said the negotiations in Washington should be used to deal with the problems of Sinai and the West Bank and Gaza. He urged the Egyptians not to give up on the Jordanians and Palestinians. At the same time, he said, the issues involving the West Bank and Gaza should not be allowed to impede progress toward an Egyptian-Israeli peace treaty.

In the meeting with Carter, Boutros Ghali took the floor for the Egyptians to make the case for linkage, or the "correlation" between the two agreements, as he was fond of calling it. After Egypt and Israel reached agreement, he asked, what pressure would there be on Israel to do anything about the West Bank and Gaza? If Egypt received some advantages in Sinai, the Palestinians must also have something. Otherwise Egypt would be isolated in the Arab world. This could jeopardize the approximately $2 billion that Egypt was receiving from Saudi Arabia. Al-Baz interjected the thought that the opposition to Camp David had already peaked in the Arab world and that within a few months King Hussein would be ready to join the talks. Carter concluded by repeating that he was committed to finding a solution to the West Bank and Gaza but that he did not want to risk the treaty between Egypt and Israel because of problems with Jordan or the Palestinians.

OPENING BIDS

For several days after these initial meetings the talks dragged on without any breakthroughs. The technicians were able to make some headway on the annexes, but the problems at the political level remained. Carter began to show signs of impatience. He was thinking of flying to the Middle East in late October, and even hoped, unrealistically, to be able to preside over the signing of the Egyptian-Israeli peace treaty at that time. An Arab summit was being talked about for early November, and Carter wanted to pin down the treaty before it convened. He also had his eye on the congressional elections.[9]

To speed up the talks, Carter decided to meet both delegations on October 17. Dayan complained about three issues: the language on priority of obligations in the treaty; the linkage between the treaty talks and the West Bank–Gaza issues; and Egypt's reluctance to speed up normalization. Then, in a shrewd gesture seemingly calculated to win Carter's support, Dayan announced that Israel was prepared to accelerate withdrawal to the interim line in Sinai. (The Camp David Accords called on Israel to pull back its forces from about two-thirds of Sinai within nine months of signing a peace treaty.) The town of Al-Arish, which had great symbolic value to Sadat, could be returned within two months instead of the nine envisaged in the framework agreement. Carter was pleased and saw the offer as a welcome sign of Israeli flexibility. In return, Carter agreed to talk to the Egyptians about moving quickly on normalization; he undertook to resolve a technical problem involving the location of the interim line; and he agreed to consider helping to finance the withdrawal of the Israeli military from Sinai, but not the cost of removing the settlers.

A few hours later Carter met with the Egyptian delegation. Kamal Hassan Ali informed the president that agreement had been reached on the delineation of limited-force zones in Sinai. Boutros Ghali then argued the case for some correlation between the treaty negotiations and the Palestinian question. In particular, he put forward the idea of establishing diplomatic relations in stages that would somehow be related to progress on the West Bank and Gaza. First would come the formal recognition of Israel, then a chargé d'affaires would be sent to Tel Aviv, and only later would ambassadors be exchanged. Carter was unhappy with this proposal and reminded the Egyptians that Sadat had orally agreed at Camp David that ambassadors would be exchanged at the time of the interim withdrawal. He then gave the Egyptians copies of his answers to King Hussein's questions and said they should help deal with the problem of linkage.

Carter also informed the Egyptians that the Israelis were prepared to accelerate withdrawal to Al-Arish. Now, he said, the Egyptians seemed to be backsliding on the timing of sending their ambassador to Tel Aviv. He argued that Egypt should reciprocate Israel's constructive attitude on

withdrawal by agreeing to an early exchange of ambassadors. Carter
ended the talks by asking the Egyptians to tell President Sadat of his
desire to visit the Middle East, before November 1 if possible.

Carter was now back in the middle of the negotiations. On October
20 he held a sometimes acrimonious meeting with the Israeli delegation.
He charged that Israel was ignoring the fact that the Egyptian-Israeli
framework was part of a broader commitment to work for a settlement
on the West Bank and Gaza as well. Barak asked if Carter thought the
treaty should be made contingent on whether an agreement could be
reached on the West Bank. Carter said that was not his intention. After
all, the West Bank formula might fail because of the actions or inactions
of third parties, in particular the Jordanians or Palestinians. But, Carter
asked, what if Israel was the party responsible for the failure of the West
Bank framework? Did Israel think that in those circumstances the treaty
would be unaffected? Barak answered that the treaty must be legally
independent of whatever happened on the West Bank and Gaza, even
though some degree of political linkage might exist. Carter then told the
Israelis that he was sure he could get Sadat to agree to an exchange of
ambassadors within one month of the interim withdrawal. Dayan asked
if the United States could write a letter guaranteeing that the treaty
would be carried out.

On the same day that Carter was having his difficult talk with the
Israelis, Assistant Secretary Saunders was in Jerusalem meeting with
Prime Minister Begin. He had previously been to Amman to deliver
Carter's answers to Hussein. He had also stopped in Riyadh and was
planning to meet with West Bank Palestinians.

First Saunders reported to Begin on Hussein's attitude, which was not
entirely negative. The king had told Saunders that he was not ready to
make a decision on entering negotiations until after the Baghdad summit
in early November, but that he would encourage Palestinians in the West
Bank to cooperate with the Camp David process. The Saudis had said
they would adopt a neutral attitude.

Begin complained that the Americans seemed to have great understanding for the political problems of Arab leaders, but none for his own. He
had been bitterly attacked by some of his oldest friends in the Irgun.
The Americans should appreciate the concessions he had already made
for peace. Then he told Saunders to convey to Carter his "deep sadness."
There had been no prior consultation with Israel over the answers to

King Hussein. Begin proceeded to launch into a point-by-point criticism of the answers, emphasizing what he considered to be all the deviations from Camp David that they contained. He attacked the United States for repeating its own position on Jerusalem, and for other statements of American positions that differed from his own. These positions, all well known to the Arabs, would, in Begin's view, harden their negotiating stance and lead them to expect American pressure on Israel. Although Carter's signature was on the answers to Hussein, Begin and his colleagues preferred to speak of the "Saunders document," and for several weeks Saunders was the target of a harsh campaign in the Israeli press.

Despite these contretemps with the Israelis in Washington and in Jerusalem, agreement *ad referendum* was reached on the text of the treaty. Each delegation had to refer back to its own capital for final approval, but the basic elements of the treaty were seemingly all in place. The Egyptians, however, had proposed during the talks that a parallel letter be signed by Sadat and Begin dealing with the West Bank and Gaza. The letter should coincide with the treaty and would commit the two parties to conclude the negotiations on the West Bank and Gaza by a fixed date, with elections to be held within three months after the treaty was signed.

Egypt also mentioned in the negotiations its special responsibility for Gaza, a reminder of Sadat's interest in the "Gaza-first" option whereby self-government would first be established in Gaza and only later in the West Bank, after King Hussein joined the negotiations. Al-Baz referred to this as a ploy to scare King Hussein and the Palestinians, in essence telling them that if they did not get into the negotiations soon they would be left out. He argued strongly that Israel should take a number of unilateral steps in Gaza before the withdrawal to the interim line in Sinai was completed.

Carter wrote to Sadat on October 22, spelling out the terms of the treaty as negotiated in Washington. He asked that Sadat accept the text in its current form, and that in addition he agree to a letter committing Egypt to send an ambassador to Israel within one month of the interim withdrawal. Carter repeated that he had asked the Israelis to withdraw more rapidly to the interim line than was called for at Camp David. Carter concluded the letter by saying he would like to visit the Middle East for the treaty signing, which he hoped could be at a very early date. A similar letter was sent to Begin. Carter noted that he did not yet have

Sadat's approval to send an ambassador to Israel within one month of the interim withdrawal, but he hoped that Sadat would have a positive attitude.

Sadat's reply came on October 24. He was willing to accommodate Carter on several points, including the exchange of ambassadors, provided some changes could be made in the text of the treaty. Egypt could not agree to permanent force limits in Sinai. Up to twenty-five years would be acceptable. (Carter noted, "Not a problem.") Second, article 6 of the treaty, the priority of obligations issue, made it seem as if Egypt's commitments to Israel were greater than those to the Arab League.[10] The language of the treaty should not downgrade Egypt's obligations under previous agreements. (Carter noted, "A problem.") Third, the treaty must clearly say that Egypt has sovereignty over Sinai. (Carter wrote, "Okay.")

A letter from Begin arrived the same day. In it the Israeli prime minister complained at length about the answers provided to King Hussein. The full transcript of Begin's talk with Saunders was appended to the letter. Then Begin reviewed the dispute over settlements in the West Bank and Gaza, noting that he had told the president there were plans to add several hundred families to the settlements in Judea and Samaria even during the three-month moratorium.

Meanwhile Dayan and Weizman were in Israel seeking to win cabinet approval for the draft treaty. They ran into considerable criticism, but nonetheless Begin pressed for cabinet support of the existing draft and won a sizable majority on October 26. For reasons of his own, and perhaps as a reward to some of the hard-line cabinet members, Begin accompanied the announcement of the cabinet's decision on the treaty with a decision to "thicken" settlements in the West Bank.

Carter was furious. He perfunctorily congratulated Begin on the cabinet vote and then commented on the decision to thicken settlements: "At a time when we are trying to organize the negotiations dealing with the West Bank and Gaza, no step by the Israeli government could be more damaging." In his own handwriting Carter added, "I have to tell you with gravest concern and regret that taking this step at this time will have the most serious consequences for our relationship."

In light of these developments, it was somewhat ironic that the Nobel peace prize was awarded the next day to both Begin and Sadat. Some of Carter's aides were bitter that the president was not included, but for the moment the more important problem was that peace itself seemed to be slipping away. Reports had even reached Washington that Sadat was about to withdraw his delegation and break off the talks. Carter contacted him and convinced him not to take any rash action, but the mood at the White House was gloomy. At a minimum, Carter would not be able to make his hoped-for trip to the Middle East before the end of the month.

During the last days of October the American team became increasingly aware that the Israelis were insisting on a very narrow definition of self-government for the Palestinians in the West Bank and Gaza. Dayan, in an unusually frank session with Vance on October 30, conveyed the most recent Israeli cabinet decisions on the treaty, and then went on to talk about the West Bank problem. Israel, he said, was prepared to talk to Egypt only about the "modalities" for holding elections. It would be a mistake to get into the question of the "powers and responsibilities" of the elected self-governing authority. To do so would open a Pandora's box. The Egyptians would inevitably argue that state lands should be under the control of the self-governing authority; Israel would reject that. Far better to limit the talks to holding elections; then Israel could work out with the Palestinians the powers of the body to which they had been elected.

The next day Dayan made many of these same points before the Egyptian delegation. He presented a strong case for limiting the discussions between Egypt and Israel to the question of how to organize the elections in the West Bank and Gaza. Otherwise the talks would drag on indefinitely. Al-Baz, speaking for the Egyptians, disagreed. The Palestinians had to know, he argued, what they were voting for. Unless the powers and responsibilities were defined in advance, the elections would be seen as a fraud. It would not be easier to grapple with this problem later. Dayan, who knew his prime minister well, said he would refer this issue to Begin if the Egyptians insisted. But he could tell them now that if Israel did consent to discuss powers and responsibilities, the negotiators would spend years trying to reach agreement.

When Carter read the accounts of these meetings, he was outraged. He saw them as further evidence of Israeli backsliding from the commitments made at Camp David. Vice President Mondale, Secretary Vance, National Security Adviser Brzezinski, and Hamilton Jordan, Carter's chief of staff, were called to the White House on November 1 for a strategy session. They decided to slow down the pace of the negotiations, to review Israel's commitments under the Camp David Accords, and to develop a series of steps to bring pressure on Begin to live up to those commitments. Responses to Israeli requests for arms could be delayed, and several other steps could be taken.

The next day Vance flew to New York for a brief meeting with Begin, who happened to be in town on his way to Canada. Dayan had earlier made it clear that Begin and the cabinet had ultimate authority and that he could do little more to resolve the disputes on remaining issues. Now, Begin found most of the treaty text acceptable but had problems with the side letter dealing with the West Bank and Gaza. Dayan and Weizman had said it should be possible to mention a target date for the holding of elections, but they did not want that date to coincide precisely with the interim withdrawal in Sinai. That would give the appearance of too much linkage. Begin, however, now said that Israel was adamantly opposed to the idea of any target date for elections. He argued that if for some reason beyond the control of Egypt and Israel the elections could not be held, that would call into question everything else, including the peace treaty. By contrast, Begin, always the legalist, found no problem in agreeing to the Egyptian request that powers and responsibilities of the self-governing authority be defined in advance of elections. On both these crucial issues, Begin ignored Dayan's advice. This was the first concrete evidence that Dayan's authority in this phase of the negotiations was much less than it had been in the preceding year.

Then Begin turned to bilateral issues. Israel would need $3.37 billion from the United States to help finance the withdrawal from Sinai, including the removal of the settlers. This aid should take the form of a loan at low interest rates. The cabinet would never approve the treaty, he said, unless the question of aid was solved first. Vance was noncommittal, refusing to give up one of the few elements of leverage the United States possessed.

As tensions rose in the U.S.-Israeli relationship, largely over the perception that Begin was diluting his already modest commitments concerning the Palestinians, pressure was mounting on Egypt to adopt a tougher position in support of Palestinian rights. The Arabs had held a summit meeting in Baghdad, and on November 5 they announced their conclusions. They criticized the Camp David Accords, and they decided that the headquarters of the Arab League was to be moved from Cairo if Egypt and Israel reached a peace treaty. The conference participants sent a small delegation to Cairo to meet with Sadat to dissuade him from continuing with the peace negotiations, but the Egyptian president refused to meet it. Instead, he publicly referred to the summit participants as "cowards and dwarfs." He would not pay any attention, he said, to "the hissing of snakes."

Still, within days the Egyptian position seemed to harden.[11] Sadat sent a message to Carter on November 8 saying there must be unequivocal agreement on what was to take place on the West Bank and Gaza. Otherwise he would be accused of making a separate deal with the Israelis and abandoning the Palestinians. Sadat was not prepared to open himself to such accusations from the other Arabs.

The time had come for the Americans to pause and assess the situation. A memorandum was prepared for Carter reviewing what Begin had been saying since Camp David about the West Bank and Gaza. On at least eight points Begin seemed to have deviated from what Carter felt was the agreed interpretation of the Camp David Accords. He noted on the memo: "To Cy and Zbig—Any aid-loan program if agreed must be predicated on Israeli compliance with Camp David agreements. J. C."

Carter met with his senior aides to review the negotiations on November 8. He was in a bad mood. Brzezinski was arguing for a tough line with Begin. He urged Carter to consider reducing aid to Israel by a certain amount for each new settlement that Begin authorized. "We do not intend to subsidize illegal settlements and we will so inform Congress." No decisions on aid should be made until Begin accepted a target date for elections.

Carter decided Vance should not go to the Middle East again as had been proposed. It was pointless for him to spend full time on a nonproductive effort. Carter had concluded that Israel wanted a separate treaty with Egypt, while keeping the West Bank and Gaza permanently. The creation of new settlements, he thought, was deliberately done to prevent Jordan and the Palestinians from joining the negotiations.[12] Carter and Vance now felt they must try to pin down the agenda for the West Bank and Gaza, even if that meant delaying the signing of an Egyptian-Israeli treaty. As usual, their sympathies were more with Sadat than with Begin.

Over the next few days the American side worked to complete the text of the treaty and all its annexes, as well as a letter on the West Bank and Gaza. Carter reviewed the entire package, and it was ready to present to the Israelis and Egyptians on November 11. In a late session at the State Department that same evening, Vance and Dayan tried to resolve some remaining issues in anticipation of a meeting between Vance and Begin in New York the next day. Dayan informed Vance that the Israeli cabinet was adamant in not agreeing to accelerate withdrawal to the interim line. He personally was inclined to accept a target date for elections in the West Bank and Gaza, but the date should not correspond to the interim withdrawal. As for the text of the treaty, Dayan seemed to be satisfied.[13]

Begin, however, was not in a conciliatory frame of mind. He refused to accept the idea of a target date, telling Vance on November 12 that Dayan had no authority to imply otherwise. He repeated his refusal to consider accelerated withdrawal. And as if he should be rewarded for his intransigence, he demanded that the aid for the withdrawal from Sinai take the form of a grant, not a loan. He had made a mistake, he said, when he earlier requested a loan and had promised that every penny of it would be repaid.

SADAT LOSES PATIENCE

Meanwhile Carter telephoned Sadat in Cairo to urge him to accept the same package. Sadat was more agitated than usual. He argued at great length that the Baghdad rejectionists should not get the upper hand. He must show that he had got something for the Palestinians, at least in Gaza, before Israel completed the interim withdrawal. He would even be willing to have the withdrawal delayed by a few months if that would allow the elections for Palestinian self-government to be held at the same time as the return of most of Sinai. Somewhat awkwardly, Sadat said he would not agree to the first phase of withdrawal without at least the beginning of self-government in Gaza. Carter made it clear he did not favor treating Gaza differently from the West Bank. Elections should be held in both areas by the end of 1979, he said.

Sadat repeated that the first phase of withdrawal should coincide with the day the Palestinians started their self-government in the West Bank and Gaza, or at least in Gaza. He accused Begin of trying to delay everything until the start of the American elections. Carter responded by urging Sadat to stop attacking Hussein and the Saudis. Sadat replied that he was punishing them for what they had done at the Baghdad summit. Give me Gaza, he pleaded. Carter was skeptical, but he agreed to try to come up with a new formulation.

Carter then called Begin in New York, pointing out that the prospects of agreement were now quite remote. Begin responded by saying that Israel had broken no promise in refusing to accelerate the withdrawal. Weizman should never have agreed to such an idea. In any case, Egypt had no right to use the Israeli decision as a pretext to refuse to send an ambassador to Israel, as Boutros Ghali had implied. Carter reassured him that Sadat would stand by his agreement to send an ambassador within one month of the interim withdrawal.

The next day Hermann F. Eilts, the U.S. ambassador to Egypt, met with Sadat and found him in an angry mood. Sadat said he and Carter were no longer speaking the same language. Egypt would not agree to peace with Israel without having reached an agreement at the same time on the West Bank and Gaza. Even if the interim withdrawal had to be delayed until November 1979, he said, that could be done if by then the Palestinians had their self-government, at least in Gaza. Sadat also said he could not accept article 6 of the draft treaty, since that made it seem as if his obligations to Israel took precedence over his obligations to his Arab allies. The only solution, he said, was for a confrontation between Carter and Begin to take place. He was planning to send his vice-president, Husni Mubarak, to see Carter the next day to discuss such a strategy.

Meanwhile a Saudi emissary arrived in Washington to meet with U.S. officials. He explained the position that the Saudis had taken in Baghdad, arguing that it would give the Saudis more influence with the radicals in the future. If only Egypt did not make a separate peace, and if there was some form of linkage, then Saudi Arabia could help defend the Camp David Accords in front of the other Arabs. But there must be some mention of ultimate Israeli withdrawal from Arab occupied territories and some mention of Jerusalem.

Several days later, on November 21, Begin telephoned Carter to say that the Israeli cabinet had voted to accept the text of the treaty and its annexes. Carter was pleased, but asked about the letter on the West Bank and Gaza. Begin replied that the cabinet had rejected the idea of setting a target date at the end of 1979 for elections in the West Bank and Gaza. And he added that there were also other problems. First, Israel wanted to resolve the question of a grant from the United States to help cover the costs of withdrawal from Sinai. Second, Israel needed assurances on oil, especially in light of the turmoil in Iran, the country from which Israel normally received its oil.

Carter tried to explain Sadat's position on the need for the interim withdrawal to coincide with the onset of self-government. Then Carter suggested that Israel might agree to delay the interim withdrawal until elections were held in the West Bank and Gaza, without setting a date for either event. Begin was surprised by this suggestion and said he would have to think about it.

Carter spoke by phone with Sadat the next day to inform him of the Israeli position. Sadat was still angry at Begin. Although he said little to Carter at the time, he was also annoyed at Carter's suggestion that the interim withdrawal might be delayed until elections were held for Palestinian self-government. Without some deadline, that could mean no withdrawal would take place at all. Sadat had suggested there might be a brief delay in withdrawal to make it coincide with the elections, but he was not ready to accept the possibility of no withdrawal at all.

Sadat remained in a foul mood for the next week. On November 28 he met with Senate Majority Leader Robert Byrd of West Virginia. Ambassador Eilts, who attended the meeting, reported that in more than 250 meetings with Sadat he had never seen the Egyptian president so emotional or upset. Two days later Eilts was handed a letter from Sadat to Carter strongly criticizing Begin for wanting only a separate peace. The talks had reached a crossroads. An Egyptian presence in Gaza was now essential. Article 6 of the treaty on priority of obligations was impossible to accept, and article 4 needed to be revised so that it did not imply permanent limits on Egyptian forces in Sinai. When Israel reneged on accelerated withdrawal, Sadat said, this upset the equation on an early exchange of ambassadors. He could no longer agree to send an ambassador to Israel one month after the interim withdrawal. Sadat also provided the Americans with the text of a sixteen-page letter he was sending to Begin.

Eilts tried to account for Sadat's temper. Egypt, he said, was feeling isolated in the Arab world. Sadat totally distrusted Begin and resented the narrow Israeli interpretation of the Camp David Accords. The debate over settlements had angered Sadat as well. The United States did not show much understanding of his problems with the other Arabs. And, Eilts concluded, Sadat was annoyed that the United States seemed to consider him the line of least resistance whenever the Israelis took a hard stand.

More constructive was Sadat's decision to send his prime minister, Mustafa Khalil, to Washington to consult with Carter. Khalil made a good impression on the Americans as a man of reason and as an able spokesman for the Egyptian side. In a meeting with Carter on December 1, Khalil pressed hard on the importance of simultaneity of Israeli withdrawal to the interim line and the establishment of the self-governing authority. He also wanted to revise article 6 of the treaty. Carter objected to the idea of revising the treaty but did suggest that interpretive notes could be appended to it.

Several days later, on December 4, Carter met with his Middle East team to review the details of the proposals Khalil had brought with him. Carter and Vance were both eager to know what Sadat's bottom line was. Would he insist on a fixed date for elections in the West Bank and Gaza? Carter favored a less precise formulation of a target date. On article 6, Carter thought Sadat might settle for some cosmetic change of words. But Carter was convinced that Sadat would insist on some explicit relationship between the implementation of the Sinai agreement and the establishment of self-government in the West Bank and Gaza. Brzezinski noted that the Camp David Accords were ambiguous on this issue of linkage, but Carter responded that Sadat was correct that some degree of linkage was implied by the agreements.[14]

Vance made it clear he did not want to make another trip to the Middle East. He suggested that Ambassador Atherton might go. Carter said there was no point in having anyone other than Vance or Mondale talk to Begin and Sadat. In a somber mood Carter said that if the negotiations failed, he wanted it to be clear that Sadat was not to blame. He wanted to be on Sadat's side. The Israelis would have nowhere else to go in any event.

Hamilton Jordan added the thought that at this point only success in the negotiations could help Carter politically. Once the treaty was signed, Carter would be in a stronger position to deal with the West Bank and Gaza issues. Carter seemed to be willing to take some political risks. He told Vance to press Israel hard, even if that ended up costing him the election and Jewish support.[15]

VANCE TO THE MIDDLE EAST

Vance set off for Cairo on December 9, 1978, with two clear objectives and one new proposal. First, he wanted to complete negotiations on the text of the treaty. Second, he wanted to make sure that the letter on the West Bank and Gaza would mention a target date of the end of 1979 for the establishment of self-government, or at least for the conclusion of the negotiations before the holding of elections.

Vance's new idea was one that originated with Carter in response to his belief that Sadat would be adamant about some form of linkage. The Camp David Accords had specified that diplomatic relations would be established after the interim withdrawal in Sinai, but there was no mention in writing about when ambassadors should be exchanged. Carter had earlier convinced Sadat that the exchange should be made right away, but after the Israelis dropped the idea of an accelerated withdrawal, the Egyptian position had become less certain.

Carter now felt it would be justified for Sadat to say that he would establish diplomatic relations after the interim withdrawal, but that the actual exchange of ambassadors would not take place until the self-governing authority in the West Bank and Gaza had been established. Sadat was likely to see considerable merit in this form of linkage, and Begin would inevitably react with horror.

Vance met privately with Sadat on December 10 and reviewed the new position on the timing of the exchange of ambassadors. As predicted, Sadat was pleased. In return, he showed some flexibility in accepting a target date instead of a fixed date for setting up the self-governing authority. He also agreed that article 6 could remain essentially unchanged, provided an interpretive note could be added making clear that this treaty did not prevail over other treaties to which Egypt was a party. In the side letter Sadat also wanted to mention the possibility that the self-governing authority might start first in Gaza, and he also inserted a provision for Egyptian liaison officers to be stationed in Gaza because of Egypt's former administrative role there.

Sadat readily informed Vance that a basis for agreement now existed but that he expected Begin to react negatively. Cheerfully, he said Vance should be ready for a big confrontation that might last for several months.

Over the next forty-eight hours the Americans hammered out a new package of documents. The treaty text was essentially unchanged, along with the annexes. Several interpretive notes were drafted. The side letter on the West Bank and Gaza was redone to reflect several of Sadat's demands. The United States agreed to draft a legal opinion of its own on the meaning of article 6, to the effect that nothing would prevent Egypt from honoring its commitments under other treaties in the event of armed attack against one of its allies. Most important, Sadat was now asked to write a letter to Carter committing himself to the exchange of ambassadors after the establishment of the Palestinian self-governing authority, at least in Gaza.

Vance and Sadat met again on December 12 to go over the entire package. At 7:45 p.m. Sadat said he was willing to accept everything in it, despite some remaining complaints by Khalil and al-Baz. But he stressed to Vance that this was as far as he could go. He pleaded with

Vance not to come back to him to ask for more concessions. In his words, there was no further room for compromise. He wanted the United States at his side in this final round. Vance said he would do his best.

As he set off for Israel Vance was aware that the three-month deadline for completing the negotiations was approaching. If at all possible, he wanted to have a package agreed on by December 17. He knew there would be some tough bargaining in Israel, but he had Carter's clear instructions to press the Israelis hard.

Vance began his meeting with Begin and his colleagues by reviewing the recent evolution of the Egyptian position. He explained that he had convinced Sadat to drop demands for changing the treaty and for a fixed date for establishing self-government. There would, however, have to be some interpretive notes to articles 4 and 6. Vance also mentioned the idea of a target date and the possibility of reaching agreement first on Gaza. Then he explained Sadat's new position on not exchanging ambassadors until after the self-governing authority was established.

Begin, always suspicious of U.S.-Egyptian collusion, looked tense during this presentation. When Vance was done, Begin did little to hide his anger. He accused Sadat of deviating from Camp David, especially on his promise to exchange ambassadors after the interim withdrawal. He rejected the idea that Egypt should have any special role in Gaza, and he maintained that Israel would never accept a target date for setting up the self-governing authority. Nor did he like the idea of interpretive notes. These seemed to dilute the strength of the peace treaty and might open loopholes for Egypt not to live up to its obligations.

Begin then went on at length to review all the concessions he had made and all the risks Israel was required to take. The United States, he said, was unfairly siding with Egypt, when it should instead be supporting Israel.

Vance eventually managed to defuse the Israeli concern over the minor issue of an interpretive note to article 4 of the treaty. Dayan even showed some interest in the idea of proceeding with autonomy in Gaza first. He also privately told Vance that there might be a way for Israel to accept the delay in the exchange of ambassadors, but that this point should not be spelled out in a letter. Any delay in exchanging ambassadors should be left vague until after the treaty was signed, and then Sadat could say whatever he wanted. On this suggestion, however, Dayan was clearly not speaking for Begin.

Vance was obliged to leave the Middle East somewhat ahead of schedule. The decision had been made to announce the normalization of relations with China, and Carter wanted him to be in Washington for the occasion. Vance had time to make only a quick stop in Cairo before he left. There he informed Sadat of Begin's angry reaction. Sadat smiled and expressed his pleasure. Vance said he had told Begin in private that the United States supported the Egyptian position.

While flying back to Washington, Vance received word that the Israeli cabinet had met and had issued the following statement: "The Government of Israel rejects the attitude and the interpretation of the U.S. government with regard to the Egyptian proposals." For once, Vance was genuinely angry. His inclination was to let the negotiations remain temporarily in limbo. An impasse had been reached, and nothing more could be done for the moment.

IMPASSE

As 1978 came to an end, the prospects for peace anywhere in the Middle East looked dim. Not only were the Egyptian-Israeli talks at an impasse, but also Iran was in turmoil. The shah's regime was on the verge of collapse, and no one in Washington seemed to know what to do about it.[16]

For the next several months American thinking about the Camp David negotiations was colored by what was happening in Iran. The strategic balance of power in the region was changing, and the positions of the negotiating parties were hardening. Israel seemed to be reacting by becoming even more insistent that the peace treaty with Egypt be independent of any commitments involving the Palestinians. Furthermore, access to Egyptian oil assumed special importance as Iranian production, hitherto Israel's main source of supply, dried up. And the spectacle of a pro-American regime in a Muslim country being swept aside by religious extremists did little to increase Israeli confidence in the long-term value of Sadat's promises.

As usual, the United States was pulled in several directions. The Iranian revolution made it increasingly important to conclude the peace negotiations between Begin and Sadat successfully. Not only was a peace treaty desirable for strategic reasons; Carter also needed a political success to offset the enormous failure in Iran. At the same time Carter sympathized with the Egyptian argument that Egypt should not be isolated from the rest of the region because of peace with Israel. If possible, Carter still wanted Sadat to be able to defend his dealings with Israel before the moderate Arab regimes. Egypt's potential role as a stabilizing force in the Arab world seemed essential now that Iran had become a new source of unrest in the region.

In brief, the American role in this last phase of the peace negotiations was heavily influenced both by Iran and by the domestic political clock. Iran provided a strategic rationale for pressing for a quick conclusion of the Camp David process; the political calendar told Carter that he would soon have to turn his attention to other matters, namely reelection. Either he needed a quick and dramatic success, or he would have to back away from further involvement in the negotiations and hope that the electorate would not accuse him of losing the chance for peace between Israel and the largest Arab country. Carter had invested so heavily in the peace process by this time that he was determined to make one last stab at agreement.

CHAPTER TWELVE

Going for Broke:
Treaty Yes, Autonomy No

When Secretary Vance left the Middle East on December 15, 1978, the talks seemed deadlocked, and Vance was frustrated. He authorized his staff to prepare a "white paper" explaining what had happened in the talks since Camp David. The obvious purpose was to answer the Israeli charge that Washington was being unfair. A draft was in fact produced on December 17 that tended to place the blame for the recent crisis on Prime Minister Begin. Some thought was given to making the document public, but in the end more cautious counsel was taken.

After returning to Washington, Vance spent the weekend at Camp David with Carter to discuss the foreign policy agenda for 1979. The president felt things were falling apart in the Middle East. Dealing with that region had also become his heaviest political burden. And it was incredibly time-consuming. But the stakes were too high to let the negotiations drop. Carter decided to "continue to move aggressively on it and not postpone the difficult discussions, even though they were costly to us in domestic politics."[1]

By mid-January the Americans were thinking of several ways of reviving the talks. Prime Minister Khalil and Foreign Minister Dayan could be invited to Washington; another summit could be arranged; a new U.S. proposal could be put forward. Most felt it would be best to resolve the minor issues before engaging the president and Vance once again. They therefore decided to send Ambassador Atherton and the State Department's legal adviser, Herbert Hansell, to the Middle East to work on articles 4 and 6 and any necessary legal interpretations. March was frequently mentioned as the time by which an agreement should be reached on the entire treaty.

On January 23, 1979, Brzezinski sent a memorandum to the president spelling out his concerns on the Arab-Israeli issue. "Events may make it difficult for us to pursue such a strategy, but I am firmly convinced for the good of the Democratic Party we must avoid a situation where we continue agitating the most neuralgic problem with the American Jewish community (the West Bank, the Palestinians, the PLO) without a breakthrough to a solution. I do not believe that in the approaching election year we will be able to convince the Israelis that we have significant leverage over them, particularly on those issues. . . . We have little time left."[2]

On February 6 Carter wrote to Begin and Sadat asking them to agree to a meeting in Washington involving Dayan, Khalil, and Vance. The talks would begin on February 21 and be held at Camp David. Vance had recommended this course of action in a memorandum to the president on February 1. There he suggested that Carter should ultimately persuade Sadat to drop the linkage of the exchange of ambassadors to the establishment of the self-governing authority in return for stronger commitments from Begin to do something on the Palestinian question. He also proposed some slight revisions of articles 4 and 6 and the text of a new letter on the West Bank and Gaza.

CAMP DAVID II

In preparation for the talks at Camp David, the Middle East team undertook one of its periodic assessments. It seemed clear that at some point Carter would have to deal directly with Begin and Sadat. Arabs and Israelis were both concerned that the United States had lost its way. The only conceivable success on the horizon for Carter in foreign policy was an Egyptian-Israeli peace treaty. Both Egypt and Israel knew the United States needed a success after Iran, and Israel had concluded that Carter would not fight hard for the West Bank.

On February 19, 1979, shortly after Secretary of Defense Brown returned from his Middle East foray, Carter assembled his Middle East team, along with Brown, Ambassador Eilts, and Ambassador Lewis. Brown gave his assessment, which boiled down to two points: everyone he had talked to was nervous about Iran, and Begin and Sadat were prepared to keep working for a peace treaty.

Carter realized he would probably have to meet again with the Egyptian and Israeli leaders. As he cast around for new ideas, he argued that Sadat should not try to speak for the West Bank. The president even speculated in front of his Middle East advisers that Sadat really "did not give a damn about the West Bank." He was more concerned with Gaza. If he would drop his interest in the West Bank, he could have his separate treaty with Israel, get something in Gaza, and embarrass Hussein.

Carter stated clearly that he did not want a public confrontation with

Israel. This was a time for progress on the overall negotiation, with details to be resolved later. Carter acknowledged that he had to take some of the blame for urging Sadat to link the exchange of ambassadors to the establishment of self-government, but Sadat would now have to drop that demand for linkage. Carter also said two mistakes had been made at Camp David. Too much emphasis had been placed on the timing of the exchange of ambassadors, and Sadat should not have agreed to negotiate in place of King Hussein if Jordan refused to join the talks.

The Saudi role was raised by Eilts, who said Sadat still wanted Saudi support but would be ready to go ahead even without it. Somewhat cavalierly, Carter said the Saudis would have nowhere else to go after the treaty was signed. "They have to work with the United States and Egypt."

The second round of talks at Camp David began on February 21. Vance, Dayan, and Khalil were the principal participants, and each was accompanied by several aides. Khalil continued to insist that Egypt could not afford to be isolated, especially with the turmoil in Iran. Any treaty must be defensible before reasonable Arab opinion. On specifics, Khalil showed some interest in holding elections only in Gaza, and he implied that the exchange of ambassadors need not necessarily be tied to West Bank and Gaza developments.

Dayan had little room for negotiating, and he repeatedly said Vance would have to deal directly with Begin on the outstanding issues. He did, however, imply that Israel might be able to make some unilateral gestures toward the Palestinians, a point the Egyptians had pressed hard.

Talks at this level seemed to hold little promise of further progress. Khalil had authority to negotiate, but Dayan did not. So Carter invited Begin to join the talks. On February 27 the Israeli cabinet rejected Dayan's recommendation that the prime minister attend, saying Begin would not participate in a summit with Khalil. Only Sadat would do. Carter was irritated but decided to ask Begin to come to Washington just to meet with him. Things now seemed to be working toward a climax.

CARTER AND BEGIN IN WASHINGTON

To prepare for his meeting with Begin, on February 28, 1979, Carter called together his top advisers—Mondale, Vance, Brzezinski, and Hamilton Jordan. Brzezinski bluntly stated that Israel seemed to want a separate peace and wanted Carter not to be reelected. Jordan agreed. Mondale drew the conclusion that Carter should therefore not confront Begin and should stand back and let things take their natural course.[3]

Begin arrived in Washington without Dayan or Defense Minister Weizman in his delegation. These comparatively moderate voices seemed to have lost Begin's confidence. Carter and Vance noted their absence with regret.

The first session between Carter and Begin took place on Friday, March 2, 1979. Begin opened with a strong argument that the United States should help Israel because only Israel stood in the path of a Soviet takeover of the whole Middle East. He maintained that Israel could help prevent a communist takeover in Saudi Arabia, and even went so far as to offer the United States an airbase in Sinai that he had already promised to return to Egypt. None of these remarks had much effect on Carter.

Next Begin turned to the outstanding issues in the negotiations. He said the talks were in a deep crisis. The American interpretations to article 6 on the priority of obligations were tantamount to making peace between Egypt and Israel contingent on the achievement of a comprehensive peace in the region. Such linkage would allow Egypt to use any pretext to tear up the treaty. Begin added that he was sure that some future Egyptian leader would recommend doing so. No interpretive notes would be acceptable. The text of the treaty must stand unchanged, whether Sadat liked it or not.

Begin then raised his objections to the side letter dealing with the West Bank and Gaza. It contained deviations from Camp David. There was no reason to separate Gaza from the West Bank, as Sadat now wanted to do, though if Egypt was prepared to drop all interest in the West Bank, Israel might consider discussing Gaza alone with Egypt. But Gaza would not then be a precedent for what might later be done on the West Bank.

Begin also introduced his own deviation from Camp David by claiming that Israel was under no obligation to discuss the West Bank unless Jordan joined the negotiations. Carter reminded him that Sadat had signed a letter, which was part of the Camp David Accords, saying that Egypt would assume the Jordanian role if Hussein did not step forward. Begin replied that the letters did not have the same value as the text of the agreement, a point Carter quickly rejected.

Next on the list of Begin's objections was the idea of setting a target date for elections to the self-governing authority. If for some reason the date was not met, Israel might be accused of violating the treaty with

Egypt, and Egypt might then break some of its commitments. Israel could not accept such linkage between the treaty and the future of the West Bank and Gaza.

Finally, Begin turned to the question of oil. Since signing the Camp David Accords, he said, Israel had lost access to Iranian oil. More than ever, Israel needed a firm guarantee from both Egypt and the United States that its oil supply would be met. If Egypt refused, Israel would not evacuate the oil fields in Sinai.

Carter was very discouraged by this meeting. There seemed to be no openings. Still, Vance was prepared to continue the talks over lunch at the State Department.

Brzezinski had made the argument to Begin that Sadat could not be pressed to renounce his commitments to Arab countries as the price of peace with Israel. That was going too far. Vance picked up on this point at lunch and told Begin that Sadat needed to be able to say the Egyptian-Israeli treaty "did not prevail over" other treaties. Begin said he did not object to that language, provided it was clear that if Egypt's treaty with Israel conflicted with its other treaty obligations, the treaty with Israel would be honored. In brief, Begin signaled a willingness to allow interpretive notes on article 6, so long as the priority of obligations went to the Egyptian-Israeli treaty. This essentially meant that Begin would say that the treaty was not meant to prevail over others, but that in practice it must do so. As Vance later wrote: "Of such are diplomatic compromises made; six months of negotiations to reach agreement with Begin on two contradictory statements in the same interpretation."[4]

Vance and his team took some time on Saturday to develop new language on article 6 and on the target date for elections in the West Bank and Gaza. The most significant alteration was tying the target date to the conclusion of the negotiations between Egypt and Israel rather than to the actual holding of elections. Meanwhile Carter had another session with his top advisers, in which he raised the possibility of going to the Middle East to bring the negotiations to a dramatic conclusion. Hamilton Jordan in particular favored it. As Carter was later to say, "My proposal was an act of desperation."[5] Later in the evening Carter had another unproductive private meeting with Begin.

A final session between the two leaders was scheduled for Sunday morning, March 4. They met against a backdrop provided by a message from Sadat, who said he was planning to come to Washington to denounce Begin for his intransigence. Carter had already begun to think the best way to proceed was for him to go to the Middle East, and he hardly welcomed the telegenic Sadat stealing the show in Washington with ringing denunciations of Israel. So an effort was made to resolve some of the issues and therefore to justify a trip by the president to the region.

Somewhat surprisingly, Begin was in a rather conciliatory mood on Sunday morning. Vance reviewed the new formulations on article 6, and after a brief discussion among the Israeli delegation in Hebrew, Begin made a minor suggestion for a change in wording and agreed to seek cabinet approval, provided the United States formally withdrew its previous legal opinion on article 6. Similarly, Begin said the new American proposal on setting a target date for concluding the negotiations on autonomy was serious and would be considered by the cabinet. After all, he commented, Egypt and Israel could assume responsibility for the timing of the negotiations, but the actual holding of elections for the Palestinian government could be blocked by "third parties." That was why he had opposed a target date for elections but could accept one for concluding the negotiations. This was a lawyer's point, but it gave Begin a pretext for changing his position without appearing to back down on a matter of principle.

The problem of oil supplies remained, along with the timing of the exchange of ambassadors, but Carter implied that he would deal directly with Sadat on both issues to find a satisfactory solution. To his surprise Carter found that the United States and Israel were now in agreement on most issues. The reason, it seemed, was not so much that Begin had been won over by Carter's argument but rather that the new American formulations went just far enough to overcome Israeli suspicions. Begin must have also realized that the moment had come to clinch the bilateral deal with Sadat.

As soon as the meeting was over, Carter sent a message to Sadat informing him that some progress had been made in the talks and that he did not want Sadat to say anything further in public, and especially not to commit himself to coming to Washington. In fact, said the president, he was considering a trip to the Middle East himself in the next few days.

The following day, March 5, 1979, the Israeli cabinet approved all the new American proposals. Carter now felt that success was at hand. A trip by him to the Middle East would produce a peace treaty and a much needed political boost.

Carter immediately decided to send Brzezinski to Cairo to see Sadat.

He wanted Brzezinski to have a broad strategic review with the Egyptian president, to inform him of the new proposals and ask for his support of them, and to tell Sadat "very privately that the President's domestic political situation was becoming more difficult and that Begin might even wish to see the President defeated."[6]

Brzezinski met with Sadat on March 6 and delivered the president's messages. Sadat made it clear that the new formulations would pose no problem for him. He was, however, reluctant to go back to the idea of sending an ambassador to Israel after the interim withdrawal.

Sadat then told Brzezinski of his most important "secret weapon"—a proposal that Carter would be allowed to convey to Begin for building a pipeline from the Sinai oil fields directly to Israel. Sadat denounced the Israelis as idiots for ignoring his proposal on Gaza, but nonetheless said he would do everything possible to make Carter's visit a big success. The treaty should be signed while Carter was in the Middle East. If all went well, Sadat would even invite Begin to Cairo for the signing. Carter was very pleased by this prospect.

Sadat then turned his anger on the Saudis, describing them as a scarecrow and a U.S. protectorate to which the Americans attached too much importance. The Saudis, he said, were indecisive and incapable of action. Sadat treated King Hussein in similar fashion, asserting that the United States should dismiss him altogether. Somewhat surprisingly, he urged the Americans to improve their relations with Iraq.

CARTER TO THE MIDDLE EAST

By the time Carter arrived in Cairo on March 7, 1979, he had every reason to believe his trip would be crowned with success. Sadat had essentially said Carter would have carte blanche to negotiate the final text of the treaty with Israel.[7]

Carter spent much of his time in Egypt celebrating the close ties between Egypt and the United States. Sadat put on an impressive show, including a train ride to Alexandria, which exposed the American president to larger and friendlier crowds than he was used to seeing at home.

Just before leaving for Israel, Carter and Secretary Vance met with Sadat and his top advisers at the Maamoura rest house near Alexandria. Carter pledged to get the best possible agreement for Egypt while in Israel and spoke as if he had Sadat's proxy in hand. Once the treaty was a reality, the United States and Egypt could plan for a "massive" government-to-government relationship in the military and economic fields. Carter also expressed the hope that the American private sector would invest in Egypt after the peace treaty was signed. In addition, Carter promised to use his maximum influence to get Jordan and Saudi Arabia to back the fait accompli of the treaty.[8]

While Carter and Sadat were congratulating each other on the achievement of peace, the Egyptian foreign ministry officials were showing anxiety. They still wanted Carter to persuade the Israelis to make some unilateral gestures to the Palestinians, and they hoped that Israel would agree to some form of special status for Egypt in Gaza. They also wanted a few minor changes in the treaty, including the replacement of a word in the notes to article 6 that they did not like. Carter and Vance promised to do their best.

Carter arrived in Israel after sundown on Saturday, March 10, 1979. He immediately drove to Jerusalem for a private dinner with Begin. To Carter's surprise, Begin made it clear that there was no chance of concluding the negotiations and signing the peace treaty while Carter was in the Middle East. The president was angry and suspected Begin of wanting him to fail. Begin was standing on procedure, arguing that the Knesset must have a chance to debate the agreement before it could be signed. Carter reminded Begin that this had not been necessary at Camp David, but Begin would not be rushed.

After all, for Begin a peace treaty with Egypt was an extraordinarily important achievement. He would not be stampeded into signing just because Carter had decided to put his prestige on the line by traveling to the Middle East. And even if Begin might agree to the text of the treaty, the Knesset did have to have its say, much as the Senate would in the United States.

Carter had little sympathy for Begin in the best of times. It was a bad start for what proved to be a difficult few days. The upbeat mood of Cairo had suddenly been replaced in Jerusalem by mutual suspicions and recriminations. And in that atmosphere, once again it seemed as if the chance for peace might be lost.

On Sunday, March 11, Carter and Begin met with their full delegations. Carter began by sketching his preferred scenario. Negotiations on the treaty text should be concluded within the next day or so; Sadat would fly to Jerusalem to sign; then Begin, Sadat, and Carter would all travel to Cairo together for a second signing ceremony.

Begin immediately poured cold water on the president's idea. The cabinet, he explained, would have to debate the matter fully, and then the Knesset would have to vote before any signature could be put on so solemn a document as a peace treaty. All this would take at least two weeks. Then Begin asked to hear the new Egyptian proposals.

Sadat and his advisers had not liked the wording of the proposed notes to article 6. The notes had been included to meet Sadat's desire to portray the Egyptian-Israeli treaty as part of the comprehensive peace mentioned in the Camp David Accords. To this end, the notes had said that article 6 of the treaty did not contravene the framework for peace agreed on at Camp David and that the treaty was not to be seen as prevailing over any other treaties to which the parties were bound. But to meet Israeli concerns, the notes went on to say these provisions did "not derogate from" the language of article 6, which in essence said that the provisions of the Egyptian-Israeli treaty would be respected without regard to actions of other parties even if a conflict arose with other obligations.

The Egyptians were bothered by the word "derogate." Carter therefore suggested that Israel accept the substitution of the following phrase: "The foregoing [the notes to article 6] is not to be construed as inconsistent with the provisions of article 6." From the Americans' standpoint, there was no substantive difference. The point was that the notes to article 6 should not be seen as changing the meaning of the treaty.

Carter also said Egypt was insisting on having liaison officers in Gaza to help prepare for self-government there. Vance then passed around the new texts of the notes to article 6 and the letter on the West Bank and Gaza.

Begin frostily replied that the United States and Israel had already agreed on the language of the notes when he was recently in Washington. Sadat had the right to object, but Begin would not budge. He rejected the new language and expected Carter to stand by the text that had been worked out in Washington. The two phrases "does not derogate from" and "is not inconsistent with" were worlds apart, he said. Article 6 was the heart of the treaty. Without it the treaty would be a sham document. Israel would not knowingly sign a sham document. At one point he said that if the words "is not inconsistent with" were used instead of "does not derogate from," it would mean that Egypt would start a war while it had a peace treaty with Israel.

Carter denied that Egypt was looking for a pretext to attack Israel. Begin then pulled out a sheaf of newspaper articles and began to read extracts from the Egyptian press that he saw as threatening to Israel.

Carter asked him what the point of such a display was. Begin referred to the terrible atmosphere in which the peace talks were being conducted and asked that the American ambassador in Cairo raise with Sadat the question of anti-Israeli articles in the Egyptian press.

Carter then asked if Begin had any counterproposals to make. Begin said no. He would stand by what had been agreed on in Washington. Begin went on to make a lengthy critique of the new note to article 6, paragraph 2. He had agreed in Washington to say in a note to the article that it should not be construed as contravening the framework for peace in the Middle East agreed to at Camp David. Sadat had wanted to add that Camp David had called for a "comprehensive peace," as in fact it did. Begin argued that by adding these two words, "comprehensive peace," Sadat was seeking a pretext to violate the treaty with Israel by making it contingent on other Arab states also making peace with Israel. Syria, he said, would then be able to render the treaty null and void by refusing to negotiate.

Toward noon Begin turned his impressive critical powers to the new letter concerning the West Bank and Gaza. He strongly objected to the possibility of implementing autonomy in Gaza first. Nor would he accept Egyptian liaison officers there. Then, for what must have been the tenth time, he objected to the term West Bank, giving a lesson to the president on the geographic and historical inappropriateness of the term and the importance of using the words Judea and Samaria. Only if Sadat were to renounce entirely his interest in those two areas, said Begin, would he agree to discuss Gaza alone with Egypt.

Other members of the cabinet joined the discussions, and for a while it seemed as if no headway would ever be made. Ariel Sharon intervened with his standard lecture on "Jordan is Palestine" and called the Hashemites the only foreigners in Jordan. He promised Carter that within twenty years one million Jews would be living in the West Bank and Gaza. No line would ever separate Israel from these areas.

After a break for lunch, the talks resumed at 3:00 p.m. Carter tried to regain Begin's confidence by promising an American guarantee of Israel's oil supply. He also said he was sure he could persuade Sadat to exchange ambassadors after the interim withdrawal if Israel would expedite the withdrawal, as originally agreed the previous November. He also said the United States would sign a memorandum of understanding with Israel on steps to be taken if Egypt violated the treaty.

Turning to bilateral U.S.-Israeli relations, Carter maintained that the two countries were equal partners. He added that what the United States did for Israel was more than balanced by what Israel did for the United States, a point that Begin had long been pressing on American audiences and that Carter did not really believe. Israel, he said, was a tremendous strategic asset to the United States, especially if it was at peace with Egypt, the other major regional friend of the United States. With these sweeteners, Carter urged the Israelis to try to find words to resolve the dispute over article 6, which eventually was done.

During a late afternoon session Begin told Carter that the Israeli cabinet would meet that evening to make its formal decisions on the matters under discussion. Then Vance could go to Cairo, and Carter could return home. In about two weeks, if all was proceeding smoothly, the Israelis might be ready to sign the treaty.

Carter responded by saying that Vance would not go to Cairo. The Egyptian position was already known to the Americans. They could conclude the negotiations right now. Begin replied that he was very tired and that the meeting should now be adjourned. Once again, the Americans felt Begin was deliberately trying to keep Carter from enjoying the fruits of his high-stakes trip to the Middle East.

Just before the meeting broke up, Carter again pleaded with Begin to try to reach agreement in the next day or so. Begin replied that the sky would not fall if agreement was not reached.

The next morning Carter and Begin and their advisers met again at 10:20 a.m. The cabinet had been in session all night, breaking up at 5:30 a.m. The Israelis looked exhausted. Carter began by making a strong case for the strategic benefits to Israel of peace with Egypt. He argued that the U.S.-Israeli relationship would grow even stronger and the United States could be even more forthcoming on aid if the peace treaty was concluded. Egypt and Israel could work together to prevent the kind of radicalism seen in Iran from spreading to the rest of the region. If the opportunity for peace was now lost, it would be hard to recover.

The Israeli cabinet had essentially confirmed the new wording of the notes to article 6, and Carter was satisfied. But the cabinet had adamantly refused to consider giving Egypt any special status in Gaza. Carter argued that its refusal would be hard for Egypt to accept. He pleaded with Begin to reconsider, but Begin refused.

The meeting broke up at 11:20 a.m. Begin and Carter left to prepare for their addresses to the Knesset. That event turned out to be somewhat less than edifying. In his remarks Carter rather undiplomatically implied that the Israeli public wanted peace more than its leaders did. During Begin's speech opposition members interrupted so frequently that it was hard to follow what was being said. Begin's old ally Geulah Cohen was ordered off the floor of the Knesset when she refused to observe parliamentary decorum. Begin seemed to enjoy the battle, but the Americans were less happy. Still, Begin had shown that he was not the most extreme hard-liner among the Israelis.

Carter went from the Knesset to a lunch with the members of the Foreign Affairs and Security Committee. During the lunch Carter revealed that he essentially had carte blanche from Sadat to conclude an agreement. Begin doubtless suspected this anyway, but now he must have become certain that Carter could be persuaded to cede on his insistence that Egypt be given a special role in Gaza.

Vance was scheduled to have one more session with the Israeli delegation on Monday afternoon, March 12. Carter hoped that the remaining problems on Gaza, on oil, and on the timing of withdrawal from Sinai and the exchange of ambassadors could all be settled.

Begin opened the meeting by saying that the cabinet had been in session for two hours and had decided to reconfirm its position on all issues. There would be no further changes from the Israeli side. Israel needed, he said, a clear-cut Egyptian promise to sell 2.5 million tons of oil to Israel each year. Begin did say he would agree to consider an Egyptian proposal to start the autonomy talks in Gaza, but this issue could not be included in the side letter. Nor could any mention be made of Egyptian liaison officers. Even on article 6 Begin insisted that the words "comprehensive peace" be removed from one of the notes, arguing that otherwise the treaty would appear to depend on the action of other Arab parties in making peace with Israel.

Begin did suggest that some expedited withdrawal to the interim line might be possible, but only if Sadat agreed to send an ambassador to Israel shortly thereafter. From this point on, the discussion quickly deteriorated. Begin accused the Americans of always showing an understanding of Sadat's concerns but never of his. Sharon harshly interjected that the Egyptians would never be allowed into Gaza in any form. They would only try to stir up the local population. Even the usually moderate Dayan and Deputy Prime Minister Yigal Yadin seemed to think Carter should not support the Egyptian claim to a special role in Gaza.

Vance tried to salvage the situation by urging that both the Gaza and oil issues be dropped from the agreement. Neither had been included in the Camp David Accords, and both could be dealt with later. Begin said oil was a matter of life and death and could not be left out of the agreement. Nor would Israel agree now to put in writing its willingness to accelerate withdrawal to the interim line.

To the surprise of the Americans, Begin then said that the talks were over and a joint communiqué should be issued announcing that some progress had been made, but that some questions still needed to be resolved. A text to this effect, obviously prepared well in advance, was passed over to Vance for his agreement.

Carter was immediately informed of the outcome of the talks. He decided there was no point for him to stay in Israel any longer. Begin clearly did not want an agreement at this time. The president ordered his plane to be prepared to return directly to Washington. But the hour was late, and to get all the presidential party and its luggage assembled in time would be difficult. Reluctantly Carter agreed to spend the night in Jerusalem, but he was a bitterly disappointed man.

FINALE

When the Americans reconvened at the King David Hotel, the mood was gloomy. No one saw much point in trying to come up with new formulations on the outstanding issues. Most of the Americans drifted off to have dinner together. No working sessions were planned.

Toward 9:00 p.m. one of Dayan's associates called Vance to suggest that the secretary should invite Dayan over for an informal talk. Dayan, it turned out, had been caucusing with members of the cabinet who were unhappy with the way the negotiations seemed to be ending. Dayan had got Begin's permission to see Vance. Weizman was apparently threatening to resign if the peace treaty was jeopardized by Begin's obstinacy.

Dayan made several suggestions and confirmed that most of the cabinet would accept the U.S. proposals on guaranteeing Israel's supply of oil and for accelerated Israeli withdrawal to an interim line in Sinai. In return for those concessions, Dayan suggested that the side letter should omit reference to Gaza as a special case and to a role for Egyptian liaison officers there. He urged Carter to meet again with Begin the next morning to put these proposals forward as new American suggestions. Meanwhile Dayan would try to prepare the way with Begin. Vance agreed to try, and for several hours the American team worked on a new set of proposals.

While Vance and Dayan were working to prevent a collapse of the talks, Carter's press secretary, Jody Powell, was briefing the press on the situation as it stood at 9:00 p.m. He painted a bleak picture, and this was the basis for the pessimistic accounts that most Americans read in their papers on Tuesday, March 13.[9]

By the time the American press accounts were being digested, the situation had already changed. Carter met with Begin alone on Tuesday morning; they were then joined by Dayan and Vance. Begin, as usual, held back from making a complete commitment to the new proposals. If Egypt accepted them, and if Sadat agreed to an early exchange of ambassadors, Begin would recommend the new proposals to the Knesset. Carter knew that was tantamount to having Begin's agreement. Pressing his luck a bit, he asked Begin if Israel would agree to undertake some unilateral gestures to improve the atmosphere for the Palestinians in the West Bank and Gaza. This issue was of great importance to the Egyptians. Begin said he would sympathetically consider this request. Carter finally knew he had an agreement in hand.

Carter then flew directly to Cairo, where he met with Sadat at the airport. Sadat's aides still had some objections, but Sadat was in no mood to quibble.[10] He had promised the president a success, and he was prepared to say that agreement had now been reached on all issues. At 5:00 p.m. Carter said that full agreement had been reached, and he placed a call to Begin from the airport to tell him so. Begin agreed to go to the cabinet the next day for final approval, but the outcome was no longer in doubt.

Carter and Sadat then walked out on the tarmac to tell the awaiting press corps that a peace agreement had been concluded. After so many ups and downs, and after the previous evening's pessimistic briefing, many of the journalists were amazed—and somewhat irritated that their previous day's stories would look bad.

On the plane back to Washington Carter's political aides were ecstatic. At long last Carter could point to a major foreign policy achievement that would be genuinely welcomed by most Americans. The foreign-policy advisers were a bit less jubilant, thinking as always of the many problems that lay ahead. Most of all, they were exhausted and grateful that the talks were over, at least for the moment. When they arrived at Andrews Air Force Base later that evening, a large crowd was waiting to congratulate Carter and Vance. It had been quite a day, starting in Jerusalem and ending in Washington.

SIGNING THE PEACE TREATY

The comprehensive Middle East peace that Carter had originally hoped for was still far off, but the largest of the building blocks in that design, the Egyptian-Israeli peace, was nearly a reality. Carter was ambivalent about whether the peace treaty would by itself bring stability to the Middle East, or whether it would set in motion an inevitable process that would widen the circle of peace around Israel. He certainly did not believe it could make matters worse than they already were.

Before the treaty signing, a few remaining issues had to be resolved. Ezer Weizman visited Washington to work out the new phases of withdrawal and to appeal successfully for additional military assistance.[11] Other bilateral U.S.-Israeli questions remained to be answered. In particular, how would the United States guarantee Israel's supply of oil if Egyptian oil was not available to meet Israel's requirements? And what would the United States promise to do if Egypt violated the treaty? What provision should be made for the contingency that UN peacekeeping forces would not be available for the Sinai after Israeli withdrawal? On all these points the United States had to find solutions. In some instances the final wording was not worked out until the actual day the peace treaty was signed.

But the problems of the draftsmen and mapmakers would not stand in the way of the signing ceremony on March 26, 1979. Carter was joined by Begin and Sadat on the north lawn of the White House. A large audience was invited to attend. Many political debts were paid that day. Egyptians and Israelis mingled freely and expressed hopes that peace might be at hand. Across the street in Lafayette Park some Palestinians and their supporters held a small demonstration against the treaty, a reminder that the next phase of negotiations would encounter opposition. But the day was one of optimism and good feeling, and it was crowned that evening by a magnificent banquet on the south lawn of the White House.

The formal Egyptian-Israeli agreement consisted of a thick file of documents that few people would ever read in their entirety. (See appendix G for the key documents.) Besides the text of the treaty, there were three annexes dealing with security arrangements, maps, and normal relations between the parties. Seven interpretive notes were attached to the basic documents. Sadat and Begin also signed a letter to Carter concerning negotiations on the West Bank and Gaza issues. Carter added in his own handwriting an explanatory note to the letter saying, "I have been informed that the expression 'West Bank' is understood by the Government of Israel to mean 'Judea and Samaria.'"

Sadat signed another letter to Carter promising that a resident ambassador would be sent to Israel within one month of the interim withdrawal. Carter conveyed this information to Begin in a letter, and Begin acknowledged its receipt. Carter also wrote to both Sadat and Begin to spell out what the United States would do to help monitor the security arrangements in Sinai and how the United States would use its best efforts to organize a multinational peacekeeping force if UN troops were unavailable.

On the day of the signing of the peace treaty, Vance and Dayan also put their signatures to a memorandum of agreement. Most of the commitments made in this document were hedged with qualifications, but it put the weight of the United States behind Israel in the event that Egypt violated the treaty. Promises made as part of previous memorandums of understanding were reaffirmed. An agreement on oil supply was signed at the same time.[12]

As for military aid to Israel, Secretary Brown wrote to Weizman committing the United States to $3 billion to help construct new airfields in the Negev. Of that amount, $800 million would be in the form of grants. The United States also informed Israel that it was prepared to act positively on a number of weapons systems that had been requested earlier. (During the negotiations Carter had deliberately held off making major decisions on arms so that he would have some remaining leverage over both Israel and Egypt.)

Brown wrote a similar letter to the Egyptian minister of defense, promising $1.5 billion in aid over the next three years. A list of military equipment that Egypt would be allowed to purchase was appended to this letter. Inevitably, a few loose ends were handled by memoranda for the record written by the legal adviser or other participants in the negotiations. None of the memos changed the basic outline of what had been agreed upon. They largely involved putting the United States on record with an interpretation of some ambiguous point in the treaty or in the annexes, or recording some informal understanding that had been reached after the text of the treaty had been completed.

At the last minute Carter was also required to write a secret letter to Begin affirming what Begin and Sadat had orally agreed upon on

March 26 concerning oil supplies. Carter also wrote to Egyptian Prime Minister Khalil to inform him of the results of his discussions with Begin about unilateral gestures toward Palestinians in the West Bank and Gaza.

Khalil, who had not known of the U.S.-Israeli memorandum of agreement until the last moment, wrote two letters to Vance spelling out sixteen reasons why Egypt rejected it. The day after the peace treaty was signed, Khalil also wrote to Carter protesting that Carter had not done enough to commit Begin to take positive actions in the West Bank and Gaza. But these were faint notes that attracted little attention, and Carter had long ago learned that Sadat would not make an issue out of such matters.[13]

ASSESSING THE TREATY NEGOTIATIONS

Complex diplomatic initiatives rarely work out quite the way their authors anticipate. Midcourse corrections are part of the normal negotiating process. For American presidents in particular, the intrusion of domestic political considerations is also part of the game. In light of these realities, one cannot judge results by the standard of initial designs or theoretical abstractions.

Instead one must look at the Egyptian-Israeli peace treaty in its political context. What more might have been achieved, given the very real constraints operating on all the parties? Could positive aspects of the agreement have been enhanced? Could the negative ones have been minimized? Why was Carter unable to make headway on the West Bank and Gaza? Why did he seem to care less about those areas than he did about Sinai?

First, Egypt and Israel were talking to each other and were ready to make decisions. The other Arabs were either opposed to the process or were sitting on the sidelines to see what would be offered them. Carter felt more of an obligation to Sadat because Sadat had taken risks for peace.

Second, the chance for a successful negotiation between Egypt and Israel was much greater than between Israel and any of the other Arab parties. Two disengagement agreements had already been signed in 1974 and 1975. Direct talks between the parties had shown that the distance between them on bilateral issues was not large. Carter's involvement could plausibly help bridge the remaining gap.

Third, Egypt was the most powerful Arab country. Peace between Egypt and Israel would not make war impossible in the Middle East, but it would dramatically change its nature. The danger of U.S.-Soviet confrontation would be reduced as well. On these grounds even a separate peace had immense strategic value for the United States.

Finally, one must frankly admit, the American political system makes it difficult for a president to tackle a problem like that of the Palestinians. Presidential authority in foreign affairs is theoretically extensive, but in practice it is circumscribed by political realities. And the Palestinian question has proved to be so controversial that most presidents have been reluctant to get deeply involved in it. Sadat, who was genuinely popular with the American public, was, in Carter's view, worth a fight with Begin. But the Palestinians had no domestic constituency, and when Sadat seemed less concerned about their fate than about Sinai, Carter found it impossible to be more demanding than the leader of the largest Arab country.

Among the participants, Carter had come to the negotiations with the least knowledge of the issues and with the greatest capacity to evolve in his understanding. The Middle East was important in his view, but he did not have fixed ideas on exactly how the problems should be solved. The engineer in him seemed to want the grand design of a comprehensive peace; left to his own devices, he might have remained wedded to that appealing notion. But he could not build the edifice alone, and so he began to concentrate on the part that was most feasible.

The idealist in Carter also played a role. The president deeply believed that men of goodwill could resolve problems by talking to one another. At Camp David he initially thought he would need only to get Sadat and Begin together and help them to overcome their mutual dislike. The agreement itself would then be worked out by the two leaders in a spirit of compromise and accommodation. The depth of their distrust, even hatred, was hard for him to understand. Begin's fixation on Judea and Samaria was especially hard for him to grasp. Finally, it was Carter who was forced to reexamine his assumptions and change his approach in the face of Begin's intransigence and Sadat's apparent willingness to settle for a bilateral deal.

The politician in Carter was slow to make his entry into the negotiations. For most of the first year domestic politics rarely seemed to concern the president as he tackled the Middle East problem. He was sometimes reckless in his disregard for public opinion, and he probably would have done better to have engaged in less controversy with Israel in public in the first months of his term. In retrospect, his behavior gained him little on the Arab side and may have helped marginally in Begin's rise to power. As time wore on, Carter, and especially his advisers, came to believe he was paying a heavy price for his involvement in the Arab-Israeli imbroglio. They also saw the Egyptian-Israeli peace treaty as one of the few potential successes that could boost the president's prestige at home and abroad.[14] By early 1979 politics had come to the fore in the decisions leading to the final push for peace. Soon after the peace treaty was signed, Carter turned over the next phase of Middle East diplomacy to a special negotiator, Robert Strauss, fully expecting him to help cover the president's political flanks as the campaign for reelection got under way.

THE AUTONOMY TALKS

The negotiations concerning the West Bank and Gaza were bound to be complicated. First of all, the Palestinians (and Jordanians) were adamant that they would not participate in the talks, so Egypt had to play the part of uninvited stand-in for them. Second, Egypt and Israel could not agree what they were negotiating about. Sadat was not very concerned with details or language, but he and his colleagues saw the negotiations as preparing the way, in stages, for the Palestinians to govern themselves, with limits on their control over foreign and defense policy only. Not surprisingly, the Egyptians fastened on those parts of Camp David that spoke of an elected "self-governing authority"; an interim period that should serve as a transition to a final agreement based on UN resolution 242; the withdrawal of Israeli forces to designated locations; and the "powers and responsibilities" of the elected Palestinian authority.

Begin, who felt that he had originated the idea of Palestinian "autonomy"—he did not like the term "self-governing authority"—had a very different notion of what the negotiations were all about. While he had agreed to postpone an Israeli claim to sovereignty during an interim period, he had not agreed to abandon such a claim. Indeed, when asked what would come after five years of Palestinian autonomy, Begin had a simple answer. Israel would at that point assert its claim to sovereignty; if the Arabs agreed, that would settle the matter. If they did not agree, autonomy would continue indefinitely. And during this prolonged period of autonomy, Israeli settlements would continue to be built in "Judea and Samaria"; East Jerusalem was not to be part of the autonomy plan at all; land and water resources would not automatically come under the control of the self-governing authority, since autonomy applied only to persons, in Begin's view, not to territory.

Insofar as Carter and Vance had developed their thinking on Palestinian issues, they tended to agree more with the Egyptian interpretation of Palestinian self-government as a transitional stage. Carter was on record as supporting the right of Palestinians from East Jerusalem to participate in elections for the self-governing authority; his views on the importance of a freeze on settlement activity were well known; and his interpretation of 242 was that Israel was obliged to withdraw, at the end of the transitional period, from most, if not all, of the West Bank and Gaza as the quid pro quo for Palestinian recognition of Israel's right to live in peace within secure and recognized boundaries. For some of the Americans involved in the negotiations, the fact that autonomy would apply to the entire West Bank and Gaza would provide the Palestinians with a sort of presumptive territorial claim when the time came to settle the "final status" of the territories. This was a point also made by some of Begin's right-wing critics, who saw in the autonomy idea the germ of a Palestinian state.

Whatever Carter's views on these matters might be, he was not inclined to engage his time and efforts in this next round of negotiations. Vice President Mondale and Hamilton Jordan had long urged Carter to find a more "political" negotiator, and Robert Strauss, fresh from his success as special trade negotiator, seemed to fit the bill. The fact that he knew little about the Middle East was not seen as a major problem.

Strauss's tenure as special negotiator was brief and uneventful. At one point he thought the problem of Jerusalem should be tackled head on, presumably on the theory that if the toughest problem could be solved first, all else would fall into place. But by fall 1979, with Carter's reelection prospects in question, Strauss left to head the reelection effort.

If Carter needed any reminding that the Palestinian issue was political dynamite at home he had only to reflect on the fate of his UN ambassador, Andrew Young. In August discussions were taking place about the possibility of amending UN Resolution 242 to make it more palatable to the Palestinians. Needless to say, the Israelis were intensely suspicious of any such move.

In his capacity as head of the Security Council, Young met with the PLO representative to see if a formula could be found that would bring the PLO to accept UN Resolution 242. Neither Carter nor Vance was informed of the meeting. Young personally appealed to the Israeli UN ambassador to keep the meeting quiet, but that was not to be. Vance was furious that Young had told the Israeli ambassador about the meeting before informing Washington and insisted to Carter that Young be replaced, which he was by his deputy, Donald McHenry.

The Andrew Young affair may have angered Israel's supporters, but it was the Iranian seizure of American hostages at the U.S. embassy in Tehran on November 4, 1979, that accelerated Carter's political decline. Unable to win their release by diplomacy and hesitant to use force, the president soon found himself trapped in the White House with the unresolved hostage problem confronting him day in and day out. Every night on the evening news the countdown went on—"This is day xxx of the hostages' captivity in Iran." As he struggled to cope with this most debilitating of foreign-policy crises, Carter had little time for Palestinian autonomy.

To replace Strauss, Carter selected another lawyer-negotiator with good credentials in the Jewish community, Sol Linowitz. With the experience of negotiating the Panama Canal treaty to his credit, Linowitz was a skilled professional, but he lacked familiarity with the complex details of the Arab-Israeli peace process. He also found himself dealing with an Israeli cabinet minus Moshe Dayan, who broke with Begin precisely over the latter's restrictive view of autonomy.[15] Similarly on the Egyptian side, the negotiators, except for Mustafa Khalil, showed little flexibility, correctly arguing that they had no mandate from the Palestinians to decide on details. At most, they were prepared to develop broad principles for the transitional period, setting in motion a process that would lead to some form of Palestinian self-determination, a far cry from Begin's vision of perpetual autonomy.

Not surprisingly, little progress was made on the toughest issues, although Linowitz had some success in resolving many of the more technical ones.[16] In the spring of 1980, while Linowitz was struggling to find common ground between Egypt and Israel on Palestinian autonomy, Carter's fortunes hit a new low with the abortive mission to rescue the hostages in Tehran. Vance, who had recommended against the operation, resigned and was replaced as secretary of state by Edmund Muskie, a senator from Maine.

Toward the end of the Carter administration, Linowitz reached the point where he felt that substantial progress had been made. But no agreement had been reached on such sensitive issues as whether East Jerusalem Palestinians could participate in the elections to the self-governing authority or as whether there would be a freeze on constructing new settlements, and only a hint had been given that some degree of shared authority over future development of water and land resources might be possible. In brief, on issues of vital importance to the Palestinians, the negotiations had not produced much. And without the direct participation of the Palestinians in the negotiations, Egypt would be reluctant to go much further in dealings with Israel. Thus for much of the next ten years, until finally the Palestinians joined the peace talks as full participants in 1991, the part of Camp David that dealt with the future of the West Bank and Gaza remained essentially a dead letter.

Carter's overwhelming defeat in November 1980 rendered hypothetical the notion that a reelected Carter might have turned his considerable abilities to completing the process started at Camp David. Instead, on January 20, 1981, a few minutes before the hostages were finally released from their captivity in Tehran, Carter turned over the office of the president to Ronald Reagan, like him a former governor and an outsider to the world of Washington. But in most other ways Reagan was to be a very different kind of president.

CONCLUSIONS

Jimmy Carter was unique among American presidents in the depth of his concern to find a peaceful resolution of the conflict between Israel and its Arab neighbors. More than any other foreign-policy issue, the Middle East occupied his time and energies.

At the beginning of his administration he knew little about the intricacies of the problem. But he felt the challenge of tackling an issue that had eluded solutions in the past. And he no doubt felt that American interests would be well served if peace could be brought to the Middle East.

As time went on Carter came to know many of the leaders in the Middle East, and he turned his extraordinary capacity for mastering detail to the negotiations between Egypt and Israel. He pored over maps of Sinai to identify lines for the interim withdrawal. He personally drafted the first version of the Egyptian-Israeli framework agreement at Camp David. And twice he put his political reputation on the line by engaging in summit negotiations that could easily have failed.

In the end Carter was able to preside over the signing of the Egyptian-Israeli peace treaty, perhaps the most noteworthy foreign-policy achievement of his administration. Yet he gained little in domestic political terms for these efforts, and some would argue that he even weakened his political base.

It does nothing to diminish Carter's achievement in the Middle East to acknowledge that he built on firm foundations laid by Presidents Richard Nixon and Gerald Ford, and especially by the remarkable diplomatic efforts of Henry Kissinger in brokering three Arab-Israeli agreements during 1974–75. Carter was also ably served by his secretary of state, Cyrus Vance, who deserves much of the credit for patiently shaping the Camp David Accords and the text of the peace treaty.

Carter's initiatives would have come to naught had the leaders of Egypt and Israel been unwilling to accept American mediation and to make peace between their two countries. At no point did Carter forcefully impose American views on either side, though often he was able to change the positions of either Prime Minister Begin or President Sadat, especially Sadat. American leadership was certainly a necessary condition for the success of the negotiations, but it was not sufficient. The parties to the conflict had to be ready for agreement.

Throughout the Egyptian-Israeli peace negotiations, Sadat maintained he needed to demonstrate that he had achieved something for the Palestinians. He repeatedly said he was not prepared for a "separate peace." What he wanted from Begin was a simple statement that Israel was willing to return Arab territory captured in the 1967 war in exchange for peace, recognition, and security from the Arabs. Also, he hoped for some form of commitment from Israel to Palestinian rights, including the right of self-determination. This commitment, of course, Begin would not give.

In retrospect, it is clear that Sadat and Carter both overestimated the role that Egypt could play in laying the groundwork for a negotiated settlement of the Palestinian issue. Both misread the attitudes of King Hussein and the Palestinian leaders. Both misjudged the part that the Saudis might be willing to take in the negotiations. Neither took Syria sufficiently into account.

Even with these errors it might have been possible to carry out the provisions of the Camp David Accords if the idea of self-government for the Palestinians in the West Bank and Gaza could have been given real content. For example, if Carter had succeeded in getting Begin's agreement to a freeze on settlement activity, if the self-governing authority had been given control over land and water resources, if genuinely free elections, including the right to vote for Palestinians living in East Jerusalem, had been promised, and if the military occupation authority had been abolished, then it might have been possible to attract Palestinians into the negotiating process.

But none of these measures proved feasible while Begin was prime minister, and thus the concept of autonomy was devalued in the eyes of those who were most crucial in determining its viability. When Begin refused to budge on these matters, neither Sadat nor Carter could find a way to persuade him to change his mind. It remained to be seen if Ronald Reagan would choose to pick up where Carter had left off, or whether he had other ideas in mind. In light of the deterioration in U.S.-Soviet relations after the Soviet invasion of Afghanistan late in 1979, it seemed likely that Reagan would accord much more attention to East-West issues than to Arab-Israeli peace talks.

Carter had been slow to recognize the depth of Begin's attachment to the West Bank and Gaza. He had also been slow to understand the linkage issue.[17] Once Egypt and Israel were at peace, Begin had few remaining incentives to deal constructively with the Palestinian question. Sadat did feel strongly about the need for linkage, and for many months he had tried to establish some explicit connection between what would happen in bilateral Egyptian-Israeli relations and the Palestinian negotiations. But when put under pressure by Carter, in the face of Begin's intransigence, and when confronted with hostility from other Arab leaders, Sadat resigned himself to accepting the separate agreement that he had hoped to avoid when he first set off for Jerusalem in November 1977.

PART FIVE

The Reagan Presidency

CHAPTER THIRTEEN

Cold War Revival: Who's in Charge?

The election of Ronald Reagan as president in November 1980 was a watershed event in American politics. Rarely had a campaign pitted two such different candidates as Reagan and Jimmy Carter against each other. Reagan, a two-term governor of California and a moderately successful movie actor, came from the conservative wing of the Republican party. He propounded two main themes: the federal government is too big and inefficient, and communism is an evil that should be fought relentlessly. Increases in defense spending were central to his foreign-policy program.

Apart from these broad principles, it was hard to know what Reagan would bring to the presidency, especially in the field of international affairs. But he certainly implied that he would break with Carter's approach to the world. No more embracing of Brezhnev, appeasing of dictators, courting of leftists, pressuring of friends. Reagan even seemed prepared to reverse course on relations with China, speaking admiringly of Taiwan in contrast to "Red China."

Even if Reagan had not come to the presidency as a determined anticommunist, recent events would have ensured that U.S.-Soviet relations would be strained. The invasion of Afghanistan late in 1979 by the Soviets was one worrisome sign that they were embarking on a more aggressive foreign policy, with implications for the Gulf region in particular. In addition, war between Iran and Iraq had broken out in September 1980, and many in Washington feared that the Soviets would try to exploit the conflict to advance into the sensitive Gulf region. With these concerns in mind, Reagan and his entourage were not inclined to press hard for movement in the Arab-Israeli peace process. In any event, Reagan's sympathies were with Israel, and Israel was in no hurry to move.

Reagan's familiarity with Hollywood seems to have introduced him, if only superficially, to personalities close to Israel. But his views on the Middle East were otherwise virtually unknown, except for a ghost-written opinion piece that had appeared during the campaign. There Reagan had displayed a strong commitment to Israel as the only reliable friend of the United States in the Middle East, because of both its democratic values and its military prowess. The contest in the Middle East was described almost exclusively in cold war terms, with scant mention of the peace process.

The only reference to the Palestinians in the article came in a warning against the creation of a radical Palestinian state on Israel's borders. The words "Camp David," "peace process," and "negotiations" were nowhere to be found. The idea of Israel and Egypt as partners in peace was missing, replaced by a description of Israel as a formidable strategic asset. Egypt, it was noted, might also be prepared to "take a front-line position in defense of Western security interests," but this possibility was clearly viewed as a "secondary" link that could not "substitute for a strong Israel in the ever-turbulent Middle East."[1]

On the surface, then, Reagan seemed likely to shift American policy in the region away from the Camp David approach toward a more muscular competition with Moscow for influence. Israel would be regarded as a strategic partner. Engaging in peace talks would be accorded lower priority than bolstering American influence in the Gulf region. American arms sales to some Arab countries, such as Jordan, might be reduced, while arms might continue to flow to Saudi Arabia. In view of campaign promises, it seemed possible that Reagan would also order the American embassy in Israel to move from Tel Aviv to Jerusalem, a highly symbolic act. In short, the Reagan agenda appeared likely to reflect the neoconservative, pro-Israeli views that were widespread among his advisers and senior officials.[2]

But Reagan was not only a pro-Israeli, anticommunist ideologue.[3] He was also remarkably uninterested in the kind of detail that fascinated his predecessor. He would seemingly be content with setting the broad lines of policy, leaving to his associates the fine points of interpretation and implementation.[4]

To say the least, Reagan evinced little interest in the nuances of Middle East policy.[5] Perhaps more than any other president, Reagan was very dependent on his staff—and on his wife, who was a keen judge of people and was fiercely determined that her husband should be protected from criticism. To get to the president, it was thought, one had to pierce the wall created by Nancy Reagan and the troika of his closest advisers—Edwin Meese, Michael Deaver, and James A. Baker III. Even a powerful cabinet member like Secretary of State Alexander M. Haig, Jr., felt frustrated in his efforts to deal with Reagan. The national security adviser, Richard Allen, was relegated to the White House basement and sent his memos to the president through the notoriously inefficient Meese. Among this group, only Secretary of Defense Caspar W. Weinberger seemed to have the kind of personal relationship with the president that allowed him regular direct access.

These three men, Haig, Weinberger, and Allen, who occupied the key foreign-policy positions in the Reagan administration, would presumably have considerable influence on how Reagan tackled Middle East issues. Haig had served in the military, as Kissinger's deputy at the White House, and as Nixon's chief of staff. He could be expected to be strongly pro-Israeli, somewhat skeptical of the peace process, and deeply suspicious of Soviet intentions in the region. On the face of it, his views and Reagan's did not seem to differ much.

Weinberger's foreign-policy views were less predictable. His prior government service had involved economic issues, and his business experience had been with Bechtel, a large construction company with extensive experience in the Middle East, including Saudi Arabia. Weinberger had spent time in Saudi Arabia and was presumably aware of Arab views. Sharing the president's conservative, anticommunist perspective, he might be counted on to boost the Saudis as a force for stability and moderation in the region.[6]

Assuming that Haig and Weinberger did indeed tilt in different directions on Middle East issues, it was anybody's guess how Reagan might decide concrete cases in the event of divided counsel. And his national security adviser seemed too weak to be an effective referee between such powerful figures as Haig and Weinberger. Similarly, Reagan's ambassador to the United Nations, Jeane Kirkpatrick, was unlikely to wield the kind of influence that comes with proximity to the president. Nonetheless, as one of the few intellectuals in the Reagan entourage, and as a committed neoconservative, her voice would be heard on occasion.[7]

Less visible, but quite important, was William J. Casey, Reagan's director of Central Intelligence. Casey had a background in intelligence from World War II, had written books on how to make money, and, by all accounts, had a penchant for covert action and an omnivorous appetite for facts and information. Rare among Reaganites, he read books. His was not, however, a reflective intelligence. He was a man of action. He had little use for abstract theorizing.[8] Given this background, one might expect that Casey would see in Israel a model ally—muscular, action oriented, anti-Soviet, and with a highly reputed intelligence service.

UNVARNISHED REAGANISM: THE FIRST YEAR

At one point during his campaign for the presidency, Reagan was quoted as saying, "Let's not delude ourselves. The Soviet Union underlies all the unrest that is going on. If they weren't engaged in this game of dominoes, there wouldn't be any hot spots in the world."[9] Such a perspective, if really an accurate reflection of Reagan's thinking, would have profound implications for his dealing with problems of the Middle East.

As president, Reagan's contribution to shaping American Middle East policy consisted primarily of injecting this theme of the Soviet instigation of regional unrest into the thinking of his subordinates. Secretary Haig, while much more attuned to nuances than the president, shared Reagan's view that the Middle East should be viewed primarily through the prism of the U.S.-Soviet rivalry.[10] Surrounding him at the State Department, and clustered at the White House and the Defense Department, was a group of like-minded newcomers with very little experience in making foreign policy. It was easy to hear top officials arguing that the most serious problem in the Middle East was the presence of twenty-plus Soviet divisions on Iran's northern border.

Early in the Reagan administration Haig began to speak of the need to try to forge a "consensus of strategic concerns" among the pro-Western regimes in the Middle East. If that meant anything at all—and the phrase was never explained clearly—it presumably meant trying to focus the attention of "our friends" in the region on the Soviet threat, while simultaneously attempting to push parochial local conflicts to the back burner. An early test case arose in the form of a decision to sell a sophisticated radar plane, called airborne warning and control system aircraft (AWACS), to Saudi Arabia.

In normal circumstances one would expect the Israelis to put up quite a fight, arguing that the presence of AWACS in Saudi Arabia could threaten their security. But if Israel and Saudi Arabia were both parts of the U.S.-sponsored strategic consensus, and if both saw the Soviet Union as the primary threat to their security, then the Israelis might be persuaded to allow the sale to go forward in the interests of strengthening the common front against the Soviets and their clients. But there was no such luck. Israel and its supporters in the United States decided to make it an all-out fight. In the end they lost. The AWACS were sold, but only after Reagan had put his prestige on the line and had gone some distance toward meeting Israeli concerns.[11] After the AWACS battle one heard far less talk of strategic consensus, and Haig himself repeatedly said the concept had never been correctly understood.

The AWACS debate was not the only sign that the pro-Israeli Reagan administration would nonetheless have disagreements with Israel. In mid-1981, on the eve of the Israeli national elections, Prime Minister Begin ordered the bombing of the Iraqi nuclear reactor on the outskirts of Baghdad. Although many in official Washington were no doubt impressed by Israel's technical prowess, and were quietly cheering Begin's bold action, open endorsement of this form of "nonproliferation" policy toward Iraq, a member state of the International Atomic Energy Agency (IAEA), would be hard to explain. So, for a moment, the United States rapped Israel's knuckles symbolically by holding up the delivery of F-16 aircraft.

In the midst of these unanticipated challenges the Reagan administration had taken comfort in the fact that Egypt under Anwar Sadat's rule seemed to be stable and friendly. But that assumption was dramatically challenged on October 6, 1981, when Sadat was gunned down by Islamic extremists. Among the charges they made against him was his orientation toward the West and his peace agreement with Israel. Sadat's successor, Husni Mubarak, was well known to the Americans, but no one could be sure if Egypt would remain stable. At worst, the peace with Israel, and therefore the final phases of Israeli withdrawal from Sinai, could be called into question, to say nothing of the Palestinian autonomy talks.

In these troubled circumstances another crisis erupted in December 1981, when Israel decided to extend Israeli law to the Golan Heights, a step just short of annexation. The Reagan administration had just signed an anti-Soviet strategic cooperation agreement with Israel at the end of November, but the agreement was suspended on December 18 as a sign of Washington's disapproval of Israel's action on Golan.[12]

In light of these developments, one might have begun to wonder wherein lay the substance of the vaunted strategic relationship with Israel. The answer was soon to be provided, at least from the Israeli perspective, by Begin's assertive defense minister, Ariel Sharon. And Lebanon was to be the testing ground.

CRISIS IN LEBANON

In the world of pure Reaganism, chronic problems such as those in Lebanon were either not worth much attention or were symptoms of Soviet mischiefmaking. No wonder White House aides had little patience for arcane discussions of the internal political dynamics of Lebanon. Who, they seemed to be saying, could keep track of all the sects and their leaders with unpronounceable names?

But Lebanon had a way of forcing itself onto the American agenda because of Israeli concerns. In early 1981 Israeli-PLO clashes had intensified across Israel's northern border. Syria had been drawn into the fray. The veteran diplomat Philip C. Habib was then called on by Reagan to try to calm things down. The United States thus found itself negotiating a cease-fire between the two archenemies, and after mid-1981 the Lebanese-Israeli border was quiet, although no one was confident that the calm could last for long.

Israeli leaders, and especially Sharon, had grander plans in Lebanon. For years the Israelis had been secretly cultivating the tough leader of one of the Christian Lebanese militias, Bashir Gemayel. With presidential elections in Lebanon slated for the second half of 1982, Israelis saw a chance to help bring their man to power. Sharon and his colleagues were also determined to crush the PLO's military presence in southern Lebanon. In some of the most dramatic scenarios, Israel might also try to drive Syrian forces out of Lebanon, inflicting a heavy blow on the leading client of the Soviet Union in the process.[13]

These possibilities were risky enough to require careful planning and an attempt at coordination with the United States. On visits to Washington, D.C., in early 1982, Israeli officials outlined their ambitious plan for Lebanon in great detail. Some State Department officials were appalled and were afraid that Sharon would get the impression from Haig's nonobjection that the United States was encouraging, or at least acquiescing, in his plan. What Haig did say, repeatedly, was that the United States would understand such a military move only in response to an "internationally recognized provocation," whatever that might mean.[14] To some, that sounded like an invitation to find a pretext to go to war. Some Israelis have claimed that Haig's statements were indeed interpreted as a "green light."[15]

During the early part of 1982 one of the key concerns in Washington was that the Egyptian-Israeli peace treaty be implemented smoothly.

This was by no means a foregone conclusion. Sadat's assassination had raised questions in Israeli minds about the durability of commitments given by Sadat. Some analysts thought Begin might be looking for a pretext to postpone the last phase of Israeli withdrawal from Sinai, particularly since such a move would put off the politically painful moment of dismantling Israeli settlements around Al-Arish and forcing the 15,000 Israelis living there to leave their homes. No one in Washington wanted a flareup in Lebanon to dampen the prospects for full implementation of the Egyptian-Israeli peace. So for several months considerable diplomatic effort went into containing the potential for conflict in Lebanon and facilitating the final withdrawal of Israeli troops from Sinai. Except for a small disputed area named Taba, all Israeli forces were removed from Sinai on April 25. When the United Nations proved unwilling to provide a peacekeeping force for Sinai, the United States took the lead in creating a multinational force, including U.S. troops. Both Egypt and Israel were satisfied with the arrangement, and it worked smoothly in ensuing years. Without much fanfare American diplomats successfully contributed to keeping Egyptian-Israeli relations on track.

As part of this effort Haig had even traveled to the region twice in January 1982 to try to breathe life into the stalled autonomy talks. But here Mubarak was showing great caution, and those efforts soon petered out. Thus, as tensions rose on the Lebanese-Israeli front, the peace between Egypt and Israel was cool, at best, and a broader negotiating process was not in sight.

Soon rumors of an Israeli move against the PLO and Syria in Lebanon were being heard regularly. By May 1982 those Americans most in the know seemed to accept the inevitability, if not desirability, of such a move.[16] All that was needed was a pretext. That came on June 3, 1982, in the form of an assassination attempt against the Israeli ambassador in London. Almost immediately it was clear that this exploit had been ordered by the notorious renegade terrorist, Abu Nidal. Whether it constituted the "internationally recognized provocation" that Haig had spoken of or not, Israel did not wait to find out. Israel struck at PLO ammunition dumps in Beirut, and the PLO retaliated by shelling towns inside Israel. Six Israeli divisions then crossed into Lebanon on June 6—"Operation Peace for Galilee"—and it was immediately clear that more that a small retaliatory raid was under way.[17]

When the Israeli invasion began, Reagan was traveling in Europe. His relations with Haig were already somewhat strained, and others in

Reagan's entourage seemed to be looking for a pretext to ease out the prickly secretary of state. Tactical differences over how to deal with Israel during the Lebanon crisis quickly emerged. One faction formed around Haig, who felt that Israel, whatever the original justification for Israel's intervention in Lebanon, should not be stopped short of destroying the PLO. Somewhat uncharacteristically, Jeane Kirkpatrick sided with Haig, normally her bitterest rival.[18] Opposed to Israel's grand design were Vice President George Bush, who was in charge of crisis management in the White House, and his close ally, Chief of Staff James Baker.[19] William Clark, who had replaced Allen as national security adviser early in 1982, also favored reining Israel in, as did Secretary of Defense Weinberger.

As the early days of the crisis passed, Sharon seemed intent on cutting off the Syrian forces and leaving them no option but a humiliating withdrawal. In this scenario President Asad might even be toppled. At a minimum, Lebanon would be out from under the Syrian thumb. This is what the Phalangist allies of Israel were most eager to see coming out of the Israeli invasion. By contrast, a defeat of the PLO that left Syria still in Lebanon was of lesser interest to the Phalange.

Sharon seems not to have counted on strong intervention from Reagan. That was a mistake. Reagan, for all his passivity, could be aroused by his advisers. When scenes of violence were brought to his attention, he would sometimes react quite emotionally. Thus, on June 9, Reagan wrote one of the harshest notes ever delivered to an Israeli prime minister:

I am extremely concerned by the latest reports of additional advances of Israel into central Lebanon and the escalation of violence between Israel and Syria. Your forces moved significantly beyond the objectives that you have described to me. The tactical advantages may be apparent, but a much more important need is to avoid a wider war with Syrian involvement, and possibly with that of the Soviets as well.

Today I received a letter from President Brezhnev which voices grave concern that a very serious situation has been created that entails the possibility of wider acts of hostility. Of course, I did not accept most of the points in his letter, but the danger of further escalation does exist.

It is now clear that escalation of Syrian-Israeli violence has occurred. I now call on you to accept a ceasefire as of 6:00 a.m. on Thursday June 10, 1982. I implore you to recommend to your government the acceptance of my proposal.

Menachem, a refusal by Israel to accept a ceasefire will aggravate further the serious threat to world peace and will create extreme tension in our relations.[20]

It is hard to believe that Reagan personally took the initiative to send such a message. More likely his aides made the case that Israel should be forced to stop, and Reagan went along.

By all accounts Haig was furious that his advice to let the Israelis finish the job was not being taken. On a whole series of issues, Reagan seemed to be ignoring his views. As early as June 14 Haig had hinted that he might resign unless Reagan gave him a clear vote of confidence. Finally, on June 25 Reagan met with Haig to accept a letter of resignation that had not been written.[21] But Haig hung on as acting secretary of state for some time, trying to steer the course of U.S. diplomacy from his retreat at the Greenbrier resort in West Virginia. Reagan, who had no stomach for confrontations, finally asked his designated secretary of state, George P. Shultz, to call Haig on July 5 and tell him to stop acting as if he were still in charge.[22]

This bizarre episode demonstrated clearly that Reagan was not only very susceptible to the influence of his advisers but was also reluctant to exercise much discipline over them. He apparently found personal confrontations unpleasant and tried hard to avoid them. With Haig's departure the Israelis feared that they had lost one of their best friends.

George Shultz, who had been Weinberger's boss at Bechtel, was viewed by Israelis with suspicion. A former secretary of both labor and the treasury, Shultz had been on Reagan's short list for secretary of state at the outset of the administration, but Richard Nixon had argued effectively on Haig's behalf.[23] During his initial confirmation hearings before the Senate in July, Shultz showed himself to be a careful, well-informed person, who seemed attentive to the nuances of the Middle East regional setting. He addressed the Palestinian issue in a forthright manner, thus confirming for some his pro-Arab reputation.[24]

As secretary of state, Shultz immediately turned his attention to the long-neglected peace process. In his view the Israeli invasion of Lebanon would destroy the chance for peace unless the United States took a new initiative. He was also worried about the impact of the invasion on the still-fragile Egyptian-Israeli relationship. Thus on July 17 he quietly convened a working group of senior officials to start planning for a "fresh start" on Arab-Israeli peacemaking.[25]

While supporting a resumption of peace diplomacy, Shultz did not look favorably on Yasir Arafat and the PLO. In his view Arafat should get no reward for leaving Beirut. But the moment the fighting in Lebanon was over and the PLO was on its way to a new location, Shultz was determined to have a peace initiative in place, and the initiative would not be postponed until the problems of Lebanon were resolved. Also, it would bear the imprint of the president, thereby giving it more authority. Reagan's willingness to go along with this approach was growing as he witnessed the Israeli shelling of Beirut. On July 30 Shultz showed Reagan a draft of the new peace initiative. Later that afternoon, National Security Adviser Clark called Shultz to say, "The president's friendship for Israel is slipping. Enough is enough."[26]

During much of August 1982 the United States, once again with the energetic assistance of Philip Habib, tried to bring the fighting in Lebanon to an end and to arrange for the evacuation of PLO fighters from Beirut.[27] An American military contingent was even sent to Lebanon as part of an international force to help oversee the PLO departure. Habib not only helped to end the bloodshed but also successfully pressed for the election of Bashir Gemayel as Lebanon's next president. To secure the PLO's departure from Lebanon, he also made explicit written commitments to the PLO that assurances had been obtained from the Israelis about the safety of Palestinian civilians left behind after the PLO's departure.[28]

THE REAGAN PLAN

By late August 1982 the Reagan administration seemed to be on the verge of success in the midst of the Lebanese agony, with a pro-Western president about to be inaugurated in Beirut, the Syrians badly battered in the Bekaa valley of eastern Lebanon, and the PLO driven from the country. (The Soviets, meanwhile, had shown themselves unable to do much to help their clients and suffered a loss of political prestige at a crucial moment in the revived cold war atmosphere of the early 1980s.)

Already on August 13 Shultz had won the president's approval of his "fresh start" initiative. Shultz felt Reagan was finally getting involved in Middle East policymaking. The following day he even arranged to have senior officials "role play" the likely reactions of Begin, Mubarak, and King Hussein to the new initiative. Watching the president's awakened interest, Meese observed that Reagan had been ready for this moment a year earlier, but Haig had kept him away from Middle East issues.[29]

With the PLO on its way out of Beirut, and the United States in a position of apparent diplomatic strength, Shultz urged the president to seize the moment to outline the new plan for a diplomatic settlement of the Israeli-Palestinian conflict. Shultz anticipated that the Israelis, in particular, would react negatively, but he nonetheless felt the United

States could help to shape the postwar agenda. On September 1, 1982, Reagan gave his first and only major speech on the Arab-Israeli conflict (see appendix H).

The core of the initiative was still Camp David, but with important substantive additions. Whereas Camp David had been vague on the so-called final status of the West Bank and Gaza after a transitional period, Reagan said the United States would oppose both Israeli annexation and an independent Palestinian state. The U.S. preference, he said, was for some form of association between the West Bank, Gaza, and Jordan. Lest any doubt remain, Reagan said the United States believed that the withdrawal provision of UN Resolution 242 should apply to the West Bank and Gaza, a position completely at odds with Begin and the Likud party's policy.

Within days the United States spelled out its views in greater detail. During the transitional period, for example, the United States would support a freeze on Israeli settlements. Palestinians should have real authority over land and resources; and Palestinians living in East Jerusalem should be allowed to vote in elections for a self-governing authority. As for the "final status" negotiations, the United States went on record as favoring the view that the extent of Israeli withdrawal from occupied territories should be influenced by the extent and nature of the peace and security arrangements offered in return. These were not positions likely to win approval from Begin. They did not. Begin reacted angrily to the Reagan Plan, as it inevitably was dubbed.[30]

The Reagan initiative clearly shifted the spotlight from Egypt to Jordan and the Palestinians. Syria was left out in the cold. Begin rejected the proposal immediately because it called for eventual Israeli relinquishment of most of the occupied territories as the price for peace. The Arab response was, on the whole, less categorical. Questions were asked, some positive noises were heard, and it was widely rumored that King Hussein (and Arafat as well) had been briefed in advance on the initiative and had indicated general approval.[31]

Shortly after the Reagan initiative the Arab states held a summit meeting in Fez, Morocco, and adopted a Saudi proposal that came to be known as the Fez plan. Though different in content from the Reagan proposal, the Fez plan at least gave the United States and the Arabs something to talk about.

The Reagan administration's decision to launch an initiative on the Palestinian issue, albeit with a strong Jordanian tilt, was predicated on the belief that the problems of Lebanon were on their way toward solution. Even before the war in Lebanon, some in the bureaucracy had been making the case for a revived peace effort. Sharon had told the Americans he would solve the Palestinian issue his way—by moving tanks into Lebanon. Once the PLO was crushed, the Palestinians in the West Bank would become pragmatic and ready to deal with existing realities.

The shortcomings of Sharon's vision became abundantly clear within weeks of the Reagan initiative. The comforting belief that Lebanon's travails were nearly over was literally and figuratively blown away with the assassination by pro-Syrian elements of Bashir Gemayel on September 14, 1982. General Sharon, who had discussed with Gemayel a plan for "cleansing" Lebanon of Palestinians, now saw a danger that Israel's long-term investment would be lost with Bashir's death. He pressed the leadership of the Lebanese Forces (a Christian militia) and the Phalange party to respect the deals he had arranged with Bashir and to prepare for "immediate action." In the circumstances Israel had great leverage over the Phalange, including the ability to withhold or grant support for the candidacy of Bashir's brother, Amin, as president.[32]

Some of the details of what happened next are not entirely clear, but the broad outline is known. Units of the Lebanese Forces militia under the command of Eli Hobeika moved into two Palestinian refugee camps, Sabra and Shatila, on the southern outskirts of Beirut. There, under the eyes of their Israeli allies, they systematically murdered as many as eight hundred Palestinian civilians. This massacre led to a strong reaction everywhere, including in Israel. Five months later Sharon and several other officers were censured for their role in not preventing the massacres and were removed from their posts.[33]

The American response to the Sabra and Shatila massacres was to put Lebanon and its ills back at the top of the agenda. American military forces, which had been withdrawn after the departure of the PLO, were returned to the Beirut area to protect the refugee camps and to provide visible backing for the embattled Lebanese government. To negotiate an Israeli-Lebanese agreement that would lead to the withdrawal of both Israeli and Syrian forces became a priority of U.S. diplomacy, to be pursued in parallel, or even before, the Reagan Plan for the West Bank and Gaza.[34] Shultz's hope that Arab-Israeli peace talks could avoid becoming hostage to Lebanon's ills was increasingly in doubt.

COURTING KING HUSSEIN

King Hussein, the object of the Reagan initiative in its first phase, began to watch how the Americans handled the Lebanese imbroglio as a test of how serious they were likely to be in dealing with the Palestinian issue. He, like many Arabs, felt that unless the Americans could get the Israelis out of Lebanon, there would be little chance of dislodging them from the West Bank. President Reagan further undermined the chances of success for his initiative by saying publicly that nothing could be done on the Palestinian question until agreement was reached on Lebanon.[35] For those who had opposed the Reagan initiative from the outset—and that included Begin, Asad, and the Soviets—this statement was an invitation to make things in Lebanon as difficult as possible, to ensure that "another Camp David," as the Syrians labeled the Reagan initiative, would not succeed.

King Hussein visited Washington in December 1982 for talks with President Reagan. In an effort to persuade the king to support the Reagan initiative, the president wrote two letters to him spelling out promises and commitments, including a supply of arms, if Hussein would agree to enter negotiations. Reagan also promised that he would convince Israel to freeze settlement activity in the West Bank once negotiations with Jordan began and that the transitional period might be shortened to less than five years.

By all accounts, Hussein was tempted, but he felt the need for Palestinian support. On occasion, however, the king left the impression that he would proceed without Arafat if the latter proved to be intransigent. Shultz, who was primarily in charge of the negotiations, was never quite sure what to make of King Hussein's comments. But he felt that the State Department "Arabists" tended to be too optimistic in their assessments.[36]

Talks between Jordan and the PLO took place over the next several months. Finally, in April 1983 the king concluded that there was no basis for developing a joint negotiating position with the PLO. The Jordanians blamed pro-Soviet hard-liners in Arafat's entourage for this inability to reach an agreement. Jordan, too, came under direct Soviet pressure not to go along.[37] On April 10, 1983, the king called Reagan to tell him that his talks with Arafat had failed. He was not prepared to move on his own. The same day he officially announced that Jordan could not accept the Reagan initiative, stating, "We in Jordan, having refused from the beginning to negotiate on behalf of the Palestinians, will neither act separately nor in lieu of anybody in Middle East peace negotiations."[38] For the moment, the Reagan Plan seemed dead.

LEBANESE-ISRAELI PEACE?

For much of the remainder of 1983, Arab-Israeli peacemaking became, from the American perspective, synonymous with trying to forge a viable Lebanese-Israeli agreement as a step toward the withdrawal of both Israeli and Syrian forces from Lebanon. Secretary Shultz, who had shown reluctance to engage directly in the shuttle-style travels of his predecessors, went to the Middle East to put the final touches on the Lebanese-Israeli accord. In part he did so to respond to the expressed concerns of Egyptian President Mubarak. Shultz was skeptical about Syria's role and tried to enlist Saudi support to pressure Damascus. He also ran into problems with the Israelis, who were unwilling to abandon their ally, Major Saad Haddad, in southern Lebanon. Despite all the obstacles, however, Shultz's shuttle seemed to pay off. On May 17, 1983, Lebanon and Israel signed an agreement that was just short of a peace treaty.

But the agreement was stillborn. Israeli withdrawal was made dependent on Syrian withdrawal, and Asad (who commanded a sizable constituency inside Lebanon) would not tolerate such a condition. Already the United States and Syria seemed to be on a collision course. In April the American embassy had been bombed with devastating effectiveness.[39] Americans traced the bombing to Lebanese allies of Iran, perhaps with some Syrian involvement as well. During the summer, fighting resumed in Beirut, and Arafat defiantly returned to the northern Lebanese city of Tripoli. Syria, by now fully rearmed by the Soviets, became increasingly assertive in Lebanon, including against the PLO.

As the violence mounted, the Israelis began to disengage from the Shouf mountains overlooking Beirut, leaving the American contingent near the airport exposed to hostile attacks. Before long the U.S. Marines found themselves, in their lightly defended positions, drawn into inter-Lebanese battles. The peacekeeping mission was gradually being eroded, and the United States was becoming a cobelligerent on the side of the Lebanese Christian forces. On October 23, at a time of mounting tension between the United States and Syria, a truck loaded with explosives drove into the compound of the American contingent of the multinational peacekeeping force. The effect was devastating. Two hundred forty-one

American servicemen were killed.[40] Simultaneously, French and Israeli units were attacked by suicide truck bombs.

Within days of the attack on the American troops in Beirut, President Reagan signed National Security Decision Directive 111, thereby reviving the strategic cooperation agreement that had been suspended in December 1981.[41] According to some accounts, Under Secretary of State Lawrence S. Eagleburger had concluded earlier in the year that close cooperation with Israel was essential for American policy in Lebanon to succeed. In reaching this conclusion, he was influenced by the decision taken by the new Israeli defense minister, Moshe Arens, to withdraw Israeli troops from central Lebanon, an action of great strategic importance that had been undertaken without coordination with Washington. Eagleburger seemed to hope that by restoring the strategic cooperation agreement, the Reagan administration would be better able to influence Israeli decisions that impinged on American interests. By November 1983, Joint Political-Military Group meetings had been agreed upon to develop areas of strategic cooperation.

Adding urgency to the rebuilding of U.S.-Israeli ties was the emergence of new leadership in Israel. To the surprise of many, on September 15, 1983, Menachem Begin, suffering from the recent death of his wife and seemingly depressed over the outcome of the war in Lebanon, announced his resignation and entered a period of seclusion that continued until his death in 1992. His replacement was Yitzhak Shamir, whose early political career had been with the Stern Group (Lehi), which had won him a reputation for extremism and violence. Relegated to the margins of Israeli political life in the early years after independence, Shamir spent some years in the Israeli intelligence service, Mossad, returning to politics in the 1970s as a member of Begin's party. At the time of the Camp David Accords he served as speaker of the Knesset; after Dayan resigned as foreign minister in October 1979, Begin hesitated before offering the post to Shamir, but eventually did so in March 1980.[42]

Now, with Begin's departure from the scene, Shamir won the Likud's endorsement to take his place. Instead of Begin and Sharon the Americans now found themselves dealing with Shamir and Arens, a change that some felt would be for the better.

Whatever the prospect for improved relations with Israel might have been, the situation in Lebanon offered little hope for Reagan and Shultz. After the October bombings, American policy became more overtly aimed at punishing Syria. On December 4, 1983, two American planes were shot down by the Syrians, with one pilot killed and one captured.[43]

By early 1984, when the politics of reelection were uppermost in the minds of some of the president's advisers, Reagan made a decision, over the opposition of Shultz, that the Marines should be "redeployed offshore." Critics termed the decision "cut and run." Whichever words one chose, the facts were the same. Reagan, who had pinned American prestige on a stable settlement in Lebanon, was removing the most tangible sign of that commitment.[44] Henceforth Lebanon would be left primarily to the squabbles of its internal factions and its two powerful neighbors.

A MISSED OPPORTUNITY?

Election years rarely witness serious initiatives for Arab-Israeli peace by American presidents. Their priorities lie elsewhere. Controversy, an inevitable corollary of any serious U.S. initiative in the region, is shunned. Pleas from Arab regimes for arms and diplomatic support are put off until after the elections.[45]

The year 1984 did not, however, prove to be entirely wasted. Early in 1984 Egypt was readmitted to the Islamic Conference, a sign that it was no longer isolated because of its peace agreement with Israel. A month later Mubarak and King Hussein made a joint appearance in Washington with President Reagan, which was symbolically important, even if Egypt's overt support for the PLO caused some ill feeling in American circles. In Israel, midyear elections produced a near standoff between Labor and Likud, resulting in a unity coalition of both parties and a rotating premiership. For the first two years Shimon Peres would be in the top job. Beginning in October 1986 Yitzhak Shamir would serve out the remaining two years of the term as prime minister. Throughout, Yitzhak Rabin would serve as minister of defense. As unusual as such an arrangement might seem, it did mean that the second Reagan administration would be dealing with Israelis in power who did not automatically exclude the key elements of Resolution 242 and its practical interpretation as spelled out by Reagan in September 1982. Indeed, it soon became clear that Peres and King Hussein were eager to explore areas for cooperation and were looking to Washington for help against the common adversaries of the Reagan Plan—the Likud, Syria, and the PLO.

This combination of regional developments, plus Reagan's extraordinary electoral victory over Walter Mondale in November 1984, seemed to set the stage for a new round of American involvement in the peace process. Rarely had conditions been better for trying to press forward with some version of an Israeli-Jordanian deal, provided that enough Palestinian support could be found to give the exercise an aura of legitimacy in Arab eyes.

During the fall of 1984 the new assistant secretary of state for Near Eastern affairs, Richard Murphy, had spent six weeks in the region probing for possible openings on the peace front. King Hussein gave the impression of being ready to proceed, perhaps without the PLO, and for the first time he did not insist on knowing the outcome of negotiations before joining the process. If that became a solid Jordanian position, it could radically change the prospects for peace, especially with a Labor-led coalition in power in Israel. Shultz began to be more hopeful about the long-stalled peace diplomacy.[46]

Arab leaders had often expressed the hope that they could deal with a reelected Republican president. This nostalgic view stemmed largely from the perception of the second Eisenhower term, and especially Dwight D. Eisenhower's tough treatment of the Israelis during and after the Suez crisis of 1956. Now, in 1985, the Arabs were again dealing with a popular, reelected Republican. So, one by one, Arab leaders trekked to Washington in the first half of 1985. First came King Fahd of Saudi Arabia, followed a month later by Egyptian President Husni Mubarak. Most important, King Hussein arrived in Washington at the end of May.

Much of Egyptian and Jordanian policy at the time was aimed at evoking a positive American response to a joint Jordanian-PLO position that had been formalized in a carefully worded statement signed on February 11, 1985.[47] In many ways the Jordanian-PLO position could be construed as a new attempt to respond belatedly to the 1982 Reagan initiative. Both parties announced that their common goal was the creation of a Jordanian-Palestinian confederation, to be established once Israel had fully withdrawn from occupied territory. They pledged to negotiate as a joint delegation within the framework of an international conference.

Shultz was wary of the idea of an international conference. As envisaged by the Arabs, such a conference could become a lopsided means of pressuring Israel for concessions. Even Peres would not accept such an arrangement, and his Likud partners were much more hostile to the idea. At most, Shultz would consider a symbolic conference to open the way to direct negotiations. Until Jordan made clear that the PLO would remain in the shadows and the international conference would not become a barrier to direct negotiations, Shultz would show little interest in the new Jordanian-PLO accord.[48]

Although the February 11, 1985, agreement raised more questions than it answered in the minds of the Reagan administration, the Jordanian attempt at clarification was reassuring. During their visit to Washington in May, Jordanian officials stated that the concept of confederation was really much closer to "federation," with responsibility for foreign affairs and defense clearly understood by both parties to be vested in Amman. The Jordanians, moreover, played down the importance of the international conference, stressing instead the need for U.S. contact with a group of Jordanians and Palestinians. They also made it clear that they thought the PLO could be brought to the point of accepting Resolution 242, perhaps in return for some form of American recognition of Palestinian self-determination within the framework of a confederation with Jordan.[49]

However tempted some American officials may have been to press forward with an initiative in these seemingly propitious circumstances, there were three offsetting considerations. In the first place, President Reagan was on record saying, in March 1985, that the United States did not want to participate in Arab-Israeli peace negotiations, despite the Camp David commitment for the United States to be a "full partner" in subsequent phases of the peace talks.[50] Reagan and Shultz repeatedly said that the problem was not for the United States to talk to the parties but to get the parties to talk to each other. Direct negotiations became something of a slogan, especially among key senators and representatives. The administration could not ignore these sentiments. Indeed, Hussein was told there was no chance for congressional approval of an arms package for Jordan unless he committed himself to direct negotiations with Israel.

A second problem in bringing the United States into a more active role in support of King Hussein's approach was reportedly Secretary Shultz's sense of disillusionment with most of the Arab leaders he had dealt with during 1982–83. He seemed to think that they wasted the opportunity provided by the Reagan plan and that their words could not always be counted on. The PLO, in particular, was not a fit partner for peace talks, in his view, although he did believe that Palestinians from the West Bank and Gaza would have to be included in a Jordanian delegation. But the idea of having Assistant Secretary Murphy meet with a joint Jordanian-Palestinian delegation proved to be controversial. As King Hussein saw it, such a meeting would set the stage for the PLO to accept UN Resolution 242; there would then be further contacts between the United States and a Jordanian-PLO delegation; next there would be an international conference; and only at that point would there be negotiations with Israel. Shultz, in contrast, insisted that any American meeting with a Jordanian-Palestinian delegation should be followed immediately by contacts with the Israelis.[51]

A third inhibition on American policy came from a concern for the political standing of Prime Minister Peres. During his first year in office he had become popular. The withdrawal of Israeli forces from Lebanon had been welcomed by a war-weary populace. Efforts to curb raging inflation were progressing, though with considerable pain. His management of the economy was turning out well for Peres. Quiet diplomacy with Jordan seemed to be laying the groundwork for a kind of condominium over the West Bank and Gaza at the expense of the PLO. Some American officials wanted to help Peres position himself for a showdown with the Likud. This desire led them to advise against anything that could be viewed as causing a strain in U.S.-Israeli relations, such as American dealings with the PLO or American support for Palestinian self-determination.

A practical test of American policy emerged during the summer. The Jordanians wanted to proceed with the idea of an American exploratory meeting with a joint Jordanian-PLO delegation. On July 19 King Hussein had met secretly with Peres in London to discuss his strategy. He had gone over a long list of possible Palestinian participants who might be part of a joint Jordanian-Palestinian delegation. Shultz was informed of the meeting by the Israelis on August 5. Peres was not enthusiastic about a preliminary U.S.-Jordanian-Palestinian meeting but would not oppose it strongly so long as no PLO members participated.

On August 9 Shultz informed Reagan of the state of play. Reagan was firm in his opposition to American officials meeting with anyone even vaguely connected to the PLO. Meanwhile, Foreign Minister Shamir sent a message to the White House expressing his adamant opposition to the idea of the Americans meeting with any Palestinians. Shultz pressed Reagan for a decision, and finally was given authority to allow Murphy to meet with a joint Jordanian-Palestinian delegation only if that led immediately to direct negotiations with Israel.[52]

The Jordanian response was noncommittal. Essentially the Jordanians said that an initial meeting should take place, and then next steps could be considered. As the Jordanians were quick to point out, their reply was almost a verbatim repetition of a long-standing American response to the Arabs' question of what would happen once negotiations with Israel began.

To try to organize a preliminary meeting between the United States and a joint Jordanian-Palestinian delegation, the Jordanians forwarded a list of seven names of possible Palestinian members of the delegation, from which the Americans were expected to select four. The Israelis had said they had no objection to two of the seven names but were quick to label the others as PLO. The Americans objected to at least three of the names, but, more important, they kept asking for assurances that any preliminary talks would be accompanied by a clear Jordanian-Palestinian commitment to direct negotiations with Israel.[53] Jordan, eager not to offend Syria, was not prepared to abandon the idea of an international conference in favor of U.S.-sponsored direct bilateral negotiations.

Despite these difficulties, for a moment in the summer of 1985 the United States seemed about to take the plunge. Assistant Secretary Murphy was sent to the Middle East, and members of a joint Jordanian-Palestinian team were assembled in Amman to meet him; but at the last moment he was told not to proceed with the meeting. Reagan's conditions could not be met, and Shultz therefore had to scrap the idea of a meeting. According to Shultz, Reagan had been immovable on the points of excluding the PLO and insisting on direct negotiations. But it is far from clear how hard anyone tried to persuade Reagan, and in any event Shultz was beginning to detect signs that the situation in the region was moving away from the possibility of productive peace talks.[54]

King Hussein made a final effort to persuade the Americans in the fall. He had been told that there was no chance of winning congressional support for a big new arms package for Jordan—something Reagan had promised the king in writing in December 1982—unless Jordan committed itself to direct negotiations. At his speech to the UN General Assembly, the king did make such a commitment, saying, "We are ready to negotiate with Israel under suitable, acceptable supervision, directly and as soon as possible, in accordance with Security Council Resolutions 242 and 338."[55] One month later the U.S. Senate rebuffed the king's request on arms, stipulating that no major sale could be concluded until "direct and meaningful" negotiations with Israel had begun. In the face of continuing congressional hostility to the sale, the administration finally withdrew the nearly $2 billion arms package for Jordan, on February 3, 1986.

October proved to be a disastrous month for Jordanian-PLO relations, as well as for Hussein's initiative. The month began with a spectacular Israeli bombing attack on Arafat's headquarters in Tunis, ostensibly in retaliation for a PLO attack on several Israelis in Cyprus a few days earlier. On October 5 King Hussein and Prime Minister Peres met secretly in London to develop a plan for joint rule in the West Bank.[56]

While Arafat was being abandoned by King Hussein, he was also being challenged by radicals from within his own organization. On October 7 a minor faction of the PLO—the Palestine Liberation Front of Abul Abbas—had the idea to hijack an Italian cruise ship, the *Achille Lauro*. Before the incident was over, one elderly American, confined to his wheelchair, had been murdered and thrown overboard. (The Syrians, eager to discredit the PLO, recovered the body on their coast and dutifully returned it to the American government, thus providing conclusive proof that the victim had been shot.[57]) At about the same time Jordan and the PLO failed to reach agreement on terms that would have allowed for a meeting of a joint Jordanian-PLO delegation with the British foreign secretary.

President Asad must have watched all these events with great satisfaction. He had opposed the February 11, 1985, agreement from the outset. He had labeled the U.S. efforts to arrange direct talks under its own auspices as tantamount to another Camp David, and now he found the Jordanian-PLO alliance coming apart. So Asad, working closely with the Jordanian prime minister, Zaid al-Rifai, encouraged the development of a working alliance with Jordan. The king was obliged to acknowledge past Jordanian misdeeds in allowing anti-Syrian terrorist groups to operate from his territory. Thus the stage was set for a Syrian-Jordanian rapprochement and a break between Jordan and the PLO, which was not long in coming.[58] On February 19, 1986, the king spelled out in graphic detail the reasons for the breakdown of coordination with the PLO.[59] The February 11, 1985, accord had lasted barely one year.

In retrospect, it seems clear that the Americans had never been enthusiastic about dealing with a joint Jordanian-PLO delegation. As one Jordanian minister put it early in the discussions in Washington, Jordan tried to stress that the PLO was relatively weak and therefore could be pressured to make concessions. The American reply, he said, was that if the PLO was weak, it should be excluded entirely from the diplomatic process.[60] Finally, when King Hussein began to conclude that the PLO was a liability in his dealings with Israel, Syria, and Washington, and that it was recreating a substantial presence in Jordan, he moved to sever the tie. In retrospect, Shultz concluded that neither Hussein nor Peres was politically strong enough to deliver the concessions needed to make the peace process work, even though their own thinking was not far apart.[61]

COVERT DEALINGS WITH IRAN

American involvement with the Arab-Israeli conflict can never be entirely isolated from other developments in the Middle East. In complex ways, events in Lebanon, Libya, and Iran all came to be entwined with Arab-Israeli diplomacy. If there was a connecting thread among these geographically remote locations, it was terrorism. By the mid-1980s the Reagan administration had become obsessed with the battle against terrorism, especially of the state-sponsored variety. And the three states topping the list of suspects were Syria, Iran, and Libya. All were actively involved in Lebanon, some with Lebanese groups and some with militant Shiites.

Already in 1984 Americans were falling victim to terrorist attacks. Malcolm Kerr, the president of the American University of Beirut and a leading specialist on Middle East affairs, was gunned down in cold blood in January 1984. Two months later the head of the CIA station in Lebanon, William Buckley, was kidnapped. In succeeding months, on into 1985, 1986, and 1987, fourteen more Americans were kidnapped from the streets of Beirut and held hostage. And terrorist attacks on airlines and airports claimed more lives.

Given the tough rhetoric of the Reagan administration against terrorism, the United States might have been expected to lash out at the states thought to be sponsoring such attacks. But only once did that happen, when Libya was held responsible for the bombing in Berlin that took two American lives. On April 14, 1986, American planes bombed Tripoli, nearly killing President Muammar Qaddafi in the process.

Curiously, Iran was treated quite differently from Libya, even though its involvement with the hostage takers in Lebanon was beyond doubt. During the spring of 1985, just as the joint Jordanian-PLO strategy was getting off the ground, some officials in Washington were beginning to debate the merits of trying to improve relations with Iran.[62] The rationale at the outset was presented in anti-Soviet terms. Iran was a large, important country that had not chosen sides in the cold war rivalry. After Ayatollah Khomeini left the scene, some argued, there would be a struggle for power, with pro-Soviet elements having a chance to gain the upper hand. The United States should therefore find some way to establish contacts with Iranians who were not pro-Soviet.[63]

On July 3, 1985, David Kimche, the director general of the Israeli Foreign Ministry, met at the White House with Robert McFarlane, Reagan's most recent national security adviser.[64] Israel had maintained some useful contacts in Iran after the revolution, and Kimche now offered to put these at the disposal of the United States in pursuit of the policy of improving relations with Iran. He told the Americans that at some point the Iranians, who were locked into a costly war with Iraq, would almost certainly ask for arms.[65] Within days of this conversation President Reagan was briefed on the Kimche conversation and reportedly gave general approval to the policy of cultivating "moderate" elements in Iran. During August Israel made a large shipment of American-made antitank missiles to Iran, and several weeks later an American hostage was released in Beirut. The "arms for hostages" exchange had begun.

Throughout most of 1986 the United States became more and more involved with Iran. Over the opposition of both his secretary of state and secretary of defense (who rarely agreed on much at all), and without their knowledge, Reagan signed an intelligence finding on January 17 that authorized the sale of American arms to Iran. Israel was to serve as the conduit. The moment of high drama—and even strange humor—came in May when McFarlane, accompanied by his National Security Council staff aides Oliver North and Howard Teicher, as well as Peres's adviser on terrorist affairs, Amiram Nir, traveled secretly to Tehran. As a symbol of their desire for a new relationship with the "moderates" in Iran, they took with them a chocolate cake with a small gold key on top of it—direct from a Tel Aviv bakery!

McFarlane soon learned that his Iranian counterparts were interested only in getting more arms and had no desire to discuss broad strategic issues or to deliver more hostages as a sign of their good intentions. He returned to Washington empty handed, although his energetic assistant, Oliver North, continued to press forward with the policy, developing in the process an innovative way of financing another of the president's pet projects, aid to the Nicaraguan Contras, which Congress had prohibited.

Finally, after the release of two more American hostages in Beirut, and the taking of an additional three, the news of McFarlane's secret visit to Tehran the previous May was published, and on November 25, 1986, the White House was obliged to confirm that arms had been sent to Iran, with the proceeds illegally diverted to the Contras. A political scandal of unprecedented proportions ensued, leading eventually to indictments against McFarlane; his successor as national security adviser, John Poindexter; and Oliver North. Reagan, who professed ignorance about the diversion of funds to the Contras, was weakened by the affair.

How, if at all, did the Iran-Contra affair affect American policy toward the Arab-Israeli conflict? First, just as the Jordanian-Palestinian initiative was getting off the ground in 1985, the attention of the White House was turning to the sensitive issue of the opening to Iran, and Israel was to play a key part in the strategy. This was no time to press the Israelis to be particularly forthcoming toward the Jordanians or Palestinians. In fact, the Israelis were in an excellent position to embarrass the Reagan administration if they ever had reason to do so.

Second, as the flow of arms from Israel to Iran got under way in 1985, Arab governments began to take notice and assumed a degree of American complicity. Simultaneously, the United States was openly tilting toward Iraq in the Iran-Iraq war. How could the two strands of policy be reconciled? At a time when American credibility was important for the possible success of the peace process, Egypt and Jordan seem to have developed doubts about the reliability of the United States.

Third, the initiative toward Iran caused deep divisions in the upper echelons of the American government, which Reagan was unwilling or unable to resolve. Divided counsels on the Middle East undermined a coherent policy toward the peace process. In the end, however, the Iran-Contra affair cannot be credited with causing the failure to exploit a possible opening in the peace process in 1985–86. But it did contribute to the erosion of American credibility at a crucial moment, weakening the president and perhaps leading to his further disengagement from foreign-policy issues as he approached the end of his second term.

CHAPTER FOURTEEN

Return to Realism: Shultz Tries Again

From the moment he became secretary of state in 1982, George Shultz had been the dominant architect of the Reagan administration's approach to the Arab-Israeli peace process. But on related matters in the Middle East, such as Lebanon and the Iran-Iraq war, he was not able to get his way so easily. Secretary of Defense Weinberger had persuaded the president to withdraw American troops from Lebanon early in 1984, a move that Shultz had opposed, and Casey, McFarlane, Poindexter, and North had been able to conduct the covert "arms-for-hostages" operation in 1985 and 1986, which both Shultz and Weinberger had objected to.

The Iran-Contra scandal clearly strengthened Shultz's hand in dealing with the White House. After firing Poindexter and North, Reagan could hardly afford to lose his respected secretary of state as well. The new national security adviser, Frank Carlucci, who took over in January 1987, was an experienced team player. He brought a degree of professionalism to the National Security Council that had been sorely lacking in previous years.

One sign of the new coherence in top-level policy circles came with the decision to support Kuwait's request early in 1987 to provide protection for its tankers from Iranian air attacks. For several years the United States had been tilting toward Iraq, and considerable concern had developed late in 1986 that Iran might be able to mount a major ground offensive in southern Iraq that would bring Iranian troops to the borders of Kuwait and Saudi Arabia. Shultz and Weinberger saw in the Kuwaiti request for "reflagging" of eleven of their tankers a chance to erase the stain of Iran-Contra and to signal to the Iranians that a threat to the oil-rich states of the Arabian peninsula would be of direct concern to the United States.

Besides wanting to restrain Iran, the United States was hoping to rebuild its damaged credibility with a number of Arab states. The fact that Kuwait had also requested, and received, Soviet help was another reason for a swift American response. By mid-July 1987 the United States was routinely escorting Kuwaiti tankers to the northern end of the Gulf and, equally surprising, was hard at work with the Soviet Union on a UN Security Council resolution calling for a cease-fire in the seven-year-old war. Resolution 598 was passed the same day that the first U.S-escorted Kuwaiti convoy sailed through the Gulf.[1]

On the whole, the reflagging operation was remarkably successful. At modest cost, and with relatively few risks, the United States helped to create conditions in which Iran finally felt compelled to accept a cease-fire—or in the words of Ayatollah Khomeini, "to drink poison"—thus ending the Middle East's costliest war to date. American prestige in the Arab world, which had sunk to a low point after the Iran-Contra revelations, was at least partially restored. Adding to the improved atmosphere in U.S.-Arab relations was an appreciation, especially in Jordan, that the United States had gradually been adjusting its position on the question of convening an Arab-Israeli peace conference.

REDISCOVERING THE INTERNATIONAL CONFERENCE

In early 1986, after the break between Jordan and the Palestine Liberation Organization, King Hussein had placed renewed emphasis on the idea of an international conference. He had always maintained that he needed either the PLO or Syria to provide cover for his talks with Israel. If the PLO was now out of the picture, it was all the more important that Syria be given an incentive to go along with any diplomatic efforts. Hence the need for an international conference of some sort. Inevitably, that would mean some degree of Soviet participation as well, an issue the Reaganites were still unenthusiastic about. American hostility to the idea of an international conference was partly rooted in the notion that such an arrangement would bring the Soviet Union back into the Middle East, from which it had supposedly been absent since Kissinger's maneuvering of 1973–74.[2]

In late 1985 Shimon Peres, still in the role of prime minister, had begun to speak positively about some type of international forum or sponsorship of direct Arab-Israeli negotiations. His expressed conditions for a conference were that it not be empowered to impose solutions and that the Soviet Union should restore diplomatic relations with Israel before the conference.

About the same time as the modification in the Israeli position, Shultz also began to hint that the administration's previous opposition to the idea of an international conference was weakening. As early as September

23, 1985, Shultz had tried out some ideas on King Hussein, who at that moment was not much interested. But Shultz was clearly edging toward the idea of some type of international "event" to accommodate Arab concerns. He was also beginning to think about how the idea of sovereignty could be reconceptualized to accommodate the complexities of the relations binding Israel, the Palestinians, and Jordan. Various forms of mixed and overlapping sovereignty seemed to him the key to overcoming the impasse over Israeli withdrawal from occupied territories.[3]

Without much fanfare, the international conference reappeared on the Arab-Israeli diplomatic scene as a potentially live issue. Quiet diplomacy then took over, with professional American diplomats trying to develop a basis of agreement between Israel and Jordan.

During much of 1986 Jordanian-Israeli contacts increased. King Hussein met with Defense Minister Yitzhak Rabin near Strasbourg in April.[4] Subsequently Jordan closed down PLO offices in Amman, and Jordan and Israel both encouraged the development of "Village Leagues" as alternative sources of leadership to that of the PLO-oriented nationalist leadership in the West Bank. Branches of the Cairo-Amman bank were opened in the West Bank, and a pro-Jordanian newspaper was set up in Jerusalem. The United States threw its support behind so-called quality-of-life measures, presumably on the theory that improved living standards would produce Palestinian political moderation.[5]

On the political front, however, the international conference remained of importance to Jordan, if only to help legitimize the de facto arrangements that were under way with Israel. In October 1986, as part of the rotation agreement between Labor and Likud, Yitzhak Shamir became prime minister. Peres took over as foreign minister, and Rabin stayed on as defense minister. Shamir had been kept informed of the contacts with Jordan but was unlikely to share Peres's enthusiasm for dealing with the king. Peres, however, was determined to press ahead, and by the spring of 1987 was within sight of an important breakthrough.

Jordan had firmed up its ties with Syria, to the point that an emissary of King Hussein met with Shultz on April 7, 1987, to say that Syria was prepared to attend an international conference of the sort Jordan had been proposing. Shultz was skeptical, but he realized that the Soviets might now be ready to help.[6]

Meanwhile King Hussein and Israeli Foreign Minister Peres met secretly in London to work out the principles for convening an international conference. Agreement was reached on April 11, 1987. Jordan and Israel both supported the idea that a conference would not have plenary powers. It could not impose its views or veto the results of bilateral negotiations that would take place under the umbrella of the conference. Both countries agreed there would be a ceremonial opening with representatives of the permanent members of the UN Security Council and those regional parties to the conflict that had accepted Resolution 242. One sticky issue, the question of what would happen in the event of a deadlock in the bilateral negotiations, the so-called referral issue, was finessed for the moment.[7]

On the day that Peres and Hussein reached agreement, an aide to Peres met with Shultz to plead with him to make the new document the core of an American initiative. Only in that way might Shamir be persuaded to accept it. Shultz refused to play this kind of game and insisted that Peres present his own agreement to Shamir before the United States would take any position on it. On April 20 Peres told Shultz that Shamir had been briefed, and two days later Shamir told Shultz that he totally rejected the London document.[8]

Shamir's rejection of the idea of a nonbinding international conference was rooted in his determination never to cede an inch of the historic Land of Israel—in practice, this meant no Israeli withdrawal from the West Bank. Moreover, the fact that Peres had negotiated the agreement behind Shamir's back ensured it of a frosty reception. Shultz was simply not prepared to take sides in this internal dispute, and a visit by Moshe Arens on Shamir's behalf on April 24 seems to have convinced Shultz not to embrace the London document. Still, he felt that Shamir had made a mistake, and he was encouraged to see that Hussein's idea of a conference was approaching his own.[9]

As a coda to this phase of diplomacy, a final effort was made, this time in collaboration with Shamir, to find some form of international sponsorship for Israeli-Jordanian talks. In mid-June Shamir had hinted to Shultz that he might consider some type of international meeting to endorse direct negotiations with Jordan. Shultz sent his aide, Charles Hill, to Israel in late July to explore this idea further. On August 6 an emissary from Shamir came to see Shultz to inform him that Shamir had met with Hussein. Shamir was still opposed to an international conference, but he would not object if the permanent members of the UN Security Council met to endorse direct Arab-Israeli negotiations. Shamir reported that his meeting with Hussein had gone well. Shortly thereafter, however,

Shultz heard from Hussein about the same meeting. Hussein characterized Shamir as "hopeless."[10]

In September Peres suggested to Hill the idea that Mikhail Gorbachev and Ronald Reagan, as part of their upcoming summit meeting, might invite Shamir and King Hussein to meet with them. Shultz was well disposed toward the idea, and Reagan was briefed on it on September 11. The president did not immediately agree, and Shultz sensed he was growing weary of the Middle East. Finally, on September 23 Reagan gave the green light.[11]

Shultz flew to the Middle East in October 1987 while en route to Moscow to put the finishing touches on arrangements for a U.S.-Soviet summit meeting in Washington before the end of the year. While in Jerusalem he persuaded Shamir to agree in principle to the idea of an American-Soviet invitation to come to Washington at the time of the summit, along with King Hussein, to receive a joint U.S.-Soviet blessing for direct negotiations.

The next day, October 19, Shultz presented the idea to King Hussein in London. The United States had made little advance preparation with Jordan, in contrast to its numerous exchanges during the fall with the Israelis. The king, who was about to host an Arab summit in Amman, was politically unable even to hint at an interest in an idea that would be ridiculed by the other Arabs. He also had no reason to think the Soviets would agree to the idea, and the Syrians, who were only mentioned as an afterthought as possible participants in the adventure, would certainly say no. So the king found himself put in the position of saying no to the Americans, a fact that was duly leaked to a pro-Israeli columnist a few months later.[12]

In normal times Hussein's hesitation would have been the last word on the peace process for the Reagan administration. With both American and Israeli elections slated for November 1988, Washington had little appetite for continuing to grapple with the seemingly intractable Arab-Israeli conflict. When the Arab summit was held in Amman in early November, it even seemed as if the Arabs had turned their backs on the Palestinian question. The Gulf, it appeared, was a much greater worry, and Arafat found himself the odd man out among the assembled Arab potentates. Even the acceptance of Egypt back into the fold, which most members of the Arab League endorsed, seemed driven more by Gulf concerns than by a desire to coordinate the diplomacy of Arab-Israeli peacemaking with Cairo.

THE INTIFADA AND THE SHULTZ INITIATIVE

During Israel's twenty-year domination of the West Bank and Gaza, there had never been trouble-free times. But the costs of the occupation had not been judged excessive by Israeli governments, and a semblance of normal life existed on most days for the growing numbers of Israeli settlers, and for the Palestinians, some 100,000 of whom had jobs in the Israeli economy as of 1988. Then on December 9, 1987, an unusually nasty series of incidents took place in Gaza, sparking large-scale Palestinian protests. Within days West Bank Palestinians joined the "uprising," or *intifada*,[13] as it was to be called, and even Israeli Arabs showed support. It soon became clear that something qualitatively new was happening. The previously quiescent Palestinians of the West Bank and Gaza were coming of political age, and with a vengeance.[14]

Though caught by surprise by the timing of the uprising and by how quickly it spread, the PLO had long been cultivating support in the occupied territories, and pro-PLO networks existed and were backed by the generally pro-PLO sentiment of the population. Before long, coordination between the Unified National Leadership of the Uprising, as the internal leadership referred to itself, and the PLO seemed to be far reaching.[15]

By January 1988 the Israelis were acknowledging that they had an unprecedented situation on their hands. Defense Minister Rabin took a strong law-and-order approach, publicly sanctioning a policy of beatings and breaking of bones as part of an attempt to frighten the young Palestinians who threw rocks and Molotov cocktails at heavily armed soldiers. Within days images of savage Israeli beatings of Palestinian youngsters were a part of the American evening television news. Public reaction was strong. Even from within the normally pro-Israeli American Jewish community there was an outpouring of criticism and concern.

Several developments then took place that convinced Secretary of State Shultz to reengage his prestige in trying to get Arab-Israeli peace talks started.[16] First, in a six and one-half page letter to Shultz dated January 17, 1988, Shamir hinted that the Israeli position on "autonomy" for the Palestinians might be softening. Second, American Jewish leaders, as well as some Israeli politicians, began to urge Shultz to become more actively involved. Third, President Husni Mubarak of Egypt came to Washington to make a forceful and convincing plea that American leadership was urgently needed to ward off a radicalization of the entire region.

Shultz approached the challenge methodically. He did not make a flamboyant speech, nor did he hold out great hopes of a breakthrough. But he did begin to explore ideas with all the parties, this time including Syria, the Soviets, and some individual Palestinians, as well as with Jordan and the Israelis. At the end of his second trip to the region in as many months, on March 4, 1988, Shultz formalized his initiative in a proposal he described as a "blend of ideas" designed to repackage and streamline the Camp David Accords.[17] (See appendix I.)

The Shultz initiative, as it was immediately labeled, was certainly the most important U.S. involvement in Arab-Israeli peacemaking since Reagan's peace initiative in September 1982. In essence, Shultz outlined the conventional goal of a comprehensive peace to be achieved through direct bilateral negotiations based on Resolutions 242 and 338. But Shultz added a new element with what he called the "interlock" between the negotiations on the transitional period for the West Bank and Gaza and the negotiations on "final status." Shultz had long felt that the time scale envisioned in Camp David should be compressed, and his initiative explicitly ensured that it would be.

The Palestinian issue, according to Shultz, should be addressed in negotiations between an Israeli delegation and a Jordanian-Palestinian delegation. Six months would be set aside for negotiating transitional arrangements. In the seventh month negotiations on the final status of the West Bank and Gaza would start—regardless of the outcome of the first phase of negotiations. A target date of one year for negotiating the final status of the territories was mentioned. Assuming that agreement could be reached on transitional arrangements, a transitional period would begin at an early date and would continue for three years. The United States, Shultz said, would participate in both sets of negotiations and would put forward a draft agreement on transitional arrangements for the consideration of the parties.

Preceding the bilateral negotiations between Israel and a Jordanian-Palestinian delegation, there would be an international conference. The secretary general of the United Nations would invite the regional parties and the permanent members of the Security Council.[18] All participants in the conference would have to accept Resolutions 242 and 338. Although the negotiating parties, by agreement, might report to the conference from time to time, the conference would have no power to impose its views or to veto the results of the negotiations.

Shultz also said that Palestinians should be represented in a combined Jordanian-Palestinian delegation. That delegation would deal with the Palestinian issue in its entirety, and those negotiations would be independent of any other negotiation.

In the months that followed his initiative, Shultz doggedly tried to wear down the opponents of his initiative in both Israel and the Arab world. His biggest problem was Prime Minister Shamir, who blasted the idea of an international conference—which Shultz saw as a marginal part of his initiative—in no uncertain terms. Shamir also rejected the "interlock" concept, claiming it was contrary to Camp David. As Shamir correctly noted, the Camp David Accords had made the "final status" talks dependent on prior success in reaching agreement on transitional arrangements. Under Shultz's proposal the talks on final status would begin whether or not agreement had been reached on an interim period, thus providing little incentive for the Palestinians to negotiate seriously on the initial transitional stage. The prospects for success in resolving the final-status issues were not bright, since, as Shamir said publicly, the exchange of territory for peace was foreign to him.[19]

Israeli criticism of the Shultz initiative was well publicized, even though Peres publicly welcomed the American effort. On the Arab side, King Hussein went to great lengths not to be put in the position of saying no to Shultz. He asked questions, sought clarifications, played hard to get, referred publicly to the importance of including the PLO in the game, and generally tried to keep his shrinking options open.

The Palestinian response was more categorical. Though pleased to see the United States responding to the uprising, the Palestinian leaders were unhappy with the second-class treatment they were given in the Shultz plan. They saw themselves as being assigned, at best, to the role of junior partner to Jordan.

The Soviet Union was also unenthusiastic about a central feature of the Shultz plan, the international conference. Whereas Shamir professed fears that the conference would become authoritative and would work to undermine the Israeli position, the Soviet concern was just the opposite. The international conference, as envisaged by the Americans, appeared to the Soviets to be only symbolic. The Soviets wanted a real role in the negotiating process, not just an opportunity to legitimize a made-in-America initiative that would ultimately leave them on the sidelines.

Syria, likewise, was cool to the Shultz proposal. Only Mubarak, whose country was already at peace with Israel, openly endorsed the new American plan.[20]

In the face of these obstacles the Shultz plan never had much chance of complete success. Nonetheless, it had wide support in American public opinion. There was little criticism of any features of the proposal, except for some sour words from Henry Kissinger about the whole idea of an international conference. Shultz and his colleagues were no doubt hopeful that they would get a lucky break and that a negotiating process might be started on their watch. But they also spoke of other purposes behind the initiative. Most important, they wanted to influence Israeli public opinion. With the prospect of peace negotiations with their Arab neighbors, the Israeli public, it was hoped, would vote in the scheduled fall 1988 elections for a leadership committed to compromise positions. That possibility might, of course, prove to be wishful thinking; much would depend on Shultz's producing an acceptable Arab partner for peace talks. Still, the American intention was to help shape the political debate in Israel so that the elections would become a referendum, of sorts, on peace.

The Shultz plan depended crucially on cooperation with King Hussein. During four trips to the Middle East in the first half of 1988, Shultz had tried to persuade Hussein, and had even reached out, without much success, to Palestinians in the West Bank. On July 31, however, the foundations of the Shultz initiative collapsed, when King Hussein, in an official statement, relinquished all Jordanian legal and administrative ties to the West Bank, stating bluntly that henceforth the PLO would be responsible for the Palestinians living there.[21]

A U.S.-PLO DIALOGUE?

With Jordan at least temporarily out of the picture, one might have thought the United States would lose interest in pursuing Arab-Israeli peace initiatives. Especially in an election year, attention was bound to be focused elsewhere. But each day the news from Israel brought more images of violence and radicalization of the Palestinians, particularly among the youth, as well as signs of increasing Islamic militancy. No one in Washington was comfortable with the worsening situation between Israel and the Palestinians. But what could be done, especially prior to both Israeli and American elections?

The idea of establishing direct contacts between Washington and the

PLO had frequently been explored in previous years. Insofar as there was episodic interest in the idea among American officials, the goal was to moderate the PLO position on peace with Israel and open the way for direct participation by legitimate Palestinian representatives in negotiations.[22] At least grudgingly, most American policymakers accepted the fact that the PLO was the most widely supported spokesman for the Palestinians. Only King Hussein was ever seen as a possible alternative. So, in one way or another, most administrations had tried to develop some contacts with the PLO.

As early as 1974 Kissinger had authorized meetings between the PLO and Vernon Walters, then with the CIA. In Beirut, intelligence operatives had maintained contacts for purposes of exchanging information on security. On occasion, diplomatic messages were exchanged in these channels. But after Kissinger's 1975 pledge that the United States would not recognize or negotiate with the PLO unless the PLO acknowledged Israel's right to exist and accepted Resolution 242, official contacts had been rare. The pledge had not stopped intermediaries from exchanging messages, sometimes with authorization and sometimes on their own.[23] But no ongoing, high-level, openly acknowledged relationship had ever existed between the United States and the PLO.

Few would have expected the pro-Israeli Reagan or the equally pro-Israeli Shultz to alter this policy. And these two men would probably argue that, in fact, they did not. Yet it was on their watch, in the waning days of the Reagan presidency, that the United State finally agreed to begin an official dialogue with the PLO.

According to the standard version of what happened, the PLO, in danger of being marginalized as the *intifada* gained momentum, and under pressure from both the Arab states and the Soviets, finally met the well-known American conditions, and therefore the dialogue began.[24] That is only part of the story.

As early as April 1988 a small group of American Jewish leaders began to explore the possibility with the Swedish government of meeting with the PLO to formulate a well-developed statement of the PLO's commitment to a peace settlement with Israel.[25] The Swedish foreign minister, Sten Andersson, had been a good friend of Israel during his career, but had been appalled by what he had seen during a visit to Israel and the occupied territories. Thus he set about trying to build bridges between Palestinians and Israelis, but soon settled on the idea of starting with a meeting between PLO leaders and prominent American Jews.

He informed George Shultz of his intentions. Hearing no objections, Andersson quietly went forward with his plans.

By his own account Shultz was not much interested in this exercise in private diplomacy, apparently paying little attention to it until later in the year.[26] He did, however, hold Andersson in high regard and took him seriously as a professional diplomat who could be trusted. This recognition proved to be important in the last phases of establishing the dialogue.

Meanwhile another track of private diplomacy opened up, to explore formulations the PLO and the United States might agree upon, initially in private, that would meet the political needs of both sides for beginning talks. The impetus for this initiative came from a Palestinian-American, Mohamed Rabie, shortly after King Hussein announced his decision to break legal ties to the West Bank.[27] Rabie was convinced that the PLO would now be ready to accept the American conditions if it could be assured in advance that an official dialogue would ensue, along with some expression of American support for the idea of Palestinian self-determination.[28]

By mid-August this initiative had been reviewed with the State Department. Draft statements that the PLO might make, and a corresponding American reply, had been reviewed.[29] The American attitude toward the initiative, to be conveyed to the PLO, was spelled out as follows:

—There has been no change in what it will take for the United States to agree to deal with the PLO.

—The United States and the PLO have come close to agreement in the past, only to see the chance slip away. If a serious effort is to be made now, there must be clarity on both sides. Ambiguity would be counterproductive, especially on the eve of Israeli elections.

—If the PLO made the kind of statement the United States required, talks could begin right away. For political reasons certain things may be easier to do after the U.S. elections, but there is no need to wait.

—Any conditional clause accompanying a statement of acceptance of Resolution 242 will not be accepted by the United States. Whatever conditions the PLO wishes to state should be done in a separate paragraph. The United States needs a "clean" acceptance of 242.

—The proposed U.S. statement seems fairly close to what the United States might be willing to say, but it will have to be reviewed personally by Secretary Shultz at the appropriate time.

—This initiative is worthwhile "if the PLO is serious." A very small group will be in charge of the initiative on the American side and will be available at all times. No other channel is pursuing this course.[30]

Shortly thereafter Rabie left for Tunis, where he presented the documents and the idea of the initiative to Arafat and other top PLO leaders. After lengthy talks he returned to Washington in early September with PLO approval of a slightly revised formulation, conditional on the United States making a statement that would approximate the sample that had been discussed with, but not yet approved by, Washington.[31] This information was immediately passed to State and was received with interest. Shultz felt he could help the next administration by starting the dialogue, but he was not prepared to endorse Palestinian self-determination, which he saw as a code word for a Palestinian state, as the necessary price.

For the Reagan administration the issue now arose of whether to tip its hand on what it would say in exchange for the PLO's acceptance of 242, its recognition of Israel's right to exist, and its renunciation of terrorism. Over the ensuing weeks news came from Tunis of impatience to hear the official American position. In mid-September the Soviets were informed by the PLO of the initiative, which they reportedly supported.

On September 16 Shultz made a major speech to a pro-Israeli group at the Wye Plantation in Maryland. He explained why the United States would not endorse the idea of Palestinian self-determination if it were seen as meaning an automatic right to statehood. He did add, however, that in negotiations the Palestinians were "free to argue for independence." But negotiations were the key thing.[32]

As frustrations began to mount on both sides, Shultz authorized that an oral message be conveyed to Rabie for Arafat on September 23, 1988. It stated: "We welcomed the receipt of the initiative, which we recognize as a serious effort. This issue has been given careful consideration and will continue to be seriously discussed. We expect to provide our reaction in six weeks or so." In brief, the American response to the proposed PLO statement would be sent after the Israeli and American elections.[33] But already one could detect that the Reagan administration was not passively awaiting PLO compliance. It was signaling a positive attitude and was reiterating that talks would in fact begin as soon as the well-known conditions were met. Previously, the stated policy was that talks could not take place unless the PLO accepted the American conditions, but even PLO acceptance of those conditions would not necessarily result in an official dialogue. Now it was explicitly stated that talks would follow immediately on the PLO's acceptance of the American terms.

In an effort to avoid having this initiative wither in the intervening weeks, the PLO provided a glimpse of its plans. On October 19 the PLO conveyed the position that it intended to take at the upcoming meeting of the Palestine National Congress (PNC). It would accept the principle of a two-state solution to the conflict, anchoring its acceptance in UN Resolution 181 of 1947, which had called for the partition of Palestine into two states and had been rejected by the Arabs at the time. In addition, the PLO would accept 242 and 338 as the basis for an international conference, along with the recognition of the rights of the Palestinian people, including their right to self-determination. The PLO would also condemn terrorism. After adopting these positions officially, the PLO would make the statement the United States wanted, and then the United States should respond.

On the basis of this information, several problems could be foreseen. The PLO still seemed to be insisting on American acceptance of Palestinian self-determination as the price for accepting 242. While condemning terrorism, the PLO was not willing to renounce it. Also, Israel's right to exist was not explicitly mentioned.

Shortly after receiving this message, the administration was told by the Jordanians that Arafat was no longer insisting on recognition of the Palestinian right to self-determination. If Israeli withdrawal could be achieved, and with the Jordanian legal claim to the territories annulled, the Palestinians would become the ruling authority in any territory vacated by Israel. While logical, the Jordanian position was not automatically credited as an accurate reflection of the PLO position.

With the Palestine National Congress scheduled to meet in November, Arafat conveyed some uneasiness about the reliability of the channel being used to communicate between Washington and Tunis.[34] More to the point, most likely, he was disappointed by what he was hearing. Shultz was not willing to tip his hand until after the PNC had met.

As that meeting approached, results of the Israeli and American elections came in. The Israeli elections again produced a standoff between the Likud and Labor parties, which in due course led to a Likud-led coalition with Labor, but this time without a rotation of the premiership and with Moshe Arens as foreign minister instead of the more dovish Shimon Peres, who moved over to the finance ministry. Rabin stayed on as defense minster, so Labor continued to hold influential posts in the cabinet. But foreign-policy decisions would henceforth be solidly under Shamir's control.

The American elections were more conclusive than those in Israel just a few days earlier. Vice President George Bush defeated Governor Michael Dukakis of Massachusetts in a landslide. A narrow window was now open during which a U.S.-PLO agreement might still be reached before the Reagan administration left office. Bush was especially eager that this be done before he was sworn in, but he did not play an important role in the decisions concerning the PLO.

When Arafat convened the PNC from November 12 to 15, he succeeded in pushing through his political program and in declaring the existence of a Palestinian state with himself as president.[35] The state was presumably to be established alongside Israel in the West Bank and Gaza. The PLO appeared to be accepting 242, but not unconditionally. And some of the language in the political document continued to express old slogans. Shultz was unimpressed.

Meanwhile the Swedish initiative was beginning to bear fruit. An initial meeting of PLO representatives and American Jewish leaders had been held in late November, and agreement had been reached on a general political statement. It took the form of an agreed interpretation of the recent PNC resolutions. The culmination of this effort was to be a public meeting of the American Jewish leaders with Arafat in Stockholm during which the new statement would be released. Before the meeting Andersson contacted Shultz to ask if he could convey anything of importance to Arafat. Shultz, who had just turned down Arafat's request for a visa to come to the United Nations on grounds that the PLO was a terrorist group, decided nonetheless to respond to Andersson.[36]

GETTING THE WORDS RIGHT

In a letter dated December 3, 1988, Shultz conveyed the long-awaited American position, along with a text of exactly what Arafat would have to say to meet the American conditions. In his letter Shultz made it clear he would not bargain further over the language. He also noted that the PLO could add other points to the basic statement, but that these should not condition or contradict its acceptance of the U.S. conditions. Finally, Shultz added that nothing in his letter should imply that the United States was prepared to recognize an independent Palestinian state. (See appendix J.)

The proposed PLO statement conveyed to Arafat by Andersson on December 7 read as follows:

As its contribution to the search for a just and lasting peace in the Middle East, the Executive Committee of the Palestine Liberation Organization wishes to issue the following official statement:

1. That it is prepared to negotiate with Israel a comprehensive peace settlement of the Arab-Israeli conflict on the basis of United Nations resolutions 242 and 338.

2. That it undertakes to live in peace with Israel and its other neighbors and to respect their right to exist in peace within secure and internationally recognized borders, as will the democratic Palestinian state which it seeks to establish in the West Bank and the Gaza Strip.

3. That it condemns individual, group and state terrorism in all its forms, and will not resort to it.

4. That it is prepared for a moratorium on all forms of violence, on a mutual basis, once negotiations begin.[37]

In return, Shultz promised, the United States would announce that it was prepared to begin substantive discussions with the PLO. The United States would recognize that the representatives of the Palestinians would have the right in the course of negotiations to raise all subjects of interest to them. Then, Shultz said, an American official would answer a planted question about whether the Palestinians could table their position on statehood, to which the answer would be "Yes, the Palestinians, as far as we are concerned, have the right to pursue an independent state through negotiations." This response was as close as Shultz would go to saying that Palestinians had a right to self-determination. In response to a PLO request, Shultz also agreed to answer a question on the international conference as follows: "The U.S. has long made its support for direct negotiations clear, but we remain prepared to consider any suggestion that may lead to direct negotiations toward a comprehensive peace. The initiative proposed by Secretary Shultz in the beginning of the year called for an international conference to begin direct negotiations. Any conference of this type must be organized so that it does not become an alternative to direct negotiations."

Arafat responded in two ways to Shultz's message. He told Andersson that he personally agreed to the language proposed by Shultz, and he even put his signature to the proposed text.[38] (See appendix J for Arafat's response.) But he added that he would have to seek agreement from the other members of the PLO Executive Committee. Then, in public, Arafat issued the statement that had been worked out between his representatives and the American Jewish leaders on November 21. Its operational language came close to meeting Shultz's concerns, but not quite. Instead of unconditionally accepting UN Resolutions 242 and 338 as the basis for negotiations with Israel, Arafat added the right of the Palestinians to self-determination as another basis for the conference, implying that this condition would have to be accepted in advance by the other participants, something that neither the United States nor Israel was prepared to do. Furthermore, though Arafat did "reject and condemn" terrorism in all its forms, he did not renounce it or pledge not to engage in it in the future. These may have seemed like verbal squabbles to some, but to Shultz they mattered. Perhaps most positive and significant, Arafat did state openly that the PLO "accepted the existence of Israel as a state in the region," a formulation he had not used before.

The next step in the process of trying to get Arafat to utter the magic words came during his appearance before a special session of the United Nations held in Geneva on December 13, 1988. Arafat had encountered some opposition within the PLO Executive Committee to the idea of using the precise language that Shultz had provided to Andersson. Nayif Hawatmeh was particularly hostile to the idea. Thus Arafat sent word to the Swedes that he would use the Shultz formulation in his speech, but it would be scattered throughout the text.[39] This message was apparently not clearly conveyed to the Americans, who were expecting to hear the exact words they had agreed upon.

As Arafat worked his way through his long and rambling speech, he made the point about "rejecting" and "condemning" terrorism in all its forms, but he did not "renounce" it.[40] Toward the end of the speech, Arafat addressed the issues of 242 and Israel's right to exist. The wording was complicated in Arabic but is probably best translated as follows:

The PLO will work to achieve a comprehensive peaceful settlement among the parties to the Arab-Israeli conflict, including the Palestinian state, Israel and other neighboring states, within the framework of the international conference for peace in the Middle East, in order to achieve equality and a balance of interests, especially the right of our people to liberation and national independence, and respect for everyone's right to exist, to peace and to security, according to Resolutions 242 and 338.

Some State Department officials listening to the speech felt that though Arafat had come close to doing so, he had not specifically mentioned negotiations with Israel or Israel's right to exist, nor had he renounced terrorism. Shultz and his influential assistant, Charles Hill, reacted negatively.[41] They had expected verbatim compliance and felt the speech was another sign that Arafat could not be trusted. The Swedes acknowledged that the speech did not meet the American conditions, but they felt it had almost done so. All Shultz would agree to was that Arafat could try one more time.

During the day on December 14 many people weighed in with Arafat—the president of Egypt, the Saudis, the Swedes, individual Americans—to try to persuade him to utter the exact words that Shultz was insisting on. Finally, in the company of several rich Palestinian businessmen who were in telephone contact with the State Department to check on acceptable wording, Arafat agreed to hold a press conference, where he finally said, in English (see appendix K for the full text):

Yesterday . . . I also made a reference to our acceptance of resolutions 242 and 338 as the basis for negotiations with Israel within the framework of the international conference. . . . In my speech also yesterday, it was clear that we mean . . . the right of all parties concerned in the Middle East conflict to exist in peace and security and, as I have mentioned, including the state of Palestine, Israel and other neighbors according to the resolution 242 and 338.

As for terrorism, I renounced it yesterday in no uncertain terms, and yet, I repeat for the record that we totally and absolutely renounce all forms of terrorism, including individual, group, and state terrorism.

Shultz finally agreed that Arafat had met the American conditions and so informed Colin Powell, the national security adviser, who then sought the president's approval to announce that the U.S-PLO discussions could begin at the level of the American ambassador in Tunisia. Reagan reportedly gave his consent quite easily. On December 14 the United States finally lifted the ban on dealing with the PLO. (See appendix K.) At least the incoming Bush administration would not have to wrestle with the problem of opening a dialogue. It, however, would face the equally daunting task of giving substance to the talks and relating them to the broader peace process.

ASSESSING THE REAGAN ERA

Reagan remained a popular figure throughout most of his presidency. He was widely credited with restoring American self-confidence after the gloom of the Carter years. More tangibly, he presided over the last phase of the cold war. By the time he left office, the world seemed a safer place as the two great nuclear powers began to reduce their bloated arsenals of weapons of mass destruction. On the economic front, many Americans were better off as the 1980s came to an end, but many at the lower rungs of the economic ladder were poorer than ever. By most measures the gap between rich and poor had grown significantly. And then there was the deficit. For all of Reagan's talk about the virtues of a balanced budget, never once did he submit one, nor did Congress come close to passing one. As a result, interest on the national debt had become the second largest item in the budget by 1989.

For most Americans these were the bread-and-butter issues that counted as they thought about the 1980s. But they were also aware that Reagan had blundered badly with his "arms for hostages" initiative in 1985–86. Some might even remember the horrifying scenes of Beirut being bombed, the Sabra and Shatila massacres, and the explosions in Beirut in 1983 that took the lives of more than three hundred Americans, more than died in any other Middle East situation under any American administration. Reagan and his top officials, however, never seemed to be blamed for such disasters, which led to the accusation that this was a "Teflon presidency."

Few broad overviews of the Reagan presidency take note of his Arab-Israeli diplomacy. No such monument as Camp David sticks in collective memory when Reagan's Middle East policy is evoked. Some would even say that there was no policy toward Arab-Israeli peace during the Reagan period. But that is manifestly untrue. Reagan, with Shultz as his mentor, gave one of the most carefully crafted speeches ever on American policy toward the Arab-Israeli conflict. A decade later it still set the parameters of American policy by both embracing and extending the Camp David Accords. At the time it enjoyed broad bipartisan support. Even the American Israel Public Affairs Committee (AIPAC) felt compelled to praise the speech, despite Begin's ferocious rejection of it. But if Reagan was unexcelled as a speechmaker, he and his aides failed to devise a strategy for translating words into practical diplomatic steps. In their defense, it can be said that even a brilliant strategist might have found it difficult to move the Likud governments of Begin and Shamir from their entrenched positions.

Still, in both 1983 and 1985, and especially the latter, Reagan and Shultz might have inched the peace process forward had they shown more drive and determination. Nothing like Kissinger's intense shuttle diplomacy, or Carter's summitry, was tried until early 1988, by which point time was running out. So the Reagan period produced little in the way of tangible progress toward Arab-Israeli peace, although several helpful additions to the Camp David framework were put forward by Shultz. On balance, Israel and its neighbors were no closer to agreement in 1988 than they had been in 1980.

Perhaps the most one can say is that things had not deteriorated beyond repair. Egypt and Israel were still at peace, even though the temperature of the relationship was tepid. The Palestinians were engaged in a sustained rebellion against the Israeli occupation, which convinced Jordan's King Hussein to pull back from the exposed position he had adopted in 1987. The long-pursued Jordan option was dead. But the Palestinians were signaling a willingness to accept explicitly Israel's existence as a state in the region, provided they could establish their own ministate alongside it in the West Bank and Gaza. This position, long discussed by Palestinians in private, finally came into the open in 1988 and, through a tortuous diplomatic effort cautiously encouraged by Shultz, led to the opening of a U.S.-PLO dialogue, one of the greatest surprises of the Reagan era.

The prospects for Arab-Israeli peace, however, did not advance during the 1980s under Reagan, and in one dimension the objective situation became more difficult. At the time of the signing of the Camp David Accords, about 10,000 Israeli settlers lived in the West Bank and Gaza (in addition to another 100,000 or so in the Greater Jerusalem area). Before Reagan, all American presidents had maintained that Israeli settlement activities in the occupied territories were not only illegal under the terms of the Fourth Geneva Convention but were obstacles to peace. Reagan, apparently influenced by the legal arguments of Eugene Rostow, professor of international law at Yale and a prominent spokesman for neoconservative, pro-Israeli views, switched position on settlements.[42] Henceforth American policy was that Israeli settlements in the occupied territories were not illegal, although they were still viewed as obstacles to peace.

Reagan's change of policy on settlements was not the reason that the number of Israeli settlers in the occupied territories grew to nearly 100,000 by 1992. But the permissive American attitude certainly encouraged the determined settlement policy of Shamir and Sharon. Some even concluded in the early 1980s that settlement activity had gone so far that a negotiated Israeli-Palestinian agreement was no longer possible.[43] Even those who resisted this conclusion acknowledged the difficulty of dealing with the large number of Israeli settlers living beyond the "green line." Reagan personally never seemed to worry much about this issue, because he was essentially uninvolved with the details of trying to advance the peace process. But his successor was to inherit the settlements issue as a major complication both in U.S.-Israeli relations and in the revived peace process of the 1990s.

It is hard not to conclude that Reagan's disengaged style as president, his lack of curiosity, and his passivity on issues related to the Middle East were impediments to creative U.S. peace diplomacy.[44] He was unwilling or unable to discipline his quarreling subordinates (Lebanon); he tolerated actions taken in his name that seemed to undercut his ostensible policies (Iran-Contra); he had no sense of strategy for dealing with Arabs and Israelis, except to make the Israelis feel secure and the Arabs almost desperate. Fortunately, during his watch the Soviet Union began to unravel, so his weaknesses and oversimplifications did not prove to be disastrous. And in his way he did lend his prestige to steps that his successor might build on.

When a president is passive and uninvolved, how much can his secretary of state hope to achieve? Shultz clearly dominated diplomatic moves toward the Arab-Israeli conflict throughout his tenure. During the last two years he was in charge of all aspects of foreign policy and was heading a team of considerable ability. Bureaucratic bickering came to an end. On some Middle East issues, such as the reflagging of Kuwaiti tankers, a policy of nuance was carried out successfully. But on Arab-Israeli matters Shultz seemed to hesitate when opportunities opened up, as in 1985. He stuck doggedly to his belief that King Hussein could be drawn into peace talks, and reassessed the situation only when his policy had clearly failed. His own formulation on an international conference was so convoluted that it failed to win support from either Arabs or Israelis, although some of the points survived in a different form under President Bush and his secretary of state, James Baker.

How much of Shultz's hesitation came from a realization that he could not count on much help from the president he served? How much came from a conviction that the Arabs needed to face up convincingly to the reality of Israel before the United States could help them? How much stemmed from a genuine admiration for the tough, pro-American Israelis with whom he dealt? How much can be attributed to domestic politics and the role of the pro-Israeli lobby? Shultz has not been communicative about his own motives, and those who worked most closely with him often found him enigmatic. But it seems fair to conclude that he admired the Israelis and was reluctant to pressure them; he became frustrated with the Arab leaders with whom he dealt and was skeptical about the wisdom of running after them unless they developed a strong commitment of their own to peace with Israel; and he shared Reagan's distrust of Soviet motives, although less so by the end of his tenure.

For both Reagan and Shultz—and they were the two key figures who counted on Arab-Israeli issues—policies emerged more often as reactions to events in the Middle East region than as part of a grand design. The Reagan initiative of 1982 was sparked by the Israeli invasion of Lebanon; the ill-conceived May 17, 1983, agreement between Israel and Lebanon was largely sponsored at Israel's behest; and the Israelis helped to plant the idea of the opening to Iran, which was then twisted and distorted by too zealous, insufficiently supervised Reaganites into an "arms for hostages" scheme and a slick means for avoiding the congressional ban on aid to the Contras in Nicaragua.

In much the same vein, the Shultz initiative of 1988 was a reaction to the *intifada*. Without the eruption of violence in the occupied territories, Shultz would probably not have devised his plan. And the opening to the PLO was a grudging reaction to King Hussein's announced relinquishment of responsibility for the West Bank.

When Reagan had strong convictions, as on how to deal with the Soviet Union, some elements of strategy became visible in the unfolding policies. But when Reagan was indifferent or uncertain, and when his advisers disagreed or were hesitant to act, policy became derivative or reactive. Not surprisingly, the record of promoting Arab-Israeli accommodation was unimpressive.

Even in the realm of U.S.-Israeli relations the legacy of the Reagan era is uncertain. Aid continued to flow at unprecedentedly high levels; Congress was unusually sympathetic to Israel; potential quarrels, such as the Pollard spying affair[45] were treated as aberrations; revelations about Israel's nuclear capabilities were ignored;[46] and the entire relationship was given a strategic rationale that had previously been missing, or had at least been less central.[47]

Many Israelis were delighted with the result. They basked in the glow of being treated as a "non-NATO ally"; American aid to the Israeli defense industry was welcomed; intelligence cooperation reached new heights. But without a vigorous peace process, the United States and Israel risked losing one of the solid links of the past. After all, the major steps in forging close U.S.-Israeli ties had come in the context of moves toward peace. Over time, would the American public and future administrations continue to provide generous support to an Israel that was not making moves toward peace with its neighbors? If the blame for the lack of peace was clearly on the Arab side, the answer might still be yes. But what if the perception was less clear? What if Israel was seen as more of an obstacle to peace than the Arabs were?[48] What if Israel's occupation of the West Bank and Gaza was seen as unjustified by a younger generation of Americans who no longer felt such close ties to Israel and who had no memory of how the conflict had come about?

President Reagan and the Likud party seemed to feel that a strong strategic alliance against the Soviet Union and its regional allies would provide enough support for U.S.-Israeli relations even without an active peace process. But what if the cold war ended and the Soviet Union was no longer a threat to the region? What then would bind the United States and Israel if not the more conventional shared values and common purposes? Could the pro-Israeli lobby alone keep the relationship intact if its strategic and moral premises were called into question? These matters never seemed to be considered during the Reagan period, and yet within a very short time U.S.-Israeli relations entered a very difficult period. Some would place the blame on Reagan's and Shultz's successors. Others would point to the overvaluation of the strategic relationship with Israel and the underinvestment in peacemaking during the Reagan era.

PART SIX

The Bush Presidency

CHAPTER FIFTEEN

Getting to the Table:
Bush and Baker, 1989–92

Rarely, if ever, has a president assumed office with a more impressive foreign affairs résumé than George Bush. Before coming to the White House in January 1989, he had been director of Central Intelligence, head of the American diplomatic mission to China, and ambassador to the United Nations, and had spent eight years as vice-president under Ronald Reagan, with special responsibility for crisis management for the National Security Council. In addition, Bush was from a political family, had served with distinction as a pilot in World War II, was a graduate of Yale, had been elected to Congress, was a successful businessman in the Texas oil patch, and had been national chairman of the Republican party.

While Bush's credentials were impressive, they gave little clue to his own deeply held views on foreign affairs. He had not been in positions where he had primary responsibility for making and articulating policy. Except for his long stint as vice-president, during which he kept any views that differed from Reagan's closely guarded, he had not, in fact, held most of his jobs for long. During his unsuccessful bid for the presidency in 1980, he had presented himself as a moderately conservative Republican but had not spelled out his views on foreign policy. For a man of wide experience, he had left few traces.

Unlike Reagan, Bush was not a skilled communicator, at least not on television. He seemed to prefer informal meetings and off-the-cuff dealings with the press to set-piece speeches. Early on it became clear he would be a hands-on president when it came to foreign policy. He, after all, knew dozens of foreign leaders; he was reasonably conversant with most major foreign-policy issues; he had an appetite for dealing with the details and personalities involved in world affairs; he was inclined to pick up the telephone at a moment's notice and talk to leaders around the world.

Bush was clearly an internationalist who saw a continuing role for American leadership as the world entered the ambiguities of the post–cold war era. Initially his internationalism was tinged with a skeptical view of the Soviet Union and its leader, Mikhail Gorbachev. Bush's hard-line stance was rather surprising in light of Reagan's own mellowing toward Gorbachev in 1987–88.

One might have concluded from Bush's background that he would use the unique powers of the presidency to conduct a foreign policy that was active in pursuit of American interests, internationalist in tone, practical in execution, and essentially aimed at upholding the status quo. Nothing in Bush's past suggested that he had a radical vision for transforming international politics. He was, in fact, often criticized for not having "the vision thing." His aides described his style as "principled pragmatism." Others saw in Bush's views a familiar state-centered, balance-of-power approach to world affairs.

With respect to the Middle East, Bush had left few hints during his career of how he felt about the Arab-Israeli conflict. It was commonly known that he had urged Reagan to take a tough line against the Israeli invasion of Lebanon in 1982. As vice-president he had gone to Saudi Arabia in the mid-1980s to urge the Saudis not to let the price of oil drop too low. He was on good terms with the Saudi ambassador to Washington, Prince Bandar ibn Sultan. And it was rumored that he did not share Reagan's emotional attachment to Israel. But none of these observations added up to much with respect to policy toward the Arab-Israeli conflict.

As secretary of state, Bush selected a close friend and political ally, James A. Baker III, formerly Reagan's chief of staff and treasury secretary, as well as the manager of Bush's successful bid for the presidency in 1988. Baker, though never running for office himself, was a quintessential politician. His strengths were alleged to be found in "deal making." If politics was the art of the possible, then Baker was a supreme politician. And he would doubtless approach diplomacy in much the same way. His lack of experience in foreign affairs counted for little compared with the excellent rapport, sometimes tinged with friendly rivalry, that he had with the president.[1] Besides, he was a quick study. Bush and Baker seemed likely to form a team that might not include many other players. Both men prized secrecy and played their cards close to the vest.

Baker had a reputation among Republicans as a "moderate." Whether this label was deserved or not, Baker was clearly not cut from neoconservative cloth. Like Bush, he was likely to be problem-oriented, tactical in his approach, and suspicious of grand theory and strategy—a manager more than a conceptualizer. Rumor had it that Baker harbored ambitions of one day becoming president, which might mean he would seek to use his time as secretary of state to preside over a series of international successes, while avoiding anything that seemed destined for failure or aroused too much controversy.

Like the president, Baker had given few hints of his views on Arab-Israeli issues. An article on Baker, published in February 1989, portrayed him as a man of great self-control and manipulative skills. His favorite pastime, it seemed, was turkey shooting, which, in Baker's words, consists of "getting them where you want them, on your terms. Then *you* control the situation, not them. *You* have the options. Pull the trigger or don't. It doesn't matter once you've got them where you want them. The important thing is knowing that it's in your hands, that you can do whatever you determine is in your interest to do."[2]

Asked in an interview shortly before his confirmation as secretary of state what leverage the United States had in the Middle East, Baker replied:

The U.S. is and can be the most influential player. But it is important that we not permit the perception to develop that we can deliver peace, that we can deliver Israeli concessions. If there is going to be lasting peace, it will be the result of direct negotiations between the parties, not something mandated or delivered by anybody from the outside, including the U.S. We must do whatever we can to enhance the prospect of the parties negotiating the problem out among themselves. It is not the role of the U.S. to pressure Israel. At the same time, it is in Israel's interest to resolve the issue. Both sides have got to find a way to give something.[3]

Most new administrations take their bearings in foreign policy from the experiences of their immediate predecessors. In the case of Bush and Baker, they had been members of an administration whose record on Arab-Israeli peacemaking was hardly distinguished. It had produced plans and initiatives but few concrete achievements. It was a fair guess that Baker, in particular, would avoid launching new substantive plans, preferring to explore procedural openings and biding his time until the parties to the conflict showed a willingness to move. Part of this cautious stance was a matter of tactics; part was no doubt politics; and part was due to competing priorities, especially in the rapidly changing arena of East-West relations.[4]

WORKING ASSUMPTIONS

If Bush and Baker shared certain ways of looking at foreign policy, including the Middle East, they certainly did not seem to have a fully developed rationale for their low-key approach to Arab-Israeli peacemaking. That was provided by a small group of like-minded aides at the State Department and the National Security Council. Most important was Dennis Ross, head of Baker's Policy Planning Staff, a specialist on U.S.-Soviet relations with a strong interest in the Middle East. Ross had worked at the Pentagon, and at the NSC under Reagan, and had then joined the Bush campaign in 1988 as a foreign-policy adviser. During the summer of 1988, just before joining the campaign, he had played an important part in developing the logic of how a new administration should tackle the Arab-Israeli conflict.

As a member of the grandly labeled "Presidential Study Group" that produced an influential pamphlet entitled *Building for Peace*, Ross associated himself with an incrementalist approach to Arab-Israeli peacemaking. From this perspective the United States should be wary of substantive plans, international conferences, and highly visible initiatives. Instead the new administration should start from the realization that the Arab-Israeli conflict was not "ripe" for resolution. The differences between the parties were too great. A premature move to negotiations would doubtless fail. So, small steps to change the political environment should receive attention. The parties should be encouraged to engage in a prenegotiation phase of confidence-building measures. And the Soviets should be left on the sidelines until they had demonstrated by their actions a willingness and an ability to play a constructive role in peacemaking by putting pressure on the Arabs and reassuring the Israelis.[5]

Another important contributor to *Building for Peace* was Richard Haass, author of a book called *Conflicts Unending*, which promoted the tautological thesis of "ripeness" as the key to negotiations.[6] (A conflict is "ripe for resolution" if it can be solved.) Haass became the head of the Middle East office on the National Security Council staff. If taken literally, his views would call for a low-profile American approach to the region. In his analysis of the Arab-Israeli conflict, the United States could err by being too active in trying to promote a settlement. That, he argued, could make a difficult situation even worse. Until the parties to the conflict were ready to negotiate, the United States should concentrate on small steps to improve the environment.[7]

This "gardening" metaphor for Middle East policy seemed founded on a belief that previous bouts of American activism had been counterproductive. They had raised Arab expectations about American pressures on Israel, caused the Israelis to adopt a defensive stance to ward off such pressures, and had made Washington the centerpiece of all diplomatic moves, instead of placing emphasis on the parties' need to deal directly with one another. Like an attentive gardener, the United States might help the ripening process by watering the plants and weeding and fertilizing, but that was pretty much the proper extent of Washington's involvement until the fruit was ripe and ready to harvest.

Critics of the "ripening" approach thought the fruit might well rot before it ever got harvested. Time did not seem to matter to the gardeners. They appeared to believe that by concentrating on procedural issues first, the hard substantive issues could be dealt with more easily at a later date. Ripening seemed to be a natural process, not something that could be advanced or impeded by political action. But what if the parties to the conflict were not uniformly hostile to the idea of a settlement, had mixed feelings, or were evenly divided? In such circumstances, should the United States sit back and wait until things were clarified, or should it try to accelerate the ripening process by deliberate interventions of its own? These questions were all unanswerable in theory. Time would tell whether they received answers in practice.

Implicit in this approach was an anti-Carter, anti-Kissinger perspective. No comprehensive plans, no high-level shuttle diplomacy were warranted in this phase of the conflict. To many Israelis this was long-awaited music; for the Arabs, this approach led to intense suspicions.[8] It was not long before these initial assumptions were put to the test.[9]

On the surface the views articulated by Bush's Middle East team seemed to indicate strong support for Israel. But there was a catch. If and when the Palestinians or Syrians ever agreed to negotiate seriously with Israel, the United States might press Israel hard to reciprocate. At the outset of the administration, however, the assumption seemed to be that it was up to the Arab parties to move further. Prime Minister Yitzhak Shamir was viewed as a tough leader who could not be expected to make any concessions to the Arabs as a down payment for negotiations. Only if negotiations were under way was there a chance of moving Shamir off dead center.

No one in the Bush administration seemed sure whether Shamir's hard-line policy toward the Arabs was primarily a tactical ploy or an accurate reflection of his deepest beliefs. On balance, the judgment seemed to be that Shamir could be moved, but only slowly and carefully.

In any event, the administration's first initiative was built on the assumption that Shamir was interested in peace and could best be dealt with by pursuing ideas that bore his prior stamp of approval.

The paradox of the Bush presidency was that this initial agenda was probably more consonant with Israeli views than that of any previous president. And yet this same administration was soon widely viewed as the most hostile ever to Israel. The change, insofar as it was real, did not reflect a change of sentiment on the part of the top decisionmakers and their advisers.

THE TEAM

All along, Bush, Baker, and Brent Scowcroft, the national security adviser, were thought to be less emotionally involved with Israel than either Reagan or George Shultz had been. But no one in 1989 would have accused them of being anti-Israeli. And apart from Bush and Baker, the top echelons of the administration were filled with figures friendly to Israel, including the secretary of defense, Richard Cheney; the deputy secretary of state, Lawrence Eagleburger; and the entire Middle East team of Ross, Haass, Daniel Kurtzer and Aaron Miller. Several members of the team could speak Hebrew quite well. But no one who knew them felt that their sympathies were with the Likud party or Shamir. Rather, the Labor party, and especially Yitzhak Rabin, the Israeli defense minister, seemed more to their liking.

During most of 1989, as the new administration was developing its approach to the Middle East, other international issues demanded much attention. Relations with the Soviet Union and Gorbachev were of particular importance, and only toward the end of 1989 were Baker and Soviet Foreign Minister Eduard Shevardnadze beginning to develop an especially close bond. Meanwhile relations with China quickly soured after the Tiananmen crackdown in June 1989. Shortly thereafter the amazing sequence of events that resulted in the collapse of all the communist regimes of eastern Europe began, culminating in the dramatic execution of the Romanian dictator Nicolai Ceauşescu in the last days of 1989. With so many significant international developments taking place in 1989, it was a wonder that the administration had time left over for the Arab-Israeli conflict. Not surprisingly, caution was the watchword of the new "confidence-building" approach to Middle East peacemaking.

Early in 1989 Shamir and Rabin were told that the Bush administration would be interested in hearing new ideas on how to revive the peace process. Rabin, in particular, saw this as an invitation to Israel to set the agenda for the next round of diplomacy. By the time Shamir arrived in Washington in early April for his first meeting with President Bush, the Israeli cabinet had adopted a four-point proposal. Its centerpiece was a call for elections in the West Bank and Gaza to select non-PLO Palestinians with whom Israel would then negotiate, according to the Camp David formula, an interim agreement on self-government.[10] Implicit in this approach was that no international conference on the Middle East would take place, a point on which Likud and Labor differed and on which the Bush administration seemed to side with Shamir, at least for the moment. Washington's initial response to these ideas was sympathetic.

On May 22, 1989, Baker spoke at the annual AIPAC convention in Washington, D.C. Baker's remarks were predictably friendly toward Israel at the outset, noting the shared commitment to democratic values and the strong strategic partnership. Baker welcomed the Shamir initiative as "an important and positive start down the road toward constructing workable negotiations." He endorsed the idea of a prenegotiations phase of talks. Only when Baker turned to the missing element in the Shamir plan, the fate of the occupied territories, did he hit a discordant note. Interpreting UN Resolution 242 as requiring the exchange of land for peace, Baker referred to "territorial withdrawal" as a probable outcome of negotiations. Then, in a pointed reference to Shamir's ideology, Baker said: "For Israel, now is the time to lay aside, once and for all, the unrealistic vision of a greater Israel. Israeli interests in the West Bank and Gaza—security and otherwise—can be accommodated in a settlement based on Resolution 242. Forswear annexation. Stop settlement activity. Allow schools to reopen. Reach out to the Palestinians as neighbors who deserve political rights." The fact that Baker immediately enunciated a comparable list of requirements for the Palestinians did nothing to warm the chilly atmosphere that descended over the pro-Israeli crowd, which only a few years earlier had heard George Shultz, from the same platform, lead the chant "Hell no, PLO."[11]

Baker's speech, besides raising Israeli worries, marked a subtle shift toward a more active effort by the Bush administration to redesign the Shamir initiative into something that might be acceptable to the Palestinians. Doing so without losing Israeli support would be difficult, to say the least. Over the next several months Baker became increasingly involved in Arab-Israeli diplomacy, probing through his diplomatic contacts for any opening.

As of mid-1989 the operational goal of American policy was to persuade the PLO to allow negotiations with Israel to begin with Palestinians who were not from within the ranks of the PLO leadership per se. The reason was simple: Shamir, it was believed, would never agree to negotiate with the PLO.[12] At the same time it would be difficult for Washington to convince the PLO to stay entirely on the sidelines. After all, the PLO's claim to be the "sole, legitimate representative of the Palestinian people" was part of the bedrock of its position. Still, by the summer of 1989 the PLO was showing signs of flexibility on this score. The PLO could stay in the shadows on two conditions: if it could select any Palestinian delegation, and if at least one delegation member was from outside the West Bank and Gaza. The PLO also felt strongly that Palestinians residing in East Jerusalem could not be excluded from the list of eligible representatives, a point on which the United States had previously expressed its agreement.

Just as the United States was trying to win PLO acceptance of Shamir's election proposal as a starting point, strains began to develop in the bilateral U.S.-PLO talks that were being conducted in Tunis. First, a leak to the press revealed that the American ambassador had been meeting with Abu Iyad, a man associated in the minds of many Americans and Israelis with terrorism, but also one who had been instrumental in bringing about the shift of PLO policy toward greater pragmatism.[13] Shortly thereafter the Fatah Congress adopted a tough line. The Palestinians thought a U.S.-PLO meeting on August 14 had involved an American ultimatum that no Palestinians from outside the occupied territories could be included in a Palestinian delegation. That was not, in fact, a correct perception of American policy, but it contributed to a growing lack of mutual confidence.

As the U.S.-PLO dialogue faded during the summer, Egypt and Sweden stepped in to try to improve the prospects for getting the PLO to go along with Baker's approach. Because President Mubarak could deal directly with the PLO leader Yasir Arafat, officials in Washington soon found this was a more effective channel than the formal U.S.-PLO dialogue, from which Arafat was excluded. Egypt then became instrumental in crystallizing the PLO position. Mubarak, for example, spelled out, on behalf of the PLO, ten points that should govern elections in the West Bank and Gaza. Baker then responded, initially through diplomatic channels, to see if common ground could be found.[14]

By late in 1989 the Egyptians had indicated that Arafat had accepted

Baker's five points.[15] The most important of these points was the notion that the Palestinians could bring to the negotiations any position related to the peace process. The precise makeup of the list of Palestinians negotiators had not been settled, but a procedure had been agreed upon that would give Israel a virtual veto, but without calling it that. In short, the United States and Egypt would produce a list of Palestinians, after consultations with the PLO, that satisfied criteria laid down by the Israelis. Israel, in turn, would not ask too many questions about the origin of the list, provided the names were acceptable. No one knew for sure if Palestinians from East Jerusalem would be acceptable to Shamir, or whether someone from outside the territories might be included. But Baker was exploring all sorts of possibilities, including Palestinians with one residence in Jerusalem and one elsewhere; Palestinians who had recently been deported by Israel, but had normally been residents of the West Bank; and so on.

ISRAELI REACTIONS

Early in 1990 Baker seemed to feel he had Egyptian and Palestinian support for his basic approach. Now he turned up the heat on Shamir to accept what Baker kept insisting was Shamir's own plan. To start the process, Baker suggested that he meet with the Israeli and Egyptian foreign ministers in Cairo. The prime minister, by now, must have had his own reservations about taking this first step onto the slippery slope, but he also had ample domestic political reasons for balking. His right-wing allies, for example, were planning to bolt the coalition if Shamir accepted the American plan; Labor was threatening to withdraw from the national unity government if he did not.

In the midst of this political acrimony the Americans became alarmed at reports of large numbers of new immigrants from the Soviet Union going to the occupied territories to live. Shamir had minimized the issue, but in so doing he had made no mention of the large number of new immigrants moving into neighborhoods of East Jerusalem. President Bush, who felt strongly that settlements were an obstacle to peace, was fully briefed, with maps, on the location of new settlers, and he apparently believed Shamir had deliberately lied to him.

Meanwhile a powerful Likud voice, that of Benjamin Begin, son of the redoubtable Menachem, came out publicly against the Baker plan. The Likud establishment then met and recommended that Shamir not accept the plan. Just after that recommendation, word came from

Washington that Bush had spoken critically of Israeli settlements in the West Bank and East Jerusalem.[16] This was no slip of the tongue. American policy had long considered East Jerusalem to be part of the occupied territories,[17] but no previous president had singled East Jerusalem out for special comment when discussing settlements. The Israeli reaction was harsh. Shamir, who almost certainly had already decided to reject the Baker plan, now had a pretext for doing so, claiming that the United States had revealed its lack of objectivity as a potential mediator. With Shamir's blunt "no," the first phase of the Bush administration's peacemaking effort was put on hold.

For a few weeks Israeli internal politics was so uncertain that it seemed possible that Labor party leader Shimon Peres might be able to form a narrow coalition without the Likud. Had that occurred, there would have been widespread satisfaction in the Bush administration. But try as he might, Peres could not lure the religious parties away from Shamir, and when the dust had settled in May 1990, Shamir was still prime minister, but this time at the head of a very right-wing cabinet from which Labor was excluded.

CHALLENGES

While the Israelis were absorbed in their internal crisis, the Arab world seemed similarly disoriented. But there the proximate cause was the end of the cold war and the loss of Soviet patronage. Iraqi president Saddam Hussein chose the occasion of a meeting in Amman, Jordan, in late February 1990 to reflect on how the end of the cold war might lead to a Pax Americana-Hebraica in the Middle East.[18] For a leader who was receiving economic and political support from the United States, and who had been quietly assisted in his eight-year-long struggle against Iran, such comments might have been considered reckless. King Hussein, among others, thought the Iraqi leader was going too far in attacking Washington, but anti-American sentiment was on the rise in the Arab world, fueled, perhaps, by a sense of vulnerability in a one-superpower world, and reflecting as well the growing appeal of Islamic radicalism with its anti-Western, anti-Israeli overtones. Whatever the cause of these sentiments, Saddam seemed to be gambling on finding a positive Arab response to his increasingly strident attacks on the United States and Israel.[19]

With the peace process in limbo and anti-American sentiment being fanned from Baghdad, it was perhaps inevitable that the U.S.-PLO

relationship would unravel. How it happened revealed the fragile underpinnings of the dialogue on both sides. First came an unusually bloody
incident in Israel, where a deranged soldier shot and killed seven
Palestinians at Rishon le Zion. Subsequent riots resulted in more Palestinian dead. The PLO, with strong international backing, launched an
appeal in the United Nations to take some action to prevent further
violence against Palestinians in the occupied territories. Arafat was keen
to come to New York to address a session of the UN. Bush and Baker
did not share his enthusiasm, and a compromise deal seems to have been
worked out. A special session of the UN would be held in Geneva,
Arafat would be allowed to make his appeal, and the United States would
support a resolution calling on the secretary general to send an envoy to
the territories.

Just as the vote was about to be held on the resolution in Geneva, a
Palestinian commando unit landed on the beach outside Tel Aviv. The
Israelis managed to intercept and neutralize the group, which consisted
of members of Abul Abbas' Palestine Liberation Front (the same group
that had been responsible for the *Achille Lauro* affair), before any civilians
were hurt, but it clearly seemed to be an intended terrorist action, at
least as defined by Israelis and Americans.[20] As such, this event seemed
to constitute a breach of the PLO pledge to renounce terrorism. In Israel
and in the United States a cry went out for the United States to break
off the dialogue with the PLO.

Under considerable political pressure at home, Bush authorized his
representative at the UN to veto the resolution on conditions in the
occupied territories, a step that infuriated Arafat and many other Palestinians. But Bush was reluctant to take the next step of ending the dialogue.
Instead he insisted that the PLO condemn the commando raid and
discipline those responsible for it. In particular, the United States wanted
action taken against Abul Abbas, who was still a member of the PLO
executive committee, although his membership was apparently frozen,
which meant that he did not participate in decisionmaking.

Arafat seemed to be in no mood to meet the American conditions.
Instead he began to spend increasing amounts of time in Baghdad, and
reports were even received that he was thinking of moving his political
headquarters there from Tunis. In mid-June, Arafat's deputy, Salah
Khalaf (Abu Iyad), expressed his concern that Arafat was coming under
Saddam's influence. The Abul Abbas raid, he maintained, had been an
Iraqi operation. Its goal was to put an end to the PLO's policy of

moderation and to its links with both Washington and Cairo. Saddam had something in mind, said Abu Iyad, something big. And he was maneuvering to get the PLO into his corner. This could only be bad, he thought, for the Palestinians. He was eager to find some way to prevent a break with Washington.[21] But it was too late. On June 20 Bush announced, more in sorrow than in anger, the suspension of the U.S.-PLO dialogue.

The summer of 1990 found American Middle East policy seemingly adrift. No one could see much future for the peace process, with an Israeli government bent on settling the occupied territories as rapidly as possible and a Palestinian movement drifting toward an alignment with an increasingly militant Iraq. And no one seemed to know what Saddam Hussein had in mind. He was making demands on the Gulf states for money and threatening Israel with chemical weapons if he was ever attacked, and by late July he began to move troops toward the Kuwaiti border to back up his demands for money. Within the region the prevailing interpretation was that Saddam was out to blackmail the Kuwaitis and Saudis by displaying his power. Egyptians, Jordanians, and Gulf leaders all advised Washington not to provoke Saddam by overreacting to his bullying. Instead talks would be held in Saudi Arabia, a deal would be struck, and Saddam would back off. But he did not. On August 2 his troops poured into Kuwait, occupying the country in a matter of hours and then annexing it, thus changing for years to come the politics of the region.

THE GULF CRISIS: AMERICA GOES TO WAR

This is not the place to analyze Saddam Hussein's motives for invading Kuwait. Nor is George Bush's response the center of this study.[22] Suffice it to say that Saddam must have calculated that Bush would not react militarily. In reaching such a conclusion, he may well have hoped that the force of Arab opinion would run so strongly against Western intervention that no Arab regime would dare collude with Washington to force Iraq to back down. This was a misreading of the Saudis and Egyptians in particular, both of whom agreed to cooperate with a massive deployment of Western, mostly American, forces in the region. And it was a misreading of George Bush, who had been raised on the lessons of Munich and did not need much coaching to conclude that American interests would suffer if Saddam Hussein got away with his bid for power.

If Saddam controlled Iraqi and Kuwaiti oil supplies directly, and if he kept troops on the Saudi border, he would in fact dominate the Gulf's vast reserves of oil and would become a one-man OPEC, able to manipulate the supply of oil to achieve whatever price he wanted. With his enormous oil revenues, he would also be able to accelerate his buildup of arms, including nuclear, chemical, and biological weapons. Before long the stage would be set for another war in the Middle East, this one involving Israel and Iraq, both possibly armed with nuclear weapons. Added to these tangible concerns were the matters of American leadership in the post–cold war world, of resistance to aggression, and of domestic political pressures on Bush to act.

While Bush methodically prepared for a war that America and its allies could not lose, Saddam tried to link his occupation of Kuwait to the Israeli occupation of Arab territories (and the Syrian occupation of Lebanon). Before asking Iraq to withdraw from territory that was rightfully Iraqi, Saddam implied, Israel and Syria should withdraw their forces. This stance was designed to win support from many in the Arab world who were inclined to see no particular difference among the three occupations and who held no special brief for the overly rich Kuwaitis in any case. Palestinians were particularly prone to grasp at Saddam's effort to link these issues, sensing the possibility that a powerful Arab savior, an echo of the great Nasser, might save them at a time when no one else seemed able to do so. Thus in Jordan and in the occupied territories, an outpouring of support for Saddam could be registered, if only briefly.

None of that support made much difference to Bush and his top aides in Washington. They were determined to oust Saddam from Kuwait, to destroy his war-making capability, to remove his weapons of mass destruction, and to do so with minimal casualties, quickly, and under the guise of UN legitimacy. On January 16, 1991, the American-led coalition launched massive air strikes against Iraq. Almost immediately it was clear the Iraqi fighting force was doomed. Saddam tried to drag Israel into the war by firing SCUD missiles at Tel Aviv. If the Israelis came into the war, Saddam believed, the Saudis, Egyptians, and Syrians would switch sides. But under considerable American pressure, Israel did not retaliate; the Arab allies in the coalition held firm; and Saddam's forces beat a hasty retreat from Kuwait at the end of February. Throughout, the Soviet Union did nothing to protect the Iraqi regime. In fact, the Soviets voted in the UN with the United States, in a graphic display of post–cold war cooperation.

What would the American-led victory, Saddam's defeat, Israeli restraint, and Palestinian support for Saddam mean for the stagnant peace process? Bush had refused to accept Saddam's effort to link the occupation of Kuwait with the Israeli occupation of the West Bank, but in a gesture toward the Arabs he had hinted on October 1, 1990, that when he had settled accounts with Saddam, he would turn his attention back toward Arab-Israeli peacemaking.[23] In March 1991 many wondered if Bush's comment had been more than idle rhetoric. Within weeks evidence began to accumulate that Bush and Baker saw an opportunity coming out of the Gulf crisis to relaunch the peace process. Indeed, Baker began to resemble a former secretary of state, Henry Kissinger, who had rushed to the region in the aftermath of another war, in 1973. Between March and October 1991 Baker made eight trips to the region, spending endless hours huddled with Syria's Hafiz al-Asad and Israel's Yitzhak Shamir. As Kissinger had done, he also touched base in Saudi Arabia and other Arab countries. But his most interesting innovation was that he began to talk with Palestinians from within the occupied territories who were known to have close ties to the PLO. Faisal Husseini and Hanan Ashrawi became his interlocutors of choice on the Palestinian side. It proved to be an important procedural shift, opening the way for Palestinian participation in the peace process despite some residual ill-feeling on both sides about the Gulf War.

ROAD TO MADRID

During the war against Iraq the Middle East team at the State Department began to think the outcome of the war might create conditions in which Arab-Israeli peace negotiations would prove possible. The reasoning went as follows. The defeat of Iraq would convince even the most die-hard Arab militants that a military solution to the Arab-Israeli conflict was impossible. The fact that the Soviet Union had cooperated with the United States during the crisis would further demonstrate that the old cold war rules of the game were being rewritten, and that the United States, more than ever, occupied the key diplomatic position. Palestinians and Jordanians, who had allowed their emotions to draw them to Saddam's side, would now realize that they had lost support among Arab regimes and that time was working against their interests. Out of weakness, therefore, the Palestinians might be expected to respond positively to any serious diplomatic overture.

American officials also hoped that patterns of cooperation forged during the Gulf War might carry over into the postwar diplomacy. On the Arab side, this would mean that Egypt, Syria, and Saudi Arabia might be expected to work in tandem to support the peace process, something that had not happened since 1974. Indeed, one of the main debates within the Bush administration was over the role to be accorded Syria in the postwar era. In public many opinion leaders were warning of the danger of embracing Hafiz al-Asad, as if he were nothing more than a somewhat shrewder version of Saddam Hussein. Asad's past record on Arab-Israeli peace provided little comfort to those who thought he might be more flexible in this round. But the weight of consensus was that Asad should be put to the test. If he agreed to negotiate with Israel, the Palestinians would almost certainly follow suit. And if Israel saw the chance of talking directly with Syria, that might provide a positive incentive to join the process. By contrast, Shamir seemed to believe nothing good could come of talking just with the Palestinians.

Shamir remained something of an enigma for the Americans. On the one hand, he had surprised many by showing great self-control during the Iraqi SCUD attacks on Israel. At the American request, he sat tight, resisting the advice of some of his own military to strike back at Iraq. On the other hand, nothing in Shamir's personality gave reason to think that the issues on which the peace process had foundered a year earlier could now be easily swept away. Still, a judgment was made that objectively Israel was more secure than it had ever been. Furthermore, the fact that the United States had rushed Patriot missiles to help defend against the SCUDs, followed by infusions of aid to offset war-related losses, would presumably create conditions in which Shamir would be reluctant to say no to George Bush.

Finally, the Middle East team realized that the American-led victory in the Gulf would inevitably enhance the leadership potential of President Bush, at least for the near term. Bush was enjoying unprecedented popularity at home. No one would seriously question his judgment in turning from the Gulf victory to Arab-Israeli peacemaking.

One lingering question remained. What national interest would the United States now serve by tackling the congealed Arab-Israeli conflict? In the Gulf, Americans could be persuaded that the combination of oil and potential Iraqi nuclear capabilities justified the expenditure of lives and money to defeat Saddam. But why should the United States, especially in the post–cold war era, take another run at the impossibly complex dispute between Israel and its Arab neighbors? Was there really any chance of success? Was the stalemate so threatening to American interests? Only a few years earlier any answer to these questions would have noted the possibility of Soviet gains and of threats to oil supplies as reasons to tackle the Arab-Israeli conflict. But the Soviet threat was now gone, and oil supplies bore no obvious relationship to the course of the Arab-Israeli dispute, at least not in 1991.

If some old answers were no longer credible, others were. For example, it had long been assumed that the Egyptian-Israeli peace would be strengthened if the peace process could be revived. In the absence of further movement in the peace process, the cool relations between Egypt and Israel might collapse altogether, at great cost to the prospects for regional stability. That remained a valid concern. Another concern was that a prolonged stalemate in the Arab-Israeli arena would result in a radicalization of opinion in both Israel and among the Palestinians. In the worst of circumstances, the conflict would be defined increasingly in religious terms, Jews against Muslims, and destroy the prospects for any settlement.

Some within the administration were also worried about the effect of a prolonged stalemate on U.S.-Israeli relations. Would the American public continue to support large outlays of aid to Israel now that the "strategic asset" argument carried so little weight? What would the effect on American opinion be of more years of TV images of heavily armed Israelis shooting at Palestinian stone throwers? Without a peace settlement Israel would look more and more like a colonial state ruling over a restless people with its own national aspirations. No one believed Israel would offer the Palestinians equal rights within the Israeli political system, since that would radically dilute the Jewishness of the state. The only alternatives to a peace settlement with territorial withdrawal would then be prolonged second-class status for the Palestinians or their expulsion from the occupied territories. Neither option seemed compatible with strong U.S.-Israeli relations. Unless the two countries could again be seen as cooperating in pursuit of peace, some felt Israel ran the risk of a sudden loss of American public support.

The clinching argument for the Middle East team, however, seems to have been more related to the prospect of a future war in the region. Without a peace settlement, some feared, another war between Israel and some coalition of Arab states was still possible. The danger of such a war had been hinted at in the recent conflict with Iraq. Surface-to-surface missiles may not have been very effective in 1991, but who could be sure that accuracies would not be improved within the decade? And what about nonconventional weapons? This time Iraq had refrained from using its chemical weapons, and it did not yet possess nuclear weapons. But would the same apply to an Arab-Israeli war fought later in the decade? No one could be sure, but it seemed prudent to try to avoid another test of arms if at all possible.

With these arguments at hand, and with a legacy of past commitments in mind, the Bush administration moved quickly to explore the new terrain in the Arab-Israeli arena. From previous experience one could presume that there would be no grand design; that the emphasis would be on procedures for getting the parties to the negotiating table; and that big, new commitments of aid would not be part of the diplomacy. The main cost to the United States was likely to be the time and energy of the secretary of state and his top aides.

On March 6, 1991, Bush addressed a joint session of Congress, saying: "We must do all that we can to close the gap between Israel and the Arab states and between Israelis and Palestinians. . . . A comprehensive peace must be grounded in United Nations Security Council Resolutions 242 and 338 and the principle of territory for peace. This principle must be elaborated to provide for Israel's security and recognition, and at the same time for legitimate Palestinian political rights. Anything else would fail the twin tests of fairness and security. The time has come to put an end to Arab-Israeli conflict." (See appendix L.)

Within days of the president's speech Baker was on his way to the Middle East for what proved to be the first of eight such trips in 1991. He stopped in Saudi Arabia, moved on to Israel, where he also met with Palestinians, and then went to Damascus. Shortly thereafter Mubarak and Asad issued a call for an international peace conference on the Arab-Israeli conflict, and Shamir responded by saying that Israel might agree to a regional conference under U.S.-Soviet sponsorship.

From this first round of talks it seemed as if an effort was under way to bring Syria into the process. The price for doing so would be some form of international conference. To win Israeli support, any such conference would have to be stripped of coercive authority, providing little more than a venue for the parties to negotiate directly. Israel would resist any UN role as well. Nor was Israel enthusiastic about European participation. All these latter points would be matters for endless hours of argumentation with Asad, but none seemed insoluble. Baker's strategy seemed to be to win Asad's agreement first, on the assumption that Israel would not then want to say no.

Baker made two more trips to the region in April, without visible results. In contrast to previous forays into Arab-Israeli diplomacy, however, this time Baker did not let his frustrations show, and he did not repeatedly threaten to drop the whole matter if the parties refused to cooperate. Both he and the president gave the impression of steady determination to get the answers they wanted.

During May 1991 a potentially difficult issue surfaced. The Israeli ambassador in Washington announced that Israel would be requesting $10 billion in American loan guarantees over the next five years to help with the absorption of new immigrants from the Soviet Union.[24] At a time when Israel was building new settlements at breakneck speed in the West Bank (and around Jerusalem), this demand raised a question in Washington of how to respond. The previous U.S.-Israeli agreement on $400 million in loan guarantees for housing had left a bitter aftertaste in Washington, since the Israelis immediately rejected the notion that these funds could not be spent beyond the green line in East Jerusalem.[25] Neither Bush nor Baker wanted to be in a position of subsidizing Israeli settlements, which they genuinely believed to be an obstacle to any future agreement between Israel and the Palestinians. Needless to say, in his many meetings with Palestinian leaders Baker was told that negotiations could not succeed unless Israeli settlements were stopped. Appearing before a House Foreign Affairs subcommittee on May 22, Baker labeled Israeli settlement activity a major obstacle to peace. Bush echoed this view the following day.[26]

During the summer Baker tried to strengthen the architecture of prospective peace talks, avoiding substance but developing a structure that had substantive implications. On May 29 the administration launched a proposal on regional arms control. This, it seemed, was designed to appeal to the Israelis by drawing several Arab states, such as Saudi Arabia, into discussions on limiting arms in the region. But the most difficult issue for Baker was to work out an acceptable formula for Palestinian representation in the peace talks. No one had ever succeeded at this task. Shamir was adamant in his refusal to deal directly with the PLO, and even a veiled role for Arafat was more than he seemed willing to accept. By contrast, most Palestinians seemed to feel that only the PLO could validate the idea of negotiating with Israel, just as in 1988 only the PLO could have legitimized the idea that Israel had a right to exist as a state within a part of the former Palestine mandate.

Conceptually, a solution to this problem was not too hard to imagine, but it would require considerable political skill to find the right balance. The starting point in the quest seemed to be the point where Baker had left off in the spring of 1990. Then the PLO had already agreed that no one from the organization would be present in the negotiations with Israel. The idea had been explored that a list of names would be drawn up by the PLO but would be put forward by Egypt. Now, in 1991, the idea of the PLO forwarding a list through Palestinians within the occupied territories gained favor. But who would be on the list? Shamir made his views clear. No one from East Jerusalem; no one from outside the occupied territories; and no one involved in terrorist actions.

A year earlier Baker had supported the Palestinians in their desire to have someone from Jerusalem and from outside the territories, but now he would not do so. The PLO had lost ground because of the Gulf War. It would have to settle for less. So a formula was devised for a joint Jordanian-Palestinian delegation, with all the Palestinians coming from the occupied territories. At the same time they would all be selected by the PLO, whose role would only barely be disguised.

On the American side, some felt that the decline of the PLO would be a desirable development in itself, not just because Shamir objected to its inclusion in the talks. The idea was widespread in Washington that the Palestinians inside the territories were more moderate, more realistic, than those on the outside. The latter, it was believed, would always feel the need to defend the rights of the exiled Palestinians, including their right to return to their original homes, an issue on which the Israelis were immovable. Although this view had some merit, it missed the point that the so-called moderates in the West Bank and Gaza had very little mass following. Insofar as they could claim to speak for the Palestinians, it was because they were seen as representing the PLO. The grass-roots leaders, by contrast, were often more radical than the PLO, sometimes on the left, sometimes as part of the growing Islamic movement. So to get the moderate Palestinians into the game, and to give them political cover, the PLO was still necessary.

Early in June Bush sent letters to Shamir, Asad, King Hussein, King Fahd of Saudi Arabia, and Mubarak spelling out his ideas for convening a peace conference in the fall. The first positive reply came on July 14—from Damascus. Within days Baker was in Syria for talks with

Asad, then on to Jordan, where King Hussein agreed to the conference idea. Hussein also publicly endorsed an idea that Mubarak had suggested: the Arabs would drop the secondary boycott of Israel once Israel agreed to stop settlements in the occupied territories.

Now Baker turned to trying to win Shamir's agreement. As an inducement Baker told Shamir that the United States would continue to honor the terms of the letter sent by President Ford to Prime Minister Rabin on September 1, 1975. That letter had promised to "give great weight to Israel's position that any peace agreement with Syria must be predicated on Israel remaining on the Golan Heights."[27] Some suspected that Baker had probably made a commitment to Asad along the lines that the United States did not recognize Israel's annexation of the Golan and felt that the terms of UN Resolution 242 should be applied there. Both American promises were tenable, although one could forsee a possible contradiction somewhere down the road. But diplomats eager to make deals are often drawn to such parallel assurances. The question is not why they are given; rather, one wonders why they are so highly valued.

Lest anyone have any doubt about his views on substance, Shamir joined the debate on July 24, 1991, stating: "I don't believe in territorial compromise. Our country is very tiny. The territory is connected to our entire life—to our security, water, economy. I believe with my entire soul that we are forever connected to this entire homeland. Peace and security go together. Security, territory and homeland are one entity."[28] In short, Shamir would not go into negotiations with any prior commitment to withdrawal. A few days later, on August 1, Shamir announced his conditional acceptance of the American proposal for a peace conference in October. All that remained was to get a list of Palestinian negotiators with whom Israel would agree to meet.

What could the Palestinians hope for from the negotiations if the PLO was to be excluded and Shamir seemed unwilling to budge on withdrawal? Perhaps the Americans could at least try to stop the Israeli settlements, or at least refuse to subsidize them. Palestinian hopes may have been raised earlier in the year when Bush had postponed the decision on the Israeli request for a $10 billion loan guarantee. For the Palestinian establishment this issue was a crucial indicator of whether Bush could be a credible intermediary. If the United States was actively subsidizing new Israeli settlements, possibly on a massive scale, Palestinians would question whether American-brokered negotiations could yield them any of their rights. By contrast, if Bush could hold the line, perhaps he could be trusted.

During August an attempted coup against Gorbachev set the stage for dramatic change in the Soviet Union. Whatever slight chance there might have been for the Soviets to play an effective role as cochairman in the peace talks came to an end. Gorbachev's own position was irretrievably weakened, and the Soviet Union began to break apart. By year's end the Communist party had been banned, Gorbachev was out of power, and each of the constituent parts of the former Soviet Union was on its way toward independence. Boris Yeltsin was the new ruler of Russia. For the Palestinians and Syrians these dramatic events were further reminders that they now stood on their own, with no major power behind them.

But Bush was gaining credibility in Arab eyes, just as the Soviets were dropping off the map. On September 6, 1991, Bush asked Congress for a 120-day delay before considering the Israeli loan request. After encountering congressional resistance, Bush went public on September 12. He spoke out forcefully against Israeli settlements and against the Israeli lobby. Within days polls showed that a large majority of the American public supported the president in his stand on the Israeli aid request.[29] By contrast, many American Jews were deeply offended by what they saw as Bush's questioning of their right to lobby on behalf of issues they believed in.

During the next few weeks Baker made additional trips to the Middle East. One could sense the beginning of the endgame. Letters of assurances were being demanded and offered.[30] (See appendix M for the text of the letter to the Palestinians.) Symbolic gestures, such as Bush's call for the repeal of the UN resolution on Zionism as a form of racism, were freely made.

Finally, on October 18 Baker was given a list of the prospective Palestinian negotiating team. On October 20 the Israeli cabinet voted to go to the conference. On October 22 Faisal Husseini announced the names of the Palestinian negotiating team, along with those, including himself, who would form an advisory group. One member of the Jordanian part of the joint team was a Palestinian from outside the territories with close family ties to Jerusalem. So the Palestinians could finally say that they had chosen a representative negotiating team, while the Israelis could say that they were not dealing with the PLO and had not recognized East Jerusalem as having the same status as the rest of the occupied territories.

THE MADRID CONFERENCE

On October 30, under the joint chairmanship of Bush and Gorbachev, the Middle East peace conference opened in Madrid (See appendix N for the text of the U.S.-Soviet invitation.) Israel, Syria, Lebanon, and a joint Jordanian-Palestinian delegation were all in attendance; so was a representative of the UN secretary general and a representative of the European Community, but far from center stage. Of greater symbolic importance was the presence of Prince Bandar ibn Sultan, the Saudi ambassador to Washington, dressed in traditional garb.

The formal speeches were unlikely to be long remembered, with the possible exception of the unusually eloquent Palestinian speech.[31] (See appendix O for Bush's speech.) But no one could ignore the symbolic—and therefore political—importance of the parties' sitting together at the negotiating table. And for the first time in recent history, the Palestinians were present speaking on their own behalf. To prove that the formal ceremonies were not the end of the road, all the parties were even persuaded to engage in a few days of face-to-face talks. The fact that no substantive progress had been made was hardly surprising. The important point was that a commitment to an ongoing negotiating process seemed to exist.

After the procedural breakthrough of getting all the parties to the negotiating table, what did Bush and Baker have in mind? They had not even hinted at any new substantive ideas, although by getting the Palestinians to the table as an almost independent party, the administration had done what no other had done before. And Bush had strongly hinted that any increase in aid to Israel would be accompanied by some conditions to slow down the pace of settlements. Otherwise Washington seemed determined to play the part of convener, but not yet that of mediator. The parties would repeatedly be brought to the negotiating table—first in Washington in December 1991, once in January, in March, and again in April 1992, to be followed by more meetings in Rome. But despite appeals from the Arabs for more substantive American involvement, Bush and Baker held back.

The reason for their reticence was not hard to discern. The Americans had always been worried about raising Arab expectations that Israeli concessions would simply be delivered by Washington. This was not going to happen. The Arab parties would have to develop positions of their own and negotiate seriously before the United States would seek to bridge differences with proposals of its own.[32] In addition, on many of the points in dispute, the Americans had no strong views of how the issues should be resolved. What they wanted was a workable agreement. Whatever the parties could agree upon would easily pass muster in Washington. At most, the administration had views of workable compromises, but it was not eager to tip its hand prematurely. So it envisaged a prolonged phase of bilateral negotiations.

Complementing the bilateral talks would be the multilateral meetings on arms control, economic development, water, refugees, and the environment. No one expected any immediate results from these talks, but some useful ideas might be explored at the expert level which would then be available to feed into the political talks at appropriate moments. In a gesture to the Russians the first round of the multilateral talks took place in Moscow on January 28, 1992. Syria did not attend, but that did not prevent some other Arab parties from participating. In the follow-on talks Israel chose not to participate in the meetings on refugees and economics because of the presence of Palestinians from outside the territories, but the meetings proceeded in any event. No party's absence from a single session, it seemed, could now torpedo the negotiating process.

If the Israelis had reason to feel gratified that the United States was not intervening in the substance of the negotiations, they had less reason for joy on the matter of the postponed loan guarantees. The 120-day deadline came and went without a decision. By mid-January 1992 congressional leaders were exploring possible compromises. In one version, Israel would receive the first year of loan guarantees, some $2 billion, but any funds spent on settlements in the occupied territories would be deducted from future amounts. A well-informed *New York Times* columnist wrote on January 17, 1992, that Shamir would be wrong to think Bush would settle for such a compromise. One way or another, Bush wanted Shamir to agree to stop settlements.[33] A few days later Shamir said there was no chance that Israel would agree to a freeze.

Domestic political realities were clearly beginning to play a role in both Washington and Jerusalem. Israeli elections were now scheduled for June 1992, as a result of the defection of small right-wing parties from Shamir's coalition. Shamir was unlikely to make concessions on settlements in the best of times, but certainly not on the eve of elections.

Normally one would expect an American president going into a reelection campaign to avoid a showdown with Congress and Israel. But foreign aid was unpopular. Bush would not lose many votes by saying no to Shamir. And it already seemed obvious that Bush would not win many votes from the American Jewish community, which increasingly saw both the president and Baker as hostile to Israel. Still, Bush did not want to alienate Israelis across the political spectrum. Instead he decided to attach conditions to the loan guarantees that he knew Shamir, but not all Israelis, would find difficult to accept. Apparently Bush hoped that Shamir's unwillingness to accept the American conditions would lead Israelis to debate the wisdom of pursuing an unrestrained policy of settling the territories. Many of the new immigrants, in particular, might blame Shamir for missing the opportunity to secure assistance that would benefit them.

Few who knew Bush and Baker believed they were indifferent to the outcome of the Israeli elections. Shamir had been a difficult leader for them to deal with. His policy on settlements and his refusal to countenance withdrawal were genuine concerns as the administration tried to foresee the future of the peace process. And Labor, after a hard-fought internal campaign, was united behind Yitzhak Rabin, a man who just might be regarded by Israelis as combining the right dose of realism and toughness to see them through the next phase of the negotiating process. To grant the loans to Shamir without conditions might well ensure Shamir's victory at the polls. That Bush and Baker did not want to do.

On February 24, 1992, shortly after Rabin's victory within the Labor party, Baker laid out the conditions for granting the $10 billion in loan guarantees.[34] Efforts by Congress to find a compromise were rejected by Bush on March 17. For the moment, the issue of loan guarantees seemed dead.[35] And until after Israeli and American elections, the negotiating process would probably be on hold as well.[36]

THE ISRAELI ELECTIONS

Israelis went to the polls on June 23 and delivered a stunning defeat to the Likud party that had ruled, almost without interruption, since 1977. Only 25 percent of the electorate cast ballots for the Likud, yielding thirty-two Knesset seats, down from forty in the 1988 elections. The defeat for Shamir was so great that he announced his intention to step down as party leader. Moshe Arens, sometimes thought to be the heir apparent, decided to retire from politics, criticizing Shamir's views on Greater Israel as he left.[37]

If the Likud was the clear loser, Rabin and his Labor party were the winners. With nearly 35 percent of the popular vote, and forty-four

Knesset seats, Rabin was in a position to forge a narrow coalition without any of the right-wing parties. Although he spent some time exploring the possibilities of creating a broad coalition, on July 13 he presented a cabinet to the Knesset that represented a coalition of Labor, the left-wing Meretz bloc, and the Shas religious party. Together these three parties held sixty-two seats, and the coalition could probably count on five Arab Knesset members as well in a future vote of confidence.

Rabin moved quickly to assert his authority. He kept the Defense portfolio for himself. As foreign minister, he named Shimon Peres, his long-time rival. But he made it clear that he, not Peres, would oversee the peace process. As head of the Israeli team negotiating with the Syrians, he named a respected Tel Aviv University academic specialist on Syria, Itamar Rabinovitch. No such change was made at the head of the Israeli team dealing with Jordan and the Palestinians.

Within days of Rabin's investiture Baker arrived in Israel to push for a resumption of peace negotiations and to prepare the way for a Rabin visit to the United States. Shortly thereafter, in a trip that symbolized the new era, Rabin traveled to Egypt for a cordial meeting with President Mubarak. Two days later Rabin announced that more than 6,000 housing units planned for the West Bank would be canceled, and subsidies on the remainder would be reduced. (Some 10,000 units well on the way to completion would be finished, so a "freeze" on settlement activity was still not in sight.)

Rabin also injected into his rhetoric a sense of urgency about finding a negotiated settlement, especially with the Palestinians. But before long he was also expressing optimism that progress could be made on the Syrian front as well.[38] Meanwhile Shamir confirmed the worst suspicions of many when he allegedly said that if he had been reelected, he would have strung out the negotiating process for at least another ten years.[39]

The changes in Israel were warmly welcomed by Bush and Baker. By playing the issue of the loan guarantees as they had, they had contributed in some degree to Shamir's defeat. Not surprisingly, then, Bush received Rabin on August 10 in Maine with a degree of warmth that had been noticeably missing from his encounters with Shamir. Although details remained to be worked out, Bush was able to tell Rabin that he would now support the loan guarantees to Israel. On October 5 both houses of Congress voted for a foreign aid appropriations bill that contained the $10 billion in loan guarantees, with Israel covering the reserve costs of some $400 million. The president retained the authority to deduct from these funds amounts that Israel might spend on settlements beyond completion of the 10,000 units already under way. On the whole, Israelis had every reason to be very pleased with the outcome of this year-long struggle over aid.

BUSH'S DECLINING FORTUNES

Throughout the early part of 1992 Bush had pressed ahead with his foreign-policy agenda, including the Middle East, as if 1992 were not an election year. After all, he faced no serious opposition for his party's nomination. His support in the polls in mid-1991, after the Gulf War victory, had been at all-time highs, and the Democratic field of candidates did not look very impressive. The cloud on the horizon was the weak state of the economy and signs of growing disenchantment with Bush's leadership.

During the primaries Bush faced a surprisingly sharp challenge from Patrick Buchanan, a conservative columnist who was able to win about one-third of the votes in the early Republican primaries. Unlike Bush, he was essentially an isolationist, a protectionist on trade issues, an opponent of foreign aid, and a sometime critic of Israel. The net effect of his challenge was probably to push Bush more to the right on domestic political issues—so-called family values.

On the Democratic side, it was clear by late spring the Governor Bill Clinton of Arkansas would be the candidate after the July party convention. Clinton had a fairly good record of governing a small, poor state, but his views on foreign policy were almost unknown. As the campaign gained momentum Clinton launched some criticism at Bush for being too tough on Israel and for attaching conditions to the loan guarantees. But Rabin's election and the renewed warmth of U.S.-Israeli relations during the summer removed the loans as a major campaign issue. Indeed, most foreign-policy issues were ignored by both parties in favor of debates over domestic priorities or questions of character. Clinton spent more time attacking Bush's role in the Iran-Contra affair and in supporting Saddam Hussein before the invasion of Kuwait than on any contemporary issue of foreign policy.

The Democratic Convention in New York proved to be surprisingly harmonious. Clinton chose as his running mate Senator Albert Gore, Jr., of Tennessee. These young Democratic candidates presented themselves as the agents of change. Initial public opinion polls showed them with a commanding lead over President Bush.

Normally the Republican Convention, which nominated Bush easily, should have given the president a significant boost in the polls. But his campaign seemed disorganized and lacking focus. Rumors began to spread that the president would call on his friend and adviser, James Baker, to take charge. On August 13 the announcement was made that Baker would become chief of staff as of August 23. As he took his farewell from the State Department, Baker seemed to be speaking with a heavy heart. He had clearly relished the role of statesman and was unhappy about leaving the Arab-Israeli peace process, in particular, at a sensitive moment.

The sixth round of peace talks convened in Washington the day after Baker and his entire top team left for the White House. Middle East policy would now be technically in the hands of Acting Secretary Lawrence Eagleburger, assisted by Assistant Secretary Edward Djerejian. Few expected much of a push from the American side as negotiations resumed on August 24.[40]

During most of September and October Bush was fully occupied with running for reelection. Despite his absence and Baker's from the negotiating process, some modest gains were made on the Syrian-Israeli front. Asad spoke publicly of the need for a "peace of the brave," consciously echoing the words of former French president Charles de Gaulle.[41] Asad's foreign minister then spoke of "total peace for total withdrawal," which for the first time indicated that Syria might go beyond merely ending the state of belligerency with Israel. By the seventh round of negotiations in late October, the Israelis had reciprocated by using the word "withdrawal" in a formal document referring to the Golan front. And Israel was working with a Syrian draft paper to try to develop a statement of joint principles to guide the negotiations. All this was fairly encouraging, but both Asad and Rabin seemed frustrated that the United States was not helping to close the deal. Also, the Palestinians, who were seeing no comparable progress in their own negotiations with Israel, were getting nervous about the possibility of Syria concluding a separate peace.

Some observers believed the conditions in the fall of 1992 were such that a major commitment of time and energy by the Bush administration might have produced significant results. But precisely because of election-year imperatives, the United States was in no position to play the role of mediator, full partner, or deal maker that it had in the past.

Finally, on November 3, 1992, the long election campaign came to an end. Despite his foreign-policy achievements, his experience, and the doubts he had raised about his opponent's character, Bush was solidly defeated in his bid for reelection. The popular vote divided 43 percent for Clinton, 38 percent for Bush, and 19 percent for independent candidate Ross Perot, resulting in a one-sided victory for the Democratic candidate in the electoral college. Once again domestic politics intruded on the conduct of American policy in the Middle East, forcing a hiatus of several months before American leadership in the peace process might once again be expected.

Unfortunately, events in the Middle East rarely conform to the needs of the American electoral calendar. During the lame-duck period from the election on November 4, 1992, to January 20, 1993, when Bill Clinton was inaugurated as president, the tensions between Israelis and Palestinians mounted rapidly. During December alone, Palestinians killed more Israelis, and Israelis killed more Palestinians, than in much of the previous year. Rabin, under domestic pressures, struck back with an unprecedented decision to deport more than 400 suspected Islamic activists to Lebanon. In another unprecedented move, Lebanon, finally governed by a cabinet with considerable popular support, refused to allow the Palestinians into Lebanon. Thus, in difficult conditions, the Palestinians remained in a sort of no-man's-land in southern Lebanon.

Coming on the last days of the eighth round of peace talks in Washington, this action cast a pall over the negotiations. Palestinian spokesmen asserted that talks would not be resumed until the deportees were returned to their homes. Rabin refused to budge. Bush could do nothing, thus ensuring that the Clinton administration would inherit a stalled peace process in need of resuscitation rather than the ongoing, institutionalized one that had continued through most of 1992.

CONCLUSIONS

Bush and Baker had come to power with an interest in the Arab-Israeli conflict, but with a determination to avoid some of the mistakes of their predecessors. They would offer no big plans, no special negotiators, no heightened expectations. The administration would probe cautiously to see if the parties were ready to move. If not, it would hold back. It would wait for the conflict to ripen.

Events in the Middle East prove to be powerful teachers. Theories do not hold up well in the face of swiftly moving realities. So it is not surprising that the administration found itself drawn into an increasingly assertive role in late 1989 and early 1990, trying to break the impasse with a proposal for Israeli-Palestinian talks on holding elections in the West Bank and Gaza. This effort failed, and failure is also part of the learning process.

The Bush administration's greatest foreign-policy error, its misreading of Saddam Hussein before his invasion of Kuwait, also set the stage for one of its greatest triumphs—the mobilization of a broad international coalition to defeat Iraq and restore Kuwait's independence. This success, in turn, opened the way for a revived and improved effort to bring Arabs and Israelis to the peace table. Bush and Baker hit on an effective division of roles. Baker was the negotiator, the deal maker, the master of details. Bush held back, but he made the hard decisions on loan guarantees and lent his constant support to his secretary of state. With considerable effort, and at some cost to Bush's domestic position, the administration attained its initial goal. Despite his defeat in November 1992, Bush was successful in winning bipartisan support for his success in bringing Arabs and Israelis to the negotiating table.[42] Clinton promised to pursue the same policy.

Bush and Baker were widely credited with realizing that the end of the cold war and the defeat of Saddam Hussein created a new opportunity for Arab-Israeli peace diplomacy. Not everyone at the time thought a major American initiative was warranted, or could succeed.[43] Baker's persistence in working out the procedures for the Madrid conference also won high marks, as did his tactical skills as a negotiator. When he left to become chief of staff in August 1992, many believed his absence would be felt. And, in fact, little further progress was made over the ensuing several months.

Bush and Baker were not as widely credited for their handling of the loan guarantee issue. Democrats tended to criticize Bush for one-sided pressure against Israel. Yet to link the provision of aid to a curtailment of settlement activity may well have been one of Bush's most important decisions. Without it, Shamir might well have been reelected, which would have cast serious doubt on the chances for the peace process. Bush's critics, most of whom were happy to see Shamir replaced by Rabin, did not seem to notice the contradiction in their own stance.

Where Bush and Baker may fairly be criticized was in their initial caution. Throughout much of 1989 they acted as if the Soviet Union still represented a serious competitor in the Middle East. They also took the comfortable path of trying to work with Shamir on structuring the peace negotiations, seeming to believe he could be cajoled toward more moderate positions. Given the short time available to any president to tackle foreign-policy issues, the loss of most of 1989 on misguided Arab-Israeli initiatives is regrettable. By the time Bush and Baker were back on track, they were already well into their third year, leaving little time to bring their efforts to fruition.

Ultimately, no president can conduct a successful foreign policy, least of all on complex matters such as Arab-Israeli negotiations, without a strong domestic base. By allowing his domestic support to fade from the historic highs of spring 1991 to the abysmal lows of late 1992, Bush ensured that he would not be able to provide the leadership necessary to move beyond the first phase of the Madrid peace talks. Fortunately, the foundations that he and Baker constructed were robust enough to survive the absence of strong American leadership, at least for a while. Because support for the negotiations was fairly strong—in the region, internationally, and in the United States—Clinton did not have to face the challenge of forging a new policy toward the Arab-Israeli conflict. Instead he could work with the structure left to him by Bush and Baker. His challenge would be to add substance to the process, to move toward concrete agreements, and to use time and circumstances to make major steps toward Arab-Israeli peace.

PART SEVEN

Conclusions

CHAPTER SIXTEEN

Challenges Facing
the Clinton Administration

With alarming regularity over the past thirty years, American presidents have found themselves dealing with Middle East crises for which they were poorly prepared. Many, but not all, of these crises have been related to the Arab-Israeli conflict. The June 1967 war, the war of attrition in 1969–70, the Jordan crisis of September 1970, the October 1973 war, the Iranian revolution in 1978–79, the Iran-Iraq war from 1980 to 1988, the Israeli invasion of Lebanon in 1982–83, the early years of the Palestinian *intifada* in 1987–88, the Iraqi invasion of Kuwait in 1990, and the subsequent war against Saddam Hussein in 1991 were enormous challenges for American foreign policy. Each evoked serious debate in Washington over the proper course of action. Each seemed to threaten some important American interest in the region. Each, to some extent, caught Washington by surprise.

The administration of Bill Clinton is in the enviable position of dealing with an ongoing Arab-Israeli peace negotiation. Since October 1991 the parties to the conflict have been in broad agreement on procedures for peace talks. What has been needed, besides direct negotiations, has been an effective mediator who can steer the negotiating teams toward realistic agreements, engage with political decisionmakers to extract command decisions, and offer both reassurance and pressure when necessary. James Baker showed what could be accomplished by such mediation in organizing the Madrid conference, but during much of the 1992 election year he and President Bush were unable to move the negotiations forward. For Clinton this means there will be less need for policy innovation than in the past and more need for effective follow-through.

THE BALANCE SHEET

The American record of managing Arab-Israeli crises and their aftermaths is mixed. On the whole, the United States has done best when it has tried hardest. From 1968 onward, successive administrations have tried to lay the foundations for peace between Israel and Egypt. In 1979 the two countries signed a peace treaty, which they have observed ever since. As its contribution to this historic achievement, the United States, under six presidents, has invested important resources—time, energy, imagination, money, military equipment—to establish a framework for peace, to get the parties involved in a negotiating process, to clinch the formal deal, and to continue to bolster the normalization of relations well after the signing of the peace treaty between the two countries.

Peace between Israel and Egypt did not come cheaply, nor was the path smooth. Several wars were fought before serious negotiations began in 1974. The bilateral peace between Israel and its most powerful Arab neighbor left many other issues unresolved. It also probably exacerbated the problems of Lebanon and initially made the Israeli-Palestinian relationship even more intractable than it had been. But the Israeli-Egyptian peace also changed the strategic picture of the region, provided something of a model for negotiations on other fronts, bolstered American influence, and ultimately helped to persuade other Arabs that diplomacy offered a better course for redressing grievances than military threats.

For the United States the economic cost of Israeli-Egyptian peace has been substantial. Since the peace treaty was signed, Congress has allocated more than $5 billion a year to the two countries. In special circumstances, additional sums have been offered. Of this total, more than half has gone for the purchase of American military equipment. Since 1985 almost all aid has been on a grant basis. In 1990 Congress even took the unusual step of agreeing to write off nearly $7 billion of Egypt's military debt from earlier years. And Congress has shown a willingness to support up to $10 billion in loan guarantees to Israel to assist with housing and immigrant absorption. Suffice it to say that no other countries in the Middle East, or anywhere else for that matter, even come close to receiving such openhanded assistance.

Apart from the important achievement of peace between Israel and Egypt, the American record is less impressive. The most promising step has been the agreement in 1991 among almost all the parties to the Arab-Israeli conflict to a formula for negotiations. Even optimists assume that the negotiations will be long and difficult, but at least procedural hurdles have been successfully overcome. Substantive agreements, however, are not yet in sight. Still, the Madrid conference and its aftermath deserve to be considered a partial success.

On the other side of the ledger are the failures and fiascoes of American Middle East policy. Some have entered the popular jargon of politics—"Irangate," for the misguided attempt to trade arms for hostages in the mid-1980s, and more recently "Iraqgate," for the policy of trying to accommodate Saddam Hussein before his invasion of Kuwait in August 1990. No simple phrase encapsulates the multiple disasters of American policy in Lebanon during the early 1980s, but the bombs that blew up the American embassy in Beirut and the Marine barracks in 1983 left graphic and tragic reminders that American failures in the Middle East can come with a heavy price in American lives. More Americans were killed in Lebanon in 1983 than in the massive war against Iraq in 1991. If one adds the prolonged agony of American hostages held in Iran and in Lebanon to the costs of failed policies, the tally is even higher.

PROTECTING NATIONAL INTERESTS

Still, for all the shortcomings of American policy in the Middle East generally, and toward the Arab-Israeli conflict in particular, American interests in the Middle East have fared surprisingly well. The great fear of Soviet dominance in the region never materialized, nor did the possibility of direct military confrontation between the two nuclear superpowers. Despite images of a "Middle East tinderbox," the region did not play the part of the Balkans earlier in the century in igniting a global conflagration. Regional conflicts, on the whole, remained confined to the region. Nuclear weapons, though present, remained in the background. Terrorism, though a persistent threat, never succeeded in changing the course of events in fundamental ways. Revolution, though often talked about, took place only in Iran. Elsewhere the state system has proved to be remarkably resilient, despite its seeming artificiality.

With respect to oil, American interests have not gone unscathed, but part of the blame must be assigned to shortsighted policies on the home front. Disruptions of oil supplies in the Middle East were bound to have some impact on price, but the exaggerated effect of the 1973–74 and 1978–79 cutbacks was in part due to flawed domestic policies and the failure to purchase adequate insurance in the form of a strategic petroleum reserve. During the 1980s and early 1990s interruptions of oil supplies from the Middle East also occurred in conjunction with Gulf crises, but better policies were in place and the impact was less. Yet, whatever the reason, the United States and the rest of the world paid an extraordinarily high price in the 1970s and early 1980s as a result of Middle East oil-supply disruptions. The recessions of the 1970s and early 1980s were directly related to the higher costs of energy.

Finally, as regards the third main American interest, Israel's security has greatly increased in the post-1967 era. By the early 1990s Israel was more secure than at any previous time in its history. More Arabs were reconciled to the idea of a Jewish state in at least a part of historic Palestine than ever before. Many Arab states were on speaking terms with Israel for the first time. And new immigrants from the former Soviet Union held out the promise of a renewal of social and economic vitality into the next century. Economic and social problems existed, but the survival of the state seemed more assured than one could have imagined thirty years earlier.

Despite this relatively positive overview of how American interests have fared in the Middle East since 1967, one should not conclude that all is well. The region remains volatile; most regimes have little mass support; opposition movements that reject the present order are widespread and are often intensely anti-American. Economic development is stalled, except in the oil sheikhdoms, and population growth puts an almost unmanageable burden on weak governments.

The Arab-Israeli conflict still generates strong passions, and the achievements of the past could be lost if, for example, the regime in Egypt changed suddenly, if radical Islamic movements gained ground, or if Israeli extremists tried to achieve their goals by force. The region is still overarmed; weapons of mass destruction are already in the arsenals of many states in the region, along with surface-to-surface missiles. Although the danger of superpower confrontation is now gone, the risk of war is still present, and in such a war American interests could still be threatened. To reconcile the American commitment to a secure Israel with the long-term need for Middle East oil, the Clinton administration will no doubt continue to see the peace process as an important part of its broader regional policy.

INGREDIENTS OF SUCCESS

To deal effectively with these challenges in the Middle East in years to come, the Clinton administration would do well to learn from the past record of success and failure. For policies to produce desirable results—such as in the drafting of UN Resolution 242 in 1967, the 1974–75 disengagement talks, the Camp David and peace treaty negotiations in 1978–79, and the diplomacy leading to the Madrid conference in 1991—certain conditions must be met.

There must be a realistic appraisal of the regional situation. To influence governments in the Middle East, politicians in Washington must be keenly aware of what is taking place there. Sustained dialogue with the parties to the conflict is the best way to develop the necessary sensitivity to the real political constraints. Dealing with the Middle East parties through intermediaries does not work well. Wishful thinking, ideological blinders, and indifference are the enemies of success in trying to take the measure of the parties to the Arab-Israeli conflict. As with medicine, correct diagnosis is the key to effective prescription.

The president and his top advisers must be involved and must work in harmony. Unless the prestige and power of the White House are clearly behind American policy initiatives, leaders in the Middle East will not take them seriously. This is one reason that special envoys from Washington rarely succeed. Bureaucratic rivalries and presidential disengagement will also weaken the credibility of any U.S. policy. When policies have succeeded, Nixon and Kissinger, Carter and Vance, Bush and Baker were seen to be working closely together. Failures are associated with the Kissinger-Rogers rivalry, the Brzezinski-Vance disagreement over Iran in 1978, and the long-running Shultz-Weinberger arguments over policy toward Lebanon and arms to Arab countries. In these latter cases presidents who were ambivalent or uninterested allowed those quarrels to undermine their policies. Had they cared enough, however, each president had the power to end these feuds. One of the few unquestioned powers of a president is to fire any top adviser who does not meet his standards. Bureaucratic rivalries are commonplace, but presidents do not have to put up with them indefinitely.

The domestic basis of support for American policy in the region must be constantly developed. Presidents must work with Congress and must explain their purposes to the American public, especially if the costs of the policy are likely to be substantial. Presidents who are unskillful in managing the domestic politics of foreign policy will undermine their own purposes. The ability to mobilize support seems to be very much tied to context: Lyndon Johnson had broad backing for his Middle East policy in 1967, while he was losing support for his Vietnam policy; Richard Nixon won praise for his foreign policy, while losing his base over Watergate; Jimmy Carter succeeded in his Arab-Israeli diplomacy, while simultaneously losing ground over Iran and the hostage crisis; Ronald Reagan was universally praised for his September 1, 1982, speech on the Middle East, and universally criticized for the Iran-Contra fiasco; George Bush won domestic laurels in the war against Iraq, only to see his standing in the polls drop within a matter of months. The lesson must surely be that high-level attention to the home front is a constant preoccupation. No president can assume that Congress and public opinion will back him for long. At the same time policy toward the Arab-Israeli conflict cannot simply reflect the pro-Israeli tone of domestic politics without losing credibility with the Arab parties to the conflict. The president should seek a domestically sustainable policy of evenhandedness, even if it will always be somewhat precarious unless the peace process is moving forward.

Success as a mediator requires a feeling both for process—the procedures for bringing the parties to the negotiations—and for substance. Issues rarely arise that are devoid of substantive implications. The questions of who comes to the negotiating table, the structure of the agenda, and the symbols associated with the peace process are all likely to convey powerful substantive messages to the parties in the Middle East. The United States cannot advance the search for peace between Israel and the Arabs by simply playing the role of mailman; nor can it design a blueprint and impose it on reluctant parties. In between these extremes lies the proper role for the United States—catalyst, energizer, friend, nag, technician, architect. Some of each of these roles has been necessary whenever the United States has succeeded in bridging the gaps between Arabs and Israelis. Carrots and sticks must both be used, sometimes together, to influence reluctant parties. Public acrimony is usually counterproductive, although a display of presidential temper is sometimes useful to underscore serious intent. Threats to abandon the peace process are effective only with the weakest parties, and often lack credibility in any case.

There must be a substantial investment in quiet diplomacy, in "prenegotiation" exploration of the terrain, before deals can be cut. Formal settings, conferences, and direct negotiations are important for symbolic purposes, but most progress is made in secret talks with the top leadership in the region. Presidential letters, memoranda of understandings, and private commitments will all be part of the process of nudging parties toward agreement. Leaks of sensitive information and offhand remarks can complicate delicate negotiations. Tight discipline is needed. Words have consequences. Not everything can be discussed in public, although excessive secrecy can also backfire. Each participant in the negotiating process need not be told exactly the same thing, but any deliberate deception will prove counterproductive. One should assume that much of what one says will eventually be leaked by someone. All the more reason to avoid duplicity.

Pressure sometimes succeeds, but it must be skillfully exerted. Part of the conventional wisdom about U.S.-Israeli relations is that pressure on Israeli governments is bound to backfire. But the record suggests a much more complex reality. True, pressures do not always produce desired results and may sometimes stiffen resistance. Pressure on Israel can also produce domestic controversy and adverse congressional reactions. But at one time or another, each president has tried to persuade Israel to take some action by implying that refusal would be costly. In a surprising number of instances, such efforts at influence have succeeded, often with an added sweetener of rewards for compliance. The same has been true of dealings with Arab parties. To succeed in influencing parties to the Arab-Israeli conflict, the United States must ask for feasible concessions, while wielding both carrots and sticks as incentives.

Timing is crucial for successful negotiations. The American political calendar does not allow much time for launching initiatives and seeing them through to completion. Also, the parties in the region may not be ready to move when the politicians in Washington are. One reason crises are so often followed by initiatives is that crises tend to convince all parties to agree that something new must be tried. Those who argue for a passive stance, in the belief that time will work in favor of accommodation, have the burden of evidence against them. The deliberate policy of doing nothing in the period 1970–73 led to a major war; the stalemate of the 1980s led to the *intifada* and may have helped create the atmosphere in the Arab world that led Saddam Hussein to believe he could get away with his invasion of Kuwait. To say that each of these crises was followed by peace initiatives is hardly a recommendation for deliberately provoking crises. Policy that reacts only to crises is extremely dangerous. Carter demonstrated in 1977 that it was not necessary to wait for an explosion before taking an initiative. Too often, however, initiatives have come only in the aftermath of wars or violence. Clinton will have the opportunity to tackle the Arab-Israeli conflict without the prod of an imminent crisis, but rather at a moment of some expectancy that positive results can be achieved through negotiations. Only Carter among recent presidents inherited such a propitious moment.

CHANGING OF THE GUARD

These guidelines may seem noncontroversial, but translating them into practice proves to be extremely difficult. One reason is the relatively rapid turnover in top positions in the U.S. government. Little experience is accumulated. Continuity is rare. Even the record of past commitments is often hard to discover after a new administration takes over.

Since 1967 seven presidents have occupied the Oval Office. Only Reagan managed to complete two full terms. These seven presidents appointed ten secretaries of state, nine directors of central intelligence, eleven secretaries of defense, and twelve national security advisers. During this same period nine different assistant secretaries for Near Eastern and South Asian Affairs have served, as have nine directors of the Middle East office of the National Security Council. On average, then, the top personnel in charge of Middle East policy changes about every three or four years. Ambassadors to key Middle East countries are rotated with about the same frequency.

The turnover in high places in Washington contrasts starkly with the amazing continuity sometimes found in the Middle East. Yitzhak Rabin was chief of staff in Israel during the 1967 war, ambassador to Washington during the Jordan crisis, prime minister during the second disengagement negotiations, defense minister during the *intifada*, and again prime minister in 1992. As a result, he is likely to know more about the history of American involvement in Arab-Israeli diplomacy than most American diplomats. Similarly, Syria's Hafiz al-Asad has ruled without interruption as president since 1970 and was already defense minister in 1967. He also knows intimately the dossier of recent peace diplomacy, most of which he has opposed and often helped to undermine. King Hussein has been acquainted with every American president since Eisenhower and often seems to despair that every few years he must invest all over again in winning the trust of a new team in Washington. Even the indomitable Yasir Arafat has managed to stay on top of the PLO since 1969. He has outlasted most American peace initiatives.

INITIAL PREDISPOSITIONS

If Americans cannot compete with Middle Easterners in the length of their tenure, the depth of their direct knowledge of the issues, and their study of history, where can they get their bearings? This book places emphasis on two main sources: the predispositions that policymakers bring with them to office, and the views that they acquire on the job. Because of the short tenure in high positions, American policymaking reflects an almost continual process of bringing in new people and educating them in the realities of the Middle East (and the ways of Washington concerning the Middle East). Formal positions on substantive issues change relatively little, but policies, representing tactical judgments, change quite often.

Predispositions relevant to Arab-Israeli diplomacy come in many forms, but for analytical purposes they can be grouped into three clusters. Do the president and his team tend to see Arab-Israeli issues in their regional context or in a broader global context? Are they inclined to attach a high priority to Arab-Israeli issues, or would they prefer to leave these issues on the back burner? Are their sympathies primarily with Israel, or are they relatively evenhanded in their views? These predispositions may be related to other views that have to do with the state of U.S.-Soviet relations (for earlier presidents), the possibility of finding a solution to age-old disputes, and the place of domestic politics in the management of Arab-Israeli diplomacy. But context, salience, and sympathies are a good starting point for characterizing the views of the presidential team that deals with Arab-Israeli issues.

Nixon and Reagan were clearly globalists in their approach to the Middle East. The contest with Moscow was never far from their thoughts. Carter was much more of a regionalist. Bush, Johnson, and Ford were somewhere in between. Clinton is likely to see the region in regional terms, but against the backdrop of global changes in the world economy and the process of democratization.

For Johnson and Reagan the Middle East was rarely a top priority, except in moments of crisis. Nixon tended to see the Middle East as explosive but was persuaded by Kissinger not to be too eager to push for a settlement. After the October 1973 war Nixon, Ford, and Carter were all prepared to deal with the Arab-Israeli issue as a matter of top priority, as was Bush after the war against Iraq. Clinton is unlikely to treat the Arab-Israeli issue as his top priority, but it will not be far from the most important cluster of issues on his foreign-policy agenda.

Johnson and Reagan were no doubt the most pro-Israeli presidents. Nixon, Ford, Carter, and Bush seemed more evenhanded. Among secretaries of state, Henry Kissinger, Alexander Haig, and George Shultz were strong supporters of Israel as an important ally, whereas Dean Rusk, William Rogers, Cyrus Vance, and James Baker took a more evenhanded stance.

If these characterizations of initial predispositions are fairly accurate, they nonetheless cannot convey a full sense of the views of these key decisionmakers. Over time, nuances are added, more information is absorbed, personal relations develop, commitments are made, and lessons are drawn that modify these initial views. Shultz, for example, began his tenure as secretary of state with a reputation for being evenhanded, but later he was seen by the Israelis as their closest friend. And yet it was also Shultz who, in the last weeks of his reign, opened the dialogue with the PLO.

The easiest of these predispositions to change is the sense of priority one brings to the analysis of the Arab-Israeli situation. When tensions rise, or violence erupts, it is quite easy for presidents and secretaries of state to turn their attention to the Arab-Israeli conflict. Nixon and Kissinger immediately changed their assessment of the priority due to the Arab-Israeli dispute when war broke out on October 6, 1973. Alternatively, if the costs of activism seem too great, a president can try to disengage from Arab-Israeli diplomacy, as Carter did in mid-1979.

It seems to be somewhat harder for leaders to shift from a globalist to a regionalist perspective, or vice versa. Such views tend to be fairly well established as part of an overall approach to foreign policy. And yet Kissinger, the quintessential globalist, found himself avidly absorbing information about Middle East politics once he decided to engage in sustained negotiations with the parties to the conflict. Similarly, Bush was initially fairly hard line in dealing with the Soviet Union in the Middle East, but suddenly the Soviet Union collapsed and Bush and Baker found a regionalist perspective quite congenial. Only Carter moved somewhat in the opposite direction. After the Iranian revolution and the Soviet invasion of Afghanistan in 1979, and in the midst of his own reelection campaign, Carter adopted a tough anti-Soviet line. He termed Israel a strategic asset in the struggle to contain Soviet influence, said that he opposed a Palestinian state because it would be an outpost of Soviet influence, and generally adopted a position that was closer to that of Ronald Reagan than to his own earlier stance.

Sympathies seem to change least of all. Pro-Israeli officials do not stop sympathizing with Israel, but they may come to appreciate the need to cultivate relations with Arab leaders as well. This seems to have been true of Reagan, who never wavered in his support for Israel, but who also sold AWACS aircraft to Saudi Arabia, tilted toward Iraq, and authorized the opening of a dialogue with the PLO. Nixon, who seemed to have little emotional affinity for the Jewish state, nonetheless adopted policies, in large measure because of his global outlook, that were very pro-Israeli. Bush, who developed a reputation for being anti-Israeli, endorsed an Israeli proposal for Palestinian elections; crushed Iraq, Israel's principal Arab foe; sidelined the PLO from the official negotiations; continued economic and military support for Israel at all-time levels despite the end of the cold war; and found no trouble in patching up quarrels with Israel once Shamir had been replaced as prime minister by Rabin.

In short, no president and no secretary of state has remained narrowly bound by initial sympathies. All have come to realize that effective mediation requires an ability to deal with leaders on both sides of the conflict, whatever one's personal preferences might be. Thus, although such preferences resist the kind of change that other views may undergo, they also seem least important in the setting of policy. It will long be debated by serious Israelis, for example, whether the ostensibly pro-Israeli Kissinger and Reagan did more for Israel's long-term security than Carter and Bush did.

ON-THE-JOB TRAINING

In learning how to deal with the Middle East, American officials must assess past performance and draw lessons about what has worked and what has failed. On the whole, Americans agree on the successful cases: the adoption of UN Resolution 242; the Egyptian and Syrian disengagement agreements; Camp David and the Egyptian-Israeli peace treaty; and the Madrid conference and its aftermath. The problem with these successes is that they cannot easily be replicated. The lessons to be learned tend to be general ones, not specifically related to the context of existing problems. And by their nature, successes change the environment, leaving new problems in their wake.

Failures are another matter. They leave strong impressions about what not to do. Once a tactic is judged to have failed in one context, it will be hard to argue that it should be tried again in another. In the annals of Arab-Israeli diplomacy it is widely believed that the Rogers Plan of 1969 was a mistake; that the U.S.-Soviet joint communiqué of October 1, 1977, calling for a resumption of the Geneva conference was an error; that the May 17, 1983, agreement between Lebanon and Israel was fatally flawed; and that the deployment of U.S. forces to Lebanon in 1982 should never be repeated. No one has made a career in Washington in recent years by trying to argue that the Rogers Plan had some positive elements that eventually led to the Egyptian-Israeli peace treaty, or that it failed because it was undercut from within the Nixon administration as much as for any other reason. Few have questioned that the October 1, 1977, communiqué was misguided, and for years the standard rebuff to anyone suggesting that the Soviet Union should be involved in Middle East diplomacy was the example of the fate of that effort.

Other Middle East cases are harder to judge. Was the Jordan crisis a success or failure? Some of both, one could contend. King Hussein was strengthened; allies of the Soviet Union were checked; the crisis was contained. But the lessons drawn were the source of subsequent problems. Complacency set in; confidence grew in Israeli military prowess as the key to stability; and Arab frustrations were ignored. The "success" in handling the Jordan crisis led, in part, to the "failure" to anticipate the October 1973 war. But that "failure" in turn set the stage for the "success" of the disengagement talks. In brief, lessons of history are invariably drawn, but involve highly subjective judgments. Still, they serve as powerful guidelines in intrabureaucratic discussions.

Accumulated experience with Middle East diplomacy does not suggest a single correct method for pursuing the peace process. Each president has had a somewhat distinctive style. Johnson limited himself to spelling out the general principles for a peace settlement, while insisting that Israel should be allowed to hold captured Arab lands as bargaining leverage to achieve peace. The logic of that approach has rarely been questioned by his successors. Nixon, influenced by Kissinger, initially opted for a policy of confronting the Soviets in the region before tackling the Arab-Israeli conflict. Then, after the 1973 war, Nixon and Kissinger developed the technique of step-by-step shuttle diplomacy. Carter began with a comprehensive design but was obliged to scale back to a more modest, through still impressive, goal of peace on one front. Reagan and Haig preached a doctrine of strategic consensus, which had few regional supporters; then in 1982 Reagan gave a speech that spelled out as clearly as has ever been done what the United States would support in an Arab-Israeli settlement. The speech was not connected to a strategy, and the Reagan years saw little real progress in peacemaking, but the vision spelled out in that speech has informed policymaking ever since. Finally, Bush and Baker, after one false start, perfected the art of the deal, bringing all the parties to accept the architecture of a negotiating process. On the whole, this is an impressive record, to which Clinton will almost certainly be tempted to add his own contribution.

SUBSTANTIVE BUILDING BLOCKS

Over time presidents and their advisers have spoken less about the substance of an Arab-Israeli agreement and more about process. This "procedural bias" stems from a belief that big plans do not work, that they are too controversial, that they become targets of opposition rather than frameworks for agreement. Yet many of the most impressive monuments of American peacemaking in the Middle East are precisely sketches of both the content of peace and the process for achieving it. UN Resolution 242, which is still seen as a foundation for any Arab-Israeli peace, is essentially a statement of the main substantive trade-off that will have to be negotiated: the withdrawal of Israeli forces from territory occupied in 1967 in return for recognition, peace, and security arrangements for Israel. If 242 had flaws, they were primarily the total disregard of the Palestinians (a substantive issue that was dealt with through procedural arrangements in later years) and the feeble mechanism designed to promote peace (a UN-designated envoy without any powers). Besides providing the basis for the Egyptian-Israeli peace, UN Resolution 242 and its "land for peace" trade-off will almost certainly be at the core of a future Syrian-Israeli agreement.

The Camp David Accords went further than Resolution 242 in addressing the Palestinian issue. Their chief innovation was to call for an interim agreement between Israel and the Palestinians based on the concept of self-government or autonomy. The reason for this approach was that neither Israelis nor Palestinians seemed able to agree on more than such an interim step. The architects of Camp David also hoped that the experience of the "transitional" period would make the issues of a final settlement more tractable. Although Camp David is not explicitly the agreed basis for the negotiations between Israel and the Palestinians, the central idea of a two-stage negotiation, starting with interim self-government for the Palestinians, has been accepted by all the parties to the Madrid conference.

Reagan's substantive legacy was his elaboration on the missing part of Camp David—namely, what lay beyond the transitional period. Without going into great detail, Reagan said that the United States would not support Israeli annexation of the West Bank and Gaza or a fully independent Palestinian state. Instead the United States would favor some form of association between the occupied territories and Jordan. In one way or another, that is likely to be the outline of any future Israeli-Palestinian-Jordanian peace agreement.

The main substantive contribution of the Bush administration did not come in the form of plans or speeches. In the course of organizing the Madrid conference, Bush and Baker began to deal with the Palestinians as a full partner in the negotiations. This ostensibly procedural step had substantive implications, although these remain to be elaborated in the course of negotiations. Bush also returned to the emphasis on freezing Israeli settlement activity during the negotiating process. Carter had tried and failed to win this point. Bush, wielding the big stick of $10 billion in loan guarantees, was taken more seriously. Indeed, one of Bush's major contributions to the peace process was the boost he gave to the unseating of the ideologically rigid Yitzhak Shamir and his replacement by the more pragmatic Yitzhak Rabin. For the first time since 1977, Israel was governed by a cabinet committed to UN Resolution 242 in its original meaning—the exchange of land for peace, in conditions of security and mutual recognition, on all fronts of the conflict. Even Bill Clinton noted that Rabin's election was the most important contribution to the peace process in the year following the Madrid conference, although he gave George Bush no credit for pushing Shamir to the sidelines.[1]

FUTURE PROSPECTS

By 1992 the United States had succeeded in launching a new round of negotiations, more promising in architectural design and in scope than any before. The general framework for negotiations could be distilled from previous positions—mainly 242 and Camp David—but the road map to peace was sketchy at best.

Almost certainly, the United States will be called on to help elaborate the contents of future peace agreements if the negotiations are to succeed. Nothing in the historical record suggests that the parties will reach agreement if left alone in direct negotiations.

In many ways the American role in the future should be easier to play than in the past. The Soviet Union as a rival and potential spoiler is no more. The globalist bias that often adversely affected American policy in the Middle East has lost its rationale. With it has gone the notion that Israel is a strategic ally of such importance that it must be supported at all costs.[2] Public backing for Israel remains high, but the White House is under little pressure to offer Israel a blank check. Public opinion, if not Congress, is more prone than ever to support an evenhanded stance toward the Arab-Israeli conflict. Such an atmosphere provides a degree of tactical flexibility for a president seeking to find common ground between Arabs and Israelis.

Perhaps most encouraging for the peace process is the evidence that many Israelis and many Arabs are tired of the conflict and are finally ready for a historic compromise. Without such sentiment in the region, the United States can do little to promote peace. The Israeli elections in 1992 brought to power a government committed to swift movement in the negotiations, in contrast to the go-slow approach of the Shamir government.

The record of the peace process since 1967 shows that progress is not incremental or continuous. More frequently, long periods of stalemate have been succeeded by bursts of activity that have produced substantial changes in the nature of the Arab-Israeli conflict. Then the parties seem to need some time to absorb the results, to ready themselves for another major move, to build support on the domestic front.

One can credibly argue that the 1980s represented an unusually long lull in the peace process and that the stage is set in the early 1990s for significant breakthroughs. One possibility would be moves toward a Syrian-Israeli treaty, based on full peace and recognition for Israel, extensive security arrangements to reduce the chance of surprise attack, and Israeli recognition of Syrian sovereignty on the Golan Heights. All these principles could be implemented over a period of years.

On the Israeli-Palestinian front the prospects for an overall agreement are less promising. But some form of interim agreement, which would allow Palestinians extensive authority to govern themselves in the West Bank and Gaza, while Israel retained control over security, seems feasible. Eventually the very complex problem of Israeli settlements and the status of East Jerusalem will have to be confronted, but they may be finessed in the interim stage by common consent. And if progress is made on the Syrian and Palestinian negotiating fronts, the Lebanese and Jordanians will not be far behind.

For the peace process to move ahead in these uniquely hopeful circumstances, American leadership will be needed. That prospect is somewhat challenged by a revival of isolationist sentiment in the United States. This attitude affects Middle East policy less than other foreign-policy issue areas, but it places a limit on any initiative that is likely to require substantial resources. As a result, the United States, while still playing the key mediating role, will have to find partners who can help underwrite steps toward peace, toward regional development, and toward arms control.

As the peace process moves along, the United States will also be confronting other, related challenges in the Middle East. How should the next president deal with assertive Islamic movements? What is the place for democracy in this part of the world? Can economic development be accelerated, as in east Asia, as a complement to peacemaking and democratization? Can arms control make headway in a region where conflicts are so endemic? And can anything be done to prevent the proliferation of weapons of mass destruction in the region? All these new concerns will demand attention alongside the traditional peace process agenda. And even that agenda will have to address in creative ways the problems of regional security, confederal arrangements, the linkage between interim steps and subsequent stages of negotiations, and the future of Jerusalem, issues that have been ignored for too long.

Time is of the essence, not so much because peace must be achieved suddenly or not at all. Rather, the process is likely to take time, which means that political leaders in the region must be able to show results early and often if they are to retain the necessary support. This is especially true in Israel, where opinion is still deeply divided, and among the Palestinians, where public sentiment plays a larger part than in most Arab regimes. A prolonged stalemate in the peace process will frustrate moderates on both sides of the conflict, lead to public disinterest in the United States, and will set the stage for future crises in a radicalized Middle East whose oil resources will be increasingly important for the industrialized West.

Thus the peace process, with an increasing emphasis on the substantive elements of future peace agreements, is likely to be a priority for President Clinton and his foreign-policy team. The record suggests that Clinton's own predispositions will matter in the shaping of policy toward the Arab-Israeli conflict, even though by now there is a fairly strong consensus on the peace process and its rationale. Still, in those moments when judgment is called for, when crises clarify choices, and when trade-offs must be made, the person occupying the Oval Office makes a difference.

If presidents play their parts well, they can help advance the peace process. If they falter, they risk jeopardizing American interests. For better or worse, they will not be allowed to ignore the region for long. Their understanding of the basic issues of the Arab-Israeli conflict and their ability to learn from experience will be the keys to whether presidents become statesmen. If they do, they stand a good chance of contributing to the long-sought goal of Arab-Israeli peace.

PART EIGHT

Appendixes

APPENDIX A

United Nations Resolutions 242 and 338

The Security Council,

Expressing its continuing concern with the grave situation in the Middle East,

Emphasizing the inadmissibility of the acquisition of territory by war and the need to work for a just and lasting peace in which every State in the area can live in security,

Emphasizing further that all Member States in their acceptance of the Charter of the United Nations have undertaken a commitment to act in accordance with Article 2 of the Charter,

1. *Affirms* that the fulfillment of Charter principles requires the establishment of a just and lasting peace in the Middle East which should include the application of both the following principles:

    (i) Withdrawal of Israeli armed forces from territories occupied in the recent conflict;

    (ii) Termination of all claims or states of belligerency and respect for and acknowledgement of the sovereignty, territorial integrity and political independence of every State in the area and their right to live in peace within secure and recognized boundaries free from threats or acts of force;

2. *Affirms further* the necessity

    (a) For guaranteeing freedom of navigation through international waterways in the area;

    (b) For achieving a just settlement of the refugee problem;

    (c) For guaranteeing the territorial inviolability and political independence of every State in the area, through measures including the establishment of demilitarized zones;

3. *Requests* the Secretary-General to designate a Special Representative to proceed to the Middle East to establish and maintain contacts with the

States concerned in order to promote agreement and assist efforts to achieve a peaceful and accepted settlement in accordance with the provisions and principles of this resolution;

4. *Requests* the Secretary-General to report to the Security Council on the progress of the efforts of the Special Representative as soon as possible.

UN SECURITY COUNCIL RESOLUTION 338, OCTOBER 22, 1973

The Security Council

1. *Calls upon* all parties to the present fighting to cease all firing and terminate all military activity immediately, no later than 12 hours after the moment of the adoption of this decision, in the positions they now occupy;

2. *Calls upon* the parties concerned to start immediately after the cease-fire the implementation of Security Council Resolution 242 (1967) in all of its parts;

3. *Decides* that, immediately and concurrently with the cease-fire, negotiations start between the parties concerned under appropriate auspices aimed at establishing a just and durable peace in the Middle East.

APPENDIX B

Joint U.S.-USSR Working Paper, Fundamental Principles (The Rogers Plan), October 28, 1969

Israel and the UAR,

In consideration of their obligations under the Charter of the United Nations,

Confirming their obligations under Security Council Resolution 242 of November 22, 1967 and expressing their readiness to implement it in good faith in all of its provisions,

Recognizing the inadmissibility of the acquisition of territory by means of war,

Recognizing also the need to establish a just and lasting peace in the Middle East under the terms of which each State in this area can live in security,

Agree that their representatives under the auspices of Ambassador Jarring will follow the procedures the parties utilized at Rhodes in 1949 to work out without delay, starting on the basis of the following provisions, a final and reciprocally binding accord on ways of implementing Security Council Resolution 242 of November 22, 1967 to establish a just and lasting peace.

Point 1

The parties, in reaching a final accord (contained in a final document or documents) on a package settlement on the basis of these Fundamental Principles, would determine a timetable and procedures for withdrawal of Israeli armed forces from UAR territory occupied during the conflict of 1967 to boundaries to be delineated in accordance with Point 3 as well as an agreed plan for interrelated fulfillment of all other provisions of Security Council Resolution 242.

Point 2

The state of war and belligerency between Israel and the UAR would be terminated and a formal state of peace would be established between them, and both parties would refrain from acts inconsistent with the state of peace and the cessation of the state of war.

In particular:

1. No aggressive action by the armed and other forces—land, sea, or air—of either party would be undertaken or threatened against the people or the armed forces of the other.

2. Both parties would undertake to do all in their power to ensure that acts of hostility and belligerency whether by government agencies, personnel, or private persons or organizations will not originate from and are not committed from within their respective territory.

3. Both parties would refrain from intervening directly or indirectly in each other's domestic affairs for any political, economic, or other reasons.

4. Both parties would confirm that in their relations with each other, they will be guided by the principles contained in Article 2, paragraphs 3 and 4 of the UN Charter.

Point 3

The parties would agree on the location of the secure and recognized boundary between them, which would be shown on a map or maps approved by the parties which would become part of the final accord. In the context of peace, including the *inter alia* agreement between the parties on the establishment of demilitarized zones, on practical security arrangements in the Sharm al-Shaykh area for guaranteeing freedom of navigation through the Strait of Tiran, and on practical security arrangements and final disposition of Gaza, the former international boundary between Egypt and the mandated territory of Palestine would become the secure and recognized boundary between Israel and the UAR.

Point 4

For the purpose of ensuring the territorial inviolability of the parties and guaranteeing the security of the recognized boundary, the parties, following the procedures set forth in the last preambular paragraph of this document, would work out an agreement on:

(a) Zones to be demilitarized and procedures of ensuring their demilitarization;

(b) Practical security arrangements in the Sharm al-Shaykh area to assure freedom of navigation through the Strait of Tiran; and

(c) Practical security arrangements for and final disposition of Gaza.

Point 5

The parties would agree and the Security Council would reaffirm:

(a) That the Strait of Tiran is an international waterway; and

(b) That the principle of free navigation for vessels of all countries, including, Israel, applies to the Strait of Tiran and the Gulf of Aqaba.

Point 6

The UAR would affirm that, in its exercise of sovereignty over the Suez Canal, the ships of all nations, including Israel, will have the right of freedom of navigation without discrimination or interference.

Point 7

The parties would agree to abide by the terms of a just settlement of the refugee problem as agreed upon in the final accord between Jordan and Israel, and to participate as Ambassador Jarring may deem desirable in working out the terms of said settlement.

Point 8

The UAR and Israel would mutually agree to respect and acknowledge each other's sovereignty, territorial integrity, inviolability and political independence and each other's right to live in peace within secure and recognized borders free from threats or acts of force.

Point 9

The final accord would be recorded in a document which is to be signed by the parties and immediately deposited with the UN. After the parties have deposited such a document, the Secretary General of the UN would be requested by the parties immediately to inform the Security Council and all UN Member States to that effect.

In the implementation of the final accord, it would be understood by the parties that their respective obligations would be reciprocal and interdependent. The final accord would provide that a material breach of that accord by one of the parties shall entitle the other to invoke the breach as a ground for suspending its performance in whole or in part until the breach shall be cured. From the moment of deposit, the document would become binding on the parties and irrevocable, and implementation and observance by the parties of the provisions of the accord would begin.

Point 10

Both parties would agree that the final accord, including the map or maps delineating the final boundaries, would be submitted to the Security Council for its endorsement.

* * *

It would be understood that the accord between the UAR and Israel would be paralleled by an accord between Jordan and Israel, which would include agreement on a just solution of the refugee problem. Implementation of both accords would begin only after agreement had been achieved on the entire package.

It would also be understood that France, the United Kingdom, the United States and the Union of Soviet Socialist Republics would submit and support an appropriate Security Council resolution and pledge that they would concert their future efforts to help the parties abide by all of the provisions of the final accord or accords.

APPENDIX C

Letter from President Ford to Prime Minister Rabin, September 1, 1975

SECRET

His Excellency
Yitzhak Rabin
Prime Minister of Israel

Dear Mr. Prime Minister:

I wish to inform you that the U.S. recognizes that the Israeli-Egyptian Interim Agreement entailing withdrawal from vital areas in the Sinai constitutes an act of great significance on Israel's part in the pursuit of final peace and imposes additional heavy military and economic burdens on Israel.

I want to assure you that the U.S. will make every effort to be fully responsive within the limits of its resources and Congressional authorization and appropriation on an ongoing and long-term basis to Israel's military equipment and other defense requirements as well as to Israel's economic aid needs, all of this based on the requests submitted by Israel, joint studies and previous U.S. Presidential undertakings.

Further to those undertakings, it is my resolve to continue to maintain Israel's defensive strength through the supply of advanced types of equipment, such as the F-16 aircraft. The United States Government agrees to an early meeting to undertake a joint study of high technology and sophisticated items, including the Pershing ground-to-ground missiles with conventional warheads, with the view to giving a positive response. The U.S. Administration will submit annually for approval by the U.S. Congress a request for military and economic assistance in order to help meet Israel's economic and military needs. Realizing as I do the importance of the Interim Agreement to the Middle Eastern situation as a whole, the U.S. will make every possible effort to assist in the establishment of

The text comes from Michael Widlanski, ed., *Can Israel Survive a Palestinian State?* (Jerusalem: Institute for Advanced Strategic Political Studies, 1990), pp. 120–21.

conditions in which the Agreement will be observed without being subjected to pressures or deadlines.

In the spirit of the special relationship existing between the United States and Israel and in light of the determination of both sides to avoid a situation in which the U.S. and Israel would pursue divergent courses in peace negotiations, the U.S. will take the position that these are negotiations between the parties. As I indicated to you in our conversation on 12 June 1975, the situation in the aftermath of the Israeli-Egyptian Interim Agreement will be one in which the overall settlement can be pursued in a systematic and deliberate way and does not require the U.S. to put forward an overall proposal of its own in such circumstances. Should the U.S. desire in the future to put forward proposals of its own, it will make every effort to coordinate with Israel its proposals with a view to refraining from putting forth proposals that Israel would consider unsatisfactory.

The U.S. will support the position that an overall settlement with Syria in the framework of a peace agreement must assure Israel's security from attack from the Golan Heights. The U.S. further supports the position that a just and lasting peace, which remains our objective, must be acceptable to both sides. The U.S. has not developed a final position on the borders. Should it do so it will give great weight to Israel's position that any peace agreement with Syria must be predicated on Israel remaining on the Golan Heights. My view in this regard was stated in our conversation of September 13, 1974.

Sincerely,

Gerald R. Ford

APPENDIX D

Joint Communiqué by the Governments of the United States and the Union of Soviet Socialist Republics, October 1, 1977

Having exchanged views regarding the unsafe situation which remains in the Middle East, U.S. Secretary of State Cyrus Vance and Member of the Politbureau of the Central Committee of the CPSU, Minister for Foreign Affairs of the U.S.S.R. A. A. Gromyko have the following statement to make on behalf of their countries, which are cochairmen of the Geneva Peace Conference on the Middle East:

1. Both governments are convinced that vital interests of the peoples of this area, as well as the interests of strengthening peace and international security in general, urgently dictate the necessity of achieving, as soon as possible, a just and lasting settlement of the Arab-Israeli conflict. This settlement should be comprehensive, incorporating all parties concerned and all questions.

The United States and the Soviet Union believe that, within the framework of a comprehensive settlement of the Middle East problem, all specific questions of the settlement should be resolved, including such key issues as withdrawal of Israeli Armed Forces from territories occupied in the 1967 conflict; the resolution of the Palestinian question, including insuring the legitimate rights of the Palestinian people; termination of the state of war and establishment of normal peaceful relations on the basis of mutual recognition of the principles of sovereignty, territorial integrity, and political independence.

The two governments believe that, in addition to such measures for insuring the security of the borders between Israel and the neighboring Arab states as the establishment of demilitarized zones and the agreed stationing in them of U.N. troops or observers, international guarantees of such borders as well as of the observance of the terms of the settlement can also be established should the contracting parties so desire. The

The text comes from "U.S., U.S.S.R. Issue Statement on the Middle East," *Department of State Bulletin*, vol. 77 (November 7, 1977), pp. 639–40. The statement was issued in New York City.

United States and the Soviet Union are ready to participate in these guarantees, subject to their constitutional processes.

2. The United States and the Soviet Union believe that the only right and effective way for achieving a fundamental solution to all aspects of the Middle East problem in its entirety is negotiations within the framework of the Geneva peace conference, specially convened for these purposes, with participation in its work of the representatives of all the parties involved in the conflict including those of the Palestinian people, and legal and contractual formalization of the decisions reached at the conference.

In their capacity as cochairmen of the Geneva conference, the United States and the U.S.S.R. affirm their intention, through joint efforts and in their contacts with the parties concerned, to facilitate in every way the resumption of the work of the conference not later than December 1977. The cochairmen note that there still exist several questions of a procedural and organizational nature which remain to be agreed upon by the participants to the conference.

3. Guided by the goal of achieving a just political settlement in the Middle East and of eliminating the explosive situation in this area of the world, the United States and the U.S.S.R. appeal to all the parties in the conflict to understand the necessity for careful consideration of each other's legitimate rights and interests and to demonstrate mutual readiness to act accordingly.

APPENDIX E

The Camp David Accords, September 17, 1978

<hr>

A FRAMEWORK FOR PEACE IN THE MIDDLE EAST
AGREED AT CAMP DAVID

Muhammad Anwar al-Sadat, President of the Arab Republic of Egypt, and Menachem Begin, Prime Minister of Israel, met with Jimmy Carter, President of the United States of America, at Camp David from September 5 to September 17, 1978, and have agreed on the following framework for peace in the Middle East. They invite other parties to the Arab-Israeli conflict to adhere to it.

Preamble

The search for peace in the Middle East must be guided by the following:

—The agreed basis for a peaceful settlement of the conflict between Israel and its neighbors is United Nations Security Council Resolution 242, in all its parts.

—After four wars during thirty years, despite intensive human efforts, the Middle East, which is the cradle of civilization and the birthplace of three great religions, does not yet enjoy the blessings of peace. The people of the Middle East yearn for peace so that the vast human and natural resources of the region can be turned to the pursuits of peace and so that this area can become a model for coexistence and cooperation among nations.

—The historic initiative of President Sadat in visiting Jerusalem and the reception accorded to him by the Parliament, government and people of Israel, and the reciprocal visit of Prime Minister Begin to Ismailia, the peace proposals made by both leaders, as well as the warm reception of these missions by the peoples of both countries, have created an unprecedented opportunity for peace which must not be lost if this generation and future generations are to be spared the tragedies of war.

—The provisions of the Charter of the United Nations and the other accepted norms of international law and legitimacy now provide accepted standards for the conduct of relations among all states.

—To achieve a relationship of peace, in the spirit of Article 2 of the United Nations Charter, future negotiations between Israel and any neighbor prepared to negotiate peace and security with it, are necessary for the purpose of carrying out all the provisions and principles of Resolutions 242 and 338.

—Peace requires respect for the sovereignty, territorial integrity and political independence of every state in the area and their right to live in peace within secure and recognized boundaries free from threats or acts of force. Progress toward that goal can accelerate movement toward a new era of reconciliation in the Middle East marked by cooperation in promoting economic development, in maintaining stability, and in assuring security.

—Security is enhanced by a relationship of peace and by cooperation between nations which enjoy normal relations. In addition, under the terms of peace treaties, the parties can, on the basis of reciprocity, agree to special security arrangements such as demilitarized zones, limited armaments areas, early warning stations, the presence of international forces, liaison, agreed measures for monitoring, and other arrangements that they agree are useful.

Framework

Taking these factors into account, the parties are determined to reach a just, comprehensive, and durable settlement of the Middle East conflict through the conclusion of peace treaties based on Security Council Resolutions 242 and 338 in all their parts. Their purpose is to achieve peace and good neighborly relations. They recognize that, for peace to endure, it must involve all those who have been most deeply affected by the conflict. They therefore agree that this framework as appropriate is intended by them to constitute a basis for peace not only between Egypt and Israel, but also between Israel and each of its neighbors which is prepared to negotiate peace with Israel on this basis. With that objective in mind, they have agreed to proceed as follows:

A. *West Bank and Gaza*

1. Egypt, Israel, Jordan and the representatives of the Palestinian people should participate in negotiations on the resolution of the Palestinian problem in all its aspects. To achieve that objective, negotiations relating to the West Bank and Gaza should proceed in three stages:

(a) Egypt and Israel agree that, in order to ensure a peaceful and orderly transfer of authority, and taking into account the security concerns of all the parties, there should be transitional arrangements for the West Bank and Gaza for a period not exceeding five years. In order to provide full autonomy to the inhabitants, under these arrangements the Israeli military government and its civilian administration will be withdrawn as soon as a self-governing authority has been freely elected by the inhabitants of these areas to replace the existing military government. To negotiate the details of a transitional arrangement, the Government of Jordan will be invited to join the negotiations on the basis of this framework. These new arrangements should give due consideration both to the principle of self-government by the inhabitants of these territories and to the legitimate security concerns of the parties involved.

(b) Egypt, Israel, and Jordan will agree on the modalities for establishing the elected self-governing authority in the West Bank and Gaza. The delegations of Egypt and Jordan may include Palestinians from the West Bank and Gaza or other Palestinians as mutually agreed. The parties will negotiate an agreement which will define the powers and responsibilities of the self-governing authority to be exercised in the West Bank and Gaza. A withdrawal of Israeli armed forces will take place and there will be a redeployment of the remaining Israeli forces into specified security locations. The agreement will also include arrangements for assuring internal and external security and public order. A strong local police force will be established, which may include Jordanian citizens. In addition, Israeli and Jordanian forces will participate in joint patrols and in the manning of control posts to assure the security of the borders.

(c) When the self-governing authority (administrative council) in the West Bank and Gaza is established and inaugurated, the transitional period of five years will begin. As soon as possible, but not later than the third year after the beginning of the transitional period, negotiations will take place to determine the final status of the West Bank and Gaza and its relationship with its neighbors, and to conclude a peace treaty between Israel and Jordan by the end of the transitional period. These negotiations will be conducted among Egypt, Israel, Jordan, and the elected representatives of the inhabitants of the West Bank and Gaza. Two separate but related committees will be convened, one committee, consisting of representatives of the four parties which will negotiate and agree on the final status of the West Bank and Gaza, and its relationship with its neighbors, and the second committee, consisting of representatives of Israel and representatives of Jordan to be joined by the elected representatives of the inhabitants of the West Bank and Gaza, to negotiate the peace treaty between Israel and Jordan, taking into account the agreement reached on the final status of the West Bank and Gaza. The negotiations shall be based on all the provisions and principles of UN Security Council Resolution 242. The negotiations will resolve, among other matters, the location of the boundaries and the nature of the security arrangements. The solution from the negotiations must also recognize the legitimate rights of the Palestinian people and their just requirements. In this way, the Palestinians will participate in the determination of their own future through:

(1) The negotiations among Egypt, Israel, Jordan and the representatives of the inhabitants of the West Bank and Gaza to agree on the final status of the West Bank and Gaza and other outstanding issues by the end of the transitional period.

(2) Submitting their agreement to a vote by the elected representatives of the inhabitants of the West Bank and Gaza.

(3) Providing for the elected representatives of the inhabitants of the West Bank and Gaza to decide how they shall govern themselves consistent with the provisions of their agreement.

(4) Participating as stated above in the work of the committee negotiating the peace treaty between Israel and Jordan.

2. All necessary measures will be taken and provisions made to assure the security of Israel and its neighbors during the transitional period and beyond. To assist in providing such security, a strong local police force will be constituted by the self-governing authority. It will be composed of inhabitants of the West Bank and Gaza. The police will maintain continuing liaison on internal security matters with the designated Israeli, Jordanian, and Egyptian officers.

3. During the transitional period, representatives of Egypt, Israel, Jordan, and the self-governing authority will constitute a continuing committee to decide by agreement on the modalities of admission of persons displaced from the West Bank and Gaza in 1967, together with necessary measures to prevent disruption and disorder. Other matters of common concern may also be dealt with by this committee.

4. Egypt and Israel will work with each other and with other interested parties to establish agreed procedures for a prompt, just and permanent implementation of the resolution of the refugee problem.

B. *Egypt-Israel*

1. Egypt and Israel undertake not to resort to the threat or the use of force to settle disputes. Any disputes shall be settled by peaceful means in accordance with the provisions of Article 33 of the Charter of the United Nations.

2. In order to achieve peace between them, the parties agree to negotiate in good faith with a goal of concluding within three months from the signing of this Framework a peace treaty between them, while inviting the other parties to the conflict to proceed simultaneously to negotiate and conclude similar peace treaties with a view to achieving a comprehensive peace in the area. The Framework for the Conclusion of a Peace Treaty Between Egypt and Israel will govern the peace negotiations between them. The parties will agree on the modalities and the timetable for the implementation of their obligations under the treaty.

C. *Associated Principles*

1. Egypt and Israel state that the principles and provisions described below should apply to peace treaties between Israel and each of its neighbors—Egypt, Jordan, Syria and Lebanon.

2. Signatories shall establish among themselves relationships normal to states at peace with one another. To this end, they should undertake to abide by all the provisions of the Charter of the United Nations. Steps to be taken in this respect include:

(a) full recognition;

(b) abolishing economic boycotts;

(c) guaranteeing that under their jurisdiction the citizens of the other parties shall enjoy the protection of the due process of law.

3. Signatories should explore possibilities for economic development in the context of final peace treaties, with the objective of contributing to the atmosphere of peace, cooperation and friendship which is their common goal.

4. Claims Commissions may be established for the mutual settlement of all financial claims.

5. The United States shall be invited to participate in the talks on matters related to the modalities of the implementation of the agreements and working out the timetable for the carrying out of the obligations of the parties.

6. The United Nations Security Council shall be requested to endorse

the peace treaties and ensure that their provisions shall not be violated. The permanent members of the Security Council shall be requested to underwrite the peace treaties and ensure respect for their provisions. They shall also be requested to conform their policies and actions with the undertakings contained in this Framework.

For the Government of the Arab Republic of Egypt:

A. Sadat

For the Government of Israel:

M. Begin

Witnessed by:

Jimmy Carter,
President of the
United States of America

FRAMEWORK FOR THE CONCLUSION OF A PEACE TREATY BETWEEN EGYPT AND ISRAEL

In order to achieve peace between them, Israel and Egypt agree to negotiate in good faith with a goal of concluding within three months of the signing of this framework a peace treaty between them.

It is agreed that:

The site of the negotiations will be under a United Nations flag at a location or locations to be mutually agreed.

All of the principles of UN Resolution 242 will apply in this resolution of the dispute between Israel and Egypt.

Unless otherwise mutually agreed, terms of the peace treaty will be implemented between two and three years after the peace treaty is signed.

The following matters are agreed between the parties:

(a) the full exercise of Egyptian sovereignty up to the internationally recognized border between Egypt and mandated Palestine;

(b) the withdrawal of Israeli armed forces from the Sinai;

(c) the use of airfields left by the Israelis near El Arish, Rafah, Ras en Naqb, and Sharm el Sheikh for civilian purposes only, including possible commercial use by all nations;

(d) the right of free passage by ships of Israel through the Gulf of Suez and the Suez Canal on the basis of the Constantinople Convention of 1888 applying to all nations; the Strait of Tiran and the Gulf of Aqaba are international waterways to be open to all nations for unimpeded and nonsuspendable freedom of navigation and overflight;

(e) the construction of a highway between the Sinai and Jordan near Elat with guaranteed free and peaceful passage by Egypt and Jordan; and

(f) the stationing of military forces listed below.

Stationing of Forces

A. No more than one division (mechanized or infantry) of Egyptian armed forces will be stationed within an area lying approximately 50 kilometers (km) east of the Gulf of Suez and the Suez Canal.

B. Only United Nations forces and civil police equipped with light weapons to perform normal police functions will be stationed within an area lying west of the international border and the Gulf of Aqaba, varying in width from 20 km to 40 km.

C. In the area within 3 km east of the international border there will be Israeli limited military forces not to exceed four infantry battalions and United Nations observers.

D. Border patrol units, not to exceed three battalions, will supplement the civil police in maintaining order in the area not included above.

The exact demarcation of the above areas will be as decided during the peace negotiations.

Early warning stations may exist to insure compliance with the terms of the agreement.

United Nations forces will be stationed: (a) in part of the area in the Sinai lying within about 20 km of the Mediterranean Sea and adjacent to the international border, and (b) in the Sharm el Sheikh area to ensure freedom of passage through the Strait of Tiran; and these forces will not be removed unless such removal is approved by the Security Council of the United Nations with a unanimous vote of the five permanent members.

After a peace treaty is signed, and after the interim withdrawal is complete, normal relations will be established between Egypt and Israel, including: full recognition, including diplomatic, economic and cultural relations; termination of economic boycotts and barriers to the free movement of goods and people; and mutual protection of citizens by the due process of law.

Interim Withdrawal

Between three months and nine months after the signing of the peace treaty, all Israeli forces will withdraw east of a line extending from a

point east of El Arish to Ras Muhammad, the exact location of this line
to be determined by mutual agreement.

For the Government of the Arab Republic of Egypt:

> *A. Sadat*

For the Government of Israel:

> *M. Begin*

Witnessed by:

> *Jimmy Carter*
> President of the United States of America

LETTER FROM ISRAELI PRIME MINISTER MENACHEM BEGIN TO PRESIDENT JIMMY CARTER, SEPTEMBER 17, 1978

Dear Mr. President:

I have the honor to inform you that during two weeks after my return
home I will submit a motion before Israel's Parliament (the Knesset) to
decide on the following question:

If during the negotiations to conclude a peace treaty between Israel
and Egypt all outstanding issues are agreed upon, "are you in favor of
the removal of the Israeli settlers from the northern and southern Sinai
areas or are you in favor of keeping the aforementioned settlers in those
areas?"

The vote, Mr. President, on this issue will be completely free from
the usual Parliamentary Party discipline to the effect that although the
coalition is being now supported by 70 members out of 120, every
member of the Knesset, as I believe, both on the Government and the
Opposition benches will be enabled to vote in accordance with his own
conscience.

Sincerely yours,

> *Menachem Begin*

LETTER FROM PRESIDENT JIMMY CARTER TO EGYPTIAN PRESIDENT ANWAR EL-SADAT, SEPTEMBER 22, 1978

Dear Mr. President:

I transmit herewith a copy of a letter to me from Prime Minister Begin
setting forth how he proposes to present the issue of the Sinai settlements
to the Knesset for the latter's decision. In this connection, I understand

from your letter that Knesset approval to withdraw all Israeli settlers from Sinai according to a timetable within the period specified for the implementation of the peace treaty is a prerequisite to any negotiations on a peace treaty between Egypt and Israel.

Sincerely,

Jimmy Carter

Enclosure:
Letter from Prime Minister Begin

LETTER FROM EGYPTIAN PRESIDENT ANWAR EL-SADAT
TO PRESIDENT JIMMY CARTER, SEPTEMBER 17, 1978

Dear Mr. President:

In connection with the "Framework for a Settlement in Sinai" to be signed tonight, I would like to reaffirm the position of the Arab Republic of Egypt with respect to the settlements:

1. All Israeli settlers must be withdrawn from Sinai according to a timetable within the period specified for the implementation of the peace treaty.

2. Agreement by the Israeli Government and its constitutional institutions to this basic principle is therefore a prerequisite to starting peace negotiations for concluding a peace treaty.

3. If Israel fails to meet this commitment, the "Framework" shall be void and invalid.

Sincerely,

Mohamed Anwar El Sadat

LETTER FROM PRESIDENT JIMMY CARTER TO ISRAELI
PRIME MINISTER MENACHEM BEGIN, SEPTEMBER 22, 1978

Dear Mr. Prime Minister:

I have received your letter of September 17, 1978, describing how you intend to place the question of the future of Israeli settlements in Sinai before the Knesset for its decision. Enclosed is a copy of President Sadat's letter to me on this subject.

Sincerely,

Jimmy Carter

Enclosure:
Letter from President Sadat

LETTER FROM EGYPTIAN PRESIDENT ANWAR EL-SADAT TO PRESIDENT JIMMY CARTER, SEPTEMBER 17, 1978

Dear Mr. President:

I am writing you to reaffirm the position of the Arab Republic of Egypt with respect to Jerusalem:

1. Arab Jerusalem is an integral part of the West Bank. Legal and historical Arab rights in the City must be respected and restored.

2. Arab Jerusalem should be under Arab sovereignty.

3. The Palestinian inhabitants of Arab Jerusalem are entitled to exercise their legitimate national rights, being part of the Palestinian People in the West Bank.

4. Relevant Security Council Resolutions, particularly Resolutions 242 and 267, must be applied with regard to Jerusalem. All the measures taken by Israel to alter the status of the City are null and void and should be rescinded.

5. All peoples must have free access to the City and enjoy the free exercise of worship and the right to visit and transit to the holy places without distinction or discrimination.

6. The holy places of each faith may be placed under the administration and control of their representatives.

7. Essential functions in the City should be undivided and a joint municipal council composed of an equal number of Arab and Israeli members can supervise the carrying out of these functions. In this way, the City shall be undivided.

Sincerely,

Mohamed Anwar El Sadat

LETTER FROM ISRAELI PRIME MINISTER MENACHEM BEGIN TO PRESIDENT JIMMY CARTER, SEPTEMBER 17, 1978

Dear Mr. President:

I have the honor to inform you, Mr. President, that on 28 June 1967—Israel's Parliament (The Knesset) promulgated and adopted a law to the effect: "the Government is empowered by a decree to apply the law, the jurisdiction and administration of the State to any part of Eretz Israel (land of Israel-Palestine), as stated in that decree."

On the basis of this law, the Government of Israel decreed in July

1967 that Jerusalem is one city indivisible, the Capital of the State of Israel.

Sincerely,

Menachem Begin

LETTER FROM PRESIDENT JIMMY CARTER TO EGYPTIAN PRESIDENT ANWAR EL-SADAT, SEPTEMBER 22, 1978

Dear Mr. President:

I have received your letter of September 17, 1978, setting forth the Egyptian position on Jerusalem. I am transmitting a copy of that letter to Prime Minister Begin for his information.

The position of the United States on Jerusalem remains as stated by Ambassador Goldberg in the United Nations General Assembly on July 14, 1967, and subsequently by Ambassador Yost in the United Nations Security Council on July 1, 1969.

Sincerely,

Jimmy Carter

LETTER FROM EGYPTIAN PRESIDENT ANWAR EL-SADAT TO PRESIDENT JIMMY CARTER, SEPTEMBER 17, 1978

Dear Mr. President:

In connection with the "Framework for Peace in the Middle East," I am writing you this letter to inform you of the position of the Arab Republic of Egypt, with respect to the implementation of the comprehensive settlement.

To ensure the implementation of the provisions related to the West Bank and Gaza and in order to safeguard the legitimate rights of the Palestinian people, Egypt will be prepared to assume the Arab role emanating from those provisions, following consultations with Jordan and the representatives of the Palestinian people.

Sincerely,

Mohamed Anwar El Sadat

LETTER FROM PRESIDENT JIMMY CARTER TO ISRAELI PRIME MINISTER MENACHEM BEGIN, SEPTEMBER 22, 1978

Dear Mr. Prime Minister:

I hereby acknowledge that you have informed me as follows:

A) In each paragraph of the Agreed Framework Document the

expressions "Palestinians" or "Palestinian People" are being and will be construed and understood by you as "Palestinian Arabs."

B) In each paragraph in which the expression "West Bank" appears, it is being, and will be, understood by the Government of Israel as Judea and Samaria.

Sincerely,

Jimmy Carter

LETTER FROM SECRETARY OF DEFENSE HAROLD BROWN TO ISRAELI DEFENSE MINISTER EZER WEIZMAN, ACCOMPANYING THE DOCUMENTS AGREED TO AT CAMP DAVID, RELEASED SEPTEMBER 29, 1978

September 28, 1978

Dear Mr. Minister:

The U.S. understands that, in connection with carrying out the agreements reached at Camp David, Israel intends to build two military airbases at appropriate sites in the Negev to replace the airbases at Eitam and Etzion which will be evacuated by Israel in accordance with the peace treaty to be concluded between Egypt and Israel. We also understand the special urgency and priority which Israel attaches to preparing the new bases in light of its conviction that it cannot safely leave the Sinai airbases until the new ones are operational.

I suggest that our two governments consult on the scope and costs of the two new airbases as well as on related forms of assistance which the United States might appropriately provide in light of the special problems which may be presented by carrying out such a project on an urgent basis. The President is prepared to seek the necessary Congressional approvals for such assistance as may be agreed upon by the U.S. side as a result of such consultations.

Harold Brown

Carter's Answers to King Hussein, October 1978

1. *Does the United States intend to be a full partner in negotiations regarding the West Bank and Gaza and the Palestinian question in general? At what stage of the negotiations will the United States participate and in what role?*

Yes, the United States will be a full partner in all the Arab-Israeli peace negotiations, leading to the achievement of a just, lasting and comprehensive Middle East peace.

The United States will use its full influence to see that the negotiations are brought to a successful conclusion.

President Carter will continue to take an active personal part in the negotiations.

2. *What does the Framework agreement mean in its paragraph (A)1, where it refers to "the representatives of the Palestinian people?"*

No comprehensive definition is attempted. In some cases, the representatives of the inhabitants of the West Bank and Gaza are specified. In one case, it is clear that "other Palestinians as mutually agreed" refers to representatives from outside the West Bank and Gaza and need not be citizens of Egypt or Jordan. Palestinians who are citizens of Egypt or Jordan may, of course, be members of the negotiating teams representing those countries. In other cases, the self-governing authority itself is mentioned.

The United States interprets the phrase "the representatives of the Palestinian people" not in terms of any single group or organization as representing the Palestinian people, but as encompassing those elected or chosen for participation in negotiations. It is expected that they will accept the purposes of the negotiations as defined in United Nations Security Council Resolution 242, and in the framework of a settlement will be prepared to live in peace and good neighbourly relations with Israel.

The text comes from a typed copy made available by the government of Jordan. The only point missing from this version is President Carter's signature at the bottom of the last page.

3. Why has the duration of five years been chosen for the transition period in the West Bank and Gaza?

The idea of a five-year transitional period for the West Bank and Gaza was an American suggestion which was first put to the parties in the summer of 1977. The key point is the concept of a transitional period—not the precise duration of five years which has been suggested and agreed.

We believe a transitional process of several years—at the outset of which the Israeli military government and its civilian administration will be withdrawn and a self-governing authority established for the West Bank and Gaza inhabitants—can demonstrate that the practical problems arising from a transition to peace can be satisfactorily resolved. We see the transitional period as essential to build confidence, gain momentum and bring about the changes in attitude that can assure a final settlement which realizes the legitimate rights of the Palestinian people while assuring the security of Israel and of the other parties.

4(A). What is the geographical definition of the "West Bank" and of Gaza in the view of the United States Government? Is Arab Jerusalem and its surrounding Arab areas incorporated into Israel after June 1967 included in the definition of the "West Bank"?

In the view of the United States the term "West Bank and Gaza" describes all of the area west of the Jordan River under Jordanian administration prior to the 1967 war and all of the area east of the western border of the British Mandate of Palestine which, prior to the 1967 war, was under Egyptian control and is known as the Gaza Strip.

With respect to negotiations envisaged in the Framework agreement, we believe a distinction must be made between Jerusalem and the rest of the West Bank because of the City's special status and circumstances. We would envisage, therefore, a negotiated solution for the final status of Jerusalem that could be different in character in some respects from that of the rest of the West Bank.

The final status of Jerusalem should not be prejudged by the unilateral actions undertaken in Jerusalem since the 1967 war. The full United States position on Jerusalem remains as stated by Ambassador Goldberg in his address to the United Nations General Assembly on 14 July 1967, and by Ambassador Yost to the Security Council on 1 July 1969.

4(B). At the end of the five years of transitional arrangements, what would be the status of the West Bank and of Gaza from the point of view of sovereignty?

The final status of the West Bank and Gaza, including the question of sovereignty, should be determined on the basis of Security Council Resolution 242 in all its parts in negotiations among Jordan, Egypt, Israel and the elected representatives of the inhabitants of the West Bank and Gaza, which should begin not later than the third year after the beginning of the transitional period. Under the terms of the Framework agreement, the outcome of those negotiations—including determining the issue of sovereignty—shall be submitted to a vote by the elected representatives of the inhabitants of the West Bank and Gaza for ratification or rejection.

Since the negotiation of the peace treaty between Israel and Jordan and the negotiations on the final status of the West Bank and Gaza are interrelated, the Framework provides that representatives of the inhabitants of the West Bank and Gaza should participate in both these negotiations.

Thus Palestinians will participate in each negotiation to resolve the final status of the West Bank and Gaza.

4(C). *What is the United States' position regarding these questions?*
The view of the United States on the geographical definition of the term "West Bank and Gaza" is stated in paragraph 4(A) above. The United States' position regarding the question of sovereignty in the West Bank and Gaza is expressed in paragraph 4(B) above.

4(D). *Will any Israeli forces remain in any part of the West Bank and of Gaza after the transitional period of five years? If so, by what right and with what justification?*
Security arrangements after the five-year interim period in the West Bank and Gaza, including the question of the possible retention of Israeli security personnel and the duration of any such presence, must be dealt with in the negotiations on the final status of the West Bank and Gaza that are to begin no later than the third year after the beginning of the transitional period.

4(E). *What is the United States' position regarding these questions?*
The United States believes that the agreement on the final status of the West Bank and Gaza must meet the legitimate aspirations of the Palestinian people and provide for Israel's security needs. The United States would not oppose, if agreed to by the parties, the stationing in the West Bank and Gaza of limited numbers of Israeli security personnel in specifically designated areas, and with a defined role, as one element in providing for the security of Israel.

5. During the transitional period of self-government in the West Bank and Gaza, under what higher supervisory authority would the self-governing authority operate? Would it be a United Nations or a similar neutral international supervisory authority? What source would finance the budgetary needs of the self-governing authority? What would be the extent of its powers? What would constitute the limitations on its powers?

The Framework provides that the parties, i.e., Egypt, Israel and Jordan, with Palestinians in the Egyptian and Jordanian delegations, "will negotiate an agreement which will define the powers and responsibilities of the self-governing authority to be exercised in the West Bank and Gaza." Thus the self-governing authority in the transitional period is established by an international agreement among the three parties. The agreement will define the powers of the self-governing authority and provide full autonomy for the inhabitants. Nothing in the Framework excludes the parties from deciding, should they so agree, to give a supervisory or other role to a United Nations or similar neutral international authority or to decide that there should be no supervisory authority. In addition, during the transitional period, representatives of Egypt, Israel, Jordan and the self-governing authority will constitute a continuing committee which may deal with matters of common concern. Methods of financing of the self-governing authority were not discussed at Camp David and remain to be set out in the agreement among the parties.

6(A). Where the document refers to the self-governing authority which is to be constituted in the West Bank–Gaza area, does the jurisdiction of this authority extend to the part of Jerusalem which had been part of the West Bank when it fell under occupation as well as other annexed area around it, both in terms of territory and people?

As stated above, the issue of the status of Jerusalem was not resolved at Camp David and must be dealt with in subsequent negotiations. The questions of how the Arab inhabitants of East Jerusalem relate to the self-governing authority remains to be determined in the negotiations on the transitional arrangements.

6(B). What is the United States' position on this question?

In those negotiations the United States will support proposals that would permit Arab inhabitants of East Jerusalem who are not Israeli citizens to participate in the elections to constitute the self-governing authority and in the work of the self-governing authority itself. It is probably not realistic to expect that the full scope of the self-governing authority can be extended to East Jerusalem during the transitional period. Such an outcome would not, however, prejudge the final status of Jerusalem, which must be resolved in the negotiations that are to begin no later than the third year after the beginning of the transitional period.

7(A). *At the end of the five-year transitional period, what would be the status of occupied Arab Jerusalem?*

The status of the West Bank and Gaza, and their relationship with their neighbors, as well as peace between Israel and Jordan, will be determined in the negotiations referred to in paragraph A.I.(c) of the Framework. The United States believes that the status of that portion of Jerusalem which Israel occupied in 1967 should be resolved in those negotiations.* The Framework envisages that these negotiations will involve Egypt, Israel, Jordan and the elected representatives of the inhabitants of the West Bank and Gaza.

7(B). *What is the United States' position on this matter?*

The position of the United States on Jerusalem is stated in Paragraph 4(A) above. The final status of Jerusalem should not be prejudged by the unilateral actions undertaken in Jerusalem since the 1967 war. Whatever solution is agreed upon should preserve Jerusalem as a physically undivided city. It should provide for free access to the Jewish, Muslim, and Christian holy places without distinction or discrimination for the free exercise of worship. It should assure the basic rights of all the City's residents. The holy places of each faith should be under the full authority of their representatives.

8(A). *What would happen to the Israeli settlements in the occupied areas during and after the transitional period? What would happen to the properties acquired and construction made there and what would their status be?*

The Framework does not deal with the status of Israeli settlements in the occupied areas, nor with the properties acquired or construction made there. The powers and responsibilities of the self-governing authority, which will exercise full autonomy on the West Bank and Gaza during the transitional period, will be defined in an agreement to be negotiated between Egypt, Israel, Jordan and, as provided in the Framework, Palestinians from the West Bank and Gaza or other Palestinians as mutually agreed to be on Egyptian and Jordanian national delegations.

*Provisions regarding Jerusalem could be included in the agreements that emerge from either or both of these negotiations. (This note appears in the original text.)

The question of the Israeli settlements in the West Bank and Gaza, and their relationship with the self-governing authority during the transitional period, will have to be dealt with in the course of those negotiations. The Framework also provides for a continuing committee, including representatives of Egypt, Israel, Jordan, and the self-governing authority, which may deal with outstanding matters of common concern during the transitional period.

The question of the Israeli settlements and their status after the transitional period would be a matter for discussion during the negotiations regarding the final status of the West Bank and Gaza referred to in paragraph A.1.(c).

8(B). *What will be Israel's obligation, during the coming period until the end of the transitional period, regarding the policy of settlement?*
It is the position of the United States that Israel should refrain from creating new settlements on the West Bank while negotiations are under way on the establishment of the self-governing authority. These negotiations will determine the question of existing settlements as well as any new settlement activity during the transitional period.

8(C). *What is the United States' position regarding both of the above questions?*
The United States' position is that settlements established during a military occupation are in violation of the Fourth Geneva Convention on the Protection of Persons in Time of War. However, in a relationship of peace, the parties to the peace should define the mutual rights of inhabitants to do business, to work, to live, and to carry on other transactions in each other's territory.

9(A). *Will the Israeli citizens who reside at present in the settlements be eligible for participation in the establishment of the self-governing authority and its subsequent activities?*
Israeli citizens residing in settlements on the West Bank and Gaza could participate in the establishment of the self-governing authority only as members of the Israeli negotiating delegation; there is no provision for their separate participation. Their participation, if any, in the self-governing authority must be determined in the negotiations for the transitional regime.

9(B). *What will be the status of the Israeli citizens residing in the West Bank and Gaza during the transitional period and will there be any, and if so what would their status be after the end of the transitional period?*

The negotiations under paragraph A.1.(b) defining the powers and responsibilities of the authority will deal with the status of Israeli settlements on the West Bank and Gaza and, accordingly, with the status of Israeli citizens residing in them. Whatever number that might remain beyond the transitional period, and their status, would presumably be agreed in the negotiations concerning the final status of the West Bank and Gaza envisaged under paragraph A.1.(c).

10(A). *At the end of the five-year transitional period, will the inhabitants of the West Bank and Gaza exercise in freedom the right of self-determination in order to decide their political future?*
The Framework provides for the elected representatives of the inhabitants of the West Bank and Gaza to participate fully in the negotiations that will determine the final status of the West Bank and Gaza and, in addition, for their elected representatives to ratify or reject the agreement reached in those negotiations. The Framework further provides that the solution from the negotiations must also recognize the legitimate rights of the Palestinian people and their just requirements. The wide acceptability of the results of this process is in the interest of all parties and is directly related to its being carried out "in freedom." In this respect, at the time the process described above is taking place, a strong local police force will exist and will be responsible to the self-governing authority to ensure that there is no interference in the political process that ensures these rights.

10(B). *What is the United States' position on this question?*
The United States supports the right of the Palestinians to participate in the determination of their own future, and believes that the Framework provides for such participation in all the important steps in determining the future of the West Bank and Gaza. The United States believes that paragraph A.1.(c) (2) does not preclude the holding of an election by the inhabitants of the West Bank and Gaza, after the conclusion of an agreement on the final status of the West Bank and Gaza, for the express purpose of electing representatives to whom that agreement will be submitted for a vote.

11(A). *What solution does the Framework Agreement envisage for the problem of the Palestinians living outside the occupied areas as refugees and for the restoration of their rights?*
Paragraph A.4. of the Framework provides that Egypt and Israel will work together with other interested parties to agree on a resolution of the

refugee problem. Implementation of the procedures agreed upon is to be prompt, just and permanent.

Paragraph A.3. of the Framework provides for a continuing committee to decide on arrangements for the admission to the West Bank and Gaza of persons displaced from those areas in 1967.

In addition, as the political institutions of self-government take shape on the West Bank and Gaza through negotiations among the parties the relationship between those institutions and the Palestinians living outside the area would be addressed.

11(B). *What does the United States regard as the basis for the solution of this question? How does it define these rights?*
The United States believes that a resolution of the refugee problem should reflect applicable United Nations Resolutions. Any program for implementation must provide those refugees living outside the West Bank and Gaza a choice and opportunity in settling themselves permanently in the context of present-day realities and circumstances.

12. *What does the Framework Agreement envisage for the future of the rest of the occupied Arab territories? What is the United States Government's position on this question?*
The Framework states that it is intended to constitute a basis for peace between Israel and each of its other neighbors. It further states that the objective is a just, comprehensive, and durable peace and that each negotiation must carry out all the provisions and principles of United Nations Security Council Resolutions 242 and 338. Paragraph C.1. specifically states that the principles of the Framework should apply to treaties between Israel and Jordan, Syria, and Lebanon in addition to Egypt. Concerning the West Bank in particular, paragraph A.1.(c) requires negotiations based on all the provisions and principles of Resolution 242 which will resolve, among other matters, the location of boundaries. The United States continues to advocate a comprehensive peace involving all of Israel's neighbors. As regards the possibility of negotiations for a peaceful settlement between Israel and Syria, the United States will support the application of all the principles and provisions of Resolution 242 to such a settlement.

13. *In the definition of the security requirements in the area, does the United States Government endorse the principle of reciprocity on these requirements or does the United States Government regard these requirements to be one sided only?*

The United States fully endorses the principle of reciprocity as applied to security requirements in the context of Middle East peace negotiations. The preamble of the Framework specifically refers to reciprocity as the basis on which the parties can agree to special security arrangements. The Framework also refers to the security concerns "of all parties" and to the security of "Israel and its neighbors."

14. *As Security Council Resolution 242 is stated to be the basis of any negotiations for the settlement of the West Bank–Gaza and other aspects of the conflict, what would the United States Government do in the event of conflicting interpretations between the negotiating parties particularly in view of the United States Government's previous interpretations of Security Council Resolution 242 and commitments based thereon which were the basis of acceptance by Jordan of the said Resolution?*

The United States will, first, adhere to its own consistent interpretation of Resolution 242, and in particular to its interpretation that the withdrawal provision of that resolution applies on all fronts. In the event of conflicting interpretations among the negotiating parties, the United States will seek, as it did during the intensive negotiations at Camp David, to bring about a consensus among the parties and will make known its own interpretations as required to bring about resolution of the conflict. The interpretations of the United States remain those it has held since 1967.

APPENDIX G

Egyptian-Israeli Peace Treaty, March 26, 1979

TREATY OF PEACE BETWEEN THE ARAB REPUBLIC
OF EGYPT AND THE STATE OF ISRAEL

The Government of the Arab Republic of Egypt and the Government of the State of Israel;

Preamble

Convinced of the urgent necessity of the establishment of a just, comprehensive and lasting peace in the Middle East in accordance with Security Council Resolutions 242 and 338;

Reaffirming their adherence to the "Framework for Peace in the Middle East Agreed at Camp David," dated September 17, 1978;

Noting that the aforementioned Framework as appropriate is intended to constitute a basis for peace not only between Egypt and Israel but also between Israel and each of its other Arab neighbors which is prepared to negotiate peace with it on this basis;

Desiring to bring to an end the state of war between them and to establish a peace in which every state in the area can live in security;

Convinced that the conclusion of a Treaty of Peace between Egypt and Israel is an important step in the search for comprehensive peace in the area and for the attainment of the settlement of the Arab-Israeli conflict in all its aspects;

Inviting the other Arab parties to this dispute to join the peace process with Israel guided by and based on the principles of the aforementioned Framework;

Desiring as well to develop friendly relations and cooperation between themselves in accordance with the United Nations Charter and the principles of international law governing international relations in times of peace;

Agree to the following provisions in the free exercise of their sovereignty, in order to implement the "Framework for the Conclusion of a Peace Treaty Between Egypt and Israel":

Article I

1. The state of war between the Parties will be terminated and peace will be established between them upon the exchange of instruments of ratification of this Treaty.

2. Israel will withdraw all its armed forces and civilians from the Sinai behind the international boundary between Egypt and mandated Palestine, as provided in the annexed protocol (Annex I), and Egypt will resume the exercise of its full sovereignty over the Sinai.

3. Upon completion of the interim withdrawal provided for in Annex I, the Parties will establish normal and friendly relations, in accordance with Article III(3).

Article II

The permanent boundary between Egypt and Israel is the recognized international boundary between Egypt and the former mandated territory of Palestine, as shown on the map at Annex II, without prejudice to the issue of the status of the Gaza Strip. The Parties recognize this boundary as inviolable. Each will respect the territorial integrity of the other, including their territorial waters and airspace.

Article III

1. The Parties will apply between them the provisions of the Charter of the United Nations and the principles of international law governing relations among states in times of peace. In particular:

    a. They recognize and will respect each other's sovereignty, territorial integrity and political independence;

    b. They recognize and will respect each other's right to live in peace within their secure and recognized boundaries;

    c. They will refrain from the threat or use of force, directly or indirectly, against each other and will settle all disputes between them by peaceful means.

2. Each Party undertakes to ensure that acts or threats of belligerency, hostility, or violence do not originate from and are not committed from within its territory, or by any forces subject to its control or by any other forces stationed on its territory, against the population, citizens or property of the other Party. Each Party also undertakes to refrain from organizing,

instigating, inciting, assisting or participating in acts or threats of belligerency, hostility, subversion or violence against the other Party, anywhere, and undertakes to ensure that perpetrators of such acts are brought to justice.

3. The Parties agree that the normal relationship established between them will include full recognition, diplomatic, economic and cultural relations, termination of economic boycotts and discriminatory barriers to the free movement of people and goods, and will guarantee the mutual enjoyment by citizens of the due process of law. The process by which they undertake to achieve such a relationship parallel to the implementation of other provisions of this Treaty is set out in the annexed protocol (Annex III).

Article IV

1. In order to provide maximum security for both Parties on the basis of reciprocity, agreed security arrangements will be established including limited force zones in Egyptian and Israeli territory, and United Nations forces and observers, described in detail as to nature and timing in Annex I, and other security arrangements the Parties may agree upon.

2. The Parties agree to the stationing of United Nations personnel in areas described in Annex I. The Parties agree not to request withdrawal of the United Nations personnel and that these personnel will not be removed unless such removal is approved by the Security Council of the United Nations, with the affirmative vote of the five Permanent Members, unless the Parties otherwise agree.

3. A Joint Commission will be established to facilitate the implementation of the Treaty, as provided for in Annex I.

4. The security arrangements provided for in paragraphs 1 and 2 of this Article may at the request of either party be reviewed and amended by mutual agreement of the Parties.

Article V

1. Ships of Israel, and cargoes destined for or coming from Israel, shall enjoy the right of free passage through the Suez Canal and its approaches through the Gulf of Suez and the Mediterranean Sea on the basis of the Constantinople Convention of 1888, applying to all nations. Israeli nationals, vessels and cargoes, as well as persons, vessels and cargoes destined for or coming from Israel, shall be accorded non-discriminatory treatment in all matters connected with usage of the canal.

2. The Parties consider the Strait of Tiran and the Gulf of Aqaba to be international waterways open to all nations for unimpeded and non-suspendable freedom of navigation and overflight. The Parties will respect each other's right to navigation and overflight for access to either country through the Strait of Tiran and the Gulf of Aqaba.

Article VI

1. This Treaty does not affect and shall not be interpreted as affecting in any way the rights and obligations of the Parties under the Charter of the United Nations.

2. The Parties undertake to fulfill in good faith their obligations under this Treaty, without regard to action or inaction of any other party and independently of any instrument external to this Treaty.

3. They further undertake to take all the necessary measures for the application in their relations of the provisions of the multilateral conventions to which they are parties, including the submission of appropriate notification to the Secretary General of the United Nations and other depositaries of such conventions.

4. The Parties undertake not to enter into any obligations in conflict with this Treaty.

5. Subject to Article 103 of the United Nations Charter, in the event of a conflict between the obligations of the Parties under the present Treaty and any of their other obligations, the obligations under this Treaty will be binding and implemented.

Article VII

1. Disputes arising out of the application or interpretation of this Treaty shall be resolved by negotiations.

2. Any such disputes which cannot be settled by negotiations shall be resolved by conciliation or submitted to arbitration.

Article VIII

The Parties agree to establish a claims commission for the mutual settlement of all financial claims.

Article IX

1. This Treaty shall enter into force upon exchange of instruments of ratification.

2. This Treaty supersedes the Agreement between Egypt and Israel of September, 1975.

3. All protocols, annexes, and maps attached to this Treaty shall be regarded as an integral part hereof.

4. The Treaty shall be communicated to the Secretary General of the United Nations for registration in accordance with the provisions of Article 102 of the Charter of the United Nations.

Done at Washington, D.C. this 26th day of March, 1979, in triplicate in the English, Arabic, and Hebrew languages, each text being equally authentic. In case of any divergence of interpretation, the English text shall prevail.

For the Government of the Arab Republic of Egypt:

A. Sadat

For the Government of Israel:

M. Begin

Witnessed by:

Jimmy Carter
President of the
United States of America

AGREED MINUTES TO ARTICLES I, IV, V AND VI AND ANNEXES I AND III OF TREATY OF PEACE

Article I

Egypt's resumption of the exercise of full sovereignty over the Sinai provided for in paragraph 2 of Article I shall occur with regard to each area upon Israel's withdrawal from that area.

Article IV

It is agreed between the parties that the review provided for in Article IV(4) will be undertaken when requested by either party, commencing within three months of such a request, but that any amendment can be made only with the mutual agreement of both parties.

Article V

The second sentence of paragraph 2 of Article V shall not be construed as limiting the first sentence of that paragraph. The foregoing is not to be construed as contravening the second sentence of paragraph 2 of Article V, which reads as follows:

"The Parties will respect each other's right to navigation and overflight for access to either country through the Strait of Tiran and the Gulf of Aqaba."

Article VI(2)

The provisions of Article VI shall not be construed in contradiction to the provisions of the framework for peace in the Middle East agreed at Camp David. The foregoing is not to be construed as contravening the provisions of Article VI(2) of the Treaty, which reads as follows:

"The Parties undertake to fulfill in good faith their obligations under this Treaty, without regard to action or inaction of any other Party and independently of any instrument external to this Treaty."

Article VI(5)

It is agreed by the Parties that there is no assertion that this Treaty prevails over other Treaties or agreements or that other Treaties or agreements prevail over this Treaty. The foregoing is not to be construed as contravening the provisions of Article VI(5) of the Treaty, which reads as follows:

"Subject to Article 103 of the United Nations Charter, in the event of a conflict between the obligations of the Parties under the present Treaty and any of their other obligations, the obligations under this Treaty will be binding and implemented."

Annex I

Article VI, Paragraph 8, of Annex I provides as follows:

"The Parties shall agree on the nations from which the United Nations force and observers will be drawn. They will be drawn from nations other than those which are permanent members of the United Nations Security Council."

The Parties have agreed as follows:

"With respect to the provisions of paragraph 8, Article VI, of Annex I, if no agreement is reached between the Parties, they will accept or support a U.S. proposal concerning the composition of the United Nations force and observers."

Annex III

The Treaty of Peace and Annex III thereto provide for establishing normal economic relations between the Parties. In accordance therewith, it is agreed that such relations will include normal commercial sales of oil by Egypt to Israel, and that Israel shall be fully entitled to make bids for Egyptian-origin oil not needed for Egyptian domestic oil consumption, and Egypt and its oil concessionaires will entertain bids made by Israel, on the same basis and terms as apply to other bidders for such oil.

For the Government of Israel:

M. Begin

For the Government of the Arab Republic of Egypt:

A. Sadat

Witnessed by:

Jimmy Carter
President of the
United States of America

LETTER FROM ISRAELI PRIME MINISTER MENACHEM BEGIN AND EGYPTIAN PRESIDENT ANWAR EL-SADAT TO PRESIDENT JIMMY CARTER, MARCH 26, 1979

Dear Mr. President:

This letter confirms that Egypt and Israel have agreed as follows:

The Governments of Egypt and Israel recall that they concluded at Camp David and signed at the White House on September 17, 1978, the annexed documents entitled "A Framework for Peace in the Middle East Agreed at Camp David" and "Framework for the conclusion of a Peace Treaty between Egypt and Israel."

For the purpose of achieving a comprehensive peace settlement in accordance with the above-mentioned Frameworks, Egypt and Israel will proceed with the implementation of those provisions relating to the West Bank and the Gaza Strip. They have agreed to start negotiations within a month after the exchange of the instruments of ratification of the Peace Treaty. In accordance with the "Framework for Peace in the Middle East," the Hashemite Kingdom of Jordan is invited to join the negotiations. The Delegations of Egypt and Jordan may include Palestinians from the West Bank and Gaza Strip or other Palestinians as mutually agreed. The purpose of the negotiation shall be to agree, prior to the elections, on the modalities for establishing the elected self-governing authority (administrative council), define its powers and responsibilities, and agree upon other related issues. In the event Jordan decides not to take part in the negotiations, the negotiations will be held by Egypt and Israel.

The two Governments agree to negotiate continuously and in good faith to conclude these negotiations at the earliest possible date. They also agree that the objective of the negotiations is the establishment of the self-governing authority in the West Bank and Gaza in order to provide full autonomy to the inhabitants.

Egypt and Israel set for themselves the goal of completing the negotiations within one year so that elections will be held as expeditiously as possible after agreement has been reached between the parties. The self-governing authority referred to in the "Framework for Peace in the Middle East" will be established and inaugurated within one month after it has been elected, at which time the transitional period of five years will begin. The Israeli military government and its civilian administration will be withdrawn, to be replaced by the self-governing authority, as specified in the "Framework for Peace in the Middle East." A withdrawal of Israeli armed forces will then take place and there will be a redeployment of the remaining Israeli forces into specified security locations.

This letter also confirms our understanding that the United States Government will participate fully in all stages of negotiations.

Sincerely yours,

For the Government of Israel:

M. Begin
Menachem Begin

For the Government of the Arab Republic of Egypt:

A. Sadat
Mohamed Anwar El-Sadat

Note: President Carter, upon receipt of the Joint Letter to him from President Sadat and Prime Minister Begin, has added to the American and Israeli copies the notation:

"I have been informed that the expression 'West Bank' is understood by the Government of Israel to mean 'Judea and Samaria'."

This notation is in accordance with similar procedures established at Camp David.*

---

*Explanatory note with the original documents.

LETTER FROM PRESIDENT ANWAR EL-SADAT
TO PRESIDENT JIMMY CARTER, MARCH 26, 1979

Dear Mr. President:

In response to your request, I can confirm that, within one month after the completion of Israel's withdrawal to the interim line as provided for in the Treaty of Peace between Egypt and Israel, Egypt will send a resident ambassador to Israel and will receive a resident Israeli ambassador in Egypt.

Sincerely,

A. Sadat
Mohamed Anwar El-Sadat

LETTER FROM PRESIDENT JIMMY CARTER TO ISRAELI
PRIME MINISTER MENACHEM BEGIN, MARCH 26, 1979

Dear Mr. Prime Minister:

I have received a letter from President Sadat that, within one month after Israel completes its withdrawal to the interim line in Sinai, as provided for in the Treaty of Peace between Egypt and Israel, Egypt will send a resident ambassador to Israel and will receive in Egypt a resident Israeli ambassador.

I would be grateful if you will confirm that this procedure will be agreeable to the Government of Israel.

Sincerely,

Jimmy Carter
Jimmy Carter

LETTER FROM ISRAELI PRIME MINISTER MENACHEM BEGIN
TO PRESIDENT JIMMY CARTER, MARCH 26, 1979

Dear Mr. President:

I am pleased to be able to confirm that the Government of Israel is agreeable to the procedure set out in your letter of March 26, 1979 in which you state:

"I have received a letter from President Sadat that, within one month after Israel completes its withdrawal to the interim line in Sinai, as provided for in the Treaty of Peace between Egypt and Israel, Egypt will send a resident ambassador to Israel and will receive in Egypt a resident Israeli ambassador."

Sincerely,

M. Begin
Menachem Begin

LETTERS FROM PRESIDENT JIMMY CARTER TO EGYPTIAN PRESIDENT ANWAR EL-SADAT AND ISRAELI PRIME MINISTER MENACHEM BEGIN, MARCH 26, 1979*

Dear Mr. President: [Prime Minister]:
I wish to confirm to you that subject to United States Constitutional processes:

In the event of an actual or threatened violation of the Treaty of Peace between Egypt and Israel, the United States will, on request of one or both of the Parties, consult with the Parties with respect thereto and will take such other action as it may deem appropriate and helpful to achieve compliance with the Treaty.

The United States will conduct aerial monitoring as requested by the Parties pursuant to Annex I of the Treaty.

The United States believes the Treaty provision for permanent stationing of United Nations personnel in the designated limited force zone can and should be implemented by the United Nations Security Council. The United States will exert its utmost efforts to obtain the requisite action by the Security Council. If the Security Council fails to establish and maintain the arrangements called for in the Treaty, the President will be prepared to take those steps necessary to ensure the establishment and maintenance of an acceptable alternative multinational force.

Sincerely,

Jimmy Carter
Jimmy Carter

*Separate but identical letters were sent to President Sadat and Prime Minister Begin.

APPENDIX H

President Ronald Reagan's Speech and Talking Points, September 1, 1982

===

TEXT OF PRESIDENT REAGAN'S SPEECH, TELEVISED FROM THE OVAL OFFICE

My fellow Americans, today has been a day that should make us proud. It marked the end of the successful evacuation of the P.L.O. from Beirut, Lebanon. This peaceful step could never have been taken without the good offices of the United States and, especially, the truly heroic work of a great American diplomat, Ambassador Philip Habib. Thanks to his efforts, I'm happy to announce that the U.S. Marine contingent helping to supervise the evacuation has accomplished its mission. Our young men should be out of Lebanon within two weeks. They, too, have served the cause of peace with distinction and we can all be very proud of them.

But the situation in Lebanon is only part of the overall problem of conflict in the Middle East. So, over the past two weeks, while events in Beirut dominated the front page, America was engaged in a quiet, behind-the-scenes effort to lay the groundwork for a broader peace in the region. For once, there were no premature leaks as U.S. diplomatic missions traveled to Mideast capitals and I met here at home with a wide range of experts to map out an American peace initiative for the long-suffering peoples of the Middle East, Arab and Israeli alike.

It seemed to me that, with the agreement in Lebanon, we had an opportunity for a more far-reaching peace effort in the region and I was determined to seize that moment. In the words of the scripture, the time had come to "follow after the things which make for peace."

Tonight, I want to report to you on the steps we've taken and the prospects they can open up for a just and lasting peace in the Middle East.

The text of the speech comes from the *New York Times*, September 2, 1982. The talking points accompanied a letter sent by President Reagan to Prime Minister Menachem Begin of Israel. The same points were presented to Arab governments. See *New York Times*, September 9, 1982.

America has long been committed to bringing peace to this troubled region. For more than a generation, successive U.S. administrations have endeavored to develop a fair and workable process that could lead to a true and lasting Arab-Israeli peace. Our involvement in the search for Mideast peace is not a matter of preference, it is a moral imperative. The strategic importance of the region to the United States is well known.

But our policy is motivated by more than strategic interests. We also have an irreversible commitment to the survival and territorial integrity of friendly states. Nor can we ignore the fact that the well-being of much of the world's economy is tied to stability in the strife-torn Middle East. Finally, our traditional humanitarian concerns dictate a continuing effort to peacefully resolve conflicts.

When our Administration assumed office in January 1981, I decided that the general framework for our Middle East policy should follow the broad guidelines laid down by my predecessors.

There were two basic issues we had to address. First, there was the strategic threat to the region posed by the Soviet Union and its surrogates, best demonstrated by the brutal war in Afghanistan; and, second, the peace process between Israel and its Arab neighbors. With regard to the Soviet threat, we have strengthened our efforts to develop with our friends and allies a joint policy to deter the Soviets and their surrogates from further expansion in the region, and, if necessary, to defend against it. With respect to the Arab-Israeli conflict, we've embraced the Camp David framework as the only way to proceed. We have also recognized, however, that solving the Arab-Israeli conflict, in and of itself, cannot assure peace throughout a region as vast and troubled as the Middle East.

Our first objective under the Camp David process was to insure the successful fulfillment of the Egyptian-Israeli peace treaty. This was achieved with the peaceful return of the Sinai to Egypt in April 1982. To accomplish this, we worked hard with our Egyptian and Israeli friends, and eventually with other friendly countries, to create the multinational force which now operates in the Sinai.

Throughout this period of difficult and time-consuming negotiations, we never lost sight of the next step of Camp David, autonomy talks to pave the way for permitting the Palestinian people to exercise their legitimate rights. However, owing to the tragic assassination of President Sadat and other crises in the area, it was not until January 1982 that we were ale to make a major effort to renew these talks. Secretary of State Haig and Ambassador Fairbanks made three visits to Israel and Egypt early this year to pursue the autonomy talks. Considerable progress was made in developing the basic outline of an American approach which was to be presented to Egypt and Israel after April.

The successful completion of Israel's withdrawal from Sinai and the courage shown on this occasion by Prime Minister Begin and President Mubarak in living up to their agreements convinced me the time had come for a new American policy to try to bridge the remaining differences between Egypt and Israel on the autonomy process. So, in May, I called for specific measures and a timetable for consultations with the Governments of Egypt and Israel on the next steps in the peace process. However, before this effort could be launched, the conflict in Lebanon pre-empted our efforts. The autonomy talks were basically put on hold while we sought to untangle the parties in Lebanon and still the guns of war.

The Lebanon war, tragic as it was, has left us with a new opportunity for Middle East peace. We must seize it now and bring peace to this troubled area so vital to world stability while there is still time. It was with this strong conviction that over a month ago, before the present negotiations in Beirut had been completed, I directed Secretary of State Shultz to again review our policy and to consult a wide range of outstanding Americans on the best ways to strengthen chances for peace in the Middle East.

We have consulted with many of the officials who were historically involved in the process, with members of the Congress, and with individuals from the private sector, and I have held extensive consultations with my own advisers on the principles that I will outline to you tonight.

The evacuation of the PLO from Beirut is now complete. And we can now help the Lebanese to rebuild their war-torn country. We owe it to ourselves, and to posterity, to move quickly to build upon this achievement. A stable and revived Lebanon is essential to all our hopes for peace in the region. The people of Lebanon deserve the best efforts of the international community to turn the nightmares of the past several years into a new dawn of hope.

But the opportunities for peace in the Middle East do not begin and end in Lebanon. As we help Lebanon rebuild, we must also move to resolve the root causes of conflict between Arabs and Israelis.

The war in Lebanon has demonstrated many things, but two consequences are key to the peace process:

First, the military losses of the P.L.O. have not diminished the yearning of the Palestinian people for a just solution of their claims; and second, while Israel's military successes in Lebanon have demonstrated that its armed forces are second to none in the region, they alone cannot bring just and lasting peace to Israel and her neighbors.

The question now is how to reconcile Israel's legitimate security concerns with the legitimate rights of the Palestinians. And that answer can only come at the negotiating table. Each party must recognize that the outcome must be acceptable to all and that true peace will require compromises by all.

So, tonight I'm calling for a fresh start. This is the moment for all those directly concerned to get involved—or lend their support—to a workable basis for peace. The Camp David agreement remains the foundation of our policy. Its language provides all parties with the leeway they need for successful negotiations.

I call on Israel to make clear that the security for which she yearns can only be achieved through genuine peace, a peace requiring magnanimity, vision and courage.

I call on the Palestinian people to recognize that their own political aspirations are inextricably bound to recognition of Israel's right to a secure future.

And I call on the Arab states to accept the reality of Israel, and the reality that peace and justice are to be gained only through hard, fair, direct negotiation.

In making these calls upon others, I recognize that the United States has a special responsibility. No other nation is in a position to deal with the key parties to the conflict on the basis of trust and reliability.

The time has come for a new realism on the part of all the peoples of the Middle East. The State of Israel is an accomplished fact; it deserves unchallenged legitimacy within the community of nations. But Israel's legitimacy has thus far been recognized by too few countries, and has been denied by every Arab state except Egypt. Israel exists. It has a right to exist in peace, behind secure and defensible borders, and it has a right to demand of its neighbors that they recognize those facts.

I have personally followed and supported Israel's heroic struggle for survival ever since the founding of the state of Israel 34 years ago. In the pre-1967 borders, Israel was barely 10 miles wide at its narrowest point. The bulk of Israel's population lived within artillery range of hostile Arab armies. I am not about to ask Israel to live that way again.

The war in Lebanon has demonstrated another reality in the region.

The departure of the Palestinians from Beirut dramatizes more than ever the homelessness of the Palestinian people. Palestinians feel strongly that their cause is more than a question of refugees. I agree. The Camp David agreement recognized that fact when it spoke of the legitimate rights of the Palestinian people and their just requirements. For peace to endure, it must involve all those who have been most deeply affected by the conflict. Only through broader participation in the peace process, most immediately by Jordan and by the Palestinians, will Israel be able to rest confident in the knowledge that its security and integrity will be respected by its neighbors. Only through the process of negotiation can all the nations of the Middle East achieve a secure peace.

These then are our general goals. What are the specific new American positions, and why are we taking them?

In the Camp David talks thus far, both Israel and Egypt have felt free to express openly their views as to what the outcome should be. Understandably, their views have differed on many points.

The United States has thus far sought to play the role of mediator. We have avoided public comment on the key issues. We have always recognized, and continue to recognize, that only the voluntary agreement of those parties most directly involved in the conflict can provide an enduring solution. But it has become evident to me that some clearer sense of America's position on the key issues is necessary to encourage wider support for the peace process.

First, as outlined in the Camp David accords, there must be a period of time during which the Palestinian inhabitants of the West Bank and Gaza will have full autonomy over their own affairs. Due consideration must be given to the principle of self-government by the inhabitants of the territories and to the legitimate security concerns of the parties involved.

The purpose of the five-year period of transition which would begin after free elections for a self-governing Palestinian authority is to prove to the Palestinians that they can run their own affairs, and that such Palestinian autonomy poses no threat to Israel's security.

The United States will not support the use of any additional land for the purpose of settlements during the transitional period. Indeed, the immediate adoption of a settlement freeze by Israel, more than any other action, could create the confidence needed for wider participation in these talks. Further settlement activity is in no way necessary for the security of Israel and only diminishes the confidence of the Arabs that a final outcome can be freely and fairly negotiated.

I want to make the American position well understood: The purpose of this transition period is the peaceful and orderly transfer of authority from Israel to the Palestinian inhabitants of the West Bank and Gaza. At the same time, such a transfer must not interfere with Israel's security requirements.

Beyond the transition period, as we look to the future of the West Bank and Gaza, it is clear to me that peace cannot be achieved by the formation of an independent Palestinian state in those territories. Nor is it achievable on the basis of Israeli sovereignty or permanent control over the West Bank and Gaza.

So the United States will not support the establishment of an independent Palestinian state in the West Bank and Gaza, and we will not support annexation or permanent control by Israel.

There is, however, another way to peace. The final status of these lands must, of course, be reached through the give-and-take of negotiations. But it is the firm view of the United States that self-government by the Palestinians of the West Bank and Gaza in association with Jordan offers the best chance for a durable, just and lasting peace.

We base our approach squarely on the principle that the Arab-Israeli conflict should be resolved through negotiations involving an exchange of territory for peace. This exchange is enshrined in United Nations Security Council Resolution 242 which is, in turn, incorporated in all its parts in the Camp David agreements. U.N. Resolution 242 remains wholly valid as the foundation stone of America's Middle East peace effort.

It is the United States' position that—in return for peace—the withdrawal provision of Resolution 242 applies to all fronts, including the West Bank and Gaza.

When the border is negotiated between Jordan and Israel, our view on the extent to which Israel should be asked to give up territory will be heavily affected by the extent of true peace and normalization and the security arrangements offered in return.

Finally, we remain convinced that Jerusalem must remain undivided, but its final status should be decided through negotiations.

In the course of the negotiations to come, the United States will support positions that seem to us fair and reasonable compromises, and likely to promote a sound agreement. We will also put forward our own detailed proposals when we believe they can be helpful. And, make no mistake, the United States will oppose any proposal—from any party and at any point in the negotiating process—that threatens the security of Israel. America's commitment to the security of Israel is ironclad and, I might add, so is mine.

During the past few days, our Ambassadors in Israel, Egypt, Jordan and Saudi Arabia have presented to their host governments the proposals in full detail that I have outlined here today.

Now I am convinced that these proposals can bring justice, bring security and bring durability to an Arab-Israeli peace.

The United States will stand by these principles with total dedication. They are fully consistent with Israel's security requirements and the aspirations of the Palestinians. We will work hard to broaden participation at the peace table as envisaged by the Camp David accords. And I fervently hope that the Palestinians and Jordan, with the support of their Arab colleagues, will accept this opportunity.

Tragic turmoil in the Middle East runs back to the dawn of history. In our modern day, conflict after conflict has taken its brutal toll there. In an age of nuclear challenge and economic interdependence, such conflicts are a threat to all the people of the world, not just the Middle East itself. It's time for us all, in the Middle East and around the world, to call a halt to conflict, hatred and prejudice; it's time for us all to launch a common effort for reconstruction, peace and progress.

It has often been said—and regrettably too often been true—that the story of the search for peace and justice in the Middle East is a tragedy of opportunities missed.

In the aftermath of the settlement in Lebanon we now face an opportunity for a broader peace. This time we must not let it slip from our grasp. We must look beyond the difficulties and obstacles of the present and move with fairness and resolve toward a brighter future. We owe it to ourselves, and to posterity, to do no less. For if we miss this chance to make a fresh start, we may look back on this moment from some later vantage point and realize how much that failure cost us all.

These, then, are the principles upon which American policy toward the Arab-Israeli conflict will be based. I have made a personal commitment to see that they endure and, God willing, that they will come to be seen by all reasonable, compassionate people as fair, achievable, and in the interests of all who wish to see peace in the Middle East.

Tonight, on the eve of what can be a dawning of new hope for the people of the troubled Middle East—and for all the world's people who dream of a just and peaceful future—I ask you, my fellow Americans, for your support and your prayers in this great undertaking.

TEXT OF TALKING POINTS SENT TO PRIME MINISTER BEGIN BY PRESIDENT REAGAN

General Principles

A. We will maintain our commitment to Camp David.

B. We will maintain our commitment to the conditions we require for recognition of and negotiation with the P.L.O.

C. We can offer guarantees on the position we will adopt in negotiations. We will not be able, however, to guarantee in advance the results of these negotiations.

Transitional Measures

A. Our position is that the objective of the transitional period is the peaceful and orderly transfer of authority from Israel to the Palestinian inhabitants.

B. We will support:

The decision of full autonomy as giving the Palestinian inhabitants real authority over themselves, the land and its resources, subject to fair safeguards on water.

Economic, commercial, social and cultural ties between the West Bank, Gaza and Jordan.

Participation by the Palestinian inhabitants of East Jerusalem in the election of the West Bank–Gaza authority.

Real settlement freeze.

Progressive Palestinian responsibility for internal security based on capability and performance.

C. We will oppose:

Dismantlement of the existing settlements.

Provisions which represent a legitimate threat to Israel's security, reasonably defined.

Isolation of the West Bank and Gaza from Israel.

Measures which accord either the Palestinians or the Israelis generally recognized sovereign rights with the exception of external security, which must remain in Israel's hands during the transitional period.

Final Status Issues

A. U.N.S.C. Resolution 242

It is our position that Resolution 242 applies to the West Bank and Gaza and requires Israeli withdrawal in return for peace. Negotiations must determine the borders. The U.S. position in these negotiations on the extent of the withdrawal will be significantly influenced by the extent and nature of the peace and security arrangements offered in return.

B. Israeli Sovereignty

It is our belief that the Palestinian problem cannot be resolved [through] Israeli sovereignty or control over the West Bank and Gaza. Accordingly, we will not support such a solution.

C. Palestinian State

The preference we will pursue in the final status negotiation is association of the West Bank and Gaza with Jordan. We will not support the formation of a Palestinian state in those negotiations. There is no foundation of political support in Israel or the United States for such a solution. The outcome, however, must be determined by negotiations.

D. Self-Determination

In the Middle East context the term self-determination has been identified exclusively with the formation of a Palestinian state. We will not support this definition of self-determination. We believe that the Palestinians must take the leading role in determining their own future and fully support the provision in Camp David providing for the elected representatives of the inhabitants of the West Bank and Gaza to decide how they shall govern themselves consistent with the provision of their agreement in the final status negotiations.

E. Jerusalem

We will fully support the position that the status of Jerusalem must be determined through negotiations.

F. Settlements

The status of Israeli settlements must be determined in the course of the final status negotiations. We will not support their continuation as extraterritorial outposts.

Additional Talking Points

1. Approach to Hussein

The President has approached Hussein to determine the extent to which he may be interested in participating.

King Hussein has received the same U.S. positions as you.

Hussein considers our proposals serious and gives them serious attention.

Hussein understands that Camp David is the only base that we will accept for negotiations.

We are also discussing these proposals with the Saudis.

2. Public Commitment

Whatever the support from these or other Arab States, this is what the President has concluded must be done.

The President is convinced his positions are fair and balanced and fully protective of Israel's security. Beyond that they offer the practical opportunity of eventually achieving the peace treaties Israel must have with its neighbors.

He will be making a speech announcing these positions, probably within a week.

3. Next Procedural Steps

Should the response to the President's proposal be positive, the U.S. would take immediate steps to relaunch the autonomy negotiations with the broadest possible participation as envisaged under the Camp David agreements.

We also contemplate an early visit by Secretary Shultz in the area.

Should there not be positive response, the President, as he has said in his letter to you, will nonetheless stand by his position with proper dedication.

APPENDIX I

The Shultz Initiative, March 4, 1988

I set forth below the statement of understanding which I am convinced is necessary to achieve the prompt opening of negotiations on a comprehensive peace. This statement of understandings emerges from discussions held with you and other regional leaders. I look forward to the letter of reply of the Government of Israel in confirmation of this statement.

The agreed objective is a comprehensive peace providing for the security of all the states in the region and for the legitimate rights of the Palestinian people.

Negotiations will start on an early date certain between Israel and each of its neighbors which is willing to do so. These negotiations could begin May 1, 1988. Each of these negotiations will be based on the United Nations Security Council Resolutions 242 and 338, in all their parts. The parties to each bilateral negotiation will determine the procedure and agenda at their negotiation. All participants in the negotiations must state their willingness to negotiate with one another.

As concerns negotiations between the Israeli delegation and the Jordanian-Palestinian delegation, negotiations will begin on arrangements for a transitional period, with the objective of completing them within six months. Seven months after transitional negotiations begin, final status negotiations will begin, with the objective of completing them within one year. These negotiations will be based on all the provisions and principles of United Nations Security Council Resolution 242. Finally status talks will start before the transitional period begins. The transitional period will begin three months after the conclusion of the transitional agreement and will last for three years. The United States will participate in both negotiations and will promote their rapid conclusion. In particular, the

Text of the letter that Secretary of State George P. Shultz wrote to Prime Minister Yitzhak Shamir of Israel outlining the American peace proposal. A similar letter was sent to King Hussein of Jordan. See *New York Times*, March 10, 1988.

United States will submit a draft agreement for the parties' consideration at the outset of the negotiations on transitional arrangements.

Two weeks before the opening of negotiations, an international conference will be held. The Secretary General of United Nations will be asked to issue invitations to the parties involved in the Arab-Israeli conflict and the five permanent members of the United Nations Council. All participants in the conference must accept United Nations Security Council Resolutions 242 and 338, and renounce violence and terrorism. The parties to each bilateral negotiation may refer reports on the status of their negotiations to the conference, in a manner to be agreed. The conference will not be able to impose solutions or veto agreements reached.

Palestinian representation will be within the Jordanian-Palestinian delegation. The Palestinian issue will be addressed in the negotiations between the Jordanian-Palestinian and Israeli delegations. Negotiations between the Israeli delegation and the Jordanian-Palestinian delegation will proceed independently of any other negotiations.

This statement of understandings in an integral whole. The United States understands that your acceptance is dependent on the implementation of each element in good faith.

Sincerely yours,
George P. Shultz

APPENDIX J

*Letter from Secretary of State George P. Shultz
to Swedish Foreign Minister Sten Andersson,
December 3, 1988*

Note: Shultz's letter was accompanied by two attachments. One was the text of a statement that the PLO should make to meet the known American conditions. The copy provided here contains the PLO handwritten changes that were agreed on after Swedish mediation. Arafat signed the revised version, reproduced here, and gave it to Andersson with a note saying that it had his approval and that "we will work to have it issued officially after being presented to the Executive Committee."

The second attachment consisted of a statement that the United States would be prepared to make in response to the proposed PLO statement. The original of that statement is not available, but a translation from the Arabic, as noted by the PLO, is provided.

THE SECRETARY OF STATE

WASHINGTON

December 3, 1988

Dear Sten:

I received through Ambassador Wachtmeister your message
concerning the meeting in Stockholm next Tuesday. I greatly
appreciate the constructive approach which you are taking
toward this issue.

The attached papers constitute my reply to the question you
raised in your message. I want to make three points in this
regard:

-- First, we will not engage in any effort to make this
the start of a negotiation over language; in other
words, we will not accept counter-drafts.

-- Second, I am aware that the PLO may wish to add,
following the statement that we have proposed,
certain positions to which they feel committed and
from which they would claim their basic statement is
derived. We would have no objection to their doing
so, provided those positions neither condition nor
contradict their acceptance of our conditions.

-- Third, nothing here may be taken to imply an
acceptance or recognition by the United States of an
independent Palestinian state.

You may share this letter with your visitor if you believe
it would be useful.

Sincerely yours,

George P. Shultz

Attachments:
As stated above.

His Excellency
Sten Andersson,
Minister of Foreign Affairs of Sweden,
Stockholm.

PROPOSED PLO STATEMENT

*assuming the role of
the provicinal government
of the state
of Palestine*

As its contribution to the search for a just and lasting
peace in the Middle East, the Executive Committee of the
Palestine Liberation Organization wishes to issue the following
official statement:

1. That it is prepared to negotiate with Israel a
comprehensive peace settlement of the Arab-Israeli conflict/on
the basis of United Nations resolutions 242 and 338.

*within th framework
of th international
conference*

2. That it undertakes to live in peace with Israel and its xx
other neighbors and to respect their right to exist in peace
within secure and internationally recognized borders, as will
the democratic Palestinian state which it seeks to establish in
X the West Bank and the Gaza Strip. *the palestinian occupied territories
in 1967*

3. That it condemns individual, group and state terrorism in
all its forms, and will not resort to.it.

X 4. That it is prepared for a moratorium on all forms of
violence, on a mutual basis, once negotiations begin.

(American draft of proposed PLO statement, provided by Secretary of
State George Shultz to Swedish Foreign Minister Sten Anderson, with
hand-written changes from Palestinian side.   December 6, 1988)

PROPOSED AMERICAN STATEMENT

The P.L.O. today issued a statement in which it accepted U.N. Security Council Resolution 242 and 338 and recognized Israel's right to exist and renounced the use of force. As a result, the United States is prepared to begin substantive discussions with representatives of the P.L.O. The United States believes that the negotiations to reach a peaceful settlement of the Arab-Israeli conflict must be based on resolutions 242 and 338 and calls on all parties to renew their efforts in the search for peace without delay. The United States recognizes that the representatives of the Palestinian people have the right to raise in negotiation all subjects of interest to them.

Questions to be answered by Secretary Shultz:*

Q. Does your statement mean that the Palestinians can put on the negotiating table their position on a Palestinian state?

A. Yes, the Palestinians, as far as we are concerned, have the right to pursue their desire to establish an independent state through negotiations. It is through the process of negotiation and direct exchange between the concerned parties that a lasting result can be achieved.

(After Swedish mediation, the U.S. agreed to another question and answer)

Q. Do you agree that negotiations should take place within the framework of an international conference?

A. The United States has long made its support for direct negotiations clear, but we remain prepared to consider any suggestion that may lead to direct negotiations toward a comprehensive peace. The initiative suggested by Secretary Shultz in the beginning of the year called for an international conference to begin direct negotiations. Any conference of this type must be properly organized so that it does not become an alternative to direct negotiations.

*The PLO notes indicate that Secretary Shultz was to provide these answers personally, but this was denied by the American side. In reality, it was the American ambassador to the UN who provided these clarifications.

As its contribution to the search for a just and lasting peace
in the Middle East, the Executive Committee of the Palestine
Liberation Organization, assuming the role of the Provisional
Government of the State of Palestine wishes to issue the following
official statement:

1. That it is prepared to negotiate with Israel within the framework
of the International Conference a comprehensive peace settlement
of the Arab-Israeli conflict on the basis of U.N. resolutions
242 and 338.

2. That it undertakes to live in peace with Israel and other
neighbours and to respect their right to exist in peace within
secure and internationally recognized borders, as will the
democratic Palestinian State which it seeks to establish in the
Palestinian occupied territories since 1967.

3. That it condemns individual, group and State terrorism in all
its forms, and will not resort to it.

APPENDIX K

Statements by Yasir Arafat and George Shultz, December 14, 1988

STATEMENT BY YASIR ARAFAT, GENEVA

Let me highlight my views before you. Our desire for peace is a strategy and not an interim tactic. We are bent to peace come what may.

Our statehood provides salvation to the Palestinians and peace to both Palestinians and Israelis. Self-determination means survival for the Palestinians.

And our survival does not destroy the survival of the Israelis as their rulers claim.

Yesterday in my speech, I made a reference to the United Nations resolution 181 [on the partition of Palestine] as the basis for Palestinian independence. I also made a reference to our acceptance of resolutions 242 and 338 as the basis for negotiations with Israel within the framework of an international conference. These three resolutions were endorsed at our Palestinian National Council session in Algiers.

In my speech also yesterday it was clear that we mean our peoples' right to freedom and national independence according to resolution 181 and the right of all parties concerned in the Middle East conflict to exist in peace and security and, as I have mentioned, including the state of Palestine and Israel and other neighbors according to the resolution 242 and 338.

As for terrorism, I renounced it yesterday in no uncertain terms, and yet I repeat for the record that we totally and absolutely renounce all forms of terrorism, including individual, group and state terrorism. Between Geneva and Algiers, we have made our position crystal clear.

Any more talk such as the Palestinians should give more—you remember the slogan, the Palestinians should give it more—or it is not enough, or the Palestinians are engaging in propaganda games and public relations exercise will be damaging and counterproductive.

The text for both statements comes from the *Washington Post*, December 15, 1988.

Enough is enough. Enough is enough. Enough is enough. All remaining matters should be discussed around the table and within the international conference.

Let it be absolutely clear that neither Arafat nor any [one else] for that matter can stop the intifada, the uprising. The intifada will come to an end only and only when practical and tangible steps have been taken toward the achievement of our national aims and the establishment of our independent Palestinian state.

In this context, I expect the EEC [European Economic Community] to play a more effective role in promoting peace in our region. They have political responsibility, they have moral responsibility and they can deal with it.

Finally, I declare before you and I ask you to kindly quote me on that: We want peace. We want peace. We are committed to peace. We want to live in our Palestinian state and let live.

STATEMENT BY GEORGE SHULTZ, WASHINGTON, D.C.

The Palestine Liberation Organization today issued a statement in which it accepted U.N. Security Council Resolutions 242 and 338, recognized Israel's right to exist in peace and security and renounced terrorism. As a result, the United States is prepared for a substantive dialogue with PLO representatives.

I am designating our ambassador to Tunisia as the only authorized channel for that dialogue. The objective of the United States remains, as always, a comprehensive peace in the Middle East.

In that light, I view this development as one more step toward the beginning of direct negotiations between the parties, which alone can lead to such a peace.

Nothing here may be taken to imply an acceptance or recognition by the United States of an independent Palestinian state. The position of the United States is that the status of the West Bank and Gaza cannot be determined by unilateral acts of either side, but only through a process of negotiations. The United States does not recognize the declaration of an independent Palestinian state.

It is also important to emphasize that the United States' commitment to the security of Israel remains unflinching.

APPENDIX L

Excerpts from Speech by President George Bush, March 6, 1991

. . . Our commitment to peace in the Middle East does not end with the liberation of Kuwait. So tonight, let me outline four key challenges to be met.

First, we must work together to create shared security arrangements in the region. Our friends and allies in the Middle East recognize that they will bear the bulk of the responsibility for regional security. But we want them to know that just as we stood with them to repel aggression, so now America stands ready to work with them to secure the peace.

This does not mean stationing U.S. ground forces on the Arabian Peninsula, but it does mean American participation in joint exercises involving both air and ground forces. It means maintaining a capable U.S. naval presence in the region, just as we have for over 40 years. Let it be clear: Our vital national interests depend on a stable and secure gulf.

Second, we must act to control the proliferation of weapons of mass destruction and the missiles used to deliver them. It would be tragic if the nations of the Middle East and Persian Gulf were now, in the wake of war, to embark on a new arms race. Iraq requires special vigilance. Until Iraq convinces the world of its peaceful intentions—that its leaders will not use new revenues to rearm and rebuild its menacing war machine—Iraq must not have access to the instruments of war.

And third, we must work to create new opportunities for peace and stability in the Middle East. On the night I announced Operation Desert Storm, I expressed my hope that out of the horrors of war might come new momentum for peace. We've learned in the modern age, geography cannot guarantee security and security does not come from military power alone.

All of us know the depth of bitterness that has made the dispute between Israel and its neighbors so painful and intractable. Yet, in the

The text comes from the *Washington Post*, March 7, 1991.

conflict just concluded, Israel and many of the Arab states have for the first time found themselves confronting the same aggressor. By now, it should be plain to all parties that peacemaking in the Middle East requires compromise. At the same time, peace brings real benefits to everyone. We must do all that we can to close the gap between Israel and the Arab states and between Israelis and Palestinians. The tactics of terror lead nowhere. There can be no substitute for diplomacy.

A comprehensive peace must be grounded in United Nations Security Council Resolutions 242 and 338 and the principle of territory for peace. This principle must be elaborated to provide for Israel's security and recognition, and at the same time for legitimate Palestinian political rights. Anything else would fail the twin tests of fairness and security. The time has come to put an end to Arab-Israeli conflict.

The war with Iraq is over. The quest for solutions to the problems in Lebanon, in the Arab-Israeli dispute, and in the gulf must go forward with new vigor and determination. And I guarantee you: No one will work harder for a stable peace in the region than we will.

Fourth, we must foster economic development for the sake of peace and progress. The Persian Gulf and Middle East form a region rich in natural resources with a wealth of untapped human potential. Resources once squandered on military might must be redirected to more peaceful ends. We are already addressing the immediate economic consequences of Iraq's aggression. Now, the challenge is to reach higher to foster economic freedom and prosperity for all the people of the region.

By meeting these four challenges we can build a framework for peace. . . .

APPENDIX M

James Baker's Letter of Assurance to the Palestinians, October 18, 1991

The Palestinian decision to attend a peace conference to launch direct negotiations with Israel represents an important step in the search for a comprehensive, just and lasting peace in the region. The United States has long believed that Palestinian participation is critical to the success of our efforts.

In the context of the process on which we are embarking, we want to respond to your request for certain assurances related to this process. These assurances constitute U.S. understandings and intentions concerning the conference and ensuing negotiations.

These assurances are consistent with United States policy and do not undermine or contradict United Nations Security Council resolutions 242 and 338. Moreover, there will be no assurances provided to one party that are not known to all the others. By this we can foster a sense of confidence and minimize chances for misunderstandings.

As President Bush stated in his March 6, 1991 address to Congress, the United States continues to believe firmly that a comprehensive peace must be grounded in United Nations Security Council Resolutions 242 and 338 and the principle of territory for peace. Such an outcome must also provide for security and recognition for all states in the region, including Israel, and for legitimate political rights of the Palestinian people. Anything else, the President noted, would fail the twin tests of fairness and security.

The process we are trying to create offers Palestinians a way to achieve these objectives. The United States believes that there should be an end to the Israeli occupation which can occur only through genuine and meaningful negotiations. The United States also believes that this process should create a new relationship of mutuality where Palestinians and Israelis can respect one another's security, identity, and political rights. We believe Palestinians should gain control over political, economic and other decisions that affect their lives and fate.

Direct bilateral negotiations will begin four days after the opening of the conference; those parties who wish to attend multilateral negotiations will convene two weeks after the opening of the conference to organize those negotiations. In this regard, the United States will support Palestinian involvement in any bilateral or multilateral negotiations on refugees and in all multilateral negotiations. The conference and the negotiations that follow will be based on UN Security Council Resolutions 242 and 338.

The process will proceed along two tracks through direct negotiations between Israel and Arab states and Israel and Palestinians. The United States is determined to achieve a comprehensive settlement of the Arab-Israeli conflict and will do its utmost to ensure that the process moves forward along both tracks toward this end.

In pursuit of a comprehensive settlement, all the negotiations would proceed as quickly as possible toward agreement. For its part, the United States will work for serious negotiations and will also seek to avoid prolongation and stalling by any party.

The conference will be co-sponsored by the United States and the Soviet Union. The European Community will be a participant in the conference alongside the United States and the Soviet Union and be represented by its Presidency. The conference can reconvene only with the consent of all the parties.

With regard to the role of the United Nations, the UN Secretary General will send a representative to the conference as an observer. The co-sponsors will keep the Secretary General apprised of the progress of the negotiations. Agreements reached between the parties will be registered with the UN Secretariat and reported to the Security Council, and the parties will seek the Council's endorsement of such agreements. Since it is in the interest of all parties for this process to succeed, while this process is actively ongoing, the United States will not support a competing or parallel process in the United Nations Security Council.

The United States does not seek to determine who speaks for Palestinians in this process. We are seeking to launch a political negotiating process that directly involves Palestinians and offers a pathway for achieving the legitimate political rights of the Palestinian people and for participation in the determination of their future. We believe that a joint Jordanian-Palestinian delegation offers the most promising pathway toward this end.

Only Palestinians can choose their delegation members, which are not subject to veto from anyone. The United States understands that members of the delegation will be Palestinians from the territories who agree to negotiations on two tracks, in phases, and who are willing to live in peace with Israel. No party can be forced to sit with anyone it does not want to sit with.

Palestinians will be free to announce their component of the joint delegation and to make a statement during the opening of the conference. They may also raise any issue pertaining to the substance of the negotiations during the negotiations.

The United States understands how much importance Palestinians attach to the question of east Jerusalem. Thus, we want to assure you that nothing Palestinians do in choosing their delegation members in this phase of the process will affect their claim to east Jerusalem, or be prejudicial or precedential to the outcome of negotiations. It remains the firm position of the United States that Jerusalem must never again be a divided city and that its final status should be decided by negotiations. Thus, we do not recognize Israel's annexation of east Jerusalem or the extension of its municipal boundaries, and we encourage all sides to avoid unilateral acts that would exacerbate local tensions or make negotiations more difficult or preempt their final outcome. It is also the United States position that a Palestinian resident in Jordan with ties to a prominent Jerusalem family would be eligible to join the Jordanian side of the delegation.

Furthermore, it is also the United States position that Palestinians of east Jerusalem should be able to participate by voting in the elections for an interim self-governing authority. The United States further believes that Palestinians from east Jerusalem and Palestinians outside the occupied territories who meet the three criteria should be able to participate in the negotiations on final status. And, the United States supports the right of Palestinians to bring any issue, including east Jerusalem, to the table.

Because the issues at stake are so complex and the emotions so deep, the United States has long maintained that a transitional period is required to break down the walls of suspicion and mistrust and lay the basis for sustainable negotiations on the final status of the occupied territories. The purpose of negotiations on transitional arrangements is to effect the peaceful and orderly transfer of authority from Israel to Palestinians. Palestinians need to achieve rapid control over political, economic, and other decisions that affect their lives and to adjust to a new situation in which Palestinians exercise authority in the West Bank and Gaza. For its part, the United States will strive from the outset and encourage all parties to adopt steps that can create an environment of confidence and mutual trust, including respect for human rights.

As you are aware with respect to negotiations between Israel and Palestinians, negotiations will be conducted in phases, beginning with talks on interim self-government arrangements. These talks will be conducted with the objective of reaching agreement within one year. Once agreed, the interim self-government arrangements will last for a period of five years. Beginning the third year of the period of interim self-government arrangements, negotiations will take place on permanent status. It is the aim of the United States that permanent status negotiations will be concluded by the end of the transitional period.

It has long been our position that only direct negotiations based on U.N. Security Council Resolutions 242 and 338 can produce a real peace. No one can dictate the outcome in advance. The United States understands that Palestinians must be free, in opening statements at the conference and in the negotiations that follow, to raise any issue of importance to them. Thus, Palestinians are free to argue for whatever outcome they believe best meets their requirements. The United States will accept any outcome agreed by the parties. In this regard and consistent with longstanding US policies, confederation is not excluded as a possible outcome of negotiations on final status.

The United States has long believed that no party should take unilateral actions that seek to predetermine issues that can only be resolved through negotiations. In this regard the United States has opposed and will continue to oppose settlement activity in the territories occupied in 1967, which remains an obstacle to peace.

The United States will act as an honest broker in trying to resolve the Arab-Israeli conflict. It is our intention, together with the Soviet Union, to play the role of a driving force in this process to help the parties move forward toward a comprehensive peace. Any party will have access to the co-sponsors at any time. The United States is prepared to participate in all stages of the negotiations, with the consent of the parties to each negotiation.

These are the assurances that the United States is providing concerning the implementation of the initiative we have discussed. We are persuaded that we have a real opportunity to accomplish something very important in the peace process. And we are prepared to work hard together with you in the period ahead to build on the progress we have made. There will be difficult challenges for all parties. But with Palestinians' continued commitment and creativity, we have a real chance of moving to a peace conference and to negotiations and then on toward the broader peace that we all seek.

APPENDIX N

U.S.-Soviet Invitation to the Mideast Peace Conference in Madrid, October 18, 1991

After extensive consultations with Arab states, Israel and the Palestinians, the United States and the Soviet Union believe that an historic opportunity exists to advance the prospects for genuine peace throughout the region. The United States and the Soviet Union are prepared to assist the parties to achieve a just, lasting and comprehensive peace settlement, through direct negotiations along two tracks, between Israel and the Arab states, and between Israel and the Palestinians, based on United Nations Security Council Resolutions 242 and 338. The objective of this process is real peace.

Toward that end, the president of the U.S. and the president of the USSR invite you to a peace conference, which their countries will co-sponsor, followed immediately by direct negotiations. The conference will be convened in Madrid on 30 October 1991.

President Bush and President Gorbachev request your acceptance of this invitation no later than 6 p.m. Washington time, 23 October 1991, in order to ensure proper organization and preparation of the conference.

Direct bilateral negotiations will begin four days after the opening of the conference. Those parties who wish to attend multilateral negotiations will convene two weeks after the opening of the conference to organize those negotiations. The co-sponsors believe that those negotiations should focus on region-wide issues such as arms control and regional security, water, refugee issues, environment, economic development, and other subjects of mutual interest.

The co-sponsors will chair the conference which will be held at ministerial level. Governments to be invited include Israel, Syria, Lebanon and Jordan. Palestinians will be invited and attend as part of a joint Jordanian-Palestinian delegation. Egypt will be invited to the conference

This is the complete text of the invitation to the Madrid peace conference held on October 30, 1991, obtained by the *Jerusalem Post*. The invitation was jointly issued by the United States and the Soviet Union to Israel, Syria, Jordan, Lebanon, and the Palestinians.

as a participant. The European Community will be a participant in the conference, alongside the United States and the Soviet Union and will be represented by its presidency. The Gulf Cooperation Council will be invited to send its secretary-general to the conference as an observer, and GCC member states will be invited to participate in organizing the negotiations on multilateral issues. The United Nations will be invited to send an observer, representing the secretary-general.

The conference will have no power to impose solutions on the parties or veto agreements reached by them. It will have no authority to make decisions for the parties and no ability to vote on issues or results. The conference can reconvene only with the consent of all the parties.

With respects to negotiations between Israel and Palestinians who are part of the joint Jordanian-Palestinian delegation, negotiations will be conducted in phases, beginning with talks on interim self-government arrangements. These talks will be conducted with the objective of reaching agreement within one year. Once agreed the interim self-government arrangements will last for a period of five years. Beginning the third year of the period of interim self-government arrangements, negotiations will take place on permanent status. These permanent status negotiations, and the negotiations between Israel and the Arab states, will take place on the basis of Resolutions 242 and 338.

It is understood that the co-sponsors are committed to making this process succeed. It is their intention to convene the conference and negotiations with those parties who agree to attend.

The co-sponsors believe that this process offers the promise of ending decades of confrontation and conflict and the hope of a lasting peace. Thus, the co-sponsors hope that the parties will approach these negotiations in a spirit of good will and mutual respect. In this way, the peace process can begin to break down the mutual suspicions and mistrust that perpetuate the conflict and allow the parties to begin to resolve their differences. Indeed, only through such a process can real peace and reconciliation among the Arab states, Israel and the Palestinians be achieved. And only through this process can the peoples of the Middle East attain the peace and security they richly deserve.

APPENDIX O

Excerpts from President George Bush's Address to the Mideast Peace Conference, Madrid, Spain, October 30, 1991

Peace will only come as the result of direct negotiations, compromises, give-and-take. Peace cannot be imposed from outside by the United States or anyone else. While we will continue to do everything possible to help the parties overcome obstacles, peace must come from within.

We come here to Madrid as realists. We don't expect peace to be negotiated in a day, or a week, or a month, or even a year. It will take time. Indeed, it should take time—time for parties so long at war to learn to talk to one another, to listen to one another. Time to heal old wounds and build trust. In this quest, time need not be the enemy of progress.

What we envision is a process of direct negotiations proceeding along two tracks, one between Israel and the Arab states, the other between Israel and the Palestinians. Negotiations are to be conducted on the basis of U.N. Security Council Resolutions 242 and 338.

The real work will not happen here in the plenary sessions, but in direct bilateral negotiations. This conference cannot impose a settlement on the participants or veto agreements. And just as important, the conference can only be reconvened with the consent of every participant. Progress is in the hands of the parties who must live with the consequences.

Soon after the bilateral talks commence, parties will convene as well to organize multilateral negotiations. These will focus on issues that cross national boundaries and are common to the region: arms control, water, refugee concerns, economic development. Progress in these fora is not intended as a substitute for what must be decided in the bilateral talks. To the contrary, progress in the multilateral issues can help create an atmosphere in which longstanding bilateral disputes can more easily be settled.

For Israel and the Palestinians, a framework already exists for diplomacy. Negotiations will be conducted in phases, beginning with talks on interim self-government arrangements. We aim to reach arrangement

Text comes from the *New York Times*, October 31, 1991

within one year. And once agreed, interim self-government arrangements will last for five years. Beginning with the third year, negotiations will commence on permanent status.

No one can say with any precision what the end result will be. In our view, something must be developed, something acceptable to Israel, the Palestinians and Jordan, that gives the Palestinian people meaningful control over their own lives and fate and provides for the acceptance and security of Israel.

We can all appreciate that both Israelis and Palestinians are worried about compromise, worried about compromising even the smallest point for fear it becomes a precedent for what really matters. But no one should avoid compromise on interim arrangements for a simple reason: nothing agreed to now will prejudice permanent status negotiations. To the contrary, these subsequent negotiations will be determined on their own merits.

Peace cannot depend upon promises alone. Real peace—lasting peace—must be based upon security for all states and peoples, including Israel. For too long, the Israeli people have lived in fear, surrounded by an unaccepting Arab world. Now is the ideal moment for the Arab world to demonstrate that attitudes have changed, that the Arab world is willing to live in peace with Israel and make allowances for Israel's reasonable security needs.

We know that peace must also be based on fairness. In the absence of fairness, there will be no legitimacy, no stability. This applies above all to the Palestinian people, many of whom have known turmoil and frustration above all else. Israel now has an opportunity to demonstrate that it is willing to enter into a new relationship with its Palestinian neighbors: one predicated upon mutual respect and cooperation.

Throughout the Middle East, we seek a stable and enduring settlement. We've not defined what this means. Indeed, I make these points with no map showing where the final borders are to be drawn. Nevertheless, we believe that territorial compromise is essential to peace. Boundaries should reflect the quality of both security and political arrangements. The United States is prepared to accept whatever the parties themselves find acceptable. What we seek, as I said on March 6, is a solution that meets the twin tests of fairness and security.

Notes

CHAPTER ONE

1. The formative works on bureaucratic politics are Graham Allison, *Essence of Decision: Explaining the Cuban Missile Crisis* (Little, Brown, 1971); and Morton Halperin, *Bureaucratic Politics and Foreign Policy* (Brookings, 1974). For an excellent critique, see Robert Art, "Bureaucratic Politics and American Foreign Policy: A Critique," *Policy Sciences*, vol. 4 (1973), pp. 467–90.

2. See Mitchell Geoffrey Bard, *The Water's Edge and Beyond: Defining the Limits to Domestic Influence on United States Middle East Policy* (New Brunswick, N.J.: Transaction Publishers, 1991).

3. See William B. Quandt, *Camp David: Peacemaking and Politics* (Brookings, 1986), pp. 6–29.

4. For a more detailed discussion of these three approaches, see William B. Quandt, *Decade of Decisions: American Policy toward the Arab-Israeli Conflict, 1967–1976* (University of California Press, 1977), pp. 3–28.

5. See Daniel Yergin, *The Prize: The Epic Quest for Oil, Money and Power* (Simon and Schuster, 1991).

6. See Raymond A. Bauer and Kenneth J. Gergen, eds., *The Study of Policy Formulation* (Free Press, 1968), p. 15.

7. Charles E. Lindblom, "The Science of 'Muddling Through,' " *Public Administration Review*, vol. 19 (Spring 1959), pp. 79–88.

8. John Steinbruner, *The Cybernetic Theory of Decision: New Dimensions of Political Analysis* (Princeton University Press, 1974), pp. 109–24.

9. Ernest May, *"Lessons" of the Past: The Use and Misuse of History in American Foreign Policy* (Oxford University Press, 1973).

10. Merle Miller, *Plain Speaking: An Oral Biography of Harry S. Truman* (Berkley Publishing, 1973).

11. Lynn E. Davis, *The Cold War Begins: Soviet-American Conflict over Eastern Europe* (Princeton University Press, 1974).

12. Alexander L. George, "The Case for Multiple Advocacy in Making Foreign Policy," *American Political Science Review*, vol. 66 (September 1972), pp. 751–85; and Irving L. Janis, *Victims of Groupthink: A Psychological Study of Foreign Policy Decisions and Fiascoes* (Houghton Mifflin, 1972).

CHAPTER TWO

1. Abba Eban, *An Autobiography* (Random House, 1977), pp. 354–55, gives an account of Johnson's early concern with Israel. Among Johnson's close friends

who were strong supporters of Israel were Arthur Krim, president of United Artists and chairman of the Democratic National Party Finance Committee, and his wife Mathilde; Abraham Feinberg, president of the American Bank and Trust of New York; Abraham Fortas, Supreme Court Justice; and Arthur Goldberg, ambassador to the United Nations. See Donald Neff, *Warriors for Jerusalem: The Six Days That Changed the Middle East* (Simon and Schuster, 1984), pp. 80–85, 156–58.

2. The report prepared in the fall of 1966 by Ambassador Julius Holmes contained this theme.

3. Lyndon Baines Johnson Library, oral history project, Lucius Battle interviewed by Paige Mulhollan, November 14, 1968, p. 36; and author's conversation with Battle. David Nes, who was in charge of the embassy in Cairo between Battle's departure and the arrival of Richard Nolte, wrote to a colleague in the State Department on May 11, 1967, stating: "We seem to have driven Nasser to a degree of irrationality bordering on madness, fed, of course, by the frustrations and fears generated by his failures domestic and foreign. Our debate here revolves around where he will strike next—Libya, Lebanon? . . . In brief, we now face all the dangers inevitably flowing from having pushed Nasser into a financial and food corner and from endeavoring to thwart him within his first two 'concentric circles.' Now we have the showdown I referred to last October." David Nes to Rodger Davies, May 11, 1967, secret (declassified November 14, 1984).

4. See Michael Brecher, *Decisions in Israel's Foreign Policy* (Yale University Press, 1975), pp. 359–61, for a review of these threats. The best documented, and the one that was carried by UPI and showed up in the *New York Times* on May 13, consisted of a background briefing on May 12, 1967, by the Israeli head of military intelligence, Aharon Yariv. John Cooley, *Green March, Black September: The Story of the Palestinian Arabs* (London: Frank Cass, 1973), p. 160, quotes from a tape of the briefing: "I could say we must use force in order to have the Egyptians convince the Syrians that it doesn't pay [to let the Palestinians carry out attacks across Syria's borders]. . . . I think that the only sure and safe answer to the problem is a military operation of great size and strength." Some analysts have mistakenly assumed that it was Chief of Staff Yitzhak Rabin who made the "threat" against Syria. See *Middle East Record, 1967*, vol. 3 (Jerusalem: Israel Universities Press, 1971), p. 187.

5. Although Israeli threats to take action against Syria were not very precise in this period, it does appear that some retaliatory action was contemplated. Michael Brecher, *Decisions in Crisis: Israel, 1967 and 1973* (University of California Press, 1980), p. 36, states that on May 7, 1967, "Israel's Cabinet decided that if Syria did not heed her public warnings and if all other noncoercive methods of persuasion failed, Israel would launch a limited retaliation raid." For the Egyptian reaction, see Mohamed Heikal [in Arabic, Muhammad Hassanayn Haykal], *1967: Al-Infijar* (Cairo: Markaz al-Ahram, 1990), pp. 445–56.

6. Heikal, *1967: Al-Infijar*, pp. 371–72, greatly exaggerates when he implies that Johnson was obsessed with Nasser and engaged in a conspiracy to bring him down.

7. Stephen Green, *Taking Sides: America's Secret Relations with a Militant Israel* (William Morrow, 1984), pp. 204–11.

8. On this incident, which in the words of Yitzhak Rabin caught Israel "with its pants down," see Avner Yaniv, *Deterrence without the Bomb: The Politics of Israeli Strategy* (Lexington, Mass.: Lexington Books, 1987), pp. 84–85.

9. Some, including Egypt's then–foreign minister, Mahmoud Riad, have maintained that Egypt only asked that UNEF be withdrawn from the border area, not Sharm al-Shaykh. That may have been the intention behind the initial requests, but Egyptian commanders in the field made it clear that the UNEF contingent at Sharm al-Shaykh should also leave. Riad's own letter to U Thant on May 18 requested the removal of UNEF from the territory of the UAR. See Mahmoud Riad, *The Struggle for Peace in the Middle East* (Quartet Books, 1981), p. 18; and "Report of the Secretary-General on the Withdrawal of the United Nations Emergency Force, June 26, 1967," reprinted in John Norton Moore, ed., *The Arab-Israeli Conflict*, vol. 3: *Documents* (Princeton University Press, 1974), p. 756. U Thant has been criticized for acceding too hastily to the Egyptian request, for not referring the question to the General Assembly, in short, for not calling Nasser's bluff. See, for example, Nadav Safran, *Israel: The Embattled Ally* (Harvard University Press, 1978), 394–95. Heikal, *1967: Al-Infijar*, pp. 457–74, argues that Nasser did initially favor only a partial withdrawal of UNEF, while Abd al-Hakim Amr ['Āmir], the head of the armed forces, wanted UNEF to leave completely. There are many indications from Egyptian sources that the Nasser-Amr rivalry was a serious problem throughout this whole period. For a good overview of the relevant facts, see Richard B. Parker, "The June 1967 War: Some Mysteries Explored," *Middle East Journal*, vol. 46 (Spring 1992), pp. 184–96.

10. Lyndon Baines Johnson, *The Vantage Point: Perspectives of the Presidency, 1963–1969* (Rinehart, Holt and Winston, 1971), p. 290; and M. Gilboa, *Six Years, Six Days* (in Hebrew) (Tel Aviv: Am Oved, 1968), p. 144.

11. Harold Saunders, a staff member of the National Security Council (NSC) at this time, was responsible for compiling the White House documents on the 1967 crisis for the Johnson Library. In a reflective cover memorandum entitled "The Middle East Crisis: Preface," December 20, 1968, top secret (declassified October 14, 1983), Saunders notes that "we 'decided' at the outset of the crisis to try to restrain Israel from trying to settle its own problems militarily. . . . The alternative was to let the Israelis do as they had so often done before—respond militarily on their own. This alternative was rejected, almost out of hand. . . . I had the impression that President Johnson himself, though he wanted to avoid war, was profoundly skeptical that we would succeed in rallying practical international support for keeping the Straits open. If we failed, our last hope was to negotiate with Nasser's Vice President. If that didn't work, we would be left to open the Straits in direct confrontation with the whole Arab world."

12. Gilboa, *Six Years, Six Days*, p. 145; and *Middle East Record, 1967*, vol. 3, pp. 194, 196.

13. The text of the February 11, 1957, aide memoire can be found in Moore, *Arab-Israeli Conflict*, vol. 3: *Documents*, pp. 638–39. On February 24, 1957, Eban

sought a clarification from Dulles to the effect that Israel could invoke the right to self-defense under article 51 of the UN Charter if its ships were attacked. Dulles agreed with Eban's position. The public manifestation of this "assent" was somewhat vague. Golda Meir spoke at the UN on March 1 and stated that Israel would exercise its inherent right of self-defense if armed force was used to interfere with Israeli shipping in the Strait of Tiran. Henry Cabot Lodge, the American ambassador to the United Nations, took note of this declaration and said that it did not seem "unreasonable." Eban was unhappy with this formulation, and therefore Eisenhower wrote to Ben Gurion on March 2, 1957, saying that Israel would "have no cause to regret" its withdrawal from Sinai and that the expressed Israeli views were "reasonable." All the relevant texts can be found in Nina J. Noring, ed., *Foreign Relations of the United States, 1955–1957: Arab-Israeli Dispute, 1957* (Government Printing Office, 1990), pp. 254–348.

14. Michael Brecher, *Decisions in Israel's Foreign Policy*, p. 375, quoting Ambassador Avraham Harman to Assistant Secretary Battle.

15. Gilboa, *Six Years, Six Days*, p. 123, quoting Rostow to Harman, May 20. Michael Bar-Zohar, *Embassies in Crisis: Diplomats and Demagogues behind the Six-Day War* (Prentice-Hall, 1970), p. 56, confirms this.

16. Gilboa, *Six Years, Six Days*, p. 145; Brecher, *Decisions in Israel's Foreign Policy*, p. 375; Bar-Zohar, *Embassies in Crisis*, p. 68. The full text of the Johnson letter is in Department of State telegram 198955, May 21, 1967, secret (declassified May 24, 1990).

17. In mid-October 1969 Abba Eban submitted an article to the *New York Times Magazine* that was prepared for publication but was withdrawn at the last moment. A copy of the galley proofs are in the author's possession and they differ in significant ways from Eban's later account in his autobiography. His words concerning the May 21 letter in the draft were: "Nothing could have been less promising than these early reports. Indeed, it was their lack of virile purpose and Johnsonian authenticity which had swayed my decision to go to Washington. This was not Johnson language; a frightened bureaucrat bleated from every line. Nothing except the signature seemed to have anything to do with the firm and candid personality which Israel had respected throughout all of his vicissitudes—and ours—at home and in the world."

18. The original draft of the letter, with Johnson's own corrections and additions, is available from the Johnson Library (declassified May 8, 1981.) See also Mohamed Heikal, *The Cairo Documents: The Inside Story of Nasser and His Relationship with World Leaders, Rebels, and Statesmen* (Doubleday, 1973), p. 243. Nolte delivered the letter, plus a more substantive "note verbale," which warned of war by miscalculation, to the Egyptian foreign minister, Mahmoud Riad. Three areas of concern were emphasized: continuing guerrilla activities against Israel from Syrian territory, withdrawal of UNEF, and troop buildups. The note went on to say, "We are convinced that any interference whatever with these international rights [of free and innocent passage in the strait for ships of all nations] could have the gravest international consequences." For the "note verbale," see Department of State telegram 199710, May 22, 1967, confidential (declassified January 4, 1990).

19. Rusk added a message to the Israelis suggesting that UNEF be transferred to the Israeli side of the border.

20. Johnson, *Vantage Point*, pp. 290–91.

21. Johnson did take one step on May 22 that had continuing importance during the crisis: he ordered the Sixth Fleet, with two aircraft carriers, the *Saratoga* and the *America*, to the eastern Mediterranean.

22. Brecher, *Decisions in Israel's Foreign Policy*, p. 378.

23. "President's Decisions Israeli Aid Package 23 May 1967," top secret (declassified May 9, 1983). A subsequent decision was made to approve the sale of gas masks. See *The Department of State during the Administration of President Lyndon B. Johnson, November 1963–January 1969*, vol. 1: *Administrative History*, pt. 4, chap. 4, section H-1, secret (declassified September 16, 1983), pp. 20, 33. According to the same source (p. 45), Eugene Rostow believed the United States had pulled the Israelis back from preemptive strikes on May 23. The United States had also asked Israel not to test the closure of the strait by sending its flagships through. Therefore, Rostow felt, an enormous responsibility fell on the United States.

24. "The United States Calls for Restraint in the Near East: Statement by President Johnson," *Department of State Bulletin*, vol. 56 (June 12, 1967), p. 870.

25. Brecher, *Decisions in Israel's Foreign Policy*, p. 381, refers to Evron's cable on why the United States was planning to take its case to the United Nations.

26. Johnson, *Vantage Point*, pp. 291–92.

27. Ibid., p. 291; and Eugene V. Rostow, *Peace in the Balance: The Future of American Foreign Policy* (Simon and Schuster, 1972), pp. 259–60. The Israeli ambassador had already called on Eisenhower on May 24, presumably to remind the former president of the commitments that had been made in 1957 concerning the strait.

28. "Record of National Security Council Meeting held on May 24, 1967 at 12 noon—Discussion of Middle East Crisis," top secret (declassified October 14, 1983). On September 10, 1992, additional portions of this document were declassified. The intriguing points are that CIA Director Helms categorically asserted that there were no nuclear weapons in the area, while General Earle Wheeler, chairman of the Joint Chiefs, was "more skeptical." Later in the discussion the president returned to the question of "what we would do after relying on Israeli forces. General Wheeler noted that a long war would hurt the Israeli economy. At that point we would have to decide whether we were going to send in forces and confront Nasser directly." The next section of the transcript is still classified.

29. Johnson, *Vantage Point*, p. 292; Gilboa, *Six Years, Six Days*, p. 143; and Bar-Zohar, *Embassies in Crisis*, p. 98.

30. Bar-Zohar, *Embassies in Crisis*, p. 123; Gilboa, *Six Years, Six Days*, pp. 145–46; and interview with Eugene Rostow, February 17, 1969.

31. Bar-Zohar, *Embassies in Crisis*, p. 125.

32. During the NSC meeting on May 24, Wheeler said that "it would be harder to open the Gulf of Aqaba than we had at first thought. Because of the two Egyptian submarines in the Red Sea, we would need a ASW [artisubmarine

warfare] unit, the nearest of which is now in Singapore—two weeks away."
Shortly thereafter "a brief discussion of possible presence of unconventional
weapons followed." "Record of National Security Council Meeting held on May
24, 1967 at 12 noon—Discussion of Middle East Crisis," p. 3, top secret
(declassified October 14, 1983).

33. These messages were sent at the instigation of the chief of staff, Yitzhak
Rabin, who was eager to force an American decision. Either Johnson would have
to commit himself to concrete action or Israel would be free to act on its own.
See Yitzhak Rabin, *The Rabin Memoirs* (Little, Brown, 1979), pp. 86–89; Gideon
Rafael, *Destination Peace: Three Decades of Israeli Foreign Policy. A Personal Memoir*
(Stein and Day, 1981), pp. 144–45; Eban, *Autobiography*, pp. 348–49; and Steven
L. Spiegel, *The Other Arab Israeli Conflict: Making America's Middle East Policy from
Truman to Reagan* (University of Chicago Press, 1985), p. 450, note 95, for a
slightly different version.

34. Brecher, *Decisions in Israel's Foreign Policy*, p. 386; and, with more detail,
Brecher, *Decisions in Crisis*, pp. 130–32; Bar-Zohar, *Embassies in Crisis*, p. 109; and
Moshe Dayan, *Moshe Dayan: Story of My Life* (William Morrow, 1976), p. 329.

35. Brecher, *Decisions in Israel's Foreign Policy*, pp. 386–87; and Bar-Zohar,
Embassies in Crisis, pp. 112–13. Eugene Rostow called in Egyptian Ambassador
Kemal and warned that Egypt must not attack Israel. The Soviets were also
asked to use their influence to restrain Nasser, which they reportedly did. Heikal,
Cairo Documents, p. 244; Gilboa, *Six Years, Six Days*, pp. 145–46; Brecher, *Decisions
in Israel's Foreign Policy*, p. 387; and Bar-Zohar, *Embassies in Crisis*, pp. 111–12.

36. While Eban was making his pitch at the State Department, the CIA had
received an alarmist report presented by an Israeli intelligence official to the CIA
station chief in Tel Aviv. It warned of a Soviet takeover of the region if Nasser
was not forced to back down. Interview with Richard Helms, June 8, 1992.

37. Brecher, *Decisions in Israel's Foreign Policy*, pp. 387–88. Harman saw Eugene
Rostow and Joseph Sisco.

38. Bar-Zohar, *Embassies in Crisis*, p. 114–15. We now know that the Egyptian
military, in particular Abd al-Hakim Amr, had issued orders for the Egyptian
air force to carry out air strikes on the morning of May 27. The Israelis must
have gotten wind of this. According to Egyptian sources, Nasser countermanded
the order on May 26. See Muhammad Fawzi, *Harb al-Thalatha Sanawat, 1967–70:
Mudhakirat al-Fariq Awal Muhammad Fawzi* (The Three-Year War, 1967–70:
Memoirs of General Muhammad Fawzi) (Cairo: Dar al-Mustaqbal al-Arabi, 1984),
p. 123; and Abd al-Muhsin Kamil Murtaji, *Al-Fariq Murtaji Yarwa al-Haqa'iq*
(General Murtaji Narrates the Facts) (Beirut: Al-Watan al-Arabi, 1976), pp. 79–81.
Also, Heikal, *1967: Al-Infijar*, pp. 573–75.

39. See Tom Wicker, *JFK and LBJ: The Influence of Personality upon Politics*
(William Morrow, 1968), pp. 195–99.

40. Eban, *Autobiography*, pp. 349–51; Brecher, *Decisions in Israel's Foreign Policy*,
pp. 389–90; and Bar-Zohar, *Embassies in Crisis*, p. 115.

41. The previous evening, May 25, 1967, Johnson had met with Helms and
Wheeler to discuss a recent Israeli intelligence assessment that was viewed as
alarmist. The president had asked for the Israeli assessment to be "scrubbed

down." On May 26 a joint CIA-DIA (Defense Intelligence Agency) assessment was ready. It concluded that Israel would gain air superiority in Sinai within twenty-four hours if Israel took the initiative, and within two to three days if Egypt struck first. The assessment went on to conclude that the Egyptian defense lines would be breached within several days. Interview with Richard Helms, June 5, 1992.

42. Gilboa, *Six Years, Six Days*, pp. 146–47; and Brecher, *Decisions in Israel's Foreign Policy*, p. 390. Bar-Zohar, *Embassies in Crisis*, p. 117, claims that McNamara expressed his opposition to the multilateral naval fleet at this meeting.

43. The Johnson Library files for the 1967 crisis contain a complete review of the commitments made in 1957. Presumably this document, dated February 26, 1957 (declassified October 19, 1982), was provided by the Israelis and summarizes the understandings reached with Dulles. This must be one of the documents reviewed by policymakers, who appear not to have been fully aware of the extent of the American commitment, especially the acknowledgment that Israel had the right to use force to reopen the Strait of Tiran if it was ever closed by force.

44. "Memorandum for the President: Your Conversation with the Israeli Foreign Minister," May 26, 1967, secret (declassified and sanitized, August 30, 1982).

45. McNamara did not oppose the president's policy, however.

46. See Rusk's handwritten draft using these words, Johnson Library (declassified June 27, 1983). This key sentence was used frequently in later communications, sometimes in slightly different forms. The Israelis spent considerable time trying to figure out if the message constituted a subtle form of encouragement to act on their own. To Rusk, it seems, it did not. Rusk's handwritten draft was edited by Johnson, who added the phrase "We cannot imagine that it will make this decision" right after the "go alone" sentence. This became the aide-memoire handed to Eban during the meeting that evening. See marked-up draft of the aide-memoire, Johnson Library, May 26, 1967, secret (declassified September 21, 1983).

47. The view was expressed that no overt act of aggression had yet occurred. Until Egypt resorted to the use of armed force, according to this argument, the U.S. commitment to Israel would not be activated.

48. The above summary is from rough notes of the meeting taken by Harold Saunders, May 26, 1967. See also Neff, *Warriors for Jerusalem*, pp. 142–43, especially for the text of Walt Rostow's memo for the president in preparation for this meeting. Rostow stated, among other things, that Eban would want to know "what can you offer right now better than a pre-emptive [Israeli] strike."

49. Jonathan Trumbull Howe, *Multicrises: Sea Power and Global Politics in the Missile Age* (MIT Press, 1971), pp. 362–67. Howe interviewed an unnamed White House source (John Roche), who stated that Johnson was stalling Eban because he had just been shown the memo of the Dulles-Eban talks of 1957 and wanted to check its authenticity.

50. Evron recalled Johnson as having said that without congressional approval for any action taken, Johnson would be "just a six-foot-four-inch friend of Israel."

He went on to say that "Israel is not a satellite of the United States. Nor is the United States a satellite of Israel." In retrospect, Evron felt that this was Johnson's way of saying that Israel was on its own. The message was less clear, he believed, when Johnson spoke to Eban, relying on the State Department briefing papers, shortly after this meeting. Interview with Ephraim Evron, June 4, 1992.

51. Brecher, *Decisions in Israel's Foreign Policy*, pp. 390–91, provides the full text of Evron's official account of his meeting with Johnson.

52. "Memorandum of Conversation, May 26, 1967," secret/nodis (drafted by Joseph Sisco, sanitized and declassified September 21, 1983). See also Brecher, *Decision in Israel's Foreign Policy*, p. 392. Johnson, *Vantage Point*, p. 293, says he told Eban the United States would use "any and all means" to open the strait. The official transcript reports on pp. 7–8 that Eban, choosing his words carefully, said, "I would not be wrong if I told the Prime Minister that your disposition is to make every possible effort to assure that the Strait and the Gulf will remain open to free and innocent passage? The President responded, yes." Earlier in the conversation, however, Johnson did say that the United States would pursue "any and all means" to reopen the strait. The difference between these two formulations—"every possible effort" and "any and all means"—became a source of controversy between the two governments a few days later.

53. Interview with Eugene Rostow, February 17, 1969; and Howe, *Multicrisis*, pp. 362–67. Howe quotes White House aide John Roche to the effect that Johnson said after his meeting with Eban: "[Israel is] going to hit them." Roche's account can be found in his oral history interview with the Johnson Library, July 16, 1970, tape 2, p. 68. Just after the meeting with Eban, Johnson took a call from Ambassador Goldberg in New York. This conversation must have led Goldberg to ask for an urgent meeting of his own with Eban, who was transiting New York on his way back to Tel Aviv. The two met at the Waldorf Astoria. Goldberg, speaking authoritatively, underscored the point the president had made about the necessity for congressional support for any U.S. action. Goldberg offered his personal opinion that this meant that the United States could do nothing militarily to help Israel. Rafael, *Destination Peace*, p. 145, provides part of this story. In addition, see the oral history interview with Arthur Goldberg, LBJ Library, March 23, 1983, p. 22. In the same interview Goldberg claims that Johnson had asked him to take charge of the crisis because Rusk had disqualified himself by making anti-Israel remarks earlier in his career (p. 16).

54. Brecher, *Decisions in Israel's Foreign Policy*, pp. 398, provides the text of this message: "The Soviets stated that if Israel starts military action, the Soviet Union will extend help to the attacked States. . . . As your friend, I repeat even more strongly what I said yesterday to Mr. Eban: Israel just must not take pre-emptive military action and thereby make itself responsible for the initiation of hostilities." Johnson then requested a two-to three-week delay before Israel would resort to force to open the strait. The original draft of the message had said "It is essential that Israel not. . . ." From his Texas ranch, Johnson strengthened this to read "Israel just must not. . . ." He also suggested including the following language: "Without exception our Congressional leaders have made it clear that

preemptive actions would find no support here." Memorandum from Jim Jones to Walt Rostow, May 27, 1967 (declassified and sanitized, September 21, 1983).

55. Brecher, *Decisions in Israel's Foreign Policy*, p. 400. Brecher, *Decisions in Crisis*, p. 146, claims that this message had a significant impact on Eshkol's thinking and probably kept the cabinet from deciding on war that day.

56. Interview with Daniel P. Levitt, law clerk for Justice Fortas in 1967, on August 8, 1991. Levitt indicated that he believed but could not confirm that Johnson had asked Fortas to play the role of "informal intermediary" with Israel.

57. See Laura Kalman, *Abe Fortas: A Biography* (Yale University Press, 1990), p. 301; and, from the same source (Levitt), Robert Shogan, *A Question of Judgment: The Fortas Case and the Struggle for the Supreme Court* (Bobbs-Merrill, 1972), p. 139.

58. On Robert Kennedy's position, see Dean Rusk, *As I Saw It* (Norton, 1990), p. 385: "Bobby Kennedy, then a Senator from New York, told McNamara and me, 'I don't know what you fellows in Washington think about the attitude of my Jewish friends in New York, but they don't want any part of this [U.S.-led multilateral fleet].' "

59. National Archives, presidential diaries, April 1, 1967, to June 30, 1967 (microfilm, part II, reel 9), especially May 27–31, 1967.

60. Interview with Walt Rostow, October 16, 1991; and Walt Rostow, *The Diffusion of Power: An Essay in Recent History* (Macmillan, 1972), pp. 417–19.

61. On May 30, 1967, Rusk and McNamara prepared a joint memorandum for the president that recommended a number of steps to "test" Egyptian intentions regarding the blockade. For example, consideration was given to a plan for sending an Israeli-owned ship into the Gulf of Aqaba. "If that passed without interference, we might attempt passage with a more 'strategic' cargo (e.g., oil). Within this period, such tests would involve no armed escort and no counteraction in the event passage was refused. The purpose would be to clarify the limits of UAR policy and to build a public case for support of free passage" (p.4). A stronger military option was also being considered. In both cases, consultation with Congress would be essential. "While it is true that many Congressional doves may be in the process of conversion to hawks, the problem of 'Tonkin Gulfitis' remains serious" (p.6). The memo concluded with the note that military contingency planning with the United Kingdom would be under way by the end of the week of June 5. LBJ Library, "Memorandum for the President," secret, May 30, 1967 (partially declassified September 27, 1991).

62. Johnson, *Vantage Point*, p. 294; Bar-Zohar, *Embassies in Crisis*, pp. 159–60; and Brecher, *Decisions in Israel's Foreign Policy*, pp. 338, 413. The full text of Eshkol's message, which Walt Rostow characterized as "somber" in a covering note to Johnson, has never been published. According to one source, Eshkol did refer to "the intelligence cooperation which you have authorized." Brecher, who has seen the letter, quotes the following sentences from it: "One of the difficulties that I face is that I must call on my people to meet sacrifices and dangers without being able fully to reveal certain compensatory factors such as the United States commitment and the full scope of your determination on the matter of the Straits of Tiran" (p. 338). Eshkol also referred to the need to stand up to Nasser soon,

noting the effect he was having on Jordan. "President Nasser's rising prestige has already had serious effects in Jordan. . . . The time is ripe for confronting Nasser with a more intense and effective policy of resistance" (p. 413). This latter point impressed Rostow, and probably the president as well. Reacting to this same Eshkol message, Harold Saunders wrote to Walt Rostow on May 31 and urged him to consider a "quite different alternative," presumably to that of the multilateral fleet. In a recently declassified portion of the message, Saunders notes that the British and Canadians "are wobbling" and the "Eshkol's message suggests that we may be up against this choice sooner rather than later." "Memorandum for WWR," secret (declassified, October 14, 1992).

63. Brecher, *Decisions in Israel's Foreign Policy*, p. 414; Gilboa, *Six Years, Six Days*, p. 197; and Bar-Zohar, *Embassies in Crisis*, p. 160. According to Rabin, *Rabin Memoirs*, p. 95, the report of this conversation between Rostow and Evron had a significant effect on Eshkol, who interpreted it as meaning that he could not count on Johnson to take firm action.

64. Transmittal of "Yost's first Report" from Walt Rostow to the president, received LBJ Communications Center in Texas, May 30, 1967, at 2:17 p.m., secret (declassified June 27, 1983).

65. Heikal, *Cairo Documents*, p. 245; Brecher, *Decisions in Israel's Foreign Policy*, p. 420; and Bar-Zohar, *Embassies in Crisis*, p. 168. Anderson's report of his talk with Nasser reached Washington on June 2. See Department of State telegram, Lisbon 1517, June 2, 1967, top secret (declassified September 3, 1982). Nasser told Anderson that Egypt would not attack, but expected the Israelis to strike. Nasser said that "he was confident of the outcome of a conflict between Arabs and Israelis."

66. Bar-Zohar, *Embassies in Crisis*, pp. 160–61.

67. Interview with Evron, November 5, 1991.

68. Bar-Zohar, *Embassies in Crisis*, p. 157, states that on May 30, after Jordan threw in its lot with Egypt, Walt Rostow expressed the opinion that he no longer saw a political solution.

69. Brecher, *Decisions in Israel's Foreign Policy*, p. 417. See also Ian Black and Benny Morris, *Israel's Secret Wars: A History of Israel's Intelligence Services* (Grove Weidenfeld, 1991), p. 537, referring to an interview with Amit, who claims he went to Washington "to tell [the Americans] that we were going to war, and to hear their reaction."

70. Letter to William B. Quandt from Abba Eban, July 26, 1990. Eban, *Autobiography*, pp. 384–85, gives a more extensive account of this message but without any mention of Evron or Fortas by name. According to Eban, an American close to Johnson (Fortas) reportedly said, "If Israel had acted alone without exhausting political efforts it would have made a catastrophic error. It would then have been almost impossible for the United States to help Israel and the ensuing relationship would have been tense. The war might be long and costly for Israel if it broke out. If Israel had fired the first shot before the United Nations discussion she would have negated any possibility of the United States helping her. Israelis should not criticize Eshkol and Eban; they should realize that their restraint and well-considered procedures would have a decisive influence

when the United States came to consider the measure of its involvement." Fortas reportedly understood that "time was running out and that it was a matter of days or even hours." But Fortas believed that "if the measures being taken by the United States prove ineffective, the United States would now back Israel." Abba Eban, *Personal Witness: Israel through My Eyes* (Putnam's, 1993), p. 405, repeats this account, this time naming Fortas.

Johnson and Fortas spoke at 8:43 p.m. on May 28, according to the president's daily calendar. Johnson tried again to call Fortas on May 31, but Fortas was in Puerto Rico. See also Shimon Peres, *David's Sling* (Random House, 1970), p. 236, where he writes: "As the month of May approached its end, it became clear that there was no longer any prospect of a maritime operation through the Straits. Even in certain circles in Washington the view was heard that the only one able to find a way out of the impasse was Israel herself. This view reached the ears of Jerusalem."

71. Brecher, *Decisions in Israel's Foreign Policy*, p. 417, indicates that Eban had also seen Amit's report, with its judgment that "there is a growing chance for American political backing if we act on our own." Eitan Haber, *Today War Will Break Out: The Reminiscences of Brigadier General Israel Lior* (Jerusalem: Edanim/ Yediot Aharonot, 1987) (in Hebrew), p. 213, notes that on June 1 Eban concluded that there was no longer any need to wait for U.S. action. His change of mind was seen by some as providing a green light for military action. According to Haber, Yariv had already reached the conclusion that the United States was not serious about the maritime fleet and that therefore Israel was free to act on its own (pp. 205–06).

72. Johnson, *Vantage Point*, p. 294, without naming Evron, reveals part of this incident. The rest is based on interviews with participants.

73. By contrast, the American embassy in Cairo strongly felt that the Egyptians would react militarily to any attempt to reopen the strait. See cable on May 26, 1967 (Cairo 8007, secret), May 28, 1967 (Cairo 8093, secret), and June 3, 1967 (Cairo 8432, secret), all declassified on January 4, 1990.

74. Interview with Evron, December 30, 1974. Notes of this meeting were made by Harold Saunders, who was present, and have been consulted as well.

75. Evron was busy on June 3. Early in the morning, he presented a long list of Israel's military needs to McNamara, who implied that the arms could never get to Israel in time, since the war would be quickly over. Evron read this as a hint that the United States was confident that Israel would win and that there was no need to wait for American action. Later in the day Evron saw Rusk, who, during a very cordial meeting, gave him Johnson's letter to Eshkol. That same evening he dined with Walt Rostow, who talked at some length about what should be done in the region after the war was over. In his view, these three senior American officials, all aware of his and Amit's messages, had several chances that day to warn Israel not to take military action, but instead they talked as if war was a foregone conclusion. Interview with Evron, November 5, 1991.

76. According to Evron, this was the closest Johnson came to responding to the messages from him and Amit that time was running out and Israel might have to act soon. By acknowledging these signals, he thought Johnson was saying

to Israel that "the red light has turned to amber." Interview with Evron, October 22, 1991.

77. Interview with Richard Helms, June 8, 1992. Amit told Helms that Israel needed nothing from the United States except the supply of arms already agreed upon, diplomatic support, and holding the Soviets at bay if necessary. Amit interpreted his and Ambassador Harman's recall to Jerusalem on June 1 as an indication that the decision for war was imminent. In Amit's view, Nasser was not planning a ground attack, but Israel could not afford to wait for his next move. The economic costs were too great, and the political pressures on Eshkol were intense. In addition, there was the possibility of an Egyptian air strike, perhaps at the Dimona nuclear reactor. According to Shlomo Aronson, *The Politics and Strategy of Nuclear Weapons in the Middle East: Opacity, Theory, and Reality, 1960–1991. An Israeli Perspective* (State University of New York Press, 1992), p. 109, an Egyptian aircraft had overflown Dimona on May 17, 1967, on a reconnaissance flight. Aronson makes an elaborate argument that Nasser's primary objective in the crisis that led to the June 1967 war was to put Egypt in a position to strike at Dimona before Israel acquired nuclear-tipped surface-to-surface missiles. Eshkol was reportedly preoccupied with the possible threat to Dimona. See Haber, *Today War Will Break Out*, p. 161.

78. Letter from President Johnson to Prime Minister Eshkol. Available with cover memorandum, June 3, 1967, from the Johnson Library, secret (declassified April 5, 1982), with the intriguing note from Walt Rostow that "It may be urgent that we put this letter on record soon." See also Brecher, *Decisions in Israel's Foreign Policy*, p. 420. Bar-Zohar, *Embassies in Crisis*, p. 175, also printed part of this text. Dayan, *Moshe Dayan*, pp. 345–46, states that a letter from Johnson was read to the ministerial defense committee meeting on June 4 at which the decision for war was made.

79. Department of State telegram 297977, June 3, 1967, p. 3, secret (declassified January 9, 1990).

80. Levitt to Quandt, August 8, 1991; and Kalman, *Abe Fortas*, p. 301.

81. Nasser had sent Johnson a letter on June 2, which reached the president the following day, that agreed to the visit of Muhieddin, but was, in the words of Walt Rostow, otherwise "quite uncompromising." See Rostow memo to Johnson, June 3, 1967, with text of Nasser letter, secret (declassified August 27, 1982), Johnson Library. Anderson's discouraging report of his talk with Nasser also reached the president at about this time.

82. Gilboa, *Six Years, Six Days*, p. 199. A participant in the meeting noted that Amit reported that the United States would bless whatever Israel did if it succeeded in getting rid of Nasser. See also Andrew Cockburn and Leslie Cockburn, *Dangerous Liaison: The Inside Story of the U.S.-Israeli Covert Relationship* (HarperCollins Publishers, 1991), pp. 145–46, quoting from Eshkol's cabinet secretary. For the original source, see Haber, *Today War Will Break Out*, pp. 216–18. Amit's own version is that he said something to the effect that the United States would not mourn if Israel struck at Egypt (interview, June 4, 1992). Amit also told the cabinet members that the "Red Sea Regatta" should not be taken seriously. During the subsequent June 4 cabinet meeting, when the

decision to go to war was officially taken, Eshkol said that Johnson had now softened his stand and would give Israel political support. See Brecher, *Decisions in Crisis*, p. 167.

83. Outgoing telegram, Department of State, Circular to Arab Capitals, Eyes Only for Ambassador from Secretary, June 3, 1967, 7:17 p.m., secret (declassified January 4, 1990). "You should not assume that the United States can order Israel not to fight for what it considers to be its most vital interests. We have used the utmost restraint and, thus far, have been able to hold Israel back. But the 'Holy War' psychology of the Arab world is matched by an apocalyptic psychology within Israel. Israel may make a decision that it must resort to force to protect its vital interests. In dealing with the issues involved, therefore, we must keep in mind the necessity for finding a solution with which Israel can be restrained. . . . It will do no good to ask Israel to accept the present status quo in the Strait because Israel will fight and we could not restrain her. We cannot throw up our hands and say that, in that event, let them fight while we try to remain neutral."

84. Merle Miller, *Lyndon: An Oral Biography* (Putnam's, 1980), p. 480. The formal Israeli cabinet decision to go to war was taken at the end of a seven-hour meeting on June 4, which ended about mid-afternoon Israeli time. If this anecdote is true, Feinberg must have based his report to Johnson on the prior decision in principle to go to war on June 5 taken by the Israeli "inner cabinet," first on June 2 and again on June 3. Evron termed the Feinberg story "bunk" in an interview on October 22, 1991. No one in the United States, he said, knew at that point when exactly the war would begin.

CHAPTER THREE

1. On the second day of the war, Arthur Goldberg forwarded to the White House a message from Israeli Prime Minister Eshkol, conveyed to him through the chief justice of Israel: "Eshkol 'hopes you understand' the action taken by Israel; that it resulted from a judgment that their security situation had so deteriorated that their national existence was imperiled. Eshkol strongly hopes that we will take no action that would limit Israeli action in achieving freedom of passage through the Gulf of Aqaba. They understand your difficulties in achieving this result; and are prepared to handle the matter themselves." See memo from Rostow to Johnson, June 6, 1967, 11:00 a.m., secret (declassified August 23, 1982).

2. Memorandum for the record, National Security Council Meeting, June 7, 1967, secret (declassified August 27, 1982). "The president said 'he was not sure we were out of our troubles.' He could not visualize the USSR saying it had miscalculated, and then walking away. Our objective should be to 'develop as few heroes and as few heels as we can.' It is important for everybody to know we are not for aggression. We are sorry this has taken place. We are in as good a position as we could be given the complexities of the situation. We thought we had a commitment from those governments, but it went up in smoke very quickly. The President said that by the time we get through with all the festering problems we are going to wish the war had not happened."

3. "Memorandum for the Record: Walt Rostow's Recollections of June 5, 1967," November 17, 1968, top secret (declassified October 23, 1984), p. 3: "I might just say parenthetically that President Johnson has never believed that this war was ever anything else than a mistake by the Israelis. A brilliant quick victory he never regarded as an occasion for elation or satisfaction. He so told the Israeli representatives on a number of occasions. However, at the time, I should say that, war having been initiated against our advice, there was a certain relief that things were going well for the Israelis. . . . It did look as though we would not be put in a position of having to make a choice of engaging ourselves or seeing Israel thrown into the sea or defeated. That would have been a most painful moment and, of course, with the Soviet presence in the Middle East, a moment of great general danger."

4. Interview with McGeorge Bundy, December 11, 1968.

5. Clark Clifford was called in to help determine how the war had begun. He quickly concluded that the Israelis had preempted. In the words of Walt Rostow: "his view was that the Israelis had jumped off on minimum provocation in a very purposeful effort to deal with air power and then go after the UAR armies which of course had assembled in the Sinai. It was his judgment at the time as I recall that it was a straight Israeli decision to deal with the crisis by initiating war, although we were all conscious of the provocations at the Straits of Tiran and mobilization in the Sinai." "Memorandum for the Record: Walt Rostow's Recollections of June 5, 1967," p. 3.

6. Jonathan Trumbull Howe, *Multicrises: Sea Power and Global Politics in the Missile Age* (MIT Press, 1971), p. 70.

7. Ibid., p. 90 (interview with Rusk).

8. Ibid., pp. 91, 93, where Rusk states that an immediate cease-fire, favored by the United States, would have left Israel only fifty miles inside Sinai.

9. Johnson was informed on June 7, 1967, of the views of a high-ranking Israeli official who had informed his American counterpart that "the Syrians will get their blow as we deal with each country in turn." The same official raised the question of what the United States had in mind for Nasser when the war was over. This was taken as more than a veiled hint that Israel would like to consider joint action to remove Nasser from power.

10. Clark Clifford, a member of the President's Foreign Intelligence Advisory Board, was asked to determine who was responsible for the *Liberty* attack. According to the notes of the NSC Special Committee meeting on June 9, 1967, Clifford reported that it was "inconceivable that it was an accident." A marginal note says that "President agreed 100%" (declassified August 12, 1985). For more on the *Liberty* affair, see James M. Ennes, Jr., *Assault on the Liberty: The True Story of the Israeli Attack on an American Intelligence Ship* (Random House, 1979); James Bamford, *The Puzzle Palace: A Report on America's Most Secret Agency* (Houghton Mifflin, 1982), pp. 217–29; Hirsch Goodman and Ze'ev Schiff, "The Attack on the *Liberty,*" *Atlantic Monthly*, September 1984, pp. 78–84; and letters to the editor, *Atlantic Monthly*, December 1984, pp. 7–8. Many American officials believed at the time of the Liberty attack that Israel had acted deliberately. In later years some participants in the crisis claimed that intelligence information

showed that the Israeli pilots knew they were attacking a ship flying the American flag. Several motives have been suggested by those who believe the attack was deliberate. The one most frequently cited is that Israel was planning its assault on the Golan Heights and did not want the United States to have evidence that Israel was deliberately breaking the UN cease-fire.

11. Lyndon Baines Johnson, *The Vantage Point: Perspective of the Presidency, 1963–1969* (Holt, Rinehart and Winston, 1971), pp. 301–02.

12. See "Memorandum for the Record: Hot Line Meeting June 10, 1967," top secret, October 22, 1968 (partially declassified February 22, 1982, and February 2, 1993).

13. Dean Rusk, *As I Saw It* (Norton, 1990), pp. 386–87.

14. Mohamed Heikal, *1967: Al-Infijar* (Cairo: Markaz al-Ahram, 1990), p. 371–75, 439, 651; and Mahmoud Riad, *The Struggle for Peace in the Middle East* (Quartet Books, 1981) p. 37. Once the war was under way, some Israelis apparently reached the conclusion that the United States wanted Israel to "finish with Nasser once and for all." See Eitan Haber, *Today War Will Break Out: The Reminiscences of Brigadier General Israel Lior* (Jerusalem: Edanim/Yediot Aharonot, 1987) (in Hebrew), p. 238, quoting the views of Yosef Tekoah of the Israeli Foreign Ministry.

15. Stephen Green, *Taking Sides: America's Secret Relations with a Militant Israel* (William Morrow, 1984) pp. 204–11; and Green, *Living by the Sword: America and Israel in the Middle East, 1968–87* (Brattleboro, Vt.: Amana Books, 1988), p. 235.

16. An equally unproven account of Johnson giving the Israelis some encouragement to go to war comes from Wilbur Crane Eveland, a disgruntled former CIA agent. In *Ropes of Sand: America's Failure in the Middle East* (Norton, 1980), p. 324, he states that Johnson asked James Angleton, a mysterious figure at CIA who was in charge of both counterintelligence and Israeli affairs, to "inform Evron that the U.S. would prefer Israeli efforts to lessen the tension but would not intervene to stop an attack on Egypt. This American position stipulated that there must be no Israeli military action against Jordan, Syria, or Lebanon." Angleton was strongly pro-Israeli and may well have played some role in the crisis, especially during the visit of Meir Amit, but once again the evidence is simply not there and Evron completely denies the story.

17. The CIA received a report of undetermined reliability in June 1967 from a "medium level Soviet official" who stated that "the USSR had wanted to create another trouble spot for the United States in addition to that already existing in Vietnam. The Soviet aim was to create a situation in which the US would become seriously involved, economically, politically, and possibly even militarily and in which the US would suffer serious political reverses as a result of its siding against the Arabs. This grand design, which envisaged a long war in the Middle East, misfired because the Arabs failed completely and the Israeli blitzkrieg was so decisive." To this end, the USSR "had encouraged the Arabs in their hostile attitude toward Israel" (sanitized and declassified, February 28, 1984).

18. See Sydney D. Bailey, *Four Arab-Israeli Wars and the Peace Process* (St. Martin's, 1990), p. 211, based on letters to the author from Rusk. Rusk said: "It would be a serious distortion of anything said by President Johnson to Abba

Eban to suppose that the President gave Israel a 'blank cheque' or that Israel had a right to believe that Israel would have United States support whatever they decided to do." Also, see Rusk's highly informative and revealing "backgrounder" to the press on June 9, 1967, 5:05 p.m., available from the Johnson Library. According to the notes of an NSC Special Committee meeting on June 14, 1967 (declassified August 12, 1985), Rusk spoke about self-determination for the West Bank. "Israel's keeping territory would create a revanchisme for the rest of the 20th c." Rusk, *As I Saw It*, p. 385, did acknowledge that the Israelis were well informed about thinking in Washington: "One thing the Israelis have is good intelligence. If any other country ever penetrated the American government the way they did, we would probably break relations with them."

19. In drawing their conclusions about Johnson's views in this crucial period, the Israelis had several sources to draw on: Harman and Evron were in frequent contact with Fortas, who was a trusted intermediary with Johnson; Evron saw Walt Rostow in this crucial period to explore a scenario of Israel's striking to open the strait; Amit came to Washington to check with intelligence and defense officials; and a number of other friends of Israel, especially the Krims, were intimately familiar with the president's thinking in these crucial days from spending many hours each day with him. In addition, Arthur Goldberg was in regular telephone contact with the president and saw it as his responsibility to offset Rusk's alleged biases. In brief, the Israelis enjoyed access to Johnson and his inner circle that virtually no other government could count on. And they correctly concluded that Johnson would not blame them if they went to war. All of the Israeli accounts make it clear that this was a crucial consideration for Eshkol and Eban, if not for some of the generals. Before deciding on war, they wanted to be sure there would be no repeat of Suez.

20. As early as June 6, 1967, Walt Rostow had noted to the president that a simple cease-fire that left Israel in control of territory would mean that "we could use the *de facto* situation on the ground to try to negotiate not a return to armistice lines but a definitive peace in the Middle East" (declassified March 3, 1982). The following day, in a handwritten memo to the president, Walt Rostow wrote that "Bill Moyers reports via Fineberg [sic] from Eban: 1. When USSR asks withdrawal from cease-fire lines, Eban will say: NO DRAW-BACK WITHOUT DEFINI-TIVE PEACE. . . . 3. Fineberg says this is route for the President totally to *retrieve* position after 'neutrality' and all that." Rostow was referring to a statement made on the first day of the war by the State Department spokesman that the United States was "neutral in thought, word and deed." This had set off a fire storm in the pro-Israeli community, which read it as a statement of indifference.

21. Evron conveyed this point to Walt Rostow on June 5.

22. By chance, the Israeli cabinet decided that same day that it would be prepared to pull back to the international border with Egypt and Syria in return for peace and demilitarization. This decision was conveyed by Rabin to Rusk on June 22, 1967. See Yitzhak Rabin, *The Rabin Memoirs* (Little, Brown, 1975), p. 135. The West Bank would be subject to negotiations, but Israel would not commit itself to full withdrawal, and East Jerusalem had already been annexed within the expanded municipal borders of Greater Jerusalem.

23. For an excellent summary of the diplomacy of this period at the UN, see David A. Korn, *Stalemate: The War of Attrition and Great Power Diplomacy in the Middle East, 1967–1970* (Boulder, Colo.: Westview Press, 1992), pp. 31–45.

24. Ibid., pp. 84–86.

25. The text of the "agreed minute" was transmitted to the Department of State in telegram 1278, October 9, 1967, from USUN New York (secret/exdis). Reference can be found in Nina J. Noring and Walter B. Smith, "The Withdrawal Clause in UN Security Council Resolution 242 of 1967: Its Legislative History and the Attitudes of the United States and Israel since 1967," February 4, 1978 (secret), p. 5.

26. Rusk, *As I Saw It*, p. 389, said that "we never contemplated any significant grant of territory to Israel as a result of the June 1967 war." See also Donald Neff, "The Differing Interpretations of Resolution 242," *Middle East International*, September 13, 1991, pp. 16–17, which draws on classified documents from the time, including Ambassador Goldberg's commitment to King Hussein that was conveyed on November 3, 1967. To obtain Jordan's acceptance of the resolution, Goldberg gave assurances to the Jordanians that the United States would work for the return of the West Bank to Jordanian authority. When George Ball, who became U.S. ambassador to the UN in June 1968, visited the Middle East in mid-July, he was authorized by the Israelis to convey to King Hussein that they were prepared to return the West Bank, with minor modifications, to his authority in return for peace.

27. On October 24, 1967, the State Department announced that forty-eight A-4 Skyhawk jets, agreed on in February 1966, would be delivered to Israel. This came one day after the Egyptian sinking of the Israeli naval ship *Elath*. Eventually the Johnson administration agreed to sell one hundred A-4s to Israel.

28. Israeli Prime Minister Eshkol stated in *Davar*, January 24, 1969, that Johnson had effectively given him a veto over whether the United States should sell tanks to Jordan.

29. Johnson reportedly delayed announcing his tentative decision on the F-4s in the hope of interesting the Soviets in an arms-limitation agreement for the Middle East. The Soviet position was consistent and negative: before a political settlement, there could be no agreement to limit arms to the area. Just before leaving office in January 1969, Johnson finally authorized the sale of the F-4s. See Korn, *Stalemate*, p. 66, for the differing American and Israeli versions of what Johnson promised.

30. The announcement came after unsuccessful talks earlier in October between Rusk and Gromyko on limiting arms to the Middle East. The atmosphere created by the Soviet invasion of Czechoslovakia in August had made agreement in such talks unlikely. In addition, on October 8 Israeli Foreign Minister Eban presented a nine-point "peace plan" to the UN. Eban, consistent with American preferences, subsequently downplayed the need for direct negotiations and endorsed Resolution 242 as a useful set of principles "which can help the parties and guide them in their search for a solution."

31. Riad, *Struggle for Peace*, pp. 90–92; and Rabin, *Rabin Memoirs*, p. 140.

32. For evidence of Fortas's strong pro-Israeli sentiments, see Laura Kalman, *Abe Fortas: A Biography* (Yale University Press, 1990), p. 302.

33. See Joseph A. Califano, Jr., *The Triumph and Tragedy of Lyndon Johnson: The White House Years* (Simon and Schuster, 1991), pp. 204–05. Johnson's pro-Israeli sentiment did not keep him from exploding when he thought his efforts on behalf of the Jewish state were not appreciated by Israel's friends. Many American Jews had been angry at a State Department statement on June 5 that defined the U.S. position as "neutral in thought, word and deed." Johnson came under immense pressure to distance himself from that statement, and some of his advisers urged him to address a pro-Israel mass rally in front of the White House on June 7. Unless he did, said some, it could turn anti-Johnson. Spotting one such aide in the hallway outside the Oval Office, Johnson shouted at him: "You Zionist dupe! You and [Ben] Wattenberg are Zionist dupes in the White House! Why can't you see I'm doing all I can for Israel. That's what you should be telling people when they ask for a message from the President for their rally."

34. According to a high-ranking intelligence official, Angleton and the CIA chief of station in Amman tried, on the second or third day of the war, to warn the political leaders in Washington that something should be done immediately to bring about an Israeli-Jordanian understanding on Jerusalem. Otherwise, they feared, this would become an insoluble problem. Their advice was ignored.

35. The United States was not heavily dependent in 1967 on Arab oil. Walter Levy, acting as adviser to the State Department, correctly predicted that an Arab oil embargo would not be very effective.

36. Some new faces were added to the circle of Johnson's advisers once war broke out, in particular, McGeorge Bundy, who was named chairman of the Executive Committee of the National Security Council to deal with the Middle East on June 6, 1967.

CHAPTER FOUR

1. LBJ Library, June 5, 1967 (declassified December 22, 1982).

2. Richard M. Nixon, *RN: The Memoirs of Richard Nixon* (Grosset and Dunlap, 1978), p. 435. Nixon received about 17 percent of the Jewish vote in the 1968 election, compared with about 80 percent for Hubert Humphrey.

3. See I. M. Destler, *Presidents, Bureaucrats and Foreign Policy: The Politics of Organizational Reform* (Princeton University Press, 1972), pp. 121–27, for a description of the NSC under Nixon.

4. Initially this was called the Interdepartmental Group (IG).

5. Kissinger's staff consisted of several close personal assistants as well as specialists in certain geographic and functional areas. Those who participated in Middle East policy included his deputy, Alexander Haig, two special assistants, Peter Rodman and Winston Lord, and his senior Middle East specialist, Harold H. Saunders, who had been on the NSC staff since the Kennedy administration.

6. Nixon, *RN*, p. 477. Nixon expressed concern that Kissinger would have difficulty working with Arabs because of his Jewish background. Henry Kissinger, *White House Years* (Little, Brown, 1979), p. 348, said that Nixon "suspected that my Jewish origin might cause me to lean too much toward Israel."

7. Kissinger, *White House Years*, p. 348. Nixon "calculated that almost any active policy would fail; in addition, it would almost certainly incur the wrath of Israel's supporters. So he found it useful to get the White House as much out of the direct line of fire as possible."

8. Two other office directors were influential in the shaping of Middle East policy during this period: Richard Parker, in charge of Egyptian affairs, and Talcott Seelye, office director for Arab Republic Affairs (ARA), which covered Jordan, Lebanon, Syria, and Iraq. Deputy Assistant Secretary Rodger Davies was also involved in most of the policy deliberations during this period.

9. Before being named to his White House post, Kissinger had spelled out a middle-of-the-road strategy for negotiations and the disengagement of American troops from Vietnam. In an article published in January 1969, he expressed a concern that was to haunt the Nixon administration throughout its first term: "what is involved now is confidence in American promises. However fashionable it is to ridicule the terms 'credibility' and 'prestige,' they are not empty phrases; other nations can gear their actions to ours only if they can count on our steadiness." "The Viet Nam Negotiations," *Foreign Affairs*, vol. 47 (January 1969), pp. 211–34.

10. Richard M. Nixon, "Asia after Viet Nam," *Foreign Affairs*, vol. 46 (October 1967), pp. 111–25.

11. Kissinger, *White House Years*, pp. 562–64, provides his clearest assessment of the differences between his own views on the Middle East and those of Nixon. Most significantly, Nixon believed that the Soviets were strengthening their position in the region in the aftermath of the June 1967 war; Kissinger felt that their position would be undermined as long as Israel was kept strong and the Soviets' inability to satisfy Arab demands was repeatedly demonstrated.

12. Kissinger, *White House Years*, p. 347.

13. The "Nixon Doctrine" was outlined by the president on July 25, 1969, during a news conference on Guam. The first practical manifestation of the policy, "Vietnamization," was announced by Nixon in a speech delivered November 3, 1969.

14. See Nixon, *RN*, p. 343, for the "powder keg" analogy.

15. Middle East oil was, of course, an important concern, but U.S. dependence on Arab oil was still virtually nil in 1969–70; prices were comparatively low, and alternative sources seemed available. The main worry was continued supply of oil to Europe and Japan and, to a lesser degree, the repatriation of profits of American oil companies and their favorable contribution to the U.S. balance of payments.

16. It was feared that excessive pressure on Israel, such as withholding conventional arms, might accelerate Israel's search for a nuclear option. Indifference, on the other hand, might also encourage the Israelis to go ahead with their program.

17. The administration's opposition to an imposed settlement was twofold: it probably would not last for long, because the parties would have little sense of commitment to its terms and outside powers would tire of trying to enforce it; and it would be unfavorably received in this country.

18. Kissinger, *White House Years*, pp. 349–52. "I . . . doubted the advisability of American pressure for a general settlement until we could see more clearly what concessions the Arabs would make and until those who would benefit from it would be America's friends, not Soviet clients. . . . I thought the prerequisite of effective Middle East diplomacy was to reduce the Soviet influence so that progress could not be ascribed to its pressures and moderate governments gained some maneuvering room."

19. Nixon, news conference on January 27, 1969, *Department of State Bulletin*, vol. 60 (February 17, 1969), pp. 142–43.

20. This account was obtained in interviews with participants in the first NSC policy review of the Middle East. Kissinger's reaction to these State Department initiatives is found in *White House Years*, pp. 352–53. For background on the State Department proposals, including evidence that the Soviet position began to show signs of flexibility in mid-1969, see David A. Korn, *Stalemate: The War of Attrition and Great Power Diplomacy in the Middle East, 1967–1979* (Boulder, Colo.: Westview Press, 1992), pp. 150–56.

21. Prime Minister Eshkol died on February 26. Golda Meir was sworn in as head of government on March 17.

22. Hedrick Smith, "Big Four May Meet on Mideast Soon," *New York Times*, March 26, 1969, p. 11.

23. See Yaacov Bar-Siman-Tov, *The Israeli-Egyptian War of Attrition, 1969–1970: A Case Study of a Limited War* (Columbia University Press, 1980); and Korn, *Stalemate*, pp. 165–88.

24. See Kissinger, *White House Years*, p. 362–63. According to Kissinger, King Hussein was prepared to agree to fairly substantial rectifications in the borders of the West Bank if he could gain Gaza.

25. Ibid., pp. 360–62.

26. The American position in April on the terms of a settlement had been summarized in nine points and given to Ambassador Jarring. These were expanded upon subsequently, but in essence they covered the major issues:

—Agreement on the full package was necessary before implementation of any part.

—The parties must engage in more direct contact at later stages of the talks.

—There must be a contractually binding peace with international participation.

—Security considerations on both sides must be taken into account and final boundaries must not reflect the weight of conquest.

—Special arrangements would be required in Gaza.

—There should be a Jordanian economic, civil, and religious role in a unified city of Jerusalem.

—The refugee problem should be settled through negotiation, with controls and conditions, to take place over a long period, or through compensation and resettlement.

—There should be free navigation in the Suez Canal and the Gulf of Aqaba.

—Special security arrangements would be necessary at Sharm al-Shaykh.

Kissinger expressed strong reservations on these points, but managed to get

Nixon only to authorize some cosmetic alterations (*White House Years*, pp. 364–65). The main concession to Kissinger was that Sisco would not present all these points at one time to the Soviets, but rather in stages. It was also agreed that the American position would be that Israeli withdrawal to the 1967 Egyptian-Israeli border was "not necessarily excluded." See Korn, *Stalemate*, pp. 155–56.

27. This was revealed by Secretary Rogers in a news conference on June 5, 1969. "Excerpts from Transcript of News Conference by Secretary of State Rogers," *New York Times*, June 6, 1969, p. 8.

28. By now the U.S. position on several issues was more explicit:

—All territories evacuated by Israel should be demilitarized.

—The status of Gaza should be settled by negotiations including Israel, Egypt, and Jordan.

—The parties to a peace agreement would be responsible for preventing acts of force by military or paramilitary forces on their territory (for example, Egypt and Jordan would have to control the fedayeen).

—The state of war would end on the date the accord went into effect.

—The international frontier between Egypt and Israel would "not necessarily be excluded" as the final peace border.

See the summary of the U.S. and Soviet proposals provided in "U.S. and Soviet Plans on Mideast Show Some Accord but Many Differences," *New York Times*, October 19, 1969, p. 16.

29. Between July 31 and August 25 the Soviets commented on Sisco's July 15 proposals in talks held in Moscow with Ambassador Beam. No new Soviet position was forthcoming, however.

30. Israel made the formal request for the one hundred A-4s and twenty-five F-4s on September 15, 1969.

31. Kissinger, *White House Years*, pp. 368–69.

32. Ibid., pp. 370–71; Golda Meir, *My Life: The Autobiography of Golda Meir* (London: Futura, 1976), pp. 326–30; and Yitzhak Rabin, *The Rabin Memoirs* (Little, Brown, 1979), pp. 150–57. Meir mentions a request for eighty Skyhawks, but the number was, in fact, one hundred.

33. Rabin, *Rabin Memoirs*, pp. 156–57; Abba Eban, *An Autobiography* (Random House, 1977), pp. 464–65; and Gideon Rafael, *Destination Peace: Three Decades of Israeli Foreign Policy. A Personal Memoir* (Stein and Day, 1981), pp. 210–11.

34. Kissinger, *White House Years*, p. 372. Nixon's own account differs. "I knew that the Rogers Plan could never be implemented, but I believed that it was important to let the Arab world know that the United States did not automatically dismiss its case regarding the occupied territories or rule out a compromise settlement of the conflicting claims. With the Rogers Plan on the record, I thought it would be easier for the Arab leaders to propose reopening relations with the United States without coming under attack from the hawks and pro-Soviet elements in their own countries." Nixon, *RN*, p. 479.

35. Mahmoud Riad, *The Struggle for Peace in the Middle East* (Quartet Books, 1981), pp. 110–11.

36. The December 9, 1969, speech by Rogers contained most of the points

in the October 28 document. He described United States policy as "balanced," emphasizing friendly ties to both Arabs and Israelis. He referred to three principal elements of a prospective peace agreement:

—binding commitments by the parties to peace, including the obligation to prevent hostile acts originating from their respective territories.

—Rhodes-style negotiations to work out details of an agreement. Issues to be negotiated between Egypt and Israel would include safeguards in the area of Sharm al-Shaykh, the establishment of demilitarized zones, and final arrangements in Gaza.

—in the context of peace and agreements on security, Israeli forces would be required to withdraw to the international border between Egypt and Israel.

The full text of the speech can be found in "Text of Speech by Secretary Rogers on U.S. Policy in Middle East," *New York Times*, December 10, 1969, p. 8. See also Korn, *Stalemate*, pp. 158–61.

37. Nixon had authorized the presentation of the proposals for an Israeli-Jordanian agreement on December 17, but, according to Kissinger, *White House Years*, p. 376, at the same time he conveyed private assurance to Golda Meir via Leonard Garment "that we would go no further and that we would not press our proposal."

38. Points 1, 2, 4, 5, 7, 8, 9, and 10 of the October 28 document were essentially repeated in the December 18 proposal.

39. A summary of the text of the December 18 document appears in *Arab Report and Record*, December 16–31, 1969.

40. *Arab Report and Record*, December 16–31, 1969, p. 549.

41. The Soviet note was published in *New York Times*, January 13, 1970. According to Egypt's foreign minister, once Israel had rejected the proposals, there was little reason for Egypt to accept, "for it would mean further concessions within the framework of a settlement which we were doubtful the US could get Israel to accept." Riad, *Struggle for Peace*, p. 114. Moscow's rejection of the Rogers Plan came after extensive consultations with Egyptian officials in Moscow, including Vice President Anwar Sadat, Minister of War Fawzi, and Foreign Minister Riad. According to Riad, the Soviets were worried by the escalating fighting along the Suez Canal but saw no contradiction between providing arms to Egypt to liberate the Sinai and pursuing a political settlement. In fact, Leonid Brezhnev reportedly made far-reaching promises during these meetings, offering sixty Soviet pilots and SAM-3 missile batteries with their crews. Riad, *Struggle for Peace*, p. 113.

42. Korn, *Stalemate*, pp. 174–92.

43. Dayan was quoted in Raymond H. Anderson, "Israeli Jets Raid Suburbs of Cairo; Shoppers Watch," *New York Times*, January 29, 1970, p. 1, as saying that one of the purposes of the bombing raids against Egypt was to bring home to the Egyptian people the truth about the war. "We are saying, 'Now look here. Your leaders are not doing you any good.' " The same theme is picked up in comments by Prime Minister Meir, *Le Monde*, January 18–19, 1970.

44. A debate exists over what was actually decided during Sadat's visit to Moscow in December and what Nasser accomplished by his visit the following

month. See Mohamed Heikal, *The Road to Ramadan* (Quadrangle Books, 1975), pp. 83–90. See also Uri Ra'anan, "The USSR and the Middle East: Some Reflections on the Soviet Decision-Making Process," *ORBIS*, vol. 17 (Fall 1973), pp. 946–77, for the case in favor of the decision to send Soviet forces being made before Nasser's visit. Whatever the facts, most officials in Washington seemed to believe that Israel's deep penetration bombing was the cause of the stepped-up Soviet role in the fighting. They were, therefore, hesitant to support the Israeli request for more F-4s during the spring, despite the Soviet buildup. See Korn, *Stalemate*, pp. 189–97.

45. The full text of the Soviet note appears in "Nixon-Kosygin Letters," *Arab Report and Record*, March 1–15, 1970, p. 167.

46. Kissinger, *White House Years*, pp. 560–61.

47. "Nixon-Kosygin Letters," p. 168.

48. *U.S. Foreign Policy for the 1970s: A New Strategy for Peace*, A Report to the Congress by Richard Nixon, February 18, 1970 (Government Printing Office, 1970), pp. 80–81.

49. The chairman of the Joint Chiefs took the position that the one hundred A-4s should be sold but not the F-4s.

50. See Robert H. Trice, Jr., "Domestic Political Interests and American Policy in the Middle East: Pro-Israel, Pro-Arab and Corporate Non-governmental Actors and the Making of American Foreign Policy, 1966–1971," Ph.D. dissertation, University of Wisconsin, 1974, pp. 274 ff.

51. Tad Szulc, "Rogers and Dobrynin Confer for 70 Minutes on Mideast," *New York Times*, March 26, 1970, p. 3. In addition, there was a lull in the fighting along the canal in early March, which was interpreted in some quarters as the result of Soviet pressure on Nasser. Raymond H. Anderson, "Suez Lull Linked to Moves by the Big Four," *New York Times*, March 12, 1970, p. 5.

52. Rabin, *Rabin Memoirs*, pp. 169–72; and Kissinger, *White House Years*, pp. 568–70.

53. Also, Nasser had warned in mid-February that the United States would lose its economic interests in the Arab world within two years if it agreed to sell additional Phantom jets to Israel. James Reston, "Excerpts from Interview with President Gamal Abdel Nasser of the U.A.R.," *New York Times*, February 15, 1970, p. 18.

54. The record of Sisco's April 12, 1970, meeting with Nasser shows the Egyptian leader in a very bitter frame of mind. According to Sisco's report, Nasser said that he had "no confidence in the USG. US is strong and UAR sees its only security in Soviet Union, on whom it must depend completely. Nasser said he therefore prefers have dialogue through Soviets than directly with US." Despite the harsh words, Nasser, as usual, was cordial to Sisco and said that he wanted to keep the door open. He said that he was prepared to make peace with Israel but only if all Arab demands were met. See Sisco's cable reporting on the April 12, 1970, meeting, Department of State telegram, Cairo 803, April 13, 1970, secret/nodis (declassified April 3, 1990).

55. Nasser's "final" appeal, repeated in a letter to President Nixon the following day, stated: "The USA, in taking one more step on the path of securing military

superiority for Israel will impose on the Arab nation an irrevocable course from which we must draw the necessary conclusion. This will affect the relations of the USA and the Arab nation for decades, and, maybe, for hundreds of years. . . . We will not close the door finally on the USA, in spite of the offences against us, in spite of the bombs, the napalm and the Phantoms. . . . I say to President Nixon that there is a forthcoming decisive moment in Arab-American relations. There will be either rupture forever, or there will be another serious and defined beginning. The forthcoming developments will not only affect Arab-American relations alone, but will have wider and more far-reaching effects." Part of the text appears in "Nasser Appeals to Nixon on U.S. Arab Relations," *Arab Report and Record*, May 1–15, 1970, p. 276.

56. This point was repeated in a letter from President Nixon to Prime Minister Meir dated June 20, 1970, just after the second Rogers initiative had been launched. See Eban, *Autobiography*, p. 466.

57. Meir did not believe that Israel had ever accepted UN Resolution 242, although Israel's ambassador at the UN had publicly done so in 1968. Rafael, *Destination Peace*, p. 215.

58. During the second week of June a minicrisis erupted in Jordan as the Popular Front for the Liberation of Palestine, led by George Habash, seized hostages, including Americans, in two Amman hotels. On June 12 President Nixon ordered the 82d Airborne Division on alert.

59. See text of Rogers's letter to Egyptian Foreign Minister Riad, dated June 19, 1970, *New York Times*, July 23, 1970, p. 2; and "U.S. Initiative toward Peace in the Middle East," *Department of State Bulletin*, vol. 63 (August 10, 1970), pp. 178–79.

60. See Michael Brecher, *Decisions in Israel's Foreign Policy* (Yale University Press, 1975), chap. 8, for details of the Israeli response.

61. Marvin Kalb and Bernard Kalb, *Kissinger* (Little, Brown, 1974), p. 193.

62. "A Conversation with the President," Interview by John Chancellor and Howard K. Smith, July 1, 1970, *Department of State Bulletin*, vol. 63 (July 27, 1970), pp. 112–13.

63. This decision was made in response to a letter from Prime Minister Meir dated July 2, 1970, in which she appealed for help in dealing with the threat posed by the SAMs that were being moved closer to the canal. The ECM equipment was first used by the Israeli air force on July 18.

64. All the jets under the December 1968 contract had been delivered by the end of August 1970. According to Tad Szulc, "U.S. Mideast Plan Urges Both Sides to 'Start Talking,' " *New York Times*, June 26, 1970, p. 1, the Israelis were reassured that they would be allowed to purchase additional aircraft if the cease-fire proposal of June 19 were to fail or to break down.

65. Heikal, *Road to Ramadan*, pp. 93–95.

66. Egypt orally accepted the U.S. proposal "unconditionally." The subsequent formal written reply was somewhat more guarded.

67. Inasmuch as Jordan and Israel were formally respecting the cease-fire, one might ask why Jordan was included in the second Rogers initiative. The answer seems to be that the United States wanted to ensure that both Egypt and Jordan

would be committed to controlling the fedayeen, who were expected to oppose any political settlement based on the Rogers plan. In accepting the Rogers proposal of June 19, King Hussein clearly understood that he would be held responsible for preventing all acts of force from his territory. He informed his cabinet before his acceptance that this might mean further military clashes with the fedayeen.

68. Michael Brecher, *Decisions in Israel's Foreign Policy* (Yale University Press, 1975), pp. 493–94; and Ariyeh Tsimaqi, "The Message That Tipped the Balance," *Yedi'ot Aharonot*, July 31, 1970, p. 4. The letter reached Israel July 24.

69. Brecher, *Decisions in Israel's Foreign Policy*, p. 495. In addition, President Nixon stated at a news conference on July 30 that the United States was committed to "maintaining the balance of power in the Mideast. Seventy-one Senators have endorsed that proposition in a letter to me which I received today." Nixon further reassured Israel that it would face no risk of a military buildup during the cease-fire because there would be a military standstill during that period. Text of the interview in "President Nixon's News Conference of July 30," *Department of State Bulletin*, vol. 63 (August 17, 1970), pp. 185–87. A letter signed by seventy-three senators had been sent to Secretary Rogers on June 1, 1970, urging the sale of one hundred A-4s and F-4s. The text of that letter and the signatures appear in *Congressional Quarterly Weekly Report*, vol. 28 (June 5, 1970), p. 1475.

70. See Prime Minister Meir's speech to the Knesset, August 4, 1970, printed in *Jerusalem Post*, August 5, 1970, p. 3.

71. See the text of the cease-fire agreement in *Arab Report and Record*, August 1–15,1970, p. 457; and the Egyptian, Jordanian, and Israeli replies to Rogers's proposal of June 19, ibid., pp. 458–60.

72. For example, in his news conference on July 20, 1970, Nixon emphasized the importance of the peace initiative then under way, stating, "That is why we have not announced any sale of planes or delivery of planes to Israel at this time because we want to give that peace initiative every chance to succeed." *New York Times*, July 21, 1970, p. 16.

73. See William Safire, *Before the Fall: An Inside View of the Pre-Watergate White House* (Doubleday, 1975), p. 394.

CHAPTER FIVE

1. Yitzhak Rabin, *The Rabin Memoirs* (Little, Brown, 1979), p. 182, states that the United States asked Israel for permission to fly U-2 flights along the canal. "But inexplicably, the IDF military attaché in Washington received an order from a senior personage in Israel's defense establishment to notify the Americans that Israel objected to aerial photographs being taken just before the cease-fire went into effect! This bizarre cable contained an even more incomprehensible hint: if American planes attempted to take photographs of the battle zone, Israel would intercept them." See also Gideon Rafael, *Destination Peace: Three Decades of Israeli Foreign Policy* (Stein and Day, 1981), p. 230, on Dayan's apparent disinterest in the verification issue and his assumption that "in any case, he expected the Egyptians to move their missiles into the prohibited zone." Also, David A. Korn,

Stalemate: The War of Attrition and Great Power Diplomacy in the Middle East, 1967–1979 (Boulder, Colo.: Westview Press, 1992), pp. 264–68.

2. On August 12, 1970, the Department of State termed Israeli evidence of Egyptian violations "inconclusive." Several days later, on August 19, Ambassador Walworth Barbour urged the Israelis to end the public discussion of cease-fire violations and to name a representative to the Jarring talks.

3. Henry Kissinger, *The White House Years* (Little, Brown, 1979), pp. 582–85, notes that Soviet Ambassador Dobrynin had informed Rogers that the Soviets agreed to a standstill cease-fire; but while the United States and Israel spelled out what was meant by "standstill," Egypt was not informed of this understanding until one day after the cease-fire, and the Soviets were never formally made a party to the agreement.

4. According to "U.S. Affirms Report of Israeli Breaches," *New York Times*, September 17 1970, p. 19, Israel had also technically violated the standstill provision of the cease-fire by reinforcing near the canal. See also Korn, *Stalemate*, p. 269.

5. In early September 1970 U.S. intelligence sources detected what appeared to be preparations for a Soviet submarine base in Cienfuegos, Cuba. Secretary Rogers tended to dismiss the report as unimportant, but Kissinger treated it very seriously, alluding to it in a briefing in Chicago on September 16, just on the eve of the acute phase of the Jordan crisis. The story became public in Robert M. Smith, "U.S. Warns Soviets Not to Build Base for Subs in Cuba," *New York Times*, September 26, 1970, p. 1. It seems clear that the Cienfuegos incident accentuated Nixon's and Kissinger's distrust of Soviet intentions during this period. See Marvin Kalb and Bernard Kalb, *Kissinger* (Little, Brown, 1974), pp. 209–12.

6. According to Kissinger, *White House Years*, pp. 589–90, his relationship with Rogers was by now very poor. Nixon, when faced with such controversy, usually procrastinated, but the pace of events was soon to make that option untenable.

7. A fourth hijack attempt, led by Leila Khaled of the PFLP, against an El Al plane in London failed.

8. See William B. Quandt and others, *The Politics of Palestinian Nationalism* (University of California Press, 1973), pp. 124–28.

9. The PLO temporarily suspended the PFLP from the Central Committee because of the unauthorized hijackings, but welcomed it back once the fighting broke out on September 16.

10. Kissinger, *White House Years*, p. 597.

11. Ibid., pp. 602–06; and Seymour M. Hersh, *The Price of Power: Kissinger in the Nixon White House* (Summit Books, 1983), p. 235.

12. Kissinger, *White House Years*, p. 606.

13. Elmo R. Zumwalt, Jr., *On Watch: A Memoir* (Quadrangle, 1976), pp. 295–96, provides a brief account of a WSAG meeting on September 10 at which David Packard, deputy secretary of defense, argued against any form of ground involvement in the crisis by American troops.

14. Kalb and Kalb, *Kissinger*, p. 197; Henry Brandon, *The Retreat of American*

Power: The Inside Story of How Nixon and Kissinger Changed American Foreign Policy for Years to Come (Doubleday, 1973), p. 133; Frank Van der Linden, *Nixon's Quest for Peace* (Robert B. Luce, 1972), p. 77; and Kissinger, *White House Years*, pp. 610–12.

15. *Chicago Sun-Times*, September 17, 1970; and Hedrick Smith, "Nixon Hints He May Act If Outsiders Join the Fight," *New York Times*, September 19, 1970, p. 1.

16. Brandon, *Retreat of American Power*, p. 134.

17. Terence Smith, "Washington Reported Weighing $500-Million in Aid for Israelis," *New York Times*, September 18, 1970, p. 1.

18. Kissinger, *White House Years*, p. 618. The Syrians went to considerable lengths to make their intervention appear to consist of units of the Palestine Liberation Army. Tanks were hastily painted with PLA symbols.

19. The most damaging evidence of Soviet complicity in the intervention came from reports that Soviet military advisers had accompanied Syrian tank units as far as the Jordanian border.

20. Kalb and Kalb, *Kissinger*, pp. 200–01; and Kissinger, *White House Years*, p. 619.

21. See Kissinger, *White House Years*, p. 619, for a partial text of the note.

22. Hedrick Smith, "Rogers Calls for End of 'Invasion'—Note Sent to Moscow," *New York Times*, September 21, 1970, p. 1; and Kalb and Kalb, *Kissinger*, p. 202. Rogers's personal views were less hawkish. He reputedly favored a joint U.S.-Soviet effort to end the fighting but was rebuffed by Nixon and Kissinger.

23. Communications in Amman between the American embassy and the royal palace were extremely difficult. Radio and walkie-talkie were used, and the fedayeen often eavesdropped on sensitive conversations.

24. Kissinger, *White House Years*, p. 620.

25. Van der Linden, *Nixon's Quest for Peace*, pp. 81–82; and Kissinger, *White House Years*, p. 621.

26. Kissinger, *White House Years*, p. 622.

27. Ibid., p. 623. Rabin, *Rabin Memoirs*, p. 187, gives a somewhat different version. Rabin claims that Kissinger conveyed the king's request for Israeli air strikes and asked for an immediate Israeli reply. Rabin then asked what the U.S. was recommending, and Kissinger said he would have to call back. An hour later, according to Rabin, Kissinger called, saying, "The request is approved and supported by the United States government." "Do *you* advise Israel to do it?" Rabin asked. "Yes, subject to your own considerations," replied Kissinger."

28. Kissinger, *White House Years*, p. 623. See also Kalb and Kalb, *Kissinger*, pp. 202–07; and Benjamin Welles, "U.S.-Israeli Military Action on Jordan Was Envisioned," *New York Times*, October 8, 1970, p. 1.

29. Kissinger, *White House Years*, p. 625.

30. The United States had no independent aerial intelligence-collection capabilities to follow the course of the battle. It had to rely on Israeli reconnaissance flights and Israeli and Jordanian accounts of what was happening on the ground.

31. Kissinger, *White House Years*, p. 626. Kissinger asserts that he was not

entirely happy with this decision, since it might have been impossible to contact King Hussein to determine his views if the situation deteriorated sharply.

32. Israel asked for clarification of the U.S. position on seven points. This was given orally. But Adam Garfinkle seems to be correct when he challenges the conventional wisdom, as in Kalb and Kalb, *Kissinger*, p. 206, who claim that an agreement was actually reached. See Adam H. Garfinkle, "U.S. Decision Making in the Jordan Crisis: Correcting the Record," *Political Science Quarterly*, vol. 100 (Spring 1985), pp. 117–38. According to Garfinkle, "Thus, while Nixon did surely endorse Israeli air strikes into Jordan, he never 'authorized' an Israeli ground attack of any kind—even though he would have done so had it not been for Kissinger's intercession on the morning of the 21st. Nor did Nixon ever pledge in unequivocal terms that the United States would protect the Israeli rear flank against possible Soviet or Egyptian intervention, as is universally claimed in the scholarly literature" (p. 131). See also Alan Dowty, *Middle East Crisis: U.S. Decision-Making in 1958, 1970, and 1973* (University of California Press, 1984), p. 172. As Dowty notes, no "operationalization" of the American commitment took place beyond some routine Defense Department procedures (p. 173).

33. The Syrian air force, commanded by General Hafiz al-Asad, did not intervene, nor did the Iraqi troops in Jordan, confronted as they were by a full division of the Jordanian army.

34. Kalb and Kalb, *Kissinger*, p. 204, misinterpret the meaning of this message.

35. Alone among analysts of the Jordan crisis, Alexander Haig maintains that Israeli air strikes did, in fact, occur and were instrumental in turning the tide of battle. Haig initially states that Israel "may" have destroyed some Syrian tanks, but two paragraphs later states: "The Israeli air strikes, together with strong American diplomacy backed by credible military maneuvers suggesting that overwhelming United States air, sea, and ground power would be committed to the conflict if necessary, preserved King Hussein's regime, and, with it, the frazzled peace in the region." Alexander M. Haig, Jr., with Charles McCarry, *Inner Circles: How America Changed the World. A Memoir* (Warner Books, 1992), p. 251. Interviews with Joseph Sisco, Alfred L. Atherton, Harold H. Saunders, Richard Helms, and information from Israeli general Aharon Yariv, all confirm that no Israeli air strikes took place.

Nixon's own recollection of the Jordan crisis is reflected in the following anecdote. Talking to Kissinger by phone during the October 1973 war, Nixon said about the Jordan crisis: "We really—with no cards at all . . . played a hell of a game." Walter Isaacson, *Kissinger: A Biography* (Simon and Schuster, 1992), p. 517.

36. Elmo R. Zumwalt, Jr., *On Watch: A Memoir* (Quadrangle, 1976), p. 299, provides a copy of a memorandum that went to the president at this time detailing American military capabilities for action in the eastern Mediterranean.

37. Kissinger, *White House Years*, pp. 628–29; and Brandon, *Retreat of American Power*, p. 137. Kissinger decided to attend the Egyptian reception in part to improve his image with the Arabs.

38. According to Kissinger, *White House Years*, p. 631, on September 25 Israel was formally notified that "all aspects of the exchanges between us with regard

to this Syrian invasion of Jordan are no longer applicable. . . . If a new situation arises, there will have to be a fresh exchange."

39. Dowty, *Middle East Crisis*, pp. 138, 142–43, provides ample evidence that Laird, partly because of public reaction to the Cambodian crisis earlier in the year, was unenthusiastic about U.S. military intervention in the Jordan crisis.

40. The British had announced in 1968 that they would remove their military presence east of Suez by the end of 1971. This led to considerable planning within the bureaucracy on how to fill the ensuing vacuum.

41. Speech by President Podgorny, September 23, 1970. See Mohamed Heikal, *The Road to Ramadan* (Quadrangle Books, 1975), pp. 98–100, for evidence that the Soviets urged "utmost restraint" on Egypt during the Jordan crisis.

42. Rabin, *Rabin Memoirs*, p. 188. As Adam Garfinkle, "U.S. Decision Making," comments, the Hebrew version of Rabin's memoirs says the United States considered Israel's request for an umbrella commitment "with difficulty" (p. 131, note 37). Joseph Sisco, in an interview on October 18, 1991, recalled that there was no written commitment that he was aware of. The issue had been left hanging. There was ambiguity about the nature of any American commitment. In any event, diplomatic contacts with the Soviets seemed to be working, and the Soviets were showing considerable caution in the face of very blunt American pressures.

CHAPTER SIX

1. See Henry Kissinger, *The White House Years* (Little, Brown, 1979), p. 1285. "What finally got me involved in the execution of Middle East diplomacy was that Nixon did not believe he could risk recurrent crises in the Middle East in an election year. He therefore asked me to step in, if only to keep things quiet."

2. On October 12, 1970, Kissinger and Sisco gave a background briefing to the press on the post-Jordan-crisis situation in the Middle East. Sisco addressed the question of the Palestinians in the following terms: "more and more the Palestinians are thinking in terms of a given entity, wherever that may be. . . . So that if I were to look ahead over the next five years, assuming that we can stabilize this area, it would be on the basis of the Arabs having adopted a live and let live attitude, that is, willing to live alongside of Israel; Israel's meeting at least part of the Arab demands insofar as the occupied territories are concerned; and, lastly, giving expression to the Palestinian movement and very likely in the form of some entity."

3. The administration sought an understanding on the conditions under which Israel might use the new weapons.

4. William Beecher, "U.S. Officials Say Israelis Will Get 180 Modern Tanks," *New York Times*, October 24, 1970, p. 1. The supplemental defense appropriation, including $500 million in credits for Israel, was signed by Nixon on January 11, 1971.

5. Senator J. William Fulbright, chairman of the Senate Foreign Relations Committee, and not known as a particularly close friend of Israel, publicly endorsed the idea of a U.S.-Israeli security treaty as part of a settlement involving full Israeli withdrawal.

6. Hedrick Smith, "Mrs. Meir Sends a Note to Nixon," *New York Times*, December 2, 1970, p. 6.

7. Peter Grose, "Israel Still Asks Pledges by U.S.," *New York Times*, December 7, 1970, p. 11; and Hedrick Smith, "A Firm U.S. Stand on Mideast Likely," *New York Times*, December 8, 1970, p. 17.

8. Terence Smith, "U.S. Says It Would Join a Mideast Peace Force," *New York Times*, December 15, 1970, p. 3.

9. Meir speech to the Knesset, as cited in Lawrence L. Whetten, *The Canal War: Four-Power Conflict in the Middle East* (MIT Press, 1974), p. 142; and Tad Szulc, "U.S. Officials Say a Series of Commitments Won Israelis Return to Mideast Peace Talks at the U.N.," *New York Times*, January 1, 1971, p. 8. Shlomo Aronson, *The Politics and Strategy of Nuclear Weapons in the Middle East: Opacity, Theory, and Reality, 1960–1991. An Israeli Perspective* (State University of New York Press, 1992), p. 146, may have these understandings in mind when he refers to a 1971 agreement on "secure boundaries" that included American recognition of Israel's nuclear potential. But Aronson has only an interview with former Ambassador Simcha Dinitz to rely on, and no other account mentions anything about nuclear weapons.

10. The idea of a mutual thinning out of forces along the canal had first been officially raised in Washington on September 19, 1970, by Israeli Ambassador Rabin and General Aharon Yariv.

11. Little was known in Washington about Sadat when he became president. The biography prepared by the CIA was less than flattering. It prominently mentioned that Sadat had gone to the cinema on the night of the Egyptian revolution in 1952, implying that this was typical of his political style. Sadat openly discusses the incident in *Revolt on the Nile* (John Day, 1957).

12. *Arab Report and Record*, January 16–31, 1971, p. 75.

13. "Cairo Sees No Progress," *New York Times*, February 2, 1971, p. 2.

14. The text of Sadat's February 4, 1971, speech can be found in *New Middle East*, March 1971, pp. 32–35.

15. For Jarring's memorandum, along with the Egyptian and Israeli replies, see *Arab Report and Record*, March 1–15, 1971, pp. 158–59. The United States had strongly urged Israel not to include the sentence on refusing to withdraw to the pre-June 5, 1967, lines.

16. Meir's February 9, 1971, speech is reproduced in *New Middle East*, March 1971, pp. 35–39.

17. In an interview with *Newsweek* on February 15, Sadat spelled out in more detail his concept of an interim agreement. If Israel was prepared to withdraw to a line running from Al-Arish to Ras Muhammad, nearly two-thirds of the way across Sinai, he would reopen the canal within six months, extend the cease-fire, and allow international forces to remain at Sharm al-Shaykh to ensure freedom of navigation. Sadat's concept of a partial agreement was very far removed from Dayan's initial idea, but it could be assumed that this opening definition of the line of Israeli withdrawal might be softened with time. See Arnaud de Borchgrave, "A Talk with Sadat on Peace Terms," *Newsweek*, February 22, 1971, pp. 40–41.

Sadat seemed to realize that Israel would not agree to his terms, but thought perhaps he could enlist the United States on his side. Over the next several weeks he repeatedly queried Washington on its attitude to his February initiative and encouraged Nixon to take an active diplomatic role in the search for a settlement.

18. *U.S. Foreign Policy for the 1970's: Building for Peace*, A Report to the Congress by Richard Nixon, February 25, 1971 (Government Printing Office, 1971), pp. 129–30.

19. *Al-Ahram* editor Mohamed Heikal soon began a series of articles on the need to "neutralize" the United States.

20. Hedrick Smith, "Israel Denounces Plans of Jarring and U.S. on Sinai," *New York Times*, March 11, 1971, p. 1.

21. Meir interview in *The Times* (London), March 13, 1971, p. 1. Meir's comments set off a lively debate within Israel. The right-wing Gahal party accused her of being too conciliatory.

22. Raymond H. Anderson, "Egypt Proposes Truce If Israelis Pledge Pullback," *New York Times*, April 2, 1971, p. 1.

23. William Beecher, "U.S. Selling Israel 12 More F-14 Jets; Weighs New Bid," *New York Times*, April 20, 1971, p. 1.

24. Arnaud de Borchgrave, "Sadat: 'We Are Now Back to Square One,' " *Newsweek*, December 13, 1971, pp. 43–47.

25. Whetten, *Canal War*, pp. 182–83; Peter Grose, "Israeli Cabinet Briefed on Rogers Talks," *New York Times*, May 10, 1971, p. 3; and Meir speech of June 9, 1971, reported in "Israel Asks U.S. for New Arms Deal," *New York Times*, June 10, 1971, p. 9.

26. Sadat claimed subsequently in his interview in de Borchgrave's, "Sadat: 'We Are Now Back to Square One,' " that Sisco had illustratively sketched lines on a map of Sinai indicating the depth of Israeli withdrawal. Sadat suggested that UN peacekeeping forces should be stationed between the Egyptian and Israeli line.

27. These ministers included Sami Sharaf, in charge of presidential security; Sharawi Guma, minister of interior; and General Mohammed Fawzi, minister of defense.

28. For Kissinger's critique of the effort to revive the Jarring talks, see Kissinger, *White House Years*, pp. 1278–80. He termed the effort "activity for its own sake amid self-generated deadlines that could be met only by papering over irreconcilable differences that, in turn, made a blowup all the more inevitable. . . . My aim was to produce a stalemate until Moscow urged compromise or until, even better, some moderate Arab regime decided that the route to progress was through Washington."

29. See Mahmoud Riad, *The Struggle for Peace in the Middle East* (Quartet Books, 1981), pp. 203–04, for his negative view of the idea of an interim settlement and of the Bergus memorandum.

30. Kissinger, *White House Years*, pp. 1283–84, expresses his dismay at the Bergus operation. He concludes that Sadat must have thought the United States was incompetent or deceitful. Sadat later complained on many occasions that he had accepted 90 percent of the American proposal in the Bergus paper and that the United States had then ignored his reply. There seems to be little doubt that

Sadat viewed the paper as an official statement of U.S. policy. See Mohamed Heikal, *The Road to Ramadan* (Quadrangle Books, 1975), p. 146.

31. Sisco tried to persuade the Israelis to accept a two-stage agreement, with only a token Egyptian force crossing the canal. "Sisco Is Reported to Suggest a 2-Phased Israeli Withdrawal," *New York Times*, August 9, 1971, p. 2.

32. Rogers seems to have first termed 1971 the "year of decision" in the Middle East. See "Secretary Rogers' News Conference of December 23," *Department of State Bulletin*, vol. 64 (January 11, 1971), p. 43.

33. Kissinger, *White House Years*, p. 1285, dates his operational control over Middle East policy from this point. He notes that Rabin approached him in October 1971 to urge that he get personally involved in the interim accord negotiations: "He told me confidentially that Israel might be more flexible in its terms if I were involved and it had Presidential assurances that the demands would not be open-ended" (p. 1287). Kissinger was simultaneously being asked by an Egyptian emissary to meet with Heikal.

34. Henry Tanner, "U.S. Assures Israel on Sinai Memo," *New York Times*, June 30, 1971, p. 3.

35. Kissinger, *White House Years*, pp. 1280–89.

36. See Heikal, *Road to Ramadan*, pp. 140, 152–55. Kissinger, *White House Years*, p. 1276, dates the beginning of the back-channel contacts with Sadat to the spring of 1972.

37. De Borchgrave, "Sadat: 'We Are Now Back to Square One.' "

38. William Beecher, "U.S. Said to Plan to Help Israelis Make Own Arms," *New York Times*, January 14, 1972, p. 1.

39. Paul Erdman, "The True Story of a Spy Coup: How Israel Got Blueprints for France's Hottest Fighter Plane," *New York*, August 30, 1976, pp. 35–45.

40. Yitzhak Rabin, *The Rabin Memoirs* (Little, Brown, 1979), p. 209, gives an account of Meir's positions, which, he states, were confirmed a few days later by the president. But on p. 211, Rabin maintains that he never heard the president express agreement to shelving the Rogers Plan or to Israeli demands for border changes in Sinai.

41. Kissinger, *White House Years*, p. 1289. See also Rabin, *Rabin Memoirs*, pp. 206–09. The Israelis apparently understood from these exchanges that the Rogers Plan was a dead letter.

42. Peter Grose, "Israelis Approve Talks with Egypt on Opening Canal," *New York Times*, February 3, 1972, p. 1. According to Ambassador Rabin, in *Maariv*, December 1, 1972, the memorandum of understanding also acknowledged that Israel would not be expected to make a commitment on full withdrawal as part of an interim agreement.

43. *U.S. Foreign Policy for the 1970's: The Emerging Structure of Peace*, A Report to the Congress by Richard Nixon on February 9, 1972 (GPO, 1972), p. 133, which quotes Nixon's media briefing of June 18, 1971.

44. Ibid.

45. Tad Szulc, "Behind the Vietnam Cease-Fire Agreement," *Foreign Policy*, no. 15 (Summer 1974), pp. 34–41.

46. See Kissinger, *White House Years*, p. 1494, for the text of the agreement. Elsewhere Kissinger minimizes the importance of these principles, saying that he conducted a "delaying tactic" in his talks with Gromyko (pp. 1247–48). My impression is that Kissinger took the exercise somewhat more seriously, and almost certainly Nixon did. And though written in general terms, the principles did not simply parrot UN resolutions, as Kissinger implies.

47. "Basic Principles of Relations between the United States of America and the Union of Soviet Socialist Republics," May 29, 1972.

48. The texts of both the basic principles and the joint communiqué are found in *United States Foreign Policy, 1972: A Report of the Secretary of State* (April 1973), pp. 598–603.

49. Heikal, *Road to Ramadan*, pp. 183–84; and "Arab Aide's Talk with Nixon Called Factor in Sadat's Decision," *New York Times*, July 24, 1972, p. 2.

50. Uri Ra'anan, "The USSR and the Middle East: Some Reflections on the Soviet Decision-Making Process," *ORBIS*, vol. 17 (Fall 1973), pp. 946–77, has called into question whether Sadat took the initiative in asking the advisers to leave. Ra'anan raises some intriguing points but seems to underestimate Sadat's anger at the Soviets. See also David Kimche, *The Last Option: After Nasser, Arafat and Saddam Hussein. The Quest for Peace in the Middle East* (Scribner's, 1991), pp. 22–24, for another argument that Sadat and the Soviets colluded on the withdrawal of Soviet advisers as a step in Egypt's plan to go to war.

51. Nixon interview with Garnett D. Horner of the *Washington Star*, November 5, 1972; and "Statements from Pre-Election Interview with Nixon Outlining 2d-Term Plans," *New York Times*, November 10, 1972, p. 20.

52. Heikal, *Road to Ramadan*, pp. 200–02; and Henry Kissinger, *Years of Upheaval* (Little, Brown, 1982), p. 213.

53. Heikal, *Road to Ramadan*, pp. 202–03. The estate belonged to the chairman of the board of Pepsi-Cola, Donald Kendall, who was an ardent Nixon supporter and a proponent of improved U.S.-Egyptian relations.

54. Kissinger, *Years of Upheaval*, pp. 214–15.

55. Ibid., p. 222; and Rabin, *Rabin Memoirs*, pp. 215–18.

56. The premature story appeared in Marilyn Berger, "Nixon Assures Mrs. Meir of Aid," *Washington Post*, March 2, 1973, p. A21. A more complete story on Nixon's decision appeared in William Beecher, "Israelis Will Buy More Jets in U.S.; Total Is Put at 48," *New York Times*, March 14, 1973, p. 1.

57. Arafat and other top Fatah officials have always denied any direct involvement in the assassinations.

58. Kissinger, *Years of Upheaval*, p. 225. On March 26, 1973, Sadat had formed a "war cabinet" with himself as prime minister. Three days later he told Arnaud de Borchgrave of *Newsweek* that war was imminent. De Borchgrave rushed the text of the interview to Kissinger before its publication on April 9, 1973.

59. *U.S. Foreign Policy for the 1970's: Shaping a Durable Peace*, A Report to the Congress by Richard Nixon, May 3, 1973 (GPO, 1973), p. 138.

60. After returning from Moscow, Kissinger consulted with Israeli officials on Israel's reaction to the May 1972 principles. He was told that Israel was

opposed to the idea altogether, but that if such principles were announced they should call for negotiations and should only speak of Israeli withdrawal to secure and recognized borders.

61. Kissinger, *Years of Upheaval*, pp. 226–27. Kissinger concludes that Sadat had already made his decision for war in the summer of 1972 and that the meetings with Hafiz Ismail were essentially a diversionary tactic. According to a well-informed Israeli source, Kissinger had reason to believe that Egypt had decided on war. According to Moshe Zak, King Hussein had told him of the Egyptian-Syrian plan for war, and Kissinger had told the Israelis. On May 21, 1973, Dayan informed the general staff: "The IDF must prepare, by the end of the summer, for Egypt and Syria launching war against Israel, without Jordan." See *Jerusalem Post*, September 22, 1991, p. 5.

62. Richard Nixon, *RN: The Memoirs of Richard Nixon* (Grosset and Dunlap, 1978), pp. 884–86.

63. "U.S.-U.S.S.R. Joint Communiqué, June 25, 1973," *Department of State Bulletin*, vol. 69 (July 23, 1973), p. 132.

64. Kissinger was concerned by signs of Faisal's growing involvement in the Arab-Israeli conflict. He feared that Saudi activism would ultimately bring down the monarchy, which might then be replaced by a Qaddafi-like regime. Each time King Faisal made some reference to the use of oil as a weapon against the West, however, one of his aides would hasten to inform U.S. officials that such remarks were meant only for domestic Arab consumption.

65. Edward R. F. Sheehan, *The Arabs, Israelis, and Kissinger* (Reader's Digest Press, 1976), pp. 27–28.

66. See Kissinger, *Years of Upheaval*, pp. 202–03, 211–12, for a comparison of Kissinger's and Nixon's views. According to Kissinger, Nixon "deep down wanted . . . to impose a comprehensive settlement sometime during his term in office" (p. 202). For a detailed account of how Nixon saw the Arab-Israeli conflict in the early 1990s, which tends to confirm the view that he favored a comprehensive settlement, see Richard M. Nixon, *Seize the Moment: America's Challenge in a One-Superpower World* (Simon and Schuster, 1992), pp. 217–30.

67. By contrast, Nixon seemed eager to press forward on Middle East peace, warning on one occasion in early 1973 that "this thing is getting ready to blow." See Kissinger, *Years of Upheaval*, p. 211.

CHAPTER SEVEN

1. Roberta Wohlstetter, *Pearl Harbor: Warning and Decision* (Stanford University Press, 1962), provides a classic study of the misinterpretation of evidence indicating an impending surprise attack. See Alan Dowty, *Middle East Crisis: U.S. Decision-Making in 1958, 1970, and 1973* (University of California Press, 1984), pp. 207–13, for the reasons behind the American intelligence failure; and Michael Brecher, *Decisions in Crisis: Israel, 1967 and 1973* (University of California Press, 1980), pp. 174–91, on the "conception" that kept the Israeli decisionmakers from correctly interpreting Arab actions. Kissinger's reasons for the surprise can be found in *Years of Upheaval* (Little, Brown, 1982), pp. 459–67, along with the intriguing

piece of information that King Hussein, in May, had warned that Syrian and Egyptian military preparations were "too realistic to be considered maneuvers" (p. 461).

2. In an interview with Arnaud de Borchgrave, "The Battle Is Now Inevitable," *Newsweek*, April 9, 1973, pp. 44–49.

3. See excerpts of the report of the House Select Committee on Intelligence, chaired by Representative Otis Pike, as reprinted in "The Mid-East War: The System Breaks Down," *Village Voice*, February 16, 1976, pp. 78–79. (Hereafter Pike Committee report.) The full report can be found in *U.S. Intelligence Agencies and Activities: The Performance of the Intelligence Community*, Hearings before the Select Committee on Intelligence, September 11, 12, 18, 25, 30, October 7, 30, 31, 1975, 94 Cong. 1 sess. (Government Printing Office, 1975). See also the account written by the director of the Intelligence and Research Bureau of the State Department, Ray S. Cline, "Policy without Intelligence," *Foreign Policy*, no. 17 (Winter 1974–75), pp. 121–35.

4. On September 10 Sadat, Asad, and Hussein met in Cairo. Syria and Jordan agreed to restore diplomatic relations. Jordan, without being told of specific war plans, committed itself to preventing Israeli troops from attacking Syria through northern Jordan in the event of future hostilities.

5. After the air battles on September 13, Arab newspapers, especially in Beirut, carried stories about Syria's dissatisfaction with Soviet military equipment and the Soviet advisers.

6. The Watch Committee, whose task it is to evaluate intelligence for signs of impending hostilities, reached the same conclusion. See Pike Committee report.

7. Conor Cruise O'Brien, *The Siege: The Saga of Israel and Zionism* (Simon and Schuster, 1986), pp. 512–17, argues at length that Kissinger, perhaps implicitly or indirectly, encouraged Sadat to go to war. His evidence is meager, but he does rely heavily on Mohamed Heikal, *Autumn of Fury: The Assassination of Sadat* (Random House, 1983), pp. 49–50. Heikal argues that information reached Egypt through Saudi intelligence channels that Kissinger favored a "heating up" of the situation before he would be prepared to tackle it. This was supposedly confirmed in the meetings between Hafiz Ismail and Kissinger. I do not believe that Kissinger wanted Egypt to go to war. He did, on occasion, talk about the circumstances that would convince him to tackle the Arab-Israeli conflict. Those circumstances included a deterioration of the situation that would threaten American interests or an opening that would make a diplomatic effort productive. And Nixon had, of course, written an entire book, *Six Crises* (Doubleday, 1962), with the subtheme that crises could provide opportunities for solving problems. Although it may be true that Sadat calculated, correctly, that a resort to war would unblock the frozen diplomatic landscape, I do not believe that either Nixon or Kissinger deliberately encouraged Sadat to go to war.

8. Some analysts at the CIA reportedly played down evidence of Egyptian and Syrian preparations for hostilities, fearing that any such conclusions might be communicated to the Israelis and serve as a reason for a preemptive attack.

9. Richard M. Nixon, *RN: The Memoirs of Richard Nixon* (Grosset and Dunlap, 1978), pp. 920–21. "I was disappointed by our own intelligence shortcomings,

and I was stunned by the failure of Israeli intelligence. They were among the best in the world, and they, too, had been caught off guard."

10. Matti Golan, *The Secret Conversations of Henry Kissinger: Step-by-Step Diplomacy in the Middle East* (Quadrangle Books, 1976), pp. 37–39, contains a detailed account of the Israeli message. Kissinger, *Years of Upheaval*, pp. 465–66, discusses this message, which Kissinger says he did not see until the following morning.

11. Interview with high-ranking Israeli intelligence official, December 1975.

12. Israel received confirmation that the Arabs planned to attack at about 4:00 a.m. Israeli time, October 6. It was expected that hostilities would begin about 6:00 p.m. See Chaim Herzog, *The War of Atonement, October 1973* (Little, Brown, 1975), pp. 52–54.

13. This meeting was chaired by Kissinger's deputy, General Brent Scowcroft, and was attended by Defense Secretary James Schlesinger, Chairman of the Joint Chiefs of Staff Admiral Thomas Moorer, Deputy Secretary of State Kenneth Rush, CIA Director William Colby, Deputy Assistant Secretary of State for the Near East Alfred Atherton, Deputy Assistant Secretary of Defense for International Security Affairs James Noyes, and several staff members. As a member of the National Security Council staff during this period, I attended most of the WSAG meetings. The accounts of these sessions included here are based on memory, interviews with participants, and brief notes on the main substantive topics discussed at each meeting. Kissinger's memoirs, *Years of Upheaval*, also discuss these meetings in some detail. The full record is, of course, still classified, and the sources I have been able to use are in no way definitive. I have tried to concentrate on recording the themes that recurred in the discussions, on the major concepts that participants relied upon in reaching judgments, and on the mood that existed on each day of the crisis. Decisions were not usually made at WSAG meetings. Their real value lay in keeping top-level decisionmakers on the same wavelength. There was very little controversy or argument during any of the meetings.

14. See the same version in the Watch Committee report, October 6, 9:00 a.m., printed in *Village Voice*, February 16, 1976, p. 78, note 305. "We can find no hard evidence of a major, coordinated Egyptian/Syrian offensive across the Canal and in the Golan Heights area. Rather, the weight of evidence indicates an action-reaction situation where a series of responses by each side to preconceived threats created an increasingly dangerous potential for confrontation."

15. Kissinger made a point of this in his discussion with Mohamed Heikal, November 7, 1973, as translated from *Al-Anwar*, November 16, 1973, in "Interviews: Kissinger Meets Haikal," *Journal of Palestine Studies*, vol. 3 (Winter 1974), p. 213.

16. The president's phone logs do not show any conversations with Kissinger on October 6, and Kissinger makes no such reference in his memoirs. But Kissinger was adept at invoking Nixon's authority in front of other members of the administration. He presumably was in touch with Haig, but Haig himself did not talk to Nixon after noon on that day. See President Richard Nixon's daily diary, October 6, 1973.

17. Granting the Soviets most-favored nation (MFN) trading status was a key issue in the fall of 1973. Senator Henry Jackson had introduced an amendment that would withhold MFN treatment for the Soviet Union unless Soviet Jews were allowed to emigrate freely. Nixon and Kissinger opposed the amendment, arguing that quiet diplomacy would be more effective and that the Soviets would not accept such interference in their internal affairs. Ultimately the Soviets refused MFN tied to free emigration.

18. Golan, *Secret Conversations of Kissinger*, p. 64; and Marvin Kalb and Bernard Kalb, *Kissinger* (Little, Brown, 1974), pp. 462–63.

19. Kissinger subsequently told Egyptian officials that he was very impressed when they began to send messages through the back channel shortly after the war began. Interview with high-level Egyptian diplomat, April 1976. Nixon and Kissinger attached considerable importance to the possibility of improving U.S.-Arab relations after the war was over. See Kissinger, *Years of Upheaval*, pp. 481–82. Until receiving this back-channel message, says Kissinger, "I had not taken Sadat seriously."

20. Golan, *Secret Conversations of Kissinger*, p. 45.

21. Membership at WSAG meetings varied, but the following members were usually present: Kissinger, Schlesinger, Moorer, Colby, Scowcroft, Rush, Sisco, Clements, and several staff assistants. When oil was discussed, Deputy Secretary William Simon, former governor John Love of Colorado, and Charles di Bona might participate.

22. Kissinger apparently was aware that the Soviets, six hours after the war had begun, had suggested to Sadat that he accept a simple cease-fire at an early date. The Soviets had repeated the request on October 7. See William B. Quandt, "Soviet Policy in the October Middle East War," *International Affairs*, vol. 53 (July 1977), pp. 377–89, and vol. 53 (Ocober 1977), pp. 587–603; and Sadat's own account in *Al-Hawadith*, March 19, 1975, and *Al-Jumhurriyah*, October 24, 1975. See also, Mohamed Heikal, *The Road to Ramadan* (Quadrangle Books, 1975), pp. 209, 212–15.

23. Libya had recently decreed that American oil-company personnel were not free to leave the country without government permission. The erratic behavior of President Muammar Qaddafi led some U.S. officials to fear that he would order attacks against American interests and citizens. Instead, Libya cooperated in allowing Americans leaving Egypt to transit Libya, for which Qaddafi received a message of thanks.

24. The U.S. position favoring a cease-fire based on the status quo ante was opposed by a number of American ambassadors in Arab countries. Kissinger replied that if the United States called for a vote on any cease-fire resolution that was not linked to a full Israeli withdrawal, the resolution would be defeated; then a vote would be called on a cease-fire tied to withdrawal, which the United States would have to veto. This, in his view, would hurt U.S.-Arab relations worse than Scali's tentative call for a cease-fire based on the post-1967 lines. Above all, Kissinger wanted to avoid a vote in the Security Council until he could be sure of its desirable outcome. This required U.S.-Soviet agreement; Soviet agreement seemed to require Arab acquiescence.

25. Kalb and Kalb, *Kissinger*, p. 466. See also Edward N. Luttwak and Walter Laqueur, "Kissinger and the Yom Kippur War," *Commentary*, vol. 58 (September 1974), p. 36. Kissinger, in *Years of Upheaval*, p. 485, writes, "When I had bad news for Dinitz, I was not above ascribing it to bureaucratic stalemates or unfortunate decisions by superiors."

26. Kissinger arrived at 5:55 p.m. and was already well briefed on the course of the day's fighting.

27. Henry A. Kissinger, "The Nature of the National Dialogue," address delivered to the Pacem in Terris III Conference, Washington, D.C., October 8, 1973, printed in *Department of State Bulletin*, vol. 69 (October 29, 1973), pp. 525–31. In the speech, Kissinger, who discussed détente at some length, said (p. 528):

> "Coexistence, to us continues to have a very precise meaning:
> —We will oppose the attempt by any country to achieve a position of predominance either globally or regionally.
> —We will react if relaxation of tensions is used as a cover to exacerbate conflicts in international trouble spots.
> The Soviet Union cannot disregard these principles in any area of the world without imperiling its entire relationship with the United States. . . . Our policy with regard to détente is clear: We shall resist aggressive foreign policies. Détente cannot survive irresponsibility in any area, including the Middle East.

28. Kissinger, *Years of Upheaval*, pp. 491–93; and Kalb and Kalb, *Kissinger*, pp. 466–67.

29. Some have concluded from Kissinger's use of the word *blackmail* that Dinitz must have raised the specter of Israel resorting to nuclear weapons if its requests were not met. See especially Seymour M. Hersh, *The Samson Option: Israel's Nuclear Arsenal and American Foreign Policy* (Random House, 1991), pp. 228–30. I doubt that any explicit threat was made, but there was an element of nuclear blackmail intrinsic in the military situation. It was widely believed that the Israelis possessed nuclear arms and the means to deliver them, including surface-to-surface missiles. If Israel was on the verge of a military defeat, one could hardly rule out the use of such weapons. In addition, at some point early in the crisis, American intelligence did pick up signals that the Jericho missiles had been place on alert. Taken together, these facts would have led any American official to conclude that there was some relationship between Israel's likely reliance on nuclear threats and American resupply decisions. For Meir's confirmation that she was thinking of flying to Washington, see Golda Meir, *My Life: The Autobiography of Golda Meir* (London: Futura, 1976), p. 362.

30. See Kissinger, *Years of Upheaval*, pp. 495–96, including the content of his message to Dinitz informing him of the president's decision on resupply. At this point there was still no talk of an American airlift, unless an emergency need for tanks arose. Kissinger told Dinitz that everything on Israel's list except laser bombs was approved and that all losses in planes and tanks would be made up. According to Dowty, *Middle East Crisis*, p. 238, Kissinger mentioned to Dinitz

that the United States intended to keep a low profile and that charters might be used by Israel to carry supplies.

31. Insight Team of the London Sunday Times, *Yom Kippur War* (Doubleday, 1974), p. 279. Kissinger, *Years of Upheaval*, p. 499, says that he spoke to Dinitz around mid-day on October 10, who conveyed Meir's thanks for Nixon's decision on resupply. Kissinger urged Israel to push back to the prewar lines "as quickly as possible, or beyond them on at least one front. We could not stall a cease-fire proposal forever."

32. Mohamed Heikal, *The Road to Ramadan* (Quadrangle Books, 1975), pp. 223–24; and Kissinger, *Years of Upheaval*, pp. 499–500.

33. Kissinger, *Years of Upheaval*, p. 498.

34. Quandt, "Soviet Policy in the October Middle East 1973 War" (both parts), summarizes available data on the Soviet delivery of military equipment by air and sea during the war.

35. Kalb and Kalb, *Kissinger*, pp. 468–70; and Golan, *Secret Converstions of Kissinger*, p. 65. Kissinger, *Years of Upheaval*, p. 501, states that Scowcroft told Dinitz of the Soviet proposal for both major powers to abstain in the UN on a cease-fire vote and urged the Israelis to speed up their military efforts over the coming forty-eight hours. Kissinger also argues strongly that the delay in arranging for charter flights was not intended to be a form of pressure on Israel to get it to accept the cease-fire. I am not entirely convinced. Whatever Kissinger's intentions, the Israelis did feel under pressure to finish military operations quickly and without benefit of an all-out American airlift.

36. Richard M. Nixon, remarks at a Medal of Science presentation ceremony, October 10, 1973, *Weekly Compilation of Presidential Documents*, vol. 9 (October 15, 1973), pp. 1236–37. Nixon's views on the cease-fire-in-place idea are not known. He did favor a stalemate on the battlefield (Nixon, *RN*, p. 927), and he spoke to Kissinger often about the need to impose a settlement in concert with the Soviets. So Nixon would not have necessarily been averse to pressuring the Israelis, but there is no specific evidence that he tried to delay the resupply effort during this period as a deliberate form of pressure.

37. Insight Team, *Yom Kippur War*, p. 279. This has been confirmed by a highly placed Israeli source.

38. Nixon, *RN*, pp. 926–27.

39. Kissinger, *Years of Upheaval*, p. 509. The Israelis were told that a vote in the United Nations would not be scheduled before late afternoon October 13.

40. Brecher, *Decisions in Crisis*, p. 214. The decision was made on October 12 in the afternoon, Israeli time. Earlier in the day, the inner cabinet had decided to postpone a decision on an attempted crossing of the canal. Ibid., p. 173.

41. "Secretary Kissinger's News Conference of October 12," *Department of State Bulletin*, vol. 69 (October 29, 1973), pp. 532–41.

42. Kissinger, *Years of Upheaval*, pp. 512–13, describes in detail his meeting with Dinitz at 11:20 p.m., October 12. Kissinger was surprised that Israel had not launched its offensive. Dinitz attributed this to a shortage of supplies. By 1:00 p.m., with no guidance from Nixon (the presidential logs show no calls from

either Kissinger or Haig in this time period), Kissinger decided on some initial steps to speed the delivery of arms. Kalb and Kalb, *Kissinger*, p. 474; Golan, *Secret Conversations of Kissinger*, pp. 53, 61, 66–67; and Insight Team, *Yom Kippur War*, pp. 279–80. According to Defense Secretary Schlesinger, "Kissinger called me Friday night. . . . He indicated Israel was running short. To say the least, he was a little bit concerned." Interview with James Schlesinger, *Jewish Telegraphic Agency Daily Bulletin*, July 1, 1974, p. 4. In his October 26, 1973, news conference, Schlesinger stated that on October 13 "there were some who believed that the existence of the state of Israel was seriously compromised." At least one author, Nadav Safran, *Israel: The Embattled Ally* (Harvard University Press, 1978), p. 483, assumes that Kissinger was motivated by a fear that Israel might resort to nuclear weapons.

43. Kissinger, *Years of Upheaval*, pp. 516–19. See also Kissinger's talk with Heikal on November 7, 1973, "Interview: Kissinger Meets Haikal," pp. 210–15. There he refers to his proposal for a cease-fire in place, conveyed to the Soviets and the Egyptians on October 10, and the subsequent Egyptian refusal, communicated through the Soviets and the British. He describes the Israelis as furious, "but eventually they yielded" to his proposal. See also Insight Team, *Yom Kippur War*, pp. 280–82, where it is reported that the British ambassador met with Sadat a second time at 4:00 p.m., October 13, at which time Sadat gave his final word refusing the U.S. proposal. *Washington Post*, October 14, 1973, p. A1, also mentions the link between the arms-supply decision and Israel's acceptance of a cease-fire. In a press conference on October 26, 1973, Schlesinger stated: "The United States delayed, deliberately delayed, the start of its resupply operation, hoping that a cease-fire would be implemented quickly." "Secretary of Defense Schlesinger's News Conference of October 26," *Department of State Bulletin*, vol. 69 (November 19, 1973), p. 624.

44. See Walter Isaacson, *Kissinger: A Biography* (Simon and Schuster, 1992), p. 521, quoting from the transcript of a Kissinger-Haig telephone conversation early on October 13. Haig said, "He's [Schlesinger] ready to move MAC [Military Assistance Command] aircraft in there immediately. I think that would be foolish." "That would be disaster, Al," Kissinger replied. "How can he fuck everything up for a week—he can't now recoup it the day the diplomacy is supposed to start." This exchange tends to confirm the view that Kissinger did see a link between the airlift and the possibility of an early cease-fire.

45. Kissinger, *Years of Upheaval*, pp. 514, 515. At 12:30 p.m. on October 13 Kissinger was able to tell Dinitz that giant C-5As would fly directly to Israel until the charter issue was sorted out. Fourteen F-4s would also soon be on their way. See also Edward N. Luttwak and Walter Laqueur, "Kissinger and the Yom Kippur War," *Commentary*, vol. 58 (September 1974), p. 37; and Isaacson, *Kissinger*, p. 522.

46. The only other SR-71 flight took place on October 25. See Pike Committee report, p. 78.

47. It is extremely difficult to ascertain the degree to which the U.S. airlift affected Israeli strategy. From interviews with top Israeli officials, I have concluded that the impact of the airlift on strategic decisions was minimal on the Syrian

front and only slightly more significant on the Egyptian front. The crossing of the canal had been seriously recommended by Bar Lev on October 12. (See Herzog, *War of Atonement*, pp. 202–07.) After the Israeli victory in Sinai on October 14, it would have been ordered even without the assurance of U.S. resupplies. However, the crossing might not have been exploited so aggressively if arms had not been on their way. Some items, such as TOW and Maverick missiles, were being used to good effect in the last few days of the fighting and may have raised the prospect of a full defeat of the Third Army Corps. Ironically, the U.S. resupply put Israel in a position to do something that Kissinger was determined to prevent.

48. Faisal and Sadat were sent messages explaining the airlift in those terms before it became publicly known. Kissinger later used the same argument with Heikal; see "Interviews: Kissinger Meets Haikal." The Soviets were also informed in advance of the airlift and were told that the United States would stop if they ended their resupply to the Arabs.

49. From October 14 until the October 25 cease-fire, the U.S. resupply effort delivered approximately 11,000 tons of equipment, forty F-4 Phantoms, thirty-six A-4 Skyhawks, and twelve C-130 transports. Included were only four tanks on the early C-5 flight, and fewer than twenty were sent during the entire airlift. From October 26 until the airlift ended on November 15 another 11,000 tons of equipment were delivered. In all, 147 sorties were flown by C-5s, with 10,800 tons aboard, and 421 sorties by C-141s with 11,500 tons. During the same period, El AL aircraft carried about 11,000 tons of military supplies to Israel in more than 200 sorties. By November 15, the first ships were beginning to reach Israel with resupplies, and the airlift became superfluous. *Aviation Week and Space Technology*, vol. 99 (December 10, 1973), pp. 16–19, contains information on the airlift.

50. Heikal, *Road to Ramadan*, p. 224.

51. Golan, *Secret Conversations of Kissinger*, p. 67.

52. Impromptu comments by Nixon on October 15 at a Medal of Honor ceremony caused some consternation in Arab diplomatic circles. U.S. policy, he stated, is "like the policy that we followed in 1958 when Lebanon was involved, it is like the policy we followed in 1970 when Jordan was involved. The policy of the United States in the Mideast, very simply stated, is this: We stand for the right of every nation in the Mideast to maintain its independence and security. We want this fighting to end. We want the fighting to end on a basis where we can build a listing peace." *Weekly Compilation of Presidential Documents*, vol. 9 (October 22, 1973), p. 1251. The president's reference to Lebanon and Jordan raised the specter of U.S. military intervention. Nixon was presumably simply mentioning the two other Middle East crises in which he had been personally involved.

53. Heikal, *Road to Ramadan*, pp. 232–34, gives a somewhat distorted version of these talks but covers most of the main points.

54. Golan, *Secret Conversations of Kissinger*, p. 70.

55. Ibid., p. 72.

56. Kosygin left Cairo at 2:55 a.m., Washington time, on October 19.

57. Kissinger, *Years of Upheaval*, p. 542.

58. Golan, *Secret Conversations of Kissinger*, p. 75.

59. Kalb and Kalb, *Kissinger*, pp. 481, 483; and Ze'ev Schiff, *October Earthquake: Yom Kippur, 1973* (Tel Aviv: University Publishing Projects, 1974), p. 264.

60. He was accompanied by Joseph Sisco, Alfred Atherton, William Hyland, Winston Lord, and Peter Rodman. Helmut Sonnenfeldt joined the party during a refueling stop in Copenhagen. Ambassador Dobrynin also flew to Moscow aboard the secretary's aircraft.

61. Kissinger, *Years of Upheaval*, pp. 546–48.

62. See Theodore White, *Breach of Faith: The Fall of Richard Nixon* (Atheneum, 1975), pp. 328–42.

63. Nixon did send Kissinger additional instructions to seek agreement with the Soviet Union on a strategy to impose a comprehensive peace in the Middle East. Kissinger ignored the instructions. See Kissinger, *Years of Upheaval*, pp. 550–52.

64. In a side agreement both parties agreed that "appropriate auspices" meant that "the negotiations between the parties concerned will take place with the active participation of the United States and the Soviet Union at the beginning and thereafter in the course of negotiations when key issues of a settlement are dealt with." Ibid., p. 559.

65. Insight Team, *Yom Kippur War*, p. 380. At no time during the crisis did Nixon speak on the phone with any of the leaders in the Middle East.

66. Upon learning that Kissinger was stopping in Israel, Sadat invited him to come to Egypt as well. Kissinger declined, but expressed hope that he would be able to visit Cairo soon. Heikal, *Road to Ramadan*, pp. 248–49.

67. Golan, *Secret Conversations of Kissinger*, pp. 84–87, states that Kissinger hinted that Israel would not be held to strict observance of the cease-fire. Kissinger, *Years of Upheaval*, p. 569, says that he told the Israelis that a few hours' "slippage" in the cease-fire deadline while he was flying home would not be a problem. Joseph Sisco, testifying before the Committee on Foreign Affairs of the House of Representatives, December 3, 1973, stated, "The Israelis were anxious for a ceasefire at the time [October 22] the ceasefire was concluded as were the Egyptians." *Emergency Security Assistance Act of 1973*, Hearings before the Committee of Foreign Affairs of the House of Representatives, 93 Cong. 1 sess. (GPO, 1973), p. 56. See also Walter Laqueur, *Confrontation* (Quadrangle, 1974), p. 194; and *Maariv*, October 26, 1973.

68. During a stopover in London Kissinger called the Soviets, urging them to press the Syrians to call off an offensive planned for the following day.

69. Kalb and Kalb, *Kissinger*, p. 486.

70. Heikal, *Road to Ramadan*, pp. 251–52, prints the text of two of Nixon's letters to Sadat on October 24. In addition, Nixon wrote Sadat on October 23 to make it clear that the United States had only committed itself to engage in a process designed to make possible a political settlement but had not guaranteed any specific outcome of that process.

71. Kalb and Kalb, *Kissinger*, p. 488.

72. Ibid., p. 489.

73. See Kissinger, *Years of Upheaval*, pp. 575–83.

74. Nixon, *RN*, p. 938.

75. An enhanced alert status of seven Soviet airborne divisions was first noted on October 11; the alert status was altered on October 23. See "Secretary of Defense Schlesinger's News Conference of October 26," pp. 617–26.

76. One other consideration that may have contributed to the decision to call a global alert was the arrival during the evening of October 24 of an intelligence report that a suspicious Soviet ship had given off neutron emissions as it transitted the Bosphorous on October 22 on its way to Alexandria. Some thought this might indicate that the Soviets were introducing nuclear warheads into Egypt. Kissinger, *Years of Upheaval*, p. 584, mentions some "ominous signs," probably referring to this report. See also "Secretary Schlesinger's News Conference of October 26"; Raymond L. Garthoff, *Détente and Confrontation: American-Soviet Relations from Nixon to Reagan* (Brookings, 1985), p. 378; and Dowty, *Middle East Crisis*, p. 275.

77. Dayan was subsequently quoted as saying that Kissinger threatened to send U.S. forces to resupply the Third Army Corps. Other Israelis, including Eban, have contended that Kissinger stated that the Soviets might try to resupply the Egyptian forces. The latter seems more plausible, perhaps with the addition of an implied threat not to help the Israelis if they found themselves in confrontation with the Soviets over the fate of the Third Army Corps. This issue is discussed by Theodore Draper, "The United States and Israel: Tilt in the Middle East," *Commentary*, vol. 59 (April 1975), pp. 29–45, and the exchange of letters in *Commentary*, vol. 60 (September 1975), pp. 18–24. Moshe Dayan, *Moshe Dayan: Story of My Life* (William Morrow, 1976), p. 544, says the Americans "more or less" gave Israel an ultimatum to allow supplies through to the Third Army Corps but does not go into details.

78. See Richard Ned Lebow and Janice Gross Stein, "We All Lost the Cold War," draft, April 1992, chap. 12, p. 21. (To be published by Princeton University Press in 1994.)

79. According to ibid., chap. 12, Kissinger refused to comment when asked in an interview if, as was commonly believed, Nixon was unable to participate in the meeting because he had drunk too much that evening.

80. Kissinger, *Years of Upheaval*, p. 593. This meeting was the first that Nixon learned of the measures taken overnight.

81. See "Secretary Kissinger's News Conference of October 25," *Department of State Bulletin*, vol. 69 (November 12, 1973), pp. 585–94, for the complete text. The following day, October 26, Nixon held a press conference in which he discussed the alert: "We obtained information which led us to believe that the Soviet Union was planning to send a very substantial force into the Mideast, a military force. . . . When I received that information, I ordered, shortly after midnight on Thursday morning, an alert for all American forces around the world. This was a precautionary alert. The purpose of that was to indicate to the Soviet Union that we could not accept any unilateral move on their part to move military forces into the Mideast. . . . The outlook for a permanent peace is the best that it has been in twenty years. . . . Without détente, we might have

had a major conflict in the Middle East. With détente, we avoided it." "The President's News Conference of October 26, 1973," *Weekly Compilation of Presidential Documents*, vol. 9 (October 29, 1973), pp. 1287–94.

82. The debate over Kissinger's role in the October war has spawned a remarkably partisan body of writing. Kalb and Kalb, *Kissinger*, are favorable to Kissinger and erroneously portray Schlesinger as the obstacle to the airlift to Israel. Tad Szulc, "Is He Indispensable? Answers to the Kissinger Riddle" *New York*, July 1, 1974, pp. 33–39, points the finger at Kissinger instead. Luttwak and Laqueur, "Kissinger and the Yom Kippur War," try to set the record straight, but overlook the importance of the cease-fire effort of October 10–13. Gil Carl AlRoy, *The Kissinger Experience: American Policy in the Middle East* (Horizon Press, 1975), is a bitterly anti-Kissinger polemic. Golan, *Secret Conversations of Kissinger*, is better informed, but equally hostile to Kissinger. Edward R. F. Sheehan, *The Arabs, Israelis, and Kissinger: A Secret History of American Diplomacy in the Middle East* (Reader's Digest Press, 1976), is sympathetic to him. Very few writers have been able to discern Nixon's role in the formulation of U.S. policy during the war or to distinguish between those aspects of policy designed to preserve détente and those aimed at promoting a new relationship with Egypt.

83. The president's daily diary provides a detailed log of all meetings and telephone calls. For the seventeen days of the crisis that Kissinger was in Washington, he spent on average thirty-four minutes each day in private or very restricted meetings with Nixon. (This excludes cabinet meetings and briefings of congressional leaders where Kissinger was present.) In addition, they spoke by telephone about two times each day, each call averaging some six minutes. Altogether, Kissinger was in direct touch with the president for about three-quarters of an hour a day, or nearly an hour each day if the larger meetings are also counted. As chief of staff, Haig probably spent more time with Nixon, but much of that must have involved the Watergate mess.

CHAPTER EIGHT

1. Nixon was more inclined than Kissinger to consider a forceful American role in imposing a settlement in the region and was not reluctant to talk of pressuring Israel. But he was neither able nor determined to follow through on these sentiments.

2. He expressed this concern to Mohamed Heikal in Cairo on November 7, as reported by Heikal in a lengthy account of his talk with Kissinger in *Al-Anwar*, November 16, 1973, translated in "Interviews: Kissinger Meets Haikal," *Journal of Palestine Studies*, vol. 3 (Winter 1974), pp. 210–15.

3. See "Interviews: Kissinger Meets Haikal," pp. 211–12. Kissinger reportedly told Heikal that he had not dealt with the Middle East crisis before October 1973 because of his fear of failure. Not enough elements of the situation were under his control to ensure success.

4. Ibid., p. 214. "The USSR can give you arms, but the United States can give you a just solution which will give you back your territories, especially as

you [the Arabs] have been able to really change the situation in the Middle East. . . . Politics in our age is not a question of emotions; it is the facts of power."

5. Edward R. F. Sheehan, *The Arabs, Israelis, and Kissinger: A Secret History of American Diplomacy in the Middle East* (Reader's Digest Press, 1976), p. 51, refers to a coherent Arab policy based on a "quasi-alliance" between Washington and Cairo and on the promotion of American technology as a means of increasing American influence in the Arab world.

6. See William B. Quandt, "Soviet Policy in the October Middle East War," *International Affairs*, vol. 53 (July 1977), pp. 377–89, and vol. 53 (October 1977), pp. 587–603.

7. Nixon and Kissinger may also have been irritated by Moscow's unwillingness to live up to the commitment it undertook on October 20–21 to work for the immediate release of Israeli prisoners held in Egypt and Syria.

8. William B. Quandt, "Domestic Influences on U.S. Foreign Policy in the Middle East: The View from Washington," in Willard A. Beling, ed., *The Middle East: Quest for an American Policy* (State University of New York Press, 1973), pp. 263–85.

9. See Kissinger, *Years of Upheaval*, pp. 615–16.

10. William B. Quandt, "Kissinger and the Arab-Israeli Disengagement Negotiations," *Journal of International Affairs*, vol. 29 (Spring 1975), pp. 33–48.

11. In his first meeting with Kissinger, Fahmy agreed that the Third Army Corps would be resupplied only with nonmilitary items if Israel agreed to pull back to the October 22 lines. Fahmy at the time was acting foreign minister. He was named foreign minister on October 31.

12. Kissinger, *Years of Upheaval*, pp. 616–17. Kissinger did promise that Israel would not launch a military offensive from its position on the west bank of the Suez Canal. He also agreed to send a high-level representative to Cairo at an early date.

13. Ibid., pp. 619–24.

14. Kissinger met again with Prime Minister Meir on November 3. The following day the prime minister was reportedly called by Nixon's chief of staff, Alexander Haig, and by Nelson Rockefeller, who both conveyed Nixon's displeasure at her attitude. Matti Golan, *The Secret Conversations of Henry Kissinger: Step-by-Step Diplomacy in the Middle East* (Quadrangle Books, 1976), p. 111.

15. Kissinger had seen the Syrian representative to the United Nations on November 2, but there was still no channel for continuing contacts between Washington and Damascus.

16. Kissinger, *Years of Upheaval*, pp. 636–41. See also Sheehan, *Arabs, Israelis*, pp. 48–51.

17. An experienced career diplomat, Hermann Eilts, was named as American ambassador to Egypt, and American-educated Ashraf Ghorbal became Egypt's ambassador to the United States.

18. The text of the agreement can be found in Kissinger, *Years of Upheaval*, p. 641.

19. Ibid., p. 664, states, "Had I understood the mechanism of oil pricing

better, I would have realized that Saudi production cutbacks were more dangerous than the embargo since they critically affected world supply and therefore provided the precondition for the impoverishing price rise."

20. Sheehan, *Arabs, Israelis*, pp. 70–73, contains a partial transcript of the Kissinger-Faisal meeting. See also Kissinger, *Years of Upheaval*, pp. 659–66.

21. Several days later, in Peking, Kissinger spoke of Israeli "withdrawals" as part of a settlement, in a deliberate effort to signal his good intentions to the Saudis. The Israelis were not particularly pleased; they worried about Kissinger's mention of U.S. guarantees, fearing that external guarantees would become a substitute for Arab concessions. See "Secretary Kissinger's News Conference of November 12, 1973," *Department of State Bulletin*, vol. 69 (December 10, 1973), p. 713.

22. Moshe Dayan, *Moshe Dayan: Story of My Life* (William Morrow, 1976), p. 556, refers to Yariv's November 22 proposals.

23. Golan, *Secret Conversations of Kissinger*, pp. 120–21. He states that Kissinger did not use direct pressure but made his preferences known to the Israelis. See also Kissinger, *Years of Upheaval*, p. 752.

24. Kissinger, *Years of Upheaval*, p. 634, quotes Nixon as saying to the cabinet that "it might be necessary to apply pressure on Israel to avert a serious oil shortage."

25. Dayan, *Moshe Dayan*, p. 548, states that he opposed the kilometer 101 talks because he felt the United States should be involved in the negotiation.

26. Nixon wrote to Sadat on December 1, proposing that Egypt attend a conference in Geneva on December 18.

27. Sadat's reply to Nixon's invitation, dated December 8, confirmed Egypt's willingness to go to Geneva but did not mention Syria.

28. Kissinger's speech before the Pilgrims of Great Britain on December 12 discussed the October war and the energy crisis. It contained the revealing admission that "it is fair to state . . . that the United States did not do all that it might have done before the war to promote a permanent settlement in the Middle East." *Department of State Bulletin*, vol. 69 (December 31, 1973), p. 780.

29. Kissinger spent four hours with Sadat on December 13 and five hours on December 14. They discussed what they might do if Israel refused to attend the Geneva conference. Sadat also promised to work for the lifting of the oil embargo in early January.

30. Kissinger, *Years of Upheaval*, p. 759, quotes from the letter.

31. Nixon's tone in these letters was reflected in remarks he reportedly made to a group of seventeen governors on December 13. "The only way we're going to solve the crisis is to end the oil embargo, and the only way we're going to end the embargo is to get the Israelis to act reasonable. I hate to use the word blackmail, but we've got to do some things to get them to behave." Thomas O'Toole and Lou Cannon, "Jobs, Oil Put Ahead of Environment, Israel," *Washington Post*, December 22, 1973, p. A1.

32. These promises were codified in a memorandum of understanding. See David Landau, "Kissinger Obtains Jerusalem's Consent to Attend Geneva Parley," *Jerusalem Post*, December 18, 1973, p. 1.

33. Kissinger, *Years of Upheaval*, pp. 777–86. Sheehan, *Arabs, Israelis*, pp. 95–97, includes transcripts of portions of these talks.

34. Asad did agree to the opening of an American-manned interests section in Damascus. Thomas Scotes was sent to head the mission.

35. Marvin Kalb and Bernard Kalb, *Kissinger* (Little, Brown, 1974), pp. 526–27. Kissinger also told Golda Meir that Sadat was moving toward moderate views and that by talking of disengagement, Israel could put off negotiations on final borders.

36. Kissinger, *Years of Upheaval*, pp. 1249–50, reproduces the text of a memorandum that he sent to Nixon on December 19, 1973, summing up the positions of the parties on the eve of the conference.

37. Ibid., pp. 821–29; and Kalb and Kalb, *Kissinger*, pp. 534–35.

38. Kalb and Kalb, *Kissinger*, p. 539.

39. The text and map appear in "The Agreement: New Deployment of Forces along the Suez Canal," *Jerusalem Post*, January 20, 1974, p. 1, and in Kissinger, *Years of Upheaval*, p. 839 (map) and p. 1250.

40. The memorandum of understanding is described in general terms in Bernard Gwertzman, "Congressmen Get Mideast Briefing," *New York Times*, January 22, 1974, p. 1.

41. Kissinger, *Years of Upheaval*, p. 1251, provides the text. The stipulation concerning six batteries of short-range artillery later became a source of controversy. In the Israeli army, a battery consisted of six guns; in the Egyptian army, it contained twelve. The first reconnaissance flights after the implementation of the disengagement agreement found seventy-two artillery pieces on the Egyptian side and thirty-six on the Israeli. After angry Israeli complaints in late March, Sadat agreed to reduce his forces to the Israeli level of thirty-six guns.

42. Ze'ev Schiff, "After Accord Signed on Friday, Separation of Forces Begins Next Sunday, Will End in 40 Days," *Jerusalem Post*, January 20, 1974, p. 1, contains a generally accurate account of the secret provisions of the agreement. See also "Secretary Kissinger's News Conference of January 22, 1974," *Department of State Bulletin*, vol. 70 (February 11, 1974), p. 137.

43. "Secretary Kissinger's News Conference of January 3, 1974," *Department of State Bulletin*, vol. 70 (January 28, 1974), p. 78. On January 6, 1974, Defense Secretary Schlesinger raised for the first time the possible use of force if the oil embargo should continue indefinitely.

44. For details of the Jordanian proposals, see Bernard Gwertzman, "U.S. Laying Groundwork for Syrian-Israeli Talks," *New York Times*, February 10, 1974, p. 1, and Terence Smith, "Hussein Said to Urge an Israeli Pullback to Western Edge of the Jordan Valley," *New York Times*, February 15, 1974, p. 3.

45. Golan, *Secret Conversations of Kissinger*, p. 182.

46. These messages, which seemed to imply that Nixon wanted the embargo lifted for domestic political reasons, later proved an embarrassment to him. When the Saudis failed to live up to their promises to lift the embargo, Kissinger hinted that he might be obliged to release the texts of the commitments undertaken by Faisal. The Saudis responded by suggesting that they, too, might have some

embarrassing messages to release. The issue was quickly dropped. See Kissinger, *Years of Upheaval*, p. 947: "In the tenth month of his [Nixon's] torment he was still in thrall to the idea that a dramatic lifting of the embargo under his personal leadership was the cure-all for his Watergate agonies."

47. Bernard Gwertzman, "Israel and Syria to Confer in U.S.," *New York Times*, March 3, 1974, p. 1. There were sixty-five names on the list, more than some observers had expected.

48. During his visit to Washington on March 12, King Hussein had requested $130 million in budget support, in addition to other sums for military assistance. The administration at the time was considering $100 million, which was about twice the amount provided the previous year. The formal aid request for the Middle East for fiscal year 1975 was sent to Congress on April 24 and contained an uncommitted $100 million, presumably to be used as aid for Syria if diplomatic relations were resumed.

49. Dayan's visit had nearly been called off by the Israelis in protest over what they viewed as Egypt's violations of the terms of the disengagement agreement. The dispute over the violations is mentioned in "Arabs Assess Talks Progress," *Washington Post*, March 26, 1974, p. A13.

50. Joseph Alsop, "American Arms Sales to Egypt?" *Washington Post*, April 26, 1974, p. A31.

51. Nixon had met with Boumedienne at the White House on April 11 and had given a small private dinner for him in the evening. The talks had gone well, although Boumedienne pressed Nixon hard on the Syrian-Israeli disengagement and the Palestinians.

52. Kissinger sent Saunders to Saudi Arabia and Algeria to brief Faisal and Boumedienne on the talks and to ask for their support.

53. Kissinger, *Years of Upheaval*, pp. 1052–1110, gives a detailed account of the Damascus-Jerusalem shuttle. Sheehan, *Arabs, Israelis*, pp. 94–106, covers this period, including texts of some of the conversations between Kissinger and Meir. See also Golan, *Secret Conversations of Kissinger*, p. 194.

54. *Pravda*, May 20, 1974, did, however, warn Asad not to settle for half-measures.

55. Sadat fully endorsed this approach to Asad.

56. Golan, *Secret Conversations of Kissinger*, p. 196; and Bernard Gwertzman, "Syria-Israel Gain Seen by Kissinger," *New York Times*, May 9, 1974, p. 1.

57. Nixon had sent Meir a letter on May 10 expressing his concern that an agreement be reached.

58. The Americans had anticipated difficult negotiating around Quneitra and had come armed with large aerial photographs of the area. The photographs were actually used for drawing the final lines instead of maps because of their extraordinarily accurate detail.

59. Kissinger, *Years of Upheaval*, p. 1078, recounts Nixon's orders to cut off all aid to Israel. In the context of the Palestinian terrorist attack on Israelis at Ma'alot that occurred on May 15, Kissinger felt such action would be particularly inappropriate and he opposed it.

60. After four hours with Prime Minister Meir and eight with President Asad,

Kissinger reported to Nixon that May 16 had been his toughest day yet. The previous day Israel had been traumatized by the Ma'alot massacre, which had resulted in the deaths of numerous schoolchildren. This contributed to the defiant mood in Israel concerning concessions to Syria and added to the difficulty of Kissinger's task.

61. "Two Issues Said to Delay Troop-Separation Accord," *New York Times*, May 23, 1974, p. 1.

62. Sheehan, *Arabs, Israelis*, p. 126.

63. As late as June 2, Syria was still trying to make changes in the disengagement line. Israel refused.

64. For the text of the agreement, see *Arab Report and Record*, May 16–31, 1974, p. 215.

65. Kissinger, *Years of Upheaval*, pp. 1123–43; and Richard M. Nixon, *RN: The Memoirs of Richard Nixon* (Grosset and Dunlap, 1978), pp. 1007–18.

66. Sheehan, *Arabs, Israelis*, p. 132.

67. Nixon had never quite overcome his belief in the Eisenhower-Strauss plan of bringing peace to the Middle East by making the deserts bloom through the provision of fresh water produced by nuclear-powered desalting plants. Like many bad ideas, this one was difficult to kill, and the offer of nuclear power plants to Egypt and Israel was a variant of it.

68. Kissinger, *Years of Upheaval*, p. 1134.

69. Golan, *Secret Conversations of Kissinger*, pp. 214–17.

70. Kissinger did not accompany Nixon to Jordan. He flew instead to Canada for a NATO meeting.

71. Golan, *Secret Conversations of Kissinger*, pp. 220–21, claims that arms shipments were delayed as a form of pressure on Israel.

72. Egyptian-Jordanian Joint Communiqué, July 19, 1974, in Foreign Broadcast Information Service, *Daily Report: Middle East and North Africa*, July 19, 1974, p. D1.

73. Information Minister Aharon Yariv stated in July 1974, "Negotiations with the PLO would be possible should the PLO . . . declare its readiness to enter into negotiations while acknowledging the existence of the Jewish state in Israel and calling off all hostile acts against it." "Israel for the First Time, Gives Basis of Talks with Palestinians," *New York Times*, July 13, 1974, p. 1.

74. Golan, *Secret Conversations of Kissinger*, pp. 220–22.

75. During July 1974, however, Secretary of the Treasury Simon did travel to Egypt, Israel, and Saudi Arabia to discuss economic cooperation. He had little to offer but learned that the Egyptians were developing a very large appetite for American aid and technology and that the Israelis were contemplating a five-year military modernization program that would cost $4 billion a year, of which at least $1.5 billion was earmarked as American grant aid. Peace in the Middle East would not come cheaply.

76. Kissinger, *Years of Upheaval*, p. 1247, note 1, recognizes this criticism but argues that in the immediate aftermath of the October 1973 war nothing more than a step-by-step approach could have worked. I agree for that period, but I think more might have been done to build on the second disengagement agreement

if presidential authority had not been so badly undermined. In brief, American influence might have made a difference, but it was not available from mid-1974 on.

<h2 style="text-align:center">CHAPTER NINE</h2>

1. Ford shared Kissinger's suspicion of the Soviet Union. See Gerald R. Ford, *A Time to Heal: The Autobiography of Gerald R. Ford* (Harper and Row, 1979), p. 183: "Even before I became President, Kissinger had achieved significant success in easing the Soviets out of the Middle East. I thought they didn't want a bona fide settlement there and that their only aim was to promote instability, so I wanted to keep them out."

2. See Cecilia Albin and Harold H. Saunders, "Sinai II: The Politics of International Mediation," FPI Case Study 17, Johns Hopkins University, School of Advanced International Sudies, Washington, 1991, for the best detailed account of these negotiations. The authors point out that Ford himself was inclined to concentrate on the Egyptian-Israeli front, in part because it seemed more feasible in political terms (pp. 37–38).

3. Fahmy told Ford that Egypt was prepared to go ahead with another partial agreement with Israel before an Israeli-Jordanian agreement was reached. He also expressed the opinion that simultaneous negotiations on these two fronts was impossible. Ibid., pp. 29–30.

4. Ibid., p. 30, indicates that King Hussein made an important concession by accepting the idea that Israeli forces could remain behind in designated locations along the Jordan River after a disengagement agreement. This is referred to as the "leopard spots" concept.

5. See, for example, William Safire, "Arab Council of War," *New York Times*, October 31, 1974, p. 41. A more thoughtful analysis can be found in Richard H. Ullman, "After Rabat: Middle East Risks and American Roles," *Foreign Affairs*, vol. 53 (January 1975), pp. 284–96.

6. In November 1974 the International Energy Agency was established under OECD auspices. It agreed upon a program to build up oil stocks, to plan for reducing demand in the event of oil-supply interruptions, and to share oil if any member of the group was subjected to a selective embargo. By agreeing to these terms, the United States in theory became as vulnerable to an embargo as Europe or Japan.

7. For a discussion of the link between the Arab-Israeli conflict and the energy crisis, see William B. Quandt, "U.S. Energy Policy and the Arab-Israeli Conflict," in Naiem A. Sherbiny and Mark A. Tessler, eds., *Arab Oil: Impact on the Arab Countries and Global Implications* (Praeger, 1976), pp. 279–94. In a major address on energy at the University of Chicago on November 14, 1976, Kissinger maintained that the price of oil would come down only when the objective situation changed. In other words market forces, not political favors, would be the means of reducing prices.

8. Kissinger was pressed by an aggressive interviewer to state that the use of force against oil producers could not be excluded in the event of actual "strangula-

tion" of the Western economies. "Kissinger on Oil, Food, and Trade," *Business Week*, January 13, 1975, pp. 66–76. Detailed discussions of the circumstances in which force might appropriately be used appeared in Robert Tucker, "Oil: The Issue of American Intervention," *Commentary*, vol. 59 (January 1975), pp. 21–31; and Miles Ignotus [presumably Edward Luttwak], "Seizing Arab Oil," *Harper's*, March 1975, pp. 45–62.

9. An article by Hollis Chenery, vice-president of the World Bank, marked an important turning point in the debate over oil prices. See "Restructuring the World Economy," *Foreign Affairs*, vol. 53 (January 1975), pp. 242–63.

10. The joint communiqué issued on November 24, 1974, said that the search for peace in the Middle East should be based on UN Resolution 338, "taking into account the legitimate interests of all the peoples of the area, including the Palestinian people, and respect for the right to independent existence of all States in the area." *Department of State Bulletin*, vol. 71 (December 23, 1974), p. 880.

11. Matti Golan, *The Secret Conversations of Henry Kissinger: Step-by-Step Diplomacy in the Middle East* (Quadrangle Books, 1976), p. 229.

12. Ibid., pp. 229–30; and *Haaretz*, December 17, 1974.

13. Ford also weighed in with advice to the Israelis to be more flexible. See Ford, *Time to Heal*, pp. 245–46, for his view that Israel was sufficiently strong to be able to make concessions.

14. *Le Monde*, January 21, 1975.

15. On February 3, 1975, Syria and the Soviet Union issued a joint communiqué calling for the reconvening of the Geneva conference.

16. Golan, *Secret Conversations of Kissinger*, p. 232.

17. Asad's position on a second step in the Golan Height remained ambiguous. He did not appear particularly anxious for such an agreement, but neither did he preclude it.

18. Wolf I. Blitzer, "Kissinger Reveals Sadat's Twelve 'Concessions,' " *Jerusalem Post*, May 12, 1975, p. 1. According to Albin and Saunders, "Sinai II," p. 58, Sadat also gave Kissinger a fallback position to use as needed. This became a standard Sadat tactic in later negotiations.

19. Edward R. F. Sheehan, *The Arabs, Israelis, and Kissinger: A Secret History of American Diplomacy in the Middle East* (Reader's Digest Press, 1976), p. 156. See also Albin and Saunders, "Sinai II," pp. 56–58 for a summary of these points.

20. See Golan, *Secret Conversations of Kissinger*, pp. 236–38, although he incorrectly gives the date of the letter as March 19. Yitzhak Rabin, *The Rabin Memoirs* (Little, Brown, 1979), p. 256, provides a partial text of the letter, in which Ford threatens "reassessment" of U.S. policy, including relations with Israel. Ford, *Time to Heal*, p. 247, said that he was "mad as hell" at the Israelis over their negotiating tactics.

21. Sheehan, *Arabs, Israelis*, pp. 160–62, contains parts of the transcripts of these talks. It should be noted that the transcripts are not verbatim records but reconstructions of the conversations in dialogue form based on notes taken during the sessions by one of Kissinger's aides. A slightly different version of Kissinger's soliloquy can be found in Albin and Saunders, "Sinai II," pp. 69–70.

22. Before his departure Kissinger called on Golda Meir. Although she

publicly supported Rabin, she privately implied to Kissinger that Rabin had mishandled the negotiations and that she would have known how to get the cabinet and the Knesset to support an agreement.

23. Ford met with Max Fisher on March 27, 1975, to express his irritation with Israeli policy. Fisher was a wealthy Detroit businessman, a Republican, and a leader in the American Jewish community. He often served as an informal channel of communication between the United States and Israel. See Ford, *Time to Heal*, pp. 247, 286.

24. Ford interview with the Hearst newspaper chain, March 27, 1975. See Bernard Gwertzman, "Ford Says Israel Lacked Flexibility in Negotiations," *New York Times*, March 28, 1975, p. 1.

25. George Ball, "How to Avert a Middle East War," *Atlantic Monthly*, January 1975, pp. 6–11.

26. During this period Stanley Hoffmann brilliantly argued the case that it was in Israel's own interest to come up with a comprehensive peace initiative. The major flaw in his argument was that such a policy would require a strong Israeli government backed by a broad public consensus. That apparently was lacking. See "A New Policy for Israel," *Foreign Affairs*, vol. 53 (April 1975), pp. 405–31.

27. Sheehan, *Arabs, Israelis*, p. 166; and Albin and Saunders, "Sinai II," p. 79.

28. He also referred to U.S. policy as "evenhanded."

29. Ford, *Time to Heal*, p. 287, says that he publicly welcomed the letter from the senators, but "in truth it really bugged me. The Senators claimed the letter was 'spontaneous,' but there was no doubt in my mind that it was inspired by Israel. We had given vast amounts of military and economic assistance to Israel over the years and we had never asked for anything in return."

30. Sheehan, *Arabs, Israelis*, pp. 176–77.

31. Golan, *Secret Conversations of Kissinger*, p. 59; and Ford, *Time to Heal*, pp. 290–91.

32. Ford, *Time to Heal*, p. 291, says that he also offered Sadat significant amounts of economic assistance ($800 million) and C-130 transports. Offensive military equipment was ruled out because of Israel's strong objections.

33. Ford letter to Rabin, September 1, 1975, referring to their meeting of June 12, 1975. Reproduced in Michael Widlanski, ed., *Can Israel Survive a Palestinian State?* (Jerusalem: Institute for Advanced Strategic and Political Studies, 1990), pp. 120–21. According to Albin and Saunders, "Sinai II," p. 92, Ford told Rabin that he was inclined to put forward a U.S. plan.

34. Golan, *Secret Conversations of Kissinger*, p. 245; and Terence Smith, "Israel Offers Compromise to Egyptian Sinai Accords," *New York Times*, June 25, 1975, p. 1. Rabin, *Rabin Memoirs*, p. 267, states that the proposed map was approved by the Israeli negotiating team and conveyed to Egypt, where it was rejected.

35. Golan, *Secret Conversations of Kissinger*, p. 248, although he mistakenly gives the date of this meeting as early August. Bernard Gwertzman, "Kissinger Visited by Israeli Envoy for Secret Talks," *New York Times*, July 4, 1975, p. 1.

36. Albin and Saunders, "Sinai II," p. 86, note that Israel was very intent on

getting more military assistance to fund its ten-year modernization program called Matmon-B.

37. Rabin and Ford met in Bonn on July 12, after which the Israeli cabinet authorized a new negotiating position. See *Arab Report and Record*, July 1–15, 1975, p. 401; Terence Smith, "U.S. Is Considering Proposal That It Man Posts in Sinai," *New York Times*, July 13, 1975, p. 1; and Kathleen Teltsch, "Kissinger Warns Majority in UN on U.S. Support," *New York Times*, July 15, 1975, p. 1. Egypt's reply was forthcoming on July 21, but was rejected by Israel on July 27. Israel then presented an "absolutely final" position to Kissinger, who transmitted it to Sadat via Eilts on July 31. The Egyptian response reached Kissinger in Belgrade on August 3, and by August 7 Dinitz had responded with the Israeli position. During the next few days, further exchanges took place, and by mid-August United States and Israeli officials had completed work on a draft agreement. Ford then instructed Kissinger to undertake another trip to the Middle East to pin down the details of an agreement.

38. Sheehan, *Arabs, Israelis*, p. 184.

39. The text of the agreement can be found in *Department of State Bulletin*, vol. 73 (September 22, 1975), pp. 466–70. The secret part of the agreement was published in "U.S. Documents Accompanying the Sinai Accord," *New York Times*, September 17, 1975, p. 4, and "U.S.-Israeli Pact on Geneva," *New York Times*, September 18, 1975, p. 16. The map was also released by the Department of State.

40. Kissinger had kept Sadat informed of most of the commitments he was making to Israel but did not mention the Pershing missile. This irritated the Egyptians and raised doubts about other secret agreements that Kissinger might not have mentioned.

41. According to Albin and Saunders, "Sinai II," p. 100, the Israelis had sought much stronger language. The American negotiating team at the time interpreted this commitment as leaving room for contacts with the PLO.

42. This letter remained secret until published in Widlanski, ed., *Can Israel Survive?* pp. 120–21.

43. On September 29, 1975, Kissinger spoke to the Arab representatives at the United Nations. He said that the United States was prepared to work for a Syrian-Israeli second step, if that was wanted; that the United States would consider ways of working for an overall settlement; and that he would begin to refine his thinking on how the legitimate interests of the Palestinian people could be met. "Furthering Peace in the Middle East," Toast by Secretary Kissinger, *Department of State Bulletin*, vol. 73 (October 20, 1975), pp. 581–84.

44. The Saunders statement can be found in "Department Gives Position on Palestinian Issue," *Department of State Bulletin*, vol. 73 (December 1, 1975), pp. 797–800.

45. Schlesinger was dismissed by Ford on November 2, 1975, to be replaced by Donald Rumsfeld; CIA Director Colby was replaced by George Bush; and Kissinger was relieved of his position as national security affairs adviser, to be replaced by Brent Scowcroft. Moynihan resigned on February 2, 1976.

46. Even without Sinai II, of course, the level of aid for Israel and Egypt would have been substantial. The marginal cost of Sinai II should be measured as several hundreds of million dollars, not several billion. For an account of the congressional debate on Sinai II, see Bernard Gwertzman, "Senate Unit Asks Word from Ford," *New York Times*, October 1, 1975, p. 14. The House and Senate voted in favor of United States technicians in Sinai by large majorities, on October 8 and 9, respectively. Ford, *Time to Heal*, pp. 308–09, provides his rationale for increased aid to Israel: "If we provided the hardware, we could convince Israelis that they were secure. Then they might be willing to accept some risks in the search for peace."

47. Bernard Gwertzman, "Israel Indicates a Cool Reaction to Egypt's Ideas," *New York Times*, March 15, 1975, p. 1.

48. In late March the State Department repeatedly warned Syria against military intervention in Lebanon. On March 31 the former ambassador to Jordan, L. Dean Brown, was sent to Lebanon to try to promote a political settlement. Shortly thereafter a modest number of Syrian troops did enter Lebanon. The United States and Israel both augmented their military capabilities in precautionary measures. Throughout April, while Syria was working to achieve agreement that Elias Sarkis should replace President Suleiman Frangieh, riots broke out on the West Bank after the victory on April 12 of Palestinian nationalists in the municipal elections. Despite the increase of tensions, however, both the United States and Israel began to perceive the Syrian role in Lebanon as potentially stabilizing. Sarkis was elected as Lebanon's new president on May 8 but was not scheduled to take office until September. As fighting continued, Syria increased its military involvement in Lebanon in late May and early June. On June 5 Syria and Egypt withdrew their diplomatic representatives in each other's capitals.

49. A new ambassador, Frank Meloy, took over from Brown in late April. Subsequently, Brown criticized Kissinger for having discouraged Syria from sending troops into Lebanon. "We reined in the Syrians too much, in order to please the Israelis. It resulted in a lot more killing." *Arab Report and Record*, May 16–31, 1976, p. 321. Meloy was kidnapped and assassinated, presumably by dissident Palestinians, on June 16, 1976. He was replaced by an experienced Arabist, Talcott Seelye, but in short order the American diplomatic community in Beirut was reduced to a token force and Seelye returned to Washington. Two evacuations by sea were successfully carried out on June 20 and July 27, 1976, with the cooperation of the PLO. Throughout this period, discreet contacts between the United States and the PLO were undertaken in the interests of arranging for local security.

CHAPTER TEN

1. *Toward Peace in the Middle East*, Report of a Study Group (Brookings, 1975). This report was subsequently credited with steering the Carter administration toward a comprehensive approach to an Arab-Israeli peace agreement, with the Geneva Conference as the centerpiece of the strategy. It is true that Vance and Carter both read the report and many of its suggestions were incorporated into

policy, but it would be an exaggeration to say that the report served as a blueprint for the policies of the first year.

2. The rest of the Middle East team consisted of Alfred L. Atherton, Jr., the assistant secretary of state for Near Eastern and South Asian affairs and later ambassador-at-large for the peace talks; Harold H. Saunders, the director of intelligence and research at State, and later the assistant secretary for Near Eastern affairs; and me as staff member of the National Security Council. All of us had been involved with Kissinger's shuttle diplomacy and were personally well acquainted, which helped to reduce the normal State-NSC frictions and ensured a large measure of continuity with past negotiating efforts. Two other people came to play important roles as the negotiating process got under way: Hermann F. Eilts, ambassador to Cairo and an experienced Middle East hand; and Samuel W. Lewis, ambassador to Israel, who had considerable experience with the United Nations and proved to be a very popular and influential envoy to Israel.

3. For more detail, see William B. Quandt, *Camp David: Peacemaking and Politics*, (Brookings, 1986), pp. 38–40.

4. Ibid., pp. 41–43.

5. Cyrus Vance, *Hard Choices: Critical Years in America's Foreign Policy* (Simon and Schuster, 1983), p. 171.

6. See Yitzhak Rabin, *The Rabin Memoirs* (Little, Brown, 1979), pp. 292–99, for his version of the meeting. See also Jimmy Carter, *Keeping Faith: Memoirs of a President* (Bantam Books), 1982, p. 280; Zbigniew Brzezinski, *Power and Principle: Memoirs of the National Security Adviser, 1977–1981* (Farrar, Strauss, Giroux, 1983), pp. 90–91; and Vance, *Hard Choices*, p. 173.

7. "Clinton, Massachusetts: Remarks and a Question-and-Answer Session at the Clinton Town Meeting, March 16, 1977," *Public Papers of the President: Carter, 1977*, vol. 1 (Government Printing Office, 1977), p. 387.

8. Quandt, *Camp David*, p. 51.

9. See Carter, *Keeping Faith*, pp. 284–88, for his reaction to Begin.

10. See Quandt, *Camp David*, pp. 77–82; Moshe Dayan, *Breakthrough: A Personal Account of the Egypt-Israel Peace Negotiations* (Knopf, 1981), pp. 19–20; and Carter, *Keeping Faith*, p. 290.

11. Ismail Fahmy, *Negotiating for Peace in the Middle East* (Johns Hopkins University Press, 1983), pp. 216–19.

12. Quandt, *Camp David*, p. 90.

13. Ibid., p. 91.

14. Ibid., pp. 101–03.

15. Fahmy, *Negotiating for Peace*, p. 252.

16. Quandt, *Camp David*, pp. 122–23.

17. Dayan, *Breakthrough*, pp. 38–54.

18. For a review of the evidence, see Martin Indyk, *"To the Ends of the Earth": Sadat's Jerusalem Initiative* (Harvard University, Center for Middle Eastern Studies, 1984), pp. 41–43; and Quandt, *Camp David*, pp. 123–25.

19. See the letter written by Ambassador Hermann Eilts, "The Syrians Have Been Their Own Worst Enemies," *New York Times*, January 12, 1982, p. A14.

20. Quandt, *Camp David*, pp. 125–31.

21. Dayan, *Breakthrough*, p. 71.

22. Ibid., pp. 70–71.

23. Quandt, *Camp David*, pp. 139–41.

24. Fahmy, *Negotiating for Peace*, pp. 262–63.

25. See Steven L. Spiegel, *The Other Arab-Israeli Conflict: Making America's Middle East Policy, from Truman to Reagan* (University of Chicago Press, 1985), pp. 341–44.

26. Quandt, *Camp David*, p. 152.

27. Ibid., p. 156; and Vance, *Hard Choices*, p. 199.

28. Brzezinski, *Power and Principle*, pp. 115–20.

29. See Quandt, *Camp David*, p. 158; Carter, *Keeping Faith*, p. 300; and Dayan, *Breakthrough*, pp. 359–61, for the revised text of the Self-Rule proposal.

30. On August 5, 1970, Begin explained before the Knesset why he was resigning from the cabinet: "As far as we are concerned, what do the words 'withdrawal from territories administered since 1967 by Israel' mean other than giving up Judea and Samaria. Not all the territories; but by all opinion, most of them."

31. Quandt, *Camp David*, pp. 171–72.

32. Ibid., pp. 173–76.

33. Ibid., p. 201.

34. Ibid., pp. 212–14.

35. Ibid., pp. 216–17.

36. Ibid., p. 218.

37. Ibid., appendix F, p. 369.

38. Ibid., pp. 222–25.

39. Ibid., p. 222.

40. See Shibley Telhami, *Power and Leadership in International Bargaining: The Path to the Camp David Accords* (Columbia University Press, 1990), pp. 162–67.

41. Quandt, *Camp David*, pp. 242–47.

42. Ibid., pp. 247–51.

CHAPTER ELEVEN

1. On Sadat's political position at this time, see William B. Quandt, *Camp David: Peacemaking and Politics* (Brookings, 1986), p. 262.

2. "President As-Sadat Addresses U.S. News Media," Foreign Broadcast Information Service (FBIS), *Daily Report: Middle East and Africa*, September 20, 1978, pp. D1–D4. Israelis have frequently quoted Sadat's remark to prove that Begin was correct in his interpretation of what was agreed on. But Sadat was not present when the issue was discussed between Carter and Begin. When Sadat spoke on September 19, he had already been told that Begin had agreed only to a three-month freeze. Sadat is also wrong in saying that Israel had agreed not to expand settlements. That language had been dropped at Israeli insistence. According to Sadat's aides, the Egyptian president chose to play down the issue of settlements in the West Bank so as not to put pressure on Carter. He assumed that Carter would find a solution in due course.

3. On September 19, 1978, the Saudi News Agency released an official Saudi cabinet statement critical of the Camp David Accords because they did not call for full Israeli withdrawal and did not provide for Palestinian self-determination. Nonetheless, the cabinet statement went on to say that it did not dispute Egypt's right to recover Sinai. See FBIS, *Daily Report: Middle East and Africa*, September 20, 1978, p. C3.

4. See Jimmy Carter, *Keeping Faith: Memoirs of a President* (Bantam Books, 1982), p. 405, in which he notes that Begin seemed to want to keep both the peace with Egypt and the West Bank; and Cyrus Vance, *Hard Choices: Critical Years in America's Foreign Policy* (Simon and Schuster, 1983), p. 229. Begin had made some particularly hard-line public comments on the day after signing the Camp David Accords. Carter was so angry that he took Begin aside during their joint appearance before the U.S. Congress and told him, in Sadat's presence, that his remarks could cause serious problems. Interview with President Jimmy Carter, Plains, Georgia, May 22, 1985.

5. Sadat had the impression from Carter that the United States would deliver Saudi support for Camp David. See Hermann Frederick Eilts, "Improve the Framework," *Foreign Policy*, no. 41 (Winter 1980–81), p. 9.

6. Zbigniew Brzezinski, *Power and Principle: Memoirs of the National Security Adviser, 1977–1981* (Farrar, Straus and Giroux, 1983), p. 274.

7. Vance, *Hard Choices*, pp. 230–31, summarizes the answers to Hussein's questions, but mistakenly includes the point that sovereignty resides with the people in the West Bank and Gaza.

8. Vance speech in "United Nations: 33d General Assembly Convenes, Statement at the Opening Session of the U.N. General Assembly on September 29, 1978," *Department of State Bulletin*, vol. 78 (November 1978), p. 49.

9. Brzezinski, *Power and Principle*, p. 276, says that Carter had hoped to have the treaty signed by election day.

10. According to Ambassador Eilts, Sadat was irritated with the way his negotiating team in Washington had handled the language of article 6 of the treaty. This was one of the reasons he brought Mustafa Khalil more directly into the negotiations from that point on. Interview with Hermann Eilts on November 30, 1984.

11. According to Kamal Hassan Ali, after the Baghdad summit Sadat was very sensitive to the priority-of-obligations issue. This slowed up the negotiations on the Egyptian side. Interview in Cairo, February 4, 1985.

12. Carter, *Keeping Faith*, p. 409; Brzezinski, *Power and Principle*, pp. 276–77; and Vance, *Hard Choices*, p. 238.

13. The text of the November 11, 1978, draft of the treaty was leaked to the press by the Egyptians and Israelis. It is available in Meron Medzini, ed., *Israel's Foreign Relations: Selected Documents, 1977–1979*, vol. 5 (Jerusalem: Ministry of Foreign Affairs, 1981), pp. 577–81.

14. Ezer Weizman, *The Battle for Peace* (Bantam Books, 1981), p. 375, essentially agreed with Carter and Sadat when he wrote that it was naive to believe there was no link at all between the two agreements. After all, they were signed together.

15. Brzezinski, *Power and Principle*, pp. 277–78.

16. See Gary Sick, *All Fall Down: America's Tragic Encounter with Iran* (Random House, 1985), pp. 130–40.

CHAPTER TWELVE

1. Jimmy Carter, *Keeping Faith: Memoirs of a President* (Bantam Books, 1982), p. 412.

2. Memorandum from Brzezinski to Carter, January 23, 1979.

3. See Zbigniew Brzezinski, *Power and Principle: Memoirs of the National Security Adviser, 1977–1981* (Farrar, Straus and Giroux, 1983), p. 279. Brzezinski thought that Iran made it impossible for Carter to stand aside. "To let the Camp David Accords slip away would be to turn a triumph into disaster, with unforeseeable consequences for the Middle East as a whole." Carter by this time had also concluded that all that could be attained was a separate peace, followed by prolonged negotiations on the West Bank and Gaza. Carter, *Keeping Faith*, p. 413. In a memorandum to Carter written on February 28, 1979, Brzezinski had said that Begin believed he could afford a failure and Carter could not. "He believes that election year realities will increasingly weaken our hand in the negotiations." It was also clear that the United States would have to be very forthcoming on aid to get Israel to budge on the remaining issues of the treaty. Bilateral issues were now as important as Egyptian-Israeli differences.

4. Cyrus Vance, *Hard Choices: Critical Years in America's Foreign Policy* (Simon and Schuster, 1983), p. 244. The language quoted by Vance is the text as it was finally agreed on, but at this stage the Americans had proposed language to which the Egyptians later took exception.

5. Carter, *Keeping Faith*, p. 416.

6. Brzezinski, *Power and Principle*, p. 282. Carter, in an interview on May 22, 1985, did not recall having sent any such message to Sadat. Brzezinski, in an interview on June 3, 1985, recalled in some detail his conversation with Carter. Because Brzezinski was carrying a "political" message to Sadat from Carter, Vance did not object to his going to Cairo.

7. Carter had called Sadat on March 5 to tell him of Brzezinski's visit, and Sadat had promised him that the president's trip would be a great success. Carter felt he had a guarantee from Sadat that the negotiations would not fail because of any U.S.-Egyptian differences. As Carter later wrote. "Once more, I wanted Begin to have his way with particular phrases and depended on Sadat to be flexible on language and to take the long view concerning the effect of the agreement." Carter, *Keeping Faith*, p. 417.

8. While in Cairo, Carter had a strained meeting with his ambassador to Saudi Arabia, John C. West. He told West in no uncertain terms that he was disappointed with the Saudis and instructed him to be blunt in telling Crown Prince Fahd that he expected Saudi support in the future.

9. Jody Powell, *The Other Side of the Story* (William Morrow, 1984), pp. 93–97.

10. When Khalil asked Carter to try to change the text of the agreement in several places, the president replied: "For the last 18 months, I, the president of

the most powerful nation on earth, have acted the postman. I am not a proud man—I have done the best I could—but I cannot go back to try to change the language."

11. Ezer Weizman, *The Battle for Peace* (Bantam Books, 1981), p. 381; and Leon H. Charney, *Special Counsel* (New York: Philosophical Library, 1984), pp. 147–54.

12. See Moshe Dayan, *Breakthrough: A Personal Account of the Egypt-Israel Peace Negotiations* (Knopf, 1981), pp. 356–58, for the texts of these two memoranda.

13. These letters from Khalil can be found in *White Paper on Treaty of Peace between Egypt and Israel* (Cairo: Ministry of Foreign Affairs, 1979), pp. 155–77.

14. Ironically, according to public opinion polls, Carter gained very little as a result of the peace treaty. See Powell, *Other Side of the Story*, p. 102.

15. Dayan, *Breakthrough*, pp. 303–04.

16. For a solid account, including the texts of the Israeli and Egyptian proposals, see Harvey Sicherman, *Palestinian Self-Government (Autonomy): Its Past and Its Future* (Washington: Washington Institute for Near East Policy, 1991), pp. 21–34, and appendixes 6 and 7. Sicherman also includes the text of Linowitz's report to the president on the autonomy talks, dated January 14, 1981 (appendix 7). Linowitz provides an additional perspective in "The Prospects for the Camp David Peace Process," *SAIS Review*, no. 2 (Summer 1981), pp. 93–100. In a news conference on September 6, 1989, Linowitz claimed that "some 80% of the areas of responsibility to be conveyed to the self-governing authority" had been agreed upon. See "Ambassador Sol M. Linowitz's Press Conference: Middle East Peace Negotiations," *Department of State Bulletin*, vol. 80 (December 1980), p. 51.

17. Carter later showed that he understood the linkage issue quite well. In *The Blood of Abraham* (Houghton Mifflin, 1985), p. 45, he wrote: "From Begin's point of view, the peace agreement with Egypt was the significant act for Israel; the references to the West Bank and Palestinians were to be finessed. With the bilateral treaty, he removed Egypt's considerable strength from the military equation of the Middle East and thus gave the Israelis renewed freedom to pursue their goals of fortifying and settling the occupied territories and removing perceived threats by preemptive military strikes against some of their neighbors."

CHAPTER THIRTEEN

1. Ronald Reagan, "Recognizing the Israeli Asset," *Washington Post*, August 15, 1979, p. A25. The rhetorical flourishes and the line of argument suggest the influence of Joseph Churba, who became an adviser to Reagan during his 1980 campaign for the presidency. Churba may well have been the ghostwriter for this piece. See Joseph Churba, *The Politics of Defeat: America's Decline in the Middle East* (Cyrco Press, 1977), p. 97, in which the author speaks of "the conflict and tension endemic to the [Middle East] region. This condition is traceable largely to the sectarian and fragmented nature of Middle East society." Reagan's article says, "The Carter administration has yet to grasp that in this region conflict and tension are endemic, a condition traceable largely to the fragmented sectarian nature of Middle Eastern society." See also Ronald Reagan, *An American Life* (Simon and

Schuster, 1990), p. 410, on his reasons for supporting Israel. There he stresses "moral responsibility," not Israel's importance as a strategic asset.

2. Reagan won an unusually large proportion of Jewish American votes, some 39 percent, in the 1980 election. See Steven L. Spiegel, *The Other Arab-Israeli Conflict: Making America's Middle East Policy from Truman to Reagan* (University of Chicago Press, 1985), p. 397. Normally, Democratic presidential candidates can count on winning about 80 percent of the Jewish vote.

3. According to Lou Cannon, *President Reagan: The Role of a Lifetime* (Simon and Schuster, 1991), pp. 288–91, Reagan was also fascinated by the Biblical story of Armageddon, and attached special importance to the founding of the Jewish state in 1948 as a portent that Armageddon was approaching.

4. Ibid., p. 35, where Cannon states: "He could act decisively when presented with clear options, but he rarely initiated a meeting, a phone call, a proposal or an idea. He thought his staff would tell him anything he ought to know and invested most of his energy and interest in the public performances of the presidency. . . . He thought of himself as a man of principle, and he was difficult to push on the issues that mattered most to him. As president, he was at once the most malleable and least movable of men."

5. See Raymond Tanter, *Who's at the Helm? Lessons of Lebanon* (Boulder, Colo.: Westview Press, 1990), a book written by a member of the National Security Council staff. Reagan is hardly mentioned as a participant in the policy process.

6. Weinberger's views on the Middle East are best spelled out in "Defense Chief Weinberger on Peace Prospects Now," *U.S. News & World Report*, September 27, 1982, pp. 26–28. Among other points, Weinberger said, "We need several friends in the Mideast—not Israel alone, but clearly our relationship with Israel should be maintained."

7. Jeane Kirkpatrick, formerly a Democrat, attracted considerable attention in conservative circles with her article "Dictatorship and Double Standards," *Commentary*, vol. 68 (November 1979), pp. 34–45.

8. See Bob Woodward, *Veil: The Secret Wars of the CIA, 1981–1987* (Simon and Schuster, 1987), pp. 35–49, 71–88.

9. From an interview cited in Karen Elliott House, "Reagan's World," *Wall Street Journal*, June 3, 1980, p. 1.

10. On Haig's views generally, see Alexander M. Haig, Jr., *Caveat: Realism, Reagan and Foreign Policy* (Macmillan, 1984), especially pp. 20–33.

11. See Spiegel, *Other Arab-Israeli Conflict*, pp. 407–11; and Reagan, *American Life*, pp. 412, 415–16, on the AWACs fight and his anger at Begin for lobbying on Capitol Hill against the president's policy after having promised not to do so.

12. Helena Cobban, *The Superpowers and the Syrian-Israeli Conflict: Beyond Crisis Management?* (Praeger, 1991), pp. 83–84; for the text of the memorandum of understanding, see Nimrod Novik, *Encounter with Reality: Reagan and the Middle East (The First Term)* (Boulder, Colo.: Westview Press for the Jaffee Center for Strategic Studies, 1985), pp. 86–88.

13. See Ze'ev Schiff and Ehud Ya'ari, *Israel's Lebanon War* (Simon and Schuster, 1984); Itamar Rabinovich, *The War for Lebanon, 1970–1983* (Cornell University

Press, 1984); and Yair Evron, *War and Intervention in Lebanon: The Israeli-Syrian Deterrence Dialogue* (Johns Hopkins University Press, 1987).

14. Haig, *Caveat*, pp. 332–35.

15. Schiff and Ya'ari, *Israel's Lebanon War*, pp. 62–77. See also David Kimche, *The Last Option: After Nasser, Arafat and Saddam Hussein. The Quest for Peace in the Middle East* (Scribner's, 1991), p. 145: "Israel's political leaders, especially Prime Minister Begin and Defence Minister Sharon, had become convinced, during those spring months of 1982, that the Reagan administration was not averse to an operation in which the PLO, and perhaps even the Soviet-aligned Syrians, would be taught a lesson." Kimche states bluntly, on his own considerable authority, that there was no strong resistance to Sharon's plans in Washington. He quotes both Haig and Reagan as being understanding of Israel's objectives. "When Begin sent an oral message to Reagan in May 1982 warning that it might become 'imperative and inevitable' to remove this PLO threat, Haig's reaction was that the United States would probably not be able to stop Israel from attacking. And when Sharon met Haig in Washington later that month, Haig was reported to have told him: 'We understand your aims. We can't tell you not to defend your interests.' "

16. Just a week before the Israeli invasion, on May 26, 1982, Haig gave a major speech on the Middle East in which he focused on the Iran-Iraq conflict, the autonomy negotiations, and the explosive situation in Lebanon.

17. See Cobban, *Superpowers*, pp. 35–40.

18. Allan Gerson, *The Kirkpatrick Mission: Diplomacy without Apology. America at the United Nations, 1981–1985* (Free Press, 1991), pp. 138–55.

19. Ibid., p. 134.

20. Translated from the Hebrew version of the letter from Reagan to Begin, June 9, 1982, as published by Arye Naor, *Cabinet at War* (in Hebrew) (Tel Aviv: Lahav, 1986), p. 76. American officials have confirmed the essential accuracy of this version but add that Brezhnev's message was not particularly menacing. They imply that Reagan deliberately exaggerated the danger of escalation to make an impression on Begin.

21. Alexander M. Haig, Jr., *Inner Circles: How America Changed the World. A Memoir* (Warner Books, 1992), p. 547.

22. Cannon, *President Reagan*, pp. 202–04; and Haig, *Inner Circles*, pp. 547–48. Haig claims that he was on the verge of achieving agreement on PLO withdrawal from Lebanon in early July and that this effort fell apart when he was suddenly dismissed.

23. Cannon, *President Reagan*, pp. 202–05.

24. Bernard Gwertzman, "Shultz Declares Palestinian Needs Must Be Resolved," *New York Times*, July 14, 1982, p. A1.

25. George Shultz, *Turmoil and Triumph: My Years as Secreary of State* (Scribner's, 1993), pp. 85–86. The working group consisted of Robert McFarlane, Lawrence Eagleburger, Nicholas Veliotes, Robert Ames, Paul Wolfowitz, Charles Hill, William Kirby, and Alan Kreczko.

26. Ibid., p. 87.

27. Reagan, *American Life*, pp. 425–29; and Michael Deaver, *Behind the Scenes: In Which the Author Talks about Ronald and Nancy Reagan . . . and Himself* (William Morrow, 1987), pp. 165–66. Deaver takes credit for persuading Reagan, against the advice of the NSC staff, to call Begin to tell him to stop the bombing of Beirut. When Begin agreed, Reagan reportedly turned to Deaver and said, "I didn't know I had that kind of power." Also see Gerson, *Kirkpatrick Mission*, pp. 164–69, on the UN diplomacy in this period, especially the delaying tactics on the French-Egyptian proposal, which called for mutual Israeli-PLO recognition.

28. See Rashid Khalidi, *Under Siege: P.L.O. Decisionmaking during the 1982 War* (Columbia University Press, 1986), p. 177.

29. Shultz, *Turmoil and Triumph*, p. 92.

30. See Kimche, *Last Option*, p. 157, where he quotes Begin speaking to his Israeli colleagues on September 1: "We have been betrayed by the Americans, the biggest betrayal since the state was established. They have stabbed us in the back. We now have a completely different fight on our hands."

31. Veliotes had made a secret trip to Amman to brief King Hussein on August 20. Arafat was also given an advance briefing on the speech while still in Beirut. Begin was briefed by Ambassador Lewis only on August 31. Shultz, *Turmoil and Triumph*, p. 92, discloses the Veliotes mission and describes Shultz's rationale for going ahead in the face of probable Israeli opposition.

32. According to notes, made available to the author, of Sharon's meeting with Pierre Gemayal in Bikfaya on September 16, 1982, Sharon referred to his discussions with Bashir and again called for "the necessity of immediate action to prevent establishment of new facts by the present government in its final days, and the danger that hostile elements would try and modify political processes desirable to us." Some of the relevant background to this meeting is covered by Schiff and Ya'ari, *Israel's Lebanon War*, pp. 246–58.

33. For the results of the official Israeli inquiry, see *The Beirut Massacre: The Complete Kahan Commission Report* (Princeton, N.J.: Karz-Cohl, 1983).

34. See Geoffrey Kemp, "Lessons of Lebanon: A Guideline for Future U.S. Policy," *Middle East Insight*, vol. 6 (Summer 1988), pp. 57–68, on debates over the role of the multinational force from September 1982 until the withdrawal of the American contingent in February 1984.

35. See William B. Quandt, "Reagan's Lebanon Policy: Trial and Error," *Middle East Journal*, vol. 38 (Spring 1984), pp. 241–42.

36. Shultz, *Turmoil and Triumph*, p. 440.

37. The best account of the background to the king's decision can be found in two Pulitzer-prize-winning articles by Karen Elliott House: "Hussein's Decision: King Had U.S. Pledges on Peace Talks but Met a Maze of Arab Foes," *Wall Street Journal*, April 14, 1983, p.1, and "Hussein's Decision: Fears for His Kingdom, Sense of History Drove Monarch to Seek Talks," *Wall Street Journal*, April 15, 1983, p.1. According to the king, General Secretary Yuri V. Andropov had taken him aside in early December 1982 during a visit to Moscow to warn, "I shall oppose the Reagan plan, and we will use all our resources to oppose it. With due respect, all the weight will be on your shoulders, and they aren't broad enough to bear it."

38. Text of "Jordan's Statement on Its Refusal to Join the Reagan Peace Initiative," *New York Times*, April 11, 1983, p. A12.

39. Among the victims of the bombing was Robert Ames, one of the top CIA officials with responsibility for the Middle East, and one of the core group of officials who had worked closely with Secretary Shultz at the inception of the Reagan initiative.

40. For an inquiry into the reasons for the vulnerability of the U.S. Marine compound, see *Report of the DOD Commission on Beirut International Airport Terrorist Act, October 23, 1983* (Department of Defense, 1983). Before the bombing of the Marine compound, the Israelis had begun to withdraw from the Shouf area, a step on the way toward the new Israeli policy of consolidating a security presence in southern Lebanon only.

41. Cobban, *Superpowers*, pp. 87–88.

42. On Shamir, see Avishai Margalit, "The Violent Life of Yitzhak Shamir," *New York Review of Books*, May 14, 1992, pp. 18–24.

43. See John K. Cooley, *Payback: America's Long War in the Middle East* (Brassey's, 1991), pp. 94–97.

44. Kemp, "Lessons of Lebanon," p. 67. Kemp concludes that only a strong president can put a stop to squabbling between powerful cabinet members such as Shultz and Weinberger. In his words, "In the case of Lebanon the President never once ordered the Secretary of Defense to play a more assertive role in supporting U.S. policy in Lebanon. Indeed, at the height of the debate within the White House over whether or not the marines should be redeployed to ships in February 1984, Reagan's own viewpoint was difficult to discern. The decision in favor of withdrawal was made by a simple majority within the inner circle of advisors."

45. See William B. Quandt, *Camp David: Peacemaking and Politics* (Brookings, 1986), pp. 25–27.

46. Shultz, *Turmoil and Triumph*, p. 440.

47. See Quandt, ed., *Middle East*, p. 473, for the text of the February 11 agreement. Both Jordanian and Palestinian sources say that some amendments were later made to the basic text. The authorized English translation of the first principle called for "total withdrawal from the territories occupied in 1967 for comprehensive peace." The Arabic text simply said "land in exchange for peace."

48. Shultz, *Turmoil and Triumph*, p. 445.

49. On Israeli-Jordanian contacts during this period, see Adam Garfinkle, *Israel and Jordan in the Shadow of War: Functional Ties and Futile Diplomacy in a Small Place* (St. Martin's Press, 1992), pp. 109–20.

50. Text of "President's News Conference on Foreign and Domestic Issues," *New York Times*, March 22, 1985, p. A12.

51. Shultz, *Turmoil and Triumph*, p. 446.

52. Ibid., pp. 453–54.

53. Garfinkle, *Israel and Jordan*, p. 120, provides four of the names: Hanna Siniora (Jerusalem-based editor of *Al-Fajr*), Fayez Abu Rahme (a lawyer from Gaza), Sheik Abd al-Hamid Sayah (the speaker of the Palestine National Council), and Nabil Sha'ath (a political adviser to Arafat and prominent member of the

Palestine National Council). In addition, the list mentioned Khalid al-Hassan (prominent in Fatah and occasional emissary to Washington), Hatem Husseini (former PLO representative in Washington), and Salah Ta'amari (Fatah activist who had been imprisoned by Israel and had the distinction of being married to a former wife of King Hussein). Jerusalem Domestic Service, July 19, 1985, in Foreign Broadcast Information Service (FBIS), *Daily Report: Middle East and Africa*, p. 11. Neither the Americans nor the Israelis had any objections to Siniora and Abu Rahmeh. Nabil Sha'ath presented the most complicated case. For the PLO, his inclusion was essential. For Israel, it was out of the question. The Americans vacillated.

54. Shultz, *Turmoil and Triumph*, p. 454.

55. See the text of the September 27, 1985, speech in Amman Domestic Service, FBIS, *Daily Report: Middle East and Africa*, September 30, 1985, p. F3.

56. Garfinkle, *Israel and Jordan*, pp. 122–23.

57. In the denouement of the *Achille Lauro* affair, U.S.-Egyptian relations were strained as American F-14s intercepted an Egyptian airliner carrying the hijackers to Tunis, where the PLO would have allegedly put them on trial. The Egyptian plane was forced to land at a NATO base in Sicily, which caused a great outpouring of anger in Cairo and self-congratulations and boasting in the United States. On the *Achille Lauro* affair and its aftermath, see David C. Martin and John Walcott, *Best Laid Plans: The Inside Story of America's War against Terrorism* (Harper and Row, 1988), pp. 235–57; and Woodward, *Veil*, pp. 414–16.

58. Garfinkle, *Israel and Jordan*, p. 124, credits King Hussein with initiating the move toward Syria as a means of preventing Arafat from winning Syrian support while Jordan pursued its new strategy with Israel. Peres had reportedly accepted the idea of an international conference in order to give the king something to use with Syria.

59. The full text is found in Amman Television Service, February 19, 1986, FBIS, *Daily Report: Middle East and North Africa*, February 20, 1986, pp. F1–F16. According to American sources that were closely involved in the diplomacy of early 1986, a last-ditch effort was made to find a formula whereby the PLO would accept Resolution 242 unambiguously as the basis for negotiations with Israel and then would spell out its additional demands. King Hussein told the Americans that the PLO needed a quid pro quo for such a step, and the United States therefore made some concessions on how the PLO would be invited to, and represented at, an international conference. The PLO was still not prepared to accept Resolution 242. Arafat insisted that the United States endorse the Palestinian right of self-determination and open direct channels of communication to the PLO instead of negotiating through the Jordanians. The Jordanians had told the PLO that the United States would not budge on the issue of self-determination and urged the PLO to accept 242 anyway. The final meeting between Hussein and Arafat ended acrimoniously. The Jordanians and Americans concluded that the PLO was neither serious nor trustworthy. This conclusion had a significant impact on subsequent diplomatic moves. Hussein's public account does not cover all of these points, but the tone and substance of his remarks give credence to this interpretation.

60. Garfinkle, *Israel and Jordan*, p. 121, states that Jordan wanted to co-opt a weak Arafat, and Israel, much like the United States, wanted to eliminate him.

61. Shultz, *Turmoil and Triumph*, pp. 461–62.

62. According to Kemp, "Lessons of Lebanon," p. 67, the Shultz-Weinberger deadlock over Lebanon had convinced some Reaganites, especially Casey and NSC staffer Oliver North, that a capability should be developed to carry out covert actions "outside the system."

63. Many sources provide the basic chronology of what came to be known as the Iran-Contra affair. See especially *The Tower Commission Report: The Full Text of the President's Special Review Board* (Random House, 1987). Woodward, *Veil*, pp. 413–501, provides insider detail, as does Martin and Walcott, *Best Laid Plans*, pp. 227–34, 323–61. See also Kimche, *Last Option*, pp. 208–20, for his own and Israel's role in the opening to Iran.

64. McFarlane served as national security adviser from October 1982 until the end of 1985. After his retirement he remained involved with the arms for hostages affair, and when he made his infamous trip to Tehran in May 1986, he no longer held an official position in the government. By then, the national security adviser was the intensely secretive John Poindexter. See Martin and Walcott, *Best Laid Plans*, p. 331.

65. Kimche, *Last Option*, pp. 211–13.

CHAPTER FOURTEEN

1. See Thomas L. McNaugher, "Walking Tightropes in the Gulf," in Efraim Karsh, ed., *The Iran-Iraq War: Impact and Implications* (St. Martin's Press, 1989), pp. 171–99.

2. For additional reasons to be skeptical of an international conference, see Peter W. Rodman, "Middle East Diplomacy after the Gulf War," *Foreign Affairs*, vol. 70 (Spring 1991), pp. 10–18.

3. George Shultz, *Turmoil and Triumph: My Years as Secretary of State* (Scribner's, 1993), pp. 454–57, and chap. 44.

4. Adam Garfinkle, *Israel and Jordan in the Shadow of War: Functional Ties and Futile Diplomacy in a Small Place* (St. Martin's Press, 1992), pp. 128–29.

5. For more information on the efforts to create a sort of Israeli-Jordanian condominium, see Yossi Melman and Dan Raviv, *Behind the Uprising: Israelis, Jordanians, and Palestinians* (Greenwood Press, 1989), pp. 187–200.

6. Shultz, *Turmoil and Triumph*, chap. 44.

7. For the text of the London Document, see William B. Quandt, ed., *The Middle East: Ten Years after Camp David* (Brookings, 1988), pp. 475–76.

8. Shultz, *Turmoil and Triumph*, chap. 44.

9. Ibid.

10. Ibid.

11. Ibid.

12. See William Safire, "The Little King," *New York Times*, January 13, 1988, p. A23.

13. The word *intifada* in Arabic means "shaking off," as in shaking off the occupation.

14. Two seasoned Israeli journalists give their account of the early phase of the *intifada* in Ze'ev Schiff and Ehud Ya'ari, *Intifada: The Palestinian Uprising. Israel's Third Front* (Simon and Schuster, 1989).

15. See Helena Cobban, "The PLO and the Intifada," *Middle East Journal*, vol. 44 (Spring 1990), pp. 207–33.

16. By this time Shultz was fully in charge of the foreign policy of the United States. Weinberger had left in November 1987, to be replaced by Frank Carlucci. General Colin Powell then took over the job as national security adviser, Reagan's sixth in seven years. Also, Casey had died in January 1987.

17. Shultz, *Turmoil and Triumph*, chap. 47.

18. The use of the word "parties" instead of "states" suggested that the Palestine Liberation Organization might be invited to the conference.

19. Shamir's statement prompted Senators Rudy Boschwitz, Carl Levin, and twenty-eight other senators, including many friends of Israel, to write a letter to Shultz, dated March 3, 1988, expressing their concern about the Israeli position. Shamir's reply was published in "Text of Letter from Shamir on Criticism from Senators," *New York Times*, March 10, 1988, p. A10.

20. Shultz, *Turmoil and Triumph*, chap. 47, states, "I was frustrated by Shamir's inflexibility and by the fact that divided government, as had existed in Israel since late 1984, meant that no one could be held responsible and accountable." His comments on King Hussein were that he was "candid and gloomy: he again gave me nothing but wanted me to 'persevere.' " Asad put Shultz through an "exercise in agony," concluding by saying, "I can give you nothing but 'continue.' "

21. See the text of the king's speech of July 31, 1988, in Foreign Broadcast Information Service, *Daily Report: Middle East and North Africa*, August 1, 1988, pp. 39–41.

22. At the Algiers Arab Summit meeting in Algiers in June 1988, the PLO had circulated a document entitled "PLO View: Prospects of a Palestinian-Israeli Settlement." Bassam Abu Sharif, a close adviser of Arafat's, soon claimed authorship. Most American officials who took note of the document were encouraged by its content and tone but were unsure whether it truly represented a new, more moderate tendency within the PLO. For the text, see Quandt, ed., *Middle East*, pp. 490–93.

23. John Mroz, from the International Peace Academy in New York, had many talks with Arafat in 1981–82 that were conveyed to the State Department. According to Harvey Sicherman, *Palestinian Self-Government (Autonomy): Its Past and Its Future* (Washington: Washington Institute for Near East Policy, 1991), p. 37, Haig never used the channel for any official messages.

24. Congress in August 1985 added one more condition of its own. No American official could negotiate with the PLO unless the PLO met the conditions laid down in 1975—acceptance of UN Resolutions 242 and 338 and Israel's right to exist—and renounced the use of terrorism. Public Law 99-83, section 1302, August 8, 1985.

25. Among the Jewish personalities involved were Rita Hauser, a New York attorney; Stanley Sheinbaum, an economist and publisher from Los Angeles; Menachem Rosensaft, a Holocaust survivor who later regretted his participation;

Drora Kass, from the American branch of the Israeli International Center for Peace in the Middle East; and A. L. Udovitch, professor of Middle Eastern history at Princeton University, who joined the group just before the Stockholm meeting.

26. Shultz interview with Swedish reporter Susanne Palme, March 30, 1992 (made available to the author).

27. Mohamed Rabie is an economist by training and the author of a number of books, including *The New World Order: A Perspective on the Post–Cold War Era* (Vantage Press, 1992).

28. Rabie approached me on August 2, 1988, with his idea. As far as I knew then or know now, it was his own proposal, not one initiated by the PLO in Tunis. At this initial meeting we agreed to try to develop language that would meet the requirements of both sides. Rabie assumed that I had contacts in the State Department, and he assured me that he could communicate easily with the PLO leadership. Over the next several months he dealt exclusively with the PLO leadership, especially Abu Mazin, and I dealt with a handful of people in the State Department and NSC who were aware of this initiative. Rabie and I would then convey to each other whatever we had learned of importance to the success of the initiative. The main result of this effort, I believe, was to establish that both sides were interested in beginning a dialogue before the end of the Reagan administration and in demonstrating that mutually acceptable language would not be too difficult to develop. See Mohamed Rabie, "The U.S.-PLO Dialogue: The Swedish Connection," *Journal of Palestine Studies*, vol. 21 (Summer 1992), pp. 54–66.

29. The proposed text of what the PLO might say, as conveyed to the State Department on August 12, was as follows:

As its contribution to the search for a just and lasting peace in the Middle East, the Executive Committee of the Palestine Liberation Organization has met and decided to issue the following official statement:

1. That it is prepared to negotiate a comprehensive peace settlement of the Arab-Israeli conflict on the basis of United Nations resolutions 242 and 338.

2. That it considers the convening of an international conference under the auspices of the United Nations as an appropriate framework for negotiating a political settlement and ultimately achieving peace in the Middle East.

3. That it seeks to establish a democratic Palestinian state in the West Bank and Gaza strip and to live in peace with its neighbors and respect their right to live in peace.

4. That it condemns terrorism in all its forms and is prepared for a moratorium on all forms of violence, on a mutual basis, once negotiations under the auspices of an international conference begin.

These points are derived from the PLO's commitment to the following principles: all the states in the region—including Israel and a Palestinians state—are entitled to live in peace within secure and internationally recognized borders; that all peoples in the region—including the Israelis and the Palestinians—must enjoy the right of self-determination; and that no state should violate the rights of others, acquire land by force, or determine its future by coercion.

Israel's acceptance of these same principle is a precondition for meaningful negotiations to begin.

After talking at length with Rabie, the PLO made a few minor changes, most important of which was the addition of the idea that "all parties to the conflict, including the PLO, should participate in the international conference on an equal basis."

30. I conveyed these points, on behalf of the State Department, to Mohamed Rabie on August 13, 1988. I was told that they had been cleared by Shultz's office, which meant, at a minimum, Shultz's aide, Charles Hill, had cleared on them and that Shultz was informed. I did not at any point deal directly with Shultz or Hill, although my interlocutors regularly did. See Shultz, *Turmoil and Triumph*, chap. 47, for his account of these developments.

31. The PLO wanted the United States to say:

The U.S. Government welcomes the new PLO initiative and wishes to make the following statement:

1. The United States considers the PLO statement as a commitment to seek a political settlement of the Arab-Israeli conflict through peaceful means.

2. Recognizing the right of all peoples to self-determination as called for in the charter of the U.N., the United States believes that the Palestinian people have the right to self-determination, and should be enabled to do so through negotiations leading to a comprehensive peace settlement.

3. The United States believes that U.N. resolutions 242 and 338 embody the basic principle upon which a political settlement to the Arab-Israeli conflict can be established.

4. The United States considers the PLO's endorsement of U.N. resolutions 242 and 338, its condemnation of terrorism, its commitment to a political settlement through peaceful means as having removed the obstacles which in the past prevented the United States from having official contacts with the PLO.

Consequently, the U.S. government is prepared to meet with designated representatives of the PLO, the legitimate representatives of the Palestinian people, as soon as the Executive Committee names its representatives. Finally, the United States calls upon all parties to seize the opportunity to renew the search for peace without delay.

32. Shultz had been disappointed by Arafat's speech in Strasbourg on September 13. The PLO had signaled that this speech would not contain the new PLO position, but Shultz was still critical. For the text of Shultz's remarks, see "The First George P. Shultz Lecture on Middle East Diplomacy," Washington Institute for Near East Policy, September 16, 1988.

33. About this time consultations took place between the United States and the Soviet Union, and the Soviets made it clear that they were supporting the initiative. Shultz, *Turmoil and Triumph*, chap. 47, implies that he did not authorize the sending of a message to the PLO, but in fact one was sent.

34. Shultz, *Turmoil and Triumph*, chap. 47, notes that the PLO was able to communicate with him through the CIA. Arafat used this channel on occasion to clarify points but not for ongoing negotiations.

35. For an English translation of the resolutions of the Nineteenth PNC, see *Journal of Palestine Studies*, vol. 18 (Winter 1989), pp. 213–23.

36. In his interview with Susanne Palme, on March 30, 1992, Shultz said: "[The Swedish ambassador] came to me [on December 2] and asked: Sten Andersson wants to know what the PLO could say that would cause us to be willing to have a dialogue with them and what kind of response we would make if they made these statements. And so I produced a statement and an answer and [the Swedish ambassador] came to my home and got it and I told him this is strictly for Sten Andersson. I have nothing to do with the American Jews that are there, I don't want them to see it, the dialogue between them and the Palestinians is something you are running, it's something totally separate from this. . . . Sten was a person I trusted and had confidence in and so I thought if he is going to talk to Arafat and if he seems to think this is a serious possibility we will get him a statement. And we had learned some things about some PLO sensibilities from the Quandt [and Rabie] interchange. So that helped I think a little bit in the phraseology of what we said." See Shultz, *Turmoil and Triumph*, chap. 47, for more on these developments, especially his reasoning in denying a visa for Arafat to come to the United Nations.

37. This document was quite close to the draft that Rabie had brought back from Tunis in September with PLO approval, with the addition of several key words referring to not engaging in terrorism in the future. For reasons that are not clear, the PLO objected to the fourth point on the moratorium on violence—after having accepted it the previous September—and Shultz accepted this deletion. A few other word changes were also agreed upon through the Swedes, including the addition to point one that negotiations should take place "within the framework of an international conference."

38. This led American officials to believe, for a brief moment on December 7, that the breakthrough had been achieved.

39. A PLO internal account of this incident reads as follows: "Many voices were raised warning of the outcome of embarking on this step. And here too Hawatmeh played a disruptive role. He tried to contact Kuwait and others to incite our brothers to refuse it. He did the same thing within his organization; he began to dispatch letters and messengers. All of that led Abu Ammar (Arafat) to work to distance himself from the step, and for that reason he took another look at his speech to remove most of the commentary that it contained and that complied with the proposed text from the Americans. Abu Ammar feared for national unity and imagined that the DFLP [Hawatmeh's group] and the PFLP [of George Habbash] might leave the PLO which might influence the *intifada*, just as it would affect the total credibility of the PLO which desired an acceptable democratic appearance." From an internal PLO document in Arabic, p. 195.

40. In Arabic, he used the verbs *abaa* and *rafada* (condemn and reject), not *nabadha* (renounce, abandon, or forsake). Shultz felt that rejecting or condemning terrorism did not involve admitting that one had been engaged in it. In one form

or another, he wanted the PLO to say that it would stop doing something that it had been doing previously.

41. Shultz, *Turmoil and Triumph*, chap. 47, revealingly notes that he told Reagan that Arafat, in his speech, was saying in one place "'Unc, unc, unc,' and in another he was saying, 'cle, cle, cle,',' but nowhere will he yet bring himself to say, 'Uncle.' "

42. See Eugene Rostow, "Palestinian Self-Determination: Possible Futures for the Unallocated Territories of the Palestine Mandate," *Yale Law Studies in World Public Order*, vol. 5 (1979), p. 147. Rostow has made the same point about the legality of Israeli settlements in a number of other publications. This theme was picked up and popularized by George Will in his syndicated column in the early 1980s.

43. Meron Benvenisti wrote in 1983 that the clock had struck midnight. For an example of his thinking, see his essay "Demographic, Economic, Legal, Social and Political Developments in the West Bank," in *The 1987 Report: The West Bank Data Base Project* (Boulder, Colo.: Westview Press, 1987), pp. 67–80. See also Meron Benvenisti, *Conflicts and Contradictions* (Villard Books, 1986), pp. 169–82.

44. Reagan's memoirs, *An American Life* (Simon and Schuster, 1990), give many examples of his lack of care with details in discussing the Middle East. For example, Reagan says that UN Resolution 242 called on Israel "to withdraw from all the territories it had claimed after the 1967 war, including the West Bank" (p. 414); he casually interprets his September 1, 1982, initiative as supporting the right of Palestinians to "self-determination and self-government" (p. 430); and he states that Israeli settlements, which he had said were not illegal, were "in continued violation of UN Security Council Resolution 242" (p. 441). All three statements are inaccurate.

45. See Wolf Blitzer, *Territory of Lies: The Exclusive Story of Jonathan Jay Pollard. The American Who Spied on His Country for Israel and How He Was Betrayed* (Harper and Row, 1989).

46. The first account of the information provided by Mordechai Vanunu appeared in Peter Hounam and others, "Revealed: The Secrets of Israel's Nuclear Arsenal," *Sunday Times* (London), October 5, 1986, p. 1. See also Seymour M. Hersh, *The Samson Option: Israel's Nuclear Arsenal and American Foreign Policy* (Random House, 1991), pp. 307–12.

47. See Karen L. Puschel, *US-Israeli Strategic Cooperation in the Post–Cold War Era: An American Perspective* (Boulder, Colo.: Westview Press, 1992), chaps. 2–4.

48. For the first time, in November 1991, poll results showed that more Americans blamed Israel than the Arabs for the lack of progress in making peace. See Gerald F. Seib, "On Day One of Mideast Talks, Calm Prevails amid Ceremony," *Wall Street Journal*, October 31, 1991, p. A18.

CHAPTER FIFTEEN

1. On the Bush-Baker relationship, see Marjorie Williams, "His Master's Voice," *Vanity Fair*, October 1992; and John Newhouse, "Shunning the Losers," *New Yorker*, October 26, 1992, pp. 40–52.

2. Some Israelis saw this article on Baker as an early sign of his hostility to Israel. Early in the stream-of-conscious musings, Baker is quoted as wondering if it will ever be possible to get peace in the Middle East. Then, right after the comment on turkey-shooting tactics, he mentions Israel and notes that Israel is internally divided. "But creating something productive when Israel is divided internally is going to be real tough. Who knows?" See Michael Kramer, "Playing for the Edge," *Time*, February 13, 1989, p. 44. For an Israeli interpretation of how this shows Baker's hostility toward Israel, see Dore Gold, "US and Israel Enter New Era," *Jerusalem Post*, February 28, 1992, p. 9A.

3. Kramer, "Playing for the Edge," p. 30.

4. Bush's other key foreign policy appointments, Secretary of Defense Richard Cheney and National Security Adviser Brent Scowcroft, were not known to have strong views on the Middle East and seemed most likely to wield influence on U.S.-Soviet relations and arms control issues.

5. Washington Institute's Presidential Study Group, *Building for Peace: An American Strategy for the Middle East* (Washington: Washington Institute for Near East Policy, 1988).

6. Richard Haass, *Conflicts Unending: The United States and Regional Disputes* (Yale University Press, 1990), pp. 30–56.

7. Haass's views did apparently evolve somewhat. On September 13, 1991, he said that "one of the things we've learned, and it has affected a lot of my thinking, is that even when you try to think small and avoid some of the most sensitive, final status issues, a kind of step-by-step approach, you find that people see precedents everywhere." See "The Impact of Global Developments on U.S. Policy in the Middle East," *From War to Peace in the Middle East?* Sixth Annual Policy Conference (Washington: Washington Institute for Near East Policy, 1991), p. 10.

8. Arab suspicions were also heightened by the fact that the four top advisers to Bush and Baker on the Middle East were all Jewish—Dennis Ross, Richard Haass, Aaron Miller on the Policy Planning staff, and Daniel Kurtzer in the Near East Bureau. Somewhat ironically, the presence of Jews in such prominent positions did not seem to reassure some Israelis, especially Likud supporters, who soon were speaking crudely of "Baker's Jew boys" as responsible for the strains in U.S.-Israeli relations. See Margaret G. Warner, "Whose Side Are You On?" *Newsweek*, June 1, 1992, p. 57.

9. One significant development had taken place after the publication of the Presidential Study Group's *Building for Peace*. That was the onset of the U.S.-PLO dialogue. Those who had contributed to the report had taken a very skeptical attitude toward the PLO, indicating that the prospects were much better for finding a Palestinian negotiating partner for Israel from within the West Bank and Gaza, where objective circumstances imposed a kind of realism and pragmatism. But in December 1988 Shultz, with the support of both Bush and Baker, had agreed to the opening of a U.S.-PLO dialogue. From the outset Bush and Baker made it clear that they wanted the dialogue to continue, albeit with discretion. In addition, Bush and Baker rejected the proposal of the report that a special negotiator for the Middle East should be named.

10. The other three points of the Israeli proposal, which received less attention because they were less original, emphasized the need for negotiations with Arab states to conclude peace treaties, the importance of settling the refugee problem, and the necessity for the Camp David partners to renew their commitment to the agreements and to peace. For the text of the initial plan, see *Jerusalem Post*, April 14, 1989, p. 8. On May 15, 1989, *Jerusalem Post*, p. 2, published an expanded twenty-point version of the government's peace plan. This latter document is sometimes referred to as the May 14, 1989, initiative.

11. Address by Secretary Baker, "Principles and Pragmatism: American Policy toward the Arab-Israeli Conflict," *Department of State Bulletin*, vol. 89 (July 1989), p. 24. One of the members of the Baker Middle East team called the speech "reality therapy." Another said that "slight tension with Israel is the price we pay for having credibility with the Arab side."

12. Shamir may not have been prepared to negotiate with the PLO, but he did apparently establish contact in early 1989. According to Salah Khalaf (Abu Iyad), in an interview with the author in February 1989, Shamir had sent a message to him via an Arab leader. Shamir wanted to know if Abu Iyad continued to believe that a Palestinian state in the West Bank would simply be a stage on the way to the elimination of Israel. Shamir followed up by sending one of his political allies to Morocco to engage in lengthy discussions with Abu Iyad. Subsequent meetings were envisaged but never took place.

13. See, for example, Salah Khalaf (Abu Iyad), "Lowering the Sword," *Foreign Policy*, no. 78 (Spring 1990), pp. 91–112. Somewhat earlier Abu Iyad had videotaped a statement to Israelis that indicated a shift in his views toward acceptance of a two-state settlement. The tape was shown in Israel and produced extensive commentary, especially in the peace camp.

14. Baker also tried to enlist the help of the Iraqi government. On November 9, 1989, he sent a message to the Iraqi foreign minister informing him that the administration had decided to act favorably on grain credits for Iraq. Baker went on to say: "We are at a critical point in our diplomacy. The Government of Egypt is working closely with Palestinians to respond positively to our five-point framework, enabling us to get an Israeli-Palestinian dialogue launched. It would be useful if you could weigh in with them and urge them to give a positive response to Egypt's suggestions." Elaine Sciolino, "Baker Telling Iraqis of Loan Aid, Asks Help on Palestinian Talks," *New York Times*, October 26, 1992, p. A6.

15. For the text of Baker's five points, see Thomas L. Friedman, "Advance Reported on Mideast Talks," *New York Times*, December 7, 1989, p. A11.

16. See David Makovsky, *Jerusalem Post* (International Edition), March 24, 1990, p. 2.

17. In a letter attached to the Camp David Accords, Jimmy Carter had reiterated (albeit obliquely) the official policy that the United States considered East Jerusalem to be occupied territory to which the fourth Geneva Convention should apply. See William B. Quandt, *Camp David: Peacemaking and Politics* (Brookings, 1986), p. 386.

18. For the text of Saddam Hussein's speech, see Foreign Broadcast Information Service (FBIS), *Daily Report: Near East and South Asia*, February 27, 1990, pp. 1–5.

19. See Saddam's speech in which he said Iraq possessed binary chemical weapons and threatened their use against Israel if Israel were to attack Iraq. FBIS, *Daily Report: Near East and South Asia*, April 3, 1990, pp. 32–35.

20. Some Palestinians and their supporters argued that the intended target was military, that no one was hurt, and that the action had not been authorized by Arafat. Therefore, it should not be seen as a violation of the PLO's pledge not to engage in terrorism. Such arguments fell on deaf ears in Washington, partly because at about the same time an Israeli had been killed in a bomb explosion that intelligence sources traced directly to Fatah.

21. Author's interview with Abu Iyad, June 15, 1990.

22. For a generally convincing account, see, Bob Woodward, *The Commanders* (Simon and Schuster, 1991).

23. See Bush's speech before the UN General Assembly, reprinted in *New York Times*, October 2, 1990, p. A12, where he says that "in the aftermath of Iraq's unconditional departure from Kuwait, I truly believe there may be opportunities for Iraq and Kuwait to settle their differences permanently, for the states of the gulf themselves to build new arrangements for stability and for all the states and the peoples of the region to settle the conflicts that divide the Arabs from Israel."

24. The actual budgetary impact of granting the loan guarantees was difficult to assess. A small percentage of the total value of the loan—an amount to be determined on the basis of risk assessment—would have to be appropriated and set aside in a reserve fund. This amount could run from $50 to $800 million. Assuming that Israel repaid all the loans on time, there would be no further costs to the taxpayer. But if Israel defaulted, the costs would, of course, be substantial at a later date.

25. Baker and Israeli Foreign Minister Levy concluded agreement on a $400 million housing loan guarantee, after lengthy discussions, in October 1990. Within days, however, it became clear that Israel did not accept the American condition that no funds should be used in East Jerusalem. See "Israel Retracts Pledges to U.S. on East Jerusalem Housing," *New York Times*, October 19, 1990, p. A16. In the spring of 1992 a National Security Council staff member, Richard Haass, was quoted as saying that Israel had not given the administration a satisfactory reply about how it had spent the $400 million in loan guarantees. See *Haaretz*, April 15, 1992, p. A1, as reported in FBIS, *Daily Report: Near East and South Asia*, April 16, 1992, p. 36. See also David Makousky and Allison Kaplan, "What Went Wrong with the U.S. Aliya Loan Guarantees," *Jerusalem Post*, March 20, 1992, p. 5A, for further evidence that the Israeli government deliberately withheld cooperation in providing information on how the $400 million loan was being used.

26. Thomas L. Friedman, "Baker Cites Israel for Settlements," *New York Times*, May 23, 1991, p. A5. Thomas L. Friedman, "Bush Backs Baker View of Mideast Peace Barriers," *New York Times*, May 24, 1991, p. A3. According to one source, Shamir gave Baker a commitment in February 1991 not to build beyond a "baseline" rate of settlement growth in the West Bank. See *Report on Israeli Settlement in the Occupied Territories*, vol. 2 (Washington, July 1992), p. 1,

quoting a report from the Jewish Telegraphic Agency giving Baker's comments to a delegation of leaders from the American Jewish Congress on May 10, 1992.

27. See Martin Indyk, "Israel's Grand Bargain," *New York Times*, July 24, 1991, p. A21. The text of Ford's letter can be found in appendix C.

28. Linda Gradstein, "Shamir Bars Losing Territory," *Washington Post*, July 25, 1991 p. A27.

29. See "Excerpts from President Bush's News Session on Israeli Loan Guarantees," *New York Times*, September 13, 1991, p. A10. Thomas Dine of AIPAC later called September 12 a "day of infamy."

30. For the text of the U.S. "letter of understanding" given to the Israelis, see *Yedi'ot Aharonot*, September 17, 1991, p. 17, as reported in FBIS, *Daily Report: Near East and South Asia*, September 17, 1991, p. 28. For the Palestinian reply to Baker, see *Al-Dustur* (Amman), October 26, 1991, p. 26, as reported in FBIS, *Daily Report: Near East and South Asia*, October 28, 1991, p. 1.

31. For excerpts from the speeches, see "3 Speeches: The Area Is a 'Dangerous Battleground,' " *New York Times*, November 1, 1991, p. A10. A Wall Street Journal/ABC poll showed that 37 percent of Americans identified Israel as the main obstacle to peace, while 35 percent so labeled the Arabs. See Gerald F. Seib, "On Day One of Mideast Talks, Calm Prevails amid Ceremony," *Wall Street Journal*, October 31, 1991, p. A8.

32. The Palestinians put forward an initial proposal for an interim self-governing authority on January 14, 1992, and then developed a more elaborate version on March 3, 1992.

33. Leslie H. Gelb, "Bush's Ultimatum to Shamir," *New York Times*, January 17, 1992, p. A29.

34. Thomas L. Friedman, "U.S. Details Terms Israel Must Meet for Deal on Loans," *New York Times*, February 25, 1992, p. A1.

35. Thomas L. Friedman, "Bush Rejects Israel Loan Guarantees," *New York Times*, March 18, 1992, p. A11. At the same time, Baker met with Arens on March 17, 1992, to discuss reports of military technology transfers from Israel to China. A General Accounting Office report, *Report of Audit: Department of State Defense Trade Controls*, on the same topic was released in March 1992 by Sherman M. Funk, inspector general, Department of State. Some saw a mounting campaign by Bush and Baker against Israel, but the administration soon pulled back, perhaps fearing that the Israeli electorate would rally around Shamir if too much pressure was applied. For a detailed analysis of U.S.-Israeli relations in early 1992, see Leon T. Hadar, "The Last Days of Likud: The American-Israeli Big Chill," *Journal of Palestine Studies*, vol. 21 (Summer 1992), pp. 80–94.

36. Talks were held in Washington in April 1992 without results, but it was now commonplace for a PLO-related person to be in the background, coordinating with Tunis. In May 1992 multilateral talks were held: on environmental issues in Tokyo, on arms control in Washington, on economic issues in Brussels, on water in Vienna, and on refugees in Ottawa.

37. See Clyde Haberman, "Arens Faults Prime Minister's 'Greater Israel' Concept," *New York Times*, June 29, 1992, p. A3.

38. Indicative of Rabin's new tone were remarks that he made on September

3, 1992: "We should back away from illusions and seek compromises in order to reach peace or, at least, make practical moves to promote it. We should drop the illusions of the religion of Greater Israel and remember that we must take care of the Israeli people, society, culture, and economy. We should remember that a nation's strength is not measured by the territories it holds but by its faith and its ability to cultivate its social, economic, and security systems." FBIS, *Daily Report: Near East and South Asia*, September 3, 1992, p. 26. Also indicative of a new tone from Rabin was his view of Israel's importance to the United States. Rather than emphasizing the "strategic asset" argument, Rabin stressed the "peace partner" role. "The more the U.S. can say it is bringing peace to the area—assisted by Israel acting in its own interests—the more Israel will serve the mutual interest in creating stability and leaving less room for the extremists." Leslie H. Gelb, "America in Israel," *New York Times*, June 15, 1992, p. A19.

39. See Clyde Haberman, "Shamir Is Said to Admit Plan to Stall Talks 'for 10 Years,' " *New York Times*, June 27, 1992, p. A1. Subsequently, Shamir claimed that he had been misinterpreted. But even his clarifications indicated that he envisaged the "interim" agreement as lasting an indefinite time, during which Israel would continue to build settlements.

40. Bush and Baker had indicated that they would remain deeply involved in the negotiations, despite Baker's change of title. But according to Eagleburger, Baker played little role in foreign policy after going to the White House. See Don Oberdorfer, "Baker-less State Department Not in Idle, Officials Say," *Washington Post*, October 16, 1992, p. A23.

41. Asad, speaking to a delegation from the Golan Heights, reported on Syrian Radio, September 9, 1992, in FBIS, *Daily Report: Near East and South Asia*, September 9, 1992, p. 41.

42. Newhouse, "Shunning the Losers," pp. 50–51, in an otherwise quite critical article on Bush's foreign policy. Michael Kramer, "Bush's Reward for Courage," *Time*, August 3, 1992, p. 44, also gave Bush and Baker "considerable credit" for their handling of the loan guarantees and the negotiations more generally.

43. Kissinger expressed the view that the United States should not spend so much effort trying to organize negotiations that were destined to fail. Later he softened his views somewhat. See Henry Kissinger, "Land for Time in the Middle East," *Washington Post*, June 2, 1991, p. D7, and "If Not Peace, at Least Progress," *Washington Post*, October 31. 1991, p. A21. See also the harsh judgment of neoconservative thinker Irving Kristol, " 'Peace Process' That Heads Nowhere," *Wall Street Journal*, June 18, 1992, p. A16.

CHAPTER SIXTEEN

1. Trude B. Feldman, "On the First Anniversary of the Peace Talks in Madrid Bill Clinton Pledges to Maintain the Momentum," *Middle East Insight*, vol. 9 (November–December 1992), pp. 10–15.

2. Karen L. Puschel, *US-Israeli Strategic Cooperation in the Post–Cold War Era: An American Perspective* (Boulder, Colo.: Westview Press, 1992), pp. 153–54,

correctly concludes that "peace is the watershed issue that will determine whether strategic cooperation is significantly expanded in terms of aid and commitments. Certainly, when there has been demonstrable progress on the peace front, U.S. aid has followed in its wake. . . . In the absence of peace, particularly should Israel be perceived as an obstacle, it is hard to envision a US decision to significantly expand U.S.-Israeli strategic cooperation."

Selected Bibliography

Albin, Cecilia, and Harold H. Saunders. "Sinai II: The Politics of International Mediation." FPI Case Study 17. Johns Hopkins University, School of Advanced International Studies, Foreign Policy Institute, Washington, D.C., 1991.

Bailey, Sydney Dawson. *Four Arab-Israeli Wars and the Peace Process.* New York: St. Martin's Press, 1990.

Bard, Mitchell Geoffrey. *The Water's Edge and Beyond: Defining the Limits to Domestic Influence on United States Middle East Policy.* New Brunswick, N.J.: Transaction Publishers, 1991.

Bar-Siman-Tov, Yaacov. *The Israeli-Egyptian War of Attrition, 1969–1970: A Case Study of a Limited War.* New York: Columbia University Press, 1980.

Bar-Zohar, Michael. *Embassies in Crisis: Diplomats and Demagogues behind the Six-Day War.* Englewood Cliffs, N.J.: Prentice-Hall, 1970.

Beling, Willard A., ed. *The Middle East: Quest for an American Policy.* Albany: State University of New York Press, 1973.

Black, Ian, and Benny Morris. *Israel's Secret Wars: A History of Israel's Intelligence Services.* New York: Grove Weidenfeld, 1991.

Blitzer, Wolf. *Territory of Lies: The Exclusive Story of Jonathan Jay Pollard. The American Who Spied on His Country for Israel and How He Was Betrayed.* New York: Harper and Row, 1989.

Brandon, Henry. *The Retreat of American Power: The Inside Story of How Nixon and Kissinger Changed American Foreign Policy for Years to Come.* New York: Doubleday and Co., 1973.

Brecher, Michael. *Decisions in Crisis: Israel, 1967 and 1973.* Berkeley: University of California Press, 1980

———. *Decisions in Israel's Foreign Policy.* New Haven: Yale University Press, 1975.

Brzezinski, Zbigniew. *Power and Principle: Memoirs of the National Security Adviser, 1977–1981.* New York: Farrar, Straus and Giroux, 1983.

Cannon, Lou. *President Reagan: The Role of a Lifetime.* New York: Simon and Schuster, 1991.

Carter, Jimmy. *The Blood of Abraham.* Boston: Houghton Mifflin Co., 1985.

———. *Keeping Faith: Memoirs of a President.* New York: Bantam Books, 1982.

Cobban, Helena. "The P.L.O. and the Intifada." *Middle East Journal,* vol. 44 (Spring 1990), pp. 207–33.

———. *The Superpowers and the Syrian-Israeli Conflict: Beyond Crisis Management?* New York: Praeger, 1991.

Cockburn, Andrew, and Leslie Cockburn. *Dangerous Liaison: The Inside Story of the U.S.-Israeli Covert Relationship*. New York: HarperCollins Publishers, 1991.

Cooley, John K. *Payback: America's Long War in the Middle East*. New York: Brassey's, 1991.

Dayan, Moshe. *Breakthrough: A Personal Account of the Egypt-Israel Peace Negotiations*. New York: Alfred A. Knopf, 1981.

———. *Moshe Dayan: Story of My Life*. New York: William Morrow and Co., 1976.

Dowty, Alan. *Middle East Crisis: U.S. Decision-Making in 1958, 1970, and 1973*. Berkeley: University of California Press, 1984.

Eban, Abba. *An Autobiography*. New York: Random House, 1977.

———. *Personal Witness: Israel through My Eyes*. New York: G. P. Putnam's Sons, 1993.

Eilts, Hermann Frederick. "Improve the Framework." *Foreign Policy*, no. 41 (Winter 1980–81), pp. 3–20.

Ennes, James M., Jr. *Assault on the Liberty: The True Story of the Israeli Attack on an American Intelligence Ship*. New York: Random House, 1979.

Fahmy, Ismail. *Negotiating for Peace in the Middle East*. Baltimore: Johns Hopkins University Press, 1983.

Ford, Gerald R. *A Time to Heal: The Autobiography of Gerald R. Ford*. New York: Harper and Row, 1979.

Friedman, Thomas L. *From Beirut to Jerusalem*. New York: Farrar, Straus and Giroux, 1989.

Garfinkle, Adam. *Israel and Jordan in the Shadow of War: Functional Ties and Futile Diplomacy in a Small Place*. New York: St. Martin's Press, 1992.

———. "U.S. Decision Making in the Jordan Crisis: Correcting the Record." *Political Science Quarterly*, vol. 100 (Spring 1985), pp. 117–38.

Garthoff, Raymond L. *Détente and Confrontation: American-Soviet Relations from Nixon to Reagan*. Washington, D.C.: Brookings Institution, 1985.

Gerson, Allan. *The Kirkpatrick Mission: Diplomacy without Apology. America at the United Nations, 1981–1985*. New York: Free Press, 1991.

Golan, Matti. *The Secret Conversations of Henry Kissinger: Step-by-Step Diplomacy in the Middle East*. New York: Quadrangle Books, 1976.

Goodman, Hirsch, and Ze'ev Schiff. "The Attack on the Liberty." *Atlantic Monthly*, September 1984, pp. 78–84.

Green, Stephen. *Living by the Sword: America and Israel in the Middle East, 1968–87*. Brattleboro, Vt.: Amana Books, 1988.

———. *Taking Sides: America's Secret Relations with a Militant Israel*. New York: William Morrow and Co., 1984.

Haass, Richard. *Conflicts Unending: The United States and Regional Disputes*. New Haven: Yale University Press, 1990.

Haig, Alexander M., Jr. *Caveat: Realism, Reagan and Foreign Policy*. New York: Macmillan, 1984.

Haig, Alexander M., Jr., with Charles McCarry. *Inner Circles: How America Changed the World. A Memoir*. New York: Warner Books, 1992.

Heikal, Mohamed. *Autumn of Fury: The Assassination of Sadat*. New York: Random House, 1983.

———. *The Cairo Documents: The Inside Story of Nasser and His Relationship with World Leaders, Rebels, and Statesmen*. New York: Doubleday and Co., 1973.

———. *1967: Al-Infijar*. Cairo: Markaz al-Ahram, 1990.

———. *The Road to Ramadan*. New York: Quadrangle Books, 1975.

Hersh, Seymour M. *The Price of Power: Kissinger in the Nixon White House*. New York: Summit Books, 1983.

———. *The Samson Option: Israel's Nuclear Arsenal and American Foreign Policy*. New York: Random House, 1991.

Indyk, Martin. *"To the Ends of the Earth": Sadat's Jerusalem Initiative*. Cambridge, Mass.: Harvard University, Center for Middle Eastern Studies, 1984.

Insight Team of the London Sunday Times. *The Yom Kippur War*. New York: Doubleday and Co., 1974.

Isaacson, Walter. *Kissinger: A Biography*. New York: Simon and Schuster, 1992.

Johnson, Lyndon Baines. *The Vantage Point: Perspectives of the Presidency, 1963–1969*. New York: Holt, Rinehart and Winston, 1971.

Kalb, Marvin, and Bernard Kalb. *Kissinger*. Boston: Little, Brown and Co., 1974.

Kalman, Laura. *Abe Fortas: A Biography*. New Haven: Yale University Press, 1990.

Kemp, Geoffrey. "Lessons of Lebanon: A Guideline for Future U.S. Policy." *Middle East Insight*, vol. 6 (Summer 1988), pp. 57–68.

Kimche, David. *The Last Option: After Nasser, Arafat and Saddam Hussein. The Quest for Peace in the Middle East*. New York: Charles Scribner's Sons, 1991.

Kissinger, Henry. *White House Years*. Boston: Little, Brown and Co., 1979.

———. *Years of Upheaval*. Boston: Little, Brown and Co., 1982.

Korn, David A. *Stalemate: The War of Attrition and Great Power Diplomacy in the Middle East, 1967–1970*. Boulder, Colo.: Westview Press, 1992.

Lebow, Richard Ned, and Janice Gross Stein. "We All Lost the Cold War." [To be published by Princeton University Press in 1994.]

Linowitz, Sol. "The Prospects for the Camp David Peace Process." *SAIS Review*, no. 2 (Summer 1981), pp. 93–100.

Luttwak, Edward N., and Walter Laqueur. "Kissinger and the Yom Kippur War." *Commentary*, vol. 58 (September 1974), pp. 33–40.

Martin, David C., and John Walcott. *Best Laid Plans: The Inside Story of America's War against Terrorism*. New York: Harper and Row, 1988.

Meir, Golda. *My Life: The Autobiography of Golda Meir*. London: Futura, 1976.

Melman, Yossi, and Dan Raviv. *Behind the Uprising: Israelis, Jordanians, and Palestinians*. New York: Greenwood Press, 1989.

Miller, Merle. *Lyndon: An Oral Biography*. New York: G. P. Putnam's Sons, 1980.

———. *Plain Speaking: An Oral Biography of Harry S. Truman*. New York: Berkley Publishing Corporation, 1973.

Neff, Donald. *Warriors against Israel*. Brattleboro, Vt.: Amana Books, 1988.

———. *Warriors for Jerusalem: The Six Days That Changed the Middle East*. New York: Linden Press/ Simon and Schuster, 1984.

Nixon, Richard M. *RN: The Memoirs of Richard Nixon*. New York: Grosset and Dunlap, 1978.

———. *Seize the Moment: America's Challenge in a One-Superpower World*. New York: Simon and Schuster, 1992.

Novik, Nimrod. *Encounter with Reality: Reagan and the Middle East (The First Term)*. Boulder, Colo.: Westview Press for the Jaffee Center for Strategic Studies, 1985.

O'Brien, Conor Cruise. *The Siege: The Saga of Israel and Zionism*. New York: Simon and Schuster, 1986.

Parker, Richard B. "The June 1967 War: Some Mysteries Explored." *Middle East Journal*, vol. 46 (Spring 1992), pp. 177–97.

Powell, Jody. *The Other Side of the Story*. New York: William Morrow and Co., 1984.

Puschel, Karen L. *U.S.-Israeli Strategic Cooperation in the Post-Cold War Era: An American Perspective*. Boulder, Colo.: Westview Press, 1992.

Quandt, William B. *Camp David: Peacemaking and Politics*. Wahington, D.C.: The Brookings Institution, 1986.

———. *Decade of Decisions: American Policy toward the Arab-Israeli Conflict, 1967–1976*. Berkeley: University of California Press, 1977.

———. "Kissinger and the Arab-Israeli Disengagement Negotiations." *Journal of International Affairs*, vol. 29 (Spring 1975), pp. 33–48.

———. "Reagan's Lebanon Policy: Trial and Error." *Middle East Journal*, vol. 38 (Spring 1984), pp. 237–54.

Rabie, Mohamed. "The U.S.-PLO Dialogue: The Swedish Connection." *Journal of Palestine Studies*, vol. 21 (Summer 1992), pp. 54–66.

Rabin, Yitzhak. *The Rabin Memoirs*. Boston: Little, Brown and Co., 1979.

Rafael, Gideon. *Destination Peace: Three Decades of Israeli Foreign Policy. A Personal Memoir*. New York: Stein and Day, 1981.

Reagan, Ronald. *An American Life*. New York: Simon and Schuster, 1990.

Riad, Mahmoud. *The Struggle for Peace in the Middle East*. New York: Quartet Books, 1981.

Rostow, Eugene V. *Peace in the Balance: The Future of American Foreign Policy*. New York: Simon and Schuster, 1972.

Rostow, Walt. *The Diffusion of Power: An Essay in Recent History*. New York: Macmillan Co., 1972.

Rusk, Dean. *As I Saw It*. New York: W. W. Norton and Co., 1990.

Safran, Nadav. *Israel: The Embattled Ally*. Cambridge, Mass.: Belknap Press of Harvard University Press, 1978.

Schiff, Ze'ev, and Ehud Ya'ari. *Intifada: The Palestinian Uprising. Israel's Third Front*. New York: Simon and Schuster, 1989.

———. *Israel's Lebanon War*. New York: Simon and Schuster, 1984.

Sheehan, Edward R. F. *The Arabs, Israelis, and Kissinger: A Secret History of American Diplomacy in the Middle East*. New York: Reader's Digest Press, 1976.

Shultz, George. *Turmoil and Triumph: My Years as Secretary of State*. New York: Charles Scribner's Sons, 1993.

Sicherman, Harvey. *Palestinian Self-Government(Autonomy): Its Past and Its Future.* Washington, D.C.: Washington Institute for Near East Policy, 1991.

Sick, Gary. *All Fall Down: America's Tragic Encounter with Iran.* New York: Random House, 1985.

Spiegel, Steven L. *The Other Arab-Israeli Conflict: Making America's Middle East Policy from Truman to Reagan.* Chicago: University of Chicago Press, 1985.

Tanter, Raymond. *Who's at the Helm? Lessons of Lebanon.* Boulder, Colo.: Westview Press, 1990.

Telhami, Shibley. *Power and Leadership in International Bargaining: The Path to the Camp David Accords.* New York: Columbia University Press, 1990.

Vance, Cyrus. *Hard Choices: Critical Years in America's Foreign Policy.* New York: Simon and Schuster, 1983.

Wallach, Janet, and John Wallach. *Arafat: In the Eyes of the Beholder.* New York: Carol Publishing Group, 1990.

Washington Institute's Presidential Study Group. *Building for Peace: An American Strategy for the Middle East.* Washington, D.C.: Washington Institute for Near East Policy, 1988.

Weizman, Ezer. *The Battle for Peace.* New York: Bantam Books, 1981.

Whetten, Lawrence L. *The Canal War: Four-Power Conflict in the Middle East.* Cambridge, Mass.: MIT Press, 1974.

Woodward, Bob. *The Commanders.* New York: Simon and Schuster, 1991.

———. *Veil: The Secret Wars of the CIA, 1981–1987.* New York: Simon and Schuster, 1987.

Yergin, Daniel. *The Prize: The Epic Quest for Oil, Money and Power.* New York: Simon and Schuster, 1991.

Index